Please remember that this is a library book,
and that it belongs only temporarily to each
person who uses it. Be considerate. Do
not write in this, or any, library book.

Introduction to the Criminal Justice System

Second Edition

Introduction to the Criminal Justice System

Second Edition

by
Hazel B. Kerper
Late Professor of Criminal Law
Sam Houston State University

as revised by
Jerold H. Israel
Professor of Law
University of Michigan Law School

CRIMINAL JUSTICE SERIES

West Publishing Company
St. Paul • New York • Los Angeles • San Francisco

COPYRIGHT © 1972 By WEST PUBLISHING CO.
COPYRIGHT © 1979 By WEST PUBLISHING CO.
50 West Kellogg Boulevard
P.O. Box 3526
St. Paul, Minnesota 55165

Printed in the United States of America

Library of Congress Cataloging in Publication Data

Kerper, Hazel B
  Introduction to the criminal justice system.

  (West criminal justice series)
  Includes index.
  1. Criminal justice, Administration of—United States.
  I. Israel, Jerold H., 1934-   joint author.   II. Title.   III. Series: Criminal justice series.

KF9223.K46 1979   345'.73'05   79-112

ISBN 0-8299-0276-7

To my husband, with whom I practiced law,
and to our daughters,
who had to put up with two lawyers as parents.
H.B.K.

Preface

Almost every area of the criminal justice system has seen significant change since the publication of the first edition of this book. The Model Penal Code has taken on new significance in the area of substantive criminal law as more than 30 states have now adopted versions of that Code. In the area of sentencing, the move to determinate sentencing has cast an entirely new light on sentencing procedure and the structure of sentences. In the field of constitutional developments, the Burger Court has made its impact upon the Warren Court precedent; the scope of previous decisions has been limited, and new areas have been opened to constitutional regulation. State legislatures have been active in such areas as bail and speedy trial. L.E.A.A. funding has brought about a proliferation of new programs in many areas, such as pretrial diversion programs, special release on recognizance programs, and special probation programs. The changes have been so vast that what started out as an attempt to make some minor revisions has turned into a substantial rewriting of the whole book. The book has been rewritten, however within the structure of Professor Kerper's first edition, with emphasis on the topics emphasized in the first edition, with the organization of the first edition largely retained, and with as much of the personal flavor of the late Professor Kerper's style as could be retained. Above all, the second edition seeks to serve the same purpose as Professor Kerper's first edition. As Professor Kerper stated in the original preface:

> *This book is not a law book, but a book about the law. It is written for the beginning student in law enforcement, criminology and corrections, sociology, social welfare, government, and urban affairs who needs an understanding of the criminal law as a means of social control.*

A word should be added about two matters of form. When a reference is made to a footnote in the same chapter, the reference simply contains the number of the note and a *supra* or *infra*. When a reference is made to a footnote in a previous or later chapter, the reference is to note number and the page *supra* or *infra*. Throughout the footnotes, heavy use is made of the Model Penal Code (Proposed Official Draft 1962) and the various standards on the administration of criminal justice of the American Bar Association. The Model Penal Code is published by the American Law Institute, Philadelphia, Pennsylvania and the A.B.A.

Standards are published by the American Bar Association, Chicago, Illinois. Consistent with common rules of construction in the law, and the style adopted by Professor Kerper in the first edition, references to the masculine gender should be read to include the feminine unless the context clearly indicates otherwise.

I am most appreciative of the research assistance of John Spelman on Chapters Thirteen and Fourteen, the secretarial assistance of Ms. Carolyn Koyle, and the extraordinary patience of my family.

Jerold H. Israel

Ann Arbor, Michigan
February, 1979

Summary of Contents

Table of Contents

Introduction
to the
Criminal Justice System

Second Edition

Part One

Basic Elements Of Our Legal System

INTRODUCTION

The criminal justice system is the system by which society first determines what behavior must be prohibited under the criminal law and then proceeds to enforce that prohibition through a process that ultimately results in the punishment of offenders. Every citizen should understand how this system works. Crime affects the quality of life of every American, and the criminal justice system is the institution charged with direct responsibility for the control of crime. Each year millions of individuals and businesses are victims of crime. Available data indicates, for example, that a single crime, burglary, was either attempted or completed at over six million households in the year 1974.[1] On the other side, an estimated nine million persons are arrested for the commission of crimes (excluding traffic offenses). Almost two million are prosecuted for the commission of such crimes. In addition, one million young people are referred to the courts as juvenile delinquents, most for having committed criminal acts. It is almost impossible to estimate the total dollar cost of crime. We do know, however, that approximately 15 billion tax dollars are spent by our governments (federal, state, and local) in supporting the police, prosecutors, corrections departments, and other agencies involved in administering the criminal justice system.

Knowledge of how the criminal justice system operates is particularly important for those who work in the system. Law enforcement officers, probation and

---

1. All statistics cited in Part One of this book, unless otherwise indicated, come from M. Hindelang, M. Gottfredson, C. Dunn, and N. Paris, *Sourcebook of Criminal Justice Statistics—1976*, U.S. Law Enforcement Assistance Administration, Washington, D.C.: Government Printing Office 1976.

parole officers, employees of correctional institutions, and, of course, lawyers and judges cannot do their own jobs properly unless they fully understand what happens to the offender between his arrest and his return to the community. Others with less direct contact with the system also must be familiar with its operation. Welfare workers, truant officers, teachers, mental health workers, and doctors, for example, are constantly involved in one aspect or another of the criminal justice system. Charitable organizations work with offenders' families. Foster parents provide homes for children who are wards of the juvenile court. Junior Leagues and the League of Women Voters undertake studies of court operation and investigation of detention homes for young offenders. The Jaycees have chapters in penitentiaries. Members of Congress and of the legislatures of all fifty states are constantly concerned with the problems of crime and delinquency and must shape the laws which guide the operation of the criminal justice system in the United States. Every parent is concerned with how successfully the criminal justice system controls the drug problem; every retail merchant with the detection and prosecution of shop-lifting. All of these persons must of necessity inform themselves about the operation of the social institution directly charged with protecting society and rehabilitating the offender.

The criminal justice system is a creature of the law, being one part of our general legal system. Before we can understand how the criminal justice system works, we must understand how that general system operates. We must consider the general nature of the law, its structure, its functions, and its strengths and weaknesses in accomplishing those functions. We must be aware of the different kinds of laws, with particular emphasis upon those types of laws that have the most significant bearing upon the criminal justice system. Finally, we must have some familiarity with the structure and operation of the courts, and the special role they play in the development and application of the law. The three chapters of Part One cover each of these basic subjects: the nature of law, the different types of law, and the special role of the courts. Together, they provide a springboard for consideration of the special attributes of the criminal justice system. These chapters also provide the beginnings of a basic legal vocabulary that can be very helpful in discussing any aspect of the law. Most of the terms used are defined in the text, but you may also find helpful the glossary in Appendix B at the back of the book.

Chapter 1

What is Law?

To answer the question "What is Law?" we must first consider the character of a society, its organization, its social norms, the methods it has chosen to transmit those norms, and the nature of the sanctions it imposes for their violation. We will examine the need for social control, and the different means by which social control is accomplished in a society. We will determine that law is one means of social control and attempt to differentiate it from other means of social control employed in a society.

LAW AS A MEANS OF SOCIAL CONTROL

Social control, simply put, is the control of an individual's behavior so as to make it conform with the interests and expectations of society as a whole. A need for social control arises whenever men begin to live together in groups. Social control introduces order into the society and the element of *predictability* into social relations. If I can predict that you will drive down the right side of the road, I can safely drive in the other direction on the right side of the road. If I were not able to predict your behavior, at least most of the time, I would either drive erratically myself, attempting to guess where you would be driving, or I would stay off the road to avoid a head-on collision that could result in injury or death. Because there are rules (in this case, laws) which prescribe the method of driving on a public highway , the behavior of both of us is controlled and we are both able to use the public highways most of the time in safety.

There are many means by which the society controls the behavior of the individual. Law is only one of these means. It is easy to identify other means of social control, or, to state it another way, other means by which the individual is induced to conform his behavior to the needs and desires of the group. Morals, ethics, culture, tradition, habit, manners, fashion, to name a few, affect and even determine how the individual behaves. Most Americans use the fork in the right hand. When they want to cut meat, they shift the fork to the left hand and pick up the knife with the right. Englishmen and Frenchmen keep the fork in the left hand and do not have to keep shifting the fork from right hand to left. (It is said that American intelligence agents operating in Europe during World War II often give themselves away when they absent-mindedly use the fork in the right hand.) Thus, the *manners* and *habits* of Americans, Englishmen, and Frenchmen determine how they behave at the table. In a similar manner, the current *fashions* in their respective countries will largely determine what people will wear. In the famous battle between mini-skirt and midi-skirt, Americans again evidenced their separate national quality in successfully defying the French fashion houses. Our *culture*, or basic style of life, also influences various aspects of our behavior ranging from the food we eat to the movies we watch. In many instances, that culture is built around *traditions* or *customs* that are handed down from one generation to another and also control various aspects of our behavior.

The *morals* of the group often have a tremendous influence on the most significant aspects of individual behavior. The enforcement of moral codes is usually associated with religious beliefs and practices. The divorce rate among Catholics is lower than the divorce rate among many other religious groups. Orthodox Jews observe strict dietary restrictions. Seventh Day Adventists go to church on Saturday and keep their places of business open on Sunday. Other religious sects wear distinctive clothing. In every case, the individual who is identified with one or the other of the groups behaves differently than he would behave if he were not a member of that particular group. The group norms have controlled his behavior.

The *code of ethics* of doctors, lawyers, peace officers, teachers, and welfare workers determines how they will relate to their clients, other professionals in their own group, and the clients and professionals in the other groups. A doctor will not knowingly accept a patient who is being treated by another doctor except on a referral basis. Lawyers must not consult directly with the clients of other lawyers. Welfare workers are non-authoritarian in their contacts with clients; police officers impose authority. The professional behavior of the individual is thus guided by the ethical code of the group to which he belongs. This affects the relationships of the professional to his patient or client, which in turn affects the behavior of the patient or client toward the particular professional, and toward other professionals in the other groups.

Each of you can think of many examples of how morals, ethics, culture, tradition, habit, manners, and fashion affect your own behavior and that of your friends and determine or influence the way you interact with each other and with other individuals and groups. Let us now consider how the individual is induced or persuaded through such factors to act according to group norms and expectations. This consideration will throw light on the question of how law differs from other means of social control and permit us to arrive at a definition of law.

The Informal Decision Making Process.   Let us suppose that Johnny is the new boy in the sixth grade. He has just moved to a big city school from a school in a small country town. To make his problem more serious, he enters school six weeks after school has started. Johnny, like every normal boy, wants to be accepted by his classmates, and particularly he wants to be accepted by the "in-group."

Now begins a period of what the sociologist calls "testing." Johnny looks over the other boys in the class to try to find out who is in the group he wants to belong to. He picks out one of the boys and says "hello" to him on the playground. At lunch, he offers his dessert to another member of the group. At the same time the boys in the in-group and other boys and groups of boys are looking over Johnny. They notice the way he looks, the kind of clothes he wears, how he behaves toward the teacher, and how he throws a ball. They find out where he lives and what kind of car his family drives. They soon learn how much money he has in his pockets. They listen to his speech, determine that he is not a foreigner, but nevertheless talks "funny." This process of information gathering and decision making goes on for a considerable period of time during which Johnny has no way of knowing whether or not he is going to make it into the in-group.

If the in-group finds Johnny acceptable, one of the boys, usually the recognized leader of the group, will make overtures toward Johnny . He will be invited into the games, allowed to sit in a certain section of the school bus, or permitted to buy treats during recess. If they do not find him acceptable, none of these things will happen, and Johnny must settle for membership in a lesser group, or in extreme cases, will not be admitted to membership in any group.

How was Johnny's ultimate fate determined? Just what aspects of Johnny's looks, speech, behavior, skills, or family status got him into the in-group or kept him out? For that matter, what about Johnny admitted him to any other group, or kept him out of all the groups? Who made the decisions? When were they made? Was a vote taken? Did one boy, or several boys, refuse him membership in the group? If no vote was taken, who said what to whom that produced the decision to admit or reject Johnny? Maybe nobody actually *said* anything to anybody, yet Johnny was excluded from the group. How was the group decision arrived at?

If you think about it a while, you will realize that it is very difficult to answer any of these questions. Certainly Johnny will never get the answers, nor will his parents, nor the teacher, nor the principal. A social investigator would have difficulty in getting the answers. No boy in the in-group may be able to tell how the decision about Johnny was made. One may say he got the idea that Mike, the leader of the group, didn't like Johnny, or he will say that "Most of the guys just didn't want him around." Pressed for information on whether Mike or the other boys *said* they didn't want Johnny around, the answer, more often than not, will be "Nobody talked about it. I could tell they didn't like him." This will be a true statement. Without saying a word, Mike may have moved every time Johnny sat down beside him, Peter refused the offered dessert, and Jake deliberately dropped the ball thrown by Johnny. The signs were given, the signs were read, and the group decision arrived at. Nobody, least of all Johnny, will ever know just how nor why the decision was made. No appeal is provided for.

In the case of Johnny, the group punished Johnny by refusing him membership in the group. Putting it another way, it imposed negative sanctions on Johnny for his failure to meet the standards of the group, though exactly what those standards were would be very difficult to determine. The group could, of course, have rewarded Johnny by admitting him to the group, since this was something he wanted very much. In either case, it would be very difficult to say why and how the decision was made and almost impossible to identify who made it.

The decision making process in most groups is similarly informal and difficult to identify and describe. The members of the Country Club may hold a formal vote to admit or reject the new couple in town, but the reasons why any member voted for or against their admission would be hard to learn. A mother's disapproval of her child's behavior may be expressed in words or indicated by a frown and a refusal of cookies. A group may express its decision in words or just fail to act, and give no reasons. Groups give rewards and mete out punishments to individuals by informal means, unguided by rules of decision making, and often largely unaware of the factors which really shape the decisions. When the group is aware of the reasons for its decisions, it very often refuses to verbalize them even within the group, particularly if the decision is a negative one or would give rise to a suspicion of arbitrariness or prejudice. Thus, an individual may be informally punished by a group for a "crime" which neither he nor the members of the group can identify. It is sufficient that he fails in some way to measure up to the standards of the group. Conversely, an individual may be rewarded by a group for behavior which neither he nor the group could readily point to as deserving of group acceptance.

The Decision Making Process in the Law. The decision making process in the law is very different. In the first place, the law seldom rewards an individual for obeying the law. True, the individual who conforms his conduct to the dictates of the law may reap an incidental reward in that he is not arrested and called into court to answer for his behavior. But this is only incidental, and the law does not view itself, in failing to apply sanctions, as having rewarded the law-abiding citizen. The law imposes largely negative sanctions, and concerns itself with transgressors against the law. Second, unlike the other means of social control, the grounds for applying the negative sanctions are clearly identified under the law, the persons who make the decisions are determined by their official positions, the nature and extent of the sanctions which may be applied are set out, and the decision making process is governed by rules. What is even more important, all of these matters are determined *in advance*, and the offender against the law can ascertain in advance of his offense what conduct is unlawful, who will decide on his guilt or innocence, the limits of the punishment that he may receive, and the conditions under which he will be judged and sentenced.

Law is distinguishable from all other means of social control because the reasons for decision, the place of decision, the rules which govern decision making, and the limits of the sanctions are set out in advance. The individual knows before he undertakes the alleged act where, how, by whom, and under what conditions he will be judged. He knows what conduct has been declared illegal, and the limits of the punishments he may suffer. Usually, he has an appeal.

The Enforcement Process of the Law. There are some situations in which the basic processes of other agencies of social control resemble law. Thus, in a private club, the authority to establish rules may lie in a designated group of directors who resemble a legislature. Their rules may be set forth in advance, and the consequences of a violation may be a largely negative sanction (e.g., expulsion or a fine). The decision to impose such a sanction may be arrived at only after a formal hearing and the reasons for the decision may be given. Nevertheless, that process will still be lacking an essential element of the legal system; the enforcement of rules by the agencies of the political community, as opposed to the social, economic or religious community. The political community is an institution apart from other communities or groups because it involves, as Weber noted, "the forcible maintenance of orderly dominion over a territory and its inhabitants."[2] Religious groups or social groups may have considerable influence on their members, but they lack the ultimate territorial control that belongs to the political community, and it is this authority that is used to enforce the law.[3] Thus, law is defined as involving a "systematic and formal application of force by the state in support of explicit rules of conduct."[4] The word "state" in this definition means the same thing as "political community," for the "state is the supreme political community."[5] The significance is that while other rules are enforced by family or group, law is enforced by the government itself; if necessary, by the forces of the government, including the armed forces.

Before the government will enforce the law, it must initially be determined whether the law has been violated and, if so, what type of governmental sanction represents an appropriate response. In the American legal system (as in the English legal system from which it is derived), these tasks are largely those of the courts. The courts have the primary responsibility for interpreting the law and directing enforcement. They may be guided in this task by guidelines established by the legislatures, but the determination as to how those guidelines apply to the individual case is left to the courts.

Definition of Law. We now have seen the basic elements of law that distinguish it from all other means of social control. Putting those elements together, law can be defined as follows: *Law is a formal means of social control that involves the use of rules that are interpreted and are enforceable by the courts of a political community.*[6]

The Movement From Customs and Traditions to Law. All rules made by a society to insure social control are based upon value judgments made by that society. The society must identify those needs of the society which must be protected if the society is to survive. This usually requires the additional determination of which needs come first. If only some of the needs can be met, or if the needs cut up against each other, priorities must be set. For example, a society cannot have maximum order and maximum individual freedom at the same time. It must

---

2. Max Weber, *Law in Economy and Society*, ed. by Max Rheinstein, Cambridge, Mass.: Harvard University Press, 1954, p. 338.

3. If one thinks of the Jewish people before and after the establishment of Israel, the distinction can readily be seen. During the Diaspora, the Jewish people in various countries maintained themselves as a community, bound together by shared religious beliefs, customs, and traditions. They considered themselves a community and were recognized by others, including governments, as a community. However, it was not until Israel was established that there existed a political community with ultimate control over its own territories.

4. R. Redfield, *Primitive Law,* 33 Cincinnati L.Rev. 1, 3 (1964).

5. F. James Davis, Henry H. Foster, Jr., C. Ray Jeffery, E. Eugene Davis, *Society And The Law*, New York: The Free Press of Glencoe, 1962, p. 45.

6. F. Davis, et al., n. 5 *supra*, at p. 41.

make the value judgment of how much order will be sacrificed for individual freedom and how much individual freedom will be sacrificed for order. The society must decide what degree of deviance from expected norms of behavior will be accepted. In all societies a degree of deviancy which threatens the existence of the group will rarely be tolerated.

Once having made the value judgments that form the basis of its rules, the society must develop a method for insuring that the group will adhere to those rules. A primary element in achieving this object is the development of a process by which the values and norms of the society are transmitted to the individual—what we call the process of *socialization*. Means must be developed for passing on knowledge about the rules to the younger members of the group, and developing their natural acceptance of those rules. As a part of this process, means usually also must be developed for imposing fairly significant sanctions upon those who violate the more basic rules of the society. In a primitive society, group customs and traditions serve as the primary means for inculcating in the individual the value and norms of society and informing him about the acceptable limits of behavior. In a primitive society also, the sanctions for failure to adhere to those community rules are usually some form of group expression of disapproval. The most severe sanction is banishment from the group, which often is the equivalent, under the living conditions of the primitive society, to a sentence of death.

When the group is small, the process of socialization can rely primarily upon customs, traditions, and group morals; anti-social behavior can be controlled adequately by the family, tribe, or church. As the society grows, it becomes more diverse in activity and viewpoint. Informal community pressures also mean less. The constant close interrelationship of the various members of society is lost and with it goes the sting of most informal means of disapproval. Banishment or ostracism has much less impact when a person can readily move from one group to another and often feels he is not a part of any group. Finally, lines of leadership are not as well accepted. There may be one "head" for each family or tribe or one "elder" for a church group, but the society now may be composed of several tribes and churches. As these changes occur, a society will eventually move to the law as a means of socialization. What is needed is a system of formal rulemaking, capable of achieving community consensus, and carrying an effective system of sanctions in a diverse society. These are all features that can be provided by the legal system (although, as we shall see, not without countervailing costs).

FUNCTIONS OF THE LAW

Although the overall objective of law is accomplishing social control, it must perform various subsidiary functions to reach that goal. A complete list of the functions of law that foster social control would be lengthy indeed, but it is satisfactory for our purposes to examine five of the most obvious and basic functions: (1) achieving public order, (2) resolving basic value conflicts, (3) settling individual disputes, (4) allocating authority among different governmental agencies, and (5) making rules for the rulers.

Achieving Public Order. Although we often refer to the maintenance of "law *and* order" as two separate objectives, they really are part of the same process. The maintenance of the law—that is, adherence to the rules of law—should naturally also produce order. Indeed, the keeping of the peace ordinarily is viewed as the primary task of the law (as evidenced by the fact that law enforcement officers often are described as "peace officers"). Law can accomplish this task more effectively than other means of social control because, as we noted previously, it can bring to bear in its enforcement process the entire authority of the state. The enforcement machinery of the state provides tools to both prevent and punish illegal conduct. Police presence in the streets often serves to keep people from committing crimes. When laws are broken, moreover, the police are available to apprehend the violator. Once a person is taken into custody, the legal system can then turn to the courts to determine guilt and impose sentence. Finally, the legal system will provide special institutions to assist in applying that sentence. For example, if the sentence involves incarceration, that sanction may be carried out in jails or penitentiaries.

Of course, not all violations of the public order constitute crimes under the law. There also are so-called "civil" violations of the law, a concept we will explore in more detail in Chapter Two. It is sufficient to note here that the legal system also provides the machinery necessary to enforce behavioral standards found on this civil side of the law. Persons violating those standards may be subjected to various remedial requirements by the courts. These include the payment of money damages to persons injured by the violation, restoration of property improperly taken, or discontinuing activities that are found to be violative of the civil law. Courts not only can order such civil remedies, but they can ensure adherence to their civil orders by jailing persons who disobey them. Again, in the end, the law relies on the force of the state, the only body that we authorize to forcefully deprive a person of his liberty (and, in extreme cases, even his life).

Resolving Value Conflicts In Society. In a complex society, different groups are likely to have different views as to what is appropriate behavior. When those views come into conflict, it is essential to the maintenance of social order that the disagreement be resolved and that the resolution be accepted by the conflicting groups. If an acceptable resolution is not achieved, there will be inevitable confusion arising from the conflicting behavior of the different groups. In many areas, there also will be an almost inevitable attempt by one group to physically or economically force its view on the other groups. A major function of the law is in providing a means for peacefully resolving these basic value conflicts in society. Indeed, much of the process of enacting legislation involves the performance of exactly that function. Various groups with different values bring their conflicts to the legislature. In some instances, the contending groups will be dealing with the issue as to whether certain behavior should be prohibited by law. In others, it is whether certain behavior, now prohibited, should no longer be against the law. In either situation, the value conflicts come to a head and are resolved in the process of considering the enactment of a new law or the changing of an old law.[7]

As an illustration of the law's role in conflict resolution, consider the processing of a legislative proposal that the use of marijuana be legalized. In legislative

---

7. As we shall see in our discussion of judicial development of the common law in Chapters Two and Three the same type of resolution of basic values also is performed by the courts.

committees, on the floor of the senate and house, and in the news media, the pros and cons will be exhaustively discussed, sometimes quietly, more often, heatedly. Ultimately, the legislature will adopt one or the other of the opposing points of view, or a compromise will be arrived at. The legislature may do nothing, thus keeping in effect the state's existing laws making possession and use of marijuana a crime; it may remove possession and use of marijuana from the list of crimes and thus legalize its use; or it may simply reduce the penalty on the use of marijuana, which represents a kind of compromise between the conflicting positions. Either of the last two options will require a new statute, which must be passed by both legislative chambers and signed by the governor.

Of course, the controversy over marijuana does not automatically end when the law is passed or left unchanged, nor do all the people suddenly share the same value judgment about its use. Nevertheless, the law, as passed or left unchanged, expresses the dominant value judgment about the use of marijuana at the particular time and place. Once the law is passed or left unchanged, most people will abide by it. Even those who disagree with the law know that it may be changed in the future if the values of the minority become the values of the majority.

Settling Individual Disputes. Another basic function of the law is to settle individual disputes. Even though basic value conflicts have been resolved through adoption of a general rule of law, disputes arise in the course of applying that rule. These disputes may concern the interpretation of the legal standard or the facts in the particular case. The law says, for example, that if a homeowner fails to take proper care of his front steps, he will have to pay the hospital bills of one who trips and breaks a leg on those steps. But the homeowner and the injured party may disagree as to the meaning of the law (e.g., does the failure to put salt on icy steps during the winter constitute a lack of due care) or as to what happened in this case (e.g., did the owner actually put salt on the steps). The legal system is largely devoted to settling such legal or factual disputes. Indeed that is the primary function of the courts as they dispose of thousands of lawsuits each day.

The significance of dispute settlement can readily be appreciated if we consider what would happen if we did not have a peaceable method of settling disputes. Every man with a grievance against his neighbor would be tempted to "get even" through self-help. Fights would result, which would probably be joined in by family and kin of both parties. The result would be to damage the whole society as the disputes kept widening to take in more and more people and as the energy of the people became devoted to fighting each other instead of to the production of goods or protection of the state as a whole. As we will see later, it was just such a setting that led to the development of the criminal law.

Allocating Authority Among Different Governmental Agencies. The law also is charged with allocating authority among different governmental agencies. The people of a complex society must make choices as to the roles of various government agencies, and they ordinarily will express those choices in law. It is just as essential to avoid conflicts between governmental agencies as it is between individuals. While the agencies are unlikely to resolve their disputes through the use of physical force, a person subject to government regulation hardly views a society as orderly where two agencies are directing him to take opposing actions.

The need to allocate authority between different agencies becomes apparent when one thinks of all the new agencies that have come into existence in the last several years alone. Examples are agencies charged with responsibility for ensuring that the handicapped have adequate access to buildings, guarding against airplane hijackers, preventing pollution of our air and water, providing increased driving safety in automobiles, controlling sales of drugs and curing drug addiction, and putting a man on the moon. As government organization constantly changes, the law must constantly realign the division of authority among the new and old governmental agencies. Indeed, in a federal system such as ours, it also must specify the division of authority as between state and national governments.

Making Rules For The Rulers. Another important function of the law is to make rules for the conduct of persons in positions of governmental authority. When we say we believe in the rule of law, not men, we are expressing the fact that we insist that our rulers be governed by law. No official of the federal government and no state official has unlimited power. In our constitutional and statutory law we spell out what the President or the chief executive of a state can and cannot do; what the Congress or the state legislature can and cannot do; what the federal and state courts can and cannot do.

The first ten amendments to the federal Constitution, which are commonly described as our Bill of Rights,[8] are illustrative of our recognition of the need to control government officials. Because the colonists at the time of the revolution had suffered through various bad experiences with government officials, and with the courts in particular, they refused to ratify the Constitution until the first ten amendments were added. It was essential, they argued, that government officials be prohibited from using their authority to infringe upon important rights of the individual. Social order achieved at the sacrifice of those rights would not be worth its costs. Moreover, social order achieved by eliminating basic individual liberties was unlikely to survive; it only would produce another revolution against the laws and governments that deprived the citizenry of those liberties. The first ten amendments accordingly set out in great detail the rules limiting the authority of government, paying particular attention to the courts and their administration of the criminal law. Every state constitution similarly has its own "Bill of Rights," which seeks to protect the citizen in his encounters with the state government (again, with particular emphasis on the criminal justice system).

LIMITATIONS OF LAW

While the legal system has its obvious advantages in performing the five functions just discussed, it also has some significant limitations. Like all other social institutions, it operates imperfectly. Perhaps its major limitations are the following four: (1) law often cannot gain community support of its standards without the support of other social institutions; (2) even with community support, law cannot compel certain types of conduct contrary to human nature; (3) the law's resolution of disputes is dependent upon a complicated and expensive fact-finding process; and (4) law changes slowly.

---

8. These amendments and other provisions of the federal constitution are reprinted in Appendix C.

Inability to Guarantee Conformity Without Outside Institutional Support. The mere presence of a legal rule supported by the force of government does not necessarily ensure that the community will accept that rule. The most that law can do is to formally state the rule as expressing the dominant value of society and to seek to enforce it by imposing penalties against those who violate it. The success of these legal actions in achieving conformity often will depend upon the assistance supplied by non-legal institutions such as the family, church, and school. Law must depend upon these institutions for assistance in the socialization process. The family, the church, and the school transmit values to the individual, including the value of adherence to the law. If an action prohibited by law is one that generally is viewed as "wrong" according to the prevailing social values, the law will gain substantial adherence and enforcement will be relatively easy. Similarly, where the prohibited action is one that is viewed as neutral (i.e., neither clearly right nor wrong) and the legal prohibition does not impose a substantial burden on the individual, the basic cultural value of adherence to the law should combine with the threat of enforcement to achieve substantial conformity. Where, on the other hand, there is strong disagreement with the prohibition, and the activity is viewed as important to the individual, there is likely to be considerable disobedience notwithstanding a substantial effort to enforce the laws. Indeed, there are points at which the opposition will be so substantial that we will find systematic disobedience of the law by large groups of persons. Very widespread disobedience (sometimes described as "patterned evasion") usually will bring about a change in the law as it did with the repeal of prohibition.

Inability to Change Human Nature. Even where the law receives substantial support from the dominant non-legal institutions, it cannot force persons to act in certain ways that simply are contrary to human nature. The legal treatment of marriage is illustrative. The law traditionally has enunciated the dominant value that marriages should be preserved, and at various times, it has received full support in this area from such critical institutions as the church. Indeed, as late as the sixteenth century, the law of England, from which our marital law is drawn, refused to recognize the concept of divorce. While the law thus could preserve marriages in form, it hardly could force people to maintain certain aspects of the marital relationship. Even though supported by the teachings of other social institutions, it could not hope to force unwilling spouses to continue to show courtesy and respect for one another, or for that matter, even to continue to live together.

It should be noted that, while the legal system often cannot control basic human drives, that does not mean it has no impact upon activities involving those drives. Where supported by the teachings of other institutions, law arguably can exert some positive influence in encouraging restraint on the part of many individuals, although having little impact on many others. Most of our legislation prohibiting certain consensual sexual activities (e.g., homosexuality, adultery, intercourse by unmarried persons) is based on the assumption that law has this positive influence, although it is obvious that there will be substantial non-compliance as well. Much of the current debate over the retention of such legislation centers on whether the reinforcement from other institutions has so decreased as to largely eliminate the law's positive influence. Of course, assuming that the law has some positive influence in these areas, that influence may be offset by the impact of substantial non-compliance on general community respect for law. There are those who argue that the legal system as a whole is injured whenever the law seeks to control conduct that it simply cannot control, even though it acts with the support of other institutions.

Dependency Upon A Costly and Complex System of Proof. As we have seen, the law settles disputes through the judicial process. Disputes between individuals or between an individual and the state (as in criminal cases) are brought before a court, where it is determined whether there has been a violation of legal standards and, if so, what sanction should be applied to the violator. The process of making these determinations is complex, time-consuming, and costly as compared to most informal dispute-settling procedures. The legal process generally requires the participation of trained professionals representing each side of the dispute as well as a trained professional as judge. It requires that the parties establish through proofs the concrete factual situation to which the legal rules are to be applied. Establishing that fact situation often requires the production of numerous documents and witnesses. The process of determining the applicable legal standard, while it tends to be less time consuming, may also involve considerable research and effort.

The complexity of the judicial process, besides adding to the cost of the process, also introduces a potential for erroneous decision making. This is particularly true for the fact-finding aspect of the process, which is subject to natural difficulties (as well as possible misuse) in recalling past events. Situations arise when, for reasons completely out of the control of the law, considerable doubt will forever exist as to exactly what happened at a particular time and place. Witnesses may die, disappear, or moved to locations from which they cannot be compelled to return. Others may simply have forgotten or may have dim recollections. In addition, while the law seeks to prevent manipulation of the process, it is not always successful in doing so. Witnesses sometimes lie without their lies being discovered. Due to ignorance, poverty, or inadequate legal representation, parties to a lawsuit may fail to produce all the evidence in their favor. It is even possible that wrongdoers may bribe witness or arrange for them to be unavailable. In sum, while the legal process makes an earnest effort to discover the truth, this mission may be frustrated by natural events interfering with recollection and may be circumvented by the devious manipulations of those who do not want the truth to prevail.

Law Changes Slowly. Many people maintain that another limitation of the law is that it changes slowly. Others see this as one of the definite advantages of the law over alternative means of social control. The people who see law as changing too slowly point out that desirable social goals are often prevented or delayed because of outmoded laws. They point, for example, to laws relating to property ownership and collective enterprises that substantially delayed the development of beneficial economic relationships ranging from collective bargaining to condominium ownership of apartments. Those holding the opposite view call attention to the undesirable results that would be sure to follow if law changed every year, as does fashion. They note that desirable new practices eventually do receive the protection of the law, and that one test of the truly beneficial development is its ability to garner sufficient persistent support to gain recognition in the law.

In sum, the fact that law is a relatively stable force in a changing society is seen by some as a limitation on the law, by others as one of the great plus values of the law. It should be stressed, however, that while there is disagreement as to the desirable pace of change, everyone agrees as to the absolute need for change. They recognize that the law must constantly adapt to new values that achieve permanence in society. The law also must change to meet new problems presented by advances in technology. In the modern era of organ transplants, for example, the law must arrive at a new and more precise definition of death. The eternal genius of law, as some see it, has been the law's ability to so successfully adapt to various changes in society while remaining one of its most stable institutions.

THE IMPORTANCE OF LAW
IN ACHIEVING SOCIAL ORDER

We have examined several basic functions that law must accomplish in order to promote social order and several handicaps that limit its achievement of that goal. We now come to the crucial question: how well does the law perform in practice in achieving social order? In particular, to the extent that people do conform to the law, do they do so because of the influence of the law itself or of other social institutions? Nobody doubts the effectiveness of the law in regulating those areas of activity where there is no dominant sense of right or wrong and no strong drive to act in one way or another. Illustrative are the laws requiring that persons drive on the right side of the road, that money have a certain form, and that elections be held on a certain day. These are subjects that necessarily depend on law for regulation because other social institutions lack the interest or the general applicability necessary to regulate them. But what of those areas in which other institutions do set behavioral norms that the law largely incorporates? Do people conform to these norms largely because of the law or because of the socialization accomplished by those institutions? Unfortunately, there is no clear-cut answer indicating the exact contributions of law and other institutions.

Some scholars, pointing to the continuation of crime over the ages, argue that the law is of minor importance in achieving adherence to basic norms. They contend that the basic teachings as to right or wrong come from the family, church, or other social institutions, not the law, and that the threat of legal sanctions contributes little extra in gaining conformity. "After all," they argue, "we know that pickpockets picked pockets at the public hangings of other pickpockets." Other students of human behavior state that while it is easy to identify those who have ignored the edicts of the law, it is impossible to point out those who do conform their behavior to the social norms primarily because of the law. Proving the negative fact that law often does not succeed in its task of controlling behavior is easy enough. It is much more difficult to prove the affirmative fact that the law has probably worked well. There are certainly more law-abiding citizens than there are law violators and it may well be that law has played a primary role in their conformity.

It is not easy to provide empirical evidence as to the validity of either of these viewpoints. We seldom suspend the rule of law, so we really don't know what would happen in our society if we did. Certain events, however, have furnished a few clues. During the Boston police strike that brought Calvin Coolidge to national attention and ultimately to the Presidency, the city of Boston was in a shambles within hours after the police left the streets. Robbery, burglary, assault, rape, and other violent crimes increased many fold. Citizens were afraid to be on the streets; many locked themselves in their houses and refused to venture forth. Racketeers, hoodlums, and just plain criminals from all over the eastern seaboard, and later from all parts of the country, swarmed into Boston to take advantage of the fact that its citizens were without police protection. It was then that Calvin Coolidge, Governor of Massachusetts, declared the police strike itself illegal. In more recent times, a police strike in Montreal produced a similar result. A dramatic increase in all types of crime followed immediately upon the withdrawal of the police from the streets of that city. We have also witnessed substantial crime waves during electrical blackouts that left police at a considerable disadvantage in catching criminals.

The experiences of the Boston and Montreal police strikes and the electrical blackouts certainly suggest that law as symbolized by the police is a deterrent to antisocial acts. A careful examination of the change in society also suggests the same conclusion. Law must have played an increasingly significant role in gaining conformity to social standards as our society has grown more complex. When the individual lived closely within family and tribe, when he depended directly on their support for food and shelter, when earning their disapproval meant ostracism and death, the pressures on him to conform to the values and norms of the group were powerful indeed. On the other hand, family and peer group pressures are not so great in today's world, where the individual may make his living working for an impersonal corporation, have social contacts largely with strangers, and can find anonymity in the city almost without regard to the antisocial behavior in which he indulges himself. The restraints on his social conduct must come more substantially from the law.

SCOPE OF THE LAW

Social Values Expressed In Laws. In the development of a society, some rules become law; others do not. Some of the norms of the society become a part of the formal, coherent statements of rules and process that we call law; others remain in the realm of morals, manners, custom, and tradition. Some values of society are enforced by the state through its courts, which are supported by the maximum power of the state; other values are enforced, if at all, by informal group controls and by group sanctions which have behind them only the power of the particular group. This poses an interesting question: How do we determine which rules should be raised to the dignity of law, and which should not? What factors lead us to conclude that a certain norm is so important that it should be enforced by the courts, police, and other agencies of government while another must continue to depend upon group pressures and informal sanctions?

There are no absolute categories that determine precisely what norms will or will not be incorporated within the law. There are several factors, however, that serve as good signposts; they are not always controlling, but they generally point in the right direction. We will examine five of the more crucial of these factors: (1) whether the area of potential legal regulation concerns basic tasks of society; (2) whether the proposed legal rule reflects widely shared values; (3) whether the proposed rule is one about which people feel strongly; (4) whether the subject of regulation is one that requires uniformity in behavior in order to avoid dangerous conflicts; and (5) whether the proposed legal rule would impose behavioral standards that the law might have difficulty in enforcing.[9]

Essential Functions.   Achieving social control is most significant as to the performance of those tasks basic to any society. These key tasks are the gaining of food and shelter and the providing of protection against physical attack. Thus, we find that the behavioral norms adopted in primitive societies ordinarily started with prohibitions against taking another's life, food, or shelter. Closely related was the preservation of the family, which was the core organizational unit for the enjoyment of food or shelter. Almost all societies, for example, included among their early rules standards designed to preserve the family by preventing destruction of blood lines. Indeed, the prohibition against sexual relationship between immediate family members (incest) is so prevalent that it, perhaps even more than murder, is the prototype of the universally condemned offense.

If you were to review all of the major areas of legal regulation today, you would find that a majority of the regulated subjects still relate to the essential functions that concerned primitive societies—protection against physical attack, acquisition of food and shelter, and preservation of the family relationship. There are, of course, many other areas now reached by the law. The law today is concerned with protecting an individual's reputation as well as his person, with preservation of his enjoyment of entertainment as well as shelter. Nevertheless, when the decision is made as to whether a particular problem should be resolved by a legal rule, the fact that the problem relates to one of the essential functions of society will be a strong positive factor for a legal resolution. As between two areas, neither of which involves other elements suggesting legal regulation, the one relating to a basic societal function is likely to become a legal concern and the one without such a relationship is likely to be left to the control of other institutions. Comparison of two hypothetical situations, both involving innocent bystanders, is illustrative. In one situation, A's goods are stolen by B and sold to C; the issue posed is whether A or C should own the goods. In another, a school's athletic budget is cut and either A's sport or C's sport must be dropped from the program. In the first case, the related societal function (preserving property interests) is viewed as so important that the law must provide an answer—it must choose between the two innocent persons, the original owner and the later purchaser. In the second, the choice is left to school authorities and the law will not intervene. The interest of the sports participant simply is not significant enough to engage the authority of the law when there is no clearly right or wrong answer.

---

9.   Other relevant factors may include the community concern as to the degree of authority given to the government, the extent to which the enforcement agencies of government are otherwise overburdened, the extent to which law is needed to relieve other social institutions of substantial burdens that they carry in gaining adherence to behavioral norms.

General Acceptance. Although one might argue that there is less need for incorporating values within the law when those values are widely shared, the fact remains that universally accepted values are among those most commonly given legal recognition. When almost everybody agrees as to what is "right" and what is "wrong," we often desire to give the dignity of law to the "right" answer. Also, where there is a widespread acceptance of a particular value, persons who act in a contrary (i.e., "wrongful") manner tend to be viewed as committing a particularly flagrant offense, deserving the harsh sanctions that are imposed by the law. The original "common law crimes" are illustrative of this tendency to incorporate into law those standards as to which there is wide (and often deeply felt) community support. The common law crimes were offenses which the courts were ready to recognize as crimes on their own initiative (i.e., without legislation) because of the obvious criminality of the acts involved.[10] The common law crimes included many wrongdoings, such as murder and robbery, that had to be prohibited because of their relationship to the basic functions of society. But the common law also prohibited many other activities made criminal in large part because they were universally condemned by society. These included libel (injury to reputation), blasphemy, and general acts "corrupting morals," such as grave-snatching or parading naked in the streets.

Again, we must emphasize that the general condemnation of an act is only *one* factor considered by the courts or legislatures in determining whether the law should deal with that act. As we shall see shortly, not all acts prohibited by the law are generally condemned and not all generally condemned acts have been prohibited by the law. Other considerations may be more significant in a particular case. However, widespread condemnation of an act does increase the possibility that the social values prohibiting that act will be incorporated within the law.

Depth of Feeling. As we have seen, a primary function of the law is to resolve basic value conflicts between different groups in society. This function explains various laws which are based on values that obviously are not generally accepted in the community. Laws relating to the use of alcohol and marijuana, the political activities of corporations and unions, and the availability of abortions all reflect viewpoints on which society is sharply divided. The key here is that the issues are a matter of deep emotional concern to the interested parties. Where people feel especially strongly on an issue and realize that other groups disagree with equal vehemence, it often is their natural inclination to seek to have their viewpoint officially proclaimed the "correct" viewpoint through its incorporation in the law. And since at least the legislative (as opposed to the judicial) side of lawmaking is highly political, such persons often can be successful in achieving their objective, even though other criteria would suggest that the subject is not appropriate for legal regulation. Thus, a highly organized group that feels strongly on an issue can achieve legislative success even though their viewpoint lacks widespread community acceptance, the activity involved does not relate to the more basic functions of society, and the activity is not one requiring uniformity to avoid dangerous conflicts. Many of the legal regulations that have raised the most serious questions as

---

10. The nature of the common law and common law crimes will be discussed further in Chapters Two and Four.

to the effectiveness of the law are the product of just such organized pressure on the legislative process. This is true, for example, of such legislation as Sunday closing laws, and laws prohibiting the sale by the drink of alcholic beverages.[11]

Inherent Conflicts. There are areas which the law simply must take hold and regulate in order to avoid dangers that would be created by conflicting patterns of behavior. There may be no widely accepted or strongly felt views as to the rules involved, but simply a need for a uniform rule. Perhaps the best illustration of such a legal standard is the one that requires us to drive on the right side of the road. Of course, after such a rule is adopted, a proper sense of morals may require all travelers to know and obey it, but generally shared community views as to rightness or wrongness had nothing to do initially with the selection of the right side over the left. A choice simply had to be made and enforced by the only institution whose rules have a general applicability to all persons—that is, the law.

Enforcement Difficulties. We have looked so far only at those factors which favor legal enforcement of a behavioral standard. There also are substantial countervailing factors that often lead lawmakers not to incorporate a standard within the law, even though it relates to basic societal functions, is universally condemned, or otherwise has characteristics suggesting incorporation. Perhaps the most significant of these factors is the high cost that might be involved in enforcing the standard. Such costs might relate to a variety of factors, including involvement of the government in undesirable activity or straining of the fact-finding processes of the law.

Illustrative of situations presenting enforcement costs of the first type—i.e., requiring undesirable government activity—are those areas in which legal prohibitions can only be enforced through governmental invasions of privacy. In recent years, several jurisdictions have repealed laws prohibiting consensual, homosexual sodomy because, in part, they sought to avoid such enforcement costs.[12] Thus, some legislators have supported repeal while noting that they did not view homosexuality as morally acceptable and they believed their constituents almost universally shared that view. Indeed, they even acknowledged that homosexuality might, in some instances, constitute a threat to the basic societal value of family preservation. Nevertheless, they contended that the law should not prohibit consensual homosexual acts because enforcement would require methods of spying and enticement that are not appropriate for government enforcement agencies. Consensual acts ordinarily take place in private places, they argued, and enforcement of a legal prohibition against such acts would necessarily require government invasion even of bedroom privacy. The value of the legal prohibition, in their estimation, would not outweigh such costs.

---

11. It should be noted, however, that some legislation which appears to be in this category actually reflects a situation in which the law reflected a universally accepted value when adopted, but now has substantially less support (such as provisions making it a crime to use indecent language in the presence of women).

12. It is always difficult to point to a precise reason for legislative movement. Obviously, some legislators have been swayed by other factors—e.g., the view that homosexual activity is not immoral, does not threaten the family, etc. Nevertheless, costs of enforcement has been a primary consideration in the repeal movement.

In other areas, lawmakers have refused to incorporate widely accepted standards of morality because they were concerned that the fact-finding process of the law might not be suited to the application of those standards. The treatment of the good samaritan is illustrative. Everybody agrees that if one should pass by an infant helplessly struggling in a shallow pool, the "right" thing to do is to help him out. The person who stands by and callously watches the infant drown is universally condemned. Yet the law will not impose a duty on the passerby to play the good samaritan. To do so would raise various problems of proof. Surely the passerby should not be condemned if he thought the infant was playfully splashing rather than struggling in the water. Yet can a potential passerby be sure that the jury will believe him when he says that he didn't know the infant was struggling? Will persons, to avoid potential liability, be forced to take upon themselves the obligation of checking into every potentially suspicious situation? Would the passerby now be tempted to step out and help the infant even though he sees the mother nearby and believes she probably is in the process of teaching the infant not to fear the water? What if the passerby is a surgeon enroute to an essential activity, perhaps helping to save the life of another? As the situation becomes more and more complex, the legal fact-finding process must be capable of making more and more subtle distinctions. Moreover, its capacity to do so must be clear. If there is any doubt as to that capacity, persons whose actions are entirely proper will nevertheless alter their behavior so as to guard against possible fact-finding error that could result in their legal liability. In various areas, such as the treatment of the good samaritan, lawmakers have concluded that the costs involved—particularly the difficulties involved in coping with the subtle distinctions presented by the subject—are so great that they offset the desirability of granting statutory recognition to a basic moral obligation.

Overbearing costs of enforcement often include various other elements beyond those noted in our two illustrations. In some situations, such as those involving family relations, use of legal enforcement may be counter-productive to the basic object of the societal standard (e.g., preservation of the family). In other areas, moral or ethical standards are so ambiguous that their incorporation in the law would be inconsistent with the general requirement that the law provide fairly specific advance notice of the activities it prohibits. The end result is that we find many areas where the law does not incorporate widely accepted standards of morality and ethics. For example, to refuse to perform a promise deliberately made, where there has been no change in circumstance and there is no other excuse, is not in keeping with high ethical standards; but unless the promisor has received something that converted the promise into a contract, the law leaves the promisor free to ignore his promise. The law is not saying thereby that it approves the breaking of the promise or does not appreciate the injustice to the other party. It is saying only that, for a variety of reasons relating to the role of the law and its capacity to enforce societal standards, this societal standard simply is not appropriate for inclusion within the law.

POUND'S POSTULATES

If one were to attempt to list all of the values which are reflected in the rules of law, that list could well occupy most of the remaining pages in this book. There arguably are, however, a smaller range of most basic values that lie at the heart of the law. Roscoe Pound, one of the most famous of all legal scholars, addressed himself to those values in his *Jural Postulates.* [13] Pound began with the statement, "In a civilized society men must be able to assume: . . ." and went on to analyze the interests which a person living in a civilized society should be able to expect the law to secure. We will set forth here Pound's *Jural Postulates*, and then give examples of the specific ways in which the law, particularly the criminal law, attempts to protect those interests.

> **Postulate I.** *In a civilized society men must be able to assume that others will commit no intentional aggressions upon them.*

The criminal law punishes any kind of intentional injury inflicted upon one person by another. If death results, the offense is one of the homicide offenses punishable by imprisonment or, in some cases, by death. If the victim does not die, the offender may be guilty of aggravated assault if serious injury is inflicted, or of simple assault if the injury is minor. Robbery, which involves the taking of property from the person of another by putting him in fear, is punishable by long terms of imprisonment.

> **Postulate II.** *In a civilized society men must be able to assume that they may control for beneficial purposes, what they have discovered or appropriated to their own use, what they have created with their own labor, and what they have acquired under the existing social and economic order.*

The law's protection of private property carries out this postulate. Thus, a person is guilty of one of the theft offenses if he takes property in possession of another person. It is a crime to steal various kinds of property, including that which the victim had taken for himself from its natural state. For example, the law makes it a crime to take a wild horse which another person has tamed and kept in his corral for his use, or to divert to one's own fields water which another has dammed. Legal remedies are also provided for the illegal use of another's property. Indeed, the law even provides a means (patents) whereby certain ideas can be protected from the unauthorized use by another.

> **Postulate III.** *In a civilized society men must be able to assume that those with whom they deal in general intercourse of society will act in good faith and hence (a) will make good reasonable expectations which their promises or other conduct reasonably create; (b) will carry out their undertakings according to the expectations which the moral sentiment of the community attaches thereto; (c) will restore specifically, or by equivalent, what comes to them by mistake, or the failure of the presupposition of a transaction, or other unanticipated situation whereby they receive at another's expense what they could not reasonably have expected to receive under the actual circumstances.*

There are many illustrations of laws that carry out the principles expressed in Postulate III(a). Thus, the law makes it a crime to sell stock in a "salted" mine. So

---

13. Roscoe Pound. *Jurisprudence.* St. Paul, Minnesota: West Publishing Co., 1959, Vol. 1, pp. 367-456.

too, it is a crime to pass a bad check. Some states still even permit an action for damages based on a breach of promise to marry. And if a male gains a female's consent to sexual intercourse by a false promise of marriage, he will be guilty of the crime of "seduction" in some states.

The law protects the interests stated in Postulate III(b) in various ways. Thus, it requires that people who marry each other not commit adultery; that a man support his wife if he is able and that parents support their children if they are able; and that persons selling liquor refrain from selling their wares to minors.

In accordance with Postulate III(c), a person is required to return to the owner money he finds, if the owner can be located; a merchant is required to return the down payment on the refrigerator if he cannot deliver the refrigerator. An owner of real estate, under certain circumstances, may be required to pay for a road built on his premises by mistake, if he knew a mistake was being made and said nothing while the work was performed.

Postulate IV. *In a civilized society men must be able to assume that those who engage in some course of conduct will act with due care not to cast an unreasonable risk of injury upon another.*

The criminal law imposes responsibility for both reckless and negligent conduct which injures another. A primary illustration is the traffic laws, which prohibit various uses of an automobile that are likely to injure others. The most dangerous uses, driving while intoxicated and reckless driving, can lead to significant criminal sanctions and loss of license. If an accident results in serious injury and there has been a lack of due care, a damage remedy also is available to the person injured.

Postulate V. *In a civilized society men must be able to assume that others who maintain things or employ agencies harmless in the sphere of their use but harmful in their normal action elsewhere, and having a natural tendency to cross the boundaries of their proper use, will restrain them or keep them within proper bounds.*

We will see in the law of arson that a man who is lawfully burning off the weeds on his own land may be guilty of negligent burning if he lets the fire escape to his neighbor's land. Similarly, a circus must take extreme precautions that its wild animals do not get loose and cause injury to persons or property. Use of weapons is particularly closely regulated. Indeed, the requirement of due care is even applied to a police officer acting in the line of duty; he cannot use his weapon where its use will cause serious danger to innocent bystanders. In some states, even without such danger, he cannot use it unless deadly force is needed to protect against a threat to life or to arrest a dangerous felon.[14]

---

14. For further information on the subjects covered in this chapter, see F. Davis, et al., note 5 *supra*; L. Friedman, *Law and Society: An Introduction*, Englewood Cliffs, N.J.: Prentice-Hall, 1977; J.W. Hurst, *Law and Social Order In The United States*, Ithaca, N.Y.: Cornell University Press, 1977.

Chapter 2

The Classification of Laws

Law, like any other field of scholarly study, has its own system of classification. A person studying any one field of law should be aware of various other fields in the law, just as one studying one field of science (e.g., chemistry) should be aware of other scientific subjects (e.g., geology, physics, astronomy). There are three basic lines of division in the law that are particularly helpful in understanding the law governing the criminal justice system: (1) distinctions based upon the type of government, federal or state, which issues a legal standard; (2) distinctions based upon the particular governmental agency that establishes a legal standard; and (3) distinctions based upon the type of control imposed by the standard. With an understanding of these basic divisions, you can more readily appreciate the special place of the law governing the criminal justice system within the total range of the law. The divisions also ease analysis of any individual field of law, such as criminal justice, by identifying the basic sources of the law that contribute to the field.

FEDERAL AND STATE LAW

In our federal system of government, legal standards are established and enforced by both federal and state governments. Some subjects, such as the relations with foreign countries, are governed exclusively by federal law. Other fields, such as divorce, adoptions, and other family relationships, are governed exclusively by state law (except for persons living in federal territories, such as the District of Columbia). In many other fields, including that of criminal law enforcement, both federal and state law may apply to different aspects of the subject. In Chapter Four, we will discuss the division between federal and state criminal laws in some detail. It is sufficient to note at this point that both federal and state governments have their own criminal laws and their own law enforcement machinery. Each has its own courts, prosecutors, and law enforcement officers with primary responsibility for enforcing its own laws. Popular impressions notwithstanding, the Federal Bureau of Investigation does not have authority to investigate every crime that occurs within the United States.[1] The Bureau's basic police authority is limited to apprehending persons who violate federal law, although there may be cooperative efforts with state officials when both federal and state laws are violated. In areas in which both federal and state law operate, there may be occasional conflicts between the two. For example, Congress, in the exercise of its power to regulate interstate communications, may prohibit electronic eavesdropping (wiretapping) of telephone conversations except under limited circumstances.[2] A state, on the other hand, may seek to authorize local police to engage in wiretapping (for the purpose of investigating local crime) under conditions that are prohibited by the federal legislation. In such a situation, the law of the federal government controls, since our basic structure of government, as set forth in the federal constitution, makes the federal law supreme in any area which the federal government may lawfully regulate.[3] The state's interest in law enforcement eavesdropping accordingly must give way to Congress' power to protect the telephone system in the manner that it deems most appropriate. Fortunately, conflicts between federal and state legislation in the criminal justice field are fairly rare (although, as we shall see, the federal constitution does have considerable bearing on the state criminal justice systems).

FORMS OF LAW

Legal rules may be found in various forms, which depend primarily upon the particular type of governmental agency establishing the rule. Constitutional conventions, legislatures, administrative agencies and courts all establish legal rules, and each of these institutions will present the rule in a somewhat different form. Legal standards adopted by constitutional conventions are found in constitutions, standards adopted by legislatures are found in statutes, standards adopted by administrative agencies are found in administrative regulations, and standards adopted by courts are found in opinions commonly described as "case law." Not all of these forms of law have a bearing on the regulation of every legal subject, but the criminal justice system is one subject to which they all do apply (though not with equal weight). In the course of our discussion of specific laws governing the criminal justice system, we will make frequent mention of constitutions, statutes, and case law and occasional reference to administrative regulations. You should be familiar with each of these forms of law and their relationship to each other.

---

1.   A more detailed discussion of the federal law enforcement structure, including the F.B.I. is contained in Chapters Four and Fifteen.

2.   See pp. 257-59 *infra*.

3.   Article VI of the federal constitution provides: "This Constitution, and the Laws of the United States which shall be made in Pursuance thereof; and all Treaties made, or which shall be made, under the Authority of the United States, shall be the supreme Law of the Land; and the Judges in every State shall be bound thereby, any Thing in the Constitution or Laws of any State to the Contrary notwithstanding."

Constitutions. Both the federal government and the state governments have constitutions, i.e., written documents which set forth the general organization of government and basic standards governing the use of governmental authority. The federal constitution is the supreme law of the land, and its prevails over all other kinds of law, both federal and state.[4] Thus, a law in conflict with the federal constitution—whether a state constitutional provision, or a state or federal statute, administrative regulation, or case law ruling—is without legal force and will not be enforced by the courts. This preeminence of the federal constitution is reflected in the common practice of simply using the phrase "the Constitution" to refer to the federal constitution. The state constitutions are placed at a lower level in the hierarchy of the different forms of law, but they still are quite significant. Their relationship to other forms of *state* law is similar to the federal constitution's relationship to all other forms of law. State constitutional rules are supreme as compared to rules coming from all other state legal sources (e.g., state statutes) and prevail over such laws in cases of conflict.

Legislation. The state legislatures and the federal Congress are continuously adopting legal rules in the form of statutes, i.e., written statements of governing standards ordinarily enacted into law by an affirmative vote of both chambers of the legislature (i.e., Senate and House of Representatives) and acceptance by the chief executive. The legislatures may also establish legal standards through other, less frequently utilized procedures. Thus the state legislatures make law through compacts entered into by several states and the United States Senate makes law through its approval of treaties between the United States and other countries. Statutes remain the primary form of law enacted by legislatures, however, and the term "legislation," referring to law adopted by the legislature, commonly is used only with respect to statutes. The legislative bodies of local governments[5] also have lawmaking authority exercised through the enactment of "ordinances," which are the local counterparts of statutes. However, the permissible scope of the local ordinances tends to be rather limited for most subjects. In the criminal justice field, local ordinances in most states will not provide any significant rules beyond those found in state statutes.

A government's capacity to adopt legislation commonly is described as its *legislative jurisdiction.* The word "jurisdiction" refers to the legal power to take a certain type of action, and the phrase "legislative jurisdiction" therefore refers simply to the authority to enact legislation. Quite often the term "jurisdiction" is used by itself to refer to a government with legislative authority in a particular

---

4. The "supremacy clause" of the federal constitution, quoted in note 3 *supra*, establishes the supremacy of the federal constitution over state laws. The Supreme Court held in the famous decision of *Marbury v. Madison*, 5 U.S. (1 Crach) 137, 2L.Ed.60 (1803), that as between the federal constitution and laws adopted by Congress, the Constitution also reigns supreme. Congressional enactments in conflict with the Constitution, as interpreted by the courts, are deemed "unconstitutional" and therefore not enforceable. This authority of the courts to invalidate federal (and state) laws that are inconsistent with the Constitution is commonly known as the authority of judicial review. See W. Lockhart, Y. Kamisar, J. Choper, *Constitutional Law*, St. Paul, Minn.: West Publishing Co., 1975, ch. 1.

5. The term "local government" is used here to include all governments having some legislative authority over particular areas within the state, including counties, parishes, cities, townships, villages, etc.

area. Thus instead of saying that several states have adopted a particular type of legislation, commentators will note that several "jurisdictions" have adopted that legislation. In the criminal justice field, the governments with legislative authority are the state governments and the federal government. (While local governments technically also have such authority, their authority is so limited that it generally is ignored in describing the state of the law in the field.) Accordingly, when commentators or courts refer to the various "jurisdictions" operating in this field, they include the federal as well as the state governments. When they say that all or most "jurisdictions" follow a certain criminal justice rule, they are saying that all or most of a group of fifty-one jurisdictions, consisting of the fifty state governments and the federal government, follow that rule. In this book, we will use the term "jurisdictions" in a similar fashion.

Administrative Regulations.   As society has become more complex, the federal and state legislatures have recognized that they cannot keep up with the task of enacting legislation that provides complete coverage of all subjects that must be regulated by law. Accordingly, for various subjects, legislatures have enacted statutes setting forth general guidelines, and delegated to other governmental bodies the task of adopting more detailed regulations within those guidelines. The governmental bodies given this authority are commonly called administrative agencies. At the federal level, such agencies include the Interstate Commerce Commission and the National Labor Relations Board. At the state level, typical administrative agencies include the state Corrections Commission and the state Public Utilities Commission. The laws issued by administrative agencies are described by lawyers as "administrative regulations." They are enforceable by courts, provided that the agency has acted within the scope of its delegation from the legislature. In many instances, similar authority to enact legal rules has been given to the President by Congress and to a governor by a state legislature. The rules established by these executive officers pursuant to such legislative delegation of authority commonly are called "executive orders." Administrative regulations and executive orders tend to concentrate on the internal operations of government (e.g., civil service regulations) and the regulation of industry (e.g., industrial safety regulations), but, as we shall see, they do play a role in regulating some aspects of the criminal justice system.

One unusual form of administrative regulation deserves special attention in examining the criminal justice system, and that is the "court rule." When we think of judicially created legal rules, we usually focus only on legal standards established by courts in the process of deciding cases—so called "case law," which we will discuss shortly. Courts also establish new legal standards, however, through "court rules." These rules are adopted by the highest court in the particular jurisdiction for the purpose of regulating the procedures followed in the lower courts in that jurisdiction. Unlike the traditional case law, court rules are not announced in the course of resolving a lawsuit involving disagreement over lower court procedures. Rather, they are adopted on the higher court's own initiative as basically the administrative regulations for the court system. Court rules ordinarily are limited in scope to governing the procedures for presenting cases before the courts of the particular jurisdiction. Those rules may be very significant, however, in the administration of the criminal justice process, since the fairness of procedures is a key element of that process (as we shall see). Many key procedural rights of the defendant, such as the right to a prompt trial, may be governed by court rule rather than statute in a particular jurisdiction.

Case Law. The term *case law* commonly is used to describe the rules of law announced in court decisions. In many instances, the case law will be based upon an interpretation of the other sources of law already noted. The rule announced in the judicial decision will reflect the court's reading of a constitution, statute, or administrative regulation. The case law then merges, in a sense, with the other forms of law. Once the courts have interpreted a constitutional, statutory, or administrative provision, the "law" on the subject consists of both the original source and its interpretation in the case law. Moreover, the prevailing meaning of the provision is that given to it by the courts' interpretation (unless the provision is subsequently amended). Although the language as set forth in the statute, constitution, or administrative regulation might suggest a contrary interpretation to the ordinary reader, it is the interpretation of the courts—the case law—that governs.

Not all case law is based upon a court's interpretation of the other sources of law. Some of the legal standards applied in judicial decisions are based upon a court's authority to create its own rules, as needed to decide the case before it, where constitutions, statutes, or administrative regulations do not provide a relevant legal standard. Such totally judge-made law is known as the *common law*. The authority of the courts to create common law rules has a long tradition that explains, to a large extent, the extensive role played by American courts in shaping the law in various fields, including criminal justice.

The Common Law. The common law tradition dates back to a shift in the role of the English courts following the Norman Conquest of England in 1066. The Normans sought to ensure that a standard body of law was applied by the courts throughout England. Prior to that time, disputes had been resolved according to local social patterns, customs, and similar norms. The King's Court now sent its representatives throughout the country to decide cases according to the "true usage and custom" of the land. There eventually developed a common pattern of decisions which became known as the common law of England. As the judicial decisions became more numerous, the most significant were recorded in Year Books, which served as a handbook of legal principles applied by the courts of the time. When a judge faced a legal dispute essentially like one that was decided before, he could readily resolve it in light of the decisions recorded in the Year Books. When the case was somewhat different than those previously decided, he was forced to create new law, but could shape that law in light of the general principles suggested in the earlier cases.

When the English settled in the new world, they brought with them their common law rules and tradition. Later, when the colonies achieved independence, they retained the English common law rules and the authority of judges to create new rules through their development of the common law. The common law method was ideally suited to the new country because of its capacity to provide both stability and change. Since the common law developed from case to case, it readily could change to meet social and economic changes. At the same time, since courts relied on the pattern of prior decisions, there was a steady sense of direction.

Originally American courts relied largely on English decisions in developing the common law, but as the number of American decisions grew, the American courts began to rely more and more on their own decisions. At the same time, differences in social and economic conditions (and to some extent, differences in the personalities of the judges) led the courts in different states to take different views of the common law. As a result, while the English tradition produced a core of similarity, there developed significant differences in common law rules in the various states. Thus, the common law standard governing an officer's authority to arrest for minor crimes might be substantially different in Ohio and New York, although the general framework of the common law governing arrests was likely to be similar in both states.

When courts or commentators today speak of "common law rules," it is not always clear to which common law they are referring. At times, our concern is with common law as it was first incorporated in this country, i.e., the common law of England at the time of the revolution. When the United States Supreme Court contends that a provision of the federal constitution should be interpreted in light of its common law background, it is to this English common law that they usually refer. In other instances, we are concerned with the common law as it exists today. When this is the case, the diverse development of the common law among the various states makes it difficult to characterize a particular rule as a universal common law rule, applicable in all states. Accordingly, statements describing a rule as *the* common law rule of today usually means only that the rule reflects the dominant common law position, adopted in a substantial majority (but not necessarily all) of the states. In this book, the original common law will be described as the English common law. References simply to "the common law" refer to the common law in the United States and, unless we indicate otherwise, restate the dominant common law position applied in the majority of the states.

The Mix of Common Law and Legislative Law. Our country, along with other countries that followed the English common law, usually is described as having a "common law legal system." This description is used to contrast our legal system with that of the European "civil law" countries. Under the civil law system, the exclusive initial source of law is the legislative "code" (i.e., a statute or group of statutes that seek to set forth all legal standards governing a particular subject) and the courts have no common law authority.

Though the description of the Anglo-American system as a "common law legal system" notes an important distinction between it and the civil law system, that description should not lead one to ignore the fact that legislation also constitutes an important source of law in the Anglo-American system. That system is actually a "mixed" system of common law rules and statutory rules. The common law rules established by American and English courts have always been subject to displacement by legislative enactments. Indeed, the courts have authority to develop common law standards only where the legislatures have not sought to provide legislative solutions.[6] In almost every major field, there has been some legislative displacement of the common law ever since the English Parliament first became active in the passage of legislation. In various fields, such as criminal law, there has been a gradual movement toward more and more reliance on legislation. The legislative codes have been made more complete and detailed, leaving fewer matters for judicial development through the common law. This trend has been particularly noticeable over the past thirty years, as legislatures have met more frequently and have developed substantial legal staffs. Of course, the replacement of the common law by statute does not render the common law irrelevant to the future development of the law. In many instances, the statutes have done nothing more than codify (i.e., restated in statutory form) the common law rule. When interpreting such statutes, courts must rely heavily on the earlier common law decisions. Where statutes clearly have departed from the common law rule, the courts still may look to common law principles to help them understand the nature and range of the departure. Certain constitutional provisions also may be interpreted in light of their common law background. Finally, the common law developed a judicial methodology which, as discussed in Chapter Three, has been carried over to all aspects of judicial decision making, including the interpretation of constitutional and statutory provisions apart from their common law backgrounds.

METHOD OF REGULATION

Laws also can be categorized by the manner in which they seek to regulate a particular subject matter. The primary distinctions of this type are those drawn between criminal and civil laws and between procedural and substantive laws.

Criminal and Civil Law. Most persons are aware of at least some aspects of the differences between those legal rules that are part of the criminal law and those that are part of the civil law. They know, for example, that certain activities of individuals, such as theft, are designated as crimes and may result in the individual's imprisonment. They know also that other activities, such as an accident damaging another's property, also may produce court action, but the individual will be required to do no more than pay financial compensation to the owner of the property. They probably also know that the lawsuit based on the criminal act is brought by a government official, a prosecutor, and is called a criminal prosecution, while the lawsuit based on the accidental destruction of property will be brought by the owner of the property and will be called a civil suit. These differences reflect some of the more significant distinctions between the fields of criminal and civil law. In large part, those distinctions flow from the underlying difference in the objectives of the civil and criminal divisions of the law. The criminal law, simply put, is aimed at controlling wrongful acts by the imposition of punishment. The civil law, on the other hand, is not limited to dealing with wrongful acts, and where it does deal with such acts, it is not designed to impose punishment.

---

6. In our country, the common law also is subject to the legal limitations imposed by federal and state constitutions. The supremacy of the constitutions extends over all other forms of law, including the common law. Just as legislation cannot violate a constitutional limitation, neither can a common law rule.

In its very act of designating prohibited activity as a "crime," the criminal law is stating that the activity constitutes such a threat or affront to society that it deserves the highest degree of moral condemnation. The civil law, on the other hand, is not concerned primarily with "wrongful" activity. It often provides rules for adjustments of conflicting interest where neither party is at fault. Thus, it governs such matters as the division of wealth among family upon a relative's death, the creation and dissolution of marriage, and the form of arrangements between people for conducting business (e.g., partnerships, corporations). Of course, there are many areas where the civil law does deal with wrongful acts, but very often those acts, like the negligence involved in an auto accident, lack the high degree of immorality ordinarily associated with criminal acts. Finally, where the civil law does deal with activities so wrongful as to be appropriate subjects of criminal action, such as the intentional infliction of physical harm, the objective of the civil law still differs dramatically from that of the criminal law. The civil law is primarily concerned with assuring that the victim of the wrongful action is compensated for his injuries, while the criminal law seeks primarily to prevent recurrence of the act by condemning the act and inflicting punishment upon the actor.

The distinction in the objectives of the criminal and civil law readily explains the differences in the form of the legal actions used to enforce the two types of law. Since the criminal law deals with acts condemned as against the general interests of society, the legal action to enforce the criminal law quite naturally is brought by a government official, usually the prosecuting attorney, as the representative of the total community, not just the victim of the crime. The prosecutor's representative capacity is reflected in the very title of the legal action. It is not the prosecutor, Joe Brown, against the defendant, John Jones, but "The People" or "The State" or "The United States" against defendant, John Jones.[7] In the civil suit, on the other hand, since the purpose, even in dealing with wrongful acts, is only to compensate the injured party, the injured party himself brings the suit and does so in his own name. The case is titled Bill Smith (the person suing, who is called a "plaintiff") against the defendant John Jones.[8]

The distinction in the objectives of civil and criminal law also explains the differences in the remedies that may be imposed under these two divisions of the law. Both, for example, may require the losing defendant to pay money, but they measure the amount and direct the payment quite differently. In civil law, the amount paid (called "damages") will be measured by the harm done to the plaintiff[9] and will be paid to the plaintiff. In the criminal case, the amount paid (called a "fine") will be measured by the actor's fault and the need to deter recurrence of

---

7. The official title would be *State of Wyoming v. Jones*, with the letter v. standing for "versus," which means "against." Courts and commentators discussing the case often would refer to it, once the full title is given, simply by the name of the defendant—i.e., as the *Jones* case.

8. In some civil cases, the suit may be brought by the government through its legal officers, and the case may be titled, for example, *United States v. John Jones*. But the United States in such cases usually is suing as the injured party itself, rather than in the representative capacity involved in criminal cases. This would be true, for example, where John Jones' automobile accident involved damage to a government vehicle.

9. One narrow exception to this principle, beyond the scope of our analysis, is the "punitive" or "exemplary" damage award, which is available in limited types of civil actions. See D. Dobbs, *Remedies,* St. Paul, Minn.: West Publishing Company, 1973, p. 204-221.

the crime. Also, the fine will not be paid to the victim of the criminal act, but to some general fund designated by the state (e.g., the library fund or a school fund). Since the crime is prohibited as an offense against the people as a whole, the fine will be used to benefit the people as a whole.

Similar distinctions explain why only the criminal law may impose the sanction of the imprisonment. Confinement in a prison is the most drastic sanction commonly used in our society,[10] and it accordingly is limited in application to that field of law that seeks moral condemnation of the actor and his actions. Moreover, while imprisonment serves the criminal law's objective of preventing further offenses, it generally would not serve the civil law's objective of assisting the injured party. Confinement is an appropriate remedy under the civil law in a few situations, but its function there remains quite different from imprisonment. Thus, confinement in a mental hospital may be ordered when a mentally ill person poses a danger to himself or is unable to care for himself. The confinement is based, however, on the premise of helping the injured party, who is the patient. It is not designed to aid in the condemnation of his actions or to forewarn others, and it lasts only so long as the patient needs the confinement to help himself. As our later discussions will show,[11] rehabilitation also is an objective of the criminal law, but it is not, as compared with the civil commitment of the mentally ill, the basic objective of the criminal law. Indeed, many commentators would say that the sanction of imprisonment reveals that rehabilitation is, at most, a minor concern of the criminal law.

Overlap Of Criminal and Civil Law. To assist in analysis, scholars commonly separate the civil law into various branches according to the type of activity being regulated. Thus, they concentrate on such separate fields as family law (marriage, divorce, etc.), admiralty (law of the sea), inheritance (wills), business associations (partnership, corporations), and labor relations (collective bargaining, minimum wage laws, etc.). Most of these branches of the civil law have only a limited relationship to the criminal law. In almost every branch, the civil law will deal with some acts that also will be crimes. For example, in the field of labor law, some violations of the rules governing union electioneering (e.g., the use of bribes and threats) also constitute crimes. However, most of the activities covered in the civil fields will not overlap with the criminal law.

The one major exception to the limited relationship of civil and criminal law is that branch of civil law called "torts." The law of torts deals with those injuries inflicted upon a person for which the civil law awards money damages as compensation. It governs many harmful acts (e.g., automobile accidents) that are not sufficiently wrongful to constitute crimes. On the other side, the criminal law encompasses various acts (e.g., possession of burglar weapons) which cause no immediate harm and therefore are not torts. Nevertheless, there is considerable overlap in the coverage of the two fields of law. Most crimes that involve a direct infliction of injury to person or property also constitute torts. The actor not only can be prosecuted for the crime, but he also can be sued for the commission of a

---

10. Capital punishment, the taking of life, is the most drastic of all available sanctions, though not commonly used. It also may be used only in criminal cases. See p. 334 *infra*.

11. See Chapter Four.

tort in a civil action. If one commits murder, steals property, kidnaps another, intentionally burns another's house, or forges a valuable document, he is likely to be liable for damages under the civil law as well as subjected to criminal punishment. Our attention in this book will be devoted to the individual's criminal liability, but the possibility of civil liability should be keep in mind in evaluating the total response of the law to any particular wrongful act.

Substantive and Procedural Law. Another common classification of law divides it into two categories, substantive and procedural law. This classification exists apart from the criminal/civil division. Both criminal and civil law can be either procedural or substantive depending upon the particular phase of the subject which the law is treating. Substantive law lays down the basic guidelines for determining the legality of a particular act. It is the substantive law which tells us what we can and cannot do in our relationships with others. In the field of criminal law, for example, the statutes which define crimes are substantive laws. Similarly, in the field of labor relations, a law which states when a strike is or is not permitted is a substantive law. Procedural law, on the other hand, is that law which tells us how we may enforce the substantive law. It defines the process (i.e., procedures) of the law, dealing with such subjects as the method of determining whether the substantive law has been violated. In the field of criminal law, procedural law encompasses the processes followed in investigating crimes, apprehending the offender, determining his guilt or innocence, and applying the sentence ordered by the court. In the field of labor relations, procedural law would treat such matters as the manner of presenting a lawsuit to stop an unlawful strike, the necessary proof, the type of order a court can issue, and similar matters.

In analyzing the criminal justice system, we must look to both substantive and procedural law—substantive law to tell us what constitutes a crime and procedural law to tell us what we can do to enforce the substantive law. Part Two of this book will concentrate on substantive criminal law and Part Three will concentrate on procedural law. Before reaching the particulars of the law governing the criminal justice system, however, we should examine one other important aspect of our general legal system, the special role of the courts.[12]

---

12. For further information on the material covered in this chapter, see E.A. Farnsworth, *An Introduction to the Legal System of the United States*, New York: Oceana Publications, 1975; E. Morgan and F. Dwyer, *The Study of Law*, Chicago: Callaghan and Company, 1948; and B. Gavin, *Introduction To the Study of Law*, Brooklyn: Foundation Press, 1951, Chapters 3, 4, and 7.

Chapter 3

The Special Role of the Courts

As we saw in Chapter One, courts are only one of several agencies that establish legal rules. The law is created also by constitutional conventions, legislatures, and administrative agencies. What makes the courts' law-determining function unique is the position of the courts as the final decision-maker as to the meaning of the law as applied to the facts of a particular case. Whether dealing with a constitutional provision, a common law ruling, a statute, or an administrative regulation, courts have the final responsibility for interpreting that legal standard in the cases brought before them. Of course, judicial interpretations of constitutional standards can be overriden by a constitutional amendment and interpretations of statutes or administrative regulations can be overriden by adoption of new legislation, but such actions are fairly rare. In any event, the new rule announced in rejecting the court's interpretation will be the rule only for the future (subject again to the court's interpretation). The rule for the case already decided by the court will not be changed.

The role of the court as the final arbiter of the law in the particular case is especially important in the field of criminal law because the criminal system is built upon the prosecution of alleged criminals in cases brought to court. It thus differs from many areas of civil law where disputes commonly are settled by the parties without going to court. To understand the law governing the criminal justice system, one must be familiar with the structure of the courts responsible for applying the law and the means those courts utilize to determine the applicable legal rule. Chapter Three should provide the necessary background information on both of these points.

STRUCTURE OF THE COURTS[1]

Separate Federal and State Systems.   As we already have noted, in every state, we find two complete, parallel court systems, one the federal system and the other the state's own system. Thus, in the country as a whole, we have fifty-one judicial systems, fifty created under state laws and the federal system created under federal law. The federal and state systems are quite distinct, although, as we shall see, in certain types of cases, the United States Supreme Court provides a link between the two. The state courts are concerned primarily with lawsuits involving the application of state law and the federal courts with suits involving federal law. In the field of criminal law, this means that prosecution for crimes created by Congress are brought in federal courts and prosecutions for crimes established by the state legislatures are brought in the state courts.

There is nothing in the nature of federalism, with its separate state and federal laws, that demands two court systems. Canada, for example, has a Supreme Court of the Dominion and separate court systems in each of the provinces. There is no system of lower Dominion courts with special responsibility for applying national law. The courts of the provinces have responsibility for applying national law as well as provincial law. The United States Constitution would have permitted the adoption of a judicial system in this country similar to that of Canada. Article III established a Supreme Court of the United States, but granted Congress discretion as to whether to adopt a lower court system. Fearing that the state courts might be hostile to congressional legislation, Congress immediately created a lower federal court system in 1789. The lower federal court system has since been expanded over the years. It guarantees that federal crimes will be prosecuted only in federal courts. Indeed, Congress also provided that when federal officers are charged with crimes under state law in connection with their federal activities (e.g., a federal marshal charged with using excessive force in making an arrest), these prosecutions can also be transferred to federal courts to ensure that the officers will receive a fair trial.

While the attitude of state courts toward federal laws obviously has changed since 1789, the dual court system is now a well established American tradition. It has produced a complex judicial structure that requires lawyers in each state to be familiar with the special features of both federal and state courts. We will more fully describe those special features later in this chapter. First, however, we should be aware of the basic types of courts that are to be found in both the federal and state systems.

Jurisdiction.   Courts generally are classified according to their "jurisdiction." As used in connection with judicial authority, the term "jurisdiction" refers to the power of a court to hear a particular type of case.[2] If a court can deal with cases involving only a certain subject matter, such as only criminal law, it is described as

---

1.   As you examine this material, occasional references to the chart at the end of this chapter might be helpful. That chart sets forth the typical hierarchy of those courts handling criminal matters in the federal system and a typical state system.

2.   See pp. 25-26 *supra* for the somewhat different use of the term "jurisdiction" to describe the legislative capacity of governmental units. In both instances, the term refers to authority or power.

a court with jurisdiction limited to that legal field. Similarly, if its authority in such cases includes the power to conduct trials, its jurisdiction also is described as a "trial jurisdiction." The jurisdiction of each court ordinarily is set forth in the constitution or statute that creates that court. The jurisdictional divisions between courts tend to be based on four factors: (1) the distinction between trial and appellate authority; (2) the subject matter of the cases considered; (3) the seriousness of the cases considered; and (4) the type of parties involved.

The distinction between trial courts and appellate courts is recognized in all fifty-one judicial systems. The trial court holds the basic hearing on the evidence in the case, determines the applicable law, and either itself applies the law to the facts presented or directs the jury in their performance of that function. The appellate court, on the other hand, reviews the trial court's decision to ensure that the trial court did not act erroneously. It does not hold an evidentiary hearing, but proceeds to review the case based on an official record (called a transcript), which relates all that occurred at the trial.[3] The most well known example of a court with appellate jurisdiction is the United States Supreme Court. Trial court jurisdiction (sometimes also described as "original jurisdiction") is possessed by most local courts, such as the typical state "County," "Circuit," or "Superior" court.

The second jurisdictional distinction—the subject matter of the case (i.e., the field of law involved)—tends to be utilized primarily in distinguishing between different trial courts. Appellate courts ordinarily can hear all types of cases, although there are several states that have separate appellate courts for criminal and civil appeals. At the trial level, most states have established one or more specialized courts to deal with particular legal fields. The most common areas delegated to specialized courts are wills and estates (assigned to courts commonly known as probate or surrogate courts), divorce, adoption, and other aspects of family law (family or domestic relations courts), and actions based on the English law of equity (chancery courts). The federal system also includes specialized courts for such areas as customs and patents. While significant, the specialized courts represent only a small portion of all trial courts. Most trial courts are not limited to particular subjects, but may deal with all fields not specifically reserved for the specialized courts. Such trial courts commonly are described as having "general jurisdiction" since they cover the general (i.e., non-specialized) areas of the law. Criminal cases traditionally have been assigned to trial courts with general jurisdiction.[4]

The third level of division—based on the seriousness of the case—also is found at the trial level in almost all jurisdictions.[5] Both civil and criminal cases of a

---

3. The record commonly is a complete transcription of all that went on in the trial court, including the testimony of witnesses, rulings of the court, and, of course, the final decision announced by the jury or judge. The transcription is made by a court reporter or a mechanical recording device.

4. It should be noted, however, that the jurisdiction of such courts is not unlimited even as to cases within the general areas of law. All trial courts are subject to some limits on their overall jurisdiction. A court of general trial jurisdiction cannot, for example, try cases arising outside the state (or, in most cases, the judicial district) in which it sits.

5. Several states (less populous states, except for Illinois) have no courts below their general trial courts. In these states, the general trial courts are responsible for all levels of cases, although the judges may be split into separate divisions to handle major and minor cases.

minor nature commonly are assigned to one group of courts and more serious cases to another, higher level court. Those trial courts limited to minor cases are commonly described as magistrate courts since their judges are in many respects successors to the English office of the magistrate. Their jurisdiction is described as "limited" or "inferior" as compared to that of the "general trial courts," the courts which try the more serious cases. The dividing line between minor and major cases will vary from state to state. In civil cases, the dividing line commonly is drawn in terms of the amount of damages sought by the plaintiff. For example, magistrate courts will try all cases in which suit is for less than $1,000 while the general trial court will handle cases involving larger amounts. In the criminal area, the dividing line is tied initially to the legislative classification of the crime as a "felony" or "misdemeanor." The subtleties of this distinction are discussed in Chapter Four, but as rough measure the distinction can be viewed as follows: misdemeanors are crimes punishable by imprisonment of one year or less, and felonies are crimes punishable by imprisonment in excess of one year or by death. In some jurisdictions, the magistrate courts will try all misdemeanors, and the general trial court will try all felonies. In others, the magistrates court may try only lesser misdemeanors (e.g., those punishable by no more than 90 days imprisonment), with the general trial court trying the remaining, more serious misdemeanors as well as all felonies.

The fourth dividing line for allocating authority among courts—the special nature of the parties involved—is used far less frequently than the other three dividing lines. Perhaps the most common illustration of its use is found in the juvenile court. That court has jurisdiction over a variety of proscribed activities committed by persons under a specified age. Juvenile court jurisdiction includes many acts that would be criminal if committed by adults, and the juvenile courts accordingly are given special attention later in this book. At this point, it is sufficient simply to note that the allocation of juvenile cases to a specialized court is based on a combination of specialized law and the special nature of the party involved. Another illustration of a specialized court based on the special nature of one of the parties is the state court known as "the court of claims," which has jurisdiction over all suits against the state government for money damages. The federal court of military appeals is a specialized appellate court whose jurisdiction also is determined by a combination of specialized law and special parties.

Hierarchy of Courts.   When the specialized courts are put to one side, we find that a judicial system typically has three or possibly four levels of courts. This will be the hierarchy commonly applicable to criminal cases.

At the bottom level in the typical hierarchy will be the magistrate court. Judges on that court will try minor civil and criminal cases. They also will have some preliminary functions in the more serious felony cases that will eventually be tried in the general trial court. Thus a person arrested on a felony charge initially will be brought before a magistrate who will inform the arrestee of the charge against him, set bail, and screen the prosecution's case to ensure that it is sufficient to send on to the general trial court. All of these functions will be considered in later chapters, but it should be kept in mind that though the magistrate's trial jurisdiction is limited to minor cases, he often performs other, quite important functions in major cases.

At the next court level is the general trial court, which will try all major civil and criminal cases. While this court is predominantly a trial court, it also serves as an appellate court for the minor cases tried in the magistrate court. Thus, if a defendant is convicted on a misdemeanor charge in a magistrate court, his natural route of appeal is to the general trial court as the next highest court. As we shall see shortly, the appellate review in the general trial court may take a special form where the magistrate court is one we describe as a court "not of record." In most instances, however, the general trial court will review the record in the magistrate court for possible error in the same way that the appellate court at the next tier will review the trial decisions of the general trial court in major cases.

The court at the next level may be either the first of two or the only general appellate court in the judicial hierarchy. In almost half of the states and the federal system, there are two appellate tiers. The first appellate court, which would be at the third level in the hierarchy, is commonly described as the "intermediate" appellate court. The next level of appellate court is the appellate court of "last resort"; it is the highest court to which a case ordinarily can be taken.[6] These highest appellate courts frequently are titled "supreme courts," and for the sake of simplicity, we will use that title rather than the longer description of "appellate court of last resort."[7] Where a judicial system has two tiers of appellate courts, the supreme court will be at the fourth level of the hierarchy. In those states that have only one tier, there is no intermediate appellate court. The supreme court is the court at the third level of the hierarchy.

In most jurisdictions, the losing party at trial is given an absolute right to one level of appellate review, but any subsequent reviews by a higher appellate court are at the discretion of that higher court. Thus, in a system that has no intermediate appellate court, a defendant convicted of a felony in a general trial court has an absolute right to have his conviction reviewed by the next highest court, the supreme court. In a system that has an intermediate appellate court, the felony defendant's absolute right to review extends only to that intermediate court. If that court should decide the case against him, the defendant can ask the supreme court to review his case, but it need do so only at its discretion.[8] The application requesting such discretionary review is called a *petition for certiorari*. If the court decides to review the case, it issues a *writ of certiorari* directing that the record in the case be sent to it by the intermediate appellate court. Those supreme courts having discretionary appellate jurisdiction commonly refuse to grant most

---

6.   As we shall see, in some cases brought through the state court system, there may be one, even higher level of appellate review through an appeal to the United States Supreme Court. In such cases, there are five rather than four tiers of courts that consider the case.

7.   Ordinarily when the title "Supreme Court" is capitalized, the reference is to a specific supreme court. We will use the capitalized title to refer only to the United States Supreme Court.

8.   There may be a few exceptions, however, where the individual is given a right to review by both courts. Cases in which capital punishment has been imposed may be one such exception, and cases in which statutes have been held unconstitutional may be another.

petitions for certiorari, limiting their review to the most important cases. Consequently, even where a state judicial hierarchy has four rather than three levels, most civil or criminal cases will not get beyond the third level.[9]

Whether appellate review is provided by an intermediate appellate court, a supreme court, or both, the process of appellate review is basically the same. Unlike the trial judge, who sits alone, appellate judges sit in groups of at least three judges. The function of the appellate court is to review the record of the trial proceeding to determine if an error was committed. Ordinarily, in addition to the record, it considers written arguments (called "briefs") submitted by the lawyers for the parties on both sides,[10] and brief oral arguments (rarely lasting more than one hour) by those lawyers. If the appellate court finds that no error was committed at trial, it will "affirm" the decision below. If it finds there was error, and that error deprived the losing party of a fair trial, it will issue an order of "reversal." The consequences of the reversal will depend upon the nature of the error. In most instances, the court simply will require a new trial during which the error will not be repeated. In some cases, however, the order of reversal might include a direction to dismiss the case completely. That remedy would be needed in a criminal case, for example, if the appellate court concluded that the defendant's actions simply did not constitute a crime.

The appellate court will support its decision with a written opinion, authored by one of its members, setting forth the court's reasons for its order of affirmance or reversal. If a particular judge agrees with the result reached in the court's opinion but not its reasoning, he may write a separate "concurring" opinion. If he disagrees with the result, and votes against the majority's decision, he will write a dissenting opinion. The opinions of the appellate courts are very important in determining the law since they are primary record of past decisions, and, as we shall see, past decisions serve as the controlling guidelines for rulings in future cases. The opinion for the majority is most significant, of course, because it expresses the prevailing view, but a dissenting opinion may also be important. There is always the possibility that, as times change, the ideas expressed in today's dissents will gain acceptance in tomorrow's opinions for the majority.

Courts of Record. Our description of the hierarchy of courts has assumed so far that all trial courts are "courts of record," and appellate review accordingly will be on the record. There is one major exception to that assumption which we should note—the court "not of record." The division between courts of record and courts not of record originally was drawn when many trial courts lacked the mechanical capacity to maintain a complete record of their proceedings. If a court could provide such a record, the losing party could readily gain appellate review of the

---

9. Similarly, where the civil or criminal case is a minor case, within the trial jurisdiction of the magistrate court, the case is unlikely to get beyond the second level. Initial appellate review in such a case is before the second level court, the trial court. That review is granted as a matter of automatic right, but further review is likely to lie within the discretion of the remaining courts, the intermediate appellate court (if the jurisdiction has one) and the supreme court.

10. The party appealing is called the *appellant* and the party who won below is called the *appellee*. As we shall see, in criminal cases, the prosecution ordinarily cannot appeal (see p. 324 *infra*), so the appeals are almost always taken by a losing defendant (the appellant on appeal) with the prosecution as the appellee.

trial decision before the next highest court. If the record was not available, however, the higher court had no way of examining the proceedings below to determine if error was committed. Without a record, a second look at the case could only be provided by the higher court giving the case *de novo* consideration (i.e., fresh consideration). This was done by conducting a new trial called a *trial de novo*. The trial de novo was not in fact appellate review, since it did not review the decision below, but proceeded as if the case had begun in the higher court. The trial de novo simply was a substitute for appellate review, necessitated by the absence of a record.

At one time, the great majority of magistrate courts lacked the personnel to keep records and therefore were not courts of record. Today, magistrate courts are courts of record in about half of the states. Their decisions are reviewed by the next highest court, the general trial court, on the record. In the remaining states, either some or all of the magistrate courts remain courts not of record. Their decisions are reconsidered at the general trial court level through the granting of a trial de novo.

In many states, the status of the magistrate courts as courts not of record no longer is a product of the courts' inability to prepare a complete trial record. Rather, their special status tends to have been retained primarily because of concern that a losing party, particularly a criminal defendant, should be entitled to a more formal and thorough trial than is provided in such magistrate courts. As we shall see, magistrates in courts not of record often are non-lawyers who adhere to the traditional legal rules of trial only in a rather loose fashion. Indeed, over the years, the magistrate courts often have been criticized as the weakest link in the judiciary. [11] By keeping their status as courts not of record, the states with such informal magistrate courts ensure that any person convicted of a misdemeanor in those courts will have an automatic right to a new trial, a trial de novo, in the general trial court. (In practice, however, the right to a trial de novo is exercised rather sparingly, with most convicted misdemeanants accepting the limited sentences commonly imposed by the magistrate courts.)

THE FEDERAL JUDICIAL SYSTEM

Having examined the basic elements of a court system, we can now turn to a more detailed examination of the federal system and the various state systems. [12] We start with the federal system not because it is more important, but simply because it is less complicated. Indeed, in terms of numbers of cases handled, the federal system is far less significant than the state systems viewed as a group. In the criminal area in particular, the vast majority of all cases are litigated in state

---

11. Consider, for example, the President's Commission on Law Enforcement and Administration of Justice, *Task Force Report: The Courts,* Washington, D.C.: Government Printing Office p. 29: "These courts operate with the most meager facilities, with the least trained personnel, and with the most oppressive workload. Practices by judges, prosecutors and defense counsel which would be condemned in the higher courts may still be found in these courts . . . No program of crime prevention will be effective without a massive overhaul of the lower criminal courts."

12. In both areas, we will concentrate on the courts in the basic hierarchy since those are the courts involved in criminal cases. It should be kept in mind that, as we noted previously, all systems also will have some specialized courts such as the juvenile court.

courts. The federal courts ordinarily deal with only ten to fifteen percent of all felony prosecutions brought in this country and a much smaller percentage of all misdemeanors. Court systems in several individual states (e.g., California, Illinois) handle considerably more criminal litigation each year than does the entire federal court system.

Federal Magistrates.   The federal system does not have a separate magistrate court, but each of the general trial courts, the United States District Courts, employs one or more United States Magistrates who perform many of the same functions as the judges of a state magistrate court. The federal magistrates (formerly called commissioners) are judicial officers appointed by the district court. Their maximum jurisdiction is established by law, and has gradually been expanded by Congress in an effort to relieve the caseload burden placed upon district judges.[13] The primary function of the magistrates is in the criminal area since the federal courts do not receive civil cases involving small damage claims. Federal magistrates perform preliminary roles in felony cases similar to those traditionally performed by magistrates (e.g., set bail). They also have trial jurisdiction for all "minor" crimes, a category currently defined as including most federal misdemeanors.[14] This jurisdiction is subject to one major limitation—the defendant can, if he so chooses, insist upon a trial before the district court rather than the magistrate. Thus, while the federal system provides for review of the magistrate's decision on the record rather than a trial de novo reconsideration, the federal misdemeanor defendant does have the right to bypass the magistrate entirely and insist upon a trial before the general trial court such as the state misdemeanor defendant receives in jurisdictions granting trials de novo.

District Court.   The district court, which is the general trial court of the federal system, is divided into 94 judicial districts. Each state contains at least one district, with the larger states having up to four districts. Each district is described by reference to the state or geographical segment of the state in which it is located (e.g., "The United States District Court for the Eastern District of Texas"). Puerto Rico, Guam, the Virgin Islands, and the Canal Zone, also have district courts, although their jurisdiction differs somewhat from that of the district courts within the states. There currently are more than 500 authorized district court judgeships, but the Congress is constantly adding to that number as population grows and the quantity of litigation increases. The district courts have jurisdiction over all prosecutions brought under federal criminal law and all civil suits brought under federal statutes (e.g., the Sherman Antitrust Act). They also have

---

13. Another factor leading to a change in the magistrate's jurisdiction has been the change in the qualifications for that office. At one time, federal magistrates often were not lawyers and most served only part time. Today, they must be lawyers and more and more magistrates serve full time.

14. Title 18, United States Code §3401. In the federal system, misdemeanors are crimes punishable by imprisonment not exceeding one year or a fine not exceeding $1,000 or both such a fine and imprisonment. Certain misdemeanors are specifically excluded from the magistrate's trial jurisdiction, however, even though they otherwise fit within these maximum-sentence limitations. These include several crimes, such as corrupt election practices and jury tampering, that are viewed as particularly blameworthy. The district court also has authority to narrow the magistrate's jurisdiction, and some district courts have done this, insisting that certain other misdemeanors also be tried only before the district court.

jurisdiction in two important areas involving state as well as federal law. Where a citizen of one state is suing a citizen of another for more than $10,000, suit may be brought in the federal court (a supposedly more neutral court) even though the suit is based on state law. Also, of more significance to the criminal field, a state prisoner, tried and convicted under state law in state courts, may obtain relief from the federal district court if he can establish that the state courts violated certain rights guaranteed by the federal constitution. This procedure, which operates through the *writ of habeas corpus*, is discussed in Chapter Twelve. It, in effect, permits a federal general trial court to review the constitutional validity of a state conviction even though that conviction was upheld by the state's supreme court. Habeas corpus jurisdiction involving state prisoners was granted to the federal district courts during the post-civil war period, when there was considerable concern as to whether the southern state courts would give due respect to the federal constitutional guarantees.

Court of Appeals. The United States Court of Appeals is the intermediate appellate court of the federal judicial system. The court is divided into 11 "circuits," so named because judges were formerly described as having ridden the "circuit" when they traveled from one rural community to another. The first ten circuits cover a geographical area of several states each.[15] The eleventh circuit has jurisdiction solely over federal cases presented in the District of Columbia. All cases decided by district courts are appealable as a matter of right to the court of appeals for the circuit in which the district court is located.

Altogether, there are more than 125 judges on the court of appeals. Each of the circuits has at least four judges and two have more than twenty. Ordinarily, cases are heard by a randomly selected panel of three judges of the circuit. Occasionally, if a case is especially significant, it will be heard *en banc* (that is, before all of the judges of the court in the particular circuit). En banc review is particularly likely where two different panels within the same circuit have reached inconsistent results on similar issues. In the larger circuits, there are too many judges to hold an en banc hearing, so alternative procedures have been adopted to permit review of exceptional cases by a panel of more than the usual three judges but less than the full court.

Supreme Court. The appellate court of last resort in the federal system is the United States Supreme Court. It is composed of nine justices and, unlike the practice in the court of appeals, the Supreme Court hears every case en banc.[16]

---

15. The circuits are composed as follows: 1st Circuit—*Maine, New Hampshire, Massachusetts, Rhode Island, Puerto Rico;* 2nd Circuit—*New York, Vermont, Connecticut;* 3rd Circuit—*Pennsylvania, New Jersey, Delaware;* 4th Circuit—*West Virginia, Virginia, North Carolina, South Carolina, Maryland;* 5th Circuit—*Texas, Louisiana, Mississippi, Alabama, Georgia, Florida, Canal Zone;* 6th Circuit—*Ohio, Kentucky, Tennessee, Michigan;* 7th Circuit—*Wisconsin, Illinois, Indiana;* 8th Circuit—*North Dakota, South Dakota, Nebraska, Missouri, Arkansas, Iowa, Minnesota;* 9th Circuit—*Washington, Oregon, California, Nevada, Arizona, Idaho, Montana, Alaska, Hawaii;* 10th Circuit—*Wyoming, Utah, Colorado, New Mexico, Kansas, Oklahoma;* 11th Circuit—*District of Columbia.*

16. Because the Court frequently reviews key cases in which the lower courts are divided and the nine justices have differing philosophies, it is not surprising that the justices are divided on most of the Court's decisions. H.L. Mencken once observed that a "judge is a law student who marks his own exams." H.L. Mencken, *Backbone of the Herring*, New York: Alfred A. Knopf Publishing, 1941, p.

With regard to the federal system, the Supreme Court's appellate jurisdiction is total; it can review any case decided by any of the circuits of the court of appeals. In addition, as we shall see shortly, the Court also has appellate jurisdiction as to some cases heard in the state courts. With respect to both elements of its jurisdiction the Supreme Court's decision to grant review is largely discretionary. A litigant losing before a lower court has no right to have his case heard by the Supreme Court. He must seek discretionary review through a petition for certiorari, and his chances of success are slight since the Court typically grants less than 10% of the requests for review.

During the course of this book, we will refer to many decisions of the Supreme Court involving the application of the federal constitution to state or federal cases. Those decisions of the Court have the broadest impact because they govern both the state and federal judicial systems. It should be noted, however, that the Court is also influential in the criminal area simply as the final interpreter of federal statutory law which is applied in the federal courts alone. It occupies a role here quite similar to that of a state supreme court in supervising the activities of the lower courts within its judicial system. For our purposes, the Supreme Court's unique role as final arbiter of constitutional disputes throughout the country is more significant, but its other role simply as the highest court in the federal system also should be kept in mind.

STATE COURTS

While all state judicial systems utilize the three or four tier hierarchy previously described, they vary considerably in how they fill that structure. In some states, total judicial reorganization has produced a streamlined structure with a single court at each tier and the trial and intermediate appellate judges divided among uniform districts. In others, the judicial system is extremely complex, having grown gradually over the years through the occasional addition or deletion of particular courts. Generally, the degree of variety within and between state judicial systems lessens as the level of the court rises. The greatest diversity certainly is found at the lowest trial court level, among what we have described as the magistrate courts.

Magistrate Courts. The numerous state magistrate courts vary considerably in the limits on their jurisdiction, the geographical area they serve, their titles, and the qualifications of their judges. They are almost all limited in their criminal jurisdiction to misdemeanors, but many states further restrict these courts to misdemeanors punishable by no more than ninety days or six months imprisonment. In civil cases, some magistrate courts, like Michigan's District Court, can try cases involving claims as high as $10,000, but most have a jurisdictional limit of less than $1,000. As we already have noted, most magistrate courts are courts of

---

3. Of course, for most judges, sitting on trial courts or intermediate appellate courts, there are higher graders on higher courts. But even in the Supreme Court, which is the highest grader of them all, though each judge may indeed issue the final mark for his own exam, he must recognize that there are eight other justices who will be carefully reviewing his work and giving it their own grade.

record (with appellate review on the record), but there remain a substantial number not of record (with review by trial de novo).

The structure of magistrate courts varies from a statewide court divided into a series of uniform districts to a conglomeration of different local courts serving different political and geographical units. Thus, some states have a single court divided into separate districts that cover each individual county, while other states utilize a variety of different courts, with some serving cities, other townships, and others that part of a county that is not within a city or township. The traditional title for a magistrate court was the justice of the peace court, but that title today is used primarily in rural areas using non-lawyer magistrates in courts not of record. Other common titles are police court, recorder's court, county court, and city court. In some states, the magistrates must be lawyers; in others, no specialized training is needed. Where the magistrates need not be lawyers, they almost certainly serve on a part-time basis. Where they must be lawyers, some states require that they serve as magistrates only, while others permit them to continue in the private practice of law. The most common state pattern distinguishes between magistrate courts in metropolitan and rural areas. In the cities, the magistrate court will be a court of record with a full-time lawyer-judge and jurisdiction over all misdemeanors. In rural areas, on the other hand, the court is more likely to have the attributes of the traditional justice of the peace court: not of record, jurisdiction extending only up to ninety day misdemeanors, judges who lack legal training and spend most of their time at other professions.[17]

Over the years one national group after another has commented upon the importance of the magistrate courts and the need for improvement in those courts.[18] No doubt exists that such courts are the "workhorse" of the state judicial system. They dispose of the vast majority of all criminal cases since there are far more misdemeanor than felony charges. They also play an important role in the progress of felony cases. Thus, almost every person charged with a criminal offense will come before a magistrate court. Insofar as they convey an image of dispensing assembly-line justice in the big cities, or local, non-professional and somewhat biased justice in the rural areas, magistrate courts certainly can do considerable damage to the overall image of the judicial system.

---

17. The extreme diversity in the organization of lower courts sometimes can be illustrated in a single state. New York, for example, has six courts operating at the magistrate court level in different parts of the state: a Criminal Court in New York City; a District Court in Nassau and Suffolk counties; a City Court in sixty-one other cities; City Police Courts, City Justice Courts, or Recorder's Courts in another eighteen cities; and Town and Village Justice Courts in other communities. Judicial qualifications range from ten years of legal practice (New York City Criminal Court) to none (City Courts and Town and Village Justice Courts). The judges are appointed to the New York Criminal Court, but elected to the others. All have jurisdiction to try offenses within the traditional misdemeanor definition, but they have differing authority with respect to preliminary proceedings in felony cases. Appeals generally are on the record to a general trial court, but the New York City Criminal Court's decisions are appealable directly to the intermediate court of appeals. All six New York courts now provide jury trials, but they formerly differed on that point as well.

18. See note 11 *supra*. Several distinguished commissions have urged that lower courts be abolished as separate courts, and their jurisdiction exercised by general trial courts. See, e.g., the President's Commission on Law Enforcement, note 11 *supra*, at p. 33. A small group of states have substantially achieved such unification (see note 5 *supra*), but it appears unlikely that this approach will ever gain substantial support among the remaining states.

In the past decade, state legislatures have paid considerably closer attention to magistrate courts. Efforts have been made to alleviate some of the more basic difficulties facing such courts. Various measures have been enacted that should provide some relief against the pressure of tremendously heavy caseloads borne by magistrates courts in major urban centers. More judges have been added, the courts have been given additional staff members, and better quarters have been provided. In some jurisdictions, efforts also have been made to remove from the criminal justice system various offenses that traditionally constituted a major portion of the magistrate court's caseload. Thus, various jurisdictions have decriminalized public drunkenness and provided for alternative civil procedures that do not require as much judicial involvement. In a few jurisdictions, traffic cases have been largely removed from the magistrate courts and assigned to administrative agencies. Legislatures have sought to increase the professionalism of rural, non-lawyer magistrates by imposing mandatory training programs. Various other jurisdictions have either required that all magistrates be lawyers or limited non-lawyer magistrates to courts in the most sparsely settled areas. Although some legal experts oppose the use of non-lawyer judges under any circumstance, it generally is agreed that the use of such judges may be preferable to requiring citizens either to travel hundreds of miles to the nearest lawyer-judge or to wait weeks for the lawyer-judge to come to them in the course of "riding the circuit." There remain many states, including such heavily populated states as Texas, that have several counties without any resident lawyers.[19]

General Trial Courts. General trial courts are known by a variety of different titles, including superior court, circuit court, district court, and court of common pleas. New York even uses the title of supreme court, which other states reserve for their highest appellate court. Ordinarily the state will be divided into a number of judicial districts with at least one general trial court judge sitting in each district. The trial court districts tend to be much larger than the districts used for magistrate courts. In many states, there is one trial court district per county, but others combine sparsely populated counties in single multicounty districts. Although the majority of state trial court districts have no more than three judges, districts in metropolitan areas commonly have a substantial number of judges (e.g., over 170 in Los Angeles county). Where the district is quite large the judges may sit at various sites throughout the district. In some districts, the judges are divided into civil and criminal divisions, with the judges rotating between the divisions on a regular basis.

The trial jurisdiction of general trial courts usually begins where the trial jurisdiction of the magistrate court leaves off. Thus, in one state the general trial court may try only felonies, while in another it may hear major misdemeanors as well as felonies. Although the magistrate handles preliminary matters in such cases, the general trial court ordinarily is the first court to rule on major legal

---

19. The replacement of non-lawyer judges raises philosophical arguments as well as practical difficulties. There are those who strongly support the use of non-lawyer judges as a valuable asset in maintaining citizen control of the judiciary. They argue that the job of a magistrate is as much "social" as "legal," particularly in those jurisdictions in which the trial before a magistrate is without a jury and a trial de novo before the general trial court provides an opportunity for correction of any legal errors.

issues in the criminal cases that it will try. Frequently, the court's ruling will be rendered orally, with no written opinion ever issued. In this respect, the state trial judges differ dramatically from United States District Court judges, who commonly write legal opinions that are published in official reports.

Intermediate Appellate Courts.   Twenty-three states have intermediate appellate courts. These courts commonly are known simply as the court of appeals, but several states refer to the court as the appellate division of the general trial court. In most states, the court of intermediate appeals is organized as a single court which hears appeals coming from trial courts throughout the state. Some states, however, divide their appellate court into separate divisions with each serving a different multi-county district. The state intermediate courts of appeals usually have considerably more judges than the individual circuits of the federal court of appeals. (In the largest states, there are over fifty judges on the state intermediate court of appeals). Accordingly, while the state judges sit in panels of three, as do the federal judges, they generally do not also follow the federal practice of sitting en banc on significant cases.

Court of Last Resort.   The highest appellate court in the state, the court of last resort, usually is titled the supreme court, although several states call it the court of appeals. The state high courts vary in size, having either five, seven, or nine members, who often are called justices rather than judges. As with the Supreme Court of the United States, the justices of the state supreme courts commonly sit en banc rather than dividing into panels. Where the state has an intermediate appellate court, the state supreme court usually has discretion to grant only such petitions for review as it believes to merit additional judicial consideration. These state courts frequently accept jurisdiction on less than half of the petitions, although their review rate still is considerably higher than that which prevails in the United States Supreme Court. Where the state lacks an intermediate appellate court, the state supreme court is at the first appellate level and the losing party before the trial court often has an automatic right to appellate review.

Supreme Court of the United States.   Although we commonly describe the state supreme courts as the courts of last resort in state cases, they do not occupy that position for all such cases. On a matter involving the interpretation of state law, the state supreme court does indeed have the final word. But where the case involves an issue of federal law, a fifth tier is added to the judicial hierarchy: further review can be sought from the United States Supreme Court. On federal questions, the Supreme Court is the final arbiter whether the case arises in the federal or state system. Of course, the Supreme Court's appellate jurisdiction is largely discretionary, and the Court will refuse to accept jurisdiction in most federal-question cases coming from state courts. Still, Supreme Court review has been granted and has proven particularly significant in a substantial number of state criminal cases presenting federal constitutional claims. Many of the most famous Supreme Court decisions have involved cases in which convicted defendants initially had their constitutional objections rejected by state supreme courts, obtained discretionary Supreme Court review, and then gained a reversal of their convictions before that court. It should be emphasized, however, that in reviewing state court decisions, the Supreme Court is limited to the federal issue. This point has been underscored by recent cases in which a state court has held that a certain police practice violates the federal constitution, the Supreme Court has held that it does not, and the state court has then held that, in any event, the practice is still invalid because it violates the state constitution. The Supreme Court after the second state ruling was without further jurisdiction since that ruling was based solely on state law and no federal constitutional issue was presented. While a state court must accept the Supreme Court's interpretation of the federal constitution, it is free to impose a standard more protective of individual rights under its own state law.

LEGAL METHOD: DETERMINING THE LAW

As we have seen, a court's role varies somewhat depending upon whether the court is a trial court or an appellate court; but at either level, a prime responsibility of the court is to determine what legal rules should be applied to the case before it. At the trial level, the basic functions of the judicial process are to determine the relevant rules of law, establish the facts involved in the particular case, relate those facts to the relevant law, and enter a conclusion in terms of that law. The initial element of this process, determining the applicable rules of law, is the task of the judge and the judge alone. The jury may establish the facts, and apply the law to those facts, but it may use only those rules of law that the trial judge finds to be the applicable rules. On appeal, the function of the court, as we have noted, is to determine whether there has been an error at the trial. Since a significant potential source of error is the trial judge's possible reliance upon the wrong rules of law, the appellate court also must initially determine the applicable rules of law. In this section, we will examine the method used by courts, both trial and appellate, in determining those legal rules.

Stare Decisis. The starting point for any judge in ascertaining the law is an examination of prior case law. The judge must consider how courts have disposed of previous cases presenting the same or similar fact situations. In particular, the judge must determine what legal rules were applied to such cases in the past. For under the doctrine of *stare decisis*, the rules applied in prior cases are the rules to be applied to the present case. Past decisions form a *precedent*—a standard for application in similar subsequent cases—and reliance upon precedent is the key element of the judicial process for deciding questions of law. Stare decisis comes from the English common law directive, *stare decisis et non quieta movere*, "to stand by the decisions and not disturb settled points." It tells the court that if the decisions in the past have held that a particular rule governs a certain fact situation, that rule should govern all later cases presenting the same fact situation. Stare decisis is not an absolute principle; as we shall see, courts may depart from precedent on occasion. Yet stare decisis certainly states the guideline that will govern in the vast majority of all cases.

The application of the principle of stare decisis can best be understood in the context of a particular case. Assume, for example, that a garage owner is charged with the murder of a person who tried to steal one of his cars. The owner acknowledges that he shot and killed the thief, but he contends that the thief was in the process of driving the car away and he had to shoot to prevent the thief from escaping with the car. The issue before the trial court is whether the owner's claim of justification is recognized under the law. Does the law permit the owner of property to use deadly force to prevent a thief from escaping with the stolen property? In answering that question, the trial judge initially will look to the reports of prior decisions. The judge will be interested primarily in cases decided in his state, for only those decisions are encompassed by the doctrine of stare decisis. Just as each state's legislature passes its own laws, each state's courts establish its own precedents. If there are no binding precedents in its own state, the court may look to other states and find their precedents persuasive, but the court is not bound by stare decisis to follow those precedents. The same limitation applies to the decisions of the federal courts, with one exception. Since the United States Supreme Court is the final interpreter of the federal constitution and federal statutes, its rulings are binding on all lower courts, both state and federal. If the authority of an owner to use deadly force to prevent the theft of his property presented a federal constitutional issue, the trial court would look to Supreme Court decisions for relevant rulings on that issue. If not, federal cases involving murder prosecutions would be no more significant than decisions from any other jurisdiction not that of the court.

In looking for relevant case within its own state, the trial court will look primarily to appellate decisions since, as we have noted, the appellate courts are the primary source of written opinions. [20] In weighing appellate opinions, the opinions of the state supreme court will prevail over any inconsistent opinions in the state intermediate court of appeals. If there are no supreme court opinions, and the intermediate court of appeals is divided by districts, the trial court will look to opinions in that district covering its geographical area. Indeed, in the federal system, a district court is bound by stare decisis to follow only the opinions of the court of appeals for its circuit. Each circuit is treated, in effect, as its own jurisdiction, and the court of appeals for the various circuits are free to disagree with each other.

Assume that our trial judge, upon examining the opinions of the state supreme court, finds one decision mentioning the use of deadly force to stop an escaping thief, *People v. Jones*. In the *Jones* case, the supreme court had ruled that a farmer could not be held for murder when a trap-gun mounted in his barn killed a horse thief. The court's opinion in *Jones* had relied on a state statute, since repealed, that specifically permitted farmers to use deadly traps to protect barns. The court also had noted in its opinion that that statute "merely reflected the sound principle that any owner of property may take such steps as necessary to protect his property from a thief." Although the *Jones* facts are somewhat similar to those presented in the garage owner's case, the reasoning of the *Jones* opinion clearly indicates that our trial judge is not bound by stare decisis to follow the *Jones* ruling as to the permissible use of deadly force. There are two factors that "distinguish" *Jones* (i.e., removes the *Jones* precedent from the command of stare

---

20. Even if the trial courts in the particular state did issue published opinions (see p. 45 *supra*), their decisions would not necessarily be binding precedent. Although a court is bound by its own prior decisions, the different trial judges sometimes view themselves as separate courts for this purpose. Thus trial judge A will not feel bound by decisions of trial judge B. Both will be bound, however, by decisions of the appellate court of their state.

decisis as applied to the garage owner's case). First, the *Jones* decision was based on a statute no longer in effect. The statute was a crucial element of the *Jones* ruling and, without it, *Jones* no longer is precedent even as to the particular fact situation presented in the *Jones* case. Stare decisis only applies where the governing statutory rules remain the same. Second, even if the statute were still in effect, it was limited to farmers and had no application to garage owners. Once again, the doctrine of stare decisis would not apply since the earlier ruling was based on a special ground (the statute) that clearly does not govern the current case.

The garage owner in our hypothetical case probably would argue that both of these distinguishing factors should be ignored. He would point to the court's statement in *Jones* that "sound principle" permitted an owner to take any steps necessary to protect his property. Doesn't that statement suggest that the *Jones* court accepted deadly force to catch a thief even apart from the statute, that the *Jones* court would have reached the same result without the statute? The answer is that court in *Jones* may have held that view, but that statement of viewpoint was not essential to its ruling. Stare decisis requires adherence only to the court's *holding*, that is, its ruling as to those matters that had to be settled to decide the case. The doctrine does not apply to comments by the court as to matters not essential to the case before it. These comments are described as *dictum* or *obiter dictum* (i.e., side comments). They are not binding as precedent because they were not tested by the adversary arguments of the lawyers on both sides. The lawyers in *Jones* were not concerned with the rights of property owners generally; they were concerned only with the meaning of a statute referring to farmers. Any judicial comments about property owners generally was outside the reach of the statute and unnecessary to the court's ruling. The dictum may well be a casual aside that was not thoroughly explored by the court. Certainly, the *Jones* court did not have before it the garage owner's situation, which might raise quite different concerns than the special problem of protecting barns that was treated in the former statute. Accordingly, while dictum may be persuasive, it is not controlling. If there is no contrary precedent, the trial judge may follow *Jones* because he believes the dictum in that case suggests a sound approach to the problem, but the *Jones* ruling itself clearly does not require a finding in favor of the garage owner on the basis of stare decisis.

Having found that there is no binding precedent among the state supreme court rulings, the trial judge next will turn to the opinions of the intermediate court of appeals. There he finds the case of *People v. Blue*. In *Blue*, the court of appeals ruled that a street vendor could not be held for murder where he killed a thief who had attempted to escape with his cash receipts. The opinion was not based on a special statute and there was no statement in the opinion suggesting that the ruling was limited to owners of one type of property rather than another. Here is a binding precedent; the *Blue* case is not "distinguishable." Relying upon *Blue*, the trial judge will inform the jury that the law permitted the garage owner to use deadly force where such force was necessary to catch a thief. The trial judge will so direct the jury even though he may not agree with the *Blue* decision. Moreover, if the case should later reach the court of appeals, the judges there probably will take the same position. Although *Blue* may have been decided a decade ago and the current appellate judges would not have reached the same result if the case were before them as a matter of first impression, the court of appeals nevertheless is likely to adhere to the ruling of *Blue* on the principle of stare decisis.

Reasons for Stare Decisis.   At this point, one might reasonably ask why the law ordinarily requires adherence to stare decisis. Why is it that the judges in our hypothetical case will permit their decision to be governed by the "dead hand of the past" even though they might not agree with its rulings? The answer lies in five advantages that stare decisis contributes to the judicial system: efficiency; equality; predictability; the wisdom of past experience; and the image of limited authority. Each helps to explain why stare decisis, though not absolute, certainly is the mainstay in the judicial process of determining the law.

The efficiency contributed by stare decisis is easily understood if we considered what courts would do without stare decisis. In every case, each trial judge and appellate judge would have to work out his own solution to every legal question. He would have to examine all of the arguments for and against each position that might be taken on every issue. There would be no building blocks—no established rules that need not be debated—from which a court could proceed to a third or fourth level issue. In our hypothetical involving the garage owner, for example, the court would have to start at the beginning. Before it could ask whether an owner could use deadly force to stop a thief, it would have to consider extensive arguments by counsel on a series of preliminary questions. What is property, who is an owner, what is a thief, etc.? With stare decisis these questions have already been answered by past decisions and those answers will not be reexamined. Applying stare decisis, the court knows the status of the owner, the car, and the thief, and it can go on to consider the owner's authority to use deadly force when necessary to prevent the escape of the thief. If that issue too has been resolved by stare decisis, there may be other questions that have not been resolved—e.g., whether the owner must first fire a warning shot before he can shoot directly at the thief to prevent his escape. If the court should find that all of the issues presented in the case are governed by precedent, it can quickly determine the applicable law and turn its attention to other, more difficult cases that present "open issues" (i.e., issues not resolved by precedent). In sum, if stare decisis were not followed, and every issue in every case were fully reexamined, the courts would be able to dispose of far fewer cases and reach far fewer issues. It would be difficult indeed to keep up with the constant influx of new issues presented by new scientific and economic developments.

Another important attribute of stare decisis is its contribution to the equal treatment of persons in similar fact situations. Within one jurisdiction, there should be one rule of law applied to all persons in the same setting. Identical cases brought before different judges should, to the extent humanly possible, produce identical results. Two garage owners, both shooting at fleeing thiefs, should not have different rules of law applied to their cases because one was tried before Judge Jones in Los Angeles and another before Judge Smith in San Francisco. Stare decisis assists in providing uniform standards of law for similar cases decided in the same state. It provides a common grounding used by all judges throughout the jurisdiction. Of course, stare decisis is not a total solution; as we shall see, there are instances in which the trial courts will face a new issue, not governed by precedent, and different trial judges will reach different solutions. But eventually a single solution on that issue will be reached by the highest appellate court, and that solution will then be binding upon all of the lower courts through stare decisis.

Stare decisis also provides a stability and certainty that we view as essential in the operation of the law. It would be exceedingly difficult for a citizen to carry on satisfactorily many of the affairs of life if he could not count upon the continued recognition of the rules of law that have been applied in the past. A businessman would have no basis for predicting whether a pattern of action previously viewed as legal would continue to be acceptable. A police officer could not safely count on previously accepted practices in determining the legality of a pending arrest. If the courts were free to apply in each case the personal view of the particular judge or judges sitting in that case, without regard to past decisions, the conduct of a wide variety of activities would take on an added hazard of unpredictable legality. Without stability, the law could well loose its effectiveness in maintaining social order.

Stare decisis also ensures proper recognition of the wisdom and experience of the past. The doctrine is based, in part, on the premise that legal rules that have survived over the years are likely to be sound rules. As Justice Cardozo once noted, no single judge is likely to have "a vision at once so keen and so broad" as to ensure that his new ideas of wise policy are indeed the most beneficial for society. It is best, he continued, to "cling for the most part to the accumulated experience of the past, and to the maxims and principles and rules and standards in which that experience is embodied." [21] Since stare decisis is not absolute, it does not prevent the court from rejecting past precedent. However, as the standard rule, it certainly requires that a judge think long and hard before he departs from the findings of his predecessors over the years.

Finally, stare decisis serves to enhance the image of the courts as the impartial "interpreter" of the law.[22] Stare decisis decreases the leeway granted to the individual judge to settle controversies in accordance with his own personal desires. In cases where past precedent is directly on point, the judge's determination of law has largely been made for him. There is, of course, some leeway to distinguish past cases, or even to overturn them in exceptional cases, but the judge's ability to create new law is sharply restricted. Indeed, the doctrine of stare decisis indirectly serves to restrict the law-making role of the judge even in those

---

21. B. Cardozo, *The Growth of the Law*, New Haven, Conn.: Yale University Press, 1924, p. 141.

22. The early English view was that judges do not create law, but simply find it. Today, all serious students of the courts recognize that the courts do indeed make law, that they must do so in order to fulfill their function. Yet there remains concern that the court's role be that primarily of the interpreter, not the original writer of the laws. As one noted scholar put it: "Judges are expected to act more like conductors of music than composers, more like actors than playwrights. Some freedom of interpretation is allowed them, but not without limitation. Leonard Bernstein is a composer as well as a conductor, but when he leads the New York Philharmonic in Beethoven's Fifth Symphony, he is expected to play Beethoven, not Bernstein. Orson Welles is a playwright as well as an actor and director, but when he plays or directs Hamlet, he is expected to do Shakespeare, not Welles. Judges are expected to observe similar distinctions, hard though they may be to define." D. Karlen, *The Citizen in Court*, New York: Holt, Rinehart, and Winston, 1965, p. 176.

cases presenting "open issues" not resolved by past precedent. Decision making in such cases is hardly mechanical; it consists, as we shall see, of a good deal more than "finding" the law. Yet even here, in its most creative role, the court is still a far cry from being a third branch of the legislature. Its creative capacity is limited by the doctrine of stare decisis to the particular factual situation before it.[23] Anything the court may say about other problems not presented by that case is strictly dictum and may be ignored in the future. Thus, a sudden change in the composition of the judiciary, even at the highest level, should not present an equally sudden change in the substance of the law. On the one hand, the new judges are restricted by stare decisis to that which has been decided in the past. On the other hand, in dealing with new issues, they can only move forward as rapidly as the flow of cases will permit them, adding new precedent in gradual layers as new cases present new issues. Unlike a legislature, they cannot reach out to any area in which they are interested and simply announce a new code of legal regulations.[24]

The restrictions that stare decisis and the case law system impose upon judicial law-making are especially important to public acceptance of the judiciary because judicial law-making traditionally has been viewed in this country as a somewhat suspect activity. Over the years, various political commentators have suggested that there is an anti-democratic element in permitting law-making powers to be exercised by judges, who are not directly responsible to the electorate in the same way as legislators.[25] Stare decisis, at a minimum, negates the most basic concern that the authority given to judges will be so broad that, in an individual case, the idiosyncrasies of the particular judge will govern. It serves to bolster the image of a neutral, objective process of law determination. Indeed, substantially because of stare decisis and the uniformity and predictability it produces, the judicial system commonly is viewed as the one branch of government more than any other in which we have a "government of laws, not of men."

Departures from Stare Decisis. Notwithstanding its importance, stare decisis is not an absolute rule for deciding cases. Courts recognize that there are

---

23. Moreover, stare decisis helps to ensure that the judge will not be unduly biased by his personal feelings toward the parties in the lawsuit before him. The judge knows that the ruling of law he announces will apply not only to those parties, but to all other persons who present a like situation in future cases.

24. Thus, Justice Holmes once noted in distinguishing the law-making authority of the courts: "I recognize without hesitation that judges do and must legislate, but they can do so only interstitially; they are confined from molar to molecular motions." *Southern Pacific Co. v. Jensen,* 244 U.S. 205, 221, 37 S.Ct. 524, 531, 61 L.Ed. 1086 (1917) (dissenting opinion).

25. Judges are appointed for extensive terms in some jurisdictions, and in others where they are elected, they still tend to have far greater insulation from popular control than legislators. See Chapter Sixteen. Whether this makes judicial law-making somewhat inconsistent with the basic values of a democracy is a matter of debate. As we have noted, legal rules created by the courts can be overriden by the legislature with respect to future application (except for constitutional interpretations, which can only be overriden by constitutional amendment). Also, as we shall see in Chapter Sixteen, the judicial selection process often is heavily influenced by elected officials even when the judges themselves are not elected. The role of the judiciary in a democracy has been explored in a substantial group of writings, most of which are noted in J. Choper, *The Supreme Court and The Political Branches: Democratic Theory and Practice,* 122 University of Pennsylvania Law Review 810 (1974), and C. McCleskey, *Judicial Review in a Democracy: A Dissenting Opinion,* 3 Houston Law Review 354 (1966).

instances when it is appropriate to depart from precedent. In such situations, the previous decision will be *overruled*—that is, rejected as continuing precedent.[26] A new rule established in the current case will replace (i.e., overrule) the former rule established in past cases. Since decisions that overrule prior precedent often receive considerable publicity, overruling commonly is viewed as a more prevalent practice than is actually the case. The United States Supreme Court, for example, has overruled only slightly more than one hundred of its decisions in almost two centuries. Moreover, over half of these overrulings involved interpretations of the constitution, an area in which courts are more prone to overrule because there is no readily available legislative corrective process for erroneous decisions.[27] The record of overruling in state supreme courts reveals that these courts tend to be even more reluctant to reject stare decisis.

What will lead a court to overrule precedent? Of course, first and foremost, the court must conclude that the earlier ruling is incorrect. Yet, that alone will not be sufficient, since the basic thrust of stare decisis is to require adherence to past precedent without regard to the court's view of the precedent's correctness. An important additional factor will be the strength of the precedent to be overruled. It is one thing to overrule a single decision that has rarely been applied and quite another to overrule a long line of decisions consistently applied over the years. Still another relevant factor is the field of law involved. Courts tend to be more reluctant to override decisions relating to property or trade, where commercial enterprises are likely to have relied quite heavily on the prior precedent. In other areas, such as the law governing accidents, the people involved are less likely to have planned their activities in reliance upon previous legal rulings.

Still another relevant factor in overruling is the initial source of law upon which a prior ruling was based. If the earlier ruling was based on the interpretation of a statute and the legislature has not subsequently changed the statute, courts will be particularly reluctant to override the prior interpretation. The legislature's inaction suggests that whether the original interpretation was right or wrong, it has been deemed acceptable by the legislature. On the other hand, if the earlier decision was based on the court's common law authority to create law in the absence of legislation, the lack of a legislative response to the court's earlier ruling is less significant.

---

26. Since a lower court may not overrule a higher court, and precedent commonly is found in the opinions of appellate courts, the task of overruling is almost exclusively a function of appellate rather than trial courts. Among the appellate courts, most overruling decisions are rendered by the supreme court since the intermediate appellate court may not overrule a supreme court decision.

27. The difficulty of achieving constitutional amendments to override erroneous constitutional decisions has lead the Court to give stare decisis less weight in the constitutional area than in others. Thus, Justice Brandeis noted in *Burnet v. Coronado Oil & Gas Co.*, 285 U.S. 393, 406, 52 S.Ct. 443, 447, 76 L.Ed. 815 (1931): "Stare decisis is usually the wise policy, because in most matters it is more important that the applicable rule of law be settled than that it be settled right. This is commonly true even where the error is a matter of serious concern, provided correction can be had by legislation. But in cases involving the Federal Constitution, where correction through legislative action is practically impossible, this Court has often overrruled its earlier decisions. The Court bows to the lessons of experience and the force of better reasoning, recognizing that the process of trial and error, so fruitful in the physical sciences, is appropriate also in the judicial function."

Perhaps the most significant factor in overruling a prior decision is the presence or absence of changed circumstances. If a prior ruling was based upon scientific developments that have since changed, the court is less likely to feel bound by stare decisis. For example, an old common law rule held that a person could not be held for murder if his victim died more than a year and a day after he was attacked. That rule was based in part on the lack of medical expertise that could clearly trace a death to a blow inflicted more than a year and a day before the death. Today, medical science often permits us to trace a death back to an earlier blow, and several state courts accordingly have overruled the year and a day rule. Similarly, courts have overruled decisions that were based on factual assumptions as to the administration or the impact of a legal rule that have been proven inaccurate by experience over the years. As Justice Black once noted, "Courts are not omniscient. Like every other human agency, they too can profit from trial and error, from experience and reflection."[28]

The most controversial grounds for overruling a prior decision is a general change in the "spirit of the times." It generally is acknowledged that a legal rule will not and should not prevail where based on societal value judgments that have been dramatically altered. As Justice Holmes argued, using the most obvious example:

> *It is revolting to have no better reason for a rule of law than that it was so laid down in the time of Henry IV. It is still more revolting if the grounds upon which it was laid down have vanished long since, and the rule simply persists from blind imitation of the past.*[29]

Holmes' position is more easily accepted than applied. It is not always clear whether the value that gave rise to a particular rule has lost its relevance in today's society. This is particularly true when the rule sprang from a more recent vintage than the time of Henry IV. Consider, for example, the hypothetical case of *People v. Blue* noted in connection with our discussion of the garage owner who shot the thief. Assume that it was in 1840 that the appellate court had held in *Blue* that a street vendor could use deadly force to prevent a thief from escaping with his cash receipts. Has society's view of theft, the taking of life, and the right to use self-help changed so dramatically that a common law precedent like that in *Blue* should be overruled? What weight should be given to the fact that property owner now has available the assistance of a modern police department? In the 1840's, there were few daytime police forces, as most communities relied upon the understaffed constable and the night watchman. Assume that the state had capital punishment in the 1840's, but has since abolished it. Does that action suggest such a significant change in society's attitude toward preserving life that *Blue* no longer should be binding? What weight should be given to the fact that theft was punishable far more severely in 1840 than it is today? These and similar questions are not easily answered. They require that the court make difficult evaluations of the thought and will of the community. Not surprisingly, a decision as to whether to overrule a

---

28. *Green v. United States*, 356 U.S. 165, 195, 78 S.Ct. 632, 649, 2 L.Ed. 2d 672 (1958) (dissenting opinion).

29. O. Holmes, *The Path of the Law*, 10 Harvard Law Review 457, 469 (1897).

case like *Blue* is likely to divide a single appellate court and to produce quite different results from courts in different states.

Where Precedent Is Not Controlling. While the law-making role of the courts is most readily apparent in the overruling of prior decisions, it most frequently comes into play in those cases where there is no binding precedent. Stare decisis controls most cases, but there are others where there are no prior decisions directly on point. Notwithstanding the accumulation of precedent over the years, there remains many issues on which the appellate courts in a particular jurisdiction have never ruled.[30] As might be expected, a good portion of these open issues relate to new economic or scientific developments. Yet, it also is true that we do not have clear-cut answers to very basic questions in some jurisdictions. Thus, the right of the garage owner to use deadly force in our hypothetical situation still is an open issue in at least several states.

Once the court finds that there is no binding precedent, how does it determine what the relevant rule of law should be? First, it will look to any statute that might be controlling. In some cases, the statutory language, although not previously interpreted, may be so clear on its face as to provide an answer. But the "plain meaning" of a statutory provision is not always available. As Justice Holmes told us: "A word is not a crystal, transparent and unchanged, it is the skin of a living thought and may vary greatly in color and content according to the circumstances and the time in which it is used."[31] Frequently, there will be several conflicting interpretations that reasonably can be drawn from the statutory wording. Here, the court must look beyond the language to the purpose of the legislature. In interpreting federal statutes and the statutes of a few states, the court may gain assistance from the "legislative history" provided by recorded debates and committee reports. In most jurisdictions, however, such recorded history will not be available.[32] The court must infer the legislature's purpose from its reading of the statute as a whole. To do this, the court must appreciate the societal claims and demands that gave rise to the statute. Very often the judge must ask himself the following question: "In view of the overall objective of the statute, including the mischief it sought to prohibit, and its treatment of somewhat similar situations elsewhere in the statute, is it more likely than not that the legislature meant to give a particular treatment to the fact situation presented before me"? While such a question is based on objective criterion, it cannot be denied that the judge's answer may be based in part on which he views as the most appropriate implementation of sound social policy.

Where there is no binding precedent and no governing statute, the court must frame a legal standard based on its own common law authority. The process of developing that standard will involve, however, steps roughly analogous to

---

30. This is particularly true in jurisdictions lacking intermediate appellate courts.

31. *Towne v. Eisner*, 245 U.S. 418, 425, 38 S.Ct.158, 159, 62 L.Ed. 372 (1918).

32. Even where available, such records may be of limited value. As Professor Leflar has observed in speaking of congressional intent: "It is difficult to discover intent; and when you cannot discover with authority the state of mind of one man, the process of discovering the states of mind, the intents of 535 men, who make up the Federal Congress, becomes an extremely difficult matter." R. Leflar, quoted in R. Aldisert, *The Judicial Process*, St. Paul, Minn.: West Publishing Company, 1976, p. 179.

those applied where there is a statute, except that the emphasis will be upon related common law decisions rather than statutory language. The court initially will examine the rulings in cases that involve roughly similar situations. It will be looking for decisions which, while not squarely on point, are applicable by analogy. At times, such decisions will so clearly point in a single direction that the applicable standard will be obvious. Assume, for example, that in our hypothetical case involving the garage owner, there is no prior decision such as *People v. Blue*. Instead, there is the decision of *People v. Red*, which holds that a police officer cannot use deadly force to catch an escaping thief. There also is a general common law principle that in the area of crime prevention and law enforcement, the police officer ordinarily has greater authority than a private citizen. Under this principle, where the police officer lacks authority to use a particular degree of force for law enforcement purposes, a private citizen almost certainly would not be given that authority. Thus, combining the *Red* decision with this general principle, it appears that the garage owner, like the police officer, should be prohibited from using deadly force to prevent the escape of a thief. Together these sources point to a particular result in much the same way as a fairly unambiguous statutory provision.

In many cases, there may be no analogous decisions like *Red*, or there may be several analogous decisions that point in different directions. In such a situation, the court must make a choice based on history, custom, and sound social policy. Here, even more so than in statutory interpretation, the significance of the judge's personal view of sound social policy cannot be underestimated. Even though a court finds a roughly analogous precedent and that precedent logically points in a particular direction, the court is not likely to extend the rationale of that precedent if the result will produce a rule that is at odds with its view of the welfare of society. Justice Holmes captured the essence of this aspect of law-making under the common law in what is surely the most frequently quoted statement in all of our legal writings:

> *The life of the law has not been logic; it has been experience. The felt necessities of the time, the prevalent moral and political theories, intuitions of public policy, avowed or unconscious, even the prejudices which judges share with their fellow-men, have had a good deal more to do than syllogism in determining the rules by which men should be governed.*[33]

---

33. O. Holmes, *The Common Law*, Boston: Little, Brown & Company, 1891, pp. 1-2.

For further information on the material covered in the first part of this chapter (the structure of state and federal judicial systems), see Law Enforcement Assistance Administration, *National Survey of Court Organization*, Washington, D.C.: Government Printing Office, 1973 (and 1977 supplement), and H. Abraham, *The Judicial Process*, London, England: Oxford University Press, 3rd edition, 1975. For further information on the material covered in the second portion of this chapter (judicial method in determining the applicable law), see S. Mermin, *Law and the Legal System: An Introduction*, Boston: Little, Brown & Company, 1973, and E. Levi, *An Introduction to Legal Reasoning*, Chicago: University of Chicago Press, 1948.

THE HIERARCHY OF COURTS

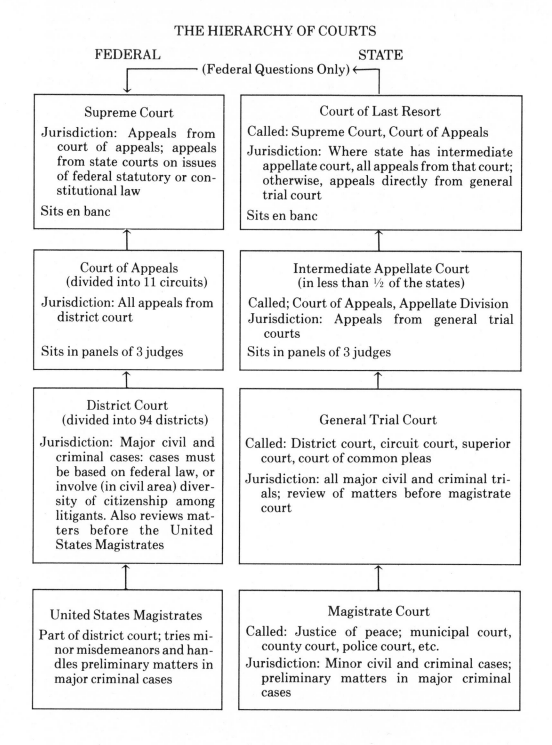

FEDERAL   STATE

(Federal Questions Only)

Supreme Court

Jurisdiction: Appeals from court of appeals; appeals from state courts on issues of federal statutory or constitutional law

Sits en banc

Court of Last Resort

Called: Supreme Court, Court of Appeals

Jurisdiction: Where state has intermediate appellate court, all appeals from that court; otherwise, appeals directly from general trial court

Sits en banc

Court of Appeals
(divided into 11 circuits)

Jurisdiction: All appeals from district court

Sits in panels of 3 judges

Intermediate Appellate Court
(in less than ½ of the states)

Called; Court of Appeals, Appellate Division
Jurisdiction: Appeals from general trial courts

Sits in panels of 3 judges

District Court
(divided into 94 districts)

Jurisdiction: Major civil and criminal cases: cases must be based on federal law, or involve (in civil area) diversity of citizenship among litigants. Also reviews matters before the United States Magistrates

General Trial Court

Called: District court, circuit court, superior court, court of common pleas

Jurisdiction: all major civil and criminal trials; review of matters before magistrate court

United States Magistrates

Part of district court; tries minor misdemeanors and handles preliminary matters in major criminal cases

Magistrate Court

Called: Justice of peace; municipal court, county court, police court, etc.
Jurisdiction: Minor civil and criminal cases; preliminary matters in major criminal cases

Part Two

The Nature of Crime and Criminal Responsibility

INTRODUCTION

Having examined the structure of the legal system generally, we are now ready to turn to that part of the law that governs the criminal justice system. We start with an exploration of the substantive criminal law—the law which defines and establishes penalties for crime. Chapter Four considers the basic elements of the concept of crime and the different categories of crimes. Chapter Five exams the common components of most offenses recognized in the criminal law. Chapters Six and Seven then consider the special aspects of several of the most significant offenses. Chapter Six concentrates on crimes against the person, such as murder and rape, while Chapter Seven concentrates on crimes against property, such as theft and arson. In the course of describing the different crimes, frequent references will be made to state statutes and decisions. Appendix A tells you how to find these sources of law and also explains the citations that you will find in the footnotes.*

---

*Since the annotated editions of the state statutes (see Appendix A *infra*) are the most readily available editions in most libraries, all of our citations will be to those editions. We will not, however, include the name of the publisher nor the term "annotated" in the citation, as almost all states now have only one major annotated edition and that will be the edition we are using. Thus, West's Annotated California Penal Code will be cited simply as "California Penal Code," McKinney's Annotated New York Penal Law will be cited as " New York Penal Law," and Smith-Hurd's Annotated Illinois statutes will be cited as "Illinois Stat.".

Chapter 4

What Is A Crime?

To understand the nature of the substantive criminal law, we must first explore the basic concepts that distinguish crimes from other violations of the law. To appreciate the range of the criminal law, we also should be aware of the many different categories of crimes. This chapter examines both of these aspects of the criminal law.

THE LEGAL DEFINITION OF CRIME

The traditional legal definition of a crime is restated in the statutes of most states. While that restatement varies slightly from jurisdiction to jurisdiction, the definition contained in the California Penal Code is typical:

> A crime or public offense is an act committed or omitted in violation of a law forbidding or commanding it, and to which is annexed, upon conviction, either of the following punishments: (1) Death; (2) Imprisonment; (3) Fine; (4) Removal from office; or (5) Disqualification to hold and enjoy any office of honor, trust, or profit in this State.[1]

Several features of this definition help to explain the legal principles underlying the concept of "crime." First, a crime, as a creature of the law, requires an act that violates the law as opposed to violating customs, religious standards, or some other means of social control.[2] There are, however, many acts that violate the law, but are not crimes. Breach of contract, for example, is illegal, yet not ordinarily criminal. To turn an illegal act into a criminal offense, further elements are

---

1.　California Penal Code §15.

2.　As the California definition notes, that behavior may be either an affirmative act (e.g., stealing another's car) or an omission, a failure to act where the law requires certain behavior (e.g., failing to file a required tax form). This distinction in the form of the act is considered in Chapter Five.

needed. The California definition also describes a crime as a "public offense".[3] A crime, in other words, is viewed as an illegality against the interests of the public as a whole as opposed to an illegality only against the individual victim of the violation. As we noted in Chapter Two, it is this factor which largely distinguishes the criminal law from the civil law and explains why the judicial enforcement of the criminal law is pursued by a public official (the prosecuting attorney) on behalf of the state. The concept of the crime as an act against the public also explains a third element of the traditional definition—that a crime is an act which may lead to the imposition of punishment.

The California provision lists five different forms of punishment. Each of these is designed to vindicate the interests of the public (largely by preventing future offenses) rather than to compensate the individual victim. As a practical matter, the court's authority to impose the second and third of the mentioned punishments (imprisonment and fine) are the crucial elements in identifying most crimes. The death penalty is limited to a narrow class of homicides which clearly are crimes. The two other categories of punishment, both relating to the holding of public office, almost always are provided for under laws that also provide for imprisonment or fine.[4] If a question arises as to whether some act prohibited by law is a crime, the court will look to the potential consequences that may be imposed upon the violator. If it finds that imprisonment or a punitive fine may be imposed, it recognizes that the behavior is viewed as an offense against the public and, hence, a crime.[5]

---

3. The word "crime" is derived from the Latin word "crimen" which means offense. Hence the words "crime," "criminal offense," and simply "offense" are often used interchangeably in describing criminal activity. We also will use these terms as synonymous terms unless the context clearly suggests otherwise. Similarly, the terms "criminal" and "offender" also will be used interchangeably.

    In some jurisdictions, the term "crime" is limited to criminal violations of state law while the term "offense" includes both those violations and local ordinance violations that may result in punishment of the offender. This characterization of local ordinance violations as something other than crimes, even though they result in punishment, has been severely criticized. See W. LaFave and A. Scott, Jr., *Criminal Law*, St. Paul, Minn.: West Publishing Co., 1972, pp.36-38. Even in those jurisdictions where this separate characterization persists, such ordinance violations are treated in almost all other respects like state criminal violations. In our use of the terms crime and offense, we will not distinguish between violations of state law and violations of ordinances. Both will be described as crimes or offenses if they contain those elements noted in the California definition of crime.

4. Recently adopted statutory definitions of crime accordingly omit any separate reference to these two categories of punishment. See, e.g., Kansas Stat. §21-3105: "A crime is an act or omission defined by law and for which, upon conviction, a sentence of death, imprisonment or fine, or both imprisonment and fine is authorized."

5. It should be noted that this statement applies only to "punitive" as opposed to "regulatory" fines. Where a statute prohibiting a particular act provides for imposing a death sentence or imprisonment upon violators, the use of these forms of punishment necessarily indicates that the statute was intended to make that act a crime. Where the statute provides only for the imposition of a fine, on the other hand, the court must carefully examine the nature of the fine in determining whether the violation is a crime. In some instances, the fine clearly is imposed as a penalty for the commission of a harmful act by a person who had a wrongful purpose. This indicates its purpose was to serve as punishment for a crime. In other cases, fines are imposed for unintentional technical violation of the law that do not cause significant harm. Here the purpose of the fine simply is to encourage greater care and, in part, to pay for the enforcement process. These latter fines often are described as "regulatory" fines since they commonly apply to heavily regulated industries (as in the case of fines imposed upon truckers for various equipment violations).

Although the concept of a criminal offense is well established today, this was not always the case. The recognition of a class of illegal acts known as crimes was a product of a gradual historical development. Society made several crucial determinations in accepting the concept of crime, some of which are still being reexamined today. First society had to determine that there were some actions that should be viewed as injurious to the public as a whole rather than just to the individual victim. This decision, in turn, was followed by the conclusion that such actions were appropriately subject to punishment. Finally, various determinations had to be made as to what punishment could legitimately be imposed. A brief review of each of these developments provides further insight into the nature of crime.

HISTORICAL DEVELOPMENT
OF THE CONCEPT OF A PUBLIC OFFENSE

Originally, the acts we now view as crimes were torts; in other words, all wrongs were originally considered to be private wrongs.[6] In the early history of the law, the state (in those days represented by the king) did not concern itself with punishing wrongs except those directed against the state, such as treason. In the case of A putting out the eye of B, it was B's responsibility to "get even," which he often did by trying to put out the eye of A. In many societies, not only was it B's responsibility to punish A, it was also the responsibility of all of B's family or kin to see that the damage done to B was punished. Sometimes, under such circumstances, A could not be found, so it became the custom to "get even" by putting out the eye of any one of A's family or kin who could be located. A blood feud developed in which every member of B's family was seeking to avenge B on any one in A's family they could find. Since A's family couldn't be expected to be happy about this, the result often was that everyone in A's family was trying to inflict injury on everyone in B's family. Such feuds could wipe out entire families on both sides.

Feuding was costly in terms of lives and property; it also destroyed the peace of the community. The king did not appreciate either consequence very much. The king saw that he was losing many good soldiers because his subjects were killing each other. So the king took over the right and the responsibility of punishing offenders. The king said in effect, "If one citizen inflicts an injury on another, the injured party must report it to me, and I will take care of punishing the wrongdoer." Conduct which resulted in injury to one of the king's subjects was declared to be an offense against the king's peace. The action brought against the offender was brought in the king's name. To this day, a crime is seen to be an offense against the "king's peace," although today the king has been replaced by

---

Violations resulting in such fines are not viewed as criminal and usually are collected through administrative agency proceedings that are quite different from criminal prosecutions.

In recent years, efforts have been made to "decriminalize" certain types of crimes by eliminating possible sentences of imprisonment, classifying the fines as regulatory, and shifting the proceedings to administrative agencies. This has been done, for example, in the area of parking violations and minor traffic violations. The legislature readily can shift its characterization of the fine in these areas to the non-punitive category because the acts involved do not present substantial fault or "culpability" (see pp. 69, 106-107 *infra*) on the part of the actor.

6.   Davis et. al., note 5, p. 7 *supra*, at ch. 8.

the state. In Texas, every criminal charge, after setting out the offense, ends with the words "against the peace and dignity of the State of Texas."

In many societies, the king also found another significant justification for the treatment of certain illegal acts as offenses against the king. In these societies, the individuals involved began to realize that blood feuds were an extremely unsatisfactory way of settling arguments. The payment of compensation gradually replaced feuding as a remedy for many wrongs. If a man stole a cow, he or his family was entitled to get a cow back from the thief. If the thief had killed the stolen cow, and had no cow at the time of the action, then, after the invention of money, the victim could collect from the thief in money the value of the cow. The king noticed this exchange of money and decided he ought to get some of it for himself. So he not only decided the punishment due the thief for breaking the king's peace, he also required that the thief or his family pay him money. The compensation for the cow went to the owner of the cow, but the fine went to the king. This was the origin of our modern system of fines in criminal cases.

One author sums up the historical development of the notion of "crime" in this way: "The concept of criminal law emerged only when the custom of private vengeance was replaced by the principle that the community as a whole is injured when one of its members is harmed. Thus the right to act against a wrongdoing was, indeed, granted to the state as the representative of the people."[7]

THE DEVELOPMENT OF PUNISHMENT

Early Forms. Punishments originally consisted of either fines, the infliction of bodily harm (known as *corporal punishment*), or execution (*capital punishment*).The primary forms of corporal punishment were branding, flogging, and mutilation. Still another early form of punishment was banishment—exclusion from the community. All of these early forms of punishment have persisted through modern times and are to be found today in at least some parts of the world. In our part of the world, however, many of these early forms of punishment have been completely or largely eliminated and new forms of punishment have been replaced them.

Modern Forms of Punishment. At the time the American colonies broke away from England, over 200 different felonies were recognized under English law, and each of the felonies was subject to capital punishment. Many of the felonies of that period, though capital offenses, were offenses we today would classify as no more than misdemeanors. Eighty percent of the executions were for property offenses, and some involved only petty theft. Executions were public affairs, attended by huge crowds, and often carried out as cruelly as possible. As might be expected, considerable dissatisfaction existed, both in this country and in England, with the heavy use of capital punishment. Courts and juries managed in various ways to avoid the imposition of the death sentence. Judges, for example, had the authority in certain crimes to reduce the sentence in their discretion to a less severe form of corporal punishment (e.g., flogging).

---

7.   R. Quinney, *Crime and Justice In Society*, Boston: Little, Brown and Company, 1969, p. 5.

Another much used form of punishment in England was transportation of convicts to overseas colonies. Certain of the American colonies were populated almost entirely by felons fleeing the harsh punishments of the motherland. (The great insistence on including the Bill of Rights in the Constitution came in large part from such colonists). The American Revolution almost created a crisis in English justice. Temporarily there was no place to send the "banished" convicts— and no place to which the fugitive from that "justice" could flee. The opening up of Australia helped to solve the problem for England. In America, banishment had been employed by the colonies during their early stages of development, but by the time of the revolution, banishment was largely unavailable as a formal sanction (although fugitives still fled to the readily available frontier).

Opposition to the traditional English form of punishments eventually led to an American invention—incarceration in a penitentiary—that became the dominant form of punishment throughout the world. Imprisonment had been initiated substantially before the late eighteenth century, but early imprisonment was used only to retain a prisoner pending trial or to hold vagrants. A new penal philosophy, developed by the Quakers of Pennsylvania, sought to replace corporal and capital punishment with the incarceration of convicted felons for long periods of time in penal institutions called prisons or penitentiaries. The Quakers established these prisons for humane reasons. The good Quakers believed that if a man were confined in solitary confinement, and permitted to meditate continuously upon his sins, he would be rehabilitated. Though in those early prisons no cruel treatment was permitted, the "Pennsylvania system" unfortunately did not result in rehabilitation of the offender. Instead there was rampant suicide and mental illness among the inmates. The concept of imprisonment attracted considerable attention, however, and it was soon followed in many states. In many jurisdictions, imprisonment was combined with corporal punishment within the prison as a means of keeping "control" over the prisoners.

Just as prisons were the primary development in penology in the 1800's, the use of probation and parole were the primary developments in the 1900's. Both involve supervised control of the convict in a community setting rather than in a prison. Under probation, the convicted person is released into the community under supervised control without first having served any time in a penitentiary. Under parole, the individual first serves a term of imprisonment and then is released for supervised control. Under both procedures, if the individual violates the terms of his supervised control, he can be imprisoned to serve the remainder of his sentence.

In the United States today, imprisonment, probation, and parole are the primary forms of punishment for all but the most petty crimes (where fines remain especially significant). Capital punishment, as we shall see,[8] has been abolished altogether in several states and is available in all others only for a single type of crime (homicide). Corporal punishment also has been abolished. Under certain circumstances, however, solitary confinement is still permitted in prisons. Loss of various rights (e.g., the right to vote) is a quite common punishment, although not viewed as a dominant form of punishment. We will discuss these various forms of

---

8.   See p. 334 *infra.*

punishment at much greater length in Chapter Thirteen. It is important at this stage merely to be aware of the general nature of the punishments used in the past and today. The nature of the various punishments imposed clearly reflects our consistent treatment of crimes as serious, wrongful acts. The severe character of most punishments, even in their modern forms, also underscores the significance of the issues that society faces when it decides to impose punishment on fellow human beings. That decision has been a matter of continuing concern to scholars studying the criminal law, and many books have been written addressed to the two basic issues presented by our use of punishment: "What are the legitimate objectives of punishment," and "What are the moral justifications for imposing punishment"? Differences in the responses that may be presented to both of these issues are extremely important, for how one answers these issues determines, in large part, the appropriate shaping of the criminal law.

THE OBJECTIVES OF PUNISHMENT

Why does society impose punishment on the individual who deviates from its norms? What does society hope to accomplish with punishment? Experts in the field commonly point to four functions as possible objectives of criminal sanctions. These are (1) retribution, (2) deterrence, (3) incapacitation, and (4) rehabilitation.

Retribution. The word retribution means "something for recompense." "An eye for an eye, a tooth for a tooth," interpreted as a command to punish the offender, has been accepted in our culture since Biblical times. It is also a natural human response. People who get hurt are inclined to hurt back. One only has to read the daily papers to realize that crimes which are currently upsetting the citizenry are drawing heavy penalties. Thus, we read that a jury in Texas returned a sentence of over 100 years against a drug pusher. The jury's response reflected the fact that the community was very upset about the drug problem. There was, however, no readily available civil remedy for the drug pusher's action, no ready means of compensating the victims of the crime. The only means of obtaining "recompense" on behalf of society was through a retributive sentence.

The situation presented by the drug offense is common to all criminal offenses. By their very nature, these are not illegalities that can readily be remedied by restitution (returning to the victim what he lost) or paying monetary compensation. How do you repay a man for the loss of an eye? How do you return stolen property that the thief has squandered? The very designation of an illegality as a crime indicates that civil remedies are likely to be inadequate. Revenge then becomes the only means of restitution—the only way to "even things up," or obtain something for recompense.

While retribution was initially recognized as the dominant objective of punishment, its validity has been a subject of considerable dispute for many years now. Opponents contend that it is barbaric and unfit for a civilized society to seek revenge; our goal in utilizing punishment should be directed solely toward controlling the future behavior of persons. Supporters of retribution respond that it is not barbaric, but morally right to hate criminals and desire to inflict retribution upon them. Other, less enthusiastic supporters of retribution argue that, right or wrong, our society's desire for retribution is a fact of life; if we do not recognize retribution, we will return to a situation in which the victim and his relatives seek their own, private vengeance. The least enthusiastic supporters of retribution argue that it should be recognized only as a minor goal of punishment. They contend that retribution should be considered only in determining what behavior requires punishment. No act should be deemed a criminal offense unless it is viewed by society as deserving retribution, but the appropriate level of punishment for the offense should be determined only on the basis of the other goals of punishment (that is, deterrence, incapacitation, and rehabilitation). It is interesting to note that the statement of purposes of the criminal law in modern codes commonly do not make a specific reference to retribution, although they do recognize the other goals of punishment.[9]

Deterrence.   When society punishes a wrongdoer, one of its main objectives is deterrence. There are two aspects to deterrence. When we punish A, we want to deter A from committing additional offenses, not only during his period of imprisonment, but after he gets out. We believe that punishment will bring about a change in the behavior of the person punished. This kind of deterrence is commonly described as "special" or "individual" deterrence. We also expect another kind of deterrence, which is described as "general" or "community" deterrence. We believe that punishing A will deter B, C, D, and all other members of the community who might consider committing the same crime. What we say is, "If these people see A punished for stealing, then they will be afraid of being punished in a similar way, and will refrain from stealing."

Considerable controversy exists as to whether punishment truly serves as a deterrent. Not all agree that punishing A will deter A, let alone that punishing A will deter B and other members of the community. In our first chapter we talked about pickpockets picking pockets while watching the hanging of pickpockets.[10] "This proves," say many, "that punishing A never deters B." But as we have

---

9.   Consider, for example, New York Penal Law §1.05:

> The general purposes of the provisions of this chapter are:
>
> 1.   To proscribe conduct which unjustifiably and inexcusably causes or threatens substantial harm to individual or public interests;
>
> 2.   To give fair warning of the nature of the conduct proscribed and of the sentence authorized upon conviction;
>
> 3.   To define the act or omission and the accompanying mental state which constitute each offense;
>
> 4.   To differentiate on reasonable grounds between serious and minor offenses and to prescribe proportionate penalties therefor; and
>
> 5.   To insure the public safety by preventing the commission of offenses through the deterrent influence of the sentences authorized, the rehabilitation of those convicted, and their confinement when required in the interests of public protection.

Note, however, R. Allen, *Retribution In A Modern Penal Law: The Principle Of Aggravated Harm*, 25 Buffalo L. Rev. 1 (1975). The author argues that while retribution is not formally recognized in section 1.05 of the New York Penal Law, various provisions of the penal law, including many that increase punishment according to the degree of harm inflicted by the crime (the "aggravated harm principle"), are justified primarily in terms of retribution. The same contention can be advanced with respect to all of the other modern codes. See also the discussion of the "hierarchy of penalties" in Chapter Five at pp. 89-91 *infra*.

10.   See p. 14 *supra*.

already pointed out, this conclusion does not necessarily follow. Certainly X number of pickpockets went on picking pockets in the crowd around the gallows, and hence were obviously not deterred by the punishments going on. But not all the persons around the gallows picked pockets. They were deterred by *something.* How many were deterred from picking pockets by the sight of pickpockets being hanged? This we never know. We catch and count only those who were not deterred. The deterrent value of punishment is very difficult to prove or disprove.

Even if it could be established that the law-abiding people were not motivated in part by a fear of punishment, that fact alone would not establish that the criminal law had no incidental deterrent effect. Critics of the deterrence theory argue that persons who abide by the law do so because of their internal inhibitions, not because they fear that they would be caught and punished if they committed crimes. Accepting that premise (which is obviously true for some people and some crimes, but certainly not all), the question arises as to how such internal inhibitions are developed. Supporters of the deterrence theory argue that the use of criminal punishment is an important factor in the development of these inhibitions. They contend that criminal punishment serves, by the publicity which attends the trial, conviction and punishment of criminals, to educate the public as to the proper distinctions between good conduct and bad. They argue that the criminal law thus reinforces our value system, developed through religion, morals, and traditions, as to what is inappropriate behavior. Indeed, it argued that the persistent infliction of punishment can eventually convince the public of the wrongfulness of acts, such as price fixing, which might not naturally be viewed as immoral or wrongful. This potential impact of punishment in creating and reinforcing self-inhibitions, and thereby preventing crime, commonly is described as the "educational" or the "general preventive" effect of punishment. Many commentators contend this aspect of the deterrence theory of punishment is the most widely accepted justification for the use of punishment today.

Incapacitation. Incapacitation means to make a person incapable of doing something. Imprisonment makes it impossible or difficult for the offender to repeat his transgression. Of course a man incarcerated in a state prison can injure a prison officer, or steal from the prison commissary or his fellow prisoners, but the fact of his being in prison keeps him away from the rest of us. We send men to prison to make it very difficult, if not impossible, for them to continue to harm society. In primitive societies, the same result was reached by banishment. We can no longer banish an offender from our society by physically ejecting him from the country, but we still practice a limited form of banishment when we place criminals in prison, restrict the persons they may associate with while on parole or probation, or keep them from holding certain jobs. Occasionally, we come closer to the original form of banishment when a prisoner is placed in solitary confinement for a limited period of time. Banishment has always been considered to be one of the most severe forms of punishment, as few men can live without the contact and support of the group. Today we rely heavily upon incapacitation—particularly through imprisonment—as an objective of punishment. As long as the offender is incarcerated, we have banished him from our midst.

Rehabilitation.   The objective of criminal sanctions that we have particularly stressed over the last several decades is that of rehabilitation of the offender.[11] "The punishment should fit not only the crime, but the criminal," we say. We thus have developed programs of treatment and resocialization in our prisons and we have promoted community-based treatment such as probation and parole. We have criminologists attempting to determine the causes of criminal behavior, and psychologists researching ways to change it. Rehabilitation is viewed as a goal, moreover, not only in determining the form of punishment, but in all aspects of the criminal justice system. The way a police officer arrests a man, and the treatment he receives in court, may have a lot to do with how successful we are going to be in his rehabilitation through the correctional process.

Although many criminologists view it as the most worthwhile goal of punishment, the rehabilitative goal has been much criticized in recent years on the ground that it simply cannot be achieved. This criticism has been bolstered by the continuously high rate of recidivism (i.e., the repeated commission of crimes) by person formerly imprisoned. As we shall see in our discussion of recidivism in Chapter Thirteen, available statistics on recidivism are not without shortcomings. Nevertheless, they clearly establish that imprisonment has failed to achieve rehabilitation in a substantial percentage of cases. Proponents of rehabilitation respond that a substantial rate of recidivism does not establish that rehabilitation cannot be achieved, but that it really hasn't been tried in earnest. Some argue that the very nature of the prison system, in particular, runs counter to the goal of reformation. They contend that the basic nature of imprisonment as a punishment must be altered, with movement toward community treatment facilities as opposed to traditional prisons. While there has been some movement in this direction, it has been slow. Some critics claim that the potential gains are too speculative to justify the extreme expense involved, while others claim that a full scale effort at rehabilitation would undercut the other necessary objectives of punishment, particularly incapacitation and deterrence.

Conflict Between The Objectives.   By and large, in determining what behavior should be deemed criminal, our emphasis is on retribution and to some extent deterrence. A person may not be declared a criminal simply because he is potentially dangerous and rehabilitation or incapacitation is desirable. He generally must have committed some harmful act in a wrongful manner. This emphasis on the harmful act, as opposed to the dangerous personality, is essential to the justifiable imposition of retribution. In stressing the harm actually done, we also promote the deterrent objective of punishment, particularly under a general preventative theory of deterrence. Thus, at the initial stage of defining the crime, the goals of retribution and deterrence will dominate. But once the law looks beyond the issue as to whether particular behavior should constitute a crime, and considers the form and degree of punishment, then it is likely that all four of the objectives of punishment may be given consideration. It also is likely, as the varying nature of

---

11.   That this objective has existed for some time is demonstrated by the State of Oregon, which in 1859 put these words into its constitution: "Laws for the punishment of crime shall be founded on principles of reformation, and not of vindictive justice."

these objectives would suggest, that the objectives may conflict in their possible application to any particular case.

If the crime is a heinous one, the goal of revenge demands a strong punishment, yet the particular offender may be one who could be rehabilitated in a relatively short period of time. The crime committed may be relatively minor, but the offender may be a psychopath, a type of person notoriously difficult to reform. The goals of incapacitation or rehabilitation may require a lengthy period of incarceration, but the insignificant nature of the crime would not permit such a severe sentence under a theory of retribution. And so it goes. Our objectives cut up against each other, and we often must choose one to the detriment of the other. This creates confusion in our criminal statutes, in the authority we give to police officers, in the way we handle the offender during trial, and especially in the way we treat him after conviction. A sentence almost always represents a kind of compromise. Our different objectives have been put in the basket, so to speak, and what comes out depends on how much of each objective is placed in that basket by the judge (or in some jurisdictions, the jury) making the sentencing decision. As one would expect from this process, what is put into the basket will vary from place to place and from time to time. The result is that we seldom know just what goal, or goals, we are trying to achieve in the case of any individual upon whom we impose punishment.

THE MORAL JUSTIFICATION FOR PUNISHMENT

We consider next the moral issue presented by society's imposition of punishment on fellow human beings. The traditional forms of punishment, as we have seen, place significant restraints upon a criminal offender. The most severe, capital punishment, eliminates life altogether. Is society justified in imposing such severe sanctions upon another human being even assuming that punishment serves the goals of retribution, deterrence, incapacitation and rehabilitation? Since punishment is being imposed, we know that society has answered this question in the affirmative, but it is important that we also understand the reasoning that has produced this "yes" answer. That reasoning explains in large part the required elements in the definition of a crime, which we will discuss in the next chapter.

Early Notions About the Causes of Wrongdoing. In the early development of social norms and the imposition of punishment for deviation from those norms, it was believed that a man offended against the social rules because (1) he had a bad, depraved mind, or because (2) he was possessed of evil spirits. In either event, punishment was obviously justified. No moral question was presented by the punishment of a man with a bad and depraved mind who deliberately transgressed against the society. If the cause of the wrongful act was that the man was possessed of evil spirits, he clearly had permitted them to usurp his will, and anyway punishing him severely was the best way to free him from them. Thus, early punishments sought both to inflict pain for the depraved mind and to exorcise the evil spirits. With the development of more advanced moral codes, a more logical justification for punishment was sought. This justification was found in the concept of "free will," which almost immediately was challenged by "determinism."

Free Will and Determinism.   At the heart of the moral justification for punishment is the idea that every man is possessed of "free will;" that he is, in other words, free to make choices. The doer of a criminal act, according to this view, always has the choice between doing the act and not doing it. If he chooses to do it knowing it is wrong, he should be held responsible for his acts.

The deterministic position, on the other hand, is that the acts of an individual are "determined" by his prior life experiences and that at any given moment he really has no power of choice. He will act, or not act, according to psychic determinants of which he is largely unaware and over which he has little or no voluntary control. According to this view, there is no justification for punishing a man for an act over which he has no control. To put it another way, crime is a social illness, and the sick offender should be treated, not subjected to severe sanctions.

If we go back to our discussion of the objectives of punishment, it is easy to see that the determinist views the objective of punishment chiefly in terms of rehabilitation of the offender. Retribution is viewed as an illegitimate goal, as is incapacitation where unaccompanied by rehabilitation. General deterrence is rejected as incapable of success, since behavior is viewed as guided by factors other than fear of punishment. Special deterrence may be accepted, but only to the extent that the "treatment" provided by punishment can modify the life experience of the individual and thus change his behavior. Indeed, the true determinist rejects the word "punishment" since it suggests the deliberate infliction of pain for wrongdoing rather than treatment for predetermined acts.

The philosopher of free will, on the other hand, accepts the rightness of retribution, sees the need for incapacitation of the wrong-doer, and supports deterrence on the theory that the free choice of the prospective criminal often can be altered by the threat of punishment. Since he accepts these goals, the free will advocate also approves the gradation of penalties according to the amount of harm done by the particular criminal act. Actually, supporters of free will not only reject the underlying theory of determinism but they often claim also that its general application in the criminal law would undermine social control. Under that theory, they argue, persons would not be responsible for their behavior even when they inflicted great injury on others and created grim danger to society as a whole. In accepting free will, the supporters do not reject rehabilitation as a legitimate goal of punishment where it can be achieved, but they reject the contention that it must be the sole or primary goal of punishment.

During the nineteenth century, the arguments on free will and determinism raged hot and heavy in the learned journals. It finally became an accepted fact that "the law believes in free will." In a case decided in 1968, Judge Wright of the Federal Court of Appeals summarized the position of law as follows:

> In the long-standing debate over criminal responsibility, there has always been a strong conviction in our jurisprudence that to hold a man criminally responsible his actions must have been voluntary, the product of a "free will." . . . In deciding responsibility for crime, therefore, the law postulates a "free will" and then recognizes known deviations.[12]

---

12.   *Salzman v. United States*, 405 F.2d 358, 368 (D.C. Cir. 1968).

As Judge Wright notes, the law starts out with an assumption of free will. A person cannot be relieved of criminal liability for a harmful act because he claims to have been so angry, irritated, hungry, or socially or economically deprived that he simply "could not control himself." On the other hand, if the circumstances were such that he physically lacked control over the injurious act, then he truly lacked free will and will not be held criminally responsible. Thus, the law will not punish an epileptic for physical actions performed in a state of seizure. Similarly, a person will not be liable for causing harm when he had no reasonable basis for believing that his acts would be harmful. Thus, if a person enters his car and drives over a neighborhood child who was hiding under the car and fell asleep there, that person will not be guilty of homicide. Although his act was a product of free will, we cannot say he caused harm of his free will because he had no reason to believe he was causing harm. (However, as we shall see, if a reasonable person under the circumstances should have suspected the child's presence and looked under the car, then the driver may be guilty of a lesser form of homicide since he willfully failed to exercise the caution we would expect from a reasonable person). Various other illustrations also could be offered of situations in which the law recognizes what Judge Wright describes as "deviations" because of the absence of truly free will. We will consider several in Chapter Five. The important point to note here is the basic premise of free will, which permits the criminal law to justify punishment as a deserved product of the individual's personal *culpability* (i.e., blameworthiness). The same concept also permits the criminal law to vary the degree of punishment according to the degree of blameworthiness of the offender.

CLASSIFICATION OF CRIMES

The substantive criminal law covers a broad range of prohibited activities. Several years ago, a study in the state of Michigan produced a list of over 3,000 different activities that constituted crimes in that state. With such extensive coverage, it is not surprising that people working in the field have sought to divide the various crimes into different categories or groups. Some of the dividing lines used in categorizing crimes have significance in the law, a particular categorization carrying with it particular legal consequences. Other lines of division are used simply as convenient guides in describing particular crimes. With the wide range of the criminal law, it often is easiest to describe a particular crime by first placing it within one or more descriptive categories and then describing the particular elements that distinguish it from other crimes in that category. In describing the crime of extortion, for example, a commentator may note initially that it is "a felony," "a crime against property," and "a former common law crime." This description will tell us the level of the crime (in terms of punishment imposed), the type of interest it is designed to protect, and its origin. With this information in hand, it will be easier to follow the remainder of the description of the extortion offense. We consider below the most significant of the various dividing lines used in classifying crimes. They will assist you not only in understanding particular crimes, but also in gaining appreciation of the range and diversity of the substantive criminal law.

Common Law and Code Offenses.   As we have seen, the common law was a body of judge-made law originally developed in England from the time of the Norman Conquest. As we also have seen, the law of crimes developed from the law of torts, a traditional common law subject. Not surprisingly therefore, the law of crimes also was developed originally by courts in the exercise of their common law authority. On a case-by-case basis, consistent with the common law traditions noted previously, the English courts created one new crime after another. By the 1600's, they had created and defined the felonies of murder, manslaughter, burglary, arson, robbery, larceny, rape and sodomy. They also had created various misdemeanors, including assault, battery, false imprisonment and perjury. At points the courts did not move fast enough for Parliament and it had to add new crimes by statute. Thus, the crime of embezzlement was first created by the Parliament rather than the courts. However, statutory offenses created by the Parliament were framed in very general terms, leaving the courts considerable room for judicial interpretation. Since the courts, in the end, usually provided the fundamental elements of definition for such statutory offenses, those offenses frequently were viewed by commentators as largely common law offenses.

Each of the thirteen original colonies, upon breaking away from England, retained the English common law crimes (including those crimes that had been initiated by Parliament, but largely developed by the English courts). Initially the American courts relied primarily on English precedent in applying those crimes. They soon began to develop and modify the common law to meet the frontier aspects of American society. Thus, in many areas, the common law of crimes in the United States began to develop a distinctly American flavor. As new states joined the Union, all except the few that had civil law tradition (e.g., Louisiana and New Mexico) followed the precedent of the thirteen original colonies. They adopted the English common law and modified it when necessary to meet the needs of American society.

Prior to the mid-1800's, almost all of the states relied upon the common law for the substance of their criminal law. In many states, the legislatures had adopted numerous statutory offenses, but these crimes did not seek to replace the common law offenses. Ordinarily the statutes merely set the maximum punishment for common law offenses, leaving the basic content of the crime to judicial determination. The legislation simply would provide, for example, that the crime of rape was punishable by a sentence up to life imprisonment. Exactly what constituted rape was left to the courts' interpretation of the common law offense of rape.

In the mid-1800's, legal reformers were attracted to the concept of codification—that is, the use of comprehensive statutes (codes) that fully defined all crimes. Underlying the codification movement was the premise that the legislature, not the court, should make the basic policy decisions involved in determining what should or should not be a crime. Instead of merely setting the penalties for crimes, the legislatures would spell out all aspects of criminal conduct. Of course, even with the code defining each element of a crime, some ambiguities would remain and the courts would still have a substantial role in interpreting the code provisions. The only crimes, however, would be those defined initially in the codes. If particular behavior did not violate a code provision, the court could not create a new common law crime and thereby render that behavior criminal. Similarly, if a code provision prohibited certain behavior, the court could not hold that the behavior was not criminal because it had not been prohibited by the common law.

The states varied in their initial approach to codification. Some were fully convinced; they adopted comprehensive codes and abolished all common law crimes. Others were half convinced; they adopted comprehensive codes, but concerned that the codes might prove inadequate, retained judicial authority to establish common law crimes. Still others retained the common law crimes, and adopted occasional statutes creating new crimes, but not comprehensive codes. Over the years, as legislatures grew more active and met more frequently, there was a continuous movement toward further codification. Today, every jurisdiction has a comprehensive code of substantive criminal offenses and only about a dozen states retain the common law as an additional source for criminal prosecution.[13] Moreover, even in those states retaining the common law crimes, the prosecution can rely on the common law offense only where the code does not include a similar offense. Since the codes in these states are sufficiently complete to encompass all major and most minor crimes, the common law offenses are infrequently utilized. Thus, even in those states that retain common law crimes, the significance of the common law today will rest, as it does in those states that have abolished the common law crimes, primarily on the helpfulness of the common law in interpreting statutory crimes.

Although the common law crimes have been replaced entirely or, in some states, almost entirely, by the crimes set forth in the codes, the common law is still helpful in interpreting those code offenses. Since the codes were drafted in light of the common law, courts tend to be heavily influenced by the common law in resolving ambiguities in the code provisions. Indeed, some courts take the position that, unless the language of the code specifically rejects the common law rule, the statutory offense will be read as largely restating the common law offense. Illustrative of the influence of the common law is a recent California decision, *Keeler v. Superior Court*,[14] involving the interpretation of the state statutory offense of murder. In that case, Mrs. Keeler, who was nine month's pregnant, was brutally assaulted by her ex-husband, who threated to "stamp it [the fetus] out of you." As a result of the assault, physicians were forced to remove the fetus. It was delivered stillborn, having suffered a fractured skull from the blows to Mrs. Keeler's abdomen. The prosecutor charged Mr. Keeler with murder under a California code provision that applies to the unlawful killing of all "human beings." The

---

13. The precise number is not clear, since the exact status of common law crimes is not settled in several states. Many states have adopted specific legislation stating that the common law shall no longer apply, while others have adopted codes which by their structure indicate a legislative intent to abolish common law crimes. Thus, all of the states listed in note 16 *infra* as following the Model Penal Code would not recognize common law crimes. In addition to those states, Arizona, California, Iowa, Nebraska, and Oklahoma have statutes or court decisions specifically rejecting common law crimes. On the other side, Alabama, Idaho, Michigan, Nevada, New Jersey, North Carolina, South Carolina, Rhode Island, and Vermont have legislation specifically recognizing the continued applicability of common law offenses. It has long been settled that there are no federal common law crimes.

14. 2 Cal. 3d 619, 87 Cal. Rptr. 481, 470 P.2d 617 (1970).

prosecutor claimed that the fetus, though killed while in its mother's womb, was nevertheless a human being since it had reached a level of development which would have permitted it to live if prematurely delivered. The California Supreme Court rejected this contention, relying largely on the traditional view of homicide under the common law. The common law held that, for the purpose of the crime of homicide, a fetus did not become a human being until it was fully born (i.e., removed from the mother's womb). The common law rule may well have been the product of an era in which medical technology lacked the capacity for successfully delivering premature infants. However, the legislature in adopting the murder statute and using the term "human being" was aware of the common law and undoubtedly intended to create a parallel statutory offense. If the legislature desired to depart from the common law definition of a human being, the court noted, it would have to do so specifically. As the *Keeler* case illustrates, even though common law crimes have been abolished, an understanding of the elements of the common law crimes still can be crucial in applying today's criminal law.

The Model Penal Code and The Changing Role Of The Codes. As we noted previously, all states now have comprehensive penal codes. These codes vary to some extent, however, in their scope. The older codes tend to concentrate primarily on setting the punishment for the various crimes. They often do not provide detailed definitions of crimes and rarely describe possible defenses to crimes (such as the justifiable use of force in self-defense). In these areas, a court is left largely to develop the law itself in light of the common law. In 1962, the American Law Institute, an association of distinguished lawyers and judges, recommended that states adopt more comprehensive criminal codes. The Institute offered as a model for the states to follow its own Model Penal Code. The Model Penal Code was designed to provide a more systematic and complete analysis of the criminal law. It dealt with defenses as well as the definitions of crimes, and it offered more complete definitions than were found in the older codes.[15]

There is probably no single development which has had such a significant impact upon the form and substance of the criminal law in this country as the Model Penal Code. Over 30 states have now adopted comprehensive codes based upon the Model Code,[16] and several others currently have commissions preparing such codes for legislative consideration. Admittedly, the state codes based upon the Model Penal Code are not identical. Most will vary from the Model Code in their definition of one or more groups of crimes, and all will utilize their own pattern of penalties for different offenses. The codes are similar, however, in their general structure, their description of the general principles of criminal law, and their definition of most offenses. Thus, if one were asked to turn to a single source

---

15. American Law Institute, *Model Penal Code, Final Proposed Official Draft*, Philadelphia, Pennsylvania: American Law Institute Executive Offices (1962). (Hereinafter referred to in the footnotes as MPC).

16. Those states are: Alaska, Alabama, Arkansas, Colorado, Connecticut, Delaware, Florida, Georgia, Hawaii, Illinois, Indiana, Iowa, Kansas, Kentucky, Louisiana, Maine, Minnesota, Missouri, Montana, New Hampshire, New Mexico, New York, North Dakota, Ohio, Oregon, Pennsylvania, South Dakota, Texas, Utah, Virginia, Washington, and Wisconsin.

to describe the substantive criminal law as its exists today, clearly the best source would be the Model Code. Most provisions of the Code reflect the current law in a substantial majority of our states. In addition to the many states that have adopted new codes largely based on the Model Code, other states with older codes, such as California and New Jersey, often rely upon the positions taken by the Model Code in interpreting their codes.

Federal and State Crimes.   In describing the criminal codes, we have concentrated so far on the state codes. The federal government also has its own criminal code which sets forth a variety of federal offenses. These crimes are prosecuted in the separate federal court system we described in Chapter Three. The federal crimes are investigated by various federal law enforcement agencies (e.g., the F.B.I. and Secret Service) and prosecuted by federal prosecutors (United States Attorneys). Persons convicted of federal crimes are sentenced to federal institutions operated by the Federal Bureau of Prisons or placed on probation under the supervision of the Federal Probation Service.[17]

The primary distinction between federal and state crimes relates to the different range of subjects they treat. A state code may reach any harmful or potentially harmful activity undertaken within the state. The limit on the state's authority is primarily geographical. A harmful act such as murder or stealing can be made a state crime so long as the act occurred within the state. The federal government's authority, in comparison, is limited by the federal consitution's restriction of federal legislation to specified subjects. Congress may deal only with activities that relate to areas specifically entrusted to the federal government by the Constitution. The most significant areas within this federal authority are: the regulation of interstate and foreign commerce; the maintenance and direction of federal service agencies such as the armed forces and the postal service; the coining and distribution of money; the imposition and collection of taxes; the enforcement of civil rights; and the regulation of federal territories (the District of Columbia, national parks, etc.). Federal criminal statutes can reach activities anywhere within the United States, but those activities must be related to these special areas of federal concern. Congress could not make murder a federal crime, for example, unless the particular type of murder related to a federal subject of regulation (e.g., involved the killing of a federal officer).[18]

Viewed in terms of their relationship to particular areas of federal authority, federal crimes tend to fall into three basic categories. First, there are those crimes that relate to the federal government's power to carry out basic federal governmental functions. Included in this category are crimes prohibiting espionage, unlawful immigration, customs violations, counterfeiting, and interference with

---

17. See Chapters Fifteen, Sixteen and Seventeen for a more complete description of the various federal agencies involved in administering the federal criminal justice system.

18. If a harmful act such as murder is committed in federally regulated territories (e.g., the District of Columbia or a national park), then the federal government can punish that act without regard to any other special federal interest in the subject matter. Accordingly, for these territories, federal law covers all types of crimes (e.g., murder, rape) whether or not the victims are government employees, the facilities used were in interstate commerce, etc. The federal authority in federal territories is essentially the same as state criminal law authority. The discussion that follows relates to federal authority outside of the federal territories.

the performance of federal officials (including bribery of federal officials, impersonation of those officials, and assaults against those officials). In some instances, crimes in this group do not simply protect federal government agencies in the performance of their functions, but they seek also to prohibit the misuse of the services provided by those agencies. Thus, the provisions relating to the mail not only protect the postal service against theft, assaults, and similar interference, but those provisions also prohibit misuse of the mails to defraud private citizens. A second, closely related category of federal offenses seeks to protect certain private facilities in which the federal government has a special interest as a result of its close regulation or financial involvement. The prime illustration of such a facility is the federally insured bank. Various offenses against such banks, including robbery and embezzlement, are federal crimes. Of course, these activities also are violations of state criminal laws, as are most of the federal crimes involving interference with federal agencies. An assault of a federal officer, for example, is a state as well as a federal crime since state law applies to all assaults occurring within the state without regard to the victim's association with the federal government. The traditional approach of the federal government has been to avoid reliance upon state laws for protection of its own personnel or of institutions of special federal concern. The use of federal criminal law ensures that the decisions involved in investigating, prosecuting and punishing such offenses will be made by federal peace officers, prosecutors, and judges, rather than state officials.

The third category of federal crimes also tends to overlap with state law. This category is composed of federal offenses based upon Congress' regulatory powers. Thus, Congress, utilizing its authority to enforce civil rights, has made it a crime for a state official to intentionally infringe upon civil liberties protected by the federal constitution. Similarly, in the exercise of its authority over commerce between the states, Congress has adopted a wide variety of criminal provisions relating to activities that extend across state lines. Kidnapping becomes a federal crime when the victim is transported over state lines, gambling becomes a federal crime when interstate communications facilities are used, and even prostitution becomes a federal crime when the participants move in interstate commerce. These activities have been made federal crimes in an effort to supplement the state criminal law. State law enforcement officers, having authority limited to their own state, often suffer disadvantages in investigating and prosecuting such criminal activities when they extend across state lines. The objective of the federal criminal law in these areas is not to usurp state law, but to lend the additional authority of the federal government to meet law enforcement problems that may often have a nationwide scope. Accordingly, the states retain exclusive responsibility for enforcement of the many basic criminal offenses, such as homicide, assault, theft, and rape, which do not involve interstate movement.

It should be emphasized that, while the federal criminal code plays a significant role in the overall enforcement of our substantive law, it is far from dominant. For those criminal activities relating to unique federal governmental functions (e.g., coining money, immigration), federal statutes clearly are the primary (and sometimes exclusive) source of prosecution. For most types of criminal activity, however, even where both federal and state law apply (as in gambling and narcotics), the vast majority of all prosecutions are based on the state codes. Overall, prosecutions under the federal code account for approximately ten percent of all felony prosecutions brought throughout the United Sates. Indeed, the total number of federal felony prosecutions is substantially less than the number of state felony prosecutions in any one of our most populous states, such as California, New York or Illinois.

Felonies and Misdemeanors.[19]   The distinction between felony offenses and misdemeanor offenses was noted in Chapter Three. We there suggested that, as a rough measure, felonies and misdemeanors could be distinguished by the maximum punishment provided for the crime: if the offense is punishable by capital punishment or imprisonment for more than one year, it is a felony; if punishable by imprisonment for less than a year or a fine alone, it is a misdemeanor. As a practical matter, this distinction will separate felonies from misdemeanors in almost all jurisdictions, but the jurisdictions do vary in their formal descriptions of the distinction.[20] All jurisdictions agree that crimes subject to capital punishment are felonies and those subject to fine alone are misdemeanors. Two different guidelines are used, however, in dividing felonies and misdemeanors where the maximum punishment is imprisonment. Some jurisdictions look to the length of imprisonment, while others look to the place of imprisonment. States relying on the length of imprisonment use the one-year dividing line previously noted. States relying on the place of imprisonment classify offenses punishable by imprisonment in penitentiaries (i.e., state prisons) as felonies and offenses punishable by imprisonment in local jails as misdemeanors. For almost all states, however, this place-of-imprisonment guideline produces the same result as the one-year dividing line. States commonly provide that all sentences of imprisonment in excess of one year must be served in penitentiaries and those of one year or less served in jails. Thus, those crimes punishable by imprisonment in a penitentiary also would meet the traditional length-of-imprisonment standard for a felony classification, and an offense punishable by imprisonment only in jail also would be a misdemeanor under that standard. It should be emphasized that under either of the two standards, the dividing line is based upon the maximum potential punishment, not the punishment actually imposed. If a person is convicted of a crime carrying a maximum punishment of several years imprisonment, he has been convicted of a

---

19. The distinction between felonies and misdemeanors was developed at common law and has been incorporated in all of the codes. At one time, all felonies were punishable by death and forfeiture of goods, while misdemeanors were punishable by fines alone. As capital punishment was limited and new forms of punishment developed, the common law was altered to meet these changes. Now both felonies and misdemeanors may be punished by fines and imprisonment.

20. What follows is a description of the general guidelines for distinguishing between felonies and misdemeanors as set forth in the various codes. Most codes also have a provision, however, stating that, notwithstanding the general guidelines, a crime is a felony or misdemeanor if it is specifically designated as such in the statutory provision defining the crime. Generally, where such a provision states that a named crime is a felony or misdemeanor, that crime would fit in the same category if the general guidelines were applied; the specific statutory designation usually adds nothing. There may be a few exceptions, however, where crimes that would be felonies under the general guidelines (i.e., crimes punishable by more than one year's imprisonment) are designated as misdemeanors in the statutory provision defining the crime. Such crimes commonly are described as "high misdemeanors." While called misdemeanors, they often are treated for procedural purposes like the felonies they would be under the general guidelines.

felony even though the judge may impose a lesser sentence of thirty days in jail or one year on probation.

The dividing line between felonies and misdemeanors has significance for various aspects of the criminal law. As we noted in Chapter Two, many states use that dividing line in distinguishing between those cases that will be tried by the magistrate courts and those that will be tried by the general trial court. In some states, the size of the jury will vary depending upon whether the crime charged is a felony (12 person jury) or misdemeanor (6 person jury). In many jurisdictions, a police officer has somewhat different authority in making arrests for felonies and misdemeanors. Several distinctions relating to the processing of felony and misdemeanor cases also will be noted in Part Three, discussing the criminal justice process.

In recent years, a number of states have adopted a new classification for very minor offenses as suggested by the Model Penal Code. The Code recommended (§1.04) that behavior punishable only by a fine be designated as a "violation," and that a violation conviction not result in any of the legal disabilities that commonly results from a criminal conviction. Several states have closely followed this proposal.[21] Other states have developed a somewhat broader grouping of minor offenses that are treated basically as misdemeanors except for certain procedural distinctions. Thus, New York has a classification called "violations" that includes all offenses punishable by a fine only or by a sentence of imprisonment that does not exceed fifteen days.[22] These new classifications have included a comparatively insignificant group of offenses such as littering, loitering, and possession of fireworks. The two classes of felony and misdemeanor remain dominant for those offenses of primary concern within the criminal justice system.

Infamous and Non-Infamous Crimes.   The word "infamous" means "without fame and good report" and was applied at common law to separate those crimes that were viewed as particularly heinous. The distinction between infamous and non-infamous crimes sometimes was drawn according to the punishment imposed, however, rather than the wicked nature of the illegal behavior. Today, the exact line of distinction varies with the use of the distinction. One use of the distinction, for example, is to determine whether a convicted person can hold public office, vote, or serve on a jury. In many states, persons convicted of infamous crimes are denied those rights (a sanction called "civil death"). Here the tendency is to look to the nature of the crime in determining whether it is infamous. Infamous crimes are often said to be those crimes reflecting the individual's "moral turpitude"—crimes in which the defendant's actions, as one court put it, were "contrary to justice, honesty, modesty, or good morals."[23] Under this standard, infamous crimes commonly include most crimes that are mala in se as opposed to mala prohibita (a distinction we will discuss shortly). The distinction between infamous and non-infamous crimes also is utilized to determine whether

---

21. See e.g., Conn. Stat. §539-27; Ohio Rev. Code §2901.02 (using term "minor misdemeanor"); Oregon Rev. Stat. §161.565.

22. N.Y. Penal Law §10.00(3). Pennsylvania uses a class designated as "summary offenses" for offenses carrying a punishment that does not exceed ninety days imprisonment. Pa. Stat. §106(c).

23. *Marsh v. State Bar of California*, 210 Cal. 303, 291 P.2d 583 (1930).

prosecution may be brought without grand jury approval of the charge. In many states and in the federal system, prosecution for infamous crimes can be brought only through an indictment, a formal charge issued by a grand jury. Here, the courts look primarily to the punishment that may be imposed for the crime rather than the nature of the behavior. Grand jury participation is thought to be necessary whenever the punishment is severe. Originally, the test was whether the punishment could include death or imprisonment at hard labor. Today, with "hard labor" no longer imposed, the emphasis is upon whether imprisonment may be served in a penitentiary. Crimes carrying a potential maximum sentence of penitentiary imprisonment or death are viewed as infamous. Since this standard is essentially the same as that for describing felonies, the infamous/non-infamous crime distinction, with respect to the use of grand jury indictments, is basically the felony/misdemeanor distinction.

Offenses Mala In Se and Mala Prohibita. The distinction between *mala in se* and *mala prohibita* crimes relates to the moral culpability of the offender. The description mala in se refers to activities that are "wrong in themselves." Mala prohibita, on the other hand, refers to acts that are wrong because prohibited by law, but not inherently evil. One who commits either type of crime has violated the law, but there is a difference between inherently wrong acts—those which by their nature every member of society would recognize to be evil—and those which are wrong only because society is seeking a certain regulatory objective. This distinction is an ancient one, and it has continued to be important in many aspects of the criminal law. Thus, in some jurisdictions, a lawyer or physician convicted of a crime that is mala in se will automatically lose his license, while his conviction for a crime mala prohibita will require a reexamination of his fitness, but not necessarily loss of the license. The distinction between the two types of offenses also may prove significant where the criminal unintentionally kills another in the course of committing a misdemeanor. In some jurisdictions, the crime automatically is raised to the level of homicide if the misdemeanor was a mala in se offense but may or may not be raised, depending upon the criminal's negligence, if the misdemeanor was a mala prohibita offense. The distinction also is useful to courts in determining the mental element required for a particular crime since mala in se offenses commonly require an intent to harm while mala prohibita offenses do not.

In most instances, crimes can readily be categorized as mala in se or mala prohibita. Most offenses which involve injury to persons or property are mala in se. All of the common law crimes, for example, fall in this category. On the other hand, most of the newer crimes that are prohibited as part of a regulatory scheme are mala prohibita. Illustrative are criminal violations of various laws requiring manufacturers to list the contents of food products. The legislature can appropriately decide that such information should be placed on the label to help the consumer, but failure to provide the information is not an act which almost any community would view as evil. This is not to say that labeling violations necessarily are mala prohibita crimes. The characterization might be different if the crime comes closer to the common law crime of false pretenses in which a person deliberately misrepresents the nature of an item (e.g., describes a glass ring as a diamond ring) in the course of selling it. The dividing line between mala prohibita and mala in se has caused particular difficulty in application to newer crimes which seek to serve the same function as some of the common law crimes. Thus, courts have divided as to whether the crime of driving while intoxicated (which certainly poses a potential danger but is not always harmful) is a mala in se or mala prohibita crime.[24]

Classification By Harm Inflicted.   Almost all of the codes, to assist in the grouping of crimes, classify them according to the type of harm inflicted. Thus, the Model Code (and state codes based upon it) use the following classifications: (1) offenses against the person (e.g., homicide, assault, kidnapping, rape); (2) offenses against property (e.g., arson, burglary, theft); (3) offenses against the family (e.g., bigamy, adultery); (4) offenses against public (governmental) administration (e.g., bribery, perjury, prison escape); (5) offenses against public order and decency (e.g., riots, loitering, prostitution). These divisions are made simply to assist in the location of particular provisions within the codes. The fact that a crime is classified as a crime against property or person does not have any legal significance. Accordingly, some of the classifications are made simply for the sake of convenience. Robbery, for example, involves a threat to property and person, but is placed with the crimes against property since it uses some of the same terms as other property crimes.

Criminological Classifications.   Criminologists use various classifications which have no special legal consequences, but are very helpful in describing different types of crimes. Perhaps the most prominent among these are "organized crime," "white collar crime," and "victimless crime."

Organized crime is very difficult to categorize. Indeed, the federal Organized Crime Control Act of 1970,[25] which provides various investigative tools and substantive criminal laws designed to reach organized crime, nowhere defines the term "organized crime." An earlier federal Act did, however, provide a useful definition of organized crime in connection with the authorization of federal grants to state agencies combatting such crime:

> Organized crime means the unlawful activities of the members of a highly organized, disciplined association engaged in supplying illegal goods and services, including but not limited to gambling, prostitution, loan sharking, narcotics, labor racketeering, and other unlawful activities of members of such organizations.[26]

Note that this definition places primary emphasis on the organizational structure that produces the crime, not simply the kind of crime involved. Not all gambling, prostitution or loan sharking can properly be described as part of organized crime. On the other hand, not all groups of persons engaged together in criminal activities have the type of organization that produces organized crime. A gang of neighborhood sneak thieves may work together in committing a series of crimes, but their

---

24. Compare *State v. Darchuck*, 117 Mont. 15, 156 P.2d 173 (1945) with *State v. Budge*, 126 Me. 223, 137 A. 244 (1927).

25. Public Law No. 90-351, 84 Stat. 922 (1970) (codified in sections scattered throughout the United States Code).

26. Section 601(b) of The Omnibus Crime Control and Safe Streets Act of 1968, codified in 42 United States Code §3701.

operation lacks the broad scope, continuity, disciplined organization, and use of public corruption that commonly characterizes organized crime.

The most familiar illustration of organized crime is that crime which flows from the operation of the organization commonly described as the "Mafia," "Cosa Nostra" or "Syndicate."[27] Considerable disagreement exists as to the precise nature of this organization. Some analysts contend that it is highly integrated, national (or even international) organization with clear lines of leadership and central control. Others claim that there simply is a series of separate crime syndicates, scattered throughout the United States, that cooperate with each other in certain aspects of their activities that require multistate operations. Under either view, however, the operation of such an organization or series of organizations reflects the basic characteristics of organized crime (whether associated with the Mafia or not)—a self-perpetuating criminal organization, supplying illegal goods and services as a major source of its income, and maintaining fairly exclusive control over those illegal activities within a particular community through the use of a variety of devices including extortion, terrorism, and corrupting public officials.

White collar crime is almost as broad a classification as organized crime, but easier to define. The category refers generally to crimes committed in the course of business activities, usually by business officials (commonly described as "white collar" workers). Some criminologists would limit the white collar category to crimes committed to benefit the business enterprise itself (e.g., price fixing) while others would include also crimes committed by white collar workers against the business enterprise (e.g., embezzlement from the company). Under either view we are dealing with crime committed by persons with solid social status, based upon their occupational position, who clearly are not driven to violate the law by social or economic deprivation.[28]

Victimless crime is the description given to crimes which involve only willing participants who desire to participate in the criminal activity. These offenses are, in other words, crimes in which the persons involved consent to the crime. Illustrative are the crimes of prostitution, gambling, and drug abuse. Whether these crimes are truly "victimless" is a matter of dispute. There obviously is not a "victim" in the sense of a participant who views himself as having suffered harm at

---

27. For varying views of this organization and organized crime generally, see President's Commission, note 11, p. 39 *supra, Task Force Report: Organized Crime;* D. Cressey, *Theft of A Nation: The Structure and Operations of Organized Crime In America,* New York: Harper & Row Publishers, 1969; J. Albini, *The American Mafia: Genesis Of A Legend,* New York: Appleton-Century-Crofts, 1971.

28. Edwin Sutherland so defined the category in his landmark book, *White Collar Crime,* New York: The Dryden Press, 1949. He used the category to refer to crimes "committed by a person of respectability and high social status in the course of his occupation." This definition and that which emphasizes benefiting the business enterprise both would exclude non-violent crimes, such as "con games" or frauds, that are perpetrated by professional criminals (who obviously are not white collar workers). Quite often, however, prosecutor's offices, in their units devoted to what they call "white collar crime," will include all crimes involving deceit, corruption or a breach of trust, without regard to the status or background of the offender. The Chamber of Commerce uses a similar concept of white collar crime in estimating that such crime costs the nation at least $40 billion each year, which is considerably more than the amount lost through violent crimes such as robberies. See *The Criminal Law Reporter,* Vol. 19, No. 2 (Washington, D.C.: Bureau of National Affairs, 1976).

the hands of another. On the other hand, the willing participant may have inflicted harm upon himself, either physically or morally. Also, victimless crimes frequently lead to other crimes that do inflict harm upon unwilling victims. Thus, prostitution has been tied in some communities to various assaultive crimes against clients and occasionally the prostitutes themselves. Similarly, drug users commonly are engaged in various other crimes (e.g., theft) to obtain money for the purchase of narcotics. Profits from gambling (often controlled by organized crime) has been used to fund various other crimes.

F.B.I. Index Crimes.   During the 1930's, the Federal Bureau of Investigation began to collect nationwide crime statistics. At the time, long before the Model Penal Code, substantive criminal law varied from state to state even more than it does today. A crime which was titled assault with the intent to murder in one state would be known as aggravated assault or armed assault in other states. To provide some uniformity for its statistical compilations (which are published annually in the Uniform Crime Reports[29]), the F.B.I. provided its own standardized definitions of key crimes, and required that local law enforcement agencies convert their local violations to those categories in reporting crimes. The standardized definitions of seven key crimes are set forth in the footnote below.[30] These seven crimes are commonly described as "Index Crimes" since they are used in the F.B.I. Part I Index which provides data on offenses "known to police." Another twenty-two offenses are included in further data provided on arrests and charges filed by

---

29. Federal Bureau of Investigation, *Crime In The United States—Uniform Crime Reports*, Washington, D.C.: Government Printing Office. The Uniform Reports are published annually. All data cited in this chapter comes from the 1976 annual report.

30.   1. *Criminal homicide.* (a) Murder and non-negligent manslaughter: All willful felonious homicides as distinguished from deaths caused by negligence. Excludes attempts to kill, assaults to kill, suicides, accidental deaths, or justifiable homicides. Justifiable homicides are limited to: (1) The killing of a person by a peace officer in line of duty; and (2) The killing of a person in the act of committing a felony by a private citizen. (b) Manslaughter by negligence: Any death which the police investigation establishes was primarily attributable to gross negligence of some individual other than the victim.
    2. *Forcible rape.* The carnal knowledge of a female, forcibly and against her will in the categories of rape by force, assault to rape, and attempted rape. Excludes statutory offenses (no force used—victim under age of consent).
    3. *Robbery.* Stealing or taking anything of value from the care, custody or control of a person by force or by violence or by putting in fear, such as strong-arm robbery, stickups, armed robbery, assauls to rob, and attempts to rob.
    4. *Aggravated assault.* Assault with intent to kill or for the purpose of inflicting severe bodily injury by shooting, cutting, stabbing, maiming, poisoning, scalding, or by the use of acids, explosives, or other means. Excludes simple assaults.
    5. *Burglary—breaking or entering.* Burglary, housebreaking, safecracking, or any breaking or unlawful entry of a structure with the intent to commit a felony or a theft. Includes attempted forcible entry.
    6. *Larceny—theft (except motor vehicle theft).* The unlawful taking, carrying, leading, or riding away of property from the possession or constructive possession of another. Thefts of bicycles, automobile accessories, shoplifting, pocket-picking, or any stealing of property or article which is not taken by force and violence or by fraud. Excludes embezzlement, "con" games, forgery, worthless checks, etc.
    7. *Motor vehicle theft.* Unlawful taking or stealing or attempted theft of a motor vehicle. A motor vehicle is a self-propelled vehicle that travels on the surface but not on rails. Specifically excluded from this category are motor boats, construction equipment, airplanes, and farming equipment.

prosecutors.[31] Standardized definitions also are used in collecting information on these crimes. It should be emphasized that all of the F.B.I. definitions are utilized only for statistical purposes; they do not constitute the legal definition of the particular crime for any jurisdiction.

The issuance of the F.B.I.'s quarterly reports on crime ordinarily attracts considerable attention. Newspapers frequently headline the upward or downward changes in the "crime rate." While the F.B.I. reports are the best available source on nationwide crime, the reader should keep in mind the limited scope of these statistics. First, the statistics include only reported crimes. There is a substantial portion of crime in the United States that is not reported to the police. Surveys indicate that the percentage of actual crimes reported to the police will vary with the particular community, the type of crime, and the general characteristics (age, sex, etc.) of the victim.[32] In many communities, less than half of the personal crimes of violence (e.g., assault, rape, robbery) are likely to be reported. On the other hand, in almost every community, a very high percentage (over 90%) of all robberies of commercial establishments are reported. Because of this "hidden" element of unreported crime, the totals in the Uniform Reports must be used with great caution in estimating the actual crime rate. Of course, if the percentages of unreported crime remain stable, a comparison of the reported crime rate from year to year is helpful. However, a sudden shift in the percentage of persons reporting crimes in a particular community can produce a dramatic increase or decrease in that community's statistics even though the actual crime rate may not have changed. Instances have been documented of shifts in police reporting practices that have substantially altered the reports for local communities.[33]

Second, the Index crimes do not include all of the most frequently committed felonies. Two of the index crimes, murder and forcible rape, are very significant crimes, but are committed far less frequently than other non-index felonies. Statistics from the California Bureau of Crime Statistics, for example, suggest that the seven most frequently committed felonies are five of the index crimes (burglary, theft, motor vehicle theft, robbery, and aggravated assault) and two non-index crimes (forgery and drug violations).[34] The Uniform Reports also include only limited information on misdemeanors, although the number of

---

31. The other offenses are: assaults that do not fall in the aggravated assault category; arson; forgery and counterfeiting; fraud (fraudulent conversion and obtaining money or property by false pretenses); embezzlement; stolen property—buying, receiving, and possessing; vandalism; weapons —carrying, possessing, etc.; prostitution and commercialized vice; sex offenses (where not covered by forcible rape, prostitution, and commercialized vice); narcotic drug laws; gambling; offenses against the family and children; driving under the influence; liquor law violations; drunkenness; disorderly conduct; vagrancy; all other offenses (all violations of state or local laws not included in the other definitions); suspicion (arrests for no specific offense and release without formal charges being placed); curfew and loitering laws (juveniles); and runaway (juvenile).

32. Law Enforcement Assistance Administration (National Crime Panel Surveys), *Criminal Victimization In The United States—1975 Report*, Washington, D.C.: Government Printing Office, 1976; *Sourcebook of Criminal Justice Statistics—1976*, note l, p. 1 *supra*, at pp. 501-530.

33. See Y. Kamisar, *How To Use Abuse—And Fight Back With—Crime Statistics*, 25 Oklahoma Law Review, 239, 242-244 (1972).

34. California Department of Justice, Bureau of Crime Statistics, *Crime and Delinquency in California*, Sacramento, California: Department of Justice, 1975, p.18 (arrest rates).

reported misdemeanors far outstrips that of felonies.[35]   Among the index crimes, only the theft offense includes misdemeanors. The remaining 22 categories used in collecting arrest statistics do, however, list arrest rates for most of the more commonly reported misdemeanors (simple assault, public drunkenness, disorderly conduct, etc.).

While the Uniform Crime Report statistics are of limited value in determining actual crime rates, they provide most useful data in analyzing various other aspects of the crime problem. They clearly establish, for example, the substantial variation in the reported crime rate as between rural and urban areas. (In 1976, for example, the rate per 100,000 inhabitants for index crimes was 5,266 for the nation as a whole, 6,073 for metropolitan areas, and 2,047 for rural areas). They also show substantial variations in the clearance of reported crimes through arrest (ranging from 79% for murder and 63% for aggravated assault to 14% for motor vehicle theft and 17% for burglary). Significant variations are also found in the percentage of charged persons who are acquitted or have the charges against them dismissed (ranging from 40% for forcible rape to 10% for driving under the influence). These and other statistics are very helpful to students of the criminal justice system, particularly those students focusing on the law governing the system. They add a perspective of size and variation that sometimes is lost in the case-by-case analysis of the law.[36]

---

35. While available statistics are limited, they typically show from three to six times as many arrests for misdemeanors as felonies. See California Bureau of Crime Statistics, *supra* note 34 at pp. 18-20.

36. For further information on the legal concepts of crime and punishment, see H. Packer, *Limits of the Criminal Sanction*, Stanford, Cal.: Stanford University Press, 1968, part I; P. Weiler, *The Reform Of Punishment* in Canadian Law Reform Commission, Studies on Sentencing, Ottawa, Canada: Information Canada, 1974. For further information on the nature of criminal activity, see E. Sutherland and D. Cressey, *Criminology*, Philadelphia, Pa.: J.B. Lippincott Company, 9th ed., 1974; H. Bloch and G. Geis, *Man, Crime, and Society*, New York: Random House, 2d ed., 1970; S. Schafer, *Introduction to Criminology*, Reston, Va.: Reston Publishing Company, 1976.

Chapter 5

The Elements Of A Crime

Before any act can be treated as a crime under the law, several elements must be present. First, a legal prohibition must be set forth in the form required by the law: the illegal act must be specifically proscribed, and a punishment for its violation must be established, in the law. Second, the definition of the crime must contain several key components. Ordinarily, there will be four such components: (1) a specified behavior (traditionally described as the element of *actus reus*); (2) a specified state of mind on the part of the actor (traditionally described as the *mens rea* element); (3) the causation of a particular harm or situation threatening harm; and (4) the absence of those circumstances recognized under the law as excusing behavior that otherwise would be criminal. In this chapter, we will consider these common elements of almost every crime.

THE LAW DEFINING THE CRIME

Underlying Policy. The first requirement for establishing a crime is that the prohibited activity clearly be described and designated as a criminal offense. To be enforced by our legal system, a criminal prohibition must have been firmly established, prior to its violation, by one of those sources of the law noted in Chapter Two.[1] Traditionally that source has been a statute, case law, or a combination of the two, although it also has been a constitutional provision for a few crimes (such as the crime of treason). Whatever the source of the law, the crime must be defined in that source and its definition must have been provided before the accused engaged in the activity for which he is being prosecuted.

The requirement of a prior legal definition is expressed in two basic statements of principle (called "legal maxims") that underlie most of our legal rules regarding the definition of crime. The first of these maxims is *Nullum Crimen*

---

1. See pp. 24-29 *supra*.

Sine Lege, which translates from the Latin as "no crime without law." The second, *Nulla Poena Sine Lege*, states the proposition that there can be "no punishment without law." These two maxims are derived from two of the primary functions of the criminal law noted in Chapter Four.[2] If the criminal law is to deter antisocial activity, it should provide persons who might engage in such activity with a warning that their actions will be subject to punishment. Advance notice as to the scope of the law also is relevant to the criminal law's emphasis upon blameworthiness as the basis for imposing retribution. Prior definition of the crime is especially important in establishing true culpability for those offenses that are mala prohibita rather than mala in se. Where the prohibited conduct is not inherently immoral, the offender has no basis for suspecting that his action is illegal unless there exists a law clearly stating that such conduct constitutes a crime. Without the warning provided by a law defining the crime, the offender can claim that he lacks moral culpability. Since his conduct is not inherently bad (the crime being mala prohibita), he should not be viewed as being at fault for failing to have anticipated a prohibition that the law had not yet established. On the other hand, when the law does define the crime in advance, the offender will have culpability; he either will have knowingly violated the law (if he knew of it beforehand) or he will have been negligent in his failure to have learned what the law prohibits.

The need for advance warning is reflected in several legal rules relating to the definition of crime. The most prominent of these are the three rules described below. The first is the *ex post facto* prohibition, found in the federal constitution and various state constitutions. The second is the so-called *void-for-vagueness* rule, which is established under the due process clauses of the federal constitution and similar provisions in various state constitutions. The third is the so-called rule of *strict interpretation* of criminal statutes, developed at the common law.

Ex Post Facto.   Article I, section 9, of the federal constitution prohibits adoption of any ex post facto law. An ex post facto law, in its purest form, is a law which retroactively makes criminal an activity that was performed before the passage of the law and was not then a crime.[3] The underlying theory of the ex post facto prohibition is that an individual should not be punished for an act which was not prohibited by law at the time he committed it. To punish a person under such circumstances is to deprive him of fair notice of the criminality of his act. As we have seen in the two legal maxims previously noted, the concept of providing a fair warning extends to both the content of an offense and the punishment that may be imposed for its violation. Accordingly, the ex post facto prohibition applies to retroactive increases in punishment as well as to retroactive expansion of the definition of a crime. It is just as much a constitutional violation to retroactively

---

2.   See pp. 63-66 *supra*.

3.   The ex post facto prohibition is to be distinguished from the *bill of attainder*, which also involves an element of retroactivity and also is prohibited by the federal constitution. The constitutional prohibition against bills of attainder bars legislation which directs that punishment be imposed upon particular individuals without affording them a trial—i.e., it prohibits a statute stating that a particular named person or group of individuals is guilty of a crime. An ex post facto law, unlike a bill of attainder, does not single out named individuals for criminal liability without a trial. Rather, it describes certain past behavior as criminal and then permits a trial to determine if a particular defendant engaged in that behavior.

increase the length of imprisonment for an offense as it is to make illegal that which was not illegal when committed. A legislature providing a new and more serious punishment for an old crime must limit that increased punishment to prospective application (i.e., to offenses committed after the date of the adoption of the legislation).[4]

Void-for-vagueness. Although the void-for-vagueness rule is not mentioned specifically in the federal constitution, it has long been recognized as an element of the due process guaranteed under the Fifth and Fourteenth Amendments of the federal constitution.[5] Under the void-for-vagueness rule, a defendant cannot be held liable for the commission of a crime if the law defines that crime in terms so vague that "men of common intelligence must necessarily guess at its meaning."[6] As Justice Holmes once noted: "Although it is not likely that a criminal will consider the text of the law before he murders or steals, it is reasonable that fair warning should be given to the world in language that the common world will understand, of what the law intends to do if a certain line is passed. To make the warning fair, so far as possible the line should be clear."[7]

When is a definition of a crime so vague as to be constitutionally void because of that vagueness? While the courts often state that the content of the crime must be clear to men of "common intelligence," they obviously do not mean that the content must be apparent to a person without legal training. The courts have always recognized that otherwise unacceptable vagueness in statutory language can be "cured" by prior case law that added specificity through its interpretation of that statutory language, yet the prior case law ordinarily would not be known to the non-lawyer. The requirement of a fair warning thus appears to be satisfied if the statutory language suggests to the average person that there is a need to seek legal advice as to the possible criminality of his proposed activity and if such advice can then provide a reasonably certain answer in light of the statutory language and case law.

The courts also have recognized that the legislative context often requires acceptance of a certain degree of ambiguity. Legislatures often are faced with a basic dilemma. If they define the subject of the offense too precisely, their language may narrow the state's scope so as to exclude behavior that logically should be within the crime's coverage. For example, if a statute defining the crime of malicious destruction of property lists each specific item of property protected by the statute (e.g., money, vehicles, clothes, etc.), it is likely that the legislature will be unable to foresee and list all of the items that should be protected. On the other hand, if a broad, "catch-all" phrase is used (e.g., "any property of value"), the

---

4. The ex post facto prohibition also bars retroactive changes in procedural or evidentiary requirements that make it easier to prove the defendant guilty. It would be a violation of the ex post facto prohibition, for example, to apply to a previously committed crime a new evidentiary rule which would reduce the degree of proof required from the prosecution to rebut an alleged defense of insanity.

5. See pp. 221-23 *infra*.

6. *Connally v. General Constr. Co.*, 269 U.S. 385, 391, 46 S. Ct. 126, 127, 70 L. Ed. 322 (1926).

7. *McBoyle v. United States*, 283 U.S. 25, 27, 51 S. Ct. 340, 341, 75 L. Ed. 816 (1931).

statute necessarily will contain some ambiguity (e.g., does it include the destruction of a student's class notes or a business' reputation?). Recognizing the need for catch-all phrasing in many areas, the courts often note that the degree of precision required to avoid the void-for-vagueness prohibition will vary with the extent to which the subject matter lends itself to precise definition. The courts will not ask for more than the legislature can reasonably provide in light of the objectives of the criminal law.

There are many decisions in every jurisdiction ruling on void-for-vagueness challenges to criminal provisions. Many commentators argue that the decisions are not always consistent in terms of the degree of ambiguity held to be acceptable or unacceptable. They stress that often the courts seem to be as concerned with the type of crime involved as with the range of the ambiguity. They note, for example, that courts apply a more stringent requirement of specificity where the crime has a bearing upon specially protected constitutional rights (e.g., freedom of speech). Thus several criminal obscenity provisions have been held invalid for a degree of vagueness that arguably would be acceptable in statutes dealing with less sensitive crimes. Another factor that may have a significant bearing upon the court's determination is the likely misuse of the statute in a pattern of arbitrary enforcement. Thus, in the famed *Lanzetta* case, the Supreme Court, in holding unconstitutional a statute aimed at criminal "gangs," noted that the statute was so broadly worded as to permit it to be used against workers who had organized for lawful union activities.[8]

Strict Construction Rule. The strict construction rule is a guideline for judicial interpretation of criminal statutes. The rule is based in large part upon concern for providing advance notice. It provides that where a statute is ambiguous as to coverage, the statute should be construed "narrowly" (i.e., strictly) so as to benefit the defendant. Where a statute is capable of two equally reasonable interpretations, and one of those interpretations would not have covered the defendant's particular activity, the narrow construction will be adopted to ensure that the defendant will not suffer as a result of the legislature's failure to make the statutory prohibition unambiguous. With the adoption of the narrow construction, a defendant will be held criminally responsible only for that behavior which obviously was prohibited under any reasonable reading of the statute.

The strict construction rule was developed during a time in England, prior to the American Revolution, when many relatively minor crimes were punished by death. To avoid imposing such an inappropriate and severe penalty, English courts often went to great lengths to find a narrow construction of a capital punishment crime under which the defendant would not be guilty of that offense. Notwithstanding a substantial reduction in the offenses punished by death, many

---

8. *Lanzetta v. State of New Jersey*, 306 U.S. 451, 59 S. Ct. 618, 83 L. Ed. 888 (1939). The statute in question made it a crime to be a "gangster," but then described a gangster as any person "not engaged in any lawful occupation, known to be a member of any gang consisting of two or more persons who have been convicted at least three times of being a disorderly person, or who has been convicted of any crime in this or any other state." The Court stressed that the statute was not limited by its terms to groups having a purpose to commit a particular crime, and the statute therefore could quite readily be used against groups who were not suspected of criminality or any illegal activities but had associates with prior convictions.

American courts during the 1800's followed the English tradition and overextended the strict construction rule. This led, in turn, to various responses designed to keep courts from adopting a strained pro-defense interpretation in the name of strict construction. In some states, the state supreme courts warned trial courts that, though penal laws were to be construed strictly, they were not to be construed so narrowly as to defeat the obvious intention of the legislature. Although the language might be somewhat ambiguous, where the context of its use clearly indicates a legislative objective to include a particular activity, the defendant has received fair notice of the intended coverage and should not be favored by a narrow interpretation. For example, where a statute prohibits defacing or erasing engine numbers on "automobiles, trucks, airplanes, or similar vehicles," strict construction does not require a reading so narrow as to exclude snowmobiles. Certainly a snowmobile could be viewed as a "similar vehicle." The crucial factor accordingly should be whether the legislative purpose would encompass snowmobiles, even though the legislation may have been adopted before such vehicles existed. That purpose often can be determined by examining the overall structure of the statute. Thus, where the prohibition against erasing engine numbers is part of a licensing statute, and snowmobiles are licensed vehicles, it is likely that the legislature meant to reach snowmobiles along with other licensed vehicles.

Some jurisdictions took the position that the old English tradition of strained interpretations was so engrained in judicial philosophy that the strict construction rule simply did more harm than good. These states adopted legislation that specifically rejected the rule. Such statutes note that the rule is "abolished" and that all criminal statutes shall be construed in the future "according to the fair import of their terms."[9] However, the same statutes also often provide that construction must be consistent with the general purposes of the criminal code, and that one of these purposes is to give "fair warning."[10] The result is that courts in these jurisdictions basically have followed a path quite similar to that followed in states that have stated that the strict construction rule remains, but should not be used to defeat a legislative purpose that is apparent on the face of the statute.

THE LAW SETTING THE PUNISHMENT

Specified Punishment. The need for a punishment set by law follows from the same policy that requires a prior definition of the crime. Fair warning requires that the individual not only be able to determine whether his behavior will be illegal, but also that he be able to determine the maximum punishment that may be imposed for such behavior. This concept is reflected in a legal maxim that serves as a companion to *Nullum Crimen Sine Lege* and *Nulla Poena Sine Lege*. That maxim, *Nullum Crimen Sine Poena*, simply notes that there shall be "no

---

9. See, e.g., Texas Penal Code §1.05(a): "The rule that a penal statute is to be strictly construed does not apply to this code. The provisions of this code shall be construed according to the fair import of their terms, to promote justice and effect the objectives of the code."

10. See, e.g., Texas Penal Code §1.02: " . . . [T]he provisions of this code are intended, and shall be construed, to achieve the following objectives: . . . (2) by definition and grading of offenses to give fair warning of what is prohibited and the consequences of violation."

crime without punishment." The prescribed penalty is, in other words, an integral part of the crime.

Penal codes of today inevitably designate penalties for the offenses specified in the code. Difficulties sometimes arise, however, where statutes dealing with the general regulation of a particular industry or profession include an isolated provision that seeks to make violation of a particular regulation a crime. At one time, the author, then an assistant prosecuting attorney, ran into such a difficulty while attempting to convict a man for practicing medicine without a license. The statutes of the state specifically prohibited practicing medicine without a license. There was no question but that the accused was performing operations, prescribing medicines, and the like, and that he had no license to do so. The entire case was before the jury when the prosecutor discovered that nowhere in the statute prohibiting practicing medicine without a license was there a provision for a criminal penalty. The law made it illegal to practice medicine without a license, but said not a word about what would happen to anyone who did! The result was that the jury was instructed to bring in a verdict for the defendant. No penalty, no crime! (Because of the unfavorable publicity, the "doctor" left the community and no further proceedings were instituted against him. At the following session, the Wyoming legislature added a penalty clause to the statute).

Code Designation of Penalties.   In about half the states, the statute defining the crime also sets forth the permissible penalties. Thus, the Michigan provision on forgery provides that a person committing that crime "shall be guilty of a felony, punishable by imprisonment in the state prison for not more than fourteen years."[11] The other half of the states follow the pattern proposed in the Model Penal Code. That Code does not fix penalties crime by crime. It divides felonies and misdemeanors into several classes, each carrying a specific maximum penalty, and then refers in the definitional section to the particular category applicable to that crime. Thus, the provision defining forgery would state simply that it is a class 2 felony. Another provision in the code, dealing exclusively with punishments, would provide that all class 2 felonies will be punishable by no more than a certain number of years of imprisonment. The advantage of this penalty structure is that it assists the legislature in comparing the penalties for different crimes. The legislature can easily compile a list of all the crimes in class 1, all those in class 2, etc. In adding a new crime, it can readily compare that crime with the offenses in the various different classes and thereby select an appropriate level for the new crime. Under a system in which the penalty is set in each individual provision, there is a tendency to ignore the relationship between offenses. Thus the federal

---

11.   Michigan Comp. Laws §750.248. It should be noted that, even in states where the punishment ordinarily is fixed in each provision of the code, there will be exceptions where reference must be made to other provisions. Thus, the Michigan Code occasionally will note only that commission of a particular crime is "a felony" or "a misdemeanor." Another provision in the code notes, however, that where a crime is designated as a felony and no specific punishment is given, the punishment shall be "imprisonment in a state prison for not more than 4 years or by a fine of not more than 2,000 dollars, or by both such fine and imprisonment." Michigan Comp. Laws §750.503. Similarly, a maximum punishment for misdemeanors (90 days and a fine of $100) is set for those crimes designated as misdemeanors without specific punishment noted in the provision defining the crime. Michigan Comp. Laws §750.504. In those states recognizing common law crimes, a similar general provision is used for such crimes. See, e.g., Michigan Comp. Laws §750.506.

criminal code, which follows a provision-by-provision approach, utilizes twelve different maximum sentences of imprisonment for felonies alone and fourteen different levels of fine. Altogether, the federal code contains 55 variations in authorized penalties. On the other hand, the proposed revision of the federal code, which would follow the Model Code format, has only five classes of felony and three of misdemeanors.

The various states following the Model Penal Code format vary in the titles given to the different classes and the maximum punishments assigned to each. Thus, Texas uses four classes of felony with the following maximum punishments: capital felonies (capital punishment); first degree felonies (life or a term of 99 years); second degree felonies (20 years and a fine not to exceed $10,000); third degree felonies (10 years and a fine not to exceed $5,000).[12] New York, on the other hand, uses five categories of felonies with the following titles and maximum punishments: class A felony (life imprisonment); class B felony (25 years imprisonment); class C felony (15 years imprisonment); class D felonies (seven years imprisonment); and class E felonies (four years imprisonment). In addition, first-degree murder is subject to a possible death penalty and all felonies may be subject to a fine not exceeding double the amount of the defendant's gain from the commission of the crime.[13]

The Hierarchy of Penalties. As you know, some offenses carry very high penalties—life imprisonment, or even death. Other offenses carry relatively mild penalties—a short stay in jail or a small fine. If I ask you how these penalties are determined, you will say, "By the legislature," and this will be a correct answer. But how does the legislature decide what criminal conduct will be severely punished by the society and what criminal conduct will be given a relatively light punishment? Is there any general pattern to be found in the way crimes are punished? Can we, for example, make a list which would show that certain kinds of crimes are apt to carry severe punishment, certain others less severe punishment, and still others very minor punishments? Saying, "Felonies have severe punishments, and misdemeanors have lighter punishments," won't help us. That would be going around in a circle, for we have already learned that felonies and misdemeanors are distinguished by the severity of the punishment. We would still have to ask the question, "Why is certain conduct classified as a felony and certain other conduct classified as a misdemeanor?"

To make our list, we will have to get at the *reason* some kinds of conduct are punished more severely than other kinds. Punishments prescribed by the legislature generally reflect the value judgments of the society concerning the seriousness of different kinds of criminal behavior. If we were to start at the top of the list with the kinds of criminal conduct that carry the most severe penalties and go on down our list to the criminal conduct which carries the lowest penalties, we would find, in most jurisdictions, a "hierarchy" or "grading" of penalties that indicates quite clearly the basic elements of these value judgments.

---

12. Texas Penal Code §§12.03—12.40.

13. New York Penal Law §§55.05, 60.05, 70.00, 80.00. The class A felony category is further divided, for other purposes, into classes A-I, A-II, and A-III.

At the top level of our hierarchy—where we have the crimes carrying the highest penalties—we would find the crime of murder in the first degree. This is the only crime which may carry the death penalty, and even then only under limited circumstances. At the next penalty level, usually authorizing life imprisonment, would be the crimes of treason, armed robbery, forcible rape, and murder in the second degree. Going on down the various levels, we usually would find assault below murder, robbery below armed robbery, burglary below robbery, theft below burglary, and so on. Most traffic offenses would be on one of the lower levels. Moving vehicle violations, however, are still likely to be on a slightly higher level than parking violations, which ordinarily would be at the very bottom (if treated as criminal offenses at all).[14]

One thing we would surely notice. Almost without exception, offenses against persons carry higher penalties (and hence would be nearer the top of the hierarchy) than offenses against property. This tells us that the society considers crimes against persons more serious (more of a threat to the society) than crimes against property. We also would notice that *the greater the damage or potential damage to the victim, the higher the penalty is apt to be*. Thus murder, which causes the death of the victim, will be punished more severely than an assault in which the victim is injured, but not killed. In robbery, property is taken by threat from the *person* of the victim, and the potential danger is far greater than in the lesser offense of theft, where the property usually is taken from the premises of another. When the robber is armed, the chances of injury are even greater; hence armed robbery is punished more severely than unarmed robbery. The offense of burglary is defined as breaking and entering into a house or other structure with intent to commit a crime. Because people live in private residences and usually are home at night, there is a greater chance that a person will be hurt during the nighttime burglary of a private residence than during the burglary of a building likely to be vacant at night. Thus many states have higher penalties for the nighttime burglary of residences than for other burglaries.

We have set forth below a brief description of the hierarchy of penalties in New York to give you one example of the lines actually drawn by a particular state legislature.[15] Different states invariably make different value judgments, however, so no two jurisdictions are exactly alike. Also, for many reasons, a logical

---

14. See note 5 at p. 59 *supra*.

15. New York lists the following offenses, among others, as *class A* felonies (life imprisonment maximum): First degree arson (causing explosion in a building likely to be inhabited); attempted murder; first degree kidnapping (including kidnapping for ransom); and murder. The following felonies are placed in the *class B* category (25 years maximum): Second degree arson (intentionally burning a building); first degree burglary (nighttime burglary of dwelling where the burglar is armed or causes physical injury to a person); second degree kidnapping; first degree rape (use of force); and first degree robbery (armed or causing serious physical injury). Offenses in the *class C* category (15 years maximum) include: Third degree arson (reckless burning of building); first degree assault (including disfiguring and causing serious injury with weapon); second degree burglary (including nighttime burglary of a dwelling); first degree forgery (forgery of stocks, bonds, and other securities); first degree grand larceny (theft by extortion); first degree promotion of prostitution (use of force or intimidation to compel a person to engage in prostitution or pimping for a prostitute less than 16 years old); second degree robbery (unarmed robbery assisted by another person); and first degree usury (professional loansharking). Illustrative *class D* felonies (7 years maximum) include: First degree abortion (non-licensed abortion of female more than 24 weeks pregnant); second degree assault (intentionally causing serious injury); third

penalty pattern may get "skewed." For example, if a state is suffering from an unusually large number of daytime burglaries and the number of nighttime burglaries is decreasing, the legislature may increase the penalty on daytime burglary without changing the penalty on nighttime burglary. In that particular state, at that time, the usual test of damage or potential damage to the victim would not explain the differences in the penalties. Nevertheless, the rule generally is that *the greater the damage or potential damage to the victim of a criminal act, the higher the statutory penalty.*

Some offenses are difficult to place in accordance with our general rule. This is particularly true of the so-called victimless crimes such as gambling, prostitution, and drug use. Many of these crimes do not involve any physical or monetary injury to the participant. The level of the penalty accordingly will be set in light of the legislature's view of the immorality of the offense and the strength of the penalty needed to deter such activities. Legislatures from different states are likely to be far apart on these judgments. Thus, in some jurisdictions, consensual homosexuality is viewed as a far more serious crime than professional gambling, while in others it is viewed as less serious. There is considerable variation also in the treatment of the sale and use of marijuana, although those differences might also reflect disagreement as to the physical harm caused by such use.

Discretionary Sentencing in the Individual Case. The principle that the law specify the punishment for a crime does not require that it specify the exact punishment which will be imposed in each particular case. If the law clearly sets forth the highest possible sentence, it gives the offender sufficient notice of the possible consequences of his violation; he certainly cannot complain if a lesser sentence is imposed in his case. Accordingly, the requirement of a specified punishment is fully satisfied by legislation that sets the maximum punishment and then leaves to the discretion of the judge and the parole board the possibility of imposing a lesser punishment in the individual case. Indeed, in most jurisdictions,

---

degree burglary (unlawful entry of any building to commit crime); first degree possession of stolen property (property valued over $1,500); first degree escape (escape from detention facility by felon); second degree forgery (forgery of will, deed, prescription, etc.); second degree grand larceny (theft of property valued in excess of $1,500); first degree perjury (giving false testimony in a judicial or administrative proceeding); second degree rape (sexual intercourse by older adult with female less than fourteen years old); third degree robbery (unarmed and unassisted robbery). The *class E* felonies (4 years maximum) including the following offenses: Second degree abortion (unlicensed abortion without regard to length of pregnancy); first degree bail-jumping (by accused felon); bigamy; falsifying business records; child abandonment; second degree criminal possession of stolen property (property valued at $250 — $1,500); second degree escape (escape from detention facility by misdemeanant); forgery of vehicle identification; first degree promotion of gambling (bookmaking or numbers receipts in excess of $5,000); third degree grand larceny (theft of property valued at $250—$1,500); incest; second degree perjury (lying in written statement submitted to public official); and third degree rape (older adult and female under 17).

Illustrative misdemeanors in the *class A* category (maximum 1 year imprisonment) include: Self-abortion by female more than 24 weeks pregnant; false advertising; third degree assault (causing non-serious injury); second degree bail-jumping (by misdemeanant); possession of burglar tools; non-support of a child; unlawful entry into a dwelling; false reporting of fire or other emergency; issuing a false financial statement; inciting to riot; petit larceny (under $250); and unauthorized use of an automobile (joyriding). *Class B* misdemeanors (3 months maximum) include: knowingly issuing a check with insufficient funds; adultery; criminal trespass; consensual sodomy; menacing (threatening to seriously injure another); public lewdness; unlawful use of drugs; and prostitution. *Violations* (15 days maximum) include: unlawful posting of advertisements; glue sniffing; indecent exposure; loitering; and patronizing a prostitute.

the law governing sentences does exactly that for almost all felonies. The penal code sets a maximum sentence of a certain period of imprisonment, but it then permits the imposition of a lesser sentence. Initially, the trial judge is given discretion to choose between imprisonment and lesser alternative sanctions such as probation. If the choice is imprisonment, the term then is set not for a single period of years, but for an "indeterminate" term, which may permit the offender to serve a substantially shorter term than the statutory maximum.

An indeterminate imprisonment term is a term that is limited by a minimum and maximum time period, but is indefinite as to the precise point of release between those extremes. The opposite of the indeterminate term is a "flat" or "determinate" term. If a judge sentences a defendant to a term of 10 years imprisonment and the person is required to serve the full 10 years, the term is flat or determinate. If, on the other hand, the judge says that the person must serve at least one year and no more than ten years, with the exact point of release to be determined in the future, then the term is indeterminate. In the vast majority of American jurisdictions, indeterminate terms of imprisonment are utilized for all felony sentences of imprisonment, except for some life sentences.[16] Ordinarily, the degree of indeterminacy is quite substantial—that is, the gap between the minimum sentence and the maximum sentence is quite large. Indeed, many jurisdictions prohibit a minimum sentence that is more than fifty percent of the maximum. Thus, if the maximum set by law is ten years, the judge cannot set a minimum of more than five years. In most cases, moreover, the judge will use a lesser minimum, perhaps setting an overall term of one to ten years.[17] After an indeterminate sentence is set, decision as to the actual time served, within the confines of the minimum and maximum, rests with the parole board. Once it concludes the prisoner is ready for release, it can release him on parole at any time after the required minimum sentence has been served. If it concludes that the prisoner is not ready for release, it can insist that he serve the full maximum term, less a statutory credit for time served without violation of prison rules ("good time").[18]

We will discuss the subjects of judicial sentencing discretion, probation, indeterminate sentences, parole, and good time credits in much greater detail in Part Three of this book. It is sufficient at this point that you are aware that these devices can (and usually do) produce a sentence in the individual case that is substantially less than the maximum set in the penal code. In light of our recent

---

16. Flat terms are used in many jurisdictions for misdemeanors. The sentence is set at a certain number of days in jail and exactly that number of days are served.

17. Technically, full indeterminacy would permit a minimum of one day, but as a practical matter, any such minimum is likely to result in incarceration for at least several months. Parole boards commonly are not willing to reach the question of parole until the person has been in prison for a period fairly close to a year. Accordingly, jurisdictions using indeterminate sentences generally insist upon a minimum sentence of at least one year. See p. 349 *infra*.

18. The "good time" credits are specified by statute or regulation as a reward for compliance with prison rules, a credit of so many days being earned for a certain period of good time. The credit is deducted from the maximum sentence to be served. Thus if a prisoner sentenced to a ten year maximum sentence receives good time credit at the rate of one month for every four month's of good time service, consistent good time service will guarantee his release at the end of eight years, even if the parole authority rejects his request for earlier release. See p. 376 *infra* for a further discussion of good time laws.

discussion of the goals of punishment in Chapter Four, we also should note briefly the relationship between those goals and this typical American sentencing structure. In large part, the structure is a product of a legislative compromise between two quite different schools of thought as to the proper emphasis in choosing among those goals.

The Compromise Between the Classical and Positivist Schools of Criminology.

The typical pattern of a statutory maximum punishment and discretion to set a lesser punishment in the individual case is derived in part from both the classical and positivist schools of criminology. The philosophy of the classical school is largely expressed in the notion that "the punishment should fit the crime." During the late eighteenth century, the Italian criminologist, Beccaria, played a particularly significant role in attempting to apply this philosophy in a systematic and scientific fashion to the process of sentencing. In an age when punishments for crimes were left largely to the whims of those in authority, he proposed a system of graded punishments that would match the harm done to the victim. Beccaria was aware that "An eye for an eye, a tooth for a tooth" can be interpreted not only to justify retribution for crime, but also to set a limit on punishments—an eye for an eye, not an eye for a tooth, or a life for an eye. Although the theory was in essence that of retribution, it also stressed a concept of "equal justice" in that the punishment would always equal the harm caused.

At about the same time that Beccaria's work began to have a substantial impact, another Italian criminologist, Lombroso, offered a different perspective of crime that was eventually to influence sentencing. Lombroso thought he had discovered the "born criminal" whom he could identify by certain "stigmata" or physical signs. When it was proved that "stigmata" were as prevalent in the halls of Oxford as they were in the Rome jails, the idea of a natural "criminal type" lost favor. Nevertheless Lombroso succeeded in shifting attention from the crime to the criminal. The theory came into being that "punishment should fit the criminal." Thus was born the idea that rehabilitation of the offender should be the objective of criminal sanctions.

The two doctrines, "punishment should fit the crime" and "punishment should fit the criminal," came into immediate conflict, for it obviously is not possible to consistently do both. Eventually a compromise of sorts was born. A statutorily prescribed maximum punishment for the crime would be set, consistent with the classical viewpoint, according to the harm done. However, when it came to sentencing the individual offender, consideration would be given for the need to achieve rehabilitation. Thus, probation would be available when it appeared at the outset that imprisonment was not needed to keep the offender from committing further criminal acts. When imprisonment was necessary, the sentence would be made indeterminate to consider the prisoner's progress towards rehabilitation during the period of imprisonment. If his development indicated he was ready to return to society, he could be released on parole prior to his having served the maximum term of imprisonment. This approach, it was argued, also took into consideration the need for deterrence, both special and general. The need for imprisonment to deter the convicted offender could be considered in the probation and parole decisions. The deterrence of other potential offenders was adequately served by the statutorily stated maximum sentence (which always existed as a potential, even though most convicted persons actually would receive lesser punishments).

The basic compromise of indeterminate sentencing did not seem to reach, however, the individual who could not be deterred or rehabilitated yet posed a continuous danger to society unless incapacitated. In some cases, the offender was so dangerous as to require incapacitation for a period longer than the maximum term indicated by the harm caused by the offense he committed. To provide for extensive incapacitation in such cases, so-called "recidivist" or "habitual offender" statutes were added to the sentencing structure. These statutes provided for a substantial extension of the statutory maximum term when the offender had several prior convictions for serious crimes. The underlying theory was that the offender's pattern of continued criminality established both a danger to society greater than that indicated merely by his last offense and a lack of any significant potential for his rehabilitation or deterrence.

Rethinking the Compromise   The compromise between the classical and positivist approaches to sentencing has always been somewhat shaky. Questions have always existed, in particular, as to the weight appropriately given to the rehabilitation goal. All jurisdictions have at least some aspects of their sentencing structure that restrict the authority of the sentencing judge and the parole board to give full weight to possible rehabilitation. Thus, jurisdictions commonly have denied the court the discretion to grant probation for various crimes (usually, the most serious, such as murder, rape, and kidnapping). Defendants charged with such offenses must be sentenced to imprisonment even though the court is convinced they are fully rehabilitated and would only be harmed by incapacitation. In many jurisdictions, the legislatures also have prescribed mandatory minimum sentences for several of these crimes. These prescribed minimums limit the judge's authority to leave as large a gap in the indeterminate sentence as he might feel to be appropriate from the viewpoint of rehabilitation. Thus, where the penal code requires a minimum of seven years imprisonment, the defendant must serve at least that time even though the judge and parole board might believe the person could be sufficiently rehabilitated to deserve parole after only a few years.[19]

In recent years, as we noted in Chapter Four, challenges to the emphasis upon rehabilitation have sharply increased. Critics have argued, in particular, that prisons do not and cannot foster rehabilitation, and prison sentences accordingly should be set strictly in terms of the other goals of punishment. To serve these goals, these critics argue, prison sentences need not be indeterminate. The traditional indeterminate sentence also has been opposed by other critics who dislike the judicial and parole board discretion inherent in indeterminate sentencing. They claim that this discretion inevitably will result in arbitrary inequalities based on the idiosyncrasies of individual decision-makers. Similar persons who have committed similar crimes, they contend, often have received different

---

19. The limitation imposed by mandatory minimums usually still leaves considerable judicial and parole board discretion, however, since the statutorily prescribed minimum ordinarily will not exceed one-third of the potential maximum. Thus, for a crime carrying a maximum sentence of 25 years, a 7 year mandatory minimum means only that the judge must impose a sentence of 7 years minimum to 25 years maximum rather than a sentence of "full" indeterminacy (1-25 years) which he might otherwise prefer.

sentences for no reason other than the fact that they were sentenced by different judges with different sentencing philosophies. In light of these and other criticisms of indeterminacy, several states have sought to sharply limit indeterminate sentences. These jurisdictions have turned largely to a "determinate" sentencing structure under which the judge sets a fixed term of imprisonment. The Califonia "presumptive-determinate" sentencing law is probably the most extensive of these provisions in eliminating discretion in the setting of prison term.[20]

The California law basically rejects the positivist approach in setting prison sentences. The opening words of the law note:

> The Legislature finds and declares that the purpose of imprisonment for crime is punishment. This purpose is best served by terms proportionate to the seriousness of the offense with provisions for uniformity in the sentences of offenders committing the same offense under similar circumstances. The Legislature further finds and declares that the elimination of disparity and the provision of uniformity of sentences can best be achieved by determinate sentences fixed by statute in proportion to the seriousness of the offense as determined by the Legislature to be imposed by the court with specified discretion.[21]

This new thrust of California law has altered the sentencing structure for all felonies that are not subject to either capital punishment or imprisonment for a life term.[22] Such offenses are divided into four categories with tripartite (three-part) alternative terms of imprisonment set for each category. These alternatives are: category one—16 months, two years or three years; category two—two, three, or four years; category three—three, four, or five years; and category four—five, six, or seven years. Burglary of a dwelling, for example, is placed in the second category, and that burglary statute therefore provides for alternative terms of two, three, or four years. The judge initially must select one of these alternatives, which becomes the basic or "core" sentence. There is no provision for indeterminacy through the use of a lesser minimum sentence and early parole. If a judge selects the three year term, for example, then the individual must serve the three years less any "good time" credits. As between the three alternatives, the middle range is presumed to be correct, and the judge must select it unless he finds, on the record, that there existed circumstances "in aggravation or mitigation of the

20. See National Institute of Law Enforcement and Criminal Justice (L.E.A.A.), *Determinate Sentencing: Reform Or Regression*, Washington D.C.: Government Printing Office (1977); A. Cassou and B. Taugher, *Determinate Sentencing In California*, 9 Pacific Law Journal 1 (1978). Other states with determinate sentencing include Arizona, Indiana, Illinois, Maryland and New Mexico. In states which have determinate sentencing without the "presumptive" feature, there is no legislative presumption favoring a particular term of years for a particular crime. The judge is permitted to set a fixed term anywhere within a range of years set by the legislature for each grade of crime. See p. 351 *infra*.

21. California Penal Code §1170(a)(1). California's rejection of indeterminacy and its emphasis on non-rehabilitative goals is not as extensive as this statement might first suggest. California still provides, for example, for substantial "good time" credits that are based in part upon participation in the prison program as well as an adherence to prison regulations. It also should be emphasized that any rejection of the rehabilitative goal extends only to imprisonment. The California trial judge usually retains other sentencing options, such as probation, that are based in large part on that goal.

22. California has six crimes in the latter category—first degree murder, kidnapping for ransom, trainwrecking, assault by a life prisoner, sabotage, and injury by explosives.

crime."[23] If mitigating circumstances exist (e.g., the defendant played a minor role in the crime), the judge may select the lowest of the three alternatives. If the judge finds aggravating circumstances (e.g., the crime involved multiple victims), he may select the highest alternative.

At first glance, California's determinate sentencing seem to provide for far less lengthy imprisonment than does indeterminate sentencing. While the maximum California core sentence for burglary of a dwelling is four years imprisonment, for example, the maximum for a similar burglary under an indeterminate sentencing statute commonly would be in the range of fifteen to twenty years. In practice, however, the minimum sentences under indeterminate sentencing will be quite low and the prisoner will be paroled soon after the minimum is served. Thus the burglary defendant who received an indeterminate sentence of two to fifteen years probably will be imprisoned for a period no longer than the core sentence imposed under the California tripartite alternatives.[24] Of course, exceptional cases exist in which the minimum is high or parole is not readily granted and the time actually served under an indeterminate sentence comes closer to the maximum set in the penal code. The California presumptive-determinate sentencing structure seeks to reach these exceptional cases with several provisions for "enhancement" of the core sentence. The enhancements may add from one to three years to the core sentence depending upon the nature of enhancement. The six basic grounds for enhancement are: (1) the possession of a firearm or use of a deadly weapon in the commission of the crime; (2) the use of a firearm; (3) intentional infliction of great bodily injury; (4) infliction of great property loss (over $25,000); (5) previous conviction of a felony for which a prison term was served; and (6) commission of multiple crimes deserving multiple punishments. In the case of certain serious felonies, when more than one ground for enhancement exists, the enhancements may be "stacked" so that considerably more than three years can be added to the core sentence.[25]

The experience with the presumptive-determinate sentencing structure is still too limited to determine how frequently the end result will be different from that which would be produced by indeterminate sentences. It is clear, however, that the difference will not be nearly as great as might be suggested by a first-glance comparison of the penal codes in states following the two different

---

23. Various illustrative circumstances are set forth in a court rule, California Rules of Court, Rules 421-422. See also note 84 at p. 351 *infra*.

24. Thus, when California had indeterminate sentencing, the median term actually served by felony offenders was less than three years. Other jurisdictions with indeterminate sentencing present similar statistics. See, e.g., *Sourcebook of Criminal Justice Statistics—1976*, note 1, p. 1 *supra*, at p. 726-729.

25. Other jurisdictions with determinate sentencing have adopted far fewer enhancements, but have provided for longer terms in the core sentence and in the few permissible enhancements (also called "extended terms"). In Illinois, for example, the range for the core determinate sentence for a class two felony (which includes burglary) is from 3-7 years. Two grounds for extended terms are recognized: (1) that the offense was accompanied by "exceptionally brutal or heinous behavior indicative of wanton cruelty" or (2) that the defendant was convicted of the same or greater class of felony within ten years (excluding time spent in custody). The extended term can result in doubling the length of the highest possible core sentence. Thus, for a class two offense, it can produce a determinate term as high as 14 years (less good time credit). See Illinois Stat. ch. 38, §§1005-8-1, 1005-8-2, 1005-8-3.2(b). See also note 84, p. 351 *infra*.

approaches. The same also is true for determinate sentencing structures that lack the presumptive feature and thus give the court broader discretion in setting the fixed term. The student must keep in mind, with respect to all jurisdictions, that the punishment prescribed in the penal code provision defining an offense does not always tell the whole story. One must be aware of the total range of applicable sentencing procedures, including several we have not yet mentioned (e.g., the "suspension" of sentences). We will examine all of these procedures in greater detail in Chapter Thirteen. At this point, having looked at the basic prerequisites as to the form of the criminal law—the requirements of prior definition of the offense and the specification of maximum penalties—we now are ready to discuss the elements of which the crime will consist.

ACTUS REUS

Every crime prohibits certain behavior, which the law describes as the *actus reus* of the crime. The phrase actus reus, which is taken from the Latin, means "the act of a criminal." However, when a court says that certain behavior constitutes the actus reus of a crime, it is not saying that any person who has engaged in that behavior will be guilty of that crime. Rather, the individual will have satisfied only the first element for conviction—the doing of the prohibited act. For criminal liability, several other elements, such as a certain frame of mind, also must have been present. In determining whether a crime has been committed, we ordinarily start with an analysis of the actus reus, as opposed to those other elements, since the actus reus is the foundation upon which the definition of the crime is built.

Policy.   The requirement that a crime include an actus reus reflects a fundamental premise of the criminal law: a person will not be punished on the basis of thoughts alone; he must have engaged in some harmful or potentially harmful behavior. To wish that an enemy were dead, to think about taking another's wallet, to contemplate burning another's property—such thoughts, though wrongful, cannot be made into crimes. To be held liable for murder, theft, or arson, the individual must undertake acts to accomplish his evil objectives. An actor *can* be held criminally liable for attempting murder, theft, or arson even if he does not successfully achieve the final results required for those crimes, but he must have taken some steps towards the accomplishment of his criminal objective.

Why is it that the law will not punish bad thoughts alone, but requires an act? Several justifications are offered for the actus reus requirement. One is that liability based upon thoughts alone is too susceptible to error in proof. Unless a person takes some action, indicating his intention, how can we be convinced beyond a reasonable doubt that he actually thought about committing a crime? Moreover, even if we could establish that the person did have such thoughts, how could we determine, without an actus reus requirement, that he seriously entertained those thoughts? Still another justification for the actus reus requirement rests on the view that the criminal law should be concerned primarily with the infliction of social harm. Thoughts alone do not cause harm or raise a significant likelihood that harm will result. The individual must take some action to either produce harm or raise a serious potential for causing harm.

Omissions.   The actus reus requirement does not necessarily require that criminal liability be based upon an affirmative act (an "act of commission"). The requirement also may be satisfied by a failure to act (an "act of omission") when the individual is under a duty to act.[26] Thus, a person may be held liable for murder by poisoning another (an act of commission) or by withholding life-saving medicine from an ill person (an act of omission). There is a significant difference, however, in the criminal law's treatment of acts of commission and acts of omission. All persons can be held liable for acts of commission, but criminal liability based upon omissions is limited to persons whose omissions violate specific legal obligations to act. As the Model Penal Code puts it, liability may not be based on an omission unless that omission violates a "legal duty" that is imposed either in the penal code itself or in another source of law, such as a civil statute.[27]

The nature of this limited criminal responsibility for omissions is illustrated by the hypothetical, noted above, in which medicine is withheld from an ill person. A person who withholds life-saving medicine, even though he has the intent that the victim die, will not be liable unless he has a special relationship to the victim that would impose a duty upon him to assist the victim. Such a relationship might exist if the actor were a person who had a contractual obligation to treat the victim (such as a physician or a nurse) or was a person charged with a general legal duty to care for the victim (e.g., a parent or spouse). A close friend or any other person without a special legal obligation to provide care would not, however, be liable for failing to assist the victim. It would not matter that the friend or bystander knew that the medicine would save the victim's life and could have provided the medicine without any significant effort. The key is that the friend or bystander has performed no act of commission causing the death of the victim, only an act of omission, and he has no legal duty to the sick person that would be violated by his act of omission.

Why is it that an omission constitutes the actus reus for a crime only when the actor has a legal duty to act? The answer lies in the basic function of the criminal law to hold liable those who are most directly responsible for causing harm. A person who performs an affirmative act that directly causes harm (as, for example, the person who poisons another) clearly establishes his primary responsibility for the act. On the other hand, acts of omission are commonly shared by many persons. When an individual dies who could have been saved by emergency medical care, it often is true that there are a number of persons who could have called for an ambulance or otherwise provided that care. It is only the person with the legal obligation to provide the care who can be said to be responsible for legally causing the death. He is the only person as to whom the law can say, "You should have acted and your failure to do so makes you as responsible as a person who caused the same harm by an affirmative act."

Voluntariness.   Even an act of commission does not satisfy the actus reus required for criminal liability if the act was involuntary — that is, an act over

---

26.   See, e.g., the California definition of crime quoted at p. 58 *supra*.

27.   MPC §2.01(3).

which the actor lacked physical control. Thus, if a man during an attack of epilepsy makes a violent movement of his arms and legs and inflicts injury on a nearby person, he will not be held criminally liable for inflicting that harm. If a driver of an automobile has a heart attack and runs over a child before he can regain control of the wheel, he will not be held criminally liable even if the child should die. In both cases, the individual was not "culpable" or "blameworthy" because he could not control his act. We assume, of course, that the man did not know he was subject to heart attacks and had not been warned against driving a car. If he had such knowledge and warning, criminal liability may be established by looking to an act as to which he did have control; in initially driving the car on the public highway, he clearly was engaging in a voluntary act, and that act may be viewed as the crucial wrongful act that eventually led to the homicide.

What kinds of acts are involuntary acts? The Model Code provision on voluntary acts, followed in the many states with penal laws based on the Code, offer three examples: (1) a reflex or convulsion, (2) a bodily movement during unconsciousness or sleep, and (3) conduct during hypnosis or resulting from hypnotic suggestion.[28] The Code also notes that an act is not involuntary simply because the individual acted out of habit and therefore was not conscious of what he was doing. In such a case, the act clearly was within the actor's physical control if he simply would have paid more attention to his actions.

MENS REA

The Nature of Mens Rea.   A second essential element of a crime is the *mens rea* of the crime. The word "mens" means mind. "Mens rea" in the criminal law means the state of mind of the actor. The mens rea requirement is the mental element required for criminal liability.[29] An old legal axiom says, "An act does not make the doer of it guilty, unless the mind also be guilty." Without a wrongful mental element, the actor is not truly culpable. Thus, both the actus reus and the mens rea are necessary elements of a crime.

Of course, the mens rea, like the actus reus, will vary from crime to crime. When we study the elements of the major crimes in the succeeding chapters we will see that the actus reus for the crime of theft is the taking of the property of another and the mens rea is the knowledge that the property belongs to another and the intent to deprive the owner of the use of that property. For the crime of manslaughter, on the other hand, the actus reus is the taking of a life, and the mens rea includes the awareness of the actor that his behavior might cause the death of another, even though he did not intend to kill. Each crime must be examined separately to determine the precise actus reus and mens rea required for that crime.

Common Levels of Mens Rea.   Although the required mens rea will vary from crime to crime, one of four basic levels of mens rea is commonly found in the vast majority of all crimes. These four different levels of awareness have always existed

---

28.   MPC §2.01(2).

29.   In penal codes based upon the Model Code, the mens rea element commonly is described as the "culpable mental state." See , e.g., New York Penal Law §15.00(b).

in the law, but they were first defined fully in the Model Penal Code. Today these definitions have been incorporated in the codes of over thirty states and are frequently relied upon by courts in other states as well. The four basic mental elements are characterized by the Code as "purpose" (called "intent" in many state codes), "knowledge," "recklessness," and "negligence."

The four basic levels of mens rea may be applied to any of three different aspects (called "material elements") of the crime. The first is the actor's physical conduct. Mens rea here relates to the actor's awareness of his physical conduct. Thus, the crime of arson requires that the actor purposely started a fire; if the fire is started accidently, the defendant does not have the required mental element as to the nature of his conduct. The second material element is the surrounding circumstances that exist apart from the individual's conduct. If a statute prohibits the knowing sale of liquor to a person under eighteen, it requires that the individual be aware of an external circumstance—the fact that the recipient is a person under eighteen. It should be emphasized that the law need not require one of the four basic levels of awareness as to every circumstance. It could provide, for example, that the seller of liquor to a minor must be aware of the fact that the item sold is liquor, but need not have any level of mens rea as to the fact that the purchaser was a minor.[30] The third possible material element is the result produced by the conduct. As we shall see, most crimes require that a certain harm has resulted from the defendant's action. The mens rea requirement for these crimes frequently focuses on the actor's mental element with respect to causing that harm. Thus, for a crime such as arson or malicious destruction of property,[31] the actor must have at least acted recklessly with respect to the type of injury that the crime prohibits.

Prior to the Model Code, courts often distinguished between the mens rea requirement for different material elements by describing crimes as requiring

---

30. It should be noted, however, that unless the statute clearly indicates otherwise, the reference to a single mental element (e.g., knowledge) in a criminal statute ordinarily will be taken as applying to all of the material elements of the crime—that is, the prohibited physical conduct, all of the required surrounding circumstances, and the required harm. Thus, New York Penal Law §15.15(1) provides:

> When the commission of an offense defined in this chapter, or some element of an offense, requires a particular culpable mental state, such mental state is ordinarily designated in the statute defining the offense by use of the terms "intentionally," "knowingly," "recklessly," or "criminal negligence" or by use of terms, such as "with intent to defraud" and "knowing it to be false," describing a specific kind of intent or knowledge. When one and only one of such terms appears in a statute defining an offense, it is presumed to apply to every element of the offense unless an intent to limit its application clearly appears.

A good illustration of a crime that distinguishes betweeen the required mental element for different elements is arson in the second degree. MPC §220.1(2). It requires that the actor purposely set a fire (the required conduct) but that he may be only reckless as to the resulting danger to property (the required result). See also pp. 169-70 *infra*.

31. Although the term "malice" literally suggests the presence of a deep seated and intense dislike, the crime of malicious destruction, like other crimes using that term, would not require actual malice against the victim of the crime. Many crimes refer to "malicious" acts yet actually require no more than extreme recklessness. Words like "malice" came to be used in the early common law because it was assumed that a person intentionally or recklessly inflicting harm acted out of ill-will. The actual presence of such a motive has never been needed, however. See also p. 135 *infra* discussing the use of the term "malice" in the context of homicide offenses, and pp. 101-02 *infra* on the law's general unwillingness to examine motive.

general intent or *specific intent.*[32] General intent refers only to the actor's mens rea as to his physical conduct. It is used to describe crimes which require that the actor intentionally do the physical act involved, but do not require that he intend the harm caused or be aware of crucial surrounding circumstances. Thus, the crime of malicious destruction of property is a general intent crime because, while it requires the causing of injury to property, the actor need not have intended that result (recklessness being sufficient). On the other hand, specific intent crimes are those in which the offender must actually have intended the result. A good illustration is first degree murder. This crime ordinarily does not apply to an accidental killing (covered by the general intent crime of manslaughter) but only to intentional killings. Another commonly used illustration of a specific intent crime is theft. That crime requires more than that the actor realize that he is taking possession of some property; he also must know that the property belongs to another (a surrounding circumstance), and he must intend a particular result, to deprive that person of his property.

Today, particularly in Model Penal Code jurisdictions, the courts are less likely to describe offenses as general intent or specific intent crimes. They ordinarily will use the Model Code terminology. Thus, they will say that the crime is one requiring recklessness or negligence as to a certain result (formerly called a general intent crime) or that the crime requires purpose or knowledge as to a result or circumstance (formerly called a specific intent crime). Our emphasis accordingly must be on achieving a complete understanding of these four levels of mens rea described in the Model Code.

Acting Purposely.[33]　Under the Model Penal Code definition, a person acts purposely with respect to a material element of an offense when:

(i) If the element involves the nature of his conduct or a result thereof, it is his conscious object to engage in conduct of that nature or to cause such a result;

(ii) If the element involves the attendant circumstances, he is aware of the existence of such circumstances or he believes or hopes that they exist.[34]

The concept of purpose is one with which we all are familiar. In the criminal law, it applies only to the actor's conduct, the harmful consequences of that conduct, or the surrounding circumstances, but not to the underlying motive for his action. If a statute makes it a crime to purposely give another narcotics, and the actor knew that the item being transferred was narcotics and intended to give it to that person, he has the necessary mens rea for the crime. The concept of purpose does not require that the court seek to determine the underlying reason for the actor's objective, whether he acted out of sympathy for the other person, greed,

---

32. Courts have been criticized for often using these terms in a vague fashion. The discussion that follows is based upon the most common usage of the terms, but it does not attempt to explain all the subtleties of the different uses of the terms. See LaFave and Scott, note 3, p. 59 *supra,* at p. 201-202.

33. As noted previously, many jurisdictions use the term "intentionally" rather than "purposely." See, e.g., Illinois Stat. ch. 38, §4-4. They define the term in the same manner as the Model Penal Code, however, and it should not be confused with the pre-Code references to intent in describing, for example, "general intent."

34. MPC §2.20(b).

hate, or some other motive. The key is the presence of the immediate objective of transfer, without regard to any other underlying objectives.

Ordinarily, if the actor has an objective to harm one victim, but accidentally harms another instead, he still will be liable under a crime prohibiting the purposeful injuring of another. The Model Code definition of "purpose" refers simply to intending the result prohibited by law, not to intending it with respect to a particular victim. The law will shift the illegal objective from one victim to another (a principle known as *transferred intent*). Thus, let us suppose that A shoots at his enemy E, but by mistake he kills his friend F. Under this definition, did A act purposely in killing his friend? The answer is "yes." Though he did not intend to kill his friend, he did intend to kill his enemy, so his conduct was purposeful as far as the end result required by law was concerned.

Acting Knowingly.   Under the Model Code definition, a person acts knowingly with respect to a material element of the offense when:

> (i)   if the element involves the nature of his conduct or the attendant circumstances, he is aware that his conduct is of the nature or that such circumstances exist;
>
> (ii) if the element involves a result of his conduct, he is aware that it is practically certain that his conduct will cause such a result.[35]

Note that the Code definition does not require absolute certainty with respect to surrounding circumstances. Assume, for example, that the penal code prohibits knowingly passing counterfeit money and the defendant passed a series of $10 bills, obtained (at a low price) from an underworld figure who had told him they were counterfeit. Can the defendant now claim that he did not knowingly pass counterfeit money because he had not seen the money being printed and therefore did not know as an actual fact that it was counterfeit? The Code answer would be "no." He certainly operated under the premise that these were counterfeit bills and we can say he was practically certain they were counterfeit. To avoid any confusion on this point, some states have altered the Model Code definition to state that "knowledge of a material fact includes awareness of the *substantial probability* that such fact exists."[36]

Acting Recklessly.   Under the Model Penal Code definition, a person acts recklessly with respect to a material element of an offense when:

> He consciously disregards a substantial and unjustifiable risk that the material element exists or will result from his conduct. The risk must be of such nature and degree that, considering the nature and purpose of the actor's conduct and the circumstances known to him, its disregard involves a gross deviation from the standard of conduct that a law-abiding person would observe in the actor's situation.[37]

This definition is particularly difficult to apply in practice, since it involves a decision as to what constitutes a "gross deviation from the standards of conduct

---

35.   MPC §2.02(2)(b).

36.   See Illinois Stat. ch. 38, §4-5.

37.   MPC §2.02(b)(c).

that a law-abiding person would observe under the circumstances."[38] Thus, a decision must be made as to what standards of conduct a law-abiding person would have followed under the particular circumstances, and a further decision must be made as to whether the accused grossly deviated from those standards. In spite of the difficulty of applying the test, it nevertheless is possible to give some examples of reckless conduct. A man fires a gun in a crowded dance hall, throws large firecrackers into a group of children, drives 80 miles an hour in a school zone, or drops heavy timbers from the roof of a building along a city street without in any way attempting to protect the people on the sidewalk below. Such reckless-ness is culpable, and if someone is injured, the person who engages in such conduct would be held responsible under a criminal statute prohibiting the reckless inflic-tion of injury.

Acting Negligently. Under the Model Penal Code definition, a person acts negligently with respect to a material element of an offense when:

> He should be aware of a substantial and unjustifiable risk that the material element exists or will result from his conduct. The risk must be of such a nature and degree that the actor's failure to perceive it, considering the nature and purpose of his conduct and the circumstances known to him, involves a gross deviation from the standard of care that a reasonable person would observe in the actor's situation.[39]

Acting negligently is distinguished from acting purposely, knowingly, or recklessly in that it does not involve a state of awareness. Negligence exists where the person should have been aware that a certain risk existed, but was not aware. While the law generallly requires actual awareness, an exception is made for crimes involving the infliction of serious bodily injury. A person may not be aware that he was creating a risk to the life or safety of another, yet if he was negligent (i.e., he should have known that he was creating such a danger), and a person is killed or seriously injured, he will be held criminally liable. Negligent acts which injure others usually are due to the fact that the actor does not care about other people's interests and simply fails to pay attention to them. The actor is suffi-ciently culpable for his failure to pay attention to impose criminal liability, at least where that lack of attention causes death or serious injury. Examples would be the driver of an automobile who fails to keep a proper look-out when crossing an intersection or the physician who forgets to take proper sanitary precautions in operating.

At common law, the distinction between recklessness and negligence was not always based on the factor of awareness. Some courts held that neither negligence nor recklessness required awareness of the risk. The primary basis for distinction was the degree of the risk involved. If the individual engaged in activity creating an especially outrageous risk, he acted recklessly. If he engaged in a less outra-geous risk, but still a risk constituting a gross deviation from the behavior of a reasonable person, he acted negligently. The Model Code, on the other hand,

---

38. Several states, noting that there is no real difference between a "law-abiding" person and a "reasonable person," have substituted the latter term for the former in adopting the MPC definition of recklessness. See, e.g., New York Penal Law §15.05(3).

39. MPC §2.02(2)(d).

describes the required degree of risk (a "gross deviation") as being identical for recklessness and negligence. The primary basis for distinction simply is the actor's awareness of the risk. The final determination as to whether the actor was negligent or reckless usually will rest upon the jury's willingness to believe the defendant was so preoccupied or ignorant that he was not aware of a risk that the reasonable person certainly would have appreciated. Most frequently the jury will assume, as the law permits it to do, that the defendant knew what a reasonable person would have known and simply did not care (i.e., he was reckless). Thus, the distinction between recklessness and negligence often has more theoretical than practical significance. If the risk meets the Code's gross deviation standard, the person is most likely to be found to have acted recklessly.

The Reasonable Person Yardstick.   In applying the "gross deviation" standard, the Model Code definitions of recklessness and negligence measure the actor's behavior against that of a law-abiding person (in the case of recklessness) or a reasonable person (in the case of negligence). Under both definitions, a person is not held to the highest humanly possible standard of conduct, but neither is he permitted to avoid responsibility where he acted in good faith but below what could reasonably be expected from him. The yardstick for judging his behavior under both definitions essentially is the response of the "reasonable person" in the same situation. Because recklessness involves the person who is aware of the risk, the Code refers to the likely response of the law-abiding person, but that standard is essentially the same reasonable person yardstick mentioned in the definition of negligence.[40] The reasonable person yardstick has a long tradition in the law. It often has been said, in various contexts, that to avoid liability, at least for the most harmful activities, a person is expected to perform according to the standards of the "ordinary prudent person," or "a man of ordinary temperament." These are all basically paraphrases of the reasonable person yardstick. The basic thrust of that yardstick is best illustrated by an examination of a simple hypothetical case.

Suppose a man is driving down the street and a child darts in front of his car. How are we to determine whether the man was either reckless or negligent, and so criminally answerable for the death of the child? We will apply the standard of the reasonable man. Although a person of extraordinarily fast reflexes could have swerved and missed the child, we will not require such extraordinarily fast reflexes from our driver. However, if an average person, paying attention to his driving, having his car under control, being able to observe the child at a sufficient distance, could have stopped and not hit the child, and our driver did not stop, then he was at least negligent according to the yardstick of the law. His conduct fell below the required standard. If he was driving 80 miles an hour in a known school zone and decided to just "take a chance" that no child would be in his path, his conduct was reckless. Not only did his conduct fall below the expected standard, there was an element in his conduct of consciously disregarding an unjustifiable risk to the life and safety of others. If he simply was not aware of the surrounding circumstances, so there was no conscious disregarding of the risk, his conduct would be negligent.

---

40.   See note 38 *supra*.

It obviously is not easy to determine exactly what conduct is reasonable, negligent, or reckless under the circumstances. The jury, made up of "ordinary persons," hears the evidence and decides on the basis of all the evidence whether the driver did or did not do all that a reasonable person could be expected to do under the circumstances. Its verdict is rendered accordingly—"not guilty" if his conduct met the standard; "guilty" if his conduct failed to measure up. The "reasonable man" is the yardstick of the law; the decision as to whether a particular individual on a particular occasion met the standard is made by his fellow "reasonable men."

Mens Rea and the Level of Punishment. As we have seen, the harm caused by a crime usually is the most significant factor in determining the level of punishment that will be authorized for the crime. Yet the mens rea also will be significant, particularly where different levels or "degrees" of the same crime are based on differences in the required mens rea.[41] In such a situation, the punishment provided is usually less for negligent and reckless acts than for knowing and purposeful acts. Unless the reckless acts were so grossly and obviously reckless that they showed utter indifference to causing harm, the person who acted recklessly or negligently has a lesser degree of culpability than the person who knowingly or purposely inflicted harm. Because there is less culpability, there is less need for a higher punishment to fulfill the objective of retribution (and, perhaps, deterrence). As Justice Holmes onced noted: "Even a dog distinguishes between being stumbled over and being kicked."[42]

Mistake of Fact. What if a person mistakenly takes the property of another believing it to be his own property? What if he destroys property of another believing it to be his own property? Assume that, in both cases, the person has made an innocent mistake of fact. Confused as to the identity of the property in question, he believed that the property was actually his property, to do with it as he pleased. That mistake may or may not excuse him from criminal liability. Whether a factual mistake constitutes a legal excuse will depend basically on the applicable mens rea and its relationship to the individual's mistaken belief. The Model Penal Code states the prevailing rule as follows: "Ignorance or mistake as to a matter of fact . . . is a defense if the ignorance or mistake negates the purpose, knowledge, belief, recklessness or negligence required to establish the material element of the offense." [43] One must, in other words, determine whether the presence of the mistake means that the mens rea required for the crime in question was not present. The mistake is relevant under the law only insofar as it establishes that there was no mens rea.

---

41. A particular offense will be divided into several degrees with the higher degree carrying a higher level of punishment. Traditionally this was done with only a few crimes such as murder, but the new codes now have first, second, and sometimes even third degrees for such diverse crimes as arson, burglary, and perjury. Quite often the distinction between the higher and lower offenses will be based on the degree of harm caused (e.g., the value of the property stolen). There will be other divisions of crimes into degrees, however, where the harm is the same for both degrees, but the level of mens rea differs. See, e.g., the discussion of arson at p. 171 *infra.*

42. O. Holmes, *The Common Law*, Boston: Little, Brown and Company, 1891, p. 3.

43. MPC §2.04.

In the first hypothetical noted above, where the man mistakenly took the property of another, any potential criminal liability would be under the crime of theft. The mens rea for theft includes knowledge that the property taken belongs to another. Our defendant obviously did not have that knowledge since he mistakenly believed that the property was his own. It matters not whether his mistake was reasonable or unreasonable; he lacked the required mens rea and therefore cannot be held liable for theft. In the second hypothetical, where the person destroyed property mistakenly believed to be his own, potential liability would be under the crime of malicious destruction of property. [44] Assume that in our jurisdiction, that crime applies to the negligent or reckless destruction of property. If the person's mistake as to the identity of the property was reasonable, that reasonableness will establish in itself that he was not negligent or reckless. It is not a violation of the reasonable person yardstick for a person to destroy property he reasonably believes to be his own. If the mistake was unreasonable—that is, if a reasonable person would not have made the same mistake under the same circumstances—then the actor clearly was negligent. A reasonable person would have been aware that the property was not his (or at least that a substantial risk existed that it was not his) and would not have destroyed it. If the actor was aware of the risk of mistaken identity, he would have been reckless. Thus, notwithstanding the honesty of his mistake, if it was an unreasonable mistake, he would be criminally liable as he still would have the necessary mens rea of either negligence or recklessness.

If our two hypotheticals are put together, we see that an honest but unreasonable factual mistake as to a material element of a crime ordinarily will negate mens rea (and constitute a defense) if the required level of mens rea is purpose or knowledge, but not if that mens rea is only negligence or recklessness. On the other hand, a reasonable mistake as to a material element ordinarily will negate any level of mens rea. There is one exceptional situation, however, where even a reasonable mistake will not suffice, and that is in the case of the so-called "strict liability" offenses.

Strict Liability.   There are some crimes that do not require any mens rea—not even negligence—as to some circumstances that are crucial in establishing the crime. These offenses are commonly described as "strict liability" crimes since they make no allowance for a reasonable mistake. Strict liability offenses tend to fall into two categories. First, there are those that involve acts that would be immoral even under those circumstances the actor reasonably but mistakenly assumed to exist. Consider, for example, the crime of "statutory rape," which prohibits consensual sexual intercourse with a female under a certain age (commonly 16 or 17). In many jurisdictions, no mens rea whatsoever is required as to the youth of the female. If the statutorily prescribed age is sixteen, and the female is under that age, the male is liable even though he mistakenly but reasonably believed that she was much older. Since the male is engaging in an activity which is frowned upon (though not illegal) even under his assumption that the female was above sixteen, he will have to "take his chances" and suffer criminal liability if

---

44.   In other states, this crime would be called "criminal mischief." See note 23, p. 170 *infra*.

mistaken. For much the same reason, many states do not require any level of mens rea as to the marital status of the married person engaged in the crime of adultery.

The so-called "regulatory crimes" are the other major group of strict liability offenses. The crimes involve heavily regulated industries, usually those distributing potentially harmful products. Illustrative are the crimes of selling liquor to minors and selling drugs in a bottle bearing an incorrect label. Both of these are crimes without regard to the reasonableness of the seller's mistakes. The tavern owner will be liable even if he reasonably believed his purchaser was an adult. The pharmacist will be liable even though the improper label was attached because of a reasonable mistake as to the contents of the bottle. The legislature desires to place considerable pressure on persons in these regulated industries to exercise every precaution in carrying on their activities. The legislature recognizes also that crimes of this type bear minor penalties and conviction does not do grave injury to the reputation of the offender. Accordingly, the legislature feels justified in establishing the regulatory crimes without requiring any mens rea as to those elements that make the prohibited activities illegal. In doing so, it has created what, in effect, is a crime that does not require fault. Such crimes have been criticized over the years as inconsistent with the basic premise that punishment should be imposed only for culpability. Nevertheless, they continue to be utilized in more and more fields that deal with widespread sales to the public. Consumer protection is thought to outweigh the need for blameworthiness as a basis for criminal liability.

HARM AND CAUSATION

The third element commonly included in the definition of a crime is the element of a harm inflicted upon some subject protected by the law. Closely related to this element is the link between it and the actus reus, reflected in the requirement that the prohibited harm has been caused by the conduct of the defendant. These two elements—that of *harm* and *causation*—are less frequently the subjects of extensive legal debate than are the elements of actus reus and mens rea. Usually there is little doubt in a particular case as to whether the harm inflicted was prohibited by the law or whether it was caused by the defendant's conduct. Nevertheless both elements are significant and they occasionally present difficult legal issues.

Required Injury. Ordinarily, a crime involves the infliction of an injury by the offender upon a protected subject matter. That protected subject matter usually is the body or property of another person. However, it also may be the government and its operations, as in the crimes of treason or bribery of a public official. The protected subject also may be the offender himself, as in the case of "victimless" crimes, such as drug abuse, where the offender is viewed as hurting himself. For some crimes, such as the distribution of obscene literature to adults, it has been suggested that the injury extends to a less tangible subject protected by the law, the moral fiber of the community and its attitudes toward sex and marriage.

Offenses commonly are classified according to the subject matter protected (crimes against the person, crimes against property, etc.). The offenses within each of these categories then often are ranked according to the degree of harm caused to the protected subject matter. Consider, for example, crimes against the person of another. If an individual intentionally assaults another and kills him, the crime is murder. If he inflicts serious bodily harm, the crime is aggravated assault. If the injury is minor, the crime is simple assault. A similar type of division is found in some jurisdictions between forcible sexual touching of the intimate parts of another (a separate crime of "sexual abuse") and forcible sexual intercourse (a more serious crime of rape).[45] In some instances, greater crimes are created out of the combination of two lesser crimes involving separate types of injury. Thus robbery consists of the combination of theft (a taking of property) and assault (the use of force or a threat of force against the person).

Crimes Aimed At Possible Future Injuries. Although most crimes require the infliction of a specified injury, there are a substantial number of exceptions. Foremost among those are the so-called *inchoate* crimes. The term "inchoate" means only partly begun, and the inchoate crimes reach activities that are the beginnings toward the completion of other crimes. Since they often reach acts involving preparation to commit some harm, the inchoate crimes sometimes also are described as "preparatory crimes." (In contrast, the crimes involving the infliction of these harms are described as "completed crimes"). The major inchoate crimes are *attempt, solicitation,* and *conspiracy.* A charge under each of these crimes will be tied to the intended commission of some completed offense. Thus, a person may be charged with an attempt to commit rape, a solicitation to commit murder, or a conspiracy to commit theft. The inchoate crimes are particularly important because they permit police to intercept persons before they can inflict the injury involved in the completed crimes, yet still charge those persons with a criminal offense.

Each of the inchoate crimes reach a different type of beginning step toward the completion of another crime. Conspiracy requires two or more persons agreeing to commit a crime and, in some jurisdictions, taking some act in furtherance of that agreement. Thus if four people plot to blow up an R.O.T.C. building and one of them purchases the material to make the bomb, they all are guilty at that point of the crime of conspiracy to commit arson. They will be subject to criminal liability even though they are apprehended before the bomb is made and before the building is blown up. Most states have a conspiracy offense that includes agreements to commit any other crime, but some limit the conspiracy offense to agreements to commit the more serious offenses.[46] Solicitation more commonly is restricted only to efforts to accomplish more serious offenses.[47] This crime consists basically of requesting or counseling another to commit a crime. The most

---

45. See, e.g., New York Penal Law §§130.35,130.65. See p. 148 *infra.*

46. The Texas conspiracy provision is typical. Texas Penal Code §15.02 provides:
    (a) A person commits criminal conspiracy if, with intent that a felony be committed:
        (1) he agrees with one or more persons that they or one or more of them engage in conduct that would constitute the offense; and
        (2) he or one or more of them performs an overt act in pursuance of the agreement.
        * * *
    (d) An offense under this section is one category lower than the most serious felony that is the object of the conspiracy, and if the most serious felony that is the object of the conspiracy is a felony of the third degree, the offense is a Class A misdemeanor.

47. Consider, e.g., Texas Penal Code §15.03:

common example is attempting to hire another to commit that crime. The crime of solicitation is completed when that other person is solicited, and it matters not that he might refuse. (If he accepts, then one would have an agreement and therefore a conspiracy, which ordinarily is punished more severely than a solicitation).[48]

The crime of attempts is, perhaps, the most complex of the inchoate offenses. Unlike conspiracy and solicitation, attempt is not limited to a single type of preparation for the commission of a crime. It covers instead a broad range of activities directed toward the accomplishment of the completed crime. Courts have been concerned, however, that if the range of acts covered is too broad, criminal liability will be imposed upon persons who do not really present a serious threat of completing their criminal objectives. A person may decide to rob a bank and may purchase a mask, but that still leaves him quite a distance from seriously undertaking the robbery. It is entirely possible that such a person will go no further toward committing the robbery. To impose criminal liability in such a case, where no harm has been committed and the individual does not pose a serious threat, would be inconsistent with the basic purposes of the criminal law. Courts accordingly have limited the application of the crime of attempts through various tests designed to determine whether the individual has made sufficient progress toward his criminal objective to show a serious intent to commit the crime. The most prominent of these tests has been incorporated in various statutory definitions of the crime of attempt: the defendant must have engaged in action that goes beyond "mere preparation" and "tends . . . to effect the commission of the crime intended."[49]

Complementing the inchoate crimes are a series of other offenses which are designed to reach specific potentially threatening situations. These crimes too do not require the infliction of an immediate harm. Indeed, in some instances, they

---

(a) A person commits an offense if, with intent that a capital felony or felony of the first degree be committed, he requests, commands, or attempts to induce another to engage in specific conduct that, under the circumstances surrounding his conduct as the actor believes them to be, would constitute the felony or make the other a party to its commission.

(b) A person may not be convicted under this section on the uncorroborated testimony of the person allegedly solicited and unless the solicitation is made under circumstances strongly corroborative of both the solicitation itself and the actor's intent that the other person act on the solicitation.

* * *

(d) An offense under this section is:

(1) a felony of the first degree if the offense solicited is a capital offense; or

(2) a felony of the second degree if the offense solicited is a felony of the first degree.

48. A person cannot be convicted for commission of more than one of the inchoate crimes. Thus, if defendant engages in solicitation, conspiracy, and other activities amounting to an attempt, all for the purpose of committing a single completed crime, he will be held liable for only the most serious of these inchoate crimes, which usually will be conspiracy. Similarly, where the ultimate criminal objective was achieved, the offender cannot be convicted of the inchoate crime of attempt or solicitation and the completed crime. In many jurisdictions, however, conspiracy is treated as a separate basis for punishment which can be combined with the completed crime. This rule is based on the view that conspiracy, because of the combination of two persons, presents a potential danger for the commission of other crimes beyond the immediate criminal objective of the participants.

49. See, e.g., Texas Penal Code §15.01.

do not require an intent to commit harm. Thus, many states make it a crime for a private person to possess a certain type of weapon (e.g., a sub-machine gun) simply because of the grave harm that may be committed through the misuse of such a weapon. Similarly, it is a crime to carry a concealed weapon without a license even if the person has the most innocent reason for carrying the weapon. Other statutes make it a crime to possess certain items only if they are possessed for illegal purposes (e.g., possession of burglar tools). These offenses are very much like inchoate offenses in that they are designed to reach a substantial step in the individual's progress toward the commission of a completed crime.

The Causal Relationship.   Where a crime is defined as requiring the infliction of some harm, it also will require that the defendant's conduct have caused that harm. After all, if the defendant did not cause the harm (and if he was not an accomplice to the person who did cause the harm), he should not be held accountable for the harm. The requirement of causation ordinarily presents few difficulties. When A shoots B through the head and B dies, there is no question that A caused B's death. On occasion, however, various intervening acts of the victim and others will raise difficult causation problems. Suppose a man assaults his wife and inflicts a minor injury. She is taken to a hopsital where an incompetent doctor performs an unnecessary operation from which she dies. Is the husband guilty of murder for having "caused" the death of his wife, or is he only guilty of assault? Suppose the wife, through a careless lack of attention to her wound, permits it to get infected and she dies as a result of the infection. Is the husband here guilty of causing the death or simply the assault? Does it matter whether the wife failed to consult a doctor? If so, does it matter whether the husband could have anticipated that failure before he attacked his wife? Suppose the husband had inflicted a mortal wound which ordinarily would cause death in a few days. In the meantime, however, another person entered the hospital and shot and killed the wife. Would the husband be liable for causing the murder in this situation?

Resolution of questions such as these is difficult and not all courts would reach the same result in each case. All do agree that the harm must have been produced in part by the defendant's conduct. There must be a showing that, "but for" the defendant's conduct, the harm would not have occurred. Such a showing is not sufficient in itself, however, to establish legal causation. For example, assume A shoots at B but misses. Fearing for his life, B then takes the next flight to Brazil, but the plane crashes and kills B. "But for" A's actions, B would not have been on that plane, yet the plane crash certainly is too remote to hold A liable for B's death. Thus courts commonly say that along with a necessary direct chain of causation, the relationship between the act and the harm must be sufficiently close to characterize the act as the "proximate cause" of the harm. In analyzing cases similar to our hypotheticals, the courts have looked to a variety of factors in determining whether the necessary proximate causation existed. Such factors include: (1) whether the actor intended to inflict serious harm; (2) whether the actor did inflict serious harm; (3) whether the intervening event was a product of "natural events" (e.g., the infection of the wound) or the action of a third person (e.g., the sloppy doctor); (4) whether any wound inflicted by an intervening event acted of its own force or in combination with the original wound in causing the death; and (5) whether the final result was foreseeable. At least where the final result could have been anticipated from the dangerous nature of the defendant's conduct, the ultimate test may be, as stated in the Model Code, whether the result was "too remote or accidental in its occurrence to have a just bearing on the actor's liability."[50] This is hardly a precise standard, but it is the best the law can do considering the complexity of the problem.

Accomplice Liability. Even where harm is clearly caused by the action of a single person, the law does not necessarily limit liability to that person. If he has been helped by others, those persons may also be liable under the theory of *accomplice liability.* The person who directly commits the crime is then described as the principal and those who assist him as the *accessories* to the crime. At common law, the rules relating to accessories were quite complex, but they have been simiplified substantially under the modern codes. Basically, a person who intends to assist the principal, shares his overall criminal objective, and renders any form of assistance will be held liable as an accessory. The accessory may perform an essential physical service (e.g., serve as a "lookout" at a bank robbery), provide material aid (furnish a gun), or simply lend his voice to the planning of the crime. He need not be at the scene nor share in the profits (although the latter factor often is important in establishing the accessory's objective of promoting the crime). Accessories are held liable for the crime committed by the principal and are subject to all of the penalties provided for that crime.[51]

CONDITIONS OR CIRCUMSTANCES THAT RELIEVE ONE OF CRIMINAL LIABILITY

The law recognizes certain conditions of the defendant or surrounding factual circumstances that will relieve the defendant of criminal viability. These conditions and circumstances are commonly described as *defenses.* As the name might suggest, they are matters to be raised initially by the defense. The prosecution is not required to negate the possible existence of a defense until the defendant asserts it.[52] In raising a defense, a defendant is saying, in effect, "I may have committed the act prohibited by law, but I cannot be convicted because of a condition or circumstance that relieves me of criminal liability." The most prominent defenses are infancy, insanity, intoxication, mistake, consent, duress, entrapment, the statute of limitations, and the justifiable use of force. For convenience of analysis, the defenses can be divided into two groups. First, there are the four defenses—infancy, insanity, intoxication and mistake—that relate to the defendant's capacity to understand what he was doing. Then there are the remaining

---

50. MPC §2.03.

51. An exception exists for the "accessory-after-the-fact," a person who lends no aid or promise of aid before the commission of the crime, but then assists the principal in avoiding detection. Under today's codes, the accessory-after-the-fact may be charged only with the separate crime of obstructing justice. See, e.g., New York Penal Law §205.50, describing the offense as "hindering prosecution" and encompassing such acts as harboring or concealing the felon, warning him as to impending apprehension, and suppressing evidence of the crime.

52. Once a defense is raised, the states vary in their requirements as to proof. Some require that the prosecution must establish beyond a reasonable doubt that the facts do not establish the defense. In other jurisdictions, at least for some defenses (most notably insanity or duress), the defendant bears the burden of convincing the jury that the defense did exist. See note 3 at p. 204 *infra.*

defenses that relate to outside circumstances rather than the condition of the defendant. We will discuss the defenses in this order. Because the defense of justifiable use of force relates primarily to the crimes of homicide and assault discussed in Chapter Six, our discussion of that defense will be reserved for the later chapter.

INFANCY, INSANITY, INTOXICATION AND MISTAKE

Age (Infancy). In the early history of the law, all persons who committed an act defined as a crime were held to be equally guilty before the law. Neither age, sex, nor unsoundness of mind could be offered as an excuse, and neither were these factors generally considered in mitigation of punishment. One of the first departures from this view came after the Church declared that a child under seven could not be guilty of sin. It followed as a natural conclusion that if a child under seven could not be guilty of sin, neither could he be guilty of a crime. The rule relieving the very young child from criminal responsibility found its way from the church courts to the courts of the King's Bench and into the common law. Of course, if a child under seven lacked the capacity of understanding needed to justify imposing criminal liability, the same might be true of a slightly older child. Accordingly, the common law soon developed a special concern for children between the ages of seven and fourteen.

At common law, a child between seven and fourteen could be held criminally responsible but only if it were affirmatively established that he understood the nature and quality of his act and knew that it was wrong. To state the rule another way, infants below the age of fourteen were presumed incapable of committing a crime, but for persons between the ages of seven and fourteen the presumption was deemed *rebuttable* (i.e., the presumption was not final, but could be overcome by contrary evidence). If it could be affirmatively shown that the child between the ages of seven and fourteen was capable of understanding the nature and quality of the act and was capable of distinguishing right from wrong, he could be held criminally responsible. Below the age of seven, the presumption that the child was incapable of committing a crime could not be rebutted.

Although the common law rule originally was adopted throughout the United States, about one-third of the states today have partially discarded it. Those states reject the concept of a rebuttable presumption and rely simply on an absolute minimum age for criminal responsibility that ranges from eight in a few states to sixteen in others.[53] Moreover, all of the states have adopted the concept of a juvenile court with special authority over all youths below a specified age (often eighteen) which usually is a higher age than the state's minimum age for criminal responsibility. If a youth below the minimum age of criminal responsibility commits an act that would otherwise be a crime, he is subject to the jurisdiction of the juvenile court. If a youth commits a criminal act while above the minimum age for criminal responsibility, but still within the juvenile court's age limitation, he also will be subject to the juvenile court's special authority. Thus, no matter whether

---

53. See LaFave and Scott, note 3, p. 59 *supra*, at p. 353 (collecting the various state statutes).

the state follows the common law rule or some other age limit on criminal responsibility, the practical cut-off age for most criminal prosecutions will be the higher age limit set under the delinquency statutes. There are, however, some exceptional cases in which a youth over the age of criminal responsibility but within the juvenile court age nevertheless may be prosecuted in criminal courts. As we shall see in a later chapter on juvenile courts, these courts are given authority to waive their exclusive jurisdiction in exceptional cases, thereby permitting criminal prosecution. Cases of waiver almost always involve juveniles over fourteen, even in those states in which the minimum age for criminal responsibility is substantially below fourteen.[54]

Insanity.   Although the law included a mental element (the *mens rea*) in the definitions of the common law crimes, it was slow in deciding just what conditions of the mind would entirely excuse the actor from criminal responsibility. That certain conditions of the mind should excuse was agreed upon quite early. Certainly, if a fourteen year old could be so lacking in understanding as to be relieved of criminal responsibility for his acts, the same could be said for at least some adults suffering from mental illness (then called a "mental disease") or mental retardation (then called a "mental defect"). The difficulty arose in determining exactly when such a person fell within this category of the legally "insane." To this day the law is still trying to arrive at an acceptable definition of legal insanity, or more precisely, an acceptable definition of the unsoundness of mind that will relieve the actor from responsibility for his criminal act. It should always be remembered that what we are dealing with here is a legal concept, although it is described by a term, "insanity," that is suggestive of medical terminology. What the law is looking for is a definition consistent with the philosophy of "free will" that underlies criminal responsibility, rather than a definition that necessarily fits the categories used by medicine.

The Wild Beast Test.   About the middle of the eighteenth century, the courts developed a standard for insanity that was called the "Wild Beast Test." It said, in effect, "that to escape punishment, the madman must be so deprived of understanding so as to know what he was doing no more than a wild beast would." Persons excused by this rule were the so-called "raving maniacs." Lesser states of mental illness were not deemed sufficient to excuse from criminal responsibility. In the case of mental defect, the test was whether the person was so retarded as to be an "idiot"—defined by one noted authority as a person who could not count twenty pence, identify his parents, or know his age.

The M'Naghten Case.   In the year 1843, a man by the name of M'Naghten shot and killed a man named Drummond. M'Naghten was suffering from a delusional psychosis and thought he was being persecuted by certain of the King's ministers, including Sir Robert Peel. (Sir Robert established the first modern police system in England, which is why English policemen are called "Bobbies.") M'Naghten, when he shot at Drummond, thought he was shooting at Peel.

---

54. See Chapter Fourteen for a more complete discussion of juvenile court jurisdiction. In several states, juveniles are automatically charged in the criminal courts on some, very serious crimes, rather than being proceeded against in the juvenile court. See p. 392 *infra*.

M'Naghten was tried and acquitted of the offense, the jury finding him not guilty by reason of insanity. Because both Drummond and Peel were popular figures in the government of that day, and because an attempt on the Queen's life had been made shortly before the Drummond killing, the acquittal of M'Naghten raised a great public outcry. The House of Lords then posed a series of questions to the Judges of the Queen's Bench concerning the nature and extent of the unsoundness of mind which would excuse the commission of a felony of this sort (murder). The answer given to the House of Lords states the famous 'M'Naghten Rule.'' This rule—or a variation of it—is still followed in most American jurisdictions.

The M'Naghten Rule.   To excuse the accused from responsibility, said the Judges, the following standard must be met: "It must be clearly proved that, at the time of committing the act, the party accused was laboring under such a defect of reason, from disease of the mind, as not to know the nature and quality of the act he was doing, or, if he did know it, that he did not know it was wrong.'' This rule is sometimes described as the "test of cognition" (i.e., referring to the mental process of gaining knowledge through both awareness and judgment), the "test of the intellect,'' or the "right and wrong test.'' Note that it does not ask whether the person can generally distinguish between right and wrong, but whether he could do so with respect to the act he committed. While the M'Naghten case itself dealt only with mental illness, the M'Naghten test soon was applied to "defects of reason" arising from retardation as well as mental illiness.

Irresistible Impulse Test.   The M'Naghten Rule did not prove to define insanity to everyone's satisfaction. It ignored the emotions, said many, and man's actions are determined as much, or more, by his emotions than by his intellect. Gradually, in a series of cases, the "Irresistible Impulse Test" was developed, usually to be applied along with the M'Naghten Rule. This test applied to a person legally sane under M'Naghten—a person who knew the nature, quality, and wrongfulness of his act—but who nevertheless, by "reason of the duress of [his] mental disease, . . . had so far lost the power to choose between right and wrong, and to avoid doing the act in question, that his free agency was at the time destroyed."[55] This was a test limited to cases of mental illness (as opposed to retardation). While M'Naghten stressed the lack of "cognitive capacity," the irresistible impulse test stressed the lack of "volition" (i.e., self control). It argued, in effect, that the person acting under an irresistible impulse was not really committing a voluntary act.

State Adoption of M'Naghten and Irresistible Impulse.   The precise status of the M'Naghten rule in American jurisdictions today is unclear. A slight majority of the states probably follow the M'Naghten rule, with about half of these states adding the irresistible impulse standard. It often is difficult to precisely characterize the relationship of a state's standard to M'Naghten since most states use somewhat different language in describing their version of the M'Naghten test. Sometimes the wording is so different from the classic statement of M'Naghten as to suggest that the state's rule may be closer in many respects to the

---

55. *Parson v. State*, 81 Ala. 577, 2 So. 854 (1887).

Model Penal Code standard (to be discussed shortly). Many states, for example, no longer require a complete impairment of the defendant's cognitive capacity, but find a substantial impairment sufficient. They also may expand upon the nature of the cognitive deficiency to include a lack of either "appreciation" or "knowledge." The New York definition of insanity is typical of this type of substantially modified M'Naghten standard:

> A person is not criminally responsible for conduct if at the time of such conduct, as a result of mental disease or defect, he lacks substantial capacity to know or appreciate either: (a) The nature and consequence of such conduct; or (b) That such conduct was wrong.[56]

The Model Penal Code Rule.   The Model Penal Code sought to combine the elements of cognitive capacity and volitional capacity in its test for legal insanity. It thus built on both the M'Naghten rule and the irresistible impulse test. It also sought to emphasize that (1) the impairment of either capaicty need not be total (by using the term "substantial"), (2) the cognitive capacity extended to understanding as well as simple awareness (by using the term "appreciate"), and (3) the lack of volitional capacity need not be the product of a sudden impluse (by referring to a lack of ability to "conform"). The Code draftsmen also sought (by including the second paragraph of the Code definition) to ensure that the test would not be utilized to build a case of legal insanity based only on the defendant's repeated criminal or anti-social acts.[57] The end result was the following standard, which has been adopted in virtually all of the federal circuits and a substantial minority of the states:

(1) A person is not responsible for criminal conduct if at the time of such conduct as a result of mental disease or defect he lacks substantial capacity either to appreciate the criminality [wrongfulness] of his conduct or to conform his conduct to the requirements of the law.

(2) As used in this Article, the terms "mental disease or defect" do not include an abnormality manifested only by repeated criminal or otherwise anti-social conduct.[58]

Criticism of the Current Tests.   We could use many pages discussing the pros and cons of the different definitions of insanity. Such a discussion is simply not feasible, however, in an introductory text of this type. You should be aware that

---

56. New York Penal Law §30.05.

57. The concern here is related to the "psychopathic personality," a psychiatric classification sometimes based in large part on the very fact that the person has behaved in an anti-social manner.

58. MPC §4.01. The word "wrongfulness" is bracketed in paragraph one as an acceptable substitute for the word "criminality." Some jurisdictions have adopted their own variations of the Model Code test. Several have eliminated the second paragraph altogether, viewing it either as unnecessary or as overly restrictive in suggesting that persons with a psychopathic personality can never be legally insane. Other jurisdictions have made modifications that move the Code test closer to the original M'Naghten and the irresistible impulse test. Thus Texas Penal Code §8.01 uses the following variation of the first paragraph of the MPC standard: "It is an affirmative defense to prosecution that, at the time of the conduct charged, the actor, as a result of mental disease or defect, either did not know that his conduct was wrong or was incapable of conforming his conduct to the requirements of the law he allegedly violated."

the subject is highly controversial. Psychiatrists in particular are highly critical of the M'Naghten standard, the irresistible impulse standard, and the Model Code standard. They contend that these standards commit a fatal error in attempting to look at special aspects of the personality of the individual, whether that be the cognitive, the volitional, or both. It is the total personality, they argue, that shapes the conduct of the individual, and the appropriate question to be asked is what impact has mental illness had on his total personality. Many psychiatrists would prefer the standard of the *Durham* case, which formerly was applied in federal courts in the District of Columbia.[59] That standard held that a person was not criminally responsible "if his unlawful act was a product of mental disease or defect." The Durham standard was subsequently replaced by the Model Penal Code test in the District of Columbia. The court there concluded that the "product" standard too frequently resulted in jurors giving "undue dominance" to the conclusions of psychiatric experts as to whether the individual was legally insane. The determination as to legal insanity, they noted, involved an "ethical and legal" rather than a "medical" conclusion.[60]

The Consequences Of An Insanity Acquittal.   When a jury finds that a defendant committed a crime, but was legally insane under the rule followed in its jurisdiction, it returns a verdict of "not guilty by reason of insanity." The law then must face the question as to what should be done with this person who committed a harmful act but was excused from criminal responsibility for that act. For most cases, it has provided a series of procedures that will result in the acquitted defendant being confined in a mental institution for a substantial period of time. Indeed, in some instances, the period of confinement may outstrip the maximum allowable period of imprisonment for the crime he committed. Many jurisdictions follow the Model Penal Code in providing that persons acquitted by reason of insanity will automatically be committed to a mental hospital for observation.[61] In other states the initial commitment lies in the discretion of the judge, although it is almost automatic in practice. Following a specified period for observation (e.g., 90 days), a hearing is held to determine whether the ex-defendant shall be committed under the standard of civil commitment. That standard authorizes commitment if a judge finds that the individual is mentally ill and presents a danger of causing injury to himself or others. Civil commitment does not automatically follow from the fact that the person was acquitted by reason of insanity. The criminal jury was concerned with the individual's mental status at the time of the crime. Civil commitment, on the other hand, looks to his mental status today. Moreover a defendant in some jurisdictions may argue that the jury's verdict only establishes a reasonable doubt as to his sanity; it does not meet the civil standard that it is more likely than not that he is insane.

---

59.   *Durham v. United States,* 214 F.2d 862 (D.C. Cir. 1954).

60.   *United States v. Brawner,* 471 F.2d 969 (D.C. Cir. 1972).

61.   MPC §4.08. In support of this provision, the drafters noted that it "not only provides the public with the maximum immediate protection, but may also work to the advantage of mentally diseased or defective defendants by making the defense of irresponsibility more acceptable to the public and to the jury."

If the ex-defendant is civilly committed (which usually is the case), he may obtain his release as soon as he no longer poses a danger to himself or others. In some states, this determination can be made by the hospital officials themselves. In most, however, the release must be approved by court order. It is common practice to test a proposed release by granting the individual conditional release, which allows him to live in the community under special supervision. Unlike a permanent release, a conditional release ordinarily does not require court approval. Where police and prosecutors have been critical of the disposition of legally insane defendants, their objections usually have focused on the release procedures. The basic complaint has been that psychiatrists are too willing to "take chances" in releasing ex-defendants without absolute assurance that they no longer are dangerous. In some jursidictions, to avoid disputes over this matter, prosecutors are notified of impending releases and given an opportunity to present their objections, if any, to the court.

Mens Rea and Insanity. Whenever a certain state of mind is an element of the offense, a mental condition which would render the accused incapable of that state of mind will negate the presence of the necessary mens rea. This is true even though the defendant's mental condition is not so severe as to relieve him from general criminal responsibility. Thus, an unsoundness of mind which would not meet the test of legal insanity may nevertheless establish the absence of the mens rea for a particular crime. This possibility is especially significant for the crime of murder, where first degree murder requires the element of premeditation. Very often, the kind of deliberate decision-making required for premeditation will not be possible due to a mental illness that falls short of establishing legal insanity. The mentally ill (but not legally insane) accused will not be liable for first degree murder, although he will still be liable for second degree murder, which requires a lesser mens rea.

Intoxication. It is commonly said that "drunkenness is no excuse for crime." This statement is only accurate if we read it as saying, "Voluntary drunkenness will not relieve one of criminal liability for a crime requiring a mens rea of recklessness or negligence." For intoxication, whether from alcohol or drugs, can indeed be an excuse when it is involuntary or when it prevents the actor from having the mens rea required for criminal liability.

Involuntary intoxication involves that rare situation where the intoxication was not self-induced. Ordinarily, this requires a showing that the individual was physically forced by others to consume an intoxicating substance or was tricked into taking such a substance by a misrepresentation that it was some other substance. If a person takes an intoxicating substance knowing what it is, but unaware of its full intoxicating capacity, his intoxication is viewed as voluntary. One is expected to be aware that alcohol and various drugs can cause intoxication. If a person is an alcoholic and claims that he lacks the capacity to refrain from drinking, his intoxication also is viewed as voluntary. Such a person, it is argued, is suffering from a self-inflicted illness. In the case of truly involuntary intoxication, the defendant will be excused from responsibility under a standard quite similar to that applied to insanity. Thus the Model Penal Code recognizes involuntary intoxication as a defense where "by reason of such intoxication the actor at the time of his conduct lacks substantial capacity either to appreciate its criminality [wrongfullness] or to conform his conduct to the requirements of law."[62] In a jurisdiction which follows the M'Naghten standard of legal insanity, involuntary intoxication will be a defense if the actor was so intoxicated that he did not know the nature and quality of his act or did not know that the act was wrong. Note that the courts here are not describing intoxication as insanity, but are simply applying a similar legal standard to a separate defense.

Whether voluntary or involuntary, intoxication may constitute a defense insofar as it prevents the actor from having the mens rea required for criminal liability. Thus where a crime requires an intention to cause a certain result and the defendant lacked that intention due to intoxication, he will not be liable for that crime. A person who killed another but was so intoxicated that he did not realize what he was doing would not be liable for the level of homicide (usually first degree murder) that requires an intent to kill. He would, however, be liable for lesser degrees of homicide that do not require such an intent (unless the intoxication was involuntary and met the applicable standard for total excuse from responsibility). Intoxication may also negate a mens rea of knowledge. Thus if a person is so intoxicated that he does not realize he is taking the property of another, he will not be liable for theft since that crime requires such knowledge.

The two levels of mens rea not negated by intoxication are negligence and recklessness. Since negligence does not require awareness of an unjustifiable risk, the intoxicated person may be negligent even though he was so intoxicated that he could not appreciate the presence or nature of the risk taken. Recklessness, on the other hand, does require an awareness of the risk, at least as defined by the Model Code. Yet the law will not recognize voluntary intoxication as a defense to a crime requiring recklessness even if the defendant was so intoxicated he did not know what he was doing. Using intoxicating substances is considered, in itself, a very risky business, automatically establishing the presence of recklessness on the part of the actor. Of course, in using intoxicating substances, the actor does not know exactly what he will do while intoxicated, but he certainly should be aware that he might lose his ability to recognize and judge his behavior as a reasonable person. The New York Code thus restated the general rule when it added the following sentence to its definition of recklessness:

> A person who creates such a risk [i.e., a risk constituting a gross deviation from the standard of conduct of a reasonable person] but is unaware thereof solely by reason of voluntary intoxication also acts recklessly with respect thereto.[63]

For most crimes involving the infliction of a permanent injury to person or property, there is some degree of the crime that requires only recklessness or negligence. Accordingly, for crimes involving such injuries, voluntary intoxication may negate the mens rea for the highest level of the crime, but it ordinarily will not relieve the person of all criminal liability. It is with these crimes in mind that it often is said that "drunkenness is no excuse."

---

62.   MPC §2.08 (4). Compare text at note 58 *supra*.

63.   See New York Penal Code §15.05(3).

Mistake. We have already seen that a mistake of fact constitutes a defense only where it negates the mens rea required for the particular crime in question.[64] What of a mistake of law? Here again we deal with a common saying that is only partially accurate, that "ignorance of the law is no excuse." Where a mistake of law results in a lack of mens rea, it actually does constitute a defense. In that situation, a mistake of law is treated in the same manner as a mistake of fact. If the person simply does not have the state of mind required by a particular crime, he cannot be held responsible for that crime no matter what the source of his mistake. If a person mistakenly believes that he is the legal owner of property and takes that property from the true owner, he has not committed theft. Since that crime requires knowledge that the property taken belongs to another, his mistake of law has negated the required mens rea. There are comparatively few crimes, however, that require knowledge of a factor, such as ownership of property, involving a legal judgment. Ordinarily, a mistake of law arises in a setting in which the defendent had the necessary mens rea for the offense charged, but claims that he should not be held liable because he honestly believed that he was not committing a crime. It was in response to such a claim that the common law developed the rule that ignorance of law was not a defense. Today, however, that rule has been modified in many jurisdictions.

The theory underlying the common law rule was that every person should learn the law. If a person was excused because of his ignorance of the law, then he would be encouraged to avoid learning what the law prohibited. But what of the person who made every reasonable effort to learn the correct rule of law, but still was led to an honest but mistaken conclusion that his acts were legal? The common law refused to establish a defense even in such a situation, reasoning that it would be too difficult to engage in a far-reaching inquiry as to whether the defendant had made every reasonable effort to learn the correct rule of law. The Model Penal Code rejected this conclusion, however, as to several situations in which government action or inaction was responsible for the defendant's inability to learn that his conduct violated the law. Section 2.04(3) of the Model Code sets forth these exceptional situations in which a mistake of law will constitute a defense to otherwise criminal conduct.

A belief that conduct does not legally constitute an offense is a defense to a prosecution for that offense based upon such conduct when:

(a) the statute or other enactment defining the offense is not known to the actor and has not been published or otherwise reasonably made available prior to the conduct alleged; or

(b) he acts in reasonable reliance upon an official statement of the law, afterward determined to be invalid or erroneous, contained in (i) a statute or other enactment; (ii) a judicial decision, opinion or judgment; (iii) an administrative order or grant of permission; or (iv) an official interpretation of the public officer or body charged by law with responsibility for the interpretation, administration or enforcement of the law defining the offense.

---

64. See p. 105 *supra.*

Most of the state codes based upon the Model Code have adopted the Model Code's rule or a somewhat narrower version of that rule. [65] Also, in a few states with older penal codes, the courts have indicated that they would recognize at least some of the exceptions noted in section 2.04(3). Thus, today, ignorance of the law is an excuse where (1) it results in a lack of mens rea, or (2) it fits one of several recognized exceptions involving governmental responsibility for the defendant's mistake.

Other Defenses

Consent. Assume that a defendant inflicted the kind of injury to the person or property of another that would ordinarily constitute a crime, but he did so with the consent of the injured party. Should that consent constitute a defense to a criminal charge? Looking only to common sense, your answer probably would vary with the particular criminal charge in question. If B asked to be killed and A obliged him, we might view A's action as less serious than some other homicides, but we hardly would want to excuse it altogether. On the other hand, if B told A to punch him in the stomach so that B could show the strength of his stomach muscles, that request probably should relieve A of any criminal responsibility for inflicting such a minor blow. Similarly, if the charge were malicious destruction of property, and the owner had consented to the destruction, we would say that the owner had not been wronged and it would be unjust to hold A criminally liable for merely complying with the owner's wishes. If we turned to the law governing consent, we would find that it generally reaches these and other common sense conclusions although its process of reasoning is sometimes quite complex.

Basically, the law recognizes consent as defense only when the presence of consent means that the actor has not inflicted the type of harm that the particular crime was designed to prevent. For each offense, one must ask: What was the crux of the public wrong prohibited by this offense—was it the infliction of harm against the will of the "victim" or the infliction of harm without regard to the "victim's" desire? There are certain areas in which the law seeks to protect the participant even against himself (e.g., use of drugs) so it is obvious that the victim's consent will not always eliminate the prohibited harm. In the area of injuries to the person, the line usually is drawn according to the seriousness of the injury involved. A person can appropriately invite some minor blow, but not the taking of his life or his disfigurement. In the area of sexual activities, similar distinctions are drawn between acts to which one can consent (intercourse) and others that remain criminal with or without consent (prostitution). In the area of property offenses, the law generally is designed to protect an owner only from a taking or destruction against his will. A person can always give away his own

---

65. Illustrative of a narrower version of the Model Code's rule is Texas Penal Code §8.03(b):

> It is an affirmative defense to prosecution that the actor reasonably believed the conduct charged did not constitute a crime and that he acted in reasonable reliance upon:
>
> (1) an official statement of the law contained in a written order or grant of permission by an administrative agency charged by law with responsibility for interpreting the law in question; or
>
> (2) a writtten interpretation of the law contained in an opinion of a court of record or made by a public official charged by law with responsibility for interpreting the law in question.

property, and his consent, in effect, does exactly that. Accordingly, consent usually eliminates criminal liability for property crimes. Of course, in this area as in others, where danger exists to a third party, the consent of the immediate "victim" is irrelevant. Thus A may agree to have B set fire to his house, but both may be guilty of a lesser degree of arson because of the threat to the community involved in using fire to destroy property.

Of course, where consent eliminates the harm that the statute would otherwise view as a public wrong, it does so only where the consent is informed and voluntary. The Model Penal Code offers the following illustrations of situations in which a consent will not meet this standard:

> *Section 2.11(3) Ineffective Consent.* Unless otherwise provided by the Code or by law defining the offense, assent does not constitute consent if:
>
> (a) it is given by a person who is legally incompetent to authorize the conduct charged to constitute the offense;
>
> (b) it is given by a person who by reason of youth, mental disease or defect or intoxication is manifestly unable or known by the actor to be unable to make a reasonable judgment as to the nature or harmfulness of the conduct charged to constitute the offense;
>
> (c) it is given by a person whose improvident consent is sought to be prevented by the law defining the offense; or
>
> (d) it is induced by force, duress or deception of a kind sought to be prevented by the law defining the offense.

Duress.   When a person is threatened with harm unless he commits a criminal act, and he therefore commits the act, he has committed the crime under coercive pressure described by the law as *duress*.[66] Duress can constitute a defense to a crime, but ordinarily will do so only when four requirements are met. First, the threat must relate to the infliction of a serious bodily injury or death. The defense of duress rests, in part, on the premise that the defendant's actions were justified because, although the defendant committed a crime, he avoided a still greater crime that was threatened by his assailant. It is not simply that he has reacted quite naturally to save himself (indeed, the threat may be against a third party rather than the defendant), but that he has served the interest of society by choosing the lesser of two evils. Of course, the relative seriousness of different crimes is difficult to measure, but the line can easily be drawn between those that

---

66. In some jurisdictions, the defense is described as that of *compulsion* rather than *duress*. See Illinois Stat. ch. 38, §7-11. The elements remain similar, however. A closely related, but much rarer defense is that of *necessity*. This defense applies to situations in which an actor, to avoid significant harm, must commit a less significant crime. Unlike duress, however, it is aimed not at a situation where the actor has been threatened by another, but where the pressure of natural physical forces compels the actor to chose between impending harm and commission of a crime. The classic case is that in which travelers, caught in a storm in a deserted area, are forced to break into a vacant dwelling (ordinarily the crime of breaking and entry, see p. 168 *infra*) in order to gain shelter. The Illinois code defines the defense of necessity as follows: "Conduct which would otherwise be an offense is justifiable by reason of necessity if the accused was without blame in occasioning or developing the situation and reasonably believed such conduct was necessary to avoid a public or private injury greater than the injury which might reasonably result from his own conduct." Illinois Stat. ch. 38, §7-13. Compare note 68 *infra* setting forth the Illinois definition of duress.

involve serious bodily harm and those that do not. Where serious bodily harm is threatened, any other crime committed to avoid it is likely to be of a lesser magnitude. The one exception is the taking of a life, and many authorities argue that duress will never excuse a killing, even where the defendant faced a threat of death.

A second element of the duress defense also reflects the concept of comparing the magnitude of the crime and the threat. The duress defense must be based on a threat so substantial that a person of "reasonable firmness" would have been "unable to resist" under the circumstances. The defendant's response thus is tested against the traditional yardstick of the law, the "reasonable person," with special emphasis on that person's quality of resistance or firmness. The response of the reasonable person obviously would consider the degree of harm caused by the crime as well as the gravity of the threat. If a person were threatened with a whipping unless he were willing to drive his assailant to a certain destination at a speed in excess of the law, we certainly would have little difficulty in finding reasonable his succumbing to the threat and violating the speed laws. On the other hand, if a person were threatened with a whipping unless he revealed a military secret that endangered the life of thousands of persons, we might well say that a person of reasonable firmness would have resisted in that situation. Of course, much will depend upon the jury's view of the facts of the case. The test is one of what the reasonable person would have done, rather than what he ideally should do, although the two concepts are frequently mixed together.

The third requirement of duress is that the threat have been immediate or imminent. This requirement is sometimes stated as a separate element of the defense and sometimes viewed as an aspect of the reasonable firmness standard. Certainly if there was ample opportunity to avoid the threatened harm, by escaping or by reporting it to the police, the defendant should have avoided it. Of course, if the individual only could escape by committing a crime, duress may be used to excuse that crime. In a series of recent cases, prison inmates have sought to excuse prison escapes on the ground that they were forced to escape in order to avoid the homosexual attacks of fellow prisoners. Generally their claims of duress have been rejected on the ground that other alternatives were available to avoid attack, but the courts have all recognized that duress can include a crime committed to escape from a threatening situation.[67]

The fourth element of the defense of duress is the requirement that the defendant not have been at fault in placing himself in a situation where it is probable that he would be subjected to a threat. If A agrees to engage in a robbery with B, and then B threatens to shoot A unless he assists in raping their victim, A cannot legitimately claim a defense of duress. When one engages in such criminal activity as robbery, he is recklessly placing himself in a position where his accomplices may threaten him if he fails to undertake further crimes. In their treatment of this element of duress, as well as others, states often vary in their definitions of the defense. Some hold that a person who is only negligent in subjecting himself to

---

67. See *Duress—Defense to Escape,* 3 American Journal of Criminal Law, 331 (1975). See also *People v. Unger,* 66 Ill.2d 333, 5 Ill. Dec. 848, 362 N.E.2d 319 (1977) (recognizing a defense where alternatives were not available).

a potentially threatening situation may still use the defense. Some limit the defense to threats against the defendant or his immediate relatives. Some states do not require that the threat involve serious bodily injury if the offense committed is only a misdemeanor. The variations simply are too great to be fully described here, but the New York statute may be offered as typical. It provides:

1. In any prosecution for an offense, it is an affirmative defense that the defendant engaged in the proscribed conduct because he was coerced to do so by the use or threatened imminent use of unlawful physical force upon him or a third person, which force or threatened force a person of reasonable firmness in his situation would have been unable to resist.

2. The defense of duress as defined in subdivision one of this section is not available when a person intentionally or recklessly places himself in a situation in which it is probable that he will be subjected to duress.[68]

Entrapment. The entrapment defense arises in situations in which an individual committed a criminal act as a result of encouragement by an undercover government agent posing as a willing participant to the crime. Under the viewpoint adopted in the federal courts and the majority of the states, the defense is treated as roughly analogous to duress. The defendant is excused from criminal liability because he is viewed as having been "coerced" into committing a crime that he would not otherwise have committed. In duress the coercion that relieves one of criminal liability comes from the threat of physical harm, while in entrapment it comes from the pressure imposed by the government's undercover agent. Not all such pressure is sufficient, however, to raise an entrapment defense. Entrapment, under the majority view, is designed to protect only those defendants who had no basic disposition to commit the crime, but were simply caught up in a government attempt to "manufacture" a crime (which it could then promptly solve). Accordingly, "a line must be drawn between the trap for the unwary innocent [entrapment] and the trap for the unwary criminal [not entrapment]."[69]

Under the majority view, the jury, in deciding whether the defense exists, must ask itself two questions: (1) whether the idea of committing the crime originated with the government agent, and (2) whether the agent then utilized tactics that induced the defendant to commit that crime even though the defendant was not otherwise disposed to commit it. If the answer to both questions is "yes," then the defense exists. The first question is naturally preliminary to the second. If the idea of committing the crime was not affirmatively planted in the mind of the defendant by the government agent—that is, if the defendant thought of committing the crime on his own initiative—then the defendant obviously has a prior disposition to commit the crime. What the government has done is nothing more than to plant a trap for the unwary criminal. Illustrative of such situations are those in which an undercover agent poses as an "easy victim" to a crime. Thus,

---

68. New York Penal Law §40.00. Compare Illinois Stat. ch. 38, §7-11: "A person is not guilty of an offense, other than an offense punishable with death, by reason of conduct which he performs under the compulsion of threat or menace of the imminent infliction of death or great bodily harm, if he reasonably believes death or great bodily harm will be inflicted upon him if he does not perform such conduct."

69. *Sherman v. United States,* 356 U.S. 369, 372, 78 S.Ct.819, 820, 2 L.Ed.2d 848 (1958).

an agent may properly pretend to be drunk, lie in the gutter with his wallet protruding from his hip pocket, and await the coming of a thief. It is not entrapment to create a situation which, from the thief's perspective, appears to provide "easy pickings."

There are, of course, many situations in which undercover agents, to effectively enforce the law, must approach suspected criminals and suggest the commission of a crime. Thus, a narcotics officer, may approach a suspected narcotics seller pretending to be a narcotics addict in need of a "fix." Similarly, a vice agent may aproach a suspected gambler and express an interest in placing a bet. In these cases, the officer may be suggesting the offense, but he is doing no more than furnishing the opportunity for the commission of the crime to one ready and willing to commit it. This is not entrapment under the second prong of the two-part test. What would be entrapment? Assume that the officer, posing as an addict, became friendly with an ex-addict who knew where narcotics might be purchased. When the ex-addict is asked by his newly found "friend" for assistance in purchasing narcotics, the ex-addict refuses to assist. The officer then feigns withdrawal symptoms, repeatedly implores the ex-addict to help a friend, and the ex-addict finally makes a purchase and delivers the drugs to his "friend." This is entrapment. The criminal design originated with the officer and the officer applied pressure that induced the ex-addict to commit a crime he was not otherwise predisposed to commit.

A substantial number of states take a somewhat different, minority view of entrapment. They contend that the defense must be recognized primarily to keep police from engaging in inappropriate activities designed to manufacture crime. For them, the crucial element is not whether the defendant in this particular case was predisposed to commit the crime, but whether the police methods were such that they posed, in general, a substantial risk of inducing criminal conduct by persons other than those who are ready to commit it. This approach to the definition is often described as formulating an "objective" test, rather than a "subjective" test, because it does not look to the background and character of the particular defendant. Its supporters claim that it emphasizes the true basis of the entrapment defense—control of police conduct. If the defense were really based on the defendant's lack of moral guilt, they argue, the defense would be available to persons induced to commit crimes by the urgings of their real friends, not simply those pressured by undercover agents. Opponents of the minority view contend that it could provide a windfall benefit to the defendant who was in fact predisposed to commit crimes but was subjected to substantial pressures. They also contend that the likelihood that police methods will encourage otherwise innocent persons to commit crimes cannot be viewed in the abstract; consideration must be given to the impact of the methods in the particular case as determined in part by the predisposition of the defendant in that case.[70]

---

70. Illustrative of a code provision following the majority approach is Connecticut Gen. Stat. §53a-15: "In any prosecution for an offense, it shall be a defense that the defendant engaged in the proscribed conduct because he was induced to do so by a public servant, or by a person acting in cooperation with a public servant, for the purpose of institution of criminal prosecution against the defendant, and that the defendant did not contemplate and would not otherwise have engaged in such conduct."

Time Limitations. Statutes of limitations prescribe the time within which a criminal action may be commenced, and thus puts a time limit upon criminal responsibility. The time limitation usually is counted from the date of the offense to the date of the filing of formal charges. In the case of crimes involving deception (e.g., embezzlement), however, the starting point may be the date the crime is discovered rather than the date it occurred. The idea behind statutes of limitations is that a man should not have to live too long under the threat of criminal action. Also, if trials are delayed too long, witnesses die and disappear, evidence is lost, parties move away, and many other things happen that make getting at the truth very difficult. It is therefore of interest to the society, as well as the accused, to hold criminal trials promptly and get them over with.[71]

Time limitations will vary from crime to crime. One offense, murder, customarily has no time limit, and states often place several other serious offenses in the same category.[72] It would serve no useful purpose to set out here the specific time limits imposed for the vast group of offenses that are subject to time limitations. These limits vary widely from state to state. Usually the time limit for felonies is longer than that for misdemeanors, and for serious felonies longer than for less serious felonies. Thus, the state may provide no time limit for murder, a time limit of 10 years for the highest level felonies five years for the remaining felonies, three years for the highest level misdemeanors, and two years for the remaining misdemeanors.[73]

The statutory time limitations are subject to certain "tolling" periods. "Tolling" means "stopping the clock." The time within which a prosecution must be brought is extended by tolling periods since such periods are not counted against the allowable time limitation. The usual reason for tolling is that the defendant cannot be found. He leaves the state or conceals himself to avoid arrest and prosecution. The statutory provisions for tolling permit the time that the defendant cannot be found or is not available to stand trial to be excluded from the

---

Illustrative of a code provision following the minority approach is Texas Penal Code § 8.06(a): "It is a defense to prosecution that the actor engaged in the conduct charged because he was induced to do so by a law enforcement agent using persuasion or other means likely to cause persons to commit the offense. Conduct merely affording a person an opportunity to commit an offense does not constitute entrapment."

71. While the protected interests are similar, the time limitations imposed by the statutes of limitations and the right to speedy trial are quite distinct. The statutes of limitations deal with the time permitted to elapse between the date of the offense and the date of the formal charge. The right to a speedy trial is concerned with the period between the bringing of charges and the trial. See p. 308 *infra.*

72. Thus New York imposes no time limit for all class A offenses, which includes first degree arson, attempted murder, first degree criminal possession of drugs, first degree criminal sale of drugs, first degree kidnapping and first and second degree murder. New York Crim. Proc. Law §30.10. California imposes no time limit for murder, kidnapping, embezzlement of public moneys, and falsification of public records. California Penal Code §799.

73. One of the less complicated provisions is Illinois Stat. ch. 38, §3-5:
    (a) A prosecution for murder, manslaughter, treason, arson, or forgery may be commenced at any time.
    (b) Unless the statute describing the offense provides otherwise, or the period of limitations is extended by Section 3-6, a prosecution for any offense not designated in Subsection (a) must be commenced within 3 years after the commission of the offense if it is a felony, or within one year and 6 months after its commission if it is a misdemeanor.

elapsed time period between the offense and the filing of charges.[74] Let us suppose, for example, that Z commits a robbery in a state where the time limitation for that offense is five years. The offense is committed on June 1, 1962. The defendant stays in the community and can be located but he is not arrested and charged with the offense. On June 1, 1964, he disappears. He cannot be found until June 1, 1970, when he again shows up in the state—he may even come back into the county where the offense occurred. Since the time from June 1, 1962 to June 1, 1970, is more than five years, you might suppose that the action against Z had "outlawed," i.e., that prosecution of the offense is now barred by the running of the statute of limitations. This would not be true. The time from June 1, 1964, when Z left the state, until June 1, 1970, when he returned, would be dropped out of the time calculation. Thus, a felony action could be commenced against Z any time before June 1, 1973—two years of the statute running from June 1, 1962 to June 1, 1964; three years running from June 1, 1970, to June 1, 1973; five years in all—the total time provided for in the statute.

In some states, under the circumstances of Z's case, the law provides that the action must be brought within a shorter time after the accused returns to the state, as for example, within a year of his return. In any event, the absence of the defendant from the state "tolled" the running of the statute of limitations and extended the time within which the action could be commenced against him after he returned.[75]

---

74. The Illinois statutory provision is typical. See Illinois Stat. ch. 38, §3-7: The period within which a prosecution must be commenced does not include any period in which:

    (a) The defendant is not usually and publicly resident within this State; or

    (b) The defendant is a public officer and the offense charged is theft of public funds while in public office; or

    (c) A prosecution is pending against the defendant for the same conduct, even if the indictment or information which commences the prosecution is quashed or the proceedings thereon are set aside, or are reversed on appeal.

75. For further information on the material covered in this chapter, see LaFave and Scott, note 3, p. 59 *supra*; M. Bassiouni, *Substantive Criminal Law,* Springfield, Ill.: Charles C. Thomas Publisher, 1978; J. Hall, *General Principles of The Criminal Law,* Indianapolis, Indiana: The Bobbs-Merill Company, 2d ed., 1960; A. Loewey, *Criminal Law In A Nutshell,* St. Paul, Minn.: West Publishing Company, 1975.

Chapter 6

Elements of the Major Crimes: Crimes Against the Person

We have seen that the legislative decision to classify certain behavior as criminal ordinarily is founded on a societal judgment that such behavior is wrongful and deserving of punishment. Of course, as the value judgments of society change, the type of behavior viewed as wrongful likewise changes. This means that the definitions of crime will vary from time to time and place to place. Yet, there are certain acts, such as treason, murder, incest, rape, robbery, burglary, and theft of valuable personal property, that almost all societies over almost all periods of history have considered wrong. These acts were among the first declared to be crimes by the early English Common Law, and they have continued to be crimes throughout the development of Anglo-American criminal law. Indeed, they have always been viewed as crimes of the most serious character, deserving severe punishment. These are the crimes we will study in this chapter and the next. Although they are the most basic offenses, their definition does vary from state to state. We will concentrate on the common law definitions which serve as the common grounding for the modern statutes and on the major variations introduced by those statutes.

THE HOMICIDE OFFENSES

The word homicide comes from the Latin noun "homo" which means "man," and a Latin verb meaning "to kill, or cause the death of." Homicide is therefore defined as "the killing of one human being by another human being."[1]

Non-Criminal Homicides.   Not all homicides are criminal, which is another way of saying that not all killings of one human being by another are blameworthy. The death of the victim may be due to accident or misfortune for which the actor cannot be blamed. Thus, a young child may suddenly jump out in front of a driver

---

1.   M. Bassiouni, p. 126 *supra,* at p. 230.

who, without negligence, is unable to stop his car in time. An errant pitch may strike a batter in just such a way as to cause his death. In these cases, where there was no intent to kill and no culpability in causing death, we describe the killing as *excused.* At other times, a killing may be intentional yet justifiable under the law. A police officer kills in self defense, or an executioner takes a life as directed by law. Here, the homicide is described as *justified.* Confusion sometimes exists as to whether a particular homicide should be described as excused or justified. The precise use of the distinction is not nearly as important, however, as the fact that placement of the homicide in either category necessarily judges it to be non-culpable and hence, non-criminal.

Criminal Homicides.   There is no single crime labeled criminal homicide. Rather, the term is used in the law to describe a group of crimes (usually two degrees of murder and manslaughter) that apply to homicides. Each of the crimes in this group has its own special elements, but they all build upon the three basic elements of any criminal homicide: (1) the death of a human being, (2) caused by the act of another human being, (3) without justification or excuse. These three elements taken together establish what is known as the *corpus delicti* of any criminal homicide offense. The phrase corpus delicti is taken from Latin and refers to proof of the "body of the crime," which basically is proof of the harm and actus reus prohibited by the particular crime.

In many jurisdictions, when there is some question as to whether a death was the product of criminal homicide, an investigation, called an *inquest,* will be held to determine if there is objective proof of the corpus delicti. When that hearing is conducted by a medical officer, it commonly is known as *coroner's inquest.* To establish the existence of the corpus delicti, the body of the deceased need not be produced, although it obviously is difficult to establish the death of a human being without a body.[2] In all but an occasional inquest, the key issue is not whether a death occurred, but whether it occurred through the deceased's own actions (e.g., whether the deceased committed suicide) or whether a death caused by another was excused or justified. If the likely presence of criminal homicide is established to the satisfaction of the coroner or other fact-finder (usually a magistrate), the case will then proceed for further investigation and prosecution under one of the crimes within the criminal homicide grouping.

Various complex legal issues may be presented in determining, at a coroner's inquest, or at a trial, whether a criminal homicide occurred. First, it must be established that a human being was killed, yet it is not always clear at what point one becomes or ceases to remain a human being. The law clearly holds that an unborn fetus is not a human being. The fetus is subject to the laws of abortion (which generally permit the abortion of the fetus with the woman's consent except in the last three months of its development). In cases involving deaths that occur at the time of birth, however, the law must identify the point at which the fetus

---

2.   Without a body, death may nevertheless be established by surrounding circumstances. See *People v. Scott,* 176 Cal.App.2d 458, 1Cal.Rptr.600 (1959). It should be noted that while the body often is offered in establishing the corpus delicti, it is not in itself the corpus delicti. The corpus delicti refers to the "body of the crime," not the body of the victim, although the two are often confused in drama and literature.

becomes a human being, now protected by the criminal laws of homicide rather than those of abortion. In other cases, at the opposite end of the spectrum, the law must ask when life ends. For example, has a nurse committed homicide when she shuts off a respiratory machine that has maintained the heartbeat of a patient whose brain has ceased to function? In both of these areas, the law today is somewhat in a state of flux.[3] The prevailing opinions seem to be that life begins when the fetus is brought forth fully from the mother and its independent circulation is established, while life ends at the cessation of the heartbeat and respiration.

To establish a criminal homicide, the prosecution also must show that the death of the human being was caused by a punishable actus reus of another person. This element of the crime may raise various issues relating to causation, omissions, and the voluntariness of acts, as suggested in Chapter Five. Finally, it must be established that the actor proceeded without justification or excuse. This element often presents the most difficult issues, particularly with respect to questions of justification. Here again we are dealing with an area of law that has been shifting in recent years.

JUSTIFIABLE HOMICIDES

As we noted previously, if a death results from a use of deadly force that is permitted under the law, the homicide is a justifiable, non-criminal homicide. This can include a broad range of homicides since the law permits one person to use deadly force against another in a variety of different situations. Some of those situations are so obvious that they require little discussion. We all recognize that deadly force can be used in the execution of a death sentence or in a battle during a war or civil rebellion. The more complex, and the most commonly raised justifications, relate to the use of deadly force in response to physical aggression or other unlawful action. These justifications include self-defense, defense of another person, defense of property, prevention of a felony, and arrest for a felony. The law governing the use of deadly force for each of these justifications varies considerably from state to state, but space permits us to discuss only those basic patterns that are followed by a substantial group of states. One also should recognize that, in any single jurisdiction, the standards relating to the different justifications will be molded together to present a consistent overall approach to the use of deadly force. The state must reconcile the limitations it applies to the use of deadly force in one area (e.g., protection of property) with the limitations its applies in other areas (e.g., arresting a person for a crime against property). For this reason, in examining the treatment of a particular justification, the reader ordinarily should be aware of the total package of laws on justification in the particular state. To assist you in gaining such an overall perspective of the area, we have set forth, at the end of this chapter, a typical grouping of the laws on justification found in one state (Texas).[4]

---

3. See, e.g., *In The Matter of Karen Quinlan,* 70 N.J. 10, 355 A.2d 647 (1976); *Keeler v. Superior Court,* 2 Cal.3d 619, 87 Cal.Rptr.481, 470 P.2d 617 (1970).

4. See addendum p. 149 *infra.*

Self-Defense. The law traditionally looks to three factors in determining whether a homicide is justified by self-defense: (1) the reasonableness of the defender's belief that he had to use deadly force to save himself; (2) whether the defender had an opportunity to retreat in safety; and (3) whether the defender was the initial aggressor in the assault that led to the use of deadly force. The first factor is treated similarly in all jurisdictions. A defender can use deadly force to protect himself only when he reasonably believes such force is necessary to save himself from imminent death or great bodily harm. The belief must be reasonable, but it need not have been accurate. If B approaches A with a gun and threatens to shoot A, A may reasonably fear that his life is in danger and respond with his own weapon. If A should kill B and later investigation reveals that B was only trying to scare A with an unloaded gun, the homicide still will be justified. Since A could not reasonably be expect to have been aware of B's true motive and the weapon's impotency, he could not reasonably have been expected to take steps other than those that appeared to be needed to save himself.

In determining whether a defender's belief as to the need for deadly force was reasonable, a fact-finder (usually the jury) must consider a variety of factors. These include the comparative size of the defender and the attacker, whether the attacker was armed, whether the attacker had a reputation as a vicious fighter, etc. The fact-finder also must recognize that the defender is under extreme emotional stress in responding to an attack. He cannot be expected to draw fine lines as to the degree of force needed to repel a threat of serious bodily harm. As Justice Holmes once noted, "detached reflection cannot be demanded in the presence of an uplifted knife."[5] The law does, however, place certain limits on what can be deemed reasonable. For example, the defender's belief must have related to immediate harm. One cannot respond with deadly force presently because he believes his assailant intends to ambush him several hours from now. The law also requires that the defender be in reasonable fear of possible death or serious bodily injury. If he fears no more than minor injuries, he cannot use deadly force. One who feels that the attacker will do no more than knock him to the ground cannot respond with deadly force simply because he does not want to suffer any kind of humiliation or injury. On the other hand, if he reasonably fears that the attacker will break his bones or disfigure him, that is sufficient without actually fearing death. Deadly force (i.e., force readily capable of causing death) can be used to respond to a threat of serious bodily injury as well as loss of life.[6]

The second factor considered in evaluating a self-defense claim—the opportunity to retreat in safety—is given somewhat different treatment in different states. In some jurisdictions, there is no special rule on retreat. On the one hand, the courts have said that there is no absolute duty to escape danger by retreating; the law will not require a non-aggressor to act in a humiliating or cowardly way. On the other hand, the judge or jury is not barred from considering the possibility of retreat as one of the many factors examined in determining the reasonableness of

---

5.   *Brown v. United States*, 256 U.S. 335, 343, 41 S.Ct.501, 502, 65 L.Ed.961 (1921).

6.   New York Penal Law § 10.00 provides a typical definition of serious bodily injury: "Physical injury which creates a substantial risk of death or which causes serious and protracted disfigurement, protracted impairment of health, or protracted loss or impairment of the function of any bodily organ."

the defender's decision to use deadly force. Thus, under this approach, the significance of the opportunity to retreat will vary with the facts of the particular case and the weight of the other circumstances supporting the reasonable use of deadly force, but the failure to retreat will not, by itself, automatically negate a claim of self-defense. Moreover, the possibility of retreat is given no weight whatsoever unless the retreat clearly could be accomplished with complete safety. Thus, retreat rarely is a factor when the attacker threatens the defender with a weapon such as a gun. No matter how fast the defender can flee, he is unlikely to be able to escape from such a threat with complete safety.

A majority of jurisdictions today, following the lead of the Model Code, have imposed an absolute requirement of retreat under some circumstances. These states reason that, though the defender is not at fault, the embarrassment he suffers in being forced to retreat is a small price to pay for saving the life that he otherwise would have to take. They accordingly hold that if the defender could have avoided the threat to himself with complete safety by retreating, and knew that he could do so, then his use of deadly force cannot be justified on the ground of self-defense. These jurisdictions do recognize certain exceptions to this rule, however. A defender is not forced to retreat from his own home. At least in this respect, a man's home is still his castle and he cannot be forced from it by an attacker. In some jurisdictions, this exception has been carried to the defender's place of business, except where the attacker was a fellow employee who also had a right to be on the premises.

If the defender in a particular case originally was an aggressor—the initiator of the fight that resulted in the homicide—then a duty of withdrawal may make the availability of self-defense even more complex. To be an aggressor, a person ordinarily must deliver the first blow or directly challenge his opponent to fight. Simply using foul language or otherwise starting a verbal dispute is not sufficient. If the aggressor initiates the dispute with deadly force, then he ordinarily cannot reclaim a right of self-defense unless he effectively withdraws from his original position as an aggressor. In some jurisdictions, he can do this only by getting across to his opponent the message that he no longer desires to fight. In others, a reasonable attempt to communicate such a message is sufficient even if the other party refuses to recognize it. Once withdrawal is achieved, if the other party persists in the battle, the former aggressor now has a "restored" right of self-defense. If the aggressor began the battle using non-deadly force, then he may not have to communicate his withdrawal although he may bear some special burdens in claiming self-defense. Since he limited his aggression to non-deadly force, his opponent should not have escalated to the use of deadly force. Both he and his opponent are at fault, and a completed withdrawal therefore may not be needed to restore the right of self-defense. However, the defender still has a special responsibility as the person who started it all, and he therefore may be required to retreat (when physically possible) even in a state that ordinarily does not require retreat. Moreover, in the case of the aggressor, that duty to retreat may include retreat from the home.

Defense Of Others.   Some states still limit the right to use deadly force in defense of another to the defender's protection of persons with whom he had some special protective relationship (e.g., spouse, child, relative, employees). Most states, however, now permit the use of deadly force to protect any other person. As with self-defense, a person defending another can use deadly force only when he reasonably believes the other is in immediate danger of death or serious bodily harm. Some state courts have held, however, that a reasonable belief will not be sufficient when the defendant went to the aid of a third person who could not lawfully have used deadly force to defend himself. Assume, for example, that A unlawfully attacks B, and B properly responds with deadly force. If C, coming upon the scene late, should go to the aid of the wrong person (i.e., A rather than B), these courts will hold that his use of force in defense of the third party will not be justified. Others argue that if C reasonably (but erroneously) thought B was the aggressor, his use of deadly force to protect A will be justified.

Defense Of Property.   Notwithstanding popular impression to the contrary, the common law and the statutory law of today both hold that deadly force may *not* be used solely to protect property. Deadly force may not be used against a mere trespasser. Neither may it be used against a thief. If a thief steals a car, the owner cannot use deadly force to stop him even if there is no other way to gain the immediate return of his property. Simply put, the law values the protection of any life, including that of a thief, over the protection of property. There are, however, various other avenues through which property can be indirectly protected with the use of deadly force. Thus, we shall see that the law authorizes the use of deadly force to prevent some dangerous felonies, including several involving the taking of property. Also, the law in many jurisdictions authorizes the use of deadly force to arrest persons who have committed crimes against property. Finally, the common law drew a distinction between the protection of property generally and the protection of a dwelling. Because of the special importance of the home as a place of security and shelter, deadly force could be used to prevent forcible entry. Today, most jurisdictions have limited this rule. Some permit deadly force to be used only when the illegal entry is believed to be for the purpose of doing harm to a person within the house. Others limit it to those forcible entries that apparently are for the purpose of committing a felony (and therefore would be burglaries).

Prevention Of Felonies.   Under the English common law, any person could use deadly force when reasonably believed to be necessary to prevent the initiation or completion of a felony. At the time, felonies were all punishable by death, and most felonies involved rather basic wrongs. As capital punishment was limited and the legislature added new felonies that often did not involve a direct infliction of serious injury, the common law rule was modified. It soon became the rule that deadly force could be used only to prevent a certain class of felonies, commonly described as "dangerous felonies" or felonies of "violence and surprise." The modern codes generally follow this modified common law rule but they vary in the felonies that they will include in the dangerous category. Almost all will include armed robbery, kidnapping, forcible rape and arson since these crimes almost always pose a threat of serious bodily harm. The states have varied, however, in their treatment of burglary. Some have favored an approach that ordinarily limits deadly force to cases in which the burglar has threatened the use of force against the occupants. The stress here is on the threat to occupants posed in the individual case. Other states, apparently believing that burglaries as a class pose as great a threat as crimes like arson and kidnapping, simply included it in the list of those crimes that automatically can be prevented or terminated through the use of deadly force. Again, the test is ordinarily one of reasonable belief. If it turns out that the reasonably suspected burglar was not a burglar, but a drunk neighbor, who thought he was breaking into his own house, the homicide still remains justified.

Arresting A Felon. At English common law, before the modern police force had been developed, any citizen could arrest a felon. Moreover, the citizen could use deadly force where needed to stop a fleeing felon, and if such force should kill the felon, the homicide was justified. The citizen took his chances as to the accuracy of his judgment, however. If it turned out that the person he had killed was not a felon, then his use of deadly force (and any resulting homicide) was not justified. This result followed even where the citizen had reasonable grounds for believing that the person he sought to arrest had committed a felony. With the development of the metropolitan police force in the nineteenth century, the law governing citizen arrests gradually changed. The general authority of citizens to arrest was restricted and their authority to use deadly force was even further limited.

In an effort to place arrest responsibility primarily upon the police, various states limited citizens to arresting for felonies which they themselves witnessed. Once this limitation was imposed, there was less concern that the citizen would arrest the wrong person. Accordingly many jurisdictions also changed their rules to justify a citizen's arrest whenever the citizen had a reasonable basis for the arrest. The citizen no longer lost the protection of the law if later investigation revealed the suspected felon had not actually committed a crime. Along with these changes in arrest authority, the citizen's power to use deadly force in exercising that authority was restricted. The citizen no longer could use such force to make any felony arrest, but only arrests for dangerous felonies such as murder, kidnapping, and rape. Often, these are the same felonies which can be prevented or terminated through the use of deadly force, so the arrest authority does not add much to the range of permissible uses of deadly force. It should be stressed, moreover, that even where the requirements are met as to the dangerous nature of the felony and the proper grounds for making the citizen's arrest, deadly force still is allowed only if the citizen reasonably believes such force is necessary to make the arrest. If a fleeing felon can be captured without the use of deadly force, then the citizen must refrain from using such force even though that would be the easiest way to make the arrest.

A police officer's authority to use deadly force in making an arrest ordinarily is much broader than that of a private citizen. The police officer starts with a more extensive power to arrest. Unlike the citizen in many jurisdictions, the police officer has authority to arrest for felonies he did not witness. A peace officer can make a felony arrest whenever he has reasonable grounds, based upon his own observations or observations of others, to believe that the person he arrests committed a felony. Since the lawfulness of the peace officer's arrest is tested solely by the existence of reasonable grounds for the arrest, the peace officer is not subject to the risk, sometimes imposed upon private citizens, of being held criminally liable if the person arrested turns out to be innocent. If the arrest was based on reasonable grounds, it is valid, and if the use of deadly force was lawful to make the arrest effective, a resulting homicide will be justified, even though it is later discovered that the suspected felon had not committed the crime.

While the states generally agree as to the proper scope of the peace officer's felony arrest authority, they are sharply divided as to the appropriate use of deadly force in exercising that arrest authority. All agree that deadly force should be used only where the officer reasonably believes he cannot make the arrest without the use of such force. Some, however, limit deadly force even then to arrests for a special group of dangerous felonies (often the same felonies which may be prevented through the use of deadly force).[7] In these jurisdictions, if an officer cannot catch a fleeing felon who has committed a non-dangerous felony (e.g., theft or forgery) without the use of deadly force, he simply must let the individual escape. Supporters of this position contend that the individual is very likely to be caught at some other time and the extra benefit of an immediate arrest is more than offset by avoidance of an unnecessary death. Since the individual has not committed a dangerous crime, there is no likelihood, they argue, that he will present a danger to life if he is not captured immediately. Of course, even in these jurisdictions, if the officer meets physical resistance in making an arrest for any crime, whether dangerous felony, non-dangerous felony, or misdemeanor, he can always use deadly force in self-defense to avoid serious bodily injury or death.

A substantial number of jursidictions still adhere to the common law rule that an officer may use deadly force where needed to arrest for any felony, with no distinction drawn between dangerous and non-dangerous felonies. Critics of this rule argue that it was developed at a time when the punishment for felonies was capital punishment and has no place in a legal system that only would impose a prison sentence if the escaping felon were caught. Supporters of the rule respond that the nature of the punishment imposed after conviction is irrelevant. After conviction, the choice is between two punishments (imprisonment and death) that both provide incapacitation and deterrence. At the time of arrest, the choice is between the possible infliction of death and the complete escape of the felon from any punishment. Supporters claim that the use of deadly force is needed to make deterrence effective by providing a realistic possibility of capture. They contend that if deadly force cannot be used in making arrests for non-dangerous felonies, the felons will be encouraged to continue committing crimes so long as they can outrun or outdrive the police. It is essential to capable law enforcement, they argue, that the officer may say "stop or I will shoot" in making an arrest for any felony.

---

7.   See p. 132 *supra.* There is considerable disagreement as to how narrowly this group of dangerous offenses should be drawn. The Model Penal Code would limit the use of deadly force to arrests for felonies themselves involving the use or threatened use of deadly force. This would exclude such offenses as burglary. See MPC §3.07. Many states with penal laws that ordinarily follow the Code put a broader grouping of crimes in the dangerous felony category. See, e.g., Illinois Stat. ch. 38, §7-5 (including burglary and any felony involving the use or threatened use of any degree of physical force against a person).

THE DIVISION OF CRIMINAL HOMICIDE INTO SEPARATE OFFENSES

In the early stages of the common law, all criminal homicides constituted the offense of murder. Subsequently, in an effort to restrict the use of the death penalty, criminal homicides were divided into two offenses, murder and manslaughter. Still later, in this country, murder was further subdivided into first degree murder and second degree murder. In some states, manslaughter was also divided into two crimes, voluntary and involuntary manslaughter. These divisions prevailed for more than a century, until the Model Penal Code proposed that the homicide offenses be substantially modified. The Code's proposal involved reorganization of first and second degree murder and addition of a new crime of negligent homicide. That proposal has not been followed by many of the states that otherwise based their new penal laws on the Model Code. The traditional division of first degree murder, second degree murder, voluntary manslaughter, and involuntary manslaughter still is utilized in a majority of the states. We will describe that division first and then turn to the Model Code variation. The overall structure of the traditional division is fairly complex, and the chart below may prove helpful in visualizing all of its parts.

Criminal Homicides

Murder (all requiring malice)		Manslaughter (no malice)	
First Degree	Second Degree	Voluntary	Involuntary
1. Intentional and premeditated killing	1. Intentional but not premeditated	1. Killing with intent to kill or to inflict grevious bodily injury but under the influence of passion caused by sufficient provocation	1. Negligent or reckless homicide
2. Killing in the course of committing a dangerous felony (e.g., rape, robbery, arson, burglary)	2. Intent to cause serious bodily injury resulting in death		2. Killing in the course of committing a dangerous misdemeanor
	3. Death by act creating grave risk of death		
	4. Killing in the course of other mala in se felonies		

Murder and Malice.   Under the traditional division, all murders require "malice aforethought." Indeed, the usual statutory definition of murder describes it as "the unlawful killing of a human being with malice aforethought." Read literally, "malice" would require an element of hatred, spite, or ill will, and "aforethought" would require that the malice had been formulated prior to the killing. At least since the middle of the sixteenth century, however, neither term has been read literally. Neither ill will nor advance planning is required for malice aforethought. An actual intent to kill, formulated on the spur of the moment with or without hatred is sufficient to establish *express* (or explicit) malice aforethought. But malice aforethought also will be *implied* (i.e., automatically assumed) from killings without an intent to kill. The common grounds for implied malice are: (1) an intent to inflict a serious bodily injury but not death; (2) a disregard for a risk so great as to show complete indifference to the sanctitiy of life (what the common law described as an "abandoned and malignant heart"); and (3) the commission of a felony which results in death. Any one of these three grounds or the intent to kill is a satisfactory mental element for the crime of murder. Each provides malice aforethought, either express or implied.

The traditional division also divides murder itself as between first degree and second degree murder. First degree murder includes those murders involving either an intent to kill accompanied by premeditation or a killing occurring during the commission of an inherently dangerous felony. All other murders (i.e., criminal homicides with express or implicit malice) will be second degree murders.[8] The distinction between first degree and second degree murder is especially important because of its impact upon the maximum punishment that may be imposed. Some first degree murders may be subject to the death penalty. All are likely to require at least life imprisonment with no possibility of parole. Second degree murders, on the other hand, often permit a term of imprisonment less than life, and even its life terms are subject to parole.

First Degree Murder: Premeditation.   The classic description of the intentional killings encompassed in first degree murder is that set forth in the California Penal Code—"all murder which shall be perpetrated by means of . . . poison, lying in wait, torture or by any other kind of willful, deliberate and premeditated killing."[9] The primary legal problems presented in applying this standard arise in the interpretation of the concept of premeditation. Obviously, the killing must be intentional. However, the terms 'premeditated" and "deliberate" and the examples of first degree murders set forth in the statute (e.g., lying in wait) suggest that the intent must have been formed some time before the commission of the offense. Premeditated murders are separated from other intentional killings because the elements of design and thought involved in premeditation and deliberation suggest a more evil person than one who kills on

---

8.   The traditional dividing line is set forth in California Penal Code §§187-189:

   §187: Murder is the unlawful killing of a human being, with malice aforethought.

   §188: Such malice may be express or implied. It is express when there is manifested a deliberate intention unlawfully to take away the life of a fellow creature. It is implied, when no considerable provocation appears, or when the circumstances attending the killing show an abandoned and malignant heart.

   §189: All murder which is perpetrated by means of a bomb, poison, lying in wait, torture, or by any other kind of willful, deliberate and premeditated killing, or which is committed in the perpetration of, or attempt to perpetrate, arson, rape, robbery, burglary, mayhem, or any act punishable under Section 288, is murder of the first degree; and all other kinds of murders are of the second degree . . . [Section 288 prohibits lewd or lascivious acts upon the body of a child under 14 years].

9.   See note 8 *supra*. California also includes a reference to a killing by bomb, a recent addition to the usual formulation.

the spur of the moment. Some courts have associated the distinction with "cold blooded killings" as opposed to that produced by the "sudden heat of passion." They recognize, however, that the facts of an actual case "may be hard to classify and may lie between the [two] poles. A sudden passion, like lust, rage, or jealousy may spawn an impulsive intent yet persist long enough and in such a way as to permit the intent to become the subject of [the] further reflection and weighing of consequences" necessary for premeditation.[10] Accordingly, few hard rules are set for evaluating the facts of the case. There is, for example, no specific length of time over which the defendant must have considered his decision to kill. A fairly sudden decision to kill may be found, in a particular case, to have been a product of sufficient reflection to constitute premeditation. In most jurisdictions, the outcome often depends on the jury's reaction that the defendant in the particular case showed a degree of "cool thought" that suggests the highest degree of culpability.

The Felony Murder Rule.   While the offender's intent and reflection are important elements in evaluating the evil quality of his action, they are not the only relevant factors. Under some circumstances a killing committed in the course of another crime may fall within the highest degree of murder although the offender acted without reflection or even the intent to kill. The traditional formula for first degree murder incorporates a limited *felony-murder* rule, which makes any killing committed in the course of a dangerous felony a first degree murder. Thus, a burglar may enter a room at night intending only to take the jewelry, and having no intent to inflict even the slightest physical harm upon any occupant of the room. He may have agreed with his confederates waiting outside that "there will be no shooting." He may not even carry a weapon. But suppose, after he enters the room, the occupant wakes up and reaches for a gun. The burglar tries to disarm the occupant and, in the struggle, the gun accidentally fires and kills the occupant. Under the traditional felony-murder rule, the burglar is guilty of first degree murder.[11]

---

10. *Austin v. United States,* 382 F.2d 129, 137 (D.C. Cir. 1969).

11. Under the traditional view of accomplice liability, the burglar's confederates also would be guilty of felony-murder. Some jurisdictions have sought to limit the felony-murder rule, however, particularly with respect to accomplice liability. Thus, New York Penal Code §125.25 provides that a person is guilty of murder when:

> 3. Acting either alone or with one or more other persons, he commits or attempts to commit robbery, burglary, kidnapping, arson, rape in the first degree, sodomy in the first degree, sexual abuse in the first degree, escape in the first degree, or escape in the second degree, and, in the course of and in furtherance of such crime or of immediate flight therefrom, he, or another participant, if there be any, causes the death of a person other than one of the participants; except that in any prosecution under this subdivision, in which the defendant was not the only participant in the underlying crime, it is an affirmative defense that the defendant:
>
> > (a) Did not commit the homicidal act or in any way solicit, request, command, importune, cause or aid the commission thereof; and
> >
> > (b) Was not armed with a deadly weapon, or any instrument, article or substance readily capable of causing death or serious physical injury and of a sort not ordinarily carried in public places by law-abiding persons; and
> >
> > (c) Had no reasonable ground to believe that any other participant was armed with such a weapon, instrument, article or substance; and

The felony-murder rule originally was based on the premise that the intent to commit a malum in se felony revealed in itself a form of malice aforethought. That evil intent then attached to all acts undertaken in the course of committing the felony. If one of these acts produced a homicide, that homicide would fit within the definition of murder because it carried with it the malice aforethought of the original crime. When this theory was first developed, the underlying felonies were themselves capital offenses, and the consequence of extending the liability of the felon to inlcude murder was not significant. Later, however, the courts and legislatures began to reconsider the theory as felonies were punished by imprisonment and more and more non-violent felonies were added to the criminal codes. Initially, almost all jurisdictions concluded that homicides committed in the course of the most dangerous felonies should be treated differently than deaths arising in the course of other malum in se felonies. Language was added specifying that deaths caused in the course of certain listed felonies would be first degree murder. Typically, these felonies were forcible rape, robbery, arson, kidnapping, burglary, and mayhem (disfigurement). In many jurisdictions, the felony murder doctrine has not been carried beyond this point. Only those felonies specified in the first degree murder statute can produce a felony-murder. Other jurisdictions held that deaths caused in the commission of other non-listed felonies can still be punished as second degree murder. In some of those jurisdictions, however, such felonies may give rise to second degree felony murder ony where they are committed in a particularly dangerous fashion. Thus, if a shoplifter happens to bump into a sales clerk, and the clerk falls in such an unusual fashion as to receive a mortal blow, the death will not be a second degree murder even though theft is a malum in se felony.

Second Degree Homicide. Under the traditional division, second degree murder includes all criminal homicides involving malice that do not fit in the first degree category. As we have just noted, in some jurisdictions, this will include certain felony-murders arising from felonies other than those specified in the first degree murder statute. In all jurisdictions, second degree murder will include such intentional killings as are not premeditated. It also will include two types of non-intentional killings. The first involves an intent to inflict grevious bodily injury but not death. In some instances, a person may strike a blow with a deadly weapon but intend to do no more than wound or maim the other party. That usually will be the intent also when the defendant attacked with his fists or feet. In such cases, there is implied malice, and any homicide that results will fall in the second degree category.

Another instance of a non-intentional second degree murder is the so-called "depraved-heart" murder. In these cases, the actor has no intent to kill or to harm. He simply is taking a risk which poses an extremely grave threat to life. The risk in such cases must be so great and unjustified that it establishes what various courts have described as a "depraved heart," "abandoned and malignant heart," or "total indifference to human life." If the risk is not of this quality, and reflects only negligence or recklessness, the crime will be manslaughter rather than second

---

(d) Had no reasonable ground to believe that any other participant intended to engage in conduct likely to result in death or serious physical injury.

degree murder. Examples of activities that have resulted in depraved heart murders are shooting into a caboose of a passing train, playing "russian roulette," and racing a car at very high speeds down a city street.

Voluntary Manslaughter. Voluntary manslaughter includes cases in which the defendant intended to kill or inflict serious bodily injury, but did not have malice because of the existence of *provocation*. What constitutes provocation varies from one jurisdiction to another, but it consists basically of some event that might well lead a reasonable man into a fit of rage and passion. If the individual suffering from such rage or passion then lashes out and kills, his action is not justified, but neither does it reflect the kind of evil intent suggested by malice.[12] Accordingly, the homicide is treated as manslaughter rather than malice. Provocation has been found in a variety of situations involving insulting conduct. These include the sight of adultery by a spouse, the uninvited infliction of a violent blow, or an illegal arrest. In most jurisdictions, words alone, no matter how insulting, do not constitute provocation.

Involuntary Manslaughter. Involuntary manslaughter encompasses cases of criminal homicide in which the actor lacked an intent to kill or cause bodily injury. The manslaughter is described as "involuntary" because the infliction of harm was not desired. Most often involuntary manslaughter involve the mental elements of criminal negligence or recklessness discussed in Chapter Five. Thus, involuntary manslaughter applied when a nightclub owner failed to provide proper exits and hundreds of people died in a fire. It also applied where a driver sought to maneuver a car with one arm down a narrow street (his other arm being in a sling).[13] Many jurisdictions also recognize a misdemeanor-manslaughter rule that is analogous to the felony-murder rule. The misdemeanor-manslaughter rule is based on premise that the commission of a misdemeanor automatically establishes criminal negligence and any death produced through the misdemeanor therefore constitutes manslaughter. Where applied, the rule is limited to commission of malum in se misdemeanors. In some jurisdictions, it is further limited to misdemeanors designed to protect against danger to the person as opposed to danger to property. Ordinarily, commission of such misdemeanors would constitute negligence on the basis of the nature of the act itself, without any help from the misdemeanor-manslaughter rule.

Model Penal Code. The Model Code instituted several changes in the traditional division among criminal homicide offenses.[14] Initially, the Code

---

12. In addition to the provocation cases, voluntary manslaughter includes other cases in which the defendant intended to kill but did so without the evil intent suggested by malice. Thus, if a defendant honestly but unreasonably kills in what he believes to be self-defense, he will be guilty of manslaughter rather than murder. The same also will be true of other honest but unreasonable misapplications of the various justifications for using deadly force.

13. See *Commonwealth v. Welansky*, 316 Mass. 383, 55 N.E.2d 902 (1944); *Bell v. Commonwealth*, 170 Va. 597, 195 S.E. 675 (1938). In some jurisdictions, special vehicle-homicide statutes have been adopted for deaths resulting from automobile accidents. These statutes apply a standard of negligence that come closer to the tort standard than the higher degree of negligence ordinarily required for criminal cases. See Michigan Comp. Law §750.323.

14. See MPC §§210.1-210.3.

eliminates the distinction between first and second degree murder. All intentional killings, whether or not premeditated, are placed in a single category of murder. Also placed in that category are depraved heart murders (described as homicides "committed recklessly under circumstances manifesting extreme indifference to the value of human life"). Criminal homicides occurring in the course of a robbery, forcible rape, arson, burglary, kidnapping, or felonious escape are presumed to fall in the depraved heart category and therefore would constitute murder. The manslaughter category, under the Code, includes provoked killings under a definition of provocation somewhat broader than the traditional view.[15] Reckless homicides are also included in the Model Code's manslaughter category. Criminal homicides involving an intent to inflict serious bodily injury are not given separate treatment. Where the weapons used and other circumstances established a depraved heart, these homicides would constitute murder as they do under the traditional division. In other instances, such homicides might involve no more than recklessness, and they then would fall within the manslaughter category. Negligent homicides are removed from the manslaughter category and treated as a separate, lower level offense called negligent homicide. Causing or aiding another in the commission of a suicide also is treated as an independent homicide offense.

As noted previously, various states that otherwise follow the Model Code have rejected the Code's division of the homicide offenses and stayed with the traditional division of first degree murder, second degree murder, voluntary manslaughter, and involuntary manslaughter. Some have adopted only part of the Code innovations, such as keeping the traditional distincitions but adding a new offense of negligent homicide. Those states that have relied more heavily on the Code proposal usually also added some of their own variations. Thus, New York divides manslaughter into two degrees, separating the reckless causation of death (a class C felony) and death caused with the intent to injure or with provocation (a class B felony).[16] Also, as we shall see in our discussion of capital punishment, some states have added new distinctions in the first degree murder category designed to separate those murders that may result in the death penalty (e.g., intentional killing of a prison guard by a person serving a life sentence).[17]

ASSAULT AND BATTERY

At common law, assault and battery were two different crimes. Today they often are merged in a single offense called "assault and battery" or simply "assault," which can be violated by either a battery or an assault. The merger has not destroyed the separate elements of each of the common law offenses and therefore it remains valuable to examine them separately.

---

15. MPC §210.3 provides: "Criminal homicide constitutes manslaughter when: (a) it is committed recklessly, or (b) a homicide which would otherwise be murder is committed under the influence of extreme mental or emotional disturbance for which there is reasonable explanation or excuse. The reasonableness of such explanation or excuse shall be determined from the viewpoint of a person in the actor's situation under the circumstances as he believes them to be."

16. New York Penal Law §125.15-20.

17. See New York Penal Law §125.27. See also pp. 334-37 *infra*.

Battery. Battery constitutes an intentional or reckless touching of another without excuse or justificiation. Although the common form of battery is the intentional punching of another, the crime does not require a significant blow that inflicts bodily injury. An offensive touching (as where a man kisses a woman against her will) also constitutes battery. The touching need not involve the body of the person committing the battery; spitting in a person's face or hitting him with a rock are also battery. Although battery usually involves a purposeful touching of another, recklessness also is a sufficient mens rea. A reckless battery would occur, for example, where the defendant threw a rock in the direction of a crowd, not hoping to hit someone, but recognizing that might well happen.

Excuse and Justification. Battery only constitutes a crime where the touching involved is not excused or justified. The most common illustration of an excused battery is the touching to which the other party consents. Thus, such activities as a football tackle, a surgeon's examination, and petting do not constitute a battery. An unconsented slight touching often is excused also where not designed to be offensive. Thus, one who pats another on the shoulder in a sign of friendship will not have committed battery even if the recipient should view the touching as offensive. As with homicide offenses, justifications for battery cover a wide variety of settings in which a person is authorized by law to strike a blow against another. Since the policy against inflicting bodily injury is less rigorous than that against causing death, there are many more circumstances justifying the use of non-deadly physical blows than deadly force.

In the area of self-defense, non-deadly force can be used to respond to any threat of the imminent use of unlawful physical force by another. Unlike the user of deadly force, the defender here need not fear death or serious bodily harm. Also, except for the aggressor, a defender with non-deadly force is not required to retreat even though he could safely avoid the threatened harm by doing so. While deadly force could not be used to protect property, non-deadly force may be used for that purpose and even to eject a person trespassing on one's land. In the prevention of crimes, non-deadly force may be used against any criminal without regard to the dangerous or non-dangerous nature of the crime. In the area of arrest, non-deadly force may be used where needed to arrest for misdemeanors as well as felonies. Other justifiable touchings include the use of force by a parent or teacher in maintaining discipline, by a prison guard in maintaining order, and by any person in preventing a suicide.[18]

18.　These and other permissible uses of physical force outside the context of self-defense, etc., are set forth in New York Penal Law §35.10:

　　The use of physical force upon another person which would otherwise constitute an offense is justified and not criminal under any of the following circumstances:

　　1.　A parent, guardian or other person entrusted with the care and supervision of a minor or an incompetent person, and a teacher or other person entrusted with the care and supervision of a minor for a special purpose, may use physical force, but not deadly physical force, upon such minor or incompetent person when and to the extent that he reasonably believes necessary to maintain discipline or to promote the welfare of such minor or incompetent person.

　　2.　A warden or other authorized official of a jail, prison or correctional institution may, in order to maintain order and discipline, use such physical force as is authorized by the correction law.

Assault. At common law an assault simply was "an unlawful attempt, coupled with present ability, to commit a battery."[19] The most common illustration was the missed punch. The common law definition did not include an attempt to frighten another person where there was no intention to actually commit the battery. Accordingly, many jurisdictions expanded the definition to include actions designed to place another in reasonable fear of a battery. Under some of the newer codes, the intent-to-frighten offense sometimes has been removed from the assault provisions and established as a separate offense called "menacing."[20]

Aggravated Assault and Battery. Ordinarily, "simple" assault and battery is a misdemeanor offense. Many states raise the level of the offense when the battery inflicts serious bodily injury or the assault or battery involved the use of a deadly weapon. Some raise the level if the victim occupied a position requiring special protection (e.g., a teacher or police officer). The higher level offense usually is described as "aggravated" assault and battery, although other states refer to the additional element in the title (e.g., "assault with a deadly weapon"). A battery that results in permanent disfigurement or loss of the use of a part of the body also constitutes a separate, higher level offense called "mayhem." When a person commits an assault in the course of attempting to complete a higher crime (e.g., rape or murder), he obviously can be held for the separate crime of attempting that higher level offense.[21] Many states, however, have created a separate, higher level assault which combines the element of assault with the intent to commit a more serious offense. Thus, California has the offenses of assault with the intent to

---

3. A person responsible for the maintenance of order in a common carrier of passengers, or a person acting under his direction, may use physical force when and to the extent that he reasonably believes it necessary to maintain order, but he may use deadly physical force only when he reasonably believes it necessary to prevent death or serious physical injury.

4. A person acting under a reasonable belief that another person is about to commit suicide or to inflict serious physical injury upon himself may use physical force upon such person to the extent that he reasonably believes it necessary to thwart such result.

5. A duly licensed physician, or a person acting under his direction, may use physical force for the purpose of administering a recognized form of treatment which he reasonably believes to be adapted to promoting the physical or mental health of the patient if (a) the treatment is administered with the consent of the patient or, if the patient is a minor or an incompetent person, with the consent of his parent, guardian or other person entrusted with his care and supervision, or (b) the treatment is administered in an emergency when the physician reasonably believes that no one competent to consent can be consulted and that a reasonable person, wishing to safeguard the welfare of the patient, would consent.

19. See, e.g., California Penal Code §240: "An assault is an unlawful attempt, coupled with a present ability to commit a violent injury on the person of another." The element of "present ability" is designed to exclude those cases where it would be impossible for the assailant to accomplish the injury. For example, assume A throws a rock at what he believes to be a person lying in a sleeping bag. Actually, there is nothing in the sleeping bag except for some blankets. A here would have the intent to commit battery, but lacks the present ability. As the hypothetical indicates, such cases would present difficult proof problems in establishing that A did really intend to strike a person. The present ability requirement avoids any mistaken convictions in such ambiguous settings.

20. See New York Penal Law §120.15: "A person is guilty of menacing when, by physical menace, he intentionally places or attempts to place another person in fear of imminent serious physical injury. Menacing is a class B misdemeanor."

21. See p. 109 *supra*.

commit murder, assault with the intent to rob, assault with the intent to rape, etc.[22]

Model Penal Code.   The Model Code introduced various innovations in defining and dividing the crime of assault and battery. These innovations have been incorporated in most of the penal laws modeled on the Code. The primary new elements of the Model Code approach are: (1) addition of battery by negligence, (2) limitation of the intent-to-frighten assault to threats of serious bodily injury, (3) addition of a separate offense of reckless endangering, and (4) addition of a separate offense of making terroristic threats that necessitate evacuation of buildings (e.g., bomb threats). The Model Code provisions are set forth below:

Section 211.1   Assault.

(1) *Simple Assault.*   A person is guilty of assault if he:

(a) attempts to cause or purposely, knowingly or recklessly causes bodily injury to another; or

(b) negligently causes bodily injury to another with a deadly weapon; or

(c) attempts by physical menace to put another in fear of imminent serious bodily harm.

Simple assault is a misdemeanor unless committed in a fight or scuffle entered into by mutual consent, in which case it is a petty misdemeanor.

(2) *Aggravated Assault.*   A person is guilty of aggravated assault if he:

(a) attempts to cause serious bodily injury to another, or causes such injury purposely, knowingly or recklessly under circumstances manifesting extreme indifference to the value of human life; or

(b) attempts to cause or purposely or knowingly causes bodily injury to another with a deadly weapon.

Aggravated assault under paragraph (a) is a felony of the second degree; aggravated assault under paragraph (b) is a felony of the third degree.

Section 211.2   Recklessly Endangering Another Person.

A person commits a misdemeanor if he recklessly engages in conduct which places or may place another person in danger of death or serious bodily injury. Recklessness and danger shall be presumed where a person knowingly points a firearm at or in the direction of another, whether or not the actor believed the firearm to be loaded.

Section 211.3   Terroristic Threats.

A person is guilty of a felony of the third degree if he threatens to commit any crime of violence with purpose to terrorize another or to cause evacuation of a building, place of assembly, or facility of public transportation, or otherwise to cause serious public inconvenience, or in reckless disregard of the risk of causing such terror or inconvenience.

RAPE AND OTHER SEXUAL OFFENSES

The crime of rape is one of the most ancient common law crimes. Traditionally, the offense has been divided into two categories. *Forcible rape* applies to sexual

---

22.   See California Penal Code §§217,220.

intercourse achieved by force or a threat of force against the will of the victim. *Statutory rape* involves sexual intercourse with a minor who is regarded by law as incapable of giving lawful consent to sexual intercourse. The term statutory rape stems from the fact that this offense was first created by statute, although the statute was so ancient that statutory rape was viewed as part of the English common law when that law was carried over to this country. Both rape offenses are limited to sexual intercourse (i.e., the penetration of the male reproduction organ into that of the female). Anal penetration (per annum) and oral penetration (per os) are separate crimes, traditionally described as "sodomy" or the "infamous crime against nature." The common modern statutory terminology for these sexual acts is "deviate sexual intercourse." In a few jurisdictions, the crimes dealing with deviate sexual intercourse basically are duplicates of those prohibiting forcible and statutory rape.[23] In most jurisdictions, deviate sexual intercourse is punishable, at least where the parties involved are of the same sex, without regard to the presence of consent or the fact that both parties are adults. However, this offense is punished at a substantially lower level than forcible deviate sexual intercourse or deviate sexual intercourse with a minor.[24]

Forcible Rape.   Under the common law, the crime of forcible rape involved three elements: (1) sexual intercourse by a male with a female who is not his wife; (2) against the will of the female; and (3) achieved by force or threat of force. Over the years, these elements have been modified and expanded by judicial decisions and new legislation. Today, to fully explain the nature of the offense, one must examine each element in detail.

Spouse Immunity.   The first element of the offense requires sexual intercourse, which we have defined as penetration of the female reproductive organ by the male organ. The courts have held that the slightest penetration is sufficient. There clearly need not be an emission. The first element also excludes from the offense forcible intercourse achieved by a husband against his wife. This exemption originally was based on the premise that the wife in marrying the husband had granted permanent consent to sexual intercourse for the duration of the marriage. Today, the exemption is usually justified on the difficulties of proof that would be involved in establishing that a particular act of intercourse was against the will of the wife. The law should not, it is argued, invade the privacy of the married couple's bedroom.[25] The exemption is not without limits, however. If the husband injured the wife in forcing the wife to have intercourse, he could be charged with battery. If he forced his wife to have intercourse with a third party, he could then

---

23.   This is the pattern proposed in the Model Penal Code, MPC §§213.1 (rape), 213.2 (deviate sexual intercourse). See also Michigan Comp. Laws §750.520a treating the different sex acts in a single crime (with several degrees) called "Criminal Sexual Conduct." See Illinois Stat. ch. 38, §11-4, combining deviate sexual intercourse with a child, sexual intercourse with a child, and lewd fondling of a child in a single offense, titled "Indecent Liberties With A Child," that replaces the former offense of statutory rape.

24.   See, e.g., Texas Penal Code §§21.02-21.09. Under Texas law, forcible rape and sexual abuse (deviate sexual intercourse) are second degree felonies, rape of a child (statutory rape) is a second degree felony, and consensual homosexual conduct is a class C misdemeanor.

25.   For this reason, some states extend the immunity of spouse to persons cohabiting together, whether or not they legally are married. See, e.g., Texas Penal Code §21.12.

be charged as an accomplice to her rape by that third person.[26] Several states recently have eliminated the exemption, permitting the husband to be convicted of raping his wife if the jury can be convinced that she had not consented.[27]

Non-Consent. The requirement that the sexual intercourse be against the female's will has resulted in the application of a series of special rules relating to the proof of rape. Some courts initially held that proof of non-consent required a showing that the woman "resisted to the utmost." This rule was soon discarded, however, as unnecessarily endangering the life of the female victim. The courts substituted a rule that resistance need only be appropriate to the circumstances of the attack, considering such factors as the relative strength of the parties, the male's use of weapons, and the futility of persistence. Many states now require no resistance whenever it is self-evident that the male threatens serious bodily harm.

Many courts also hold that, to dispute the female's claim of non-consent, she may be questioned about her prior sexual experiences when she testifies at trial. Using this authority to its fullest extent, defense counsel have often sought to "turn the tables," arguing that any woman who had sexual experience outside of marriage obviously must have encouraged (and thereby consented to) the advances of the defendant. The notoriety and publicity resulting from such cross-examinations obviously has discouraged rape victims from proceeding with charges. In recent years, courts have limited the defense authority to cross-examine on this subject, suggesting its irrelevance unless the prior sexual intercourse was with the defendant in the particular case. Several states have adopted "rape shield" laws which also restrict the admission of evidence relating to the woman's prior sexual activities.[28]

Concern that rape was easy to allege and difficult to defend against also led some states to adopt special *corroboration requirements* for proof of rape. Under these provisions, a defendant could not be convicted simply on the testimony of the alleged victim of the rape. Other evidence had to support the allegation that there had been sexual intercourse and that it had been against the will of the woman. Such evidence could include medical testimony establishing that penetration had occurred and the physical signs of a struggle (e.g., bruises, torn clothing, hysteria of the victim when reporting the offense). Corroboration requirements have been criticized as unfairly singling out one offense for special proof requirements and requiring the victim, in effect, to resist to the utmost in order to establish corroborative evidence. Today, less than a dozen states continue to impose corroboration requirements.[29]

---

26. Accomplice liability explains how some women have been convicted of rape. Where a woman assists a male in forcing intercourse upon another woman, the woman rendering assistance as well as the male would be guilty of rape.

27. See, e.g., Oregon Rev. Stat. §§163.305-163.315; New Jersey Stat. §2C: 14-5; Delaware Code §§764-772. See also Michigan Comp. Laws §750.250P permitting prosecution where the couple, at the time of the rape, "was living apart and one of them has filed for separate maintenance or divorce."

28. See V. Berger, *Man's Trial, Woman's Tribulation: Rape Cases In The Court Room,* 77 Columbia L.Rev. 1 (1977); Note, *Recent Statutory Developments In The Definition Of Forcible Rape,* 61 Virginia L.Rev. 1500 (1975).

29. See the articles cited in note 28 *supra.*

Force.   At common law, forcible rape required the use of physical force or the threatened use of force. The courts and legislatures soon recognized, however, that this requirement excluded some obvious cases in which the male achieved intercourse against the will of the female. For example, the female might be unconscious or unable to resist as a result of drugs administered by the male. Similarly, because of mental illness or retardation, the female might participate when she obviously is unable to understand what is happening. The newer codes have added these and similar situations of non-consensual intercourse to the prohibition of rape statutes.[30]

Statutory Rape.   Rape at first was limited to unlawful intercourse without the consent of the woman. An ancient English statute then added the act of intercourse with a female child under the age of ten without the limitation that the intercourse be against the will of the child. Under this new form of rape, the crime did not require the use of force or threats. Commission of the offense depended solely on the age of the victim. The offense was based on the premise that the child under ten would lack the capacity to understand the nature and implications of the sexual act. Her consent was viewed as too naive to be given legal effect, and hence the intercourse was treated as obtained against the female's will. Traditionally, this offense was punished just as severly as a forcible rape. Also, the offense was treated as one of "strict liability."[31] The male was liable even if he had reasonably assumed that the consenting female was ten or older.

The modern penal codes have retained the basic concept of statutory rape, but have departed from the common law in several areas. First, all jurisdictions have raised the statutory rape age. Ordinarily, the minimum age for legally effective consent is sixteen, seventeen, or eighteen.[32] The higher age limit has raised questions, in turn, as to the validity of the assumption that the female lacked the

---

30.   See, e.g., Texas Penal Code §21.02:
  - (a) A person commits an offense if he has sexual intercourse with a female not his wife without the female's consent.
  - (b) The intercourse is without the female's consent under one or more of the following circumstances:
    - (1) he compels her to submit or participate by force that overcomes such earnest resistance as might reasonably be expected under the circumstances;
    - (2) he compels her to submit or participate by any threat that would prevent resistance by a woman of ordinary resolution;
    - (3) she has not consented and he knows she is unconscious or physically unable to resist;
    - (4) he knows that as a result of mental disease or defect she is at the time of the intercourse incapable either of appraising the nature of the act or of resisting it;
    - (5) she has not consented and he knows that she is unaware that sexual intercourse is occurring;
    - (6) he knows that she submits or participates because she erroneously believes that he is her husband; or
    - (7) he has intentionally impaired her power to appraise or control her conduct by administering any substance without her knowledge.

31.   See p. 106 *supra*.

32.   Several states continued to use the age of twelve, which was the age commonly set in the early American statutes. See, e.g., Delaware Code, Title 11, §767.

understanding to give a valid consent. Some authorities defend the higher age limit on the ground that, even where the sixteen or seventeen year old has considerable sexual experience (and therefore is fully aware of the implications of the sexual act), continued promiscuity will be harmful to her psychic development and should not be encouraged. The law must, in effect, protect her from herself. Others support the higher age limit on the ground that the age must be set where any substantial group of females of a particular age need protection. The limit must be drawn, they argue, in light of the limited understanding often found among females of a certain age; exceptions cannot be made for more experienced females of the same age because it would be unseemly and inappropriate to examine the sexual background of each individual "victim" of statutory rape in the courtroom setting. Several states have rejected this contention that all females of a certain age must be treated similarly. They have raised the age limit but provided that the offense does not apply where the female is in the upper age range (e.g., 14-17) and the defense can establish prior promiscuous sexual intercourse.[33]

The higher age limit also has led some states to eliminate the "strict liability" aspect of statutory rape. Some jurisdictions now provide that the male shall not be liable if he "reasonably believed" the female was of the age set by law for consent.[34] Most, however, remain of the view that the male must "take his chances" in engaging in such risky activity; he will be liable, no matter how reasonable his belief, if the female was under the age limit.[35]

The raising of the age limit also has produced various changes in the levels of punishment imposed for statutory rape. Most jurisdictions no longer impose the same maximum punishment for all statutory rapes as for forcible rape. Ordinarily, the statutory rape offense is divided into two levels. When the female is under a fairly low age, such as ten or twelve, the crime is prosecuted more severely (often at the same level as forcible rape). When the female is older, but still within the statutory limit, the crime ordinarily is punished at a lesser level. Some jurisdictions also consider the age of the male in punishing statutory rape. They view the statutory rape offense as concerned primarily with the situation in which the older, more experienced male takes advantage of a young female. Accordingly, where the male and female are only a few years apart, they treat the offense as less significant.[36] When this factor is added to divisions drawn according to the age of

---

33. Jurisdictions vary in their description of this defense. Some refer to the female having "engaged promiscuously in sexual intercourse." Texas Penal Code §21.09. Others refer to the female's "want of chastity." See Tennessee Code §39-3706. Illinois recognizes the defense where the female was a prostitute or previously married. See Illinois Stat. ch. 38, §11-4(b).

34. See Illinois Stat. ch. 38, §11-4(b).

35. This position may be expressed as a general principle for all crimes involving activities with children. Thus, New York Penal Law §15.20(3) provides: "Notwithstanding any other provision of this chapter and notwithstanding the use of the term 'knowingly' in any offense defined in this chapter in which the age of a child is an element thereof, knowledge by the defendant of the age of such child is not an element of any such offense and it is no defense to a prosecution therefor that the defendant did not know the age of the child or believed such age to be the same as or greater than that specified in the statute."

36. Texas, for one, goes even farther and finds no liability where the male was no more than two years older than the female.

female, the grading of the different levels of statutory rape can be quite complex. New York for example uses four grades: (1) rape in the first degree, applicable where the female is less than eleven and punished as a class B felony (the same level as for forcible rape); (2) rape in the second degree, applicable where the female is between the ages of eleven and fourteen and the male is over eighteen, and punished as a class D felony; (3) rape in the third degree, applicable where the female is between fourteen and seventeen and the male is over twenty-one, and punished as a class E felony; and (4) an offense called sexual misconduct, applicable to cases in which the male is within four years of the highest age grouping for the female under second and third degree rape, and punishable as a class A misdemeanor.[37]

Other Sexual Offenses.   As noted at the outset of this section, the crime of rape traditionally is limited to sexual intercourse. Most states have a variety of other offenses dealing with other types of sexual activity where the actor used force or was involved with a minor under the legal age of consent. We noted previously the crimes involving deviate sexual intercourse. Similar offenses, at a lower punishment level, apply to sexual fondling of the private parts without the valid consent of the other party. These offenses commonly are described as 'sexual abuse" or, in the case of minors, "indecent liberties." Where a female takes advantage of a minor male, the crime is sometimes described as "debauching a male child." The newer statutes tend to be sex-neutral, however, and apply by their terms to the rape or sexual abuse of either males or females.

Criminal codes also include a series of provisions prohibiting certain sexual activities between consenting adults. As we noted previously, most states prohibit deviate sexual intercourse between persons of the same sex. The crime of incest commonly prohibits sexual intercourse or deviate sexual intercourse between specified relatives (usually parent and child, brother and sister, uncle and niece, and aunt and nephew). The crime of prostitution prohibits the sale of sexual services. In many jurisdictions, that offense or a related crime (e.g., "patronizing a prostitute") also includes the purchase of such services. The solicitation by the prostitute or the prospective purchaser commonly is prohibited so as to reach situations in which the transaction is not completed. A series of other offenses reach the promotion of prostitution and the operation of houses of prostitution. Some jurisdictions prohibit the open and notorious cohabitation of an unmarried man and woman. The very act of sexual intercourse between an unmarried male and female will constitute a misdemeanor (rarely enforced) in several jurisdictions. Sexual conduct between a married person and a partner other than his or her spouse generally is punished as adultery. A variety of other sexual conduct offenses also can be found, especially in the older codes. The criminal law is devoted to the enforcement of moral judgments, and there are few areas in which society has been more concerned with making such judgments than in sexual relations.[38]

---

37. New York Penal Law §§130.20-130.35.

38. For further information relating to crimes against the person generally, see the authorities cited in note 75 at p. 126 *supra.* On the homicide offenses, see also G. Fletcher, *Rethinking Criminal*

ADDENDUM: TEXAS LAWS ON JUSTIFICATION

SUBCHAPTER C. PROTECTION OF PERSONS

§9.31 Self-Defense

(a)   Except as provided in Subsection (b) of this section, a person is justified in using force against another when and to the degree he reasonably believes the force is immediately necessary to protect himself against the other's use or attempted use of unlawful force.

(b)   The use of force against another is not justified:

(1)   in response to verbal provocation alone;

(2)   to resist an arrest or search that the actor knows is being made by a peace officer, or by a person acting in a peace officer's presence and at his direction, even though the arrest or search is unlawful, unless the resistance is justified under Subsection (c) of this section;

(3)   if the actor consented to the exact force used or attempted by the other; or

(4)   if the actor provoked the other's use or attempted use of unlawful force, unless:

(A)   the actor abandons the encounter, or clearly communicates to the other his intent to do so reasonably believing he cannot safely abandon the encounter; and

(B)   the other nevertheless continues or attempts to use unlawful force against the actor.

(c)   The use of force to resist an arrest or search is justified:

(1)   if, before the actor offers any resistance, the peace officer (or person acting at his direction) uses or attempts to use greater force than necessary to make the arrest or search; and

(2)   when and to the degree the actor reasonably believes the force is immediately necessary to protect himself against the peace officer's (or other person's) use or attempted use of greater force than necessary.

(d)   The use of deadly force is not justified under this subchapter except as provided in Sections 9.32, 9.33, and 9.34 of this code.

§ 9.32. Deadly Force in Defense of Person

A person is justified in using deadly force against another:

(1)   if he would be justified in using force against the other under Section 9.31 of this code;

(2)   if a reasonable person in the actor's situation would not have retreated; and

(3)   when and to the degree he reasonably believes the deadly force is immediately necessary:

(A)   to protect himself against the other's use or attempted use of unlawful deadly force; or

---

Law, Boston, Mass.: Little Brown and Company, 1978, Chapters 4 and 5; J. Michael and H. Wechsler, *A Rationale Of The Law of Homicide,* 37 Columbia L.Rev. 701, 1261 (1937) (the legal classic in the field). On sex offenses, see M. Amir, *Patterns In Forcible Rape,* Chicago, Ill.: University of Chicago Press, 1971; M. Walker and S. Brotsky (E. & S.), *Sexual Assault: The Victim And The Rapist,* Lexington, Mass.: Lexington Books, 1976.

(B)   to prevent the other's imminent commission of aggravated kidnapping, murder, rape, aggravated rape, robbery, or aggravated robbery.

§ 9.33. Defense of Third Person

A person is justified in using force or deadly force against another to protect a third person if:

(1)   under the circumstances as the actor reasonably believes them to be, the actor would be justified under Section 9.31 or 9.32 of this code in using force or deadly force to protect himself against the unlawful force or unlawful deadly force he reasonably believes to be threatening the third person he seeks to protect; and

(2)   the actor reasonably believes that his intervention is immediately necessary to protect the third person.

§ 9.34. Protection of Life or Health

(a)   A person is justified in using force, but not deadly force, against another when and to the degree he reasonably believes the force is immediately necessary to prevent the other from committing suicide or inflicting serious bodily injury to himself.

(b)   A person is justified in using both force and deadly force against another when and to the degree he reasonably believes the force or deadly force is immediately necessary to preserve the other's life in an emergency.

SUBCHAPTER D. PROTECTION OF PROPERTY

§ 9.41. Protection of One's Own Property

(a)   A person in lawful possession of land or tangible, movable property is justified in using force against another when and to the degree the actor reasonably believes the force is immediately necessary to prevent or terminate the other's trespass on the land or unlawful interference with the property.

(b)   A person unlawfully dispossessed of land or tangible, movable property by another is justified in using force against the other when and to the degree the actor reasonably believes the force is immediately necessary to reenter the land or recover the property if the actor uses the force immediately or in fresh pursuit after the dispossession and:

(1)   the actor reasonably believes the other had no claim of right when he dispossess the actor; or

(2)   the other accomplished the dispossession by using force, threat, or fraud against the actor.

§ 9.42 Deadly Force to Protect Property

A person is justified in using deadly force against another to protect land or tangible, movable property:

(1)   if he would be justified in using force against the other under Section 9.41 of this code; and

(2)   when and to the degree he reasonably believes the deadly force is immediately necessary:

(A)   to prevent the other's imminent commission of arson, burglary, robbery, aggravated robbery, theft during the nighttime, or criminal mischief during the nighttime; or

(B)   to prevent the other who is fleeing immediately after committing burglary, robbery, aggravated robbery, or theft during the nighttime from escaping with the property; and

(3)   he reasonably believes that:

(A)   the land or property cannot be protected or recovered by any other means; or

(B)   the use of force other than deadly force to protect or recover the land or property would expose the actor or another to a substantial risk of death or serious bodily injury.

§ 9.43.   Protection of Third Person's Property

A person is justified in using force or deadly force against another to protect land or tangible, movable property of a third person if, under the circumstances as he reasonably believes them to be, the actor would be justified under Section 9.41 or 9.42 of this code in using force or deadly force to protect his own land or property and:

(1)   the actor reasonably believes the unlawful interference constitutes attempted or consummated theft of or criminal mischief to the tangible, movable property; or

(2)   the actor reasonably believes that:

(A)   the third person has requested his protection of the land or property;

(B)   he has a legal duty to protect the third person's land or property; or

(C)   the third person whose land or property he uses force or deadly force to protect is the actor's spouse, parent, or child, resides with the actor, or is under the actor's care.

§ 9.44.   Use of Device to Protect Property

The justification afforded by Sections 9.41 through 9.43 of this code applies to the use of a device to protect land or tangible, movable property if:

(1)   the device is not designed to cause, or known by the actor to create a substantial risk of causing, death or serious bodily injury; and

(2)   use of the device is reasonable under all the circumstances as the actor reasonably believes them to be when he installs the device.

SUBCHAPTER E. LAW ENFORCEMENT

§ 9.51.   Arrest and Search

(a)   A peace officer, or a person acting in a peace officer's presence and at his direction, is justified in using force against another when and to the degree the actor reasonably believes the force is immediately necessary to make or assist in making an arrest or search, or to prevent or assist in preventing escape after arrest, if:

(1)   the actor reasonably believes the arrest or search is lawful or, if the arrest or search is made under a warrant, he reasonably believes the warrant is valid; and

(2)   before using force, the actor manifests his purpose to arrest or search and identifies himself as a peace officer or as one acting at a peace officer's direction, unless he reasonably believes his purpose and identity are already known by or cannot reasonably be made known to the person to be arrested.

(b)   A person other than a peace officer (or one acting at his direction) is justified in using force against another when and to the degree the actor reasonably believes the force is immediately necessary to make or assist in making a lawful arrest, or to prevent or assist in preventing escape after lawful arrest if, before using force, the actor manifests his purpose to and the reason for the arrest or reasonably believes his purpose and the reason are already known by or cannot reasonably be made known to the person to be arrested.

(c) A peace officer is justified in using deadly force against another when and to the degree the peace officer reasonably believes the deadly force is immediately necessary to make an arrest, or to prevent escape after arrest, if the use of force would have been justified under Subsection (a) of this section and:

(1) the actor reasonably believes the conduct for which arrest is authorized included the use or attempted use of deadly force; or

(2) the actor reasonably believes there is a substantial risk that the person to be arrested will cause death or serious bodily injury to the actor or another if the arrest is delayed.

(d) A person other than a peace officer acting in a peace officer's presence and at his direct is justified in using deadly force against another when and to the degree the person reasonably believes the deadly force is immediately necessary to make a lawful arrest, or to prevent escape after a lawful arrest, if the use of force would have been justified under Subsection (b) of this section and:

(1) the actor reasonably believes the felony or offense against the public peace for which arrest is authorized included the use or attempted use of deadly force; or

(2) the actor reasonably believes there is a substantial risk that the person to be arrested will cause death or serious bodily injury to another if the arrest is delayed.

(e) There is no duty to retreat before using deadly force justified by Subsection (c) or (d) of this section.

(f) Nothing in this section relating to the actor's manifestation of purpose or identity shall be construed as conflicting with any other law relating to the issuance, service, and execution of an arrest or search warrant either under the laws of this state or the United States.

(g) Deadly force may only be used under the circumstances enumerated in Subsections (c) and (d) of this section.

§ 9.52. Prevention of Escape from Custody

The use of force to prevent the escape of an arrested person from custody is justifiable when the force could have been employed to effect the arrest under which the person is in custody, except that a guard employed by a penal institution or a peace officer is justified in using any force, including deadly force, that he believes to be immediately necessary to prevent the escape of a person from a jail, prison, or other institution for the detention of persons charged with or convicted of a crime.

Chapter 7

Elements of the Major Offenses:
Crimes Against Property

The major series of property crimes are the "theft crimes." Prior to the Model Code, this group included the separate crimes of larceny, embezzlement, and false pretense. Today, most states, following the Code, combine these separate offenses in a single crime called theft. Several additional key crimes build upon the theft offense by requiring theft plus some other elements. Perhaps the most notable crimes in this group are robbery and extortion. Before we begin to study theft and the crimes related to theft, we must consider some elementary concepts of property law that are incorporated in various property crimes. In particular, distinctions must be drawn between real and personal property and between ownership and possession.

Real and Personal Property. Many of the traditional theft offenses required the physical movement of property, which, in turn, limited their application to personal property. This limitation was not as significant as it might at first appear, however, since almost all real property except land can be physically changed to personal property. Real property is land and whatever is affixed to the land. Personal property is all other property. Real property is normally unmovable; personal property is normally movable.[1] If a house is taken off the land and put on a trailer for moving, it has been changed from real property to personal property. Crops growing on the land are real property; once they are cut, they are personal property. Oil still in the ground is real property; when it is pumped out of the

---

1. It should be noted that in property law there are two different meanings given to the term "personal property." The term can be used with reference to the physical qualities of the property as in distinguishing between personal and real property. It also can refer to the ownership of the property as in distinguishing between property owned by private persons and that owned by the government. The law of theft is concerned only with the former meaning. When it is said that theft applies to personal property, we include all movable property, whether owned by private individuals or the government.

ground and put in storage tanks, it is personal property. A lavatory is real property when it is installed in a bathroom, but it is personal property both before it is installed and after it is removed.

Ownership and Possession.   Most theft crimes are crimes against possession. This means that a person commits a crime if he takes property from another even though the victim does not own the property. Suppose Mary loans a handbag to Susie to take to a party. A masked man rips the handbag out of Susie's hand and flees. The masked man is guilty of theft even though Susie did not own the handbag. This would also be true even though Susie had "borrowed" the handbag from Mary without Mary's knowledge, or even if Susie had stolen the handbag from Mary.

In our hypothetical, Mary was the *owner* of the handbag. We would say the handbag "belonged" to her. In most situations, an owner will have *possession* of personal property as well as ownership. Possession refers to the right to exercise control over the property. When the property is physically under the control of the owner, as when Mary is carrying the handbag, the possession is *actual*. An owner may also have a form of possession, called *constructive* possession, when the property is outside the owner's immediate physical control, but he has not given up his ownership right to exercise control over the property. Thus, Mary retains constructive possession over her handbag when she takes a trip and leaves the bag at home. She also may retain constructive possession when she loans the property to another, but this will depend upon how it was surrendered. If, in the presence of Susie, she handed the bag to Susie to hold for a few moments, Mary obviously would be giving Susie temporary custody, but not real control over the property. Constructive possession would remain with Mary. On the other hand, if Mary lent Susie the bag to be taken away and used for the evening, Mary certainly would be relinquishing all possessory rights to Susie for that evening. If Susie had stolen the bag, Mary would not have voluntarily relinquished control, and the law therefore would say that she retained constructive possession of the property.

The law of theft generally protects both constructive and actual possessory interests. When the masked bandit stole the handbag, he deprived either Mary or Susie of possession. If Susie had been given the bag for the night, then she had actual possession. If she was merely given temporary custody, then Mary had constructive possession. If the property had been stolen, Mary also would have constructive possession. In any case, there has been a taking from the possession of another.

An Owner May Steal His Own Property.   Since the theft crimes protect possessory interests in property, an owner who parts with possession of his property can be a thief if he turns around and violates the possessory rights granted to others. If you own a Ford truck and rent it to James for a period of two weeks to move his furniture from one place to another, you cannot simply "remove" the truck from James possession because you need it. If you do, you are guilty of theft, and if you take it from James at gun point or by threats, of robbery. You are the owner of the truck, but James has lawful possession of it under agreement from you. Because theft is a crime against possession, you can be guilty of theft, even though your intent is to take back property which you own. You are depriving

James of a lawful interest (possession for two weeks) which you did not have a right to infringe.[2] On the other hand, if James used the truck to haul dynamite, which he had no right to do, you could retake your truck without being guilty of a theft offense since James had lost his possessory interest by violating the agreement. (This does not mean, however, that you can march onto James' property and use force to take the truck; if you do so, you might be liable for other crimes such as assault or trespass).

THE THEFT OFFENSES

Larceny.   The crime which we commonly refer to as "stealing" is the common law offense of larceny. It was one of the earliest offenses known at the common law and it also served as the springboard for the development of other theft offenses. The common law offense of larceny requires: (1) a taking of personal property, (2) from the possession of another person, (3) with knowledge that the property belongs to another and with the intent to deprive that person permanently of his interest in the property. We already have noted two concepts that are particularly important in determining the scope of the offense. Although the crime applies only to the taking of personal property, various kinds of property affixed to the land can be converted by severance from real to personal property. Similarly, while larceny requires a taking from the possession of another, the concept of possession includes constructive possession as well as actual possession. Equally significant concepts are also presented in interpreting the requirements that there be a "taking" of the property and that the actor have the specified knowledge and intent.

What Constitutes A Taking.   Initially the common law held that a taking could exist only when a person physically took hold of property in the possession of another and removed it from that person's control. The process of taking from another required the carrying away of the property, an element described as *asportation.* A literal application of the asportation element soon presented difficulties. Consider, for example, the following situation. A has a satchel of money on a table belonging to him when B, a bigger and heavier person, approaches. Knowing that the money is not his, B says, "That is my money. Don't touch it." Rather than risk a fight with B, A walks away from the satchel to go to get the police. The police get back to the scene before B has even touched the satchel. Has B "stolen" the satchel? Some early cases said "No." There has been no theft because there has been no asportation. Many states passed statutes which said that, to constitute a "taking," it is not necessary that the property be removed any distance from

---

2.   The Model Code makes this point quite clear in defining protected property as "property in which any person other than the actor has an interest which the actor is not privleged to infringe, *regardless of the fact that the actor also has interest in the property.*" MPC §223 (7) (emphasis added). The Code provision goes on to note that the property is protected "regardless of the fact that the other person might be precluded from civil recovery because the property was used in an unlawful transaction or was subject to forfeiture as contraband." Thus, it is theft to steal a gambler's money even though that money is being used unlawfully. It also is theft to steal narcotics even though the drug is "contraband" (that is, material that cannot lawfully be possessed).

the place of taking; it is sufficient that it has come into the possession of the thief.[3] In other words, a taking exists if the thief has obtained dominion over the property which deprives the previous possessor of his control, no matter for how short the period of time involved.

The taking requirement also presented difficult legal issues where the defendant had received lawful custody of the property and then decided to convert it to his own use. Some cases were resolved by relying on the concept of constructive possession. If a servant removed property from the home of his master, it was said that the property, though in the servant's custody, was still within the constructive possession of the master. The removal accordingly was a taking from the master's possession and larceny could apply. This analysis could not be extended, however, to situations in which the owner had clearly given full possession to another person. Larceny did not apply, for example, where a carriage was delivered to a blacksmith for repairs, but the blacksmith sold the carriage and kept the profits for himself. Neither did larceny apply where a depositor gave money to a bank messenger to have it deposited in his account, but the messenger ran off with the money. In both cases, the owner originally gave possession to the actor so the actor's subsequent wrongful conversion of the property to his own use could not constitute a taking from the owner's possession. The crux of the actor's wrongdoing was not an unlawful taking of property but the purposeful misuse of his lawful possession of the property. What was needed here was a new theft crime that went beyond larceny, and the Parliament began to establish such a crime as early as the sixteenth century. That crime eventually became known as embezzlement, an offense we will discuss later.

Another crime that was created as a result of the shortcomings of the taking requirement for larceny was the offense of false pretenses. When a person obtained property by fraud and deceit (e.g., assuming a false identity, or using counterfeit coins), larceny did not apply because there was no taking without the consent of the other party. The false pretenses offense, considered later in this chapter, applied notwithstanding the voluntary relinquishment of ownership by the duped party.

Knowledge Of Ownership.   Another major limitation upon the scope of the larceny offense flows from the mens rea requirement that the defendant know that the property taken does not belong to him. This requirement gives rise to the so-called "claim of right" defense to a larceny charge. If the defendant honestly believed that he had a right to the property, even though it was in the possession of another, he obviously did not know that he was taking property that belonged to another. It did not matter that his belief was mistaken or that it was unreasonable. For example, consider again the hypothetical in which you owned a Ford truck and rented it to James for a two week period. We saw that you committed a theft crime (i.e., larceny) if you simply decided to take the truck back knowing that James still had a right to use it. If you correctly concluded that James had breached his agreement by renting the truck and therefore lost his possessory rights, you would

---

3.   The Model Code reaches this situation in providing that theft exists where a person "takes" or "exercises unlawful control" over the movable property of another. See MPC §223.2, quoted *infra*. The various state provisions based on the Code use similar provisions.

not commit larceny in taking the truck back without James' permission. What if, however, you were mistaken as to the legal consequences of James' rental of the truck? What if James had not violated the agreement and still had a right to possess the truck? Indeed, what if your mistake was based on a totally unreasonable view of James' rights? In all of these situations, the outcome would still be the same provided you had a good faith belief that James no longer had a right to the truck. Even though you took property from the possession of another, you would not be guilty of larceny since you had an honest belief (a claim of right) that you alone had a right to current possession of the property.

Intent To Permanently Deprive.   To commit larceny, a person not only has to be aware that the property taken is not his, but he also must intend to permanently deprive the owner or other person in possession of his interest in that property. This mental element does not necessarily require an intent to keep or destroy the property. An intent to deprive is also satisfied by a disposition of the property that makes it probable that the owner will not recover it. Thus if A stole B's horse and rode it to the next county where he abandoned the horse, there would be sufficient likelihood of B's permanent loss to establish the necessary intent for larceny. Similarly, if A intended to return a stolen item after keeping it for so long a period that a substantial portion of its value would be lost, that also would be viewed as an intent to permanently deprive. On the other hand, if A took the item intending to use it for a brief period and then return it, he would not have committed larceny since he had no intent to permanently deprive the owner of the property.[4] He did not intend to keep the property, to use it for so long a period as to sharply reduce its value, or to dispose of it in a way that would substantially hinder its return.

The taking of property with an intent to return it was viewed by the common law as not so harmful an act as to require a criminal penalty. The typical situation would be that in which one "borrowed" an item belonging to an employer, friend, or neighbor without permission, used it for a limited purpose, and promptly returned it. Thus, A might take his neighbor B's lawn mower, cut his lawn, and return the mower. A acted improperly, but not in such a way as to require more than a civil sanction. However, with the arrival of motor vehicles and "joyriding," the states were forced to adopt special legislation making the unauthorized taking of an automobile a crime, without regard to the absence of an intent to permanently deprive.[5]

---

4.   Thus, an Illinois case held that, where a service station operator took another's automobile for the purpose of getting coffee and then returned it to the service station, he lacked the mens rea for larceny of the motor vehicle. *People v. DeStefano*, 23 Ill.2d 427, 178 N.E.2d 393 (1961).

5.   The motor vehicle offense is usually titled "unauthorized use of a vehicle" or "joyriding." All jurisdictions have extended that crime to a variety of vehicles and several have extended it to include situations in which the defendant lawfully obtained the use of the vehicle, but then used it for another purpose, although still intending to return it. New York Penal Law §165.05, which applies to all "vehicles" (defined as including aircraft and any vessel 'equipped for propulsion by mechanical means or by sail") provides:

A person is guilty of unauthorized use of a vehicle when:

1.   Knowing that he does not have the consent of the owner, he takes, operates, exercises control over, rides in or otherwise uses a vehicle. A person who engages in any such conduct

Embezzlement.   As previously noted, the crime of embezzlement is a statutory crime designed to close what the English Parliment viewed as a loophole in the larceny offense. It seeks to reach persons who lawfully received possession of the property of another and then wrongfully convert that property to their own use. The original embezzlement statute listed only certain persons in a position of trust who were subject to the statute. That list gradually has been extended, however, to encompass all persons who receive property with a duty to handle that property in a certain way on behalf of the owner, including employees, attorneys, brokers, bankers and bailees.[6] The embezzlement statutes apply only if the person in a position of trust seeks to permanently deprive the owner of the property by such activities as selling it, giving it away, or intentionally destroying it. Thus, an employee entrusted with a company car does not commit embezzlement if he merely uses the car for a personal trip.[7] The mens rea for embezzlement also is similar to that for larceny in requiring knowledge that the conversion of the property is unauthorized. Statutes commonly require an element of "fraud," which is defined as purposefully converting the property of another without an honest belief that one could legally do so. Here again, a claim of right is a defense to the criminal charge. Unlike larceny, embezzlement commonly includes the conversion of real property as well as personal property. Thus, an agent who has control over real property belonging to his employer commits embezzlement if he should sell the property without authorization and transfer the receipts to his own account.

False Pretenses.   False pretense is the other major statutory crime that was created to fill a loophole in the larceny coverage. It applies to persons (usually sellers) who induce other persons to transfer property to them by means of false representations. It is not necessary that the entire transfer be induced by the falsehood. Thus, a butcher who represents a three pound turkey as weighing four pounds commits the crime of false pretenses in obtaining the purchaser's payment for the non-existent pound. False pretenses will not apply, however, unless the

---

without the consent of the owner is presumed to know that he does not have such consent; or

2.   Having custody of a vehicle pursuant to an agreement between himself or another and the owner thereof whereby he or another is to perform for compensation a specific service for the owner involving the maintenance, repair or use of such vehicle, he intentionally uses or operates the same, without the consent of the owner, for his own purposes in a manner constituting a gross deviation from the agreed purpose; or

3.   Having custody of a vehicle pursuant to an agreement with the owner thereof whereby such vehicle is to be returned to the owner at a specified time, he intentionally retains or withholds possession thereof, without the consent of the owner, for so lengthy a period beyond the specified time as to render such retention or possession a gross deviation from the agreement.

6.   The term "bailee" as used here refers to the person who receives possession of another's property in trust for some special object or purpose. Thus, a truck driver hired to transport goods is a bailee, as is a dry cleaner who stores another's furs. The term should not be confused with the word "bail," which refers to property placed with the court to gain a defendant's release from custody pending trial. In some jurisdictions, special statutes, entitled "conversion by bailee," were enacted prior to the adoption of more comprehensive embezzlement statutes that apply to various persons in a position of trust besides bailees.

7.   Neither, of course, would he be liable for larceny. See note 4 *supra.* As for joyriding, see note 5 *supra.*

misrepresentation was as to a material past or present fact that the seller knew to be false. It is not a crime for a seller to make overly optimistic predictions or to express an overly generous estimate of the value of the property being sold. If a person selling a horse claimed that it was a "great" horse which "surely would win the big race," those statements would not constitute false pretenses even if he actually believed the horse was a poor specimen and a likely loser. The law generally does not protect the buyer against such "sellers talk" or "puffing." On the other hand, if the seller misstated the facts as to the horse's blood line or its actual medical record, then he would have committed false pretenses had those statements induced the buyer to purchase the horse.

Levels Of The Theft Offenses.   The punishment for the offenses of larceny, embezzlement and false pretenses traditionally was based on the value of the property obtained. The precise dividing line as to value has varied with the times and the jurisdiction. Prior to the 1940's, if the property illegally obtained was worth less than fifty dollars, the crime was a misdemeanor. If it was worth more than fifty dollars, the crime was a felony. During the 1950's and 1960's, the dividing line commonly was raised to one hundred dollars. Today, under the combined theft provisions of the Model Code, more than one dividing line may be used. In New York, for example, the crime is a class A misdemeanor where the value of the property obtained is less than 250 dollars, a class E felony where the property is worth between 250 and 1,000 dollars, and a class D felony when the property is worth more than 1,500 dollars. Where particular types of larceny, embezzlement, or false pretenses cause greater commercial problems or pose threats to individual safety, that criminal activity often is governed by a separate statute and punishment set at a higher level. Thus, the forgery of checks, which is a type of false pretense, is a separate, more serious crime. Larceny from the person of another (e.g., picking pockets) is treated separately because of the addition of a possible threat to the person. Because of the serious problems presented by car thefts, that activity also is treated separately in many jurisdictions.[8]

Consolidated Theft Provisions.   In recent years, a substantial majority of the states have discarded the separate crimes of larceny, embezzlement and false pretenses and have replaced them with a single, consolidated theft provision. Most of the consolidated provisions are based on the theft chapter of the Model Penal Code. The Code creates a single crime, called theft, that reaches all of the various methods of obtaining or converting property that formerly constituted larceny, embezzlement, and false pretenses. It also includes several related offenses such as receiving stolen property and extortion (commonly called blackmail). The Code provision also applies to certain activities that often did not fit under the traditional crimes, such as the use of deception to obtain services rather than property and the failure to return property received as a result of mistaken delivery by a department store. Probably the most innovative addition was a provision making it a theft to fail to dispose of property in accordance with a prior

---

8.   Car theft provisions sometimes are supplemented by special statutes making it a crime to erase motor vehicle engine numbers, to offer for sale or sell a car without an engine number, to offer or sell a car without having proper certificate of title, etc. Transporting a stolen vehicle across state lines is a federal offense under 18 United States Code §2312.

commitment (as where an employer deducts union dues from an employee's paycheck and then fails to transfer the money to the union). The various Model Code provisions establishing the consolidated theft offense are set forth below. While state provisions will vary in certain details (such as the property value dividing felonies and misdemeanors), they usually are very similar to the Code provisions.

Model Penal Code Article 223: Theft and Related Offenses[9]

Section 223.1 Consolidation of Theft Offenses; Grading Provisions Applicable to Theft Generally.

(1) *Consolidation of Theft Offenses.* Conduct denominated theft in this Article constitutes a single offense. An accusation of theft may be supported by evidence that it was committed in any manner that would be theft under this Article, notwithstanding the specification of a different manner in the indictment or information, subject only to the power of the Court to ensure fair trial by granting a continuance or other appropriate relief where the conduct of the defense would be prejudiced by lack of fair notice or by surprise.

(2) *Grading of Theft Offenses.*

    (a) Theft constitutes a felony of the third degree if the amount involved exceeds $500, or if the property stolen is a firearm, automobile, airplane, motorcycle, motorboat, or other motor-propelled vehicle, or in the case of theft by receiving stolen property, if the receiver is in the business of buying or selling stolen property.

    (b) Theft not within the preceding paragraph constitutes a misdemeanor, except that if the property was not taken from the person or by threat, or in breach of a fiduciary obligation, and the actor proves by a preponderance of the evidence that the amount involved was less than $50, the offense constitutes a petty misdemeanor.

---

9.   The following definitions, set forth in MPC §223.0, apply to this article:

    "Deprive means: (a) to withhold property of another permanently or for so extended a period as to appropriate a major portion of its economic value, or with intent to restore only upon payment of reward or other compensation; or (b) to dispose of the property so as to make it unlikely that the owner will recover it.

    "Movable property" means property the location of which can be changed, including things growing on, affixed to, or found in land, and documents although the rights represented thereby have no physical location. "Immovable property" is all other property.

    "Obtain" means: (a) in relation to property, to bring about a transfer or purported transfer of a legal interest in the property, whether to the obtainer or another; or (b) in relation to labor or service, to secure performance thereof.

    "Property" means anything of value, including real estate, tangible and intangible personal property, contract rights, choses-in-action and other interests in or claims to wealth, admission or transportation tickets, captured or domestic animals, food and drink, electric or other power.

    "Property of another" includes property in which any person other than the actor has an interest which the actor is not privileged to infringe, regardless of the fact that the actor also has an interest in the property and regardless of the fact that the other person might be precluded from civil recovery because the property was used in an unlawful transaction or was subject to forfeiture as contraband. Property in possession of the actor shall not be deemed property of another who has only a security interest therein, even if legal title is in the creditor pursuant to a conditional sales contract or other security agreement.

(c) The amount involved in a theft shall be deemed to be the highest value, by any reasonable standard, of the property or services which the actor stole or attempted to steal. Amounts involved in thefts committed pursuant to one scheme or course of conduct, whether from the same person or several persons, may be aggregated in determining the grade of the offense.

(3) *Claim of Right.* It is an affirmative defense to prosecution for theft that the actor:

(a) was unaware that the property or service was that of another; or

(b) acted under an honest claim of right to the property or service involved or that he had a right to acquire or dispose of it as he did; or

(c) took property exposed for sale, intending to purchase and pay for it promptly, or reasonably believing that the owner, if present, would have consented.

(4) *Theft from Spouse.* It is no defense that theft was from the actor's spouse, except that misappropriation of household and personal effects, or other property normally accessible to both spouses, is theft only if it occurs after the parties have ceased living together.

Section 223.2 Theft by Unlawful Taking or Disposition.

(1) *Movable Property.* A person is guilty of theft if he unlawfully takes, or exercises unlawful control over, movable property of another with purpose to deprive him thereof.

(2) *Immovable Property.* A person is guilty of theft if he unlawfully transfers immovable property of another or any interest therein with purpose to benefit himself or another not entitled thereto.

Section 223.3 Theft by Deception.

A person is guilty of theft if he purposely obtains property of another by deception. A person deceives if he purposely:

(a) creates or reinforces a false impression, including false impressions as to law, value, intention or other state of mind; but deception as to a person's intention to perform a promise shall not be inferred from the fact alone that he did not subsequently perform the promise; or

(b) prevents another from acquiring information which would affect his judgment of a transaction; or

(c) fails to correct a false impression which the deceiver previously created or reinforced, or which the deceiver knows to be influencing another to whom he stands in a fiduciary or confidential relationship; or

(d) fails to disclose a known lien, adverse claim or other legal impediment to the enjoyment of property which he transfers or encumbers in consideration for the property obtained, whether such impediment is or is not valid, or is or is not a matter of official record.

The term "deceive" does not, however, include a falsity as to matters having no pecuniary significance, or puffing by statements unlikely to deceive ordinary persons in the group addressed.

Section 223.4 Theft by Extortion.

A person is guilty of theft if he purposely obtains property of another by threatening to:

(a) inflict bodily injury on anyone or commit any other criminal offense; or

(b) accuse anyone of a criminal offense; or

(c) expose any secret tending to subject any person to hatred, contempt or ridicule, or to impair his credit or business repute; or

(d) take or withhold action as an official, or cause an official to take or withhold action; or

(e) bring about or continue a strike, boycott or other collective unofficial action, if the property is not demanded or received for the benefit of the group in whose interest the actor purports to act; or

(f) testify or provide information or withhold testimony or information with respect to another's legal claim or defense; or

(g) inflict any other harm which would not benefit the actor.

It is an affirmative defense to prosecution based on paragraphs (b), (c), or (d) that the property obtained by threat of accusation, exposure, lawsuit or other invocation of official action was honestly claimed as restitution or indemnification for harm done in the circumstances to which such accusation, exposure, lawsuit or other official action relates, or as compensation for property or lawful services.

Section 223.5 Theft of Property Lost, Mislaid, or Delivered by Mistake.

A person who comes into control of property of another that he knows to have been lost, mislaid, or delivered under a mistake as to the nature or amount of the property or the identity of the recipient is guilty of theft if, with purpose to deprive the owner thereof, he fails to take reasonable measures to restore the property to a person entitled to have it.

Section 223.6 Receiving Stolen Property.

(1) *Receiving.* A person is guilty of theft if he purposely receives, retains, or disposes of movable property of another knowing that it has been stolen, or believing that it has probably been stolen, unless the property is received, retained, or disposed with purpose to restore it to the owner. "Receiving" means acquiring possession, control or title, or lending on the security of the property.

(2) *Presumption of Knowledge.* The requisite knowledge or belief is presumed in the case of a dealer who:

(a) is found in possession or control of property stolen from two or more persons on separate occasions; or

(b) has received stolen property in another transaction within the year preceding the transaction charged; or

(c) being a dealer in property of the sort received, acquires it for a consideration which he knows is far below its reasonable value.

"Dealer" means a person in the business of buying or selling goods and includes a pawnbroker.

Section 223.7 Theft of Services.

(1) A person is guilty of theft if he purposely obtains services which he knows are available only for compensation, by deception or threat, or by false token or other means to avoid payment for the service. "Services" include labor, professional service, transportation, telephone or other public service, accommodation in hotels, restaurants or elsewhere, admission to exhibitions, use of vehicles or other movable property. Where compensation for service is ordinarily paid immediately upon the rendering of such service, as in the case of hotels and restaurants, refusal to pay or absconding without payment or offer to pay gives rise to a presumption that the service was obtained by deception as to intention to pay.

(2) A person commits theft if, having control over the disposition of services of others, to which he is not entitled, he knowingly diverts such services to his own benefit or to the benefit of another not entitled thereto.

Section 223.8 Theft by Failure to Make Required Disposition of Funds Received.

A person who purposely obtains property upon agreement, or subject to a known legal obligation, to make specified payment or other disposition, whether from such property or its proceeds or from his own property to be reserved in equivalent amount, is guilty of theft if he deals with the property obtained as his own and fails to make the required payment or disposition. The foregoing applies notwithstanding that it may be impossible to identify particular property as belonging to the victim at the time of the actor's failure to make the required payment or disposition. An officer or employee of the government or of a financial institution is presumed: (i) to know any legal obligation relevant to his criminal liability under this Section, and (ii) to have dealt with the property as his own if he fails to pay or account upon lawful demand, or if an audit reveals a shortage of falsification of accounts.

Section 223.9 Unauthorized Use of Automobiles and Other Vehicles.

A person commits a misdemeanor if he operates another's automobile, airplane, motorcycle, motorboat, or other motor-propelled vehicle without consent of the owner. It is an affirmative defense to prosecute under this Section that the actor reasonably believed that the owner would have consented to the operation had he known of it.

ROBBERY

Elements Of Robbery. Although robbery is located in the newer codes among the property crimes, it actually is a crime against both person and property. In short, robbery is a combination of an assault and a theft. The basic elements of robbery under the common law were: (1) a larceny, (2) with the stolen property taken from the victim or in the presence of the victim, and (3) with the taking accomplished by means of force or a threat of force. These elements have been incorporated, with only minor modifications, in both the older and newer state statutory provisions.[10]

We already are familiar with the first element of robbery, the commission of larceny. The use of force to obtain property will not constitute robbery unless there is a completed larceny. This means that if a person conducting a hold-up is captured before he can obtain the property from his victim, he has not committed a robbery since the element of taking needed for larceny (and robbery) is missing.[11] (The individual can be convicted of attempted robbery, however). Similarly, since a claim of right is a defense to larceny, it also is a defense to robbery. If an individual believes that he has a lawful right to property possessed by another, he does not commit robbery if he uses force or a threat of force to take that property from that other person. (However, he still may be prosecuted for assault since a claim of right is not a defense to that crime).

The second element of robbery—that the larceny be committed by taking property from the victim or in the presence of victim—rarely presents legal difficulties. Property is viewed as taken from the person of the victim if it was in his hand, the pockets of his clothing, or otherwise attached to his body (e.g., an earring). Property is viewed as taken from the presence of the victim if it was within the general proximity of his location and subject to his control. Thus, property is taken from the victim's control if the robber ties the victim up in one room of a dwelling and then helps himself to property located in another room. It would not be robbery, however, if the thief uses force to immobolize a victim at one place while his accomplice steals from the victim's house several miles away. Of course, several other crimes probably would be committed in that situation, including both assault and theft.

The major element that robbery adds to the larceny offense is the robber's use of actual force or a threat of force. The force used can take various forms. In some jurisdictions, the snatching of a purse is sufficient force, but most jurisdictions hold such a sudden movement is not sufficient. Simple purse snatching commonly is viewed as no more than a larceny from the person. On the other hand, if the owner resists the thief's efforts, and the thief then struggles with the owner, this additional use of force probably will convert the larceny into a robbery. A threat of force that puts the victim in fear of attack also will be sufficient to raise a larceny to robbery. The threat need not relate to serious bodily injury, but to any use of force (e.g., a punch) against the victim. The threat must relate to the immediate use of force, however, rather than to the use of force sometime in the

---

10.   Illustrative is New York Penal Law §160.00:

> Robbery is forcible stealing. A person forcibly steals property and commits robbery when, in the course of committing a larceny, he uses or threatens the immediate use of physical force upon another person for the purpose of:
>
> 1.   Preventing or overcoming resistance to the taking of the property or to the retention thereof immediately after the taking or;
>
> 2.   Compelling the owner of such property or another person to deliver up the property or to engage in other conduct which aids in the commission of the larceny.

11.   See p. 157 *supra*.

future. If A tells B that he will hire a gunman and have B shot unless B immediately gives him certain property, A has committed extortion, but not robbery.[12]

Degrees of Robbery.   Robbery traditionally is viewed as a serious crime because of the threat to the person as well as to property. The various degrees of the robbery offense generally are set according to the element of danger to the person rather than the value of the property taken. In New York, for example, a simple robbery is punishable as a class D felony. If the robber has the assistance of an accomplice, thereby presenting a greater threat, the offense is punishable as a class C felony. If the robber is armed with a deadly weapon or dangerous instrument (e.g., a crowbar), the offense is punishable as a class B felony. If the robber, whether armed or not, causes serious physical injury to the victim or a person who comes to the victim's assistance, the crime also is punished as a class B felony.[13] In many jurisdictions, armed robbery is subject to the highest available punishment, aside from capital punishment.

BURGLARY

Elements of Burglary.   Burglary is the most substantial of a series of offenses designed to protect the owner or other possessor of real property from unwarranted intrusions upon that property. At common law burglary consisted of: (1) breaking into and entering, (2) a residence, (3) in the nighttime, (4) with intent to commit a felony. Under the statutes of most states, this definition of burglary has been considerably broadened. In all jurisdictions, the modern offense of burglary now includes breaking into and entering any building or similar structure, whether or not a residence, and the offense can take place in the daytime as well as the nighttime. In many jurisdictions, burglary no longer requires a breaking, as it applies to an unlawful entry with or without a breaking. The required intent accompanying the entry also has been changed. In most states, it is sufficient that the actor had the intent to commit a crime of any level, including misdemeanors as well as felonies. Thus, the basic elements of burglary today are: (1) a breaking and entering (or simply an illegal entry in many jurisdictions), (2) into a building or similar structure, (3) with the intent to commit a crime.

Breaking and Entry.   A breaking at common law required the use of force to create an opening through which the burglar entered the dwelling. If the occupant had created the opening himself, it was felt that he was not entitled to the special protection of the burglary offense. (Of course, the occupant still had the protection of lesser offenses that prohibited all unlawful entries). Thus, where a thief entered the home through an open window, or by pushing upon a partially open window, there was no breaking.[14] On the other hand, if he entered through the chimney, it was a breaking because the occupant obviously could not be expected

---

12.   See M.P.C. § 223.4 at p. 162 *supra.*

13.   New York Penal Law §§160.05-160.15.

14.   There was some disagreement as to the partially opened window. If the burglar did not simply push the window open, but used a mechanical device to assist him, his action was more likely to be viewed as a breaking.

to close off the chimney and the availability of such an unusual entryway could not be taken as encouraging the entry.

Today, the emphasis in the burglary offense is on the unlawful entry rather than the breaking. Over half of the states no longer require a breaking for the basic burglary offense (although, as we shall see, the element of breaking may be required for a higher degree of burglary). It is sufficient in these states that the person enters the building unlawfully with an intent to commit a crime. If the premises are not open to the public and the defendant enters without consent, he has satisfied the element of unlawful entry even though he enters through an open window or unlocked door. Indeed, in some instances, the entry may be unlawful even where the building is open to the public. Thus, if a person lawfully has been ordered to stay out of a certain public building (e.g., a non-student ordered to stay out of a university building), he will commit burglary if he subsequently enters with an intent to commit a crime in that building. Similarly, if a part of the building is open to the public, but the individual enters into a portion closed to the public, his entry into that portion is unlawful and he can be held for burglary if that entry was made with the intent to commit a crime. Some of the newer codes go even farther and reach the person who lawfully enters a public building, but then remains unlawfully to commit a crime.[15] Thus, if a person enters a department store during regular hours, hides in the lavatory, and then emerges after closing with the intent to steal, he will have committed burglary.

Building or Structure.   All of the current codes have extended the scope of the burglary offense to protect various types of buildings besides dwellings. Most simply refer to entry into "any building." The term "building" is held to include any permanent or semipermanent structure affixed to the ground, having four walls and a roof. It encompasses, for example, the typical barn, garage, or outhouse. An Illinois case held that an outdoor telephone booth permanently attached to concrete slabs was a building that could be burglarized.[16] Because the term "building" suggests a structure affixed to the ground, many codes have included provisions encompassing other structures viewed as deserving the same protection as buildings. Thus, the New York Code provision applies to all buildings, and, in addition, to "any structure, vehicle, or watercraft used for overnight lodging of persons or used by persons for carrying on business therein."[17] Most of the codes based on the Model Code have similar provisions. The California provision refers directly to any "tent, vessel, railroad car, trailer coach as defined by the Vehicle Code, vehicle as defined by said Code when the doors of such vehicle are locked, [or] aircraft."[18] Although the modern burglary statutes are quite broad, there do remain certain enclosed areas of private property that are not within the special protection of those statutes. A fenced-in corral is not an included structure, neither is a haystack, a fenced garden, or a tennis court. An offender entering

---

15.   Thus, New York Penal Law §140.20 provides that a person is guilty of burglary if he "knowingly enters or remains unlawfully in a building with the intent to commit a crime therein."

16.   *People v. Goins,* 66 Ill.App.2d 251, 213 N.E.2d 52 (1965). See also *People v. Clemison,* 105 Cal.App.2d 679, 233 P.2d 924 (1951).

17.   New York Penal Law §140.00, based on MPC §221.0.

18.   California Penal Code §459.

illegally into such areas and taking the horses, the hay, the cucumbers, or the tennis net is guilty of theft, but not of burglary, even though he forces a gate or climbs a fence in the process. Also, as we shall see, the distinction between residences and other buildings may still be significant in the division of the burglary offense into separate degrees for punishment purposes.

Intent to Commit a Crime.   There are basically two aspects to the mens rea requirement of burglary. First, there is the mental element with respect to the lawfulness of the entry. Some jurisdictions hold that the offender must have entered the building knowing that he did not have a right to enter. Ordinarily, the very act of breaking will suggest such knowledge. On occasion, where entry was made through an unlocked door and various persons were permitted on the premises (e.g., employees), a defendant may claim successfully that, while he intended to commit a crime in the building, he did not believe his very entry into the building was unauthorized. Most often, any dispute as to the proof of the required intent will relate to the second aspect of the mens rea, the accompanying intent to commit a crime.

Every jurisdiction holds that the illegal entry must have been made with the intent to commit a crime within the building. A few jurisdictions retain the common law requirement of an intent to commit a felony. Many others, following the Model Code, extend the mens rea to include the intent to commit any crime.[19] While most burglars will have entered the building for the purpose of committing a basic felony, such as rape, robbery, or major theft, these statutes also will include those who entered to commit misdemeanors, such as a petty destruction of property or a simple assault. Several states use a standard that falls between the common law and this broader Model Code provision. They require an intent to commit a felony or any theft, whether felony or misdemeanor. As a practical matter, the addition of the intent to commit the misdemeanor of petty theft has limited significance. Most thieves will enter a building with the intent to steal as much valuable property as they can find; while they may wind up stealing property of a value less than that required for a felony, their intent upon entry will not have been so limited.

The importance of the dual mens rea requirements of burglary in establishing the special culpability of the burglar are illustrated by the following hypotheticals. First, assume a man gets very drunk at a party and decides to go home, get some beer, and return. He lives in one of a row of houses that look pretty much alike, inside and out. He goes to a house, finds the screen door latched, forces the latch, opens the door, and enters the house. In the refrigerator, he finds some beer, which happens to be his own brand. He takes the beer and goes back to the party. *Unfortunately he was in the wrong house.* Is he guilty of burglary? The answer is "No." If these facts are really true, and the jury believes them, he has not committed the offense of burglary because the necessary intent was lacking. He didn't enter a house knowing that he had no right to be there; he thought it was his own house. Neither did he enter with the intent to commit a crime. He intended to take his own beer (and later believed he was taking his own beer).

---

19.   MPC §221.1.

Now let us change the facts of our hypothetical slightly. Assume that the man also was very tired when he left the party and just wanted to get some sleep. Assume also that he recognized that the house he was trying to enter was not his own, but belonged to a neighbor who was on vacation. The man decided to sleep there anyways rather than return home, where his family might not appreciate his condition. Accordingly, he forced the latch on his neighbor's door, entered, and went to sleep on the couch. The next morning he left. Again, he has not committed burglary; although he knowingly entered the home unlawfully, he had no intent to commit a crime there. Of course, his unlawful entry is not to be excused. He probably is guilty of an offense far less serious than burglary. In those states where burglary is known as "breaking and entry with intent to commit a felony," this lesser crime might be known as "simple" breaking and entry (commonly called "B & E"). That crime involves a breaking and entry with knowledge of unlawfulness, but it does not require the intent to commit a crime on the premises. In other jurisdictions, the lesser crime might be known simply as trespassing—the knowing unlawful entry onto the premises of another.[20] Both "B & E" and "trespass" are likely to be misdemeanors, while burglary would be a felony.

The Degrees Of Burglary.   Most jurisdictions divide burglary into two or more degrees. All degrees will be felonies, but only the highest degree (first degree burglary) will carry one of the higher felony punishments. Various factors are used to divide the offense into separate degrees. Burglaries committed by persons who are armed commonly are placed in the first degree category. Some jurisdictions also place in a higher category those burglaries that involve a breaking and entry into a dwelling. For this purpose, a dwelling includes any place commonly used for lodging. It does not matter that the residents are away at the time of the entry. Some jurisdictions stress the dwelling element alone without regard to whether the entry was by breaking. Others place in a higher punishment category nighttime burglaries of dwellings. They reason that such burglaries are more dangerous (the residents are more likely to be home at night), more difficult to investigate (there is less visibility), and tend to be more frightening to victims. The latter two factors probably were the primary justifications for the common law's emphasis upon nighttime burglaries. The common law accordingly distinguished between night and day according to the available sunlight. Today, the statutory provisions usually define "nighttime" as that period between sunset and sunrise (or 30 minutes after sunset to 30 minutes before sunrise).[21]

---

20.   The trespass offense protects against more than the invasion of the home. Usually, it also extends to all enclosed property and even to non-enclosed property where the owner previously has ordered the individual not to enter. The unlawful entry into the home usually is treated as a more serious crime than those other forms of trespass.

21.   One of the more complicated divisions of burglary in separate degrees is that provided in New York Penal Law. It defines in ascending order three degrees of burglary:

§140.20: A person is guilty of burglary in the third degree when he knowingly enters or remains unlawfully in a building with intent to commit a crime therein. Burglary in the third degree is a Class D felony.

§140.25: A person is guilty of burglary in the second degree when he knowingly enters or remains unlawfully in a building with intent to commit a crime therein, and when:

1.   In effecting entry or while in the building or in immediate flight therefrom, he or another participant in the crime:

Burglary and Another Offense Committed at the Same Time.   In most states, an offender can be held guilty of both the offense of burglary and any other offense he commits after entry. Let us suppose the offender breaks and enters a house intending to steal a $5.00 ring that he particularly wants. *Circumstance 1.* He steals the $5.00 ring. He is guilty of both burglary and misdemeanor theft. *Circumstance 2.* He steals a $600.00 ring in place of, or in addition to, the $5.00 ring. He is guilty of burglary and felony theft. *Circumstance 3.* He doesn't steal anything, but he finds a woman in the house and rapes her. He is guilty of both burglary and rape. The offender can, and will be charged not only with the burglary, but with the offense actually committed, and he can be sentenced to a term in prison for each offense.

The Model Penal Code proposed a change in this rule by providing that a person may not be convicted both for burglary and for the offense which it was his purpose to commit after the burglarious entry, unless the additional offense constituted a felony of the first or second degree.[22] However most of the jurisdictions with codes based upon the Model Code have not accepted this particular recommendation.

ARSON

Elements of Arson.   At common law, arson was the unlawful burning of a dwelling house belonging to another. As in the case of burglary, contemporary statutory definitions go far beyond the behavior prohibited by the common law. Arson now includes the use of explosives as well as fire. It protects against the burning or exploding of any building, not simply dwellings. Under some circumstances, it even applies to the burning or exploding of one's own property. Finally, while the common law applied only to an intentional burning of a building, the modern provisions apply to recklessness as well. Thus, the elements of the offense today ordinarily are: (1) an intentional or reckless burning or explosion, (2) of a building owned by another person, or (3) under limited circumstances, of a building owned by the actor.

Intentional or Reckless Burning or Explosion.   Arson traditionally has been separated from other offenses involving the destruction of property because of the

---

(a) Is armed with explosives or a deadly weapon; or

(b) Causes physical injury to any person who is not a participant in the crime; or

(c) Uses or threatens the immediate use of a dangerous instrument; or

2. The building is a dwelling and the entering or remaining occurs at night.

Burglary in the second degree is a Class C felony.

§140.30: A person is guilty of burglary in the first degree when he knowingly enters or remains unlawfully in a dwelling at night with intent to commit a crime therein, and when, in effecting entry or while in the dwelling or in immediate flight therefrom, he or another participant in the crime:

1. Is armed with explosives or a deadly weapon; or

2. Causes physical injury to any person who is not a participant in the crime; or

3. Uses or threatens the immediate use of a dangerous instrument.

Burglary in the first degree is a Class B felony.

22.   MPC §221.1(2).

special dangers posed by fire. If a person intentionally destroyed part of the dwelling of another, such as by throwing a rock through a window, that conduct is punished as a misdemeanor if the damage caused is under a specified value (usually the same dollar limit applied in separating misdemeanor thefts from felony thefts).[23] On the other hand, if the same damage is caused by fire, the relevant offense is arson, which always has been viewed as a very serious felony. With the development of explosives, it followed naturally that destruction by explosives also would be included within the arson offense. In many respects, explosives pose an even greater danger than fire.

At common law, arson was limited to an intentional burning of a dwelling. If a person set a fire too close to a neighbor's house, disregarding the strong likelihood that the fire would spread, he would not be liable for arson even though the neighbor's house was destroyed by the fire. State legislatures frequently added new statutory offenses, however, that would reach such reckless destruction of property. The Model Code proposed treating the reckless damaging of property through explosion or fire as an offense within the arson grouping when the fire or explosion itself was intentionally set. [24] Many of the state codes based on the Model Code have included such reckless conduct as the lowest degree of arson.[25]

Building of Another. The property protected by the new arson statutes has been expanded from the common law in much the same manner as the property protected from burglary has been expanded. In New York, for example, the language describing the protected property is identical in the burglary and arson statutes. Both cover all buildings and "any structure, vehicle, or watercraft used for overnight lodging of persons or used by persons for carrying on business therein."[26] The various examples of included structures noted in our discussion of burglary statues would also apply to arson statutes. Most jurisdictions also have separate statutes that cover the intentional or reckless burning of personal property. There are several states, however, that bring the damaging of personal property by fire or explosion within the definition of arson.[27]

---

23. This offense was called "malicious destruction of property" under the older codes. The newer codes call it "criminal mischief." The offense commonly encompass both intentional and reckless destruction of real or personal property. See, e.g., New York Penal Law §§145.00-145.12.

24. MPC §220.1.

25. See New York Penal Law §150.05:
    1. A person is guilty of arson in the third degree when he recklessly damages a building by intentionally starting a fire or causing an explosion.
    2. In any prosecution under this section, it is an affirmative defense that no person other than the defendant had a possessory or proprietary interest in the building.
    Arson in the third degree is a class E felony.

26. New York Penal Law §150.00. See also p. 168 *supra* discussing the structures protected by burglary provisions.

27. Thus, Illinois Stat. ch. 38, §20-1 provides:
    1. A person commits arson when, by means of fire or explosive, he knowingly:
       (a) Damages any real property, or any personal property having a value of $150 or more, of another without his consent; or
       (b) With intent to defraud an insurer, damages any property or any personal property having a value of $150 or more.

Property of the Arsonist.   Under special circumstances a person exploding or burning his own property can be guilty of arson. The primary considerations are the owner's purpose and the danger posed to others. If the owner sought to destroy his property for the purpose of collecting insurance, then his use of fire or explosives would constitute arson. Because it is difficult to determine exactly what his purpose may have been, at least in those cases in which he was arrested before an insurance claim could be filed, some codes shift the burden to the owner to show that his "sole intent was to destroy or damage the building for a lawful and proper purpose." [28] Even if the owner had a legitimate purpose, however, he still may be guilty of arson if he recklessly set the fire or used the explosive in such a way as to place either other persons in danger of bodily injury or other persons' property in danger of damage. Thus, if an owner desires to raze a building located in a heavily populated area with fire or explosives, he certainly would be well advised to obtain the necessary approval of fire officials. Not only may his failure to do so be a violation of a city ordinance, but he also may find that he proceeded in such a hazardous fashion as to subject himself to serious criminal liability under the state arson statutes.

Degrees Of Arson.   The arson offense commonly is divided into two or three degrees bearing progressively higher felony-level punishment. Although the arson offense is designed to protect property, the division between the degrees usually is not based on the property damage caused by the fire or explosion. Instead, the emphasis usually is upon both the actor's mental element and the danger to persons created by the fire or explosion. Where the actor was reckless rather than purposeful in damaging the building, his conduct usually is placed in the least substantial degree of the offense. On the other hand, where the building involved was occupied, the offense is likely to be placed in the highest category (arson in the first degree). Some jurisdictions, rather than looking to actual occupancy, simply raise the level of the offense where the surrounding circumstances make it likely that a person would be in the building. When the burning was designed to defraud an insurer, that factor also may raise the level of the offense.[29]

Property "of another" means a building or other property, whether real or personal, in which a person other than the offender has an interest which the offender has no authority to defeat or impair, even though the offender may also have an interest in the building or property.

28.   Thus, New York Penal Law §150.10(2) provides: "In any prosecution under this section, it is an affirmative defense that (a) no person other than the defendant had a possessory or proprietary interest in the building, or if other persons had such interests, all of them consented to the defendant's conduct, and (b) the defendant's sole intent was to destroy or damage the building for a lawful and proper purpose, and (c) the defendant had no reasonable ground to believe that his conduct might endanger the life or safety or another person or damage another building."

29.   For further information on the crimes against property, see the authorities cited in note 75 at p. 126 *supra*. See also G. Fletcher, note 38, p. 149 *supra*, at Chapters 1 and 2; J. Hall, *Theft, Law, and Society*, Indianapolis, Ind.: Bobbs-Merrill Company, 1952, 2d ed.

Part 3

The
Criminal Justice
Process

INTRODUCTION

The criminal justice system is the system by which society first determines what
will constitute a crime and then identifies, accuses, tries, convicts, and punishes
those who have violated the criminal law. In Part Two, we considered the initial
step of establishing a substantive law of crimes. We now turn to the *criminal
justice process* through which that substantive law is applied—that is, the series
of procedures by which society identifies, accuses, tries, convicts and punishes
offenders. These procedures provide a series of stages through which the offender
passes—from investigation to arrest, to formal accusation, to determination of
guilt, to the determination of sentence, and finally to the imposition of sentence.
The chart on the following two pages presents a graphic representation of these
various stages in the criminal justice process.[1] Relying heavily on the chart, we will
present an overview of the process in the next chapter. We then will consider, in
the succeeding chapters of Part Three, each of the major stages in the process,
ending with a brief description of the alternative process provided for juveniles.

1.　Our chart is a modified version of a chart published in the President's Commission Report, *The
　　Challenge Of Crime In A Free Society*, note 11, p. 39 *supra*, at p. 8-9. Because of various changes
　　that have occurred since that chart originally was published in 1967, we have departed from the
　　original at several points.

A general view of The Criminal Justice System

This chart seeks to present a simple yet comprehensive view of the movement of cases through the criminal justice system. Procedures in individual jurisdictions may vary from the pattern shown here. The differing weights of line indicate the relative volumes of cases disposed of at various points in the system, but this is only suggestive since no nationwide data of this sort exists.

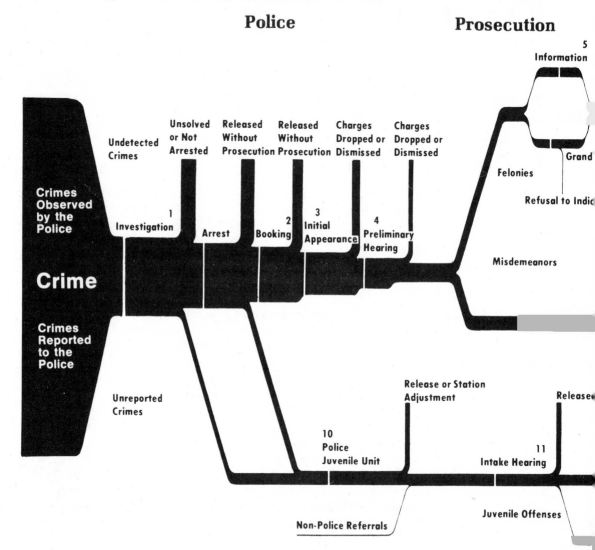

Police

Prosecution

5
Information

Undetected Crimes

Unsolved or Not Arrested

Released Without Prosecution

Released Without Prosecution

Charges Dropped or Dismissed

Charges Dropped or Dismissed

Grand

Felonies

Refusal to Indic

Crimes Observed by the Police

1 Investigation

Arrest

2 Booking

3 Initial Appearance

4 Preliminary Hearing

Misdemeanors

Crime

Crimes Reported to the Police

Unreported Crimes

Release or Station Adjustment

Release

10 Police Juvenile Unit

11 Intake Hearing

Non-Police Referrals

Juvenile Offenses

1. May continue until trial.

2. Administrative record of arrest. First step at which temporary release on bail may be available.

3. Before magistrate, commissioner, or justice of peace. Formal notice of charge, advice of rights. Bail set. Summary trials for petty offenses usually conducted here without further processing.

4. Preliminary testing of evidence against defendant. Charge may be reduced. No separate pre-

liminary hearing for misdemeanors in some systems.

5. Charge filed by prosecutor on basis of information submitted by police or citizens. Alternative to grand jury indictment.

6. Reviews whether Government evidence sufficient to justify trial. Some States have no grand jury system; others seldom use it.

Courts

Corrections

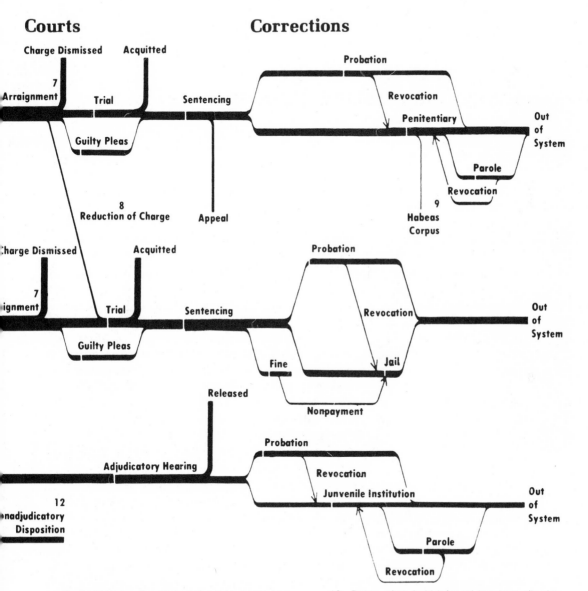

7. Appearance for plea; defendant elects trial by judge or jury (if available).

8. Charge may be reduced at any time prior to trial in return for plea of guilty or for other reasons.

9. Challenge on constitutional grounds to legality of detention. May be sought at any point in process.

10. Police often hold informal hearings, dismiss or adjust many cases without further processing.

11. Probation officer decides desirability of further court action.

12. Welfare agency, social services, counseling, medical care, etc., for cases where adjudicatory handling not needed.

Chapter 8

An Overview of the Criminal Justice Process

This chapter presents an overview of the sequence of procedures that constitute the criminal justice process. As with any overview, a certain degree of overgeneralization is inevitable. Most of the procedures will be discussed again, however, in later chapters, where various refinements are added. At this time, try to concentrate on the total picture rather than the details of the individual procedures.

Before considering our overview, you should be forewarned that there currently is no single set of criminal justice procedures uniformly used throughout the United States. Just as there is diversity among states in the definition of crime, there is diversity among states in the process used to enforce the criminal law. Indeed, there is even greater diversity in the treatment of process because procedures vary not only from state to state, but also within a single state according to the level of the offense charged. While the diversity must be taken into account, the basic sequence of procedures is so complex that it is best examined initially without regard to the many variations employed in different states. Our overview accordingly concentrates on the sequence of procedures commonly applied in most states and uses the terminology employed in most states. A few variations are noted where they are fundamental and are followed in a substantial number of states.

To assist you in following the overview, it would be helpful at the outset if you would carefully examine the chart at pages 174-175. Note that the chart follows the flow of the criminal justice process through a horizontal line which starts at the point of the commission of the crime and continues through to the convicted offender's completion of his sentence. The thickness of this horizontal line gradually narrows to indicate the decreasing number of cases involved at each succeeding stage of the process. The various lines pointing upward or downward indicate cases leaving the process. As we shall see later, the process has a "sieve effect," constantly sifting persons out of the criminal justice system before they complete all of the stages in the process. You also will note that the horizontal line eventually divides into three major prongs. The first division occurs quite early in the process and notes the beginning of the separate treatment of juveniles through the juvenile justice process. That process will be considered in Chapter Fourteen. Farther along in the flow of the criminal process, the horizontal line again divides as felonies and misdemeanors are separated. We will concentrate in our overview primarily on the processing of felonies since felonies are more serious crimes and require more complex procedures than misdemeanors. Footnotes along the way will note the key distinctions in the processing of misdemeanors.

Ongoing Procedures. Both the chart on pages 174-75 and our overview present the various procedures in the chronological order in which they tend to be used. By and large, each procedure constitutes a separate stage in the criminal justice process that follows upon the completion of a prior procedure. There are certain procedures, however, that tend to be ongoing. As the first footnote in the chart notes, investigatory procedures start at an early stage but may continue on through the time of trial. Similarly, the prosecutor's decision to go forward with a case is subject to an ongoing opportunity for review at various points throughout the overall process. The judge's review of the evidence before the jury is another step that is ongoing in the sense that it may be repeated at various points during the trial. Generally, we will discuss these ongoing procedures only at the point at which they first arise and will not consider them again at later points at which they may be repeated. Our discussion of investigatory procedures will be split, however, to consider separately pre-arrest and post-arrest investigations, since investigatory procedures may be somewhat different at these two stages of the process.

Functions Of The Process. In gaining an overview of the criminal justice process, it might be helpful to keep in mind the seven major functions that are performed by that process: (1) determining whether a crime has been committed, (2) detecting the possible offender, (3) apprehending that person, (4) providing for a review of the evidence by the prosecutor to determine whether the case against the alleged offender merits prosecution, (5) providing for a review of the prosecutor's decision by an independent agency, such as a magistrate or grand jury, (6) providing for a determination by a jury or judge as to the alleged offender's guilt, and (7) setting and administering a punishment where the alleged offender has been found guilty. Some of the steps in the criminal justice process may serve more than one of these functions, and some of the functions may be served by more than one step. Each step will be designed to perform at least one of these functions, however, and the process as a whole will perform them all.

THE STEPS IN THE PROCESSING OF A FELONY CASE

1. Commission of the Crime. Note that the flowline in our chart has its greatest thickness at the first stage, the commission of crime, and then narrows sharply at the next stage, the investigation of crime. As we already have noted, many crimes are never reported to the police, [2] and thus there are far fewer crimes investigated than committed. Where the police do learn of crime, their information usually comes, as the chart indicates, after the crime has been completed. In a limited number of situations, however, police may initiate an investigation of a crime even before it is completed. Thus, in the investigation of possible victimless crimes, as we have seen, police undercover agents may engage in various activities designed to trap the potential offender when he eventually does violate the law.[3]

2. Pre-arrest Investigation.

Once the police receive information relating to a possible crime, they then must determine (1) whether the crime actually was committed and (2), if it was committed, whether there is sufficient information pointing to the guilt of a particular person to justify arresting that person. The pre-arrest investigation is aimed primarily at making these determinations. The degree of investigation needed will, of course, vary with the circumstances. Where the officer observed a crime being committed in his presence, he usually can make an arrest "on the spot." In this situation, the pre-arrest investigation will have consisted of no more than the officer's initial observation. If the officer observes suspicious activity, but is uncertain as to exactly what has occurred, he may stop the suspect on the street and briefly question him before deciding whether to make an arrest. In this type of case, the pre-arrest investigation will have consisted of the officer's observations, some interrogation (i.e., questioning), and possibly a limited search to ensure that the suspect is not carrying a weapon.

Where the officer does not observe the commission of the crime, the pre-arrest investigation often is more complex. Initially, the officer will obtain a statement from the victim and any bystanders. Any physical evidence left at the scene of the crime may be removed and examined, sometimes by the police laboratory. Potential suspects may be visited at their homes or stopped on the street and questioned. If a suspect makes a statement, it may be verified through interviews with other persons, such as employers or friends. If the officer has reason to believe that evidence of the crime can be found in a particular location, a search of that location may be conducted (usually pursuant to a court order). In unusual cases, the police may place a suspect under surveillance or utilize the services of an undercover agent to obtain information from the suspect. In other cases, a wiretap or other form of electronic surveillance will be instituted pursuant to a court order. In still others, the officer may be required to examine documents or records obtained through the issuance of a court order.[4]

---

2. See p. 81 *supra.*

3. See p. 123 *supra.*

4. In a small percentage of cases, the pre-arrest investigation may be conducted by the prosecuting attorney rather than the police. The prosecuting attorney's primary means of investigation is the grand jury. While the most noted function of the grand jury is to review the sufficiency of the evidence supporting a criminal charge (see step 11 described *infra*), it also has authority to obtain information concerning possible criminal activities. Through the use of a subpoena (a court order issued on behalf of the grand jury), the prosecutor can compel potential witnesses to testify before the grand jury or present documents to the grand jury. This authority makes the grand jury an especially effective investigative agency in complicated cases requiring examination of countless documents and in cases involving witnesses who are uncooperative with police. Thus grand juries often are used to investigate such crimes as consumer fraud, antitrust violations, loan-sharking and political corruption.

Among the various pre-arrest investigatory procedures noted above, the most common procedures are the observation by the officer, the questioning of witnesses, and the questioning of the suspect. Even in serious felony cases, procedures such as the search of the suspect's home, wiretapping, surveillance, and scientific examination of evidence are used in only a small percentage of the investigations.

3. The Arrest. The term *arrest* has various definitions, and discussions of police practices often are confused by the failure of the discussants to agree on the meaning of that term. For the purpose of this overview, we will use a common statutory definition of "arrest"—the taking of a person into custody for the purpose of charging him with a crime. This ordinarily involves the officer's exercise of physical control over the suspect for the purpose of first transporting him to a police facility and then requesting that felony charges be filed against him.[5] Where there is no immediate need to arrest a suspect, an officer might first seek a court order, commonly called an *arrest warrant,* which authorizes the officer to make the arrest. The arrest warrant is issued by a magistrate and offers the advantage of prior judicial approval of the arrest. In the vast majority of felony cases, however, the officer will act without a warrant and will make the arrest as soon as he is convinced that he has sufficient grounds to lawfully do so. The arrest made without a court order commonly is described as a "warrantless" arrest.

Typically, contemporaneously with the arrest, the officer will search the arrestee and remove any weapons, contraband, or evidence of the crime found on his person. The arrestee then will be transported to a police precinct station, a centrally located jail, or some similar police "holding" facility. If the officer should determine, however, that the arrestee is young enough to be a juvenile under state law, he will take the arrestee directly to a juvenile facility. The description of the process from this point on assumes that the arrestee is not a juvenile. (If a juvenile arrestee is mistakenly treated as an adult and taken to the police facility, he will be transferred to a juvenile facility as soon as his true age is discovered).

4. Booking. Once the arrestee arrives at the police facility, he will be *booked.* Booking is the clerical process by which an administrative record is made of the arrest. The arrestee's name, time of arrival, and the offense involved are listed on the police "blotter" or "log" as an official record of the arrest. As part of the booking process, the arrestee ordinarily will be photographed and his fingerprints will be taken. If the means are available, his fingerprints and name will be checked against local or state-wide records to see if he is wanted for another crime. In some places, this data can also be used to ascertain whether the arrestee has a prior criminal record.

While at the police facility, the arrestee typically will be given the right to make a telephone call and will be informed of the charge on which he has been booked. He then will be placed in a "holding" room, usually some form of cell, while awaiting his presentation before a magistrate. In most places, the arrestee

---

5. In the case of a misdemeanor, the arrested person may not be transported to the police facility, but may simply be released on the street after the officer has given him a citation (similar to a traffic ticket) directing that he appear in court on a certain day.

will be searched before being placed in the "holding" room. Ordinarily this search will be more thorough than the search conducted by the officer contemporaneously with the arrest. This second search is designed primarily to make an inventory of the individual's personal belongings and to prevent the introduction of contraband into the holding area.

5. *Post-arrest Investigation.*   The timing and degree of the post-arrest investigation will vary with the fact situation. In some cases, such as where the arrestee has been caught "red-handed," there will be little post-arrest investigation. In other situations, the post-arrest investigation will involve many of the same kinds of investigative activities as could have been performed before the arrest, such as witness interviews, search of the suspect's home, viewing the scene of the crime, etc. Where the officer has sufficient grounds to justify an arrest without the evidence that might be obtained through such investigative techniques, he may use those techniques at his convenience, either before or after the arrest.

Post-arrest investigation does offer one investigative source that ordinarily is not available prior to the arrest—the person of the arrestee (who is now in custody). Thus the arrestee may be placed in a lineup where he can be viewed by witnesses, or he may be required to provide handwriting or voice samples. The arrestee also may be interrogated after having been warned of his rights. Ordinarily, investigative procedures of this type will be initiated after the arrestee is booked, although the timing will vary with the particular situation.

6. *The Decision to Charge.*   Sometime between the booking of the arrestee and his presentation before a magistrate (see step 9), there will be a review of the decision to press charges, first by the police and then by the prosecutor.[6] The review procedure varies considerably from jurisdiction to jurisdiction, both as to the participants involved and the standards they apply. Ordinarily, it starts with an arrest report that will be filled out by the arresting officer. In some places, that report must be completed before the arrestee is booked, while others simply require that it be prepared before the officer completes his shift for that day. The report will contain a narrative account of the crime and the circumstances of the arrest. It ordinarily will include a brief description of all evidence then available (e.g., witnesses, seized contraband). A higher ranking officer, such as a "desk sergeant" or precinct duty officer, then will review the report to decide whether the case should be approved for prosecution. In many instances, this officer may reduce a recommended felony charge to a misdemeanor charge or direct that the arrestee be released. The arrestee's release may be ordered because the evidence is insufficient to support a criminal charge or because the police department has a policy against pressing charges under the special circumstances of the case (e.g., an intrafamily assault). When the arrestee is released because the available evidence is insufficient, there may be a follow-up investigation and the individual may later be rearrested.

---

6.   In those cases where the arrest is made pursuant to an arrest warrant, the case often will be reviewed prior to the issuance of the warrant and a subsequent review will be unnecessary. We assume from this point on that the arrest in the case we are following was made without a warrant.

Assuming that the higher ranking officer has approved the charge, the next step in the review process is the presentation of the case to the prosecutor's office. In some jurisdictions, a prosecuting attorney commonly does not review the case until after the arrestee's initial appearance before a magistrate. In those jurisdictions, the complaint (see step 7) will be prepared and filed by the police without the prior approval of the prosecutor. In most jurisdictions, the prosecutor will review the case before the arrestee's initial appearance. The information considered by the prosecuting attorney will vary according to local practice. In some areas, the prosecutor's decision ordinarily is based solely on the police report. In others, the prosecuting attorney also will interview the arresting officer, the victim, or some other eyewitness.

The prosecuting attorney must decide whether the arrestee should be charged and, if so, whether the charge should be that recommended by the police. Of course, the prosecutor must consider the strength of the evidence. If it is not sufficient to support the charge, then the arrestee must be released or the charges reduced to meet the evidence. The prosecutor also may consider various other factors besides the weight of the evidence, such as the amount of harm caused by the crime, the victim's attitude, the criminal record of the arrestee, and the adequacy of any alternative remedies that may be utilized without invoking the criminal process (e.g., reimbursing the victim). This broad grouping of factors is considered because the prosecutor has responsibilities beyond avoiding the prosecution of the innocent. Even though the individual clearly is guilty and that guilt can be proven, the prosecuting attorney may decide that the prosecution recommended by the police would not serve the ends of justice. He may conclude that it would be more appropriate to charge a lesser offense, or even to dismiss the prosecution on condition that alternative remedies are undertaken.

7. *Filing the Complaint.* Assuming the prosecutor decides to proceed, the next step is the formal initiation of criminal prosecution through the filing of a "charging" document before a court. A charging document accuses the arrestee of committing a crime, and its filing officially makes him a "defendant" in a criminal case. The most common titles for the charging documents used in the criminal law are the "complaint," the "information," and the "indictment." Although they differ in other respects, each of thse documents will contain a statement charging the accused person with the commission of one or more specified crimes.

In most felony cases, the initial charging document is the *complaint*, which will be filed with the magistrate court prior to the arrested person's initial appearance (see step 9). At later stages in the process, an indictment or information will replace the complaint as the charging document.[7] The complaint ordinarily will set forth facts alleging that the accused, at a particular time and place, committed specified acts that constitute a violation of a particular criminal statute. The complaint must be signed by a "complainant," a person who swears under oath that he believes the facts alleged in the complaint to be true. Ordinarily, the

---

7.   In misdemeanor cases which are tried before the magistrate, the complaint ordinarily is the only charging instrument used in the case. The substitution of an indictment or information for the complaint only occurs when a case is taken before the general trial court, as in a felony cases. See pp. 36-37, 44 *supra*.

complainant will be either the victim of the crime or the investigating officer. The prosecuting attorney, in the course of reviewing the decision to charge, will make certain that the complaint is properly prepared. Once the complaint is completed and approved, it is filed with the local magistrate court, before which the arrestee will soon be presented.

8. *Magistrate Review of the Complaint.* Although the complaint is filed with the magistrate court, that court does not have authority to hold a trial in a felony case. Its function is only to handle several preliminary tasks before transferring the felony case to a trial court of general jurisdiction.[8] The first of these tasks is to determine whether there is a sufficient legal basis to support the arrest under which the defendant is being held in custody.[9] The magistrate is, in effect, reviewing the judgment of the police and prosecutor that the accused could properly be arrested and charged with the offense alleged in the complaint. This determination, usually made before the defendant's first appearance (see step 9), is an *ex parte* determination (that is, a determination made without the participation of the defense). The magistrate's decision ordinarily is based on facts presented in either the complaint itself, a supporting affidavit, or a brief oral statement given by the victim or arresting officer. As we shall see in later chapters, the magistrate need only find reasonable grounds (called *probable cause*) to believe that the arrestee committed the crime charged.[10] However, if the magistrate finds that the facts alleged do not meet this probable cause standard, he must dismiss the complaint and the arrestee must be released.

In some states, the magistrate will issue an arrest warrant after finding probable cause. The defendant, of course, already has been arrested (under a warrantless arrest) and the warrant is not being used here to obtain prior approval for the arrest (its traditional function). The warrant is issued in this setting simply to provide judicial authorization for continuing to hold the arrestee in custody. In other jurisdictions, a post-arrest issuance of the warrant is viewed as an unnecessary formality, and the magistrate's finding of probable cause will simply be noted in the case file.

9. *The First Appearance.* After the complaint has been filed and reviewed, the defendant is taken from the holding facility and presented before the magistrate. This first appearance of the defendant in court is the next major step in the criminal justice process. It usually is described simply as the "first appearance," but some jurisdictions refer to it as the "initial presentment" or the "arraignment on the warrant." [11] Almost all jurisdictions have a requirement that an arrested person be presented before the magistrate without unnecessary delay. In most

8. See pp. 36-37 *supra* on the nature and function of the magistrate court and the general trial court.

9. Where the arrest was made pursuant to a warrant (see note 6 *supra*), the magistrate will have made such a determination in issuing the warrant and another review of the arrest will not be required.

10. See pp. 267-69 *infra*.

11. This is to be distinguished from the later "arraignment" at the trial court stage (see step 13), where the defendant must enter a plea to the felony charge.

communities, the time consumed in booking, transportation, reviewing the decision to charge, preparing the complaint, and performing other preliminary matters will delay the first appearance for several hours. Indeed, in many places, unless the individual is arrested in the early morning hours, his case will not be ready for presentation to the magistrate until after the courts have closed for that day. If the community does not have a "night court," the arrested person will have to spend the night in jail before being presented the next morning. Moreover, if arrested on a Friday afternoon, he may spend three nights in jail, awaiting a first apearance on Monday morning, unless the magistrate court has a special weekend session.

The first appearance itself often is quite brief. Initially, the magistrate will make certain that the person before him is, in fact, the person whose name is stated in the complaint as the defendant. The magistrate then will inform the defendant of the charge set forth in the complaint. The magistrate also will inform the defendant of various rights that he has under the law. The scope of this advice varies from state to state. Ordinarily, the magistrate will at least inform the defendant of his right to remain silent and warn him that anything he says in court or to the police may be used against him at trial.

The defendant also will be told that he has a right to be assisted by counsel and that counsel will be appointed at the expense of the state if he is indigent (i.e., he cannot afford to hire an attorney). [12] Although the timing varies, most jurisdictions at least initiate the appointment process at the first appearance. The magistrate will determine if the defendant is financially eligible and desires the assistance of appointed counsel. He then will either make the appointment himself or notify the judge in charge of making such appointments. In many communities, lawyers employed by the office of the public defender will automatically represent almost all indigent defendants. They often begin that representation shortly after the indigent is arrested and thus are present when he appears before the magistrate. In those jurisdictions where the appointed counsel is selected from the "private bar" (i.e., those lawyers who are self-employed), the appointment process often is not completed until after the first appearance. The appointed lawyer will be available to the defendant, however, before the next stage in the process, the preliminary hearing on the complaint.

Perhaps the most important function performed by the magistrate at the first appearance is his determination of conditions that the defendant must meet to gain his release from custody pending his trial. [13] This function is commonly described as the *setting of bail.* Traditionally, the term "bail" referred to personal property that a defendant had to deposit with the court to obtain his release from custody. The property served as a guarantee that the defendant would appear at trial. If he failed to do so (i.e., "skipped bail"), his property would be forefeited to the state. Today, bail can take several forms. Occasionally, the individual will post

---

12. As we shall see in Chapter Eleven, this right may not apply to all misdemeanor cases.

13. In many places, persons arrested on misdemeanor charges do not have to wait for the first appearance to gain their release. They are released at the police facility if they promise to appear before the magistrate on a date set for first appearance. In some jurisdictions such release can be obtained only by posting a specified sum of money (commonly called "stationhouse bail"), as a guarantee for their appearance.

cash. More frequently, he will provide as a guarantee an "appearance bond"—that is, a promise to pay a certain amount of money if he fails to appear in court at a scheduled time. Ordinarily, in felony cases, the defendant's personal promise to pay (often called an "unsecured" bond) is not viewed as a sufficient guarantee. The bond must be secured by the promise of a licensed bail bondsman. The bondsman represents a company with sufficient assets to provide (for a fee) an acceptable guarantee that the bond will be payed if the defendant fails to appear.

10. Preliminary Hearing.   The next step in the criminal process is the preliminary hearing. The preliminary hearing is one of three independent "screening" processess that may be available in a felony case. [14] Each involves a review of the prosecution's evidence to safeguard against unwarranted prosecutions. They are described as "screening" procedures because they operate like a sieve to "screen-out" those prosecutions that lack substantial evidentiary support. The first of these screens is the magistrate's ex parte review of the complaint, described previously as step 8. The second screening is the preliminary hearing, which also is conducted by the magistrate, and the third is the grand jury's review of the evidence (see step 11). The availability of the preliminary hearing and grand jury review varies from state to state. Only about half the states regularly provide grand jury review. Many more states regularly provide a preliminary hearing.

The preliminary hearing will be held before a magistrate, often the same magistrate who presided at the first appearance. The magistrate's task at the preliminary hearing is to determine whether there is sufficient evidence supporting the charge to send the case forward to the grand jury (where a grand jury is used) or to the trial court. If the evidence is found sufficient, the case is "boundover" to the next stage; if the evidence is found insufficient, the charges are dismissed and the defendant is released from jail or from any bail restrictions. Unlike the magistrate's initial screening of the complaint prior to the first appearance, the preliminary hearing is an "adversary proceeding"—that is, both sides are represented. The defendant is there with counsel and is entitled to challenge the prosecution's evidence and introduce his own evidence. As a result, the preliminary hearing sometimes resembles a mini-trial. (It is at the preliminary hearing, not the trial, that television's Perry Mason won all of his cases). The prosecutor ordinarily will rely on live witnesses, rather than affidavits, in presenting the state's evidence. Those witnesses are then subject to cross-examination by the defense counsel, and the defense may also introduce its own witnesses.

11. Grand Jury Review.   The function of the grand jury, like that of the preliminary hearing, is to screen out those cases in which there is insufficient evidence to continue the prosecution. The standard applied by the grand jury, like that applied at the preliminary hearing, is commonly described as the *prima facie* evidence standard. We will discuss it at length in the next chapter. It is sufficient to note here that the grand jury must find more proof of guilt than the bare minimum needed for an arrest but less than is needed for a conviction at trial.

---

14.   In misdemeanor cases tried before the magistrate court, there will not be a preliminary hearing or a grand jury review. The only screening will be that performed by the magistrate prior to the first appearance (see step 8.) The case then will move directly to an arraignment on the complaint (see step 13), which commonly will be held in conjunction with the first appearance.

Although the basic standards of proof used at the preliminary hearing and grand jury review are similar, the two screening procedures are quite different in other respects. The grand jury is composed of a group of private citizens, ordinarily ranging from 16 to 23 persons, who are selected to review cases for a term of one to several months. Unlike the preliminary hearing, which is open to the public, the grand jury hears evidence in secret. Moreover, the evidence it hears is only that presented by the prosecutor. The defendant is not present and the defense has no opportunity to present evidence or cross-examine the prosecution witnesses. After the grand jury has heard the prosecutor's evidence, it receives from the prosecutor a proposed *indictment*. The indictment is the document which will replace the complaint at the trial level as the formal charging document in the case (see step 12). The grand jury votes on the proposed indictment, with the majority prevailing. If the majority concludes that there is sufficient evidence for the prosecution to proceed, the indictment is approved by the grand jury as a "true bill." If the grand jury majority concludes that the prosecution should not proceed, then the complaint must be dismissed and the defendant released from jail or from any bail restrictions.

12. *Filing of the Indictment or Information.* The case is now ready for presentation before the trial court. The first step involved is the filing of a new charging document. If the case was reviewed and approved by the grand jury, that document will be the indictment noted previously. In states where grand jury review is not required and the case moves directly from the preliminary hearing to the trial court, the charging document is signed by the prosecutor alone. It is then referred to as an *information*. The information or indictment will be similar in substance to the complaint. It will set forth the time, date, and place of the alleged criminal act as well as the nature of the act. The accusation will not be signed by the complainant, but by the prosecutor (information) or the prosecutor and the grand jury foreman (indictment). Ordinarily the offense alleged will be the same as that alleged in the complaint, but sometimes the precise charge will have been changed as a result of evidence brought out at the preliminary hearing or the grand jury review.

13. *Arraignment on the Information or Indictment.* Shortly after the information or indictment is filed with the trial court, the defendant is *arraigned* before that court. The arraignment is a brief process designed to serve two purposes: (1) to inform the defendant of the specific charge against him, and (2) to permit him to answer that charge by pleading not guilty, guilty, or *nolo contendere* (no-contest). At the arraignment the court will first read the information or indictment to the defendant and then ask him how he pleads. The defendant, ordinarily attended by his counsel, will then enter his plea. If defendant pleads not guilty, the case is set for trial. If the defendant pleads guilty or no-contest, the case is then set for sentence. The no-contest plea largely has the impact of a guilty plea, but does not require the defendant to admit his guilt.

Although the trial is, in many respects, the high point of the criminal justice system, most of the cases reaching the trial court will be disposed of by a guilty plea rather than a trial. Many of those guilty pleas, as we shall see later, are a product of a negotiated agreement between prosecutor and defense under which the defendant receives some concessions in response to his guilty plea. This process of negotiation is commonly called *plea-bargaining* and the resulting guilty pleas are commonly described as *negotiated pleas*.

14. Pre-trial Procedures. Assuming that the defendant pleads not guilty at the arraignment, there are a series of procedures that may then be utilized prior to the scheduled trial. Perhaps the most significant of these is the process by which each side will learn about the evidence to be presented by the other side (a process commonly described as *discovery*). Another major pretrial procedure is the defendant's presentation of various legal challenges to the prosecution. Most of these challenges are based on alleged violations of state law or the federal constitution which we will discuss in later chapters. One such challenge may be the claimed denial of a speedy trial through delay in prosecution. Another pretrial challenge may relate to certain evidence (e.g., a confession) that the prosecution intends to use but the defense believes to be inadmissible. The pretrial challenges are presented to the trial judge and are decided after a hearing before that judge.

15. The Trial. The trial is a fact-finding process aimed at determining whether the defendant is guilty or innocent of the offense charged. It is an adversary proceeding in which each side produces its evidence. [15] A neutral fact-finder then determines the facts and reaches a conclusion as to guilt or innocence based upon an application of the substantive criminal law to those facts. The defendant is entitled to have a jury sit as that neutral fact-finder, although he ordinarily can waive his right to a jury and have the trial judge sit as the finder of fact. In most states, juries in felony cases are composed of twelve persons. [16] After the jury has heard the evidence, the judge will explain to the jury the substantive law governing the crimes charged. The judge also will explain the jury's duty to assess the facts in accordance with the legal standard requiring proof of guilt beyond a reasonable doubt. The jury will reach its conclusions through its private deliberations. In most jurisdictions, the jury's final decision as to guilty or not-guilty (the jury's *verdict*) must be agreed upon by all of the jurors.

A jury that cannot reach a unanimous verdict is known as a *hung jury*. Where the jury "hangs," it is dismissed and the case ordinarily is retried before a new jury. In the vast majority of trials, however, the jury will reach a verdict of either guilty or not-guilty. If the jury finds the defendant not-guilty (i.e., "acquits" the defendant), the charges against the defendant are dismissed and he can never again be prosecuted on the same charge. If, on the other hand, the defendant is found guilty, he will then move to the next stage of the criminal justice process, the imposition of sentence.

---

15. While the same principle applies to misdemeanors, the trial in minor misdemeanor cases may be much less formal. In some localities, it is common procedure to have the prosecution represented by the arresting police officer rather than a prosecutor, at least where the defendant is not represented by a lawyer. See pp. 39, 43 *supra*, noting the criticisms of magistrate court practice.

16. The situation in misdemeanor cases may differ. In some jurisdictions, the defendant does not have a right to a jury trial in minor misdemeanor cases tried before a magistrate court. This is particularly true in those states utilizing magistrate courts that are not of record (see p. 38 *supra*) and providing a trial de novo before a general trial court. In those jurisdictions providing for jury trials in magistrate courts, the juries usually are composed of six persons rather than twelve.

16. Sentencing. Once guilt is determined either through a trial or acceptance of a guilty plea, the trial judge is obligated to impose a sentence in accordance with the statute under which defendant was convicted. As we saw in Chapter Five, most felony statutes will grant the judge considerable discretion in selecting a sentence. Thus, the judge often will have a choice between imposing a sentence of probation or imprisonment. If probation is used, the court must select appropriate standards of conduct (probation "conditions") which the defendant must adhere to while on probation. If imprisonment is selected, and the jurisdiction uses indeterminate sentences, the judge ordinarily will have considerable discretion in setting the maximum and minimum sentences. Where the state uses a presumptive-determinative sentencing structure, the judge is given less discretion, but he still must determine whether mitigating or aggravating factors justify a departure from the middle-range sentence for the particular crime. [17]

The procedure followed in imposing felony sentences will vary from state to state, but certain basic features are quite common. Ordinarily, sentencing will not be undertaken immediately upon a finding of guilt, but will be delayed for a week or more to permit the collection of information relevant to determining the proper sentencing. That information ordinarily will be brought together in a presentence report prepared by a probation officer. The prosecution and the defense also may call to the court's attention any information that they view as relevant to sentencing. There will not be a trial-type hearing, however. Witnesses will not be called, and the judge may consider information that would not be admissible at trial. [18]

17. Appeals and Collateral Attacks. Following the imposition of sentence, defendant may appeal his conviction. [19] In most jurisdictions, defendant is given an automatic right to have his conviction reviewed by an appellate court. Any further appellate review is discretionary, as explained in Chapter Three. [20] If the appellate court finds no substantial legal error in the trial court proceedings, the conviction will be affirmed. If it finds a substantial legal error was committed, the conviction will be reversed. Subsequent proceedings will then depend upon the basis for the reversal. If the appellate court relied on a ground establishing a total lack of authority to convict (e.g., no crime was committed), a new trial will not be permitted. On the other hand, if the reversal was based on an error that could be avoided in a new trial (e.g., an improper direction to the jury), a new trial will be permitted.

---

17. See pp. 95-96 *supra*. In misdemeanor cases, the magistrate ordinarily is given discretion to impose a flat sentence of imprisonment not to exceed a specified maximum of a certain number of days or months in jail. See note 16 at p. 92 *supra*.

18. In misdemeanor cases, there is likely to be no presentence report or separate hearing on sentencing. The judge is likely to impose sentence immediately upon a finding of guilt, although the defense will be given an opportunity to present any information it views as relevant to sentencing.

19. Unlike the defendant, the prosecutor has no right to appeal an adverse decision on the issue of guilt. If the defendant is acquitted, that ends the matter. On the other hand, if the charge is dismissed before trial on the basis of some legal error, the prosecution will be permitted to appeal that ruling in many, but not all states. See p. 324 *infra*.

20. See pp. 37-38 *supra*. In misdemeanor cases, the initial review may be in the form of a trial de novo, see p.39 *supra*. Appeals in misdemeanor cases ordinarily will be to the general trial court rather than the intermediate appellate court or state supreme court. See p. 37 *supra*.

If the defendant's appeal is unsuccessful, there may be a remaining avenue for challenging his conviction. In order to ensure full consideration of possible fundamental trial defects, the federal government and many states have provided systems for a collateral challenge to a conviction. The challenge is viewed as "collateral" because it does not flow out of the direct appellate process. Collateral challenges take many forms. The most common (and famous) is the *writ of habeas corpus*, a directive of the court to bring the prisoner forward so it can consider the validity of his continued detention. Collateral challenges may present only the most basic errors (e.g., certain constitutional defects) and in many states are limited to basic errors that could not be raised at trial or on appeal (e.g., the subsequent discovery that the prosecution knowingly used perjured testimony). All states also have additional procedures for presenting newly discovered evidence, but relief will not be provided unles it is quite clear that, if the new evidence had been presented at trial, defendant would have been acquitted.

18. *Probation and Parole Revocation.* Where the defendant's sentence is probation, there still may be an additional hearing in the criminal justice process —a probation revocation hearing. If the defendant is accused of violating probation by a probation officer, he will be arrested and presented before the sentencing court for a hearing on that charge. The hearing often will resemble a mini-trial, with the probation officer serving, in effect, as the prosecutor. Defendant may be represented by counsel, introduce evidence, and cross-examine witnesses produced by the probation officer. If the court finds that the probation conditions were violated, it may revoke the probation and send the defendant to prison.

If the defendant is imprisoned, either directly or as a result of a probation revocation, he may have two more hearings in the criminal justice process. The first would be a parole hearing, designed to determine if he should be released after having served the minimum term of an indeterminate sentence. Ordinarily, this is an informal hearing before the parole board. The hearing is not an adversary proceeding. The prisoner basically is allowed to present his arguments as to why he should be granted parole. He may or may not be told of adverse information and asked to respond. In many states, he will be allowed to bring in one or two witnesses (e.g., a future employer) to speak on his behalf. If the prisoner is granted parole, and is later charged with violating a condition of parole, he will then be granted a parole revocation hearing to determine whether he should be returned to prison. This hearing will be held before a hearing officer appointed by the parole board, but otherwise will resemble a probation revocation hearing.

19. *Final release.* Once a sentence is fully served, the defendant is finally released from the process. If he is on probation or parole, he is released form responsibility to comply with the conditions of probation or parole. If he is imprisoned, he will be released from custody. Since the determination of the release date involves no more than a calculation of time, no hearing is involved. The determination is made administratively by the probation, parole, or prison authorities (depending upon whether the defendant is on probation, on parole, or still in prison).

THE "SIEVE EFFECT"

As we have seen, the different thicknesses of the horizontal lines in the chart on pages 174-75 represent the volume of cases handled at each stage in the criminal justice process. Note that the primary line following the flow of felony cases narrows quite abruptly between crimes committed and crimes investigated (largely reflecting the fact that a substantial portion of crimes are not reported to the police). The flow line continues to narrow, though somewhat more gradually, through to the end of the process. This reflects a progressive reduction in the volume of cases as one moves from the beginning to the end of the process. More persons are investigated than are arrested, more arrested than charged, more charged than tried, and more tried than convicted. Indeed, as the flow line indicates, a substantial portion of the cases that enter the process at the point of investigation will not travel through even the first several steps in the process.

The continuous elimination of cases throughout the process reflects a basic function of the process—to operate as a sieve that progressively eliminates weaker cases until, at the end, the only persons left (at least theoretically) are those most clearly guilty and deserving of punishment. Like a sieve, the process is designed to provide a series of screens, each more refined than the one before, and each adding to the elimination of cases inappropriate for the final imposition of criminal sanctions. To illustrate the operation of this "sieve effect," the chart at the end of this chapter traces the route of 1,000 felony arrestees in a typical jurisdiction. In reviewing that chart, keep in mind the considerable diversity in the administration of the criminal justice process. The figures we use are those of a typical metropolitan county. They obviously vary considerably from those applicable to many other localities. The overall pattern, however, reflects the general movement of the criminal justice process in almost every jurisdiction.

Our chart follows 1,000 arrests covering a typical "mix" of felony offenses, ranging from murder to automobile theft. [21] We start with arrests because those statistics are most readily available. The "sieve effect" has, of course, begun before an arrest is made. To produce 1,000 arrests, there must have been a substantially greater number of crimes called to the attention of the police. Exactly how many reported crimes were involved would depend upon the mix of the offenses reported. For some felonies, the arrest rate is much lower than for others. For example, burglars are very difficult to apprehend unless they are "caught in the act." There ordinarily will be no eyewitness to the burglary. But even where the victim saw the offender, he probably will be able to furnish the police with no more

---

21. That mix will vary with the locality and the types of offenses placed within the felony category (e.g., whether possession of marijuana is considered a felony). Using statistics provided in the *Uniform Crime Reports*, the following mix would be fairly common for 1,000 felony arrests in a metropolitan county: murder and non-negligent manslaughter (10); negligent manslaughter (1); forcible rape (14); robbery (99); aggravated assault (102); burglary (188); larceny (275); motor vehicle theft (66); arson (6); forgery and counterfeiting (20); fraud (17); embezzlement (2); receiving stolen property (35); and narcotic drug violations (165). See *Uniform Crime Reports*, p. 80 *supra*, at pp. 173-175. Since our estimate is based on *Uniform Crime Report* definitions, see notes 30 and 31 at pp. 80-81 *supra*, and those definitions do not always distinguish between felonies and misdemeanors (see pp. 81-82 *supra*), we have placed fewer cases in categories such as larceny (which includes misdemeanors and felonies) than the statistics in the *Uniform Crime Reports* would suggest.

than a very general description since most burglaries are committed by non-acquaintances of the victim. As a result, 100 reported burglaries are likely to result in only 20-30 arrests. On the other hand, more than twice as many arrests will be made for 100 reported instances of aggravated assault. In those cases, unlike the burglary, the victim ordinarily has seen his assailant and quite frequently the assailant was an acquaintance he can identify by name. Moreover, police are more likely to receive prompt notification of an assault so they can arrive on the scene while the crime still is in progress or the trail of the assailant still is "warm." Assuming that our 1,000 arrests reflect a typical mix of felonies, they could be the product of 3,500-4,000 reported felony offenses.

The first major exit point in the processing of our 1,000 arrestees occurs shortly after the arrest when the juvenile arrestees are transferred to the juvenile justice system. The number of juvenile arrestees in our total group of 1,000 arrestees will vary with the state's maximum age limit for juvenile court jurisdiction and the crimes for which the arrests were made. The proportion of juvenile crime is very high for several property crimes (e.g., over 50% for motor vehicle theft) and fairly low for several crimes of violence (e.g., 12-15% for homicide, and 15-20% for serious assaults). Taking a typical mix of crimes and the typical age limitation, approximately 300 of our 1,000 arrestees (30%) will be juveniles.

Having transferred the juveniles, the criminal justice system now has 700 arrestees as it moves on to the next major step that eliminates a substantial number of cases—the review of the decision to charge, first by the police and then by the prosecuting attorney. The number of cases eliminated at this stage will vary according to the type of screening imposed by the prosecutor. Let us assume that we are in a jurisdiction where a fairly rigorous initial screening is applied. In such a jurisdiction, between the prosecutor and the police, approximately 20-30% of the remaining 700 cases would be terminated. The decision not to proceed would be based on such grounds as the lack of sufficient evidence, the victim's refusal to prosecute, the fact that other prosecutions are pending against the defendant (and no need exists for multiple prosecutions), and a determination that criminal prosecution would not be in the interest of justice (e.g., alternatives to criminal prosecution are preferred). We will assume that 25% of the cases involving adult arrestees (i.e., 175 cases) are eliminated on these grounds.

Upon reviewing the arresting officer's requested charge, the police and prosecutor also will find a substantial number of cases in which the charges should be reduced to misdemeanors. In some cases, the evidence will only support the lesser charge. In others, certain offenses classified as felonies are viewed as not sufficiently serious to merit a felony prosecution. Thus, in a state where shoplifting is a felony, the charges against the person arrested for the first time on that offense may routinely be lowered to the misdemeanor of petty theft. The percentage of cases in which charges are reduced to misdemeanors will vary with prosecution policy, but it commonly will fall in the range of 10-20% of the total group of adult felony arrestees. We will assume that in our typical jurisdiction charges are reduced for 75 of our 700 adult arrestees (approximately 11%). Deducting these 75 cases, which are transferred to misdemeanor processing, and the 175 cases that were dismissed outright, we now have left only 450 cases in which felony charges will be filed with the magistrate.

The next two major steps in the screening of cases are the preliminary hearing and, where available, grand jury review. Of course, the more rigorous the previous screening, the smaller the percentage of cases likely to be eliminated by these screening procedures. Nevertheless, even with careful pre-charge prosecutorial screening, the preliminary hearing and grand jury combined can result in the exclusion of 8-12% of the filed felony cases. Perhaps as many as half of the excluded cases will not leave the criminal justice system, however, but simply will be reduced to misdemeanors. If we assume the exclusion of 40 cases at this stage (approximately 9% of the 450 charges filed), we then have only 410 of the original 1,000 cases that even reach the general trial court.

Assuming that our jurisdiction has rigorous early screening, most of the 410 cases that arrive at the trial stage will continue through to a final determination as to innocence or guilt. Still, motions will be made to dismiss the prosecution on legal grounds, witnesses will become unavailable, and victims will have a change of heart. As a result, another 30 of our 410 cases (about 7%) will be dismissed at this point. This will leave us only 380 cases in which findings as to guilt or innocence will be made. Most of these cases will not go to trial, but will be resolved by a guilty plea. The percentage of guilty pleas varies with several factors, including local practice on plea negotiations. For most jurisdictions, the overall guilty plea percentage in felony cases is likely to range between 70 and 90 percent. We will assume there are 320 guilty pleas out of our remaining 380 cases (approximately 84%).

We now have left 60 cases in which guilt will be contested at trial. [22] Thus, the criminal trial, which often is viewed as the centerpiece of our criminal justice process, is in actuality a relatively unusual means of disposing of cases. Out of 1,000 persons arrested for felony offenses, only 6% will go to trial on a felony charge. [23] A substantial majority of these trials will produce guilty verdicts. For most major felonies, the trial conviction rate exceeds 70%. For some offenses (e.g., rape) it may be lower, but for others (e.g., larceny) it is substantially higher. The mix of the cases going to trial probably will contain a higher percentage of offenses with stronger acquittal rates than the original mix of offenses. Accordingly, the overall acquittal rate readily can reach the 30-40% range. We will assume that 20 cases (33⅓%) resulted in acquittals and the remaining 40 cases resulted in convictions.

When the 40 convictions at trial are added to the 320 guilty pleas, we have a total of 360 convictions out of the 410 cases that reached the general trial court. Note that not all of these convictions will be for the offense originally charged. The jury will have convicted on a lesser crime in some cases. Many of the guilty pleas also will have been to lesser charges. Indeed, in a large number of the guilty pleas, perhaps 15-25%, the charge may have been reduced to a misdemeanor. In addition to these misdemeanor convictions, the 1,000 felony arrests will also have

---

22. We must note again that there will be considerable variation from community to community. In Baltimore, where cases commonly are tried to a judge sitting without a jury, over 40% of the arrests may result in trials. At the other extreme, New York City probably set a record for non-trial dispositions several years ago with less than 600 felony trials for over 94,000 felony arrests.

23. Of course, some of those arrestees who had the charges against them initially reduced to misdemeanors may go to trial on the misdemeanor charge. Yet, the percentage of trials at all levels will still be less than 10%.

produced some misdemeanor convictions following charge reductions at the earlier screening stages. We will assume that 60 of our 360 trial court convictions were to misdemeanor charges and 80 of the 95 cases previously reduced to misdemeanors resulted in convictions.[24] Thus, out of 1,000 felony arrests, the total number of criminal convictions for all offenses will exceed 40 per cent—300 felony convictions and 140 misdemeanor convictions.[25] When only adult arrestees are considered (i.e., the 300 juvenile arrestees are excluded), the percentage of convictions is slightly above 60 per cent.[26]

The sentencing on the 400 convictions will vary, of course, with the seriousness of the crimes for which the convictions were obtained. In a typical jurisdiction, assuming a common mixture of offenses, approximately one-third of the defendants convicted of felonies will be sentenced to prison. This would mean approximately 100 persons imprisoned out of the initial group of 1,000 arrestees. The remaining 200 defendants convicted of felonies would receive probation. However, not all of these will escape incarceration. In many jurisdictions, about 15-20% of the probation sentences are combined with short jail sentences to be served before the defendant is released on probation. In the misdemeanor cases, a smaller portion of the convicted defendants will be incarcerated. Most simply will be fined or placed on probation, but the misdemeanor convictions could add another 20 persons who will receive short jail terms. Thus, out of the total group of 1,000 arrestees, approximately 160 persons will be sentenced to either a jail or prison term. When probation violations are added, the total percentage incarcerated could well reach 20 per cent.

ADMINISTRATION OF THE CRIMINAL JUSTICE PROCESS

An Integrated Process. The criminal justice process may be likened to an assembly line in an automobile factory (though it is not even remotely as efficient as an assembly line). The offender, like the car, is on a moving belt. As he passes from station to station, different people do different things to him until ultimately he comes out at the end of the line, a convicted man who has, hopefully, been "corrected." The man, like the car, may drop off the assembly line at many points and never get clear to the end. He may be taken off the line temporarily and then

---

24. Conviction rates in misdemeanor cases tend to be higher than in felony cases.

25. Of course, some of these convictions will be appealed and reversed, but the percentage involved is too slight to have a significant bearing on the overall pattern. Approximately 10-15% of the convictions (mostly the convictions in cases that were tried) will be appealed and approximately 15-20% of the appealed cases will be reversed. Some of the cases reversed will be retried and result in second convictions. Thus, the conviction rate is unlikely to be altered by more than 1 or 2% by the appellate process.

26. The available statistics suggest that this percentage is somewhat higher than that achieved by the criminal justice system in our largest cities. See, e.g., D. McIntyre and D. Lippman, *Prosecutors and Early Disposition of Felony Cases*, 56 American Bar Association Journal 1154, 1156 (1970). The best available study, the Vera Institute's, *Felony Arrests: Their Prosecution and Disposition In New York City's Courts*, New York, 1977 reported a conviction rate of 56% for felony arrests, but only slightly more than ¼ of those convictions were on felony charges. In communities where the process is not quite as overloaded (see p. 198 *infra*), the proportion of felony convictions is likely to be higher.

be put back on it. He may get entirely through the line, but by committing a new offense, flunk the final inspection. So he is "called back by the factory," taken out of circulation, and started again through the line.

Looking at the criminal justice process as similar to an assembly line, we immediately see that it is an integrated process. Like the assembly line, it is composed of a series of interlocking parts, each having an impact upon the other. Each stage of the process builds upon what was done at earlier stages, and the activity at the earlier stages is shaped in anticipation of what will occur at the later stages.

Illustrations of the integrated nature of the criminal justice process can be found throughout the everyday administration of the process. Unfortunately, perhaps the most dramatic illustrations are some near breakdowns that have been caused by a lack of overall planning when changes have been instituted in the process. To return to our assembly line analogy, if the line is changed at one point, with new items added or old ones eliminated, accommodations also must be made at other points in the process. Without corresponding changes at various points on the line, a slowdown or speedup at any one point will create a pile up of cars at an earlier or later stage. Too often, this lesson of the assembly line appears to have been forgotten in the administration of the criminal process. Let us consider a few examples.

The Supreme Court in its decision in *Gideon v. Wainwright*[27] in 1963 decreed that the right to be represented by a lawyer at a felony trial is a constitutional right. As a result, over 4,000 inmates of the Florida prison system had to be re-tried. The impact of this decision quite naturally was felt by prosecutors, judges, and defense counsel, who participate in the trial of cases. Yet it also was felt by other administrators far removed from the trial stage. About 2,000 of the inmates were not re-convicted and were set free. Florida had empty beds in its prisons for the first time in many years, and abandoned plans for constructing a new penal institution. However, county jails overflowed as prisoners awaiting new trials were brought to those jails. Moreover, no money was provided for moving and guarding these prisoners. The relationship between county and state officials reached a new low.

When the new Bail Reform Act was introduced in the District of Columbia and more defendants were able to obtain their pretrial release, the percentage of guilty pleas declined dramatically. With more trials scheduled, the average time lapse between arrest and trial increased, and the District soon faced a serious speedy trial problem. This consequence of bail reform was not unique. Experience shows that almost every new requirement introduced at any point in the criminal justice system is likely to cause some delay unless appropriate accommodations are made. If "warnings" must be given and a lawyer must be present at a lineup, the processing of the arrestee before his initial appearance takes longer. If additional questions must be asked of prospective jurors, the jury selection process slows down. If pre-sentence reports are mandatory, additional time elapses between conviction and sentence.

---

27. *Gideon v. Wainwright*, 372 U.S. 335 83S.Ct.792, 9L.Ed.2d799 (1963). See p. 278 *infra*.

To maximize the efficiency of any integrated process, whether an assembly line or the criminal justice process, the administration of the different parts of the process must be coordinated. Decisions made at any one stage of the process must take into consideration the impact upon other stages. There also must be an overall goal that will foster a consistent approach to the process as a whole. This type of coordination can be provided rather easily in an assembly plant. Achieving coordination in the administration of the criminal justice system, however, is quite a different matter. Various special features of the criminal justice system make it very difficult, if not impossible, to achieve the kind of coordination we expect in other integrated processes. Perhaps the most prominent of these features are: (1) the significant role that discretion plays in the administration of the process; (2) the division of administrative responsibility among five different professional groups (police, prosecutors, defense counsel, judges, and corrections officials); (3) the division of authority of each professional group among numerous government agencies; and (4) the extremely heavy caseloads handled throughout the system. Illustrations of the impact of these factors upon individual procedures are noted at various points throughout this book. Part Four, in particular, explores the various consequences of the divisions among the five professional groups. At this point, we intend to present no more than an overview of the general administrative difficulties caused by these factors. This overview is in many respects as significant as the overview of the legal structure of the process presented in the first part of this chapter. To fully understand a legal system, one cannot look to the law alone. Consideration also must be given to the people involved in applying it and the practical pressures under which they work.

Discretionary Authority.   It is sometimes assumed that the administration of the criminal justice process should be fairly uniform because of the dominant role that law plays in governing the process. Detailed legal regulations, specifying what must be done and how it must be done, undoubtedly contribute to a consistent, coordinated administration. However, the criminal justice process really is not subject to this type of legal regulation. Many aspects of the process are governed by detailed legal rules, but many others are left largely to the discretion of the individual official. For example, the law tells police when they may make an arrest and how they can make it, but it ordinarily does not require them to make an arrest simply because they have the legal authority to do so. The police have discretion to refuse to arrest when they feel an alternative course of action would more appropriately serve the interests of justice. Thus, police might take the position that intrafamily assaults are best handled by mediation rather than arresting the spouse who struck the first blow. Police also have discretion to determine how they will allocate their scarce investigative resources. They may, for example, choose to ignore prostitution so long as the prostitutes stay within the "red light" district of the city. Since the law leaves decisions of this type to the discretion of the police, the other professionals in the criminal justice system must be prepared to react to a full or partial exercise of police authority as the police see fit to exercise that authority. Thus, if the police decide to "crack down" on prostitutes and produce a substantial increase in arrests, other professionals adversely affected, such as the local prosecutor and jailer, may use their influence to gain police consideration of their problems, but they cannot rely on the law to force the police to change that policy to accommodate their concerns.

Broad discretionary power is not limited to the police, but extends to all of the professionals involved in the administration of the criminal justice process. The prosecutor has discretion to decide not to charge an arrested offender or to charge at a lower level than the maximum permitted by law. In many jurisdictions where larceny from a building is a felony, prosecutors commonly charge shoplifters with the lesser offense of petty larceny if the property taken is under a certain value. If a prosecutor changed his mind and decided to fully enforce the offense as a felony, that decision would have a substantial impact upon the trial courts and magistrate courts, but they would be forced to accept the decision since it would be within the prosecutor's discretionary power. Of course, judges often are given almost equally broad discretionary authority (as in sentencing) that has a direct impact upon the police, prosecutor, and corrections. Moreover, while the discretionary decisions of the other professions are subject to the control of the heads of their agencies (e.g., the chief of police), judicial discretion often is exercised by the individual judge with no higher-court control. In the corrections field, the parole board is still another agency having substantial discretionary authority that affects the operations of other participants in the administration of the process.

Division Among Professional Groups. Each of the five major professional groups participating in the criminal justice system—police, prosecutors, defense attorneys, judges, and corrections officials—has its own separate tasks to perform and, as we have seen, considerable discretion in performing those tasks. Most often, the different professionals have made little effort to coordinate their activities with those of the other professionals. Indeed, some commentators maintain that we have more than a mere lack of coordination; they maintain that the system is plagued by purposeful conflicts largely produced by rivalries among the different professional groups. Such purposeful conflicts obviously do exist in some communities on a fairly regular basis and in others in occasional cases, but in most communities, administrative inconsistencies probably are unintentional. There is no doubt, however, that lack of coordination, whether intentional or unintentional, presents a serious problem. It is, however, almost inherent in the nature of the division among the professions.

No matter what process is involved, the division of responsibility among different professional groups will almost automatically present some difficulties in achieving a coordinated administration. Different professionals will have different perspectives that naturally lead them in different directions. In many cases, the technical languages of their professionals also may create a communications gap. To return to our assembly line analogy, the different professionals concerned with the operation of the line (engineers, cost accountants, labor relations experts, and others) will almost certainly want to institute techniques and standards that are in partial conflict. Nevertheless, their efforts will be coordinated because they all have the same ultimate goal of corporate success and they all are subject through a chain of command to a central, final decision-maker, the manager of the plant. The criminal justice system has neither of these advantages. The goals of the participants differ and there is no central authority.

The diversity in the roles of the different professionals naturally produces a diversity in their immediate and long range goals. As we shall see in the next chapter, the criminal justice process is based on the assumption that two of the participants, the prosecutor and defense counsel, will be adversaries. Their roles certainly do not encourage cooperation or coordination. The judges, as neutral decision-makers, also are given a role that requires a largely independent exercise of authority. The police, prosecutor, and, perhaps, corrections official, may be seen as having roles that are more readily synchronized. Yet each has a task that gives him a somewhat different perspective. Police see crime, so to speak, "in the raw." Unlike the corrections officer, they see the victim as well as the offender. Unlike the prosecutor, they see the crime as committed in the street rather than as reported in the law office or courtroom. The prosecutor approaches the case as a lawyer (and, in most localities, as an elected official). This gives him a special responsibility to the judicial system[28] and a special perspective not shared by police or corrections officials. The corrections officer, in turn, tends to be more concerned with the offender than with the crime. He naturally will place more emphasis on rehabilitation and less on deterrence than will either the police or the prosecutor. [29]

The separate roles of the different professionals are reflected in each group's largely independent authority. The police are responsible for investigation and apprehension, the prosecutor for prosecution, the defense counsel for representation of the accused, the court for adjudication of guilt or innocence and the assessment of sentence, and the corrections officer for the administration of that sentence. The court's authority to adjudicate does give it some control over the other groups, but that control is limited in scope. The courts may make determinations as to the legality of the operations of the other professionals, and, in making those determinations, the courts may require the other professionals to desist from engaging in illegal operations or may deny them benefits obtained from such operations. However, the courts may exercise their authority only in the context of deciding cases which have been brought before them. Courts do not and may not reach out and regulate those daily operations of police, prosecutors, defense attorneys or corrections officials that are not challenged in the course of a legal dispute. Neither can courts control, even in the context of litigation, the other professionals' exercise of discretion in those areas where the law grants them that authority.

---

28. See pp. 432-33 *infra* discussing the role of the prosecutor as an officer of the court.

29. Very frequently, a lack of understanding leads the different professions to hold the others in low regard. This is less true as between prosecutors, defense counsel, and judges, who are all lawyers, have a similar training, and focus on judicial operations. The sharpest criticisms tend to arise between the police, the lawyers, and the corrections officials. Thus, defense laywers complain that police often seek to "get their man" at any cost, ignoring the basic rights of individuals. Prosecutors and judges criticize police for their failure to properly prepare cases in light of legal requirements. Police, in turn, often complain that cases really are lost because: (1) prosecutors are primarily interested in using their position as a stepping stone to higher political office or to lucrative private practices; (2) defense attorneys too often lack ethics; and (3) judges impose standards more appropriate for a "dream world," removed from reality and unresponsive to public demand. The lawyers and the police both commonly disparage the efforts of corrections, claiming that available corrections alternatives usually are ineffective. Indeed, some argue that corrections, rather than combating the increase in crime, actually contributes to it. Corrections officials, in turn, claim that they receive little cooperation from the other professions and frequently are hampered by arbitrary charging and sentencing policies of prosecutors and judges.

Governmental Divisions. Responsibility for administrating the criminal justice system not only is divided among five separate professions, but the responsibility of each professional group is further divided among a multitude of separate governmental agencies. [30] Initially, there is the division among fifty-one separate jurisdictions (i.e., each of the fifty states and the federal government). Each of these jurisdictions has its own police, prosecutor, public defender, judicial and corrections agencies. [31] Added to this initial division is the further division of authority among a variety of agencies at the state, county, municipal, and even township levels. The degree of fragmentation varies with the particular jurisdiction, but a 1974 survey found no state with less than seventy separate agencies involved in the administration of the criminal justice process. Indeed, a majority of the states had over 1,000 separate criminal justice agencies. [32]

The most fragmented component of the criminal justice system, at least when measured by the number of agencies involved, clearly is the police. In most states, we have separate police departments at the local government level (i.e., the city or township police department), at the county level (i.e., the sheriff's department) and at the state level (i.e., state police or state highway patrol). In addition, there may be specialized agencies assigned to enforce certain laws (e.g., a state narcotics bureau) or special geographical areas (e.g., park police). Prosecutorial authority tends to be more concentrated. The key official is the county prosecutor or district attorney, but many jurisdictions also grant the state attorney general and the city attorneys authority to prosecute for a limited range of offenses. [33] Public defender agencies often are located at both the state and county level. Judicial authority, as we have seen in Chapter Three, is divided among magistrate courts, general trial courts, and appellate courts. In many jurisdictions, different types of magistrate courts will exist in different parts of the state. [34] In the area of corrections, authority again is divided between local, county, and state agencies. The jail usually will be operated by a city or a county agency. The prisons will be operated by the state. Probation officers often are county employees, while parole officers are state employees.

In recent years, efforts have been made—primarily by consolidating smaller units and giving state agencies more supervisory authority—to obtain greater coordination and uniformity of operations among the different governmental agencies performing in each professional field. As we shall see in Part Four, these

---

30. For a detailed description of the various agencies, see Chapters 15 to 17. At this point we are concentrating on the general pattern of distribution of agencies, but those chapters note various important exceptions to that pattern, such as the concentration of all prosecution authority in the Attorney General's office in several states and the concentration of corrections in a single agency in others.

31. Since we are concerned here with the variety of governmental agencies, we deal only with public defender systems and not with other methods of providing for defense counsel. Of course, when private counsel is added to the public defenders office, the defense counsel profession obviously is spread over more independent units, though not all governmental units, than any of the other professions in the criminal justice system.

32. *Sourcebook of Criminal Justice Statistics—1976*, note 1, p. 1 *supra*, at pp. 38-39.

33. City attorneys commonly are limited to the prosecution of ordinance violations. See p. 59 *supra*. On the authority of state attorneys general, see pp. 426-27 *infra*.

34. See, e.g., note 17 at p. 43 *supra*.

efforts have been very successful with judicial and corrections agencies, but largely unsuccessful with police agencies. The primary obstacles to consolidating departments or increasing state supervisory authority have been: (1) the difficulties involved in gaining agreement among different governments as to the appropriate division of funding responsibilities; (2) partisan political objections to consolidations that favor elected officials of opposing parties; (3) desire for local control of the criminal justice process; and (4) at least with regard to the police, opposition to centralized authority as posing an inherent threat to political liberties. With respect to the police, and perhaps prosecutors as well, these obstacles appear insurmountable, and the inefficiency and inconsistency that results from the division of authority among a multitude of government agencies is likely to remain a persistent problem of criminal justice administration.

An Overloaded System.   Probably no factor has a greater bearing on the quality of the administration of criminal justice than the extra-ordinarily heavy caseloads borne by the vast majority of agencies administering the criminal justice process. As Professor Francis Allen has observed: "The American system of criminal justice is confronted by quantitative demands that exceed the capacities of its resources and procedures. The administration of criminal justice groans under a stifling and increasing weight of numbers—numbers of offenses, of accused persons, and of convicted offenders." [35] Of course, caseload size varies considerably from one jurisdiction to another, and from one agency to another within a jurisdiction, but there are few jurisdictions where caseloads generally do not exceed the maximum that experts view as compatible with ensuring professional standards of performance.

The caseload of the typical trial court provides a good illustration of the excessive quantitative demands placed upon criminal justice agencies. In most metropolitan areas, the felony caseload per individual judge falls within the range of 100-200 cases per year. At first glance, one might assume that a court could easily accommodate a median caseload of 150 criminal cases each year. Assuming approximately 230 potential trial days each year (i.e., excluding vacations, weekends, and holidays), a court could easily dispose of 150 criminal trials since most criminal trials do not last longer than a day. We cannot forget, however, that the criminal trial is only part of the court's responsibility. Frequently, pretrial and post-trial matters (e.g., hearings on pretrial motions and sentencing) will occupy as much of the court's time as the trial itself. Neither can we forget that the criminal docket itself is only a part of the judge's responsibility. Along with 150 criminal cases, the judge is likely to have three times that number of civil cases. With a combined criminal and civil caseload of 600 cases per judge, it becomes impossible for the court to keep its docket current if there is to be a trial in each case. The vast majority of the cases must be disposed of without trial—usually by settlements in civil cases and negotiated pleas in criminal cases.

Though heavy, the caseloads borne by the general trial courts usually are not the worst in the criminal justice system. Magistrates commonly bear a heavier burden. Individual magistrates have been known to dispose of more than 3,000

---

35. F. Allen, *Central Problems of American Criminal Justice*, 75 Michigan Law Review 813, 818 (1977).

non-traffic misdemeanor cases per year, averaging no more than 15 minutes per case. Police departments, which have a variety of time-consuming responsibilities besides the investigation of crime (e.g., traffic control), commonly face annual investigative caseloads in excess of 100 reported crimes for each officer employed. Probation officers often have been known to have such extensive caseloads that they can average little more than 15 minutes per month for each person under their supervision. At the same time, they often are required to prepare extensive presentence investigative reports to assist the court in sentencing. In prisons, overcrowding has reached the point where courts have been required to halt the addition of prisoners until living conditions are improved.

Heavy caseloads have had an impact on almost every facet of the criminal justice system. Perhaps the most obvious impact has been the increased reliance upon procedures for disposing of cases without trial. As we have seen, in most jurisdictions today, the vast majority of felony cases are disposed of by negotiated pleas of guilty. Even so, prosecutors frequently have been forced to make substantial adjustments in order to handle adequately those major felonies that do go to trial. To conserve manpower for such cases, some prosecutors simply have refused to prosecute minor crimes that they would otherwise have prosecuted. In many jurisdictions, prosecutors proceed without adequate preparation in the less serious cases. The police often follow similar policies designed to concentrate manpower on more serious problems. In many places, only a small group of officers are assigned to seeking out the large numbers of persons who have "skipped bail" on minor offenses. In the corrections field, parole boards have been forced to consider space limitations and limited supervisory resources in making parole decisions.

Notwithstanding the undesirable pressure imposed upon all aspects of the criminal justice system, heavy caseloads are likely to remain a primary feature of the system for some time. In large part, the heavy caseloads have been produced by government's inability to add personnel commensurate with the increase in crime. The primary factor preventing more substantial increases in personnel, particularly in police, prosecutor, public defender, and corrections positions, has been a lack of financing. The criminal justice system has had to compete for public funds with schools, hospitals, public health and the building of highways. By and large, these areas of expenditure have received greater support. The general legislative preference has been for projects that might change the social and economic environment that contributes to the production of crime rather than the criminal justice process, which has the more limited goal of controlling crime by apprehending and processing violators. It is unlikely that state and local governments, which furnish the primary funding for the criminal justice system, will dramatically shift their priorities in the immediate future.[36]

---

36. Helpful descriptions of the criminal justice process are included in D. McIntyre, H. Goldstein, and D. Skoler, *Criminal Justice in The United States*, Chicago, Ill.: American Bar Foundation, 1974; J. Poulous, *The Anatomy Of Criminal Justice*, Mineola, N.Y.: Foundation Press, 1976; D. Neubauer, *Criminal Justice In Middle America*, Morristown, N.J.: General Learning Press, 1974. The "sieve effect" is discussed from a different perspective in A. Blumberg, *Criminal Justice*, Chicago, Ill.: Quadrangle Books, 1967. Problems presented in achieving coordination in the administration of the criminal justice system are discussed in D. Skoler, *Organizing The Non-System*, Lexington, Mass.: Lexington Books, 1977.

The Sieve Effect—Disposition of 1,000 Felony Arrests

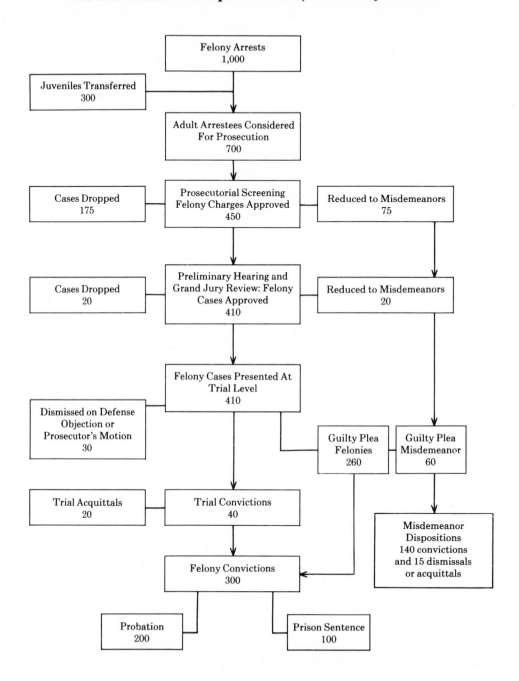

Chapter 9

Some Basic Concepts
of the Criminal Justice Process

In this chapter we will consider some basic premises that provide the theoretical foundation for the criminal justice process. These premises are: (1) that the process utilize an adversary system of decision-making, (2) that the process be accusatorial, with the burden on the state to persuade the decision-maker of the defendant's guilt, (3) that the process impose a series of screening stages with the state required to meet a progressively higher burden of proof at each stage, and (4) that the process guarantee to the defense various rights designed to ensure fairness and recognition of the dignity of the individual. Most of the specific legal rules discussed in the remaining chapters of Part Three follow from these premises.

THE ADVERSARY SYSTEM

Developments and Theory. The Anglo-American system of law is an adversary system. It is, in other words, a system which arrives at a decision by (1) having each side to a dispute present its best case and (2) then permitting a neutral decision-maker to determine the facts and apply the law in light of the opposing presentations of the two sides. In the criminal case, the opposing parties are the state, representing the victim and the general public, and the defendant. Their legal representatives are the prosecuting attorney and the defense attorney. The neutral finder of fact is usually the jury and the neutral finder of law is the judge, although the judge also will serve as the fact-finder when the jury is waived.

The adversary system developed as England moved from a rural to a more urbanized society. When the jury system was initially established in eleventh century England, jurors were persons who were likely to know the facts of a dispute, and they were directed to decide disputes based on their first-hand knowledge. As English society became more urbanized, it was no longer possible to assume that the jurors themselves would have knowledge of the case. A method had to be developed for presenting the facts to the jury. The adversary system was instituted as a means of meeting this need, with each side presenting witnesses to testify on its behalf. Gradually, the structure of the trial changed until the adversary system predominated. First-hand knowledge of the facts kept one from jury service, and jurors were directed to consider only such evidence as was introduced by the adversaries.

The adversary system is based on the theory that partisan advocacy by the two opposing sides will best lead to the determination of truth and will best promote community confidence in the decision-making process. Each side is given its day in court, its opportunity to present its side of the story. The opposing parties frame the factual issues, seek out possible evidence, choose that evidence they will present, and advance the interpretation of the law that is most favorable to their side. The decision-makers, the judge and the jury, are neutral, passive participants. They have no responsibility to go out and develop a case. Rather, they sit back and largely work with what they are given. It is assumed that material presented by the opposing sides will fully develop the relevant facts and law, thereby permitting the decision-makers to reach an impartial and rational conclusion.

Adversary vs. Inquisitorial System.   Although the adversary system has been the American system from the start, it is not the only reasonable system for determining guilt or innocence. European countries, for example, utilize the so-called inquisitorial system of justice. While the adversary theory maintains that the truth will best be discovered in the clash between the parties, the inquisitorial system is based on the premise that the truth is best discovered through a disinterested inquiry conducted by a magistrate. The European magistrate accordingly acts as an active fact-finder concerned with the discovery of evidence rather than as a passive umpire. It is the function of the magistrate, not the parties, to call witnesses and experts and to make certain that all relevant evidence is produced. Both sides are obligated to assist the court in this regard by producing such evidence as the magistrate desires, including the defendant's own testimony (which cannot be compelled in the American system due to the privilege against self-incrimination).

The inquisitorial system reduces considerably the responsibilities of the attorneys and their opportunities to exercise some initiative in the presentation of the case. Witnesses are not interviewed by the attorneys before trial, in part because they are not viewed as witnesses for either side but as witnesses appearing on behalf of the court. Similarly, witnesses testify in an uninterrupted narrative and are questioned initially by the magistrate (although European lawyers today do have the right of cross-examination common to the adversary system).

Which is the best system—the adversary or the inquisitorial? Reasonable persons obviously can disagree on that issue. Persons favoring the adversary system claim that the inquisitorial system places too much authority in the hands of the magistrate and takes from the defendant too large a portion of his control over his own destiny. Moreover, it is argued, the system appears to favor the state. Even if one can assume that the magistrate actually will be fair and impartial, the structure of the system does not convey the positive sense of neutral fact-finding that instills public confidence in the criminal justice system. The adversary system, its supporters claim, presents exactly that image—at least as it is used in this country. Each side is given an equal opportunity to present its case through its own legal advocate. The final judgment as to guilt or innocence is left not to a judge, but to the community, as represented by the jury. Moreover, to maintain public confidence in the fairness of the proceeding, the presentation of evidence, announcement of the verdict, and imposition of sentence are all public proceedings.[1]

Legal Safeguards. The adversary process rests on the premise that each side will have the capacity to fully present its case. The primary criticism of the process is that this presumed equality in capacity does not exist. The state, it is argued, has so many resources that it simply can overpower the defense. The framers of the adversary process have been sensitive to such criticism almost from the outset. The adversary process has long been subject to various legal safeguards designed to ensure that the state will not win a case simply because it has more money, more lawyers, and the superior investigative authority of the government at its disposal. In particular, the state has been required to carry the burden of proof and to establish proof beyond a reasonable doubt. Indeed, as developed in this country, the criminal justice process has included a series of screening devices which require that the state meet progressively higher standards of proof and thereby ensure that no case will even be brought to trial unless the state has substantial evidence. In addition, the defendant is given the protection of various constitutional rights designed to ensure that the prosecution acts fairly and respects the dignity of the individual. Like the concept of adversary decision-making itself, these legal safeguards also belong among the basic principles underlying the criminal justice process.

THE ACCUSATORIAL SYSTEM

The Burden of Proof. The Anglo-American system of law is shaped by an accusatorial process of proof as well as an adversary system of decision-making. The key to an accusatorial process of proof is that the party making the accusation of wrongdoing bears the burden of proving that the accusation is true. The charging instrument—in the criminal case, the complaint, indictment, or information—is viewed as no more than a statement of the belief of the accuser. It alleges that certain facts exist, but these allegations establish nothing in themselves and no assumption is made as to their accuracy. The jurors may not assume, simply because the accuser represents the state, that his allegations are true. The prosecutor, as the accuser, must persuade the jurors, by reference only to evidence produced before them, that the allegations in the charging instrument are accurate. This burden of persuading the jury is described legally as the "burden of proof."

---

1. The adversary trial also serves, according to some experts, as a better safety-valve for public indignation against offenders than an inquisitorial proceeding. The public trial with the prosecutor representing the state (and the victim) arguably better serves the psychological needs of the community than the neutral inquiry conducted by the magistrate.

Placement of the burden of proof on the prosecution means that the defendant need not establish his innocence; it is the prosecutor that must establish his guilt. The defendant can simply sit back, produce no evidence whatsoever, and be assured of his acquittal if the prosecutor has not produced sufficient evidence to convince the jury that the defendant committed the crime. Moreover, the prosecutor's evidence must be so convincing as to meet another basic standard of the criminal justice process—that the proof establish guilt beyond a reasonable doubt. That standard, which is discussed later in this chapter, makes the state's burden of proof a particularly heavy one.

Why is the burden of proof placed on the state? In part, it is simply because the state is the initiating party. In an adversary system, someone must bear the burden of persuasion, and it is logical to assign that burden to the person asking the court to take action. Thus, in a civil suit, it is the plaintiff, the person who initiates the suit and asks for damages or some other relief, who bears the burden of meeting the level of persuasion required in civil cases. But the placement of the burden of proof on the state in criminal cases also reflects other, more basic values. As the Supreme Court has noted, it is a "fundamental value determination of our system that it is far worse to convict an innocent person than to let a guilty man go free."[2] Indeed, the early English writer Blackstone, who was very influential in shaping the views of the draftsmen of the Constitution, once noted that "it is better that ten guilty persons escape than one innocent suffer." A system that views the protection of the innocent as its highest goal is invariably led to place the burden of proof on the state. Though a person is innocent, he may have difficulty in producing evidence that clearly establishes his innocence. If he were forced to carry the burden of proof, all uncertainties as to proof would be resolved against him. Where the jurors were uncertain as to whether he was guilty or innocent, they would be required to find him guilty. A guilty verdict would be based not on the prosecution's evidence establishing guilt, but only on the defendant's inability to "clear himself." The possibility of erroneously convicting the innocent would be far greater under such a system than under our system; by placing the burden on the prosecution, we permit conviction only where the jurors are affirmatively convinced of defendant's guilt by the prosecution's positive showing.[3]

The Burden of Going Forward With the Evidence. Although they often are combined, the burden of initially producing evidence is quite separate from the burden of proof. The two burdens should not be confused, as their relationships to the accusatorial process are quite different. The burden of producing evidence

---

2. *In re Winship*, 397 U.S. 358, 90 S.Ct. 1068, 25 L.Ed.2d 368 (1970).

3. The placement of the burden of proof upon the prosecution is not without limitations. There are a few defenses as to which the burden of proof may be placed upon the defendant. These only can be defenses that do not negate any basic element of the crime (mens rea, act, etc.) and that are uniquely within the knowledge of the defense. The due process clause of the Fourteenth Amendment requires that the prosecution bear the burden of proving all elements of the crime, including the absence of any "defense" that directly negates any of those elements. *Patterson v. New York*, 432 U.S. 197, 97 S.Ct. 2319, 53 L.Ed. 2d 281 (1977). The two most significant examples of defenses on which the defendant may be given the burden of proof are insanity and duress. It should be noted, however, that not all states shift the burden of proof even for the few defenses where it can be done constitutionally. Many states require that the prosecution carry the burden of disproving all defenses placed in issue, including insanity and duress.

refers only to the obligation of initially introducing evidence that places a particular issue in dispute before the jury. Ordinarily, that burden is assigned along with the burden of proof. Thus, the prosecution has the obligation of initially presenting evidence on each element of the crime as well as persuading the jury that those elements existed. For example, if the crime involved is the theft of property valued at over $100.00, the prosecution must first introduce evidence showing that the stolen item was worth more than $100.00. The prosecution cannot sit back and claim that, since the defense has not introduced any evidence suggesting the item is worth less than $100.00, it must obviously be worth more than $100.00. There are some matters, however, that the prosecution should not have to consider in its proof unless there is some evidence that the issue exists in the case. For example, the prosecution should not automatically have to introduce evidence that the defendant was not insane or was not entrapped. On these issues, largely within the special knowledge of the defendant, the defense ordinarily carries the burden of going forward with the evidence. Once the issue is raised by the defendant's evidence, the burden then shifts back to the prosecution to introduce counter evidence and persuade the jury that the defenses did not exist.[4]

Unlike the placement of the burden of proof, the placement of the burden of going forward is not of great significance in protecting the innocent. It is a matter governed primarily by the convenience of the parties in first offering proof. Any defendant wanting to raise a particular defense can readily introduce sufficient evidence to suggest that the defense might be present in the case. The key point is that the prosecutor then assumes the ultimate burden of persuasion; he must convince the jury that the defense did not exist. The basic accusatorial structure is retained, but the prosecution's burden does not come into play until the defense first comes forward with at least some evidence.

Presumption of Innocence.   The presumption of innocence is closely related to the placement of the burden of proof. Indeed, the presumption really does no more than provide an additional means of emphasizing that the burden of proof is upon the prosecution. Thus, a typical jury charge on the presumption notes:

> *A defendant in a criminal action is presumed to be innocent until the contrary is proved . . . This presumption places upon the State the burden of proving him guilty beyond a reasonable doubt.*[5]

The presumption of innocence is not what lawyers call an "evidentiary presumption."[6] It does not arise from factual inferences, statistically supported, that accused persons are in fact more likely to be innocent than guilty. It merely reflects the obvious proposition that, with the burden on the prosecution to prove guilt, the individual must be treated as innocent until that burden is met. It serves to emphasize to the jury that they must accept the basic premise of an accusatorial system—they must put aside any suspicion that might naturally arise from the

---

4.   There are, however, the few exceptions mentioned in footnote 3 *supra*.

5.   California Criminal Jury Instructions 2.90, prepared by the Committee on Standard Jury Instructions of the Superior Court of Los Angeles County.

6.   Evidentiary presumptions are discussed at p. 319 *infra*. They are legal rules relating to the proof of the existence of certain facts.

filing of a criminal charge by the state and reach their conclusion solely upon the evidence produced before them.[7]

PROGRESSIVE REVIEWS
WITH HIGHER STANDARDS OF PROOF

We saw earlier in Chapter Eight how the criminal justice process acts as a sieve, with successive screening reducing the number of cases that pass through each subsequent stage of the process. This "sieve effect" is a product, in part, of a basic objective of the criminal justice process—to avoid imposing unnecessary restraints upon innocent persons. Thus, the process is designed not only to avoid convicting the innocent but also to minimize subjecting innocent persons to the trial process or even to the restraint of an arrest. To ensure that this objective is met, the process imposes a series of progressively higher standards of proof that must be met as each further restraint is imposed upon a suspect. Thus, as the individual moves from the status of suspect, to arrestee, to defendant, and finally to convicted person, the prosecution must carry a higher and higher burden of proof, culminating in proof beyond a reasonable doubt.

Each of the standards of proof to be met by the prosecution is measured in terms of a level of belief that must be established in the mind of a reasonable person as to the guilt of the accused. The chart on page 207 sets forth in its first column the legal phrase describing each of the standards of proof. The second column notes the level of belief that each standard must rationally establish, and the third column notes the type of action that may be taken when the particular standard of proof is met.

Note that the chart describes seven different standards of proof, but only the second through the sixth standards are critical legal standards. The first standard is a standard that is always satisfied since it describes that situation in which there is no evidence reasonably pointing to the guilt of a particular person. We have included it in the chart primarily to distinguish between this no-evidence situation and the second standard of proof ("reasonable basis"), which describes the minimum level needed to impose a restraint on a particular suspect. The seventh standard is included in the chart for a similar reason. It describes absolute proof of guilt, a level never demanded by the law. We have included it primarily to illustrate the distinction between this highest of all possible standards and the sixth level ("proof beyond a reasonable doubt"), which is the standard required for conviction. Thus the issue before a court will be, depending upon the type of restraint being imposed, whether level two, three, four, five, or six has been met. Levels one and seven may be used to illustrate the lowest and highest possible standards, but neither are standards required by the law.

---

7. Thus, the Michigan Criminal Jury Instructions, 3:1:02-03 notes:

>   Basic to our system of criminal justice is the principle that a person accused of a crime is presumed to be innocent ... You must begin your deliberations with the presumption of innocence foremost in your minds. The fact that the defendant was arrested and is on trial is no evidence against him. There must be evidence introduced in this trial that convinces you of the defendant's guilt beyond a reasonable doubt. The law does not require a defendant to prove his innocence or to produce any evidence whatsoever.

STANDARDS OF PROOF AND LEVELS OF ACTION

LEGAL DESCRIPTION OF STANDARD OF PROOF	LEVEL OF BELIEF ESTABLISHED	ACTION THAT CAN BE TAKEN
1. No significant proof	complete doubt (or suspicion without factual support)	investigation not involving restraints upon the person
2. Reasonable basis	belief that there is a significant possibility that individual has committed or is about to commit a crime	temporary restraint (e.g., stopping the suspect on the street)
3. Probable cause	belief that there is a substantial likelihood that the individual committed a crime	arrest; also a variation of this standard used in some jurisdictions for issuance of information or indictment
4. Preponderance of evidence	belief, based on all of the evidence presented, that it is more likely than not, that the individual committed a crime	variation of this standard used in some jurisdictions for preliminary hearing bindover and issuance of an information
5. Prima facie case	belief, based on prosecution evidence only, that individual is so clearly guilty as to eliminate any reasonable doubt	used in some jurisdictions for issuance of indictment
6. Proof beyond a reasonable doubt	belief, considering all of the evidence presented, that individual is so clearly guilty as to eliminate any reasonable doubt	conviction for crime
7. Absolute proof of guilt	belief so certain that defendant is guilty as to eliminate even unreasoned doubts	such certainty is never needed

Acting Without Any Significant Proof.   None of the legally required standards of proof need be met until some minimal physical restraint is imposed upon the suspect. A restraint exists where a suspect is detained in a particular place or ordered to do a certain thing (e.g., stand in a lineup). It also exists if there is interference with the suspect's possession of property, as when his house is searched or his property seized. If an action taken by a government official with respect to a suspect does not involve a restraint, the government need not have the evidentiary support of even the lowest of the legal standards of proof, the "reasonable basis" standard. Non-restraint actions may be taken without any evidence pointing to the guilt of the suspect. Such actions may be based on no more than a hunch or a wild guess.

The range of non-restraint actions that police may utilize without meeting any proof requirement is best illustrated by looking at a hypothetical case. Assume that the police are investigating the reported theft of property from a warehouse. Inspection of the premises indicates that the property could have been stolen by an employee, but there are over 100 employees who could have committed the crime. With over 100 possible suspects, the police really have no significant proof against any one employee. As we shall see, they lack the reasonable basis needed to temporarily detain any particular employee or the probable cause necessary to arrest any employee of search the home of any employee. Nevertheless, they still may use investigative techniques that do not involve imposing a restraint on a particular suspect. Assume that the investigating officer decides that it would be wise to "check out" the backgrounds of the ten employees most recently hired by the warehouse. With the warehouse's permission, he may check the employee's records to obtain the names and addresses of the ten newest employees. He may then check police records to determine whether any of the ten have past arrests or convictions. He may question the neighbors of each of the ten to determine whether they had seen the employee bringing any warehouse property into his home. Indeed, they may even ask any employee if he would volunteer to give a statement as to his whereabouts at the time of the theft, etc. The officer may not, however, order the employee to appear at a certain place for the purpose of questioning. Neither, if the employee voluntarily meets him, may he require the employee to stay at that place until he asks further questions or checks the employee's statement with other persons. Such directives would involve a restraint and require that the police meet at least the "reasonable basis" standard of proof.[8]

Reasonable Basis.   The reasonable basis standard is the lowest of our legally required standards of proof. It is the standard that must be met to subject a suspect to a minor restraint, such as that involved in the temporary detention of a suspect. Actions imposing more substantial restrictions upon the suspect, such as an arrest or conviction, must be justified by a higher level of proof. The most common procedure utilizing a minor restraint is the "forcible stopping" of a

---

8.   In determining whether investigative action imposes a restraint requiring some specific proof as to possible guilt, the touchstone ordinarily is the Fourth Amendment. If the investigative technique involves a "seizure" of the person or a "search," then the Fourth Amendment will require that the police meet either the "reasonable basis" or "probable cause" standard depending upon the nature of the activity. See Chapter Ten.

suspect by a police officer on the street. We refer here to any situation in which the officer uses his authority to require the suspect to stay in the officer's presence for a short period of time. The forcible stop need not involve the actual use of physical force; the implicit threat that the officer will use force is sufficient. The forcible stop imposes less restraint on the suspect than an arrest since it involves only a temporary detention at the place of the stop. The individual is not taken into custody and transported to a holding facility for the purpose of pressing charges, which ordinarily is the procedure following an arrest. Forcible stops often are used where the officer is not certain whether the situation justifies an arrest. Thus a suspect may be stopped to be questioned, to await the arrival of an eyewitness who might identify him as the criminal, or to await the receipt of further information from headquarters that might identify him as a wanted criminal. In any of these situations, the detention is lawful only if the officer can point to a reasonable basis for holding the suspect even for a short period of time.

The reasonable basis standard has not received as much attention from the courts as the other levels of proof, and its content accordingly has not been as fully explored in court opinions.[9] However, most of the basic features of the reasonable basis standard are firmly established. First, the reasonable basis must be based upon facts and circumstances presented to the officer, not on a mere "hunch." Thus, it often is noted that the officer needs more than a "mere suspicion." Second, the reasonable basis standard, like all of our levels of proof, extends to two factors—(1) that a crime was committed and (2) that it was the suspect who committed the crime. Finally, the reasonable basis standard requires a "significant" level of probability as to the existence of each of these two factors. Unfortunately, it is not always clear as to exactly how likely it must be that the suspect committed a crime in order to meet this significant level of probability.

Judicial decisions have not drawn a precise measurement as to the degree of probability needed to establish a reasonable basis for imposing a minor restraint. They note that the probability clearly need not approximate a fifty percent possibility, yet it must be more than a "remote" possibility. To gain a better understanding of the exact degree of probability, one can only examine the cases and note what has been sufficient in one case and insufficient in another. Perhaps the easiest cases are those in which the commission of a crime is clear, but the suspect's involvement is uncertain. In such a situation, the probability of the suspect's involvement ordinarily has been sufficient if there are relevant factors that place the suspect among a comparatively small group of persons, one of whom most likely committed the crime. Consider, for example, the hypothetical we discussed in the previous section involving a theft from a warehouse. Even if it was fairly clear that the property had been stolen by an employee, since there were 100 employees, there would not be a reasonable basis for detaining any of them. A reasonable basis clearly requires more than a one out of a hundred choice that the suspect is guilty. On the other hand, if there had been only five employees with access to the stolen property, there would be a small group of persons from which the criminal apparently came. The probability as to any one of the five woud be

---

9. See pp. 238-40 *infra* discussing the key decisions in this area, and use of the stop-and-frisk procedure that gave rise to judicial consideration of the reasonable basis standard.

insufficient to arrest him or charge him with the crime, but sufficiently strong to justify his temporary detention for questioning or some other investigative purpose.[10]

Application of the reasonable basis standard causes more difficulty where the suspect is clearly identified, but uncertainty exists as to whether a crime was committed. Consider, for example, a situation in which an officer observes a young man walking the streets at 2:00 a.m. in a district with few residences, a great many retail stores, and a high burglary rate. The time, location, and fact that the individual is on foot gave rise to some suspicion, but not enough to temporarily detain him.[11] If, in addition, the individual was carrying an appliance of the type sold in several of the stores (e.g., a television set), there certainly would be a sufficient possibility that the person committed a crime to temporarily detain him.[12] The officer still would not be aware of any burglary, but the probability that the television set was stolen would be sufficient to forcibly hold the individual for a short period of time while the officer could check to determine if any of the local appliance stores had been burglarized. There may be various explanations as to why an innocent individual could be in the neighborhood at that time carrying a television set; still, the likelihood of a burglary is considerably more than a remote possibility and it should be sufficient to justify the stop.

Probable Cause: Arrest Authority.   Probable cause is the level of proof that must be met at several stages in the criminal justice process. Initially, it is the standard that must be met to sustain an arrest. The traditional definition of probable cause, as applied to justify an arrest, is set forth in *Brinegar v. United States*:

> It [*probable cause*] *has come to mean more than mere suspicion. Probable cause exists where the facts and circumstances within* ... *the arresting officers' knowledge and of which they had reasonably trustworthy information are sufficient in themselves to warrant a man of reasonable caution in the belief that an offense has been committed or is being committed [by the person to be arrested].*[13]

The essential elements of probable cause, as described in *Brinegar*, are

---

10.   Exactly how large the group may be without being too large is not clear. In part, the nature of the restraint imposed would be significant. The Uniform Rules of Criminal Procedure, in a rule relating to temporary detention of suspects for such purposes as placing them in a lineup, described the required degree of probability as "probable cause to believe that an offense has been committed by one or more *of several persons comprising a narrow focal group.*" (Emphasis added). See National Conference of Commissioners on Uniform State Laws, *Uniform Rules of Criminal Procedure*. St. Paul, Minnesota: West Publishing Company, 1974, Rule 436.

11.   Of course, the officer may always approach and seek to gain the suspect's voluntary cooperation in answering a few questions.

12.   See *Stewart v. United States*, 364 A.2d 1205 (D.C. App. 1976) (where officer observed defendant and his companion, late at night, walking in residential area at a moderate pace, and carrying various stereo components and a pillowcase containing other items, officer was justified in using force to briefly detain defendant on the street for questioning).

13.   *Brinegar v. United States*, 338 U.S. 160, 175-76, 69 S.Ct. 1302, 1310-1311, 93 LEd 1879, (1949), quoting in part from *Carroll v. United States*, 267 U.S. 132, 162, 45 S.Ct. 280, 288, 69 L.Ed. 543 (1925).

similar in several respects to the "reasonable basis" standard applied to a temporary detention. The officer must be acting upon facts and circumstances known to him, not upon a "hunch" that gives rise to "mere suspicion." Also, the rational belief justified by those circumstances must relate both to the commission of the crime and the identity of the arrested person as the offender. The primary difference between the reasonable basis and probable cause standards lies in the strength of the belief that is justified by the circumstances. As we have noted, an arrest imposes a considerably greater restraint upon the suspect than a temporary detention since it ordinarily involves taking the suspect into custody, removing him to the police station, and holding him for appearance before a magistrate. The arrest also has far greater procedural significance since it is the initial step in bringing a formal accusation against the suspect. In light of these more substantial consequences, the criminal justice process quite naturally demands that the circumstances establish a greater probability of guilt to justify an arrest than a temporary detention. The probable cause standard accordingly requires substantially greater probability than the reasonable basis standard, although, here again, the exact degree of probability required cannot be stated with mathematical precision.

Courts often speak of probable cause as requiring a rational belief that the arrestee "probably" committed the crime in question. Some commentators have relied on such phrasing to suggest that it must be "more-likely-than-not" that the arrested person committed the crime. Probable cause, they argue, means that the available information establishes a more than 50% probability that the person is guilty. An examination of the leading cases indicates, however, that a more than 50% probability is not always needed. On the other hand, it certainly is true that the degree of probability should come within a reasonable distance of a 50% probability. Illustrative is the Supreme Court case of *Wong Sun v. United States*.[14] There police learned from an informant that "Blackie Toy," the proprietor of a laundry on San Francisco's famed Leavenworth Street, had participated in the sale of heroin. The police went to "Oye's Laundry" on Leavenworth and immediately arrested the apparent proprietor, who turned out to be Blackie Toy. However, it appeared that Leavenworth, which was 30 blocks long, contained several chinese laundries and the record failed to show any reason why the police had picked the correct laundry other than by chance. The Supreme Court held the arrest invalid, noting that it could not be saved by the officers' good fortune in arresting the correct person. With several persons equally likely to fill the informer's description of Blackie Toy, there was substantially less than a 50% probability that the owner of any one laundry would be the wanted Blackie Toy. If there had been only two laundries and two proprietors who fit the description of Blackie Toy, the situation probably would have been different; in that case the probability as to each suspect would be 50% (assuming the reliability of the informant) and probable cause as to both would exist.[15]

---

14. 371 U.S. 471, 83 S.Ct. 407, 9 L.Ed. 2d 441 (1963).

15. The classic hypothetical is that of the murdered man found in a locked room with two other persons, each of whom accuses the other of committing the crime. It is generally assumed that both can be arrested in such a case, although eventually the prosecution will have to find further evidence that breaks the deadlock.

Unfortunately, it is not always as easy to estimate the degree of probability as it was in *Wong Sun*. There are many instances, for example, where the court cannot readily identify the number of persons who might meet a certain description. In such a case, a court will not ask for a mathematical analysis, but simply will insist on a showing that there is a "substantial likelihood" that the arrestee is the offender. *Brown v. United States* is typical.[16] Police there received a radio report at 4:30 a.m. that an armed robbery had just been committed by a heavily built Negro male, about 5'5" in height, driving a maroon 1954 Ford (a car then 10 years old). Shortly thereafter, 20 blocks from the robbery, the driver of a 1952 maroon Ford was stopped and arrested. The driver was black, but was 5'11" rather than the 5'5". Also he was wearing a blue jacket rather than the reported brown jacket. The court nevertheless held that the arrest was justified by probable cause. The court noted that the police could disregard the discrepancies as to height and clothing color; such variations commonly exist where an excited victim of a robbery gives a hurried description of the robber. The variation in the year of the car was explained by the similarity of the 1952 and 1954 models. The remaining, accurate portion of the description, combined with the discovery of the arrestee near the location of the robbery, was sufficient to establish probable cause. The court did not undertake a scientific evaluation of the probabilities, but simply noted that they were sufficient to establish probable cause:

> The total number of 1954 Fords meeting that description [still] being driven in 1964 was limited; still smaller was the total number being driven at 4:30 on a Monday morning, and yet smaller those driven in that immediate neighborhood at that time by heavy Negro males. Ordinary human experience alone, without resort of the law of probability, tells us this. [17]

In *Wong Sun*, the police could readily estimate how many laundries they might find on Leavenworth street. In *Brown*, on the other hand, they had no way of knowing how many others in the neighborhood were likely to fit the victim's description of the robber. In determining whether the police acted on probable cause, courts will take into consideration the limitations under which the police operate. They will not expect police to do more than make a reasonable estimate of probabilities based on their common experience. As the courts have frequently noted, probable cause is "a commonsensible rather than a technical concept." It requires that the police officer act reasonably in light of "factual and practical considerations of everyday life," not as a scientifically precise "legal technician."[18]

Probable Cause: Issuance Of A Charging Document.   Some states use probable cause as the required standard of proof that must be met to file an

---

16.   365 F.2d 976 (D.C. Cir. 1976).

17.   365 F.2d at 978.

18.   *Brinegar v. United States*, 338 U.S. 160, 175 69 S.Ct. 1302, 1310, 93 L.Ed. 1879 (1949). See also the cases discussed in A. Cook, *Probable Cause To Arrest*, 24 Vanderbilt Law Review 317 (1971).

information or indictment.[19] Thus, where the formal charge is contained in an information, state law will provide that the information can be filed with the trial court only after a magistrate has made a finding of probable cause at a preliminary hearing. Similarly, where the charge is by indictment, state law will provide that the grand jury can only indict upon a finding of probable cause. Although the standard in both instances is described simply as "probable cause," it generally is viewed as requiring somewhat more substantial factual support than the probable cause needed to justify an arrest. Since the issuance of the information or indictment ordinarily comes at a later stage than the arrest, the prosecution often will have more information relating to the suspect's possible guilt or innocence than the officer had when he made the arrest. Consider, for example, a case like the *Brown* case, where police arrested a suspect who matched a robbery victim's description of the robber. While the suspect's location, his physical characteristics, and the model and color of his car established probable cause justifying an arrest, they probably would not have been sufficient in themselves to justify issuing an indictment or information. The grand jury or magistrate examining probable cause would expect further evidence of guilt. Was the stolen property found in the car? Could the victim identify the arrested person as the robber? If such additional evidence could not be obtained, the probability of the suspect's guilt is likely to be viewed as no longer high enough to establish probable cause. While the same affirmative factors of location, physical description, and car model are present, they now must be weighed against other negative or neutral factors (e.g., the lack of eyewitness identification) that were not available to the officer at the time of the arrest.

Some experts argue that the difference in the two probable cause standards rests on more than differences in the available evidence. They contend that the probable cause required for issuing a charge simply demands a higher degree of probability than that for an arrest. While less than a 51% probability may often be permissible for an arrest, it never should be permissible, they argue, for issuance of a charge. Most magistrates undoubtedly take this view in ruling on probable cause at preliminary hearings, and many grand juries take the same position. They would not, for example, permit the issuance of an indictment or information where the evidence pointed equally to two persons as the possible offenders.[20] Nor would they permit the charge to issue in other instances where the probabilities of guilt and innocence appear to be roughly equal. Higher courts generally have not spoken on this issue, so it cannot be said with certainty that probable cause at this stage legally requires a more-than-50%-probability. Insofar as it does require that higher degree of probability, the applicable standard is quite similar to the perponderance of the evidence standard to be discussed next.

Preponderance Of The Evidence.   The preponderance of the evidence standard is the traditional standard of proof in civil cases, and it is sometimes said that

---

19.   Other states, as we shall see, require a higher standard of proof for the issuance of an information or indictment.

20.   See note 15 *supra*.

the standard has no applicability in criminal cases. Such statements are not accurate, although it is true that the preponderance standard plays a much less significant role in criminal cases. The preponderance standard assumes an adversary presentation of evidence. It directs the trier of fact to weigh the evidence on both sides and decide in favor of the side whose evidence is more convincing, even though it may be far from fully convincing. The trier of fact decides in favor of whichever side is more persuasive, although that side may have prevailed by the slightest of margins. The preponderance standard, in effect, requires a belief only that it is more-probable-than-not that a certain result is correct.[21] In civil proceedings, the preponderance standard is the standard governing the final decision on the merits. In the criminal case it has relevance primarily to preliminary matters. Since the grand jury is given only the prosecution's evidence, the preponderance standard would not apply to its decision to issue an indictment. A preliminary hearing, on the other hand, is an adversary proceeding. Both sides are given the opportunity to present evidence. Thus, where the magistrate carefully weighs that evidence and will authorize further proceedings only where the balance of evidence supports guilt, he is, in effect, applying the preponderance of the evidence standard. The preponderance standard also will be applied by the trial court in making preliminary findings of fact in conjunction with its decisions on legal issues. Thus, if the court, in determining whether a confession was obtained illegally, must decide whether the defendant was in fact physically threatened, it may decide that factual issue under a preponderance of the evidence standard. If it concludes that the police are more likely to be telling the truth when they say that no threats were made, the court will proceed on that factual assumption even though it has some reasonable doubts as to what actually occurred.[22]

Prima Facie Case. In some jurisdictions, the standard of proof required for grand jury issuance of an indictment is described as a *prima facie case* standard (i.e., presenting a case that appears "sufficient on first disclosure"). The prima facie case standard originally was a trial standard used in civil and criminal cases in determining whether a case should reach the jury. The standard has two major characteristics. First, it looks only to the evidence presented by the initiating party; in the criminal case, this means only the evidence presented by the prosecution. This factor makes the standard particularly appropriate for a grand jury proceeding since only the prosecution's evidence is presented to that body. Second, a prima facie case requires that the prosecution's evidence be reasonably sufficient under the ultimate standard of proof that will be applied at trial. In a criminal case, that standard will be proof beyond a reasonable doubt. Thus, in applying a prima facie case standard, a grand jury must ask itself whether trial

---

21.   If the evidence is equally convincing on both sides, the burden of proof controls and decision is made against the side bearing that burden.

22.   The preponderance standard also has a role in one other aspect of the criminal justice process. Where the burden of proof on a particular defense is allocated to the defendant, that burden is associated with a preponderance standard, rather than a reasonable doubt standard. Thus, where the defendant bears the burden on a defense such as duress, the jury must acquit if they find his evidence more convincing as to the existence of duress even though they have reasonable doubts as to whether duress existed. See note 3 *supra*.

jurors reasonably could find guilt beyond a reasonable doubt based on the evidence presented before the grand jury. As the California Penal Code puts it, the grand jury may indict only "when all the evidence before it, taken together, if unexplained or uncontradicted, would in its judgment warrant a conviction by a trial jury." [23] Of course, if the grand jury finds the evidence sufficient to meet this standard, they are not saying that the accused is guilty beyond a reasonable doubt. Since they have heard only the prosecution's evidence, they recognize that a jury could well reach a different conclusion once the defense presents its side of the case.

Proof Beyond A Reasonble Doubt: Its Special Role. The ultimate standard of proof in the criminal process—that required to find a person guilty—is proof beyond a reasonable doubt. This standard is the highest standard of proof required anywhere in American law. The reasonable doubt standard requires substantially greater certainty than either the preponderance of the evidence standard traditionally applied in civil cases or the "clear and convincing evidence" standard reserved for a limited class of civil claims (e.g., fraud). The use of this highest standard of proof in the criminal justice system reflects the system's special concern for avoiding mistakes which might result in the conviction of the innocent. In a civil case, a mistaken judgment favoring one party is not worse than a mistaken judgment favoring the other. Either mistake is equally bad. In the criminal case, however, we seek in particular to safeguard against a mistaken conviction even if, in so doing, we increase the probability of mistaken acquittals. It is better that a guilty man be mistakenly acquitted than an innocent man be mistakenly convicted. The theory underlying this position, and the relationship of that theory to the reasonable doubt standard, were aptly described by the Supreme Court in *In re Winship*:

> *The reasonable doubt standard . . . is a prime instrument for reducing the risk of convictions resting on factual error . . . The accused during a criminal prosecution has at stake interests of immense importance, both because of the possibility he may lose his liberty upon conviction and because of the certainty that he would be stigmatized by the conviction. Accordingly, a society that values the good name and freedom of every individual should not condemn a man for commission of a crime when there is reasonable doubt about his guilt. As we said in* Speiser v. Randall: *'There is always in litigation a margin of error representing error in fact-finding, which both parties must take into account. Where one party has at stake an interest of transcending value—as a criminal defendant in his liberty—this margin of error is reduced as to him by the process of placing on the other the burden of . . . persuading the fact-finder . . . of his guilt beyond a reasonable doubt.' . . . Moreover, use of the reasonable doubt standard is indispensable to command the respect and confidence of the community in applications of the criminal law. It is critical that the moral force of the criminal law not be diluted by a standard of proof that leaves people in doubt whether innocent men are being condemned. It is also important in our free*

---

23. California Penal Code §939.8.

*society that every individual going about his ordinary affairs have confi-
dence that his government cannot adjudge him guilty of a criminal offense
without convincing a proper factfinder of his guilt with utmost certainty.* [24]

Proof Beyond A Reasonable Doubt Defined. It is far easier to describe the
role of the reasonable doubt standard than to describe the precise degree of
certainty that the standard requires for a guilty verdict. Indeed, many appellate
courts suggest that, in charging a jury, the trial judge should best let the words
speak for themselves without embellishment—that is, the jury simply should be
told that it may not convict unless the prosecution proves, beyond a reasonable
doubt, all the elements of the crime charged.[25] Other courts have concluded that
the standard requires further definition. They usually have sought to provide a
better understanding of the standard by describing what a reasonable doubt does
and does not approximate. The following description is typical:

> *A reasonable doubt is a fair, honest doubt growing out of the evidence or
> lack of evidence in this case or growing out of any reasonable or legitimate
> inferences drawn from the evidence or the lack of evidence. It is not merely
> an imaginary doubt or a flimsy, fanciful doubt or a doubt based upon the
> mere possibility of the innocence of the defendant or a doubt based upon
> sympathy, but rather it is a fair, honest doubt based upon reason and
> common sense. It is a state of mind which would cause you to hesitate in
> making an important decision in your own personal life. By stating that the
> prosecution must prove guilt beyond a reasonable doubt, I mean there must
> be such evidence that causes you to have a firm conviction amounting to a
> moral certainty of the truth of the charge here made against this
> defendant.*[26]

It is open to debate whether such instructions place too much emphasis upon
one aspect or another of the reasonable doubt standard. Some would argue that
the reference to a doubt based upon "reason" may be misleading because it might
suggest that the doubt must be one for which the juror could clearly articulate a
rationale. A juror could well entertain a reasonable doubt based on a careful
evaluation of all of the evidence and still not be able to state the precise grounds
for the doubt. Others may argue that the reference to a "firm conviction amounting to moral certainty" tends to suggest that the juror must be completely and
totally certain, yet it is clear that absolute certainty is not needed.[27] Whether such

---

24. *In re Winship*, 397 U.S. 358, 363-64, 90 S.Ct. 1068, 1072-1073, 25 L.Ed. 2d 368 (1970).

25. See Illinois Pattern Jury Instructions, 2.03; *People v. Malmenato*, 14 Ill. 2d 52, 150 N.E. 2d 806
(1958): "Reasonable doubt is a term which needs no elaboration and we have so frequently
discussed the futility of attempting to define it that we might expect the practice to be
discontinued."

26. Michigan Criminal Jury Instructions 1:2:10.

27. Absolute certainty would exist where the evidence was so overwhelming that the trier of fact could
perceive of no way in which the facts could be other than he believes them to be. Some have argued
that this level of proof could be reached only when the trier of fact himself witnessed the crime,
and it thus can never be achieved under our system since an eyewitness, by that fact alone, would
be disqualified from serving as the neutral trier of fact.

criticisms have merit or not, they deal with subtleties that arguably have little impact upon the jurors as they consider the overall thrust of the court's instruction on reasonable doubt. The key to any definition of the reasonable doubt standard is that, as the Supreme Court stressed in *In re Winship*, it "impresses on the trier of fact the necessity of reaching a subjective state of certitude of the facts in issue."[28]

CONSTITUTIONAL SAFEGUARDS

In our initial discussion of the adversary system, we noted that the adversary system is regulated by various legal safeguards designed to ensure that it operates fairly. The most significant of these safeguards are the guarantees found in the Bill of Rights, the first ten amendments to the federal constitution. Several of the key Bill of Rights' provisions are designed in large part to guarantee that the defendant will have ample opportunity to present his case. They establish the right of the defendant to be assisted by counsel, to confront prosecution witnesses, and to compel the attendance of his own witnesses. Other provisions guarantee a neutral fact-finding process, providing, for example, a right to a public trial before an impartial jury. Still other guarantees ensure that the prosecution carries its burden of proving its case with its own resources. With the Constitution prohibiting compulsory self-incrimination, the prosecution may not build its case through the forced testimony of the defendant. Similarly, with the Constitution prohibiting double jeopardy, the prosecution may not seek to wear the defendant down through repetitive prosecutions until the state finally emerges victorious.

Several constitutional guarantees are aimed at still other aspects of fairness, not as closely related to the adversary and accusatorial elements of the criminal justice process. These guarantees are concerned primarily with values relating to the basic dignity of the individual. Thus, the Fourth Amendment prohibits an unreasonable invasion of the individual's privacy in the search for evidence. The Eighth Amendment also recognizes the dignity of the individual in prohibiting the infliction of cruel and unusual punishments and the imposition of excessive bail which unreasonably forces a person to stay in jail pending trial.

We can see from our brief survey that the Bill of Rights' guarantees play an extremely important role in shaping all aspects of our criminal justice process. These guarantees must be studied with care by any student of the criminal justice

---

28. It is this general impression that is commonly stressed by defense counsel in conveying the reasonable doubt concept to the jury. Consider, e.g., the following excerpt from a defense counsel's closing argument, taken from D. Cohen, *How to Win Cases By Establishing A Reasonable Doubt*, Englewood Cliffs, N.J.: Executive Reports Corporation, 1971, p. 106: "You see, this is not like an accident case or a suit involving real estate, where only property rights are determined. In such a case, the side which brings the suit need only produce evidence that outweighs his opponents to be successful. In those cases, if the jury makes a mistake, all that is lost is money. But in this case, if the jury makes a mistake and sends an innocent man to jail, no money in the world could ever compensate him; therefore, the law places upon the state a heavy burden of proving guilt not merely by the weight of the evidence, but by proving guilt beyond doubt. You, as intelligent civic minded people can appreciate the difference in the amount of proof required, and can now see what reasonable doubt really is. If you are not sure—if you have reservations—if you feel that the prosecution has left out a missing link; if you believe that this incident could have happened in any other way than the prosecution suggests—then you must give to my client the benefit of your uncertainty and find him not guilty. That's what reasonable doubt is all about."

process. Appendix C of this book contains selected provisions of the Constitution, including the Bill of Rights. You should carefully read (and reread) those provisions as we progress through the next several chapters. At almost every point in our discussion of the various steps in the criminal justice process, we will take note of the impact of one or more of the first ten amendments. Before reaching these specific constitutional requirements, however, you should be familiar with the general range of rights incorporated in the first ten amendments, the other constitutional provisions that make those rights applicable to all criminal proceedings throughout the United States, and the special role of the constitutional requirement of due process. These are the topics we turn to now.

The Range Of The Bill Of Rights.   When the thirteen original colonies "pooled their sovereignty" to form the union, they were determined to preserve from federal encroachment the liberties they considered essential to free men. When the original draft of the Constitution did not specifically guarantee those liberties, they refused to ratify it. It was not until the first ten amendments were added to the basic document of government that the new constitution could come into being. Those amendments guaranteed twenty-seven specific rights, and over half of those rights (seventeen to be exact) referred directly to criminal procedure. At the time of the constitution's adoption, the leading English and American philosophers viewed the basic fairness of criminal procedure as an essential measure of civilized society. Indeed, as Chief Justice Warren later noted, the fairness of criminal procedure was viewed as a primary "measure by which the quality of . . . [a] civilization may be judged."[29] A society that could treat a suspected (or convicted) criminal fairly—that could reject the view that "criminals should be fought according to their own rules" (i.e., without rules)—was a society truly concerned with the rule of law and the protection of liberty. In light of this prevailing philosophy, it was not surprising that the draftsmen of the Bill of Rights gave so much of their attention to the criminal justice process.

Almost all of the original amendments may have some bearing on the criminal justice system. Thus, the First Amendment guarantee of freedom of speech limits the activities involving speech that Congress may declare to be a crime. Similarly, the Tenth Amendment, preserving to the states rights not delegated to the federal government, may bar Congress from regulating through criminal laws certain activities of entirely local concern.[30] However, the key amendments, in terms of their potential impact upon the criminal justice system, are the Fourth, Fifth, Sixth and Eighth Amendments. Each of these contain provisions directly applicable to the administration of the criminal laws:

Fourth Amendment.   The Fourth Amendment (1) guarantees the right of the people to be secure against unreasonable searches and seizures and (2) prohibits the issuance of warrants authorizing searches or seizures in the absence of a showing of probable cause and a particular description of the place to be searched and the persons or things to be seized.

------

29.   *Coppedge v. United States*, 369 U.S. 438, 449, 82. S.Ct. 917, 923, 8 L.Ed. 2d 21 (1962).

30.   See p. 73 *supra*.

Fifth Amendment. The Fifth Amendment adds four additional rights. It provides: (1) that prosecutions for a capital or otherwise infamous offense shall be upon a presentment or indictment of a grand jury (except for certain military prosecutions); (2) that no person shall be twice put in jeopardy for the same offense; (3) that no person shall be compelled in a criminal case to be a witness against himself (the prohibition against compulsory self-incrimination); and (4) that no person shall be denied life, liberty, or property (which encompasses the imposition of all forms of criminal penalties) without due process of law.

Sixth Amendment. The Sixth Amendment includes eight rights relating to criminal procedure. It guarantees to the accused "in all criminal prosecutions" each of the following rights: (1) the right to a speedy trial; (2) the right to a public trial; (3) the right to trial by an impartial jury; (4) the right to have that jury be "of the state and district wherever the crime shall have been committed," with the district "previously ascertained by law"; (5) the right to be informed of the nature and cause of the accusation against him; (6) the right to be confronted with the witnesses against him; (7) the right to have compulsory process for obtaining witnesses in his favor; and (8) the right to have the assistance of counsel for his defense.

Eighth Amendment. The Eighth Amendment provides that: (1) excessive bail shall not be required; (2) excessive fines shall not be imposed; and (3) cruel and unusual punishment shall not be inflicted.

Application To The States. With so many provisions dealing directly with criminal procedure, one might have thought that the Bill of Rights would have had a significant impact on the administration of criminal justice from the very outset. That was not the case, however. The first ten amendments applied *only* to the federal government. The draftsmen generally were not concerned about securing their rights from violation by their state governments. Each state had its own constitution and most of those state constitutions included several guarantees similar to those found in the federal constitution. The first ten amendments were designed solely as a safeguard against the new government, the federal government. Thus, the Bill of Rights did not apply to the vast majority of the criminal prosecutions in the United States since those prosecutions were being brought under state laws in state courts.

Between 1865 and 1870, Amendments XII, XIV, and XV were added to the Constitution. These amendments were a product of the Civil War. They reflected the view that the protection of liberty within the states could not be left to the states alone. This had been proven by the treatment of blacks in the southern states. What was needed was a federal guarantee of liberty, enforced by the federal courts, against actions of state governments that violated the fundamental rights of individuals. Such a guarantee was thought to be especially necessary to protect the rights of the former slaves, both in the south and the north. The Fourteenth Amendment was designed, in particular, to provide that federal guarantee. Section 1 of the Fourteenth Amendment included the following key provision:

> *No State shall . . . deprive any person of life, liberty, or property, without due process of law.*

This provision, commonly described as the "due process clause" of the Fourteenth Amendment, served as the springboard for the eventual application to the states of almost all of the Bill of Rights' guarantees. [31]

The Supreme Court recognized from the outset that the Fourteenth Amendment's due process clause applied to state criminal procedure. When a state imposed a penal sanction—whether capital punishment, imprisonment, or a fine —it obviously was involved in taking a person's "life, liberty, or property." The crucial issue was what procedures were necessary to provide "due process." Initially, it was argued that the due process guarantee of the Fourteenth Amendment simply paralleled the due process clause in the Fifth Amendment. It was further argued that, since the Bill of Rights included a due process clause, but then proceeded to list separately such guarantees as the right to grand jury indictment, jury trial, and the assistance of counsel, those guarantees could not be included within the concept of due process. The Supreme Court promptly rejected this argument, noting that due process was a flexible concept (see, in this regard, our very next section). Accordingly, due process readily could overlap and include some of the same guarantees that were noted in the other provisions of the Bill of Rights. Having accepted this flexible view of due process, the Court soon adopted what has been described as the "fundamental rights" interpretation of due process.

Under the fundamental rights interpretation, the due process clause of the Fourteenth Amendment included all elements of procedural fairness that were "implicit in the concept of ordered liberty." The state was required, as one opinion put it, to provide the "fundamental fairness essential to the very concept of justice."[32] The essentials of fair procedure certainly included various rights that were specified in the Bill of Rights, but they did not necessarily include either all of those rights or all aspects of those rights. For example, due process might include the prohibition against self-incrimination, yet not include the requirement that felonies be prosecuted by grand jury indictment. Moreover, even as to self-incrimination, due process might not encompass the full scope of that prohibition as it was applied under the Fifth Amendment. Thus, as applied to federal courts, self-incrimination prohibited the government from forcing the defendant to testify and it also prohibited the prosecutor from making negative comments to the jury about the defendant's failure to testify. Under the original fundamental rights interpretation, due process might prohibit the states from seeking to force a defendant to testify, yet not prohibit negative comments. It was possible, in other words, for due process to only "partially incorporate" a guarantee specified in the Bill of Rights.

During the period between 1930 and 1960, the Supreme Court, applying the fundamental rights interpretation, held that various aspects of the Bill of Rights' guarantees were essential to achieving justice and therefore applicable to state

---

31. The Fourteenth Amendment also included a prohibition against any state denying "to any person within its jurisdiction the equal protection of the laws." This provision eventually also had a bearing on state criminal procedure, although not with the same impact as the due process clause.

32. *Lisenba v. California*, 314 U.S. 219, 236, 62 S.Ct. 280, 289, 86 L.Ed. 166 (1941). See also *Palko v. Connecticut*, 302 U.S. 319, 58 S.Ct. 149, 82 L.Ed. 288 (1937); *Adamson v. California*, 332 U.S. 46, 67 S.Ct. 1672, 91 L.Ed. 1903, (1947).

proceedings under the Fourteenth Amendment. Then, in the 1960s, during the tenure of Chief Justice Earl Warren, the Court expanded the fundamental rights interpretation in such a way as to produce the almost complete application of the Bill of Rights' guarantees to the states through the Fourteenth Amendment. This development was so dramatic that the press soon began to refer to it as having produced a "criminal law revolution" under the Warren Court.[33] The major innovation adopted by the Court was to reject the concept of partial incorporation of a fundamental guarantee. If a guarantee, such as the self-incrimination prohibition, was viewed as fundamental and applicable to the states, its fundamental nature would apply to all aspects of the guarantee. This position of "full incorporation" of selective rights (sometimes described as the "selective incorporation theory") required that all fundamental guarantees be applied to the states through the Fourteenth Amendment with the same force as they were applied to the federal government under the Bill of Rights.

Although a few justices still prefer the original fundamental rights approach, the selective incorporation interpretation has been applied by the Supreme Court majority to a wide variety of cases since the early 1960s. In those decisions, the Court has found fundamental and fully applicable to the states all of the specific Bill of Rights' guarantees except three. Moreover, as to two of the three—the Eighth Amendment prohibitions against excessive bail and excessive fines—the Court has indicated that they will be held fundamental as soon as the issue is presented in a case before the Court. The remaining guarantee—the right to prosecution by grand jury indictment—presents a different situation. The Court held in one of its earliest Fourteenth Amendment cases that the grand jury requirement was not fundamental, and subsequent cases over the years have reaffirmed that position.[34] Thus, it seems that, aside from this one exception of grand jury indictment, all of the Bill of Rights' guarantees will be applied to the states in their full scope through their incorporation within the Fourteenth Amendment due process clause.[35]

Due Process. We have seen how the flexible nature of the due process clause of the Fourteenth Amendment permitted the application of the Bill of Rights' guarantees to the states. The flexible nature of due process also permits the due process clauses of the Fifth and Fourteenth Amendments to perform another very important role in American constitutional law—serving as the source of various procedural rights that are not included in the other, more specific guarantees in the federal constitution. This role of the due process clauses can be traced back to the recognition of the concept of due process in the great charter of English liberties, the Magna Carta, issued by King John in 1215 under threat of civil war. In Article 39 of the Magna Carta, the King promised that: "No free man shall be

---

33. There were other elements to this criminal law revolution that are discussed in later chapters, but the adoption of the selective incorporation doctrine was the cornerstone of that "revolution. "See also Graham, note 23, p. 422 *infra.*

34. *Hurtado v. California,* 110 U.S. 516, 4 S.Ct. 292, 28 L.Ed. 232 (1884). See *Gerstein v. Pugh,* 420 U.S. 103, 95 S.Ct. 854, 43 L.Ed. 2d54 (1975) for the continued acceptance of *Hurtado.*

35. The various cases are collected in Chapter One of J. Israel and W. LaFave, *Criminal Procedure In A Nutshell,* St. Paul, Minn.: West Publishing Company, 1975.

arrested, or imprisoned or . . . proceed[ed] against, . . . unless by the lawful judgment of his peers or by the law of the land." The phrase "by the law of the land" was viewed as requiring those procedures which were accepted at that time as essential to a fair proceeding. The precise elements of a fair proceeding were left largely undefined, however, so as to permit adjustment in light of continuing developments in the law. Thus, there was developed a flexible concept of fundamental fairness, capable of growth in the continuing search for a reliable fact-finding process to be applied in an even-handed manner to all free men. The Magna Carta guarantee was reiterated in subsequent statements of basic law, including the constitutions of the first American states. Very frequently the language of the guarantee was altered to refer to proceedings in accord with the "due course of the law of the land" or simply the "due course of law." The basic concept remained the same, however, and it was this concept that was expressed by the Fifth Amendment and Fourteenth Amendment prohibitions against the denial of life, liberty, or property without the "due process of law."

As a guarantee of fundamental fairness, not tied to specific language, the due process requirement permits a court to fashion standards of fairness far beyond specific guarantees, which are restricted by both their language and, quite often, a narrow historical purpose. As Justice Frankfurter once noted: "Due process is, perhaps, the least frozen concept of our law—the least confined to history and the most absoprtive of powerful social change."[36] Where new technology presents procedural difficulties not previously encountered, constitutional challenges commonly are based on a due process analysis. Thus, where the issue arose as to whether the televising of a trial could be so disruptive as to interfere with the fairness of the proceeding, the Supreme Court analyzed the problem in light of due process.[37] Due process also is relied upon to give recognition to society's continuing development of higher standards of fairness that sometimes run counter to long standing practices. *Mayberry v. Pennsylvania* is illustrative.[38] Although trial judges traditionally have heard contempt charges involving courtroom misconduct defying their own orders, growing recognition of the need to avoid the appearance of bias (as well as actual bias) led to a due process ruling in *Mayberry* that a judge could not preside over a contempt charge arising from a highly personal attack upon the judge, even though the judge had avoided becoming "personally embroiled" in the controversy. Finally, the due process requirement

---

36. *Griffin v. Illinois*, 351 U.S. 12, 20-21, 76 S.Ct. 585, 591, 100 L.Ed. 891 (1956). The reason this is so was eloquently explained in another Frankfurter opinion defining due process:"[D]ue Process, unlike some legal rules, is not a technical conception with a fixed content unrelated to time, place, and circumstances. Expressing as it does in its ultimate analysis, respect enforced by law for that feeling of just treatment which has been evolved through centuries of Anglo-American constitutional history and civilization, 'due process' cannot be imprisoned within the treacherous limits of any formula. Representing a profound attitude of fairness between man and man, and more particularly between the inidividual and government, 'due process' is compounded of history, reason, the past course of decisions, and stout confidence in the strength of the democratic faith which we possess. Due process is not a mechanical instrument. It is not a yardstick. It is a process." *Joint Anti-Fascist Refugee Committee v. McGrath*, 341 U.S. 123, 162-63, 71 S.Ct. 624, 643-644, 95 L.Ed. 817 (1951).

37. *Estes v. Texas*, 381 U.S. 532, 85 S.Ct. 1628, 14 L.Ed. 2d 543 (1965) (holding the televising violated due process under the facts of that case).

38. *Mayberry v. Pennsylvania*, 400 U.S. 455, 91 S.Ct. 499, 27 L.Ed. 2d 532 (1971).

also provides a basis for extending the principles underlying more specific guarantees to analogous situations. Thus, the Sixth Amendment provides for a trial before an impartial jury, but it makes no reference to an impartial judge. Due process was held to fill that gap by requiring impartiality of the judge.[39] In sum, the due process guarantee often adds that extra element of growth that permits a constitutional framework adopted almost two centuries ago to be applied so easily to the criminal justice process of today.[40]

---

39. *Tumey v. Ohio*, 273 U.S. 510, 47 S.Ct. 437, 71 L.Ed. 749 (1927).

40. For additional information on the basic themes of the criminal justice process, see E. Pottkamer, *Administration of Criminal Law*, Chicago, Ill.: University of Chicago Press, 1953; H. Packer, *The Limits Of The Criminal Sanction*, Palo Alto, Cal.: Stanford University Press, 1968, pp. 149-246. For an excellent description of the criminal process in other countries, see S. Bedford, *The Faces Of Justice: A Traveller's Report*, New York: Simon and Schuster, 1961. For additional materials on the role of constitutional limitations upon criminal procedure, see J. Israel and W. LaFave, note 35 *supra*.

Chapter 10

Criminal Investigation

Traditionally, the criminal justice process is studied by analyzing the roles of the different participants in the process. The subject matter accordingly is divided into four separate topics—law enforcement, prosecution and defense, judging, and corrections. We, however, will look at the process from a different perspective. We will follow its development chronologically through each of the various stages of the process, starting with investigation and finishing with the completion of sentence. We will divide the topic according to the functions performed at the different stages—investigation, accusation, adjudication, imposition of sentence, and administration of sentence. Our emphasis will be upon the law and the practice followed in the performance of those functions rather than upon the roles of particular participants. We do not mean to ignore, however, the advantages of a role-oriented perspective. In Part Four, we will build upon the material presented in the next several chapters and look at the special roles of each of the major participants in the process.

THE RANGE OF INVESTIGATION

Variety of Police Officers. At each stage of the criminal justice process, certain professionals play a more significant role than others. At the investigatory stage, the police are given the dominant responsibility. Accordingly, we will be concerned in this chapter almost exclusively with actions taken by persons we refer to as "police officers." Who are these "police officers?" We obviously do not refer only to those government officials who have the official title of "police officer." The term police officer, as we use it, includes all government officials charged by the law with the duty to investigate and enforce criminal violations. Jurisdictions vary in the general term they use to describe such officials; some use "police officers," others "peace officers," and others "law enforcement officers." The reference under any of these descriptions is not limited by official titles. It usually will include officers in local, county, and state departments, who may be known as police officers, sheriff's deputies, or state troopers. It includes officers who have authority to enforce all criminal law and others, such as conservation officers, with authority limited to enforcing only a narrow class of laws. It includes officers whose authority extends throughout the state (or even the country, in the case of federal officers, such as F.B.I. agents), and officers whose authority is limited to offenses committed within a specially designated area (such as a park ranger). In Chapter Fifteen, we will take a closer look at the wide variety of officials who fall in the police officer category. At this point, it is sufficient that we recognize that the law governing investigations generally grants equal investigative authority to all "police officers" within a jurisdiction,[1] and, in doing so, it deals with a broad range of officials having quite different training and professional qualifications.

We also should keep in mind that most police officers only have authority to act as police officers when dealing with certain types of offenses or offenses committed in certain locations. A conservation officer, for example, may have no greater authority to arrest for a non-conservation offense than a private citizen. Members of general police departments, while they usually have authority to enforce all criminal laws, often can exercise that authority only within the boundaries of the governmental unit that employs them (sometimes described as the officer's *bailiwick*).[2] A city policeman's authority often is limited to the city, the sheriff's authority to the county, and the state trooper's authority to the state. In most jurisdictions, if an officer employed by one city should witness a crime committed in another city, he would have no greater authority to arrest for that crime than a private citizen. Indeed, in some jurisdictions, an officer who seeks to make an arrest outside his bailiwick even for a crime committed in his bailiwick is denied the special arrest authority of police officers unless he is acting pursuant to a warrant or is in hot pursuit of the criminal.[3]

---

1. Indeed, in many jurisdictions, certain investigative authority commonly associated with the police officer, such as the special arrest authority of a police officer, is given also to prosecutors or judicial officials.

2. "Bailiwick" originally referred to the bailiff's village, but it now refers to the special district or territory of any police officer.

3. This common law limitation has been rejected in many states. See, e.g., California Penal Code §803.1(a). Some have gone farther. Thus, New York authorizes a police officer to arrest anywhere in the state for crimes other than petty offenses without regard to whether the crime was committed in the officer's bailiwick. See New York Criminal Procedure Law §140.10.

   Most states have provisions authorizing an out-of-state officer to make an arrest within that state when acting in fresh pursuit of a felon fleeing from the officer's state. The arrestee must then be taken before a magistrate, who will review the validity of the arrest. If the magistrate finds the arrest is valid, the officer may take the arrestee back to the officer's state. See, e.g., New York Criminal Procedure Law §140.55, Illinois Stat. ch. 38, §107-4.

   Where a person has fled to another state and an officer cannot make an arrest in close pursuit, the fugitive may be returned through the process of extradition. Article IV, §2 of the federal constitution provides for interstate extradition, and forty-seven states have adopted the more comprehensive Uniform Extradition Act. See West's Uniform Laws Annotated, vol. 11, p. 51. Under extradition procedure, the state in which the fugitive is now located will arrest him and deliver him into the custody of the requesting state upon receiving proper proof that the fugitive had been charged with a crime in the requesting state. Extradition usually is automatic, although a governor occasionally will refuse to extradite an individual on the grounds that justice would not be served by further proceedings. The only legal grounds for objecting to extradition relate to the

In summary, when we note throughout this chapter that a police officer has certain investigative authority, keep in mind that this refers only to officials recognized as police officers under state law who are acting within an area and with respect to a crime for which they have law enforcement responsibilities.

Variations In Investigations. The functions of police investigation are to determine whether a crime has been committed, to determine who committed the crime, to apprehend that person, and to collect evidence that may be used against him at trial. As we noted in the Chapter Eight overview, police investigation may encompass a wide range of practices, including arrest, interrogation, searches, undercover surveillance, examination of records, etc. We will concentrate in this chapter only on those practices that are likely to raise legal difficulties. There are many important investigative techniques that are left largely unregulated by the law because they do not infringe upon any legally protected interests of the individual. For example, the detective who examines old newspapers to gather information about a suspect need not be concerned about probable cause, self-incrimination, or any of the other legal concepts that we will discuss in this chapter. The same position is occupied by the criminalistics officer who utilizes scientific tests to analyze evidence found in open view at the scene of the crime. Quite naturally, most of the publicity is attracted by police investigative practices that tend to be at the center of legal controversy. These are important practices, but we should keep in mind that they are only part of the total investigatory process.

Another factor to keep in mind is the varied use of the different investigative practices. The scope of the investigation in any single case will depend upon the needs of that case. A crucial factor will be the strength of the evidence available at the outset of the investigation. Far fewer investigatory steps are needed when an officer observes the crime being committed and can make an immediate arrest than when there are no eyewitnesses or eyewitnesses can provide only a vague description of the offender. Another significant factor will be the nature of the offense. Murder, burglary, embezzlement, and gambling are all violations of the criminal law, yet they are distinct types of behavior requiring different techniques to ensure effective investigation. Many of the investigative techniques most commonly dramatized on the television screen turn out in practice to be of limited value. The scientific laboratory analysis, for example, is very helpful in only a limited class of cases. For many major felonies, such as armed robbery, there rarely is any physical evidence on which the police technician can even begin to work.[4] The seriousness of the crime may also be a significant factor in determining the scope of the investigation. Some offenses may be so insignificant that police will not devote extensive resources to their investigation.[5] In other cases, the offense

---

form of the papers; the fugitive may not challenge the merits of his prosecution in the other jurisdiction.

4. Moreover, even when traces are found, they may only be useful in identifying an offender by matching the traces against samples of clothes, hair, or blood taken from a prime suspect. The police still must first identify the suspect and gain sufficient evidence against the suspect so that they will have legal authority to take the samples from him.

5. While state statutes do not specifically give police discretion to decide how extensively they will investigate a reported crime, that discretion has always been recognized as existing in the absence of a contrary statutory direction. Police are not under a legal obligation to fully investigate all

may be sufficiently significant, but the likelihood of success may be too slim to justify extensive investigation.

CONSTITUTIONAL FRAMEWORK
REGULATING INVESTIGATORY PRACTICES

The investigation of crime is one of the two stages in the criminal justice process (the trial being the other) that are most closely regulated by the Bill of Rights' guarantees. Indeed, the impact of the federal constitution is so significant that the Supreme Court decisions dealing with criminal investigations may well have been the most highly publicized group of decisions rendered by that Court over the past two decades. The limitations imposed by those decisions upon basic police investigatory techniques, such as interrogation, searches, electronic eavesdropping, and lineups, have stemmed largely from four constitutional guarantees—the Fourth Amendment provisions on searches and seizures, the Fifth Amendment right against self-incrimination, the Sixth Amendment right to the assistance of counsel, and the due process guarantees of the Fifth and Fourteenth Amendments. Although the specific requirements of these amendments will be discussed later in the chapter, you should initially be aware of their general thrust and their impact upon the trial as a result of the application of the "exclusionary rule."

The Fourth Amendment.   The Fourth Amendment to the United States Constitution reads as follows:

> *The right of the people to be secure in their persons, houses, papers, and effects, against unreasonable searches and seizures, shall not be violated, and no Warrants shall issue, but upon probable cause, supported by Oath or affirmation, and particularly describing the place to be searched, and the persons or things to be seized.*

Note that the amendment does not refer specifically to arrests. It obviously was intended to apply to arrests, however, since it refers to warrants for the "seizure" of "persons," which are arrest warrants. Accordingly, both the warrant provision and the initial provision referring to unreasonable seizures of persons have been viewed from the start as applying to arrests. In 1964, in the case of *Terry v. Ohio,*[6] the Supreme Court held that the reference to unreasonable seizures of persons went beyond arrests and also applied to the temporary detention of a person for investigation (as in a forcible stop to briefly question a person).

The Fourth Amendment, as you can see, is divided into clauses. The first clause prohibits unreasonable searches and seizures and the second deals with the

---

offenses reported, no matter how insignificant the offense or how unlikely it is that the investigation will be successful. The decision to extensively investigate can be based upon a variety of factors similar in nature to those governing the decision to prosecute. See p.   infra. Studies have shown, for example, that police in some communities will not go beyond taking the victim's report where the offense is minor (stolen hubcaps) and the identity or whereabouts of the offender is unknown.

6.   392 U.S. 1, 88 S.Ct. 1868, 20 L.Ed.2d 889 (1968).

issuance of warrants (i.e., court orders) authorizing searches and seizures. The Supreme Court has interpreted the two clauses as being closely related to each other, with the second largely dominating the first. For example, only the second clause refers to probable cause, requiring that warrants be issued only on the basis of probable cause. The first clause states that searches and seizures may not be "unreasonable," but it does not state specifically that searches or seizures are unreasonable if not based on probable cause. The Supreme Court has held, however, that the probable cause requirement generally applies to both clauses. Its analysis has been based both on the English common law background of the Fourth Amendment and the fact that the draftsmen certainly did not intend to permit government officials to evade the probable cause requirement of the warrant clause by conducting searches and seizures without warrants. The latter point is illustrated by considering the quite common police practice of making arrests without a warrant. In such cases, the seizure of the person (i.e. the arrest) must be tested by the reasonableness requirement of the Fourth Amendment's first clause. If that clause did not hold invalid an arrest without probable cause, then it would be easier to arrest without a warrant than with a warrant, and the warrant clause would be undermined. Accordingly, the Supreme Court has held that an arrest without a warrant must be based on the same type of probable cause that would be needed to gain a warrant authorizing that arrest. The same kind of analysis also has been applied to searches, and the Supreme Court has held that, at least as to the traditional search for evidence (the kind commonly covered by warrants), probable cause also is required when the search is conducted without a warrant.

In dealing with searches, where time is often available to obtain a warrant, the Court has also sought to integrate the two clauses by holding that the warrant issuance process itself is an essential element of the reasonableness required by the first clause. As we shall see, the Court has held that a search generally will be viewed as unreasonable if there was opportunity to obtain a warrant and the police failed to obtain it. Unless one of several special exceptions justifies the lack of a warrant, a search conducted without a warrant, though otherwise justified by probable cause, will be held invalid under the first clause of the Fourth Amendment. Why this emphasis upon obtaining warrants? In part, it is another reflection of the Court's concern that the first clause not be used to undermine the second clause. In part also, the emphasis on warrants reflects the Court's conclusion that the warrant procedure provides significant additional protection to the subject of a search. The determination that probable cause exists is not always easy to make, and the Court has assumed that the warrant process, by requiring the magistrate's review of the officer's probable cause determination, will produce fewer mistakes and therefore fewer searches that lack probable cause justification. In *Johnson v. United States,* the Court expressed this view as follows:

> *The point of the Fourth Amendment, which often is not grasped by zealous officers, is not that it denies law enforcement the support of the usual inferences which reasonable men draw from evidence. Its protection consists in requiring that those inferences [i.e., the probable cause determination] be drawn by a neutral and detached magistrate instead of being*

judged by the officer engaged in the often competitive enterprise of ferreting out crime.[7]

As we shall see, perhaps the greatest confusion in the area of searches centers upon defining those situations in which the *Johnson* viewpoint will prevail and warrants will be required and those situations in which countervailing needs of effective law enforcement will permit searches to be conducted without warrants.

The Right Against Self-Incrimination.   The Fifth Amendment to the United States Constitution declares, "No person shall . . . be compelled in any criminal case to be a witness against himself." This guarantee commonly is described as the "right to remain silent" or the "right against self-incrimination." The guarantee has its roots in the English opposition to the "investigation by oath" technique used by the early English Courts, including the infamous Court of the Star Chamber. That court conducted inquiries, often into the most politically sensitive crimes, by relying largely on compelled testimony. A suspect was called before the court and ordered to testify under oath. If he refused, his action was in "contempt" of the court's order, and he was subject to punishment for that contempt. If he testified, he often was questioned in such a manner that, no matter what he said, his statement would be twisted and manipulated against him. The Court of the Star Chamber was abolished in 1641, but the lessons of history were not lost on the early American settlers. The federal constitution and all but two of the original state constitutions contained prohibitions against self-incrimination.

The history behind the self-incrimination clause has been an important element in shaping its interpretation. It was clear from its language that the self-incrimination clause prohibited a prosecutor from forcing the defendant to testify at trial; the defendant could testify if he so desired, but he could not be compelled to testify. The question arose, however, as to whether the self-incrimination clause was to be read literally to bar compelled testimony only in the criminal case itself. The Supreme Court recognized that such a narrow construction would permit the evils of the Star Chamber proceeding to be duplicated in the American criminal justice process. If the defendant could be required to testify at preliminary proceedings and then have his testimony there used against him at trial, his right not to testify at trial would be meaningless. Accordingly, the Court has held that a witness can refuse to testify at a preliminary hearing, a grand jury hearing, or any other proceeding where his answers might directly furnish evidence or lead to evidence that could be used against him in a criminal case. Moreover, this right exists not simply for the person already charged with crime, but any person who could be prosecuted in the future. A witness before a Congressional committee hearing, for example, may refuse to answer an incriminating question on the basis of the Fifth Amendment even though no criminal charges are pending against him.

The self-incrimination clause initially was applied only to government attempts to compel testimony through the use of a court order to testify. In all of the proceedings in which the clause first was held applicable, the individual was

---

7.   *Johnson v. United States,* 333 U.S. 10, 14, 68 S.Ct. 367, 369, 92 L.Ed. 436 (1948).

being required to testify by a court order (a *subpoena*) and his refusal to testify, if not for the protection of the Fifth Amendment, would have resulted in criminal punishment for contempt. The compulsion in these cases came from the judicial authority to punish a refusal to comply with its orders. In *Miranda v. Arizona,*[8] a key case discussed later in this chapter, the Supreme Court held that the amendment also was applicable to another, more informal form of compulsion. The issue posed in *Miranda* was whether police use of various abusive interrogation techniques to induce a suspect to make incriminating statements violated the self-incrimination clause. Though the police had no legal authority to compel the suspect to answer their questions, their interrogation practices obviously exerted considerable psychological pressure. Examining the practices of the Star Chamber, which had included various abusive interrogation techniques, the Court concluded that the Fifth Amendment did not distinguish between "the informal compulsion exerted by law enforcement officers during in-custody questioning" and the "formal compulsion" of the court order in a judicial proceeding.[9] This ruling has had, as we shall see, a significant bearing on police investigative practices.

Sixth Amendment Right To Counsel.   The Sixth Amendment declares that, "In all criminal prosecutions, the accused shall enjoy the right to ... have the Assistance of Counsel for his defense." This guarantee was originally interpreted to mean that the defendant had a right to be assisted by counsel of his own choosing at trial. By expanding upon that interpretation in two areas, the court has given the Sixth Amendment a significant impact even at the investigatory stage. First, the Court held that the indigent accused had the same right to the assistance of counsel as his more affluent counterpart.[10] Accordingly, the indigent accused could demand that the state provide him with a lawyer, paid by the state, whenever an accused with funds could insist that he had a constitutional right to the assistance of his privately retained lawyer. Second, the Court held that the constitutional right to assistance of counsel was not limited to the trial. The Sixth Amendment refers to the "accused" and it therefore applies as soon as the suspect becomes an "accused" person through the commencement of the criminal prosecution. This occurs at the point that "adversary judicial proceedings have been initiated" by the filing of a formal charge and the presentation of the suspect before a court on that charge.[11] In the typical proceeding, this stage is reached when a complaint is filed with a magistrate and the arrested person is presented before the magistrate at the first appearance. From that point on, the suspect is an accused person, and he is entitled to the assistance of counsel at any "critical

---

8.   *Miranda v. Arizona,* 384 U.S. 436, 86 S.Ct.1602, 16 L.Ed.2d 694 (1966).

9.   The Court noted: "We are satisfied that all the principles embodied in the privilege apply to informal compulsion exerted by law-enforcement officers during in-custody questioning. An individual swept from familiar surroundings into police custody, surrounded by antagonistic forces, and subjected to the techniques of persuasion described above cannot be otherwise than under compulsion to speak. As a practical matter, the compulsion to speak in the isolated setting of the police station may well be greater than in courts or other official investigations, where there are often impartial observers to guard against intimidation or trickery." 436 U.S. at 461.

10.   This development is discussed in Chapter Eleven at pp. 277-79 *infra*.

11.   See *Kirby v. Illinois,* 406 U.S. 682, 689, 92 S.Ct. 1877, 1882, 32 L.Ed.2d 411 (1972).

stage" of the criminal proceeding—that is, any stage at which "substantial rights of the accused may be affected" and the "guiding hand of counsel" is therefore necessary.[12] Many preliminary proceedings in a criminal case, including investigatory proceedings, can be critical stages protected by the Sixth Amendment. Thus, the Supreme Court has held that the interrogation of an accused person is a critical stage because a confession given during interrogation could surely affect the accused's subsequent trial. Because of its potential for manipulation, a lineup also is a critical stage. If the police desire to use these investigative techniques after the suspect has formally become an "accused," they must grant him his right to the assistance of counsel, including the assistance of state-provided counsel if he is indigent.

Due Process.   As we saw in the last chapter, the due process clause of the Fifth and Fourteenth Amendments prohibits fundamentally unfair practices that are not barred by more specific constitutional guarantees. One basic test of due process, in judging the fairness of a particular procedure, is that the procedure be consistent with the overall criminal justice goal of avoiding the mistaken conviction of innocent persons. Thus, a prosecutor violates due process if he purposely keeps from the court evidence that would tend to establish the innocence of the defendant or he purposely uses evidence that he knows to be false. Due process similarly can be violated through the use of evidence obtained by investigative practices that render the evidence inherently unreliable. Thus, even before *Miranda v. Arizona* found the self-incrimination clause applicable to in-custody police interrogation, the Supreme Court had held that due process was violated by the use of confessions obtained through police interrogation methods that cast serious doubts on the trustworthiness of the statements they produced. Confessions obtained through the use of physical brutality or harsh psychological pressure were excluded from evidence under this rule (which later was expanded to exclude all "involuntary" statements).[13] The Supreme Court also has relied on due process of exclude eyewitness identification testimony based upon identification procedures (e.g., lineups) that were manipulated so as to produce a substantial likelihood to mistaken identification. Another element of due process, recognition of personal dignity, prohibits the use of evidence obtained by investigative practices that are so flagrant as to "shock the conscience" of a "civilized society."[14]

---

12.   See *Kirby v. Illinois,* 406 U.S. 682, 92 S.Ct. 1877, 32 L.Ed.2d 411 (1972); *Mempa v. Rhay,* 389 U.S. 128, 88 S.Ct. 254, 19 L.Ed.2d 336 (1968); *Coleman v. Alabama,* 399 U.S. 1, 90 S.Ct. 1999, 26 L.Ed.2d 387 (1970).

13.   The due process prohibition of "involuntariness" eventually approximated the prohibition against compelled self-incrimination which was later held in *Miranda* to apply to custodial interrogation of suspects. See pp. 259-60 *infra.*

14.   In the leading case, *Rochin v. California,* 342 U.S. 165, 72 S.Ct. 205, 97 L.Ed. 183 (1952), police entered without notice a home which defendant shared with others, forced open the door to defendant's bedroom, and then used a stomach pumping process to retrieve two pills the defendant had swallowed. The police actions almost certainly would have been viewed as a violation of the Fourth Amendment, but the Supreme Court had not yet held that amendment applicable to the states through the Fourteenth Amendment due process clause. See pp. 219-21 *supra.* The Court held that due process was violated and the evidence obtained by the police could not be used against the defendant at his trial.

The Exclusionary Remedy.   Assuming that a police investigative technique violates a suspect's constitutional rights, what remedies are available? Both state and federal law commonly provide for civil actions to collect money damages. The value of a civil action is limited, however, because: (1) damages generally can be recovered only upon a showing that the officer intentionally violated the suspect's constitutional rights; (2) in many jurisdictions, civil actions can be brought against the individual officer, but not his governmental employer, and the officer commonly will lack the funds to pay high damage awards; and (3) where the suspect had, in fact, committed a crime and the police illegality was not flagrant, juries tend to be rather unsympathetic to the suspect's damage claim. [15]Arguably, the more effective remedy, and certainly the more significant in terms of its impact upon the criminal justice process, is the *exclusionary remedy.* That remedy, simply put, prohibits the prosecution from using at trial evidence obtained in violation of the defendant's constitutional rights. The remedy is called the "exclusionary" remedy because the evidence is excluded from the trial. It applies to each of the constitutional provisions discussed above. Thus, if the police search the home of a murder suspect in violation of the Fourth Amendment and find a murder weapon, they cannot use that weapon in any subsequent prosecution of that suspect. If they obtained the suspect's confession through compulsion violating the suspect's right against self-incrimination, that confession cannot be used in evidence at any subsequent trial. If, after adversary judicial proceedings have started and the suspect has formally become an "accused" person, the police deny him the right to be assisted by counsel during a critical proceeding (e.g., a lineup), any evidence obtained in that proceeding will be excluded as having been acquired in violation of the Sixth Amendment right to counsel. Finally, if evidence was obtained through a procedure so unfair as to be likely to produce untrustworthy evidence (e.g., a manipulated lineup where the suspect is the only person remotely fitting the description of the offender), that evidence also will be excluded on the ground that its admission would violate due process. Moreover, in each instance, the exclusionary remedy will not be limited simply to that evidence immediately obtained through the constitutional violation. Any evidence subsequently discovered through the use of information obtained from the initial constitution violation also will be excluded.

Although we tend to refer to the exclusionary remedy as a single remedy for all constitutional violations, the theoretical justifications for the remedy differ substantially with the constitutional right violated. These differences in theory are reflected in the division among justices of the Supreme Courts as to the validity of the remedy. All of the justices have agreed that evidence obtained in violation of the self-incrimination prohibition and the due process guarantee must be excluded from a criminal trial. There has been continued disagreement, however, as to the need for the exclusion of evidence obtained in violation of the Fourth and Sixth Amendments. With respect to Fourth Amendment violations, in particular, several justices argue that the exclusionary rule should either be rejected or limited in application to cases involving flagrant violations. So far, this

---

15.   For a review of available civil remedies, see R. Spurrier, *To Preserve These Rights,* Port Washington, N.Y., Kennikat Press, 1977; S. Schlessinger, *Exclusionary Injustice,* New York, Marcel Decker, 1977.

position has not commanded the support of a majority of the justices, but it may do so in the future. In light of this possibility, it is especially important that you appreciate the differences in the underlying justifications for the rule as applied to different types of constitutional violations.

In the case of self-incrimination, exclusion is required by the plain language of the Fifth Amendment. The historical objective of the self-incrimination prohibition clearly was to keep the prosecution from using the compelled statement of the defendant. In the case of a due process violation, the language of the clause does not specifically require exclusion, but exclusion follows from the nature of the violation. For example, if due process is violated because evidence was obtained by methods likely to render it untrustworthy, the untrustworthy nature of the evidence logically dictates that it must be excluded. Exclusion of evidence obtained through a Fourth Amendment violation has been a subject of controversy because the language of the amendment does not specifically require exclusion and the impact of the remedy is to bar evidence that is trustworthy. The latter point is illustrated by our hypothetical excluding a murder weapon found in an illegal search of the defendant's home. The fact that the search was conducted without a warrant or probable cause does not make the evidence less reliable than if it were found as a result of a lawful search. There is no dispute as to where the weapon was found, and its presence in the defendant's home clearly is relevant in determining his guilt. Thus the exclusion of evidence obtained in violation of the Fourth Amendment must rest on grounds somewhat different from those applied to self-incrimination and due process violations.[16]

The key case holding the exclusionary remedy applicable to Fourth Amendment violations is *Mapp v. Ohio*.[17] Prior to that case, courts and legislatures had divided as to the need for the exclusionary rule. The federal courts and almost half of the states prohibited prosecution use of evidence obtained through unlawful searches.[18] They argued that any other rule would render the Fourth Amendment guarantee almost worthless, and that excluding the evidence was the only way to discipline the police and prevent their violation of the Fourth Amendment guarantees. The other half of the states rejected that view. They argued that, if the prosecutor were denied the use of illegally seized evidence, he often would be unable to prove his case and the guilty defendant would go free. A police officer's wrongdoing in conducting an illegal search did not justify excluding reliable evidence and thereby allowing a criminal to go free.[19] They also contended that there

---

16. Arguably this is not the case where the due process violation relates to the preservation of the dignity of the person rather than the untrustworthy nature of the evidence. See e.g., note 14 *supra*.

17. *Mapp v. Ohio,* 367 U.S. 643, 81 S.Ct. 1684, 6 L.Ed.2d 1081 (1961).

18. The federal adoption of the exclusionary rule dated back to the 1914 decision of the Supreme Court in *Weeks v. United States,* 232 U.S. 383 34 S.Ct. 341, 58 L.Ed. 652 (1914). Although the *Weeks* ruling apparently was based on the Fourth Amendment, it did not apply to the states since the Supreme Court had not yet held that Fourth Amendment protections were incorporated in the due process clause of the Fourteenth Amendment. See pp. 219-21 *supra*.

19. The most well known statement of this position is found in the opinion of Judge (later Supreme Court Justice) Benjamin Cardozo in *People v. Defore,* 242 N.Y. 13, 150 N.E. 585 (1942):

    "The criminal is to go free because the constable has blundered . . . [Under the exclusionary remedy] the pettiest peace officer would have it in his power, through overzeal or indiscretion

were other ways (e.g., civil suits and disciplinary proceedings) to discourage police illegalities. In *Mapp,* the Supreme Court majority rejected both of these arguments. It held that the exclusionary rule was required by the Fourth Amendment since its use was essential to the vindication of the individual's rights under that amendment.

The *Mapp* majority rested its conclusion as to the essential nature of the exclusionary rule on two grounds. First, it stressed the need for exclusion to deter improper police practices. The purpose of the rule, the majority noted, "is to deter —to compel respect for the constitutional guarantee in the only effectively available way—by removing the incentive to disregard it."[20] The majority rejected the suggestion that other remedies might be equally effective in this connection. It noted with approval the conclusion of a state court that "other remedies have completely failed to secure compliance with the constitutional provisions." The majority opinion also supported the exclusion of unconstitutionally seized evidence as a logical extension of the judiciary's duty to uphold the Constitution. Thus, the opinion noted:

> *There are those who say, as did Justice (then Judge) Cardozo, that under our constitutional exclusionary doctrine '[t]he criminal is to go free because the constable has blundered.' In some cases this will undoubtedly be the result. But, as was said in [a later case] 'there is another consideration—the imperative of judicial integrity.' The criminal goes free, if he must, but it is the law that sets him free. Nothing can destroy a government more quickly than its failure to observe its own laws, or worse, its disregard of the charter of its own existence. As Mr. Justice Brandeis, dissenting, said in* Olmstead v. United States: *'Our government is the potent, the omnipresent teacher. For good or for ill, it teaches the whole people by its example. . . . If the government becomes a lawbreaker, it breeds contempt for law; it invites every man to become a law unto himself; it invites anarchy.*[21]

The reasoning of *Mapp* was later extended, with little additional explanation, to evidence obtained by police investigative methods that violated an accused person's right to the assistance of counsel. Thus, in *Massiah v. United States,*[22] the Court excluded a confession obtained from an already indicted defendant who was questioned without being informed of his right to the assistance of counsel. In several states, courts have extended the exclusionary rule to

---

to confer immunity upon an offender for crimes the most flagitious. A room is searched against the law and the body of a murdered man is found. If the place of discovery may not be proved, the other circumstances may be insufficient to connect the defendant with the crime. The privacy of the home has been infringed, and the murderer goes free."

20. This deterrent function, the majority explained, adequately responded to those who challenged the validity of the exclusionary rule on the ground that it failed to assist victims of illegal searches who were innocent, were never prosecuted, and therefore had no need to exclude any illegally seized evidence. Since the function of the exclusionary rule was to prevent future violations, it served all potential victims of unconstitutional searches, whether guilty or innocent of crimes.

21. 367 U.S. at 659.

22. *Massiah v. United States,* 377 U.S. 201, 84 S.Ct. 1199, 12 L.Ed.2d 246 (1964). See p. 262 *infra* discussing the *Massiah* case.

bar evidence obtained through investigative methods that violate state law, but do not violate the federal constitution.[23]

Derivative Evidence. The exclusionary rule requires exclusion of all evidence derived by the prosecution from a constitutional violation. This includes not only evidence obtained directly from a constitutional violation, but further evidence— sometimes described as "secondary" or "derivative" evidence—that is obtained through leads furnished by the directly obtained evidence. Thus, if the police conduct an illegal search of a bookmaking operation and find records that lead them to some hidden bank accounts, both the initially discovered records and the bank accounts will be subject to the exclusionary rule. Similarly, if the police deprive a defendant of his Sixth Amendment right to counsel and consequently obtain a confession, both the confession and evidence discovered through the confession will be excluded from evidence.

The Supreme Court has explained the exclusion of secondary evidence as merely depriving the government of the "fruits of the poisonous tree." The constitutional violation is the poisonous tree and the exclusionary rule ensures that the prosecution does not benefit from the violations extension by excluding the evidentiary fruits borne by the tree. The Court has recognized, however, that there are limits in the application of the "poisonous fruits" rule. If the means of acquiring evidence are substantially removed and distinguishable from the initial violation, the secondary evidence will be admissible. Thus, in *Wong Sun v. United States,*[24] two of the defendants were arrested in violation of the Fourth Amendment. One responded immediately to his arrest by admitting his guilt and telling the police where they might find the narcotics they were seeking. The Court held that his statement and the narcotics both were fruits of the unconstitutional arrest and therefore could not be used at trial. The other defendant eventually made an incriminating statement several days after the unconstitutional arrest. In the meantime, he had been released from police custody pending trial. His statement could be used by the prosecution. Even though he might never have made the statement if he had not been arrested in the first place, his voluntary actions several days later made the "connection between the arrest and the statement . . . so attenuated as to dissipate the taint" of the original constitutional violation.

Exclusionary Rule Exceptions. There are a few narrow exceptions to the exclusionary rule. The two most significant exceptions relate to the legal doctrines of "standing" and "impeachment." The doctrine of standing says basically that a defendant has the right to object to a constitutional violation (i.e., has "standing" to object) only if he was a victim of the violation. Thus, a defendant can seek to

---

23. See, e.g., *People v. Brisendine,* 13 Cal.3d 528, 119 Cal. Rptr. 315 531 P.2d 1099 (1975) (evidence obtained through violation of state constitutional guarantee); *Johnson v. State,* 282 Md. 314, 384 A.2d 709 (1978) (evidence obtained through violation of a court rule requiring prompt presentment of an arrestee before a magistrate). The Federal Crime Control Act restricting electronic surveillance (see p. 257 *infra*), also requires exclusion of evidence obtained through violations of the Act.

24. *Wong Sun v. United States,* 371 U.S. 471, 83 S.Ct. 407, 9 L.Ed.2d 441 (1963).

exclude evidence only if his rights were violated by the unconstitutional police activity that produced the evidence. For example, if A's house is searched in violation of the constitution and evidence damaging to B is found there, B cannot prevent the use of that evidence at his trial. B lacks "standing" to object to the illegal acquisition of the evidence because he was not the victim of the search. Only the person whose privacy was invaded by the search (here A) can object to the use of the evidence obtained through the search. Moreover, that victim can only object when he himself is being prosecuted and the evidence is being used directly against him, rather than against his associates in their prosecution.

The "impeachment" doctrine refers to the right of an opposing party to introduce information showing that a witness is lying. Its impact upon the exclusionary rule arises when a defendant testifies at trial and lies as to a fact that can be disproved by reliable evidence that had been obtained unconstitutionally from the defendant. Consider, for example, *Walder v. United States.*[25] The defendant there, charged with purchasing and possessing heroin, asserted in his trial testimony that he had never handled narcotics at any time "in [his] life." In response, the prosecutor brought to the jury's attention the fact that heroin had been seized in defendant's presence two years previously. The earlier seizure had been unconstitutional, and the narcotics accordingly had been excluded from evidence at the defendant's previous trial for possession of those narcotics. The Supreme Court held that nevertheless the same evidence could be used to impeach the defendant in the current trial. As the Court reasoned, "it is one thing to say that the Government cannot make affirmative use of evidence unlawfully obtained, [but] ... quite another to say that the defendant can turn the illegal method by which evidence in the Government's possession was obtained to his own advantage and provide him with a shield against contradiction of his untruths."

Having examined the constitutional framework regulating investigatory practices, including the primary means of enforcing those constitutional regulations (the exclusionary rule), we can now turn to an examination of particular investigative practices. We start with the initial restraints imposed upon the suspect (temporary detention and arrest), then consider searches and interrogation, and finish with identification procedures. As noted previously, these procedures are only a part of the total range of investigatory practices used by the police. There are other significant techniques that we will not discuss since they present far fewer, if any, difficult legal questions.

TEMPORARY DETENTION

Stops. The stop (sometimes called a forcible stop) often is the first step taken by a police officer in dealing with a suspect. We described the stop in Chapter Nine as the use of police authority to detain a suspect in the officer's presence for a short

---

25. *Walder v. United States,* 347 U.S. 62, 74 S.Ct. 354, 98 L.Ed. 503 (1954).

period of time. A more complete definition is contained in the *Model Rules For Law Enforcement:*[26]

> "A 'stop' is a temporary detention of a person for investigation. A stop occurs when an officer uses his authority either to compel a person to halt, to remain in a certain place, or to perform some act (such as walking to a nearby location where the officer can use a radio, telephone, or call box). If a person is under a *reasonable* impression that he is not free to leave the officer's presence, a 'stop' has occurred."

The stop should be distinguished from what the *Model Rules* describe as a "contact"—"the face-to-face communication between an officer and a private person under circumstances where the person is free to leave if he wishes." The Supreme Court has held that a stop is a "seizure" of a person and it therefore is governed by the Fourth Amendment. However, since the stop does not involve the same degree of restraint as an arrest, it may be justified on a standard of probability less than the probable cause standard applied to on arrest. It requires only sufficient information to establish a "reasonable basis" for believing the suspect has committed, is committing, or is about to commit a crime. A contact, on the other hand, does not even require a reasonable basis. The officer may act without any rational basis for suspicion whatsoever. As Justice White noted in *Terry v. Ohio:*[27] "There is nothing in the constitution which prevents a policeman from addressing questions to anyone on the streets. Absent special circumstances [justifying a stop], the person approached may not be detained or frisked but may refuse to cooperate and go on his way."

Reasonable Basis. We have already described in Chapter Nine the "reasonable basis" standard (sometimes called a "reasonable suspicion" standard) needed to justify a stop. Most frequently, the reasonable basis will be provided by facts observed by the officer, such as the person's conduct (e.g., running away from an actual or possible crime scene) and location (e.g., in a high crime area at a very late hour). The officer may also rely, however, on information given to him by someone else. In *Adams v. Williams,*[28] for example, the Court approved a stop where an informant known to the officer told him that a man sitting in a nearby car was carrying narcotics and had a gun at his waist. The officer did not have enough information as to the informant's reliability to establish probable cause for an arrest, but he did have a reasonable basis to justify a forcible stop of the man in the car.

Police Conduct During A Stop. Even though the officer clearly has proper justification for a stop, he must make certain that his conduct during the stop also is within the allowable limits of the law. What may the officer do after the initial stop has been made? He certainly may detain the person—using reasonable force, if necessary—for a reasonable period while he obtains further information from another source (e.g., police headquarters) concerning the possible commission of a

---

26. Project on Law Enforcement Policy and Rulemaking, *Model Rules For Law Enforcement: Stop and Frisk,* Tempe, Ariz.: Arizona State University College of Law, 1973, p. 3.

27. *Terry v. Ohio,* 392 U.S. 1, 34, 88 S.Ct. 1868, 20 L.Ed.2d. 889 (1968) (concurring opinion).

28. *Adams v. Williams,* 407 U.S. 143, 92 S.Ct. 1921, 32 L.Ed.2d. 612 (1972).

crime. The permissible length of a stop for this purpose is unclear, but the *Model Rules* suggest a maximum period of no more than twenty minutes. Ordinarily, the officer will want to question the individual, asking him to at least identify himself and explain his presence in the area. The officer clearly has such authority, but the individual, at least in most jurisdictions, has no duty to respond. A few jurisdictions have statutes requiring the individual lawfully stopped to identify himself and account for his actions.[29] The constitutionality of such provisions is highly questionable in light of the individual's constitutional right against self-incrimination, at least insofar as the statutes require the individual to explain his conduct. Certainly, in the absence of such a statute, the individual has the legal right to refuse to respond to the officer's question. On the other hand, while such a refusal does not by itself establish probable cause to arrest, several lower court cases have suggested that it may be considered, along with other factors, as an element adding up to probable cause, depending upon the circumstances and the nature of the refusal.[30]

Frisks.   In *Terry v. Ohio,*[31] an officer observed three men who appeared to be "casing" a store for a robbery. He then approached the men and asked them their names. When the only response was a mumble, the officer spun one around and frisked him, finding a pistol in his breast pocket. The frisking procedure used in *Terry* was the standard police pat-down technique for discovering weapons. It consists of a pat-down of the outer clothing, concentrating particularly on those areas where a weapon could be concealed, such as the armpits, waist, groin area, and entire surface of the legs. If the officer feels something hard which could be a weapon, he then reaches under the clothing and removes it. The *Terry* decision upheld the frisk procedure under the circumstances of that case and laid down guidelines for its use in the future.[32]

---

29. Local ordinances frequently include such a provision. See, e.g., *People v. Defillippio,* 80 Mich.App. 197, 262 N.W.2d 921 (1977) (holding such an ordinance unconstitutional). State provisions authorizing a stop-and-frisk procedure also commonly note that the officer may demand that the suspect give his name and identify himself, but they do not impose criminal penalties for the suspect's refusal to respond. See the New York provision quoted in note 32 *infra.* Compare the California loitering provision quoted in note 30 *infra.*

30. See *Model Rules,* note 26 *supra,* at pp. 50-51. Some jurisdictions have loitering provisions that may make a refusal to identify and to account an element of a crime. See, e.g., California Penal Code §647(e):

    "Every person who commits any of the following acts is guilty of disorderly conduct, a misdemeanor: . . . Who loiters or wanders upon the streets or from place to place without apparent reason or business and who refuses to identify himself and to account for his presence when requested by any peace officer so to do, if the surrounding circumstances are such as to indicate to a reasonable person that the public safety demands such identification."

    Courts have divided as to whether such provisions violate the due process prohibition against vagueness in criminal statutes.

31. *Terry v. Ohio,* 392 U.S. 1, 88 S.Ct. 1868, 20 L.Ed.2d 889 (1968).

32. The Court found it unnecessary in *Terry* to rule upon the constitutionality of the New York statute authorizing a stop-and-frisk procedure. The New York provision (New York Criminal Procedure Law §140.50) is a typical stop-and-frisk provision. It now provides:

    1. . . . [A] police officer may stop a person in a public place located within the geographical area of such officer's employment when he reasonably suspects that such person is committing, has committed or is about to commit either (a) a felony or (b) misdemeanor defined in

The *Terry* opinion initially concluded that the frisk must be viewed as a search for Fourth Amendment purposes. The Court noted that the frisk is a considerable intrusion upon a person's privacy, possibly inflicting great indignity and arousing strong resentment. On the other hand, the frisk is not a full-fledged search of the person and its objective is to protect the officer against attack rather than to search for evidence of a particular crime. The Court reasoned that, in light of the frisk's less intrusive nature and the officer's need to protect himself, a frisk could be justified on less than the probable cause ordinarily needed for a search of the person for evidence. On the other hand, the officer could not be allowed to frisk at will, simply because he had the reasonable basis needed for a stop. The Court accordingly recognized what it described as a "narrowly drawn authority ... [permitting] a reasonable search for weapons for the protection of the police officer, where he has *reason to believe* that he is dealing with an armed and dangerous individual, regardless of whether he has probable cause to arrest." Note that the standard of probability is the same as that required for the stop—a reasonable basis—except that here the belief must relate to the suspect being armed and dangerous rather than simply to his having committed a crime. The reasonable basis may be established by a variety of factors. In *Terry,* the officer was dealing with suspected criminal activity (a robbery) that often includes the use of weapons. Other cases upholding frisks have recognized the officer's reliance on such factors as an obvious bulge in the suspect's clothing, the suspect's nervousness combined with the concealment of his hand in his pocket, and the suspect's presence in an area where people frequently carry arms.

Summons.   Falling somewhere between the typical investigatory stop and the arrest is the stop for the purpose of issuing a summons. The summons is a notice to appear in court to answer to a criminal charge. The most commonly used summons is the traffic ticket (sometimes called "citation"). In most jurisdictions, the police officer has an option of issuing a summons, rather than taking a person into custody, on a variety of misdemeanor charges.[33] The officer may stop a person suspected of committing a misdemeanor, give him a summons, and then let him

---

the penal law, and may demand of him his name, address and an explanation of his conduct.

* * *

3. When upon stopping a person under circumstances prescribed in subdivision one ... a police officer ... reasonably suspects that he is in danger of physical injury, he may search such person for a deadly weapon or any instrument, article or substance readily capable of causing serious physical injury and of a sort not ordinarily carried in public places by law-abiding persons. If he finds such a weapon or instrument, or any other property possession of which he reasonably believes may constitute the commission of a crime, he may take it and keep it until the completion of the questioning, at which time he shall either return it, if lawfully possessed, or arrest such person.

33.   New York Criminal Procedure Law §150.20 is typical of state provisions authorizing issuance of a summons (called an appearance ticket in New York). That section provides:

(1) Whenever a police officer is authorized to arrest a person without a warrant for an offense other than a felony, he may ... instead issue to and serve upon such person an appearance ticket.

(2) Whenever a police officer has arrested a person without a warrant for an offense other than a felony ..., he may, instead of bringing such person before a local criminal court, ... issue to and serve upon such person an appearance ticket ...

proceed on his way. Ordinarily, the officer may only issue a summons where he also has legal authority to arrest. Thus, he must have probable cause to believe the person has committed the crime noted in the summons. Even though probable cause is required, the stop to issue a summons is not technically treated as an arrest. The officer cannot conduct an incidental search as he could where an arrest is made, and the individual truthfully may say on an employment questionnaire that he never has been arrested.[34] While he was detained and charges were issued, he was not taken into custody as would have been the case for an arrest.

ARREST: THE PROBLEM OF DEFINITION

The Definition Of An Arrest. We have described an arrest up to this point as the act of taking a person into custody for the purpose of charging him with a crime. Although this is a standard textbook definition, even found in some state statutes, it is not without weakness. How the law labels a particular activity may depend in part upon the purpose for which the label is being applied. What is an arrest for one purpose may not be an arrest for another. One always must consider the setting in which the term "arrest" is being used. For example, various courts, in defining the civil damage action for the tort of false arrest, have included as an element of the arrest an understanding by the person arrested that he is being arrested. When the law is seeking to compensate an individual for the mental anguish produced by an illegal detention, the individual's awareness that he was being detained is obviously an important factor. On the other hand, when the law is concerned with exclusion of evidence obtained through illegal arrests, the definition of an arrest may rest more upon the officer's purpose in taking a person into custody than the detained individual's understanding of that purpose. Certainly, for example, if the officer acted without probable cause and took custody for the purpose of making an arrest, his action would not be viewed as something other than an illegal arrest simply because the arrestee was too intoxicated to understand what was happening to him.

In this chapter, we are approaching the definition of arrest from the perspective of the legal judgments that are made in the administration of the criminal justice process. In that process, the question of what constitutes an arrest is usually presented in the context of deciding whether a person had been arrested before certain evidence was discovered on his person. (If he had been, and the arrest was illegal, the evidence will be barred from trial as the fruit of the illegal arrest). For the purpose of deciding this issue, a person is viewed as having been

---

34. In recent years, officers have been encouraged to use the summons in lieu of an arrest in most misdemeanor cases. A few jurisdictions have required the officer to use the summons for all non-violent misdemeanors unless circumstances exist suggesting that (1) the individual poses a danger to himself (e.g., due to intoxication), (2) the individual will persist in the misdemeanor if not taken into custody (e.g., the trespassing demonstrator), or (3) the individual is not likely to appear in court as directed by the summons. In considering whether the person is likely to respond to the summons, the officer is directed to consider such factors as: (1) whether the individual has provided satisfactory identification; (2) whether the individual will sign a promise to appear in court as directed; (3) whether the individual lives or works in the community; and (4) whether the individual has a record of failing to appear in past cases. While "mandatory-summons" provisions are a new development as applied to misdemeanors generally, they long have been used in Motor Vehicle Codes for various traffic offenses.

arrested when the two major elements of our definition are present: (1) the police officer has taken the person into custody, and (2) the officer has done so for the purpose of possibly charging the person with the commission of a crime. Thus, while our definition is not an all inciusive definition applicable throughout the law, it is the appropriate definition for our concerns. Both elements of the definition require additional explanation, however, to distinguish the arrest from other police actions.

The Element Of Custody.   When we say that an arrest requires that a person has been taken into "custody," we mean that the officer has exercised control over the movements of that person. Ordinarily that control will include the transportation of the arrestee to a police station or other holding facility. The custody begins, however, at the initial point of detention, which may occur several minutes before the arrestee is placed in a police vehicle. It begins as soon as the officer uses his authority to restrain the suspect from moving on his way.[35] Exactly when that has occurred is not always clear, although its timing can be crucial to the validity of an arrest. Assume, for example, an officer approaches X with the intent to make an arrest, but before the officer reaches him, X does something incriminating (e.g., tries to discard narcotics). If the officer lacked probable cause as he approached X, the officer's observation of X's action may have converted what would have been an illegal arrest into a legal arrest. But the observation could only be considered in justifying the arrest if it occurred before the arrest took place, that is, before X was in custody. Whether that was the case would depend upon how the officer approached X. If the officer came forward in such a manner as to indicate X was already under restraint (e.g., with him gun drawn), then the arrest had already occurred and X's incriminating response could not be considered in justifying the arrest. If the officer approached in a manner no different from that of an officer who might merely want to engage in a few moments of conversation, then X had not yet been arrested and his incriminating action could be considered in establishing probable cause.

The Element Of Purpose.   Not every exercise of authority by a police officer that restrains the movement of another person constitutes an arrest. There are various situations in which persons are taken into custody and even transported to some facility, but there is not an arrest because the exercise of custody has no relationship to possibly charging the person with the commission of a crime. Thus, a person may be taken into custody and delivered to a mental hospital because he is acting in such a way as to indicate that he is insane and presents an immediate danger to himself. Similarly a lost child may be taken into custody and removed to a police station while the police search for his parents. In these and various other situations too numerous to list, there is the custodial element necessary for the arrest, but not the purpose of holding the person for possible prosecution.

Application of the purpose-element of an arrest becomes more difficult where detention is related to the suspect's possible commission of a crime, but it is

---

35.   State statutes referring to the point of arrest commonly emphasize this element of restraint. See, e.g., Illinois Stat. ch. 38, §107-5(a): "An arrest is made by an actual restraint of the person or by his submission to custody."

unclear whether the officer intends to charge the suspect with a crime. Consider, for example, the situation in which an individual acting suspiciously is ordered to stop by a police officer. Has the person been arrested or only temporarily detained pursuant to the officer's authority to make a stop? The distinction is important because, as we saw, a stop may be justified by a lesser standard of proof (the reasonable basis standard) than an arrest (the probable cause standard). If the suspect subsequently is ordered by the officer to enter the squad car in order to be transported to the station, we clearly have an arrest since the officer has gone beyond the limits of an on-the-street stop. But what if, in the time period between the initial detention and the entry into the car, the suspect engaged in incriminating acts needed to establish probable cause? If the initial detention was only a stop, justified by a reasonable basis, the subsequent incriminating acts established probable cause, and the arrest was valid. On the other hand, if the officer acted initially with the intent to take the person to the station for possible initiation of charges, then the detention was an arrest from the very start and probable cause cannot be established by the suspect's subsequent conduct. The officer's initial purpose thus can be very important. Yet, until that point at which the officer directs the suspect to enter the police car, we cannot really determine his purpose based upon his actions, and we therefore cannot be certain whether he intended to arrest or only to stop. Of course, if the officer states at the outset that the suspect is "under arrest," that answers our question. Most jurisdictions have statutes requiring the officer to immediately inform the arrestee that he is under arrest, except where the circumstances make that impracticable.[36]

Likelihood Of Charges.   When the courts speak of an arrest as a custodial detention for the purpose of pressing charges, they are not saying that officer must believe that charges necessarily will be filed against the person. For example, an officer may be aware, in taking into custody a person who possesses a small quantity of marijuana, that the prosecutor probably will not press charges. The officer nevertheless intends to present the person for the possible filing of charges, and that is sufficient to make the custodial detention an arrest. Some police departments have followed a pattern of regularly taking persons into custody with little likelihood of prosecution. Drunks are taken to the station to allow them to "sober-up," and prostitutes are taken to the station to keep them off the street for

---

36. See, e.g., New York Criminal Procedure Law §140.15(2): "The arresting police officer must 'inform such person of his authority and purpose and of the reason for such arrest unless he encounters physical resistance, flight, or other factors rendering such procedure impracticable." '

Other common statutory provisions relating to the method of an arrest include: (1) authorizing the officer to arrest at any hour of any day or night; (2) authorizing the use of that force necessary and reasonable to make the arrest, including deadly force in some instances (see p. 133 *supra*); (3) authorizing entry onto private premises to make an arrest. In the case of entry into a building not open to the public, the officer ordinarily must "give or make reasonable effort to give notice of his authority and purpose to an occupant" prior to entry. Once notice is given, the officer also must afford the occupant a reasonable opportunity to admit him before entering on his own initiative. However, immediate forcible entry without prior notification (called "no-knock" entry) is authorized where believed to be necessary to avoid endangering the life of the officer or other persons in the vicinity. Many states also permit such entry where surprise is viewed as necessary to prevent the destruction of evidence or to prevent the suspect from escaping. See, e.g., New York Criminal Procedure Law §120.80. The constitutionality of no-knock entry under such circumstances was upheld in *Ker v. California,* 374 U.S. 23, 83 S.Ct. 1623, 10 L.Ed2d 726 (1963).

a night. In either case, the officer's action is an arrest, and it must meet the legal requirements for an arrest. The individual is booked on a charge, and although the charge usually is dropped, the persons are presented for possible prosecutions.

We sometimes hear of arrests "for investigation" or arrests "on suspicion." In these situations, an officer takes a suspect to the police station intending to do no more than question him about a crime. At the time the person is taken into custody, there is no intent to charge him with any crime unless he should happen to confess during the interrogation. Since there is this possibility of prosecution, those arrests may be viewed as true arrests, although some scholars argue that they are simply another form of "seizure" of the person under the Fourth Amendment. No matter how they are characterized, the investigative "arrests" or "seizures" must meet the standard of probable cause required for an arrest. An "arrest on suspicion" that clearly is based on suspicion alone—and not probable cause—is illegal.

ARRESTS: BASIC LEGAL REQUIREMENTS

Requirements For A Legal Arrest. Most jurisdictions divide arrests into three categories in establishing the legal requirements for an arrest:

1. *Arrests pursuant to a warrant.* An officer may lawfully make an arrest for a misdemeanor or a felony pursuant to the direction of a lawfully issued warrant.

2. *Warrantless arrests for a felony.* An officer may make an arrest without a warrant when he has probable cause to believe that the person he is arresting has committed a felony.[37]

3. *Warrantless arrests for a misdemeanor.* Jurisdictions are divided as to the legal requirements for warrantless misdemeanor arrests. Some hold that the officer can arrest whenever he has probable cause. They thus apply the same legal standard as for a warrantless felony arrest. Others permit warrantless arrests for a misdemeanor only if the officer has probable cause and the offense was committed in his presence. Still others require probable cause alone for certain types of misdemeanors and probable cause plus commission in the officer's presence for others.

We will discuss various aspects of the requirements for each category in the next several sections. Note the one common element for each category—the arrest must be justified by probable cause. An arrest pursuant to a warrant is valid only if the warrant was lawfully issued, and a magistrate cannot lawfully issue a warrant unless he properly determines that probable cause exists. A police officer making a

---

37. There are a few exceptions to this position. For example, in Texas, an officer may arrest without a warrant for a felony only where (1) the felony was "committed in his presence or within his view," or (2) "where it is shown by satisfactory proof to a peace officer, upon the representation of a credible person, that a felony has been committed, and that the offender is about to escape, so that there is no time to procure a warrant." See Texas Code of Criminal Procedure, art. 14.01, 14.04.

felony arrest without a warrant must be operating on information that establishes probable cause. The same is true of an officer arresting for a misdemeanor, although here some states limit the officer to misdemeanors committed in his presence. Of course, aside from these state statutory requirements, probable cause also is required under the Fourth Amendment. This central role of the probable cause requirement, under both state and federal law, makes an understanding of the nature of probable cause essential to an understanding of the law of arrest. We discussed the nature of probable cause at some length in Chapter Nine, and it might be helpful at this point to review that discussion.[38]

Arrest With A Warrant. Arrest warrants ordinarily are issued by magistrates, although they can be issued by judges of other courts as well. To obtain a warrant, a police officer must file with the magistrate a sworn complaint alleging that the accused person committed a crime in a particular place within the magistrate's district. The person making the complaint (the complainant) can be either the victim of the crime or the investigating officer himself. Where an officer-complainant did not himself observe the crime, but is relying upon information furnished by others, he ordinarily will describe his accusation as based on "information and belief" as opposed to his "personal knowledge."[39] In several jurisdictions, a complaint ordinarily may be filed only if approved by the prosecuting attorney. This requirement is designed to ensure that criminal proceedings are not initiated in a case where the prosecutor does not believe that prosecution is justified. In

---

38. See pp. 210-12 *supra.* Many state statutes refer to the presence of "reasonable cause" but the courts have held that phrase has the same content as "probable cause." The two phrases often are used interchangeably in statutes and court opinions.

39. Pennsylvania Court Rule 133 sets forth a fairly typical complaint form:

   I, the undersigned do hereby state under oath (affirmation)

   (1) My name is _____ and I live at _____ ;

   (2) I accuse _____, who lives at _____, with violating the penal laws of the Commonwealth of Pennsylvania;

   or

   I accuse an individual whose name is unknown to me but who is described as _____ with violating the penal laws of the Commonwealth of Pennsylvania; . . .

   (3) The date (and day of the week) when the accused committed the offense was on or about _____ ;

   (4) The place where the offense was committed was in the County of _____ _____ ;

   (5) . . . The acts committed by the accused were _____ _____, all of which were in violation of (section) and (subsection) of the Act of _____ or the _____ _____ Ordinance of (political subdivision).

   (6) I ask that a warrant of arrest or a summons be issued and that the accused be required to answer the charges I have made;

   and

   (7) I swear to or affirm the within complaint upon my knowledge, information and belief, and sign it on _____, 19____, before _____ whose office is that of _____.

   _____
   (Signature of affiant)

most jurisdictions, prosecution approval is not a formal legal requirement, but the prosecutor generally is consulted before a felony complaint is filed.

The magistrate may not issue a warrant unless he decides that the complaint is supported by information establishing probable cause to believe the accused person committed the alleged crime. The magistrate may not simply accept the complainant's belief that probable cause exists. He must review for himself the information known to the complainant, which usually is set forth either in the complaint itself or in an accompanying affidavit. In some jurisdictions, the complainant also may testify before the magistrate. If the magistrate concludes that probable cause exists, he issues the warrant. A typical warrant is set forth below.[40] Note that it directed not only to the officer who requested the warrant, but to all officers within the state. Any police officer may make an arrest pursuant to a warrant, and he need not have a copy of the warrant in his possession.

In making an arrest pursuant to a warrant, an officer ordinarily is required to inform the arrestee of the existence of the warrant. In many jurisdictions the officer also must show the warrant to the arrestee if the arrestee makes such a request and the officer has the warrant in his possession. In other states, the arrestee must be given a copy of the warrant as soon as it is "practicable." Once the arrest is made, the officer must see to it that the warrant is returned to the magistrate along with the presentation of the arrested person. On the back of the warrant, the officer will note the time and place of the arrest.

Information from an Informant.   Perhaps the most difficult problem arising in the issuance of warrants has been the treatment of information received from informants in establishing probable cause. An informant is any person who gives an officer information relating to the commission of a crime. The information received by the officer from the informant is known as *hearsay*. When the officer relays that information to the magistrate, he is not reporting on what he himself observed but what he had heard others say (i.e., hearsay). Hearsay is acceptable in establishing probable cause, but it does present certain dangers. We are all familiar with the possibility that a person might falsely accuse another of committing a crime or might pass along to an officer rumors based on the speculation of still other persons. To ensure that arrests are not based on information coming from such unreliable informants, the Supreme Court has held that the officer must have a reasonable ground for relying on hearsay, as established by two factors: (1) circumstances suggesting that the informant is credible (i.e., a person who tells the truth); and (2) circumstances indicating that the informer himself has a reliable

---

40.   A typical warrant form is that suggested in California Penal Code, §814:

County of

The people of the State of California to any peace officer of said State:

Complaint on oath having this day been laid before me that the crime of _____ (designating it generally) has been committed and accusing _____ (naming defendant) thereof, you are therefore commanded forthwith to arrest the above named defendant and bring him before me at _____ (naming the place), or in the case of my absence or inability to act, before the nearest or most accessible magistrate in this county.

Dated at _____ (place) this   day of   , 19   .

_____

(Signature and full official title of magistrate.)

source for the information. Both factors ordinarily must be present. Even though the informant is telling the truth as he believes it to be, that does not necessarily mean that his beliefs are based on a source of information that is reliable. A person may be well respected in the community as a truthful person, yet still make an accusation entirely on speculation. On the other hand, even though a person is in a position to be a reliable source of information (e.g., he witnessed the activity in question), that is no assurance that he will give a truthful account unless he also is a credible person.

In judging hearsay reliability, based on the informant's credibility and source of information, courts carefully distinguish between different types of informants supplying information in different situations. The easiest case for establishing probable cause is that in which the informant claims to be a victim of a crime and is willing to sign a complaint or have his name used in the complaint. There is no assurance that the person is not lying, but his willingness to openly accuse another furnishes adequate indicia of his personal credibility.[41] Where the credible informant-victim also witnessed the crime, he obviously is basing his accusation on personal information rather than rumor or suspicion. Thus, both elements needed to establish the reliability of the hearsay are present. (If the crime was not observed by the victim, then the officer ordinarily must seek further information as to why the victim believes that the particular person he accused committed the crime). The non-victim eyewitness to the crime who is willing to sign a statement as to his observations is basically in the same situation as the victim. While it is possible that he may be lying, the circumstances offer sufficient indicia of credibility to permit the officer to rely on this informant's statement without additional corroboration.

Where an informant provides information relating to a crime he allegedly witnessed, but refuses to permit his identity to be disclosed, his credibility naturally is suspect. In such a case, the officer must consider various factors. Did he interview the informant, so he could personally evaluate his demeanor, or did he receive the information through an anonymous telephone call? Was the informant an ordinary, public-spirited citizen merely fearful of getting "involved" or a person who might have a motive for falsely accusing another?[42] Finally, was there independent corroboration of the informant's story through statements made by others or facts known by the officer? Without substantial corroboration, information from an anonymous informant, even one without any apparent motive for lying, is not likely to furnish sufficient basis in itself for a finding of probable cause.

The police face the greatest difficulty in relying on informants where the informant is drawn from the criminal milieu and the police will not reveal his identity. Courts are aware that criminal informants often receive concessions in

---

41. If the individual signs the complaint, he is subjecting himself to a perjury charge if he has lied. His willingness to bear that risk is another indication that he is telling what he believes to be the truth.

42. Persons with such a motive include jealous spouses or jilted sweethearts, dismissed employees, business rivals, petty offenders who want to stand well with the police, a person planning a crime who hopes to lead the police in the opposite direction, and hired informants (often call professional informers) who are paid for the information they give the police.

exchange for information that leads to a conviction. They also recognize that such informants might be tempted to fabricate information, to "frame" another, in order to obtain a benefit for themselves. Accordingly, in such cases, they always insist that the officer have significant corroborating information. In some cases, a record of reliable information given by the informant in the past will be sufficient. In others, police may have other information that demonstrates the reliability of the informant's information. Of course, it does not prove much to corroborate those portions of the informant's statement that point to facts that are open and obvious to anyone. Corroboration is most helpful when it shows that the informant obviously was in a position to have first-hand knowledge of the activities noted in his statement.

Assuming corroboration or other factors which support the reliability of the informant's information, the officer's application for a warrant must set forth those facts. The magistrate must make his own, independent determination of probable cause. He cannot do so if the officer's affidavit merely states that there is reason to believe the informant is reliable, and does not set forth those reasons. If a warrant is issued based on such a conclusionary statement, the warrant will be invalid and the arrest will be subject to legal attack. Although the officer need not reveal the informant's name, his presentation to the magistrate must include a full statement as to those facts that have led the officer to accept the informant's information as reliable.

Probable Cause and Warrantless Felony Arrests. For felony offenses, neither state law nor federal constitutional law requires that the officer obtain a warrant. Nevertheless, since there is a preference for the neutral judgment of the magistrate, the Supreme Court has indicated that, in a "marginal case," it will be more willing to find the presence of probable cause for an arrest made with a warrant than for an arrest made without a warrant. Of course, in many instances, the officer will not have time to obtain a warrant. He must make an arrest promptly or risk the possibility that the suspect will not be readily found again. In such cases, he often must make a very quick judgment as to whether probable cause exists. Indeed, sometimes he must decide in a matter of seconds whether or not he can make an arrest. The courts recognize that the officer often operates under such pressing circumstances. They note that probable cause is a "practical, nontechnical conception" that takes into consideration the pressures imposed by the need for hasty decisions.[43] Nevertheless, cases do arise where an officer has made an arrest without a warrant, been sustained on his judgment by lower courts,

---

43. The Supreme Court's position is reflected in the following statement: "These long-prevailing standards [of probable cause] seek to safeguard citizens from rash and unreasonable interferences with privacy and from unfounded charges of crime. They also seek to give fair leeway for enforcing the law in the community's protection. Because many situations which confront officers in the course of executing their duties are more or less ambiguous, room must be allowed for some mistakes on their part. But the mistakes must be those of reasonable men, acting on facts leading sensibly to their conclusions of probability. The rule of probable cause is a practical, nontechnical conception affording the best compromise that has been found for accommodating these often opposing interests. Requiring more would unduly hamper law enforcement. To allow less would be to leave law-abiding citizens at the mercy of the officers' whim or caprice." *Brinegar v. United States,* 338 U.S. 160, 69 S. Ct. 1302, 93 L. Ed. 1879 (1949).

and has finally had his action rulled unconstitutional by a narrow majority in a higher appellate court.

One of the major difficulties facing an officer is that there are few hard and fast rules as to the weight to be given to particular conduct of a suspect. Consider, for example, the flight of a suspect when approached by an officer. Flight often is viewed as an incriminating circumstance. It does not establish probable cause by itself, but it usually is an important factor that may, along with other factors, contribute to a finding of probable cause. Yet, there are circumstances under which the court will give almost no weight whatsoever to flight. In the *Wong Sun* case,[44] for example, the Supreme Court was not impressed by a suspect's flight when a federal officer attempted to gain entry to the suspect's laundry at six o'clock in the morning. The officer (who apparently was not in uniform) initially presented himself as a customer, was told that the laundry would not be open for another two hours, and then identified himself as a narcotics agent (showing his badge) and demanded entry. The suspect immediately slammed the door and started running down the hallway to his living quarters at the back of the laundry where his wife and children were sleeping. The Supreme Court stressed that the flight did not furnish the corroboration needed to support incriminating information supplied by an informant. The suspect's flight, under the circumstances, "signified a guilty knowledge no more clearly than it did a natural desire to repel an unauthorized intrusion."

Warrantless Arrests for Misdemeanors. At the common law, arrests for misdemeanors could be made without warrants only when the misdemeanor was committed in the officer's presence. At the time, the consequence of an arrest could be more significant than an eventual misdemeanor conviction. The arrestee often was kept in jail for a substantial period of time while awaiting trial. If the arrest was made pursuant to a warrant, it had the support of the magistrate's judgment. When the officer acted on his own judgment, he was more likely to be mistaken. Reliance on hearsay was viewed as particularly dangerous. Accordingly, the officer could make a warrantless arrest only when the offense was committed in his presence. In such cases, the officer's judgment as to probable cause would be made on his own observations and he was less likely to be mistaken.[45]

In recent years, many states have departed from the common law rule. They feel that the consequences of an arrest are no longer so onerous. Most misdemeanants are released on bail pending trial. Also, officers are better trained, and have more familiarity with evaluating probable cause. Some of these jurisdictions permit warrantless arrests for misdemeanors on the basis of probable cause alone. Some still require the "presence" element for most misdemeanors but create exceptions for several listed offenses (e.g., possession of drugs), where probable cause alone is enough. Others permit departure from the presence requirement under specified circumstances, such as the officer's reasonable belief that the person may cause injury unless taken into custody immediately or that the person

---

44. See note 24 at p. 236 *supra*.

45. The offense need not actually be witnessed by the officer, however. Courts have held that a misdemeanor is committed in the officer's presence if he is able to perceive it through any of his five senses—sight, hearing, touch, taste, and smell.

will not be apprehended unless he is arrested immediately. Of course, these conditions only offset the presence requirement; the officer still must have probable cause.[46]

SEARCHES

What Is A Search? A search basically is an action of a government official that invades a person's reasonable expectation of privacy. Ordinarily, it involves an officer looking at something, but a search also can be achieved through the other senses, such as listening. The key is that the observation (or other use of the senses) invaded the privacy of the person complaining about its illegality. If a court determines that the observation was of a type that the complaining party reasonably could have expected, then there has been no invasion of any privacy interest protected by the Fourth Amendment. Thus, though the Fourth Amendment refers to the right of people to be secure against unreasonable searches in their houses, not all observation into a house necessarily constitutes a search. If an officer, standing on a sidewalk, can look through the picture window of a house and see contraband in the front room, he has not conducted a search. As the Supreme Court noted in *Katz v. United States*,[47] the leading case on the definition of a search: "[T]he Fourth Amendment protects people, not places. What a person knowingly exposes to the public, even in his own home or office, is not a subject of Fourth Amendment protection."

When and where does a person have a reasonable expectation of privacy? It generally is held that you do not have such an expectation just because the property involved belongs to you. An owner of farm lands, for example, has no reasonable privacy expectation as to what is located in his open fields. Indeed, one court held that a homeowner did not have a reasonable expectation of privacy as to a marijuana plant growing in a planter in his backyard; the plant could be readily observed by delivery men and others who came to the back door.[48] Neither is there a reasonable expectation of privacy as to items in a car that can be seen by looking through the car windows. Moreover, in such cases, the officer's action does not become a search simply because a flashlight is used to observe matter otherwise open to view during the nighttime. On the other hand, a person can sometimes have a reasonable expectation of privacy even in a public place. Thus, in *Katz,* the Court noted that while a person placing a call in a public telephone booth could reasonably anticipate that others would see him, there was a search when the police used an electronic eavesdropping device to *listen* to his conversation.

---

46. As of 1975, the jurisdictions that have departed entirely from the common law presence requirement include: Colorado, Hawaii, Illinois, Iowa, Louisiana, New York and Wisconsin. States that recognize the presence requirement but create major exceptions thereto include: Connecticut, Georgia, Kansas, Maryland, Nebraska, Montana, North Carolina, Ohio, Oregon, Rhode Island, Utah, Virginia, Washington, and Wyoming. The remaining states follow the presence requirement permitting only minor exceptions, if any. One or two states still follow the earlier common law rule which limited warrantless arrests to misdemeanors that constituted a breach of the peace and were committed in the officer's presence.

47. *Katz v. United States*, 389 U.S. 347, 88 S.Ct. 507, 19 L.Ed.2d 576 (1967).

48. *People v. Bradley,* 1 Cal.3d 80, 81 Cal.Rptr. 457, 460 P.2d 129 (1969).

Closely related to the reasonable expectation of privacy concept is the "plain view" rule. Assume that an item is located in a home, office, hotel room, or some other place where it generally is not open to public view. A peace officer enters the premises in a lawful manner and sees the item. In such a case, there has been no search. So long as the officer "had a right to be in the position to have the view," the person with a privacy interest in the premises cannot complain. Indeed, the Supreme Court held that this doctrine applied when an undercover agent, posing as a prospective purchaser of narcotics, gained entry into a home and observed a narcotics transaction.[49]

The classification of an observation as a search or non-search often may be the controlling factor in judging the subsequent seizure of evidence. If the observation was not a search since it did not invade upon any reasonable expectation of privacy, then the officer need not justify the observation under the Fourth Amendment. It matters not, for example, that he lacked the probable cause needed to uphold a search. Moreover, once he observed evidence of a crime through his non-search, he then had probable cause to seize the item. He was entitled at that point to take whatever steps were needed (including entry onto private property) to take immediate possession of the evidence. If, on the other hand, the original observation was a search, and that search did not meet relevant constitutional standards, then the subsequent seizure of the evidence will also fail as the fruit of the unconstitutional search.

In most disputed cases, the police observation preceding a seizure clearly will have constituted a search. The officers will have swept through a house looking for evidence, opened the trunk of a car, or looked through a man's pockets. From this point on, we will be concerned with such cases as we examine the legal requirements for a valid search. But it should be kept in mind that not all observations are searches, and that the initial question to be considered in any search-and-seizure problem is whether there was, in fact, a search.

Legal Requirements for a Search.   The basic legal requirements for a search come primarily from the Fourth Amendment. State statutes sometimes duplicate these requirements, but rarely impose additional requirements. The law tends to divide searches into three categories.

1.   *Searches incident to a warrant.* Searches may be conducted as authorized by a lawful warrant in any type of situation.

2.   *Warrantless searches for the purpose of finding evidence.* Searches for evidence may be undertaken without a warrant only if (1) the officer has probable cause and (2) the failure to obtain a warrant is justified under certain specified exceptions. The two primary exceptions are the moving vehicle and emergency exceptions.

3.   *Warrantless searches for purposes other than finding evidence.* Warrantless searches may be conducted under limited circumstances for other purposes even though the officer may lack probable cause. The two primary

---

49.   *Lewis v. United States,* 385 U.S. 206, 87 S.Ct. 424, 17 L.Ed.2d 312 (1966).

illustrations here are the search incident to the arrest and the inventory search.

Each of these categories will be examined in more detail in the next few sections. The reader should be forewarned, however, that the legal requirements applicable to searches are highly complex, with numerous special exceptions. All we can do here is touch upon the general rules in their most common application.

Search Warrant. A search warrant is similar to an arrest warrant except that it authorizes an officer to conduct a search of certain premises rather than to arrest a certain person. Like the arrest warrant, a search warrant is issued by a magistrate on the basis of information supplied to him in sworn statements. Since nobody is being charged with a crime, the sworn statement does not take the form of a complaint, but usually is an affidavit of the investigating officer. The affidavit must establish the presence of probable cause justifying the search. The probable cause for a search relates to two somewhat different elements than the probable cause for an arrest. It must be established that there is probable cause to believe (1) that the items for which the search is conducted are connected with criminal activity, and (2) that those items can be found in the place that the police desire to search. The degree of probability required is essentially the same as that under probable cause for an arrest.[50] Here also, the officer can rely on information received from informants, but his affidavit must set forth facts indicating that the informant is credible and that his information comes from a reliable source.

The Fourth Amendment requires that the search warrant "particularly describ[e] . . . the place to be searched." Courts have held that, to meet this constitutional standard, the place to be searched must be described with sufficient certainty to enable the officer executing the warrant to distinguish that place from all other places. The description may be one used in the locality and known to the people there, such as "the old Randolph house." A technical description by lot and block number is not always required, although the best practice is to include such a description. Minor errors in description, such as incorrect street or suite number, will not invalidate a warrant if the remainder of the description makes it apparent what building or part of a building is to be searched.

The Fourth Amendment also provides that no search warrants shall issue except those "particularly describing the . . . things to be seized."[51] The degree of particularity required varies somewhat depending upon the nature of the material to be seized. Greater leeway is permitted in describing contraband (property, the possession of which is a crime). Thus, during prohibition, a description merely of

---

50. See pp. 210-12 *supra.*

51. We will assume that state law permits the warrant to authorize seizure of all types of evidentiary matter. At one time, the Supreme Court had held that an officer could only seize contraband, the fruits of a crime, or instrumentalities of the crime (i.e., items used in the commission of a crime). A warrant could not be issued to seize other items that were simply helpful evidence in proving the crime—e.g., a shoe that could be matched with prints at the scene of the crime or a letter in which the suspect acknowledged committing the crime. In *Warden v. Hayden*, 387 U.S. 294, 87 S.Ct. 1642, 18 L.Ed.2d 782 (1967), the Supreme Court rejected this limitation and held that an officer could seize such evidence. Most states, but not all, revised their statutes on search warrants to permit a search for any type of evidentiary item.

"cases of whiskey" was held to be sufficient.[52] Similarly, in describing items used exclusively for illegal purposes, the description may be more general. Thus, a warrant authorizing the search of a gambling establishment may refer to various specific items (e.g., numbers slips) and include a catch-all reference to "other similar gambling paraphernalia." By comparison, innocuous property must be described more specifically so that the executing officer will not be confused between the items sought and other property of a similar nature. A warrant authorizing the seizure of "stolen goods," without further identification of those goods, would be invalid.

The description of the items to be seized necessarily limits the scope of the search. If the description includes large items that could not be found in a drawer, the officer may not search drawers. On the other hand, if the officer in the proper course of the search inadvertently finds evidence not mentioned in the warrant, he may seize that evidence under the "plain view" doctrine.[53] The discovery must be inadvertent, however. If the warrant fails to mention a particular object, but the police knew its location and intended to seize it when they obtained the warrant, then they cannot rely on the plain view doctrine. If allowed to do so, they would be evading the requirement that warrants particularly describe the things to be seized.

Searches for Evidence Without a Warrant.   As we indicated at the outset of this chapter, the Supreme Court has held that searches generally must be made pursuant to a warrant to be deemed reasonable under the first clause of the Fourth Amendment. Indeed, the Court has stated: "Searches conducted outside the judicial process [i.e., without a warrant] . . . are *per se* unreasonable under the Fourth Amendment—subject only to a few specifically established and well-delineated exceptions."[54] Unfortunately, the number and scope of the exceptions to this "warrant-requirement" are not as clear as the Court's statement might suggest. The key exceptions are based primarily on two grounds. First, exceptions have been recognized in situations where the officer ordinarily has no opportunity to obtain a warrant before he is required to engage in a search. Second, exceptions also have been recognized where the function of the search is not to seek evidence of a crime, but to serve other purposes. A prime example of an exception based on both grounds is the frisk incident to a stop, discussed earlier in this chapter. The frisk is justified constitutionally as a limited search for the officer's self-protection rather than a search to uncover evidence of a specific crime. Moreover, as the Court noted in *Terry v. Ohio*, the frisk requires "necessarily swift action predicated upon the on-the-spot observations of the officer on the beat—which historically has not been, and as a practical matter could not be, subjected to the warrant procedure."

---

52. *Steele v. United States*, 267 U.S. 498, 45 S.Ct. 414, 69 L.Ed. 757 (1925).

53. See p. 251 *supra* discussing the plain view rule. Application of the plain view concept in this context is approved in *Coolidge v. New Hampshire*, 403 U.S. 443, 91 S.Ct. 2022, 29 L.Ed.2d 564 (1971). See also *Cady v. Dombrowski*, 413 U.S. 433, 93 S.Ct. 2523, 37 L.Ed.2d 706 (1973). Some states still follow, as a matter of state law, an older line of cases that prohibited seizure of any items not designated in the warrant.

54. *Katz v. United States*, 389 U.S. 347, 357, 88 S.Ct. 507, 514, 19 L.Ed.2d 576 (1968).

Other specific exceptions to the warrant requirement are the search incident to an arrest, the inventory search, the search of a vehicle, and the emergency search. The first two also constitute exceptions to the probable cause requirement, and we will discuss them in the next section dealing with that category of searches. The vehicle and emergency exceptions are similar in that both require probable cause and dispense only with the warrant requirement. They are recognized as exceptions primarily because the officer lacks the opportunity to obtain a warrant before the search is made. In the case of the vehicle search, the emphasis is on the situation generally presented by such searches rather than the specifics of the particular case. In the emergency situation, the emphasis is more on the lack of opportunity under the facts of the particular case.

The vehicle exception was first noted by the Supreme Court in *Carroll v. United States.*[55] Officers there, having probable cause to believe a car was carrying contraband, stopped the car on the highway and searched the interior (finding the contraband hidden behind the upholstering of the seats). The Court held that a warrant was not needed in such a case. It noted that there was a "necessary difference between a search of a store, dwelling house or other structure in respect of which a proper official warrant may be obtained, and a search of a ship, motor boat, wagon or automobile . . . where it is not practicable to secure a warrant because the vehicle can be quickly moved out of the locality or jurisdiction in which the warrant must be sought." In *Carroll,* the officer had not arrested the driver, and the question was later raised as to the validity of a warrantless search where the driver had been taken into custody. In that case, it was argued, the car could no longer be moved, and the police should be required to obtain a warrant. The Supreme Court rejected this contention in *Chambers v. Maroney.*[56] The Court noted that there was no assurance that the car would not be removed by the driver (if released), or by another person with access to the car, while the officers were seeking to obtain a warrant. Of course, the officers could impound the car, but that would also involve a Fourth Amendment seizure. Accordingly, so long as the officers had probable cause, they could proceed to search the stopped vehicle without a warrant under the *Carroll* exception to the warrant requirement. Later cases have suggested that the *Carroll* exception might not apply in highly unusual circumstances (e.g., where the police knew for some time that the car was to be searched, and the car was located in a position where it could not readily be removed).[57] Ordinarily, however, a search of a car is permissible without a warrant —provided the officers have probable cause.[58]

---

55. *Carroll v. United States,* 267 U.S. 132, 45 S.Ct. 280, 69 L.Ed. 543 (1925).

56. *Chambers v. Maroney,* 399 U.S. 42, 90 S.Ct. 1975, 26 L.Ed.2d 419 (1970).

57. See *Coolidge v. New Hampshire,* 403 U.S. 443, 91 S.Ct. 2022, 29 L.Ed.2d 564 (1970).

58. The presence of probable cause is crucial. An officer cannot search an automobile simply because he has arrested the driver. The officer must have probable cause to believe that there is evidence relating to the offense within the car. Thus, if an officer arrested a driver for driving without a license, there could be no possible probable cause for a search since there is no material evidence of the crime to be found. As we shall see in the next section, the officer might search the driver and that part of the car within his immediate control as a search incident to the arrest. He could not, however, conduct a full search of the car as was done in *Carroll* and *Chambers.*

The emergency search exception to the warrant requirement is based on the need for an immediate search that prevents the officer from seeking a warrant. So far, the courts have recognized two situations in which such an emergency exits. In *Warden v. Hayden,*[59] officers in "hot pursuit" of a wanted criminal were justified in making a warrantless search of a dwelling that the suspect had recently entered. The Fourth Amendment did not require that the officers stop in their direct pursuit of a felon to obtain a warrant simply because the felon entered a dwelling. A warrantless search was permitted, the Court noted, in any portion of the dwelling where the suspect might be hiding or weapons might be found.

Schmerber v. California[60] recognized a similar emergency exception based on a need to prevent the destruction of evidence. The police there had probable cause to believe that the defendant had operated a vehicle under the influence of alcohol and, over his objection, they had a physician take a blood sample to establish the alcoholic content of his blood. If the sample was not taken promptly, it would be of little value since the alcohol in the blood was dissipating. The Court held that, although the search of the person here had been particularly intrusive in quality, a warrant was not needed in light of the loss of evidence that surely would occur during the time needed to obtain a warrant. In later cases, the Court refused to extend this doctrine to permit a warrantless search of a dwelling on the theory that an accomplice or friend of the suspect (who was in custody) might return to the premises and destroy any evidence before a search warrant could be obtained. In *Schmerber* the evidence was certain to be lost and there were no alternatives available for preserving the evidence. Police always can protect against the return of an accomplice by posting a guard at the dwelling while they seek a warrant.

Searches Requiring Neither a Warrant Nor Probable Cause. As we noted previously, there are a few situations in which searches may be justified without either probable cause or a warrant. *Terry v. Ohio,* permitting a frisk on a reasonable basis standard, accepted one such search. Another, somewhat similar search is the search conducted incident to an lawful arrest. When an officer makes a lawful arrest, he must have probable cause to believe that the arrestee committed a crime. However, probable cause to arrest does not necessarily furnish probable cause to believe that the arrestee has on his person either evidence of the crime or a weapon. Indeed, for some offenses, such as reckless driving, there would be no material evidence of the crime that the person possibly could have in his possession. Nevertheless, the Court has permitted a full search of the person incident to arrest where the arrestee has been placed in custody. The basic justification for the search is the protection of the officer. In this situation, the Court has reasoned, a frisk is not sufficient: "It is scarcely open to doubt that the danger to an officer is far greater in the case of the extended exposure which follows the taking of a suspect into custody and transporting him to the police station than in the case of the relatively fleeting contact resulting from the typical *Terry*-stop." [61] Moreover,

---

59. *Warden v. Hayden,* 387 U.S. 294, 87 S.Ct. 1642, 18 L.Ed.2d 782 (1967).

60. *Schmerber v. California,* 384 U.S. 757, 86 S.Ct. 1826, 16 L.Ed.2d 908 (1966).

61. *United States v. Robinson,* 414 U.S. 218, 234-235, 94 S.Ct. 467, 476, 38 L.Ed.2d 427 (1973) (upholding a full search incident to an arrest for operating a motor vehicle with a revoked license).

once the officer begins the full search, he need not limit himself to seizing weapons. He also may look for (and seize) any evidence of a crime and thereby prevent any attempt by the arrested person to destroy that evidence.

While accepting the search incident to an arrest as a necessary exception to the warrant and probable cause requirements, the Court has restricted the exception so as not to completely undermine those requirements. The exception is limited to searches incident to full-custody arrests. It does not extend to the situation in which the person is stopped on probable cause for the purpose of issuing a summons. Thus, it does not apply to a traffic stop unless the officer intends to take the person to the police station (rather than release him after issuing a traffic citation).[62] Also, the search is limited to the person of the arrestee and that area within his immediate control—that is, the area within which the arrestee might reach to obtain a weapon or destroy evidence. Where a person is arrested in the living room of his home, the "search-incident" rule cannot be used to conduct a warrantless search of the entire room (although it might justify the search of a desk or other container in the room if the arrestee is standing next to it when arrested). The search also must be made at the same time as the arrest. The officer need not stop to inform the person that he is under arrest and then make the search. In the interest of self-protection, he may immediately make certain that the person is not carrying weapons. On the other hand, he may not search first, release the person, and then arrest sometime later, claiming that the search was incident to the subsequent arrest. Finally, and most significantly, the search must be incident to a *lawful* arrest. If the officer lacked probable cause justifying the arrest, the search will be invalid and evidence seized through it will be subject to the exclusionary rule.

Another search that may be made without probable cause or a warrant is the inventory search. In *South Dakota v. Opperman*,[63] the Court upheld such a search of an illegally parked automobile that had been towed to a "city impound lot." Following a standard police department policy, a police officer searched the interior of the car for valuables. In the course of that search, he found contraband in an unlocked glove compartment. The Supreme Court found that, under these circumstances, the search was reasonable. The function of the search was simply to protect any valuables in the car and to deter the owner of an impounded vehicle from raising a false claim that items were stolen while the car was in police custody. In light of this "benign, non-criminal purpose," neither probable cause nor a warrant was required. Lower courts have taken a similar approach in dealing with searches of arrestees for inventory purposes before they are placed in jail cells.

---

62. Where the stop has been made for the purpose of issuing a traffic ticket, a frisk is permissible only if the driver's actions furnish a reasonable basis for the frisk under *Terry*. However, an officer making a traffic stop may automatically order the driver out of the car. See *Pennsylvania v. Mims*, 434 U.S. 106, 98 S. Ct. 330, 54 L.Ed.2d 331 (1977). In some jurisdictions, as a matter of state law, a full search of the person is not permitted incident to a traffic arrest even if the suspect is taken into custody. See, e.g., *People v. Brisendine*, 13 Cal.3d 528, 119 Cal.Rptr. 315, 531 P.2d 1099 (1975).

63. *South Dakota v. Opperman*, 428 U.S. 364, 96 S.Ct, 3092, 49 L.Ed.2d 1000 (1976).

Search With Consent. Where voluntary consent is given, a search also may be conducted without a warrant and without probable cause. The willingness of the individual to have his privacy invaded by the search automatically renders the search reasonable—provided the individual acted voluntarily and had the authority to consent to the search of the premises. Courts note, however, that a voluntary consent will not readily be assumed, especially where the person consenting is in custody. In such a situation, to establish a valid consent, it may be necessary to show that the person was told of his right to refuse to permit the search and knowingly waived that right. Where the person was not arrested, but was simply detained pursuant to a traffic stop, warnings as to rights need not be given.[64]

In some cases, consent has been given by a person other than the defendant who is now objecting to the search of his quarters. Whether such a consent is acceptable depends on the interest of the consenting person in the premises. One party cannot waive another's right to privacy, but where that party had an equal right to use the premises, police can rely on his consent. The defendant, in effect, shared his privacy with the other person, taking the risk that the co-occupant might invite others onto the premises. Under this analysis, an apartment house manager cannot consent to the search of a tenant's apartment. Neither can a hotel clerk consent to the search of a guest's room. In both instances, the consenting party does not have an equal right to use of the premises. On the other hand, one roommate can consent to the search of a shared house. A parent similarly can consent to the search of his son's room where the son is not renting the room. Ordinarily, an employer also can consent to the search of his employee's work space.

Electronic Surveillance. The use of electronic devices, such as wiretaps and hidden microphones, to secretly eavesdrop upon and record conversations is commonly described as electronic surveillance. A search, as we have seen, does not necessarily require a physical entry onto the suspect's property, but can encompass any observation by government agents that infringes upon the suspect's reasonable expectation of privacy.[65] In the same manner, electronic surveillance also can constitute a search even though the placement of the listening device does not require an entry onto the suspect's property. The crucial question is whether the surveillance constitutes an invasion of a reasonable expectation of privacy. As a general rule, there is such an invasion (and therefore a search) where electronic surveillance is used to eavesdrop on a private conversation without the advance consent of any of the parties to the conversation.

The Supreme Court has held, in a series of cases, that electronic surveillance should not be viewed as a search simply because one party to a conversation is surprised to learn that another has arranged to record that conversation.[66] If A speaks to B, an undercover agent, and B later relays that conversation to a police officer, there certainly has been no search. A may have anticipated that B could

---

64. *Schneckloth v. Bustamonte,* 412 U.S. 218, 93 S.Ct. 2041, 36 L.Ed.2d 854 (1973).

65. See p. 250 *supra.*

66. *United States v. White,* 401 U.S. 745, 291 S.Ct. 1122, 28 L.Ed.2d 453 (1971); *Lopez v. United States,* 373 U.S. 427, 83 S.Ct. 1381, 10 L.Ed.2d 462 (1963); *On Lee v. United States,* 343 U.S. 747, 72 S.Ct. 967, 96 L.Ed. 1270 (1952).

keep a secret, but his mistaken expectation is certainly not the type of privacy interest protected by the Fourth Amendment. If B were wired for sound, A's privacy interest would be no different. He simply is in a somewhat worse position because B can now use the recording to corroborate his account of the conversation. The same would be true if B were wired for sound in such a way as to permit a police officer to monitor their conversation. A takes his chances on B in each case, and he had no reasonable expectation of privacy whether B simply reveals the conversation to others, records it, or assists in having others monitor it.

Where, on the other hand, neither A nor B are aware of the electronic eavesdropping, there then is an invasion of a reasonable expectation of privacy. People are not required to anticipate that their telephone will be tapped or that "electronic bugs" may be located in a place (e.g., a home) where it appears safe to carry on a private conversation. Of course, the fact that the electronic surveillance constitutes a search does not necessarily make it illegal. Like all searches, an electronic search will be acceptable constitutionally if the requirements of the Fourth Amendment (e.g., warrant authorization, probable cause) are met. In the case of electronic surveillance, however, special statutory requirements imposed by the Congress in the Crime Control Act of 1968 also must be met.[67]

The Crime Control Act extends to both state and federal electronic surveillance conducted without the consent of one of the parties to the conversation. It requires, consistent with the Fourth Amendment, that the surveillance be authorized by a warrant, issued upon probable cause, that specifies the telephone to be tapped or the place at which the hidden "bug" will be placed. The warrant also must specify the nature of the conversations sought to be intercepted, and it must limit the length of the surveillance, with an initial maximum of thirty days. The Crime Control Act also imposes various requirements beyond those derived from the Fourth Amendment. The use of electronic surveillance is limited to the investigation of certain crimes (primarily felonies involving violence, drugs, or organized crime activities). Application for a warrant must be approved by designated prosecution officials at the state and federal levels. The application must show that other investigative procedures have been tried and have failed, or that they reasonably appear to be unlikely to succeed or too dangerous to try. Following the completion of surveillance, parties to the conversations recorded must be given notice of the surveillance.

The use of non-consensual electronic surveillance has been a highly controversial subject both as to its effectiveness as an investigative tool and its impact on individual liberties. The Crime Control Act has been subject to periodic attack in Congress, but efforts to sharply limit the scope of the Act have failed. States can utilize non-consensual electronic surveillance only if they adopt legislation patterned upon the federal legislation. A substantial number of states have not done so, and non-consensual electronic surveillance by state officers is illegal in those states.[68]

---

67.   18 United States Code §2510-2520.

68.   See National Commission For The Review of Federal And State Laws Relating To Wiretappng And Electronic Surveillance, *Commission Studies*, Washington, D.C.: Government Printing Office, 1976, at p. 6: "By the end of 1974, a total of 22 States and the District of Columbia had

POLICE INTERROGATION

The Nature of Interrogation. The questioning of suspects is a valuable police investigative tool, used in a variety of situations. The purpose of police interrogation will vary with the situation. In some cases, the police are confident of the suspect's guilt and hope to obtain a confession or at least a partially incriminating statement (called an admission).[69] In other cases, the officer may be uncertain as to the suspect's guilt and simply is looking for an innocent explanation of some suspicious circumstances. The place and length of the interrogation also will vary. The interrogation may consist of no more than a few questions asked on the street or it may involve questioning over a period of several hours at the police station. The technique of the interrogation also may vary from simple, direct questioning to the use of subtle psychological ploys.[70] The law governing interrogations thus must deal with a variety of different types of interrogations. Initially, the Supreme Court, relying on the due process clause, sought to apply a case-by-case approach in determining the constitutionally permissible range of interrogations. In the mid-1960's, the Supreme Court decision in *Miranda v. Arizona* largely dispensed with that approach, as the Court sought to set forth a series of general guidelines governing police interrogations.[71]

The Miranda Decision. In its *Miranda* opinion, the Supreme Court actually dealt with four separate cases. In each case, the defendant had been questioned by police officers after having been arrested and taken to a police station. In each case, the interrogation lasted at least two hours before the defendant confessed. In none of the cases had the defendant been given a full warning of his rights prior to the interrogation. As the Court viewed the cases, each involved "incommunicado interrogation of individuals in a police-dominated atmosphere resulting in self-

---

provided statutory procedures for court-approved electronic surveillance for criminal investigations that were consistent with Title III standards (Arizona, Colorado, Connecticut, Delaware, Flordia, Georgia, Kansas, Maryland, Massachusetts, Minnesota, Nebraska, Nevada, New Hampshire, New Jersey, New Mexico, New York, Oregon, Rhode Island, South Dakota, Virginia, Washington, Wisconsin). While some jurisdictions adopted the Title III procedures almost verbatim, there have frequently been variances in State legislation, reflecting local efforts to account for differences in the structure of the State judiciary as well as the needs of local law enforcement. Some States have adopted standards considerably more restrictive than those of Title III. The statute adopted in the State of Washington, and a statute adopted in Pennsylvania in 1975, are so restrictive, in fact, as to make electronic surveillance a relatively impractical tool in law enforcement."

69. A confession is a statement in which the suspect admits that he committed the crime. An admission is a statement acknowledging the truth of certain facts that are incriminating, but not the commission of the crime. Thus, if a person admits that he was present at the scene of an assault, but denies that he participated, that is an admission. If he admits his participation, his statement then is a confession. The law governing interrogation does not distinguish between the two types of statements. Either type is excluded from evidence if obtained in violation of the defendant's constitutional rights.

70. Thus, in the *Miranda* case (discussed *infra*), the Court noted the use of the "friendly-unfriendly" or "Mutt and Jeff" technique of station-house interrogation. One officer appears to be the relentless investigator, convinced of the suspects guilt, and anxious to "send him away." Another officer, appearing to be more friendly, encourages the suspect to confide in him so he can assist the suspect in "holding off" the more aggressive, unfriendly investigator.

71. *Miranda v. Arizona*, 384 U.S. 436, 86 S.Ct. 1602, 16 L.Ed.2d 694 (1966). The Court was divided 5-4 in this case and some justices have continued to express doubts as to the wisdom of the majority opinion.

incriminating statements without full warnings of constitutional rights." Under such circumstances, the Court concluded, there had been a violation of defendant's right against self-incrimination, and that constitutional violation required that the defendant's confession be excluded from evidence. Where police used custodial interrogation, the Court noted, it would automatically assume that the interrogation violated the suspect's right against self-incrimination unless the prosecution could establish that the suspect was given a full warning of his rights and he voluntarily waived those rights and agreed to be questioned.

The Miranda Warnings. The warning of rights required by *Miranda* includes each of the following elements:

1. The suspect must be told that he has a right to remain silent.

2. The suspect must be told that anything that he says can be used against him in court (described at points in the opinion as "can and will" be used against him).

3. The suspect must be told that he has the right to consult with a lawyer and to have a lawyer with him during any interrogation.

4. The suspect, must be told that if he is indigent (i.e., lacks the funds to hire a lawyer), a lawyer will be appointed at the state's expense to represent him.

The *Miranda* warnings must be given in clear and unequivocal terms that the individual can understand. Most police departments have developed a standard warning that officers recite prior to engaging in what may be viewed as custodial interrogation. If the warnings are not given, the prosecution may not excuse that failure on the ground that the suspect already was aware of his rights. The purpose of the warnings is not only to inform the suspect of his rights, but also to overcome the compulsive atmosphere of custodial interrogation by indicating a police willingness to recognize those rights.

Waiver of the Miranda Rights. *Miranda* notes that if the suspect indicates that he wishes to remain silent, the police may not persist in interrogation. Similarly, if the suspect asks for a lawyer, the police must arrange for his consultation with counsel before the interrogation begins. Note, however, that the police have no obligation under *Miranda* to arrange for counsel if they decide not to interrogate. As a practical matter, police generally assume that the lawyer will advise the suspect not to give information, and they therefore treat the request for a lawyer as effectively barring interrogation.

Miranda recognizes that the suspect can voluntarily waive his rights to remain silent and be assisted by a lawyer. In such a case, the statement obtained through custodial interrogation will not have been obtained in violation of the privilege against self-incrimination. Of course, the waiver must continue throughout the interrogation. The *Miranda* opinion stressed that, "if the individual indicates in any manner ... during questioning that he wishes to remain silent, the interrogation must cease." Prior to *Miranda,* the Supreme Court had indicated that a variety of police interrogation practices—such as threats of physical violence, denial of food, use of psychological coercion, and forced hypnosis or narcosis —constituted a violation of due process. If a suspect initially waived his *Miranda* rights, but the police then found it necessary to use any such techniques to get him to confess, their very use of those techniques would indicate that the suspect had terminated his waiver and the interrogation should have ceased. On the other hand, if the suspect orally waived his rights and then refused to permit officers to take notes, a closer question would be presented. Courts have held that, under some circumstances, such a refusal does not establish a termination of the initial waiver.[72]

Because of its concern over the coercive nature of custodial interrogation, the *Miranda* majority noted that "a heavy burden rests on the Government to demonstrate that the defendant knowingly and intelligently waived his privilege against self-incrimination and his right to retained or appointed counsel." Waiver cannot be established by the suspect's failure to affirmatively state that he desired to remain silent. A verbal acknowledgment of his understanding and willingness to speak must be present. Police often seek to obtain a written waiver, although such a formal waiver is not essential. A simple statement, such as "I might as well tell you about it," may be sufficient.[73] In determining whether the waiver was made knowingly and voluntarily, courts will consider such factors as the suspect's education, the influence of liquor or drugs, and mental illness or retardation. It is not essential that the suspect appreciated the seriousness of the crime charged. It is sufficient that he was aware of his *Miranda* rights and nevertheless desire to talk.

Custodial Interrogation. The *Miranda* rules apply only to "custodial interrogation." The Court in *Miranda* clearly indicated, however, that the custodial element was not limited to the situation in which the police removed a suspect to a police facility for questioning. Although each of the four *Miranda* cases involved police station interrogation, the Court noted that the compulsion requiring Fifth Amendment protection also could arise in other interrogation settings. Accordingly "custodial interrogation" was defined as interrogation occurring when a suspect "is taken into custody or otherwise deprived of his freedom in a significant way." Such significant detention can occur on the street, at a suspect's home or place of employment, or in a squad car, as well as at the police station. The trial court must, in each instance, examine the surrounding circumstances. If the police visit a person at his home or place of business and simply ask him to answer certain questions, that questioning generally will not be viewed as custodial in nature. The compulsion stressed by *Miranda* ordinarily is not present where the person is in familiar surroundings and the police have indicated he will be detained only for a few moments. On the other hand, questioning in the home did constitute custodial interrogation under the special circumstances of *Orozco v. Texas.*[74] There, four police officers, two detectives and two uniformed officers, entered defendant's boarding house room (apparently without knocking) at 4:00 a.m. and immediately asked him two questions about his presence at the scene of a shooting and his ownership of a pistol and its location. The Supreme Court held that Orozco had been subjected to custodial interrogation even though he had been "in his own

---

72. Compare *Frazier v. United States*, 419 F.2d 1161 (D.C. Circ. 1969) with *Frazier v. United States*, 476 F.2d 891 (D.C. Cir. 1973).

73. *United States v. Boykin*, 398 F.2d 483 (3d Cir. 1968).

74. *Orozco v. Texas*, 394 U.S. 324, 89 S.Ct. 1095, 22 L.Ed.2d 211 (1969).

bed, in familiar surroundings." The location of the questioning was an important factor, but not necessarily conclusive.[75]

Most courts have held that brief questioning incident to a stop (as opposed to an arrest), does not require the *Miranda* warnings. They acknowledge that the individual has been detained, but not that the *Miranda* opinion specifically stated that the rules announced there were "not intended to hamper . . . [g]eneral on the scene questioning as to facts surrounding a crime." In such situations, the *Miranda* opinion noted, "the compelling atmosphere inherent in the process of in-custody interrogation is not necessarily present." Courts have been careful however, to look at the facts of the particular case. If the officer actually used force to make the stop or engaged in lengthy, rigorous questioning, a court is more likely to hold that *Miranda* applies even though the person has not yet been arrested.

Of course, even if the person clearly is under arrest, *Miranda* only applies if there has been interrogation. The *Miranda* opinion noted that "volunteered statements . . . are not barred by the Fifth Amendment and their admissibility is not affected in our holding today." The police have no duty to interrupt a volunteered statement to warn the individual of his rights. Moreover, if the volunteered statement is not clear, an officer's attempt simply to obtain a clarification ordinarily will be viewed as a "threshold question" that does not constitute interrogation under *Miranda*. On the other hand, if the officer clearly seeks to expand upon the scope of the volunteered statement, his questions are likely to be viewed as interrogation subject to *Miranda*.

Sixth Amendment Limitations. As we noted previously, once adversary judicial proceedings have been initiated, a suspect must be viewed as an "accused" person for the purpose of the Sixth Amendment. He then is entitled to the assistance of a lawyer at any critical stage of the criminal proceeding, and questioning designed to obtain incriminating statements certainly is a critical stage. Thus, once the suspect is an accused—that is, charges have been filed and he has been presented before a magistrate—he is entitled to the assistance of a lawyer without regard to the application of *Miranda*. If he does not specifically waive that right, his statement must be excluded even though it was not a product of custodial interrogation. *Massiah v. United States*[76] is illustrative. The defendant there had been indicted and released on bail pending trial. A codefendant, acting at the request of the police, engaged defendant in an incriminating conversation that was recorded electronically. *Miranda* obviously would not apply to such a case since the defendant was not in custody at the time of interrogation. However, the defendant was an accused person for Sixth Amendment purposes since he had been indicted. He obviously had not waived his right to counsel since he did not even know that he was being questioned by a government agent. Accordingly, his

---

75. In *Oregon v. Mathiason*, 429 U.S. 492, 97 S.Ct. 711, 50 L.Ed.2d 714 (1977) the Court held that, under the circumstances of that case, interrogation at the police station had not been custodial interrogation. There the suspect voluntarily came to the police station after a policeman requested that they meet at some convenient place; he was immediately told that he was not under arrest, and he was allowed to leave at the close of the interview, even though he had admitted committing the crime.

76. *Massiah v. United States,* 377 U.S. 201, 84 S.Ct. 1199, 12 L.Ed.2d 246 (1964).

statement was obtained in violation of the Sixth Amendment and could not be used at his trial.

The Impact Of Miranda. Few decisions of the Supreme Court have been more controversial than *Miranda*. The decision was praised by many who claimed that it recognized the realities of interrogation and took essential steps to safeguard the Fifth Amendment privilege against self-incrimination. It was opposed by others who viewed it as unnecessary and likely to "handcuff" the police in solving crimes. Dire predictions that the decision would make confessions impossible to obtain certainly have not been realized. Available empirical studies show that many suspects still confess. Some argue that they do so either because of a guilty conscience or a belief that their prompt acknowledgment of guilt may help them when a court sets their sentence. Others claim that they do so because they do not understand or appreciate the *Miranda* warnings, too often read in a rapid-fire fashion by their interrogators.

Of course, *Miranda* has had some impact upon the ability of police to obtain confessions. Available evidence suggests that some lips have been sealed by *Miranda* and some cases have been lost as a result.[77] There is disagreement, however, as to the number of such cases or their impact upon police morale. Some say *Miranda*, at least initially, led the police to adopt a "what's the use" approach to investigations. Others argue that the limitations imposed by *Miranda* have led to more efficient detective work. Officers have been willing, they claim, to put in more time in pains-taking routine, checking and rechecking files, making door to door canvasses for potential witnesses, etc. In *Harris v. New York*,[78] the Supreme Court held that a confession obtained in violation of *Miranda*, but otherwise trustworthy, could be used under the impeachment exception to the exclusionary rule.[79] Thus, while the illegally obtained confession could not be used to prove the defendant's guilt, it could be used on cross-examination if his testimony at trial was inconsistent with the confession. Despite predictions that *Harris* would undermine *Miranda*, it appears to have had little impact on police adherence to the *Miranda* rules.

IDENTIFICATION PROCEDURES

Identification procedures tend to fall into two categories. First, there are the scientific procedures which seek to match physical evidence taken from the suspect's person with similar evidence found at the scene of the crime. These procedures include the comparison of fingerprints, blood samples, clothing fiber, hair, and similar items. The second group of identification procedures are designed to determine whether an eyewitness to the crime can identify the suspect as the criminal. The primary procedures in this category are the lineup, the showup, and

---

77. Miranda's case was not one of these. On retrial, he was convicted of rape and kidnapping without the use of the confession excluded by the Supreme Court decision. See *State v. Miranda*, 104 Ariz. 174, 450 P.2d 364 (1969).

78. *Harris v. New York*, 401 U.S. 222, 91 S.Ct. 643, 28 L.Ed.2d 1 (1971).

79. See p. 237 *supra*. If the statement is obtained in violation of due process, indicating that it is untrustwrothy, it cannot be used in any fashion at trial. See *Mincey v. Arizona*,   U.S.   , 98 S.Ct. 2408, 57 L.Ed.2d 290 (1978).

the photographic display. A lineup involves the presentation of several persons, including the suspect, to the eyewitness for possible identification. The showup involves the presentation of the suspect alone to the eyewitness. The photographic display involves the presentation of pictures of several persons, including the suspect, for possible identification. Eyewitness identification procedures are likely to present much more serious legal problems than the scientific procedures. Those problems relate primarily to the Sixth Amendment and due process guarantees of the federal constitution. Neither type of identification procedure presents any self-incrimination difficulties. Admittedly, the suspect is compelled to physically present himself in the lineup and showup and to give up a part of himself in the taking of certain scientific samples. He is not, however, being required to give "testimony" against himself, and the self-incrimination clause applies only to the compelled production of evidence of a testimonial or communicative nature.[80] A procedure which results only in the taking of physical evidence may be subject to the Fourth Amendment requirement of reasonableness, but it does not violate the Fifth Amendment.[81]

Sixth Amendment Limitations.   As we have noted, once adversary judicial criminal proceedings have started, the Sixth Amendment entitles the accused to the assistance of counsel at all subsequent "critical stages" of the criminal justice process. If an accused person is in custody and directed by police (or court order)[82] to participate in an identification procedure, is he entitled to the assistance of counsel? The answer depends on the nature of the procedure. The Supreme Court has held that an identification procedure is not a "critical stage" if it involves largely mechanical tasks that can accurately be explored at trial so as to reveal any misidentification. There is no crucial need for the lawyer to be present at the moment that such an identification procedure is used since the lawyer can adequately protect his client at trial. All of the scientific identification procedures meet this standard and therefore are not "critical stages" for Sixth Amendment purposes. As the Court noted in discussing those procedures in *United States v. Wade*: "Knowledge of the techniques of science and technology is sufficiently available, and the variables in techniques few enough, that the accused has the opportunity for a meaningful confrontation of the Government's case at trial through the ordinary processes of cross-examination of the Government's expert witnesses and the presentation of his own experts."[83]

---

80.   *Schmerber v. California*, 384 U.S. 757, 86 S.Ct 1826, 16 L.Ed.2d 908 (1966).

81.   Since the individuals required to submit to lineups or to give blood samples have been arrested on the basis of probable cause, Fourth Amendment requirements ordinarily are met without difficulty. Of course, if any of the identification procedures flow from an unconstitutional arrest, the results of the procedure may be excluded as the fruit of the poisonous tree. See p.   *supra*. See also *Davis v. Mississippi*, 394 U.S. 721, 89 S.Ct.1394, 22 L.Ed.2d 676 (1969) (where 24 youths were detained for questioning and fingerprinting in an unconstitutional dragnet arrest, fingerprints of youth matching those at the scene of crime were excluded as fruits of Fourth Amendment violation).

82.   Ordinarily a person in custody will simply be directed by police to participate. If he refuses, a court order may be obtained directing him to do so. A failure to obey the court would be punished as contempt of court.

83.   *United States v. Wade*, 388 U.S. 218, 227-28, 87 S.Ct. 1926, 1932-33, 18 L.Ed.2d 1149 (1967).

United States v. Ash[84] held that the photographic display also belonged in the non-critical stage category although it involved a less mechanical process than the scientific identification procedures. There still was adequate opportunity to challenge any misidentification at trial since the entire photographic display could be reproduced there. The jury could see what the witness saw, noting the comparative features of the persons in the pictures and other factors reflecting on the quality of the test presented by the display. Moreover, since the accused was not himself present when the display was shown to the eyewitnesses, the procedure did not present the element of a trial-type confrontation that suggested the need for a lawyer.

In *Wade*, the Court held that the lineup, unlike the procedures noted above, was a "critical stage" for Sixth Amendment purposes.[85] The failure of the prosecution to afford the defendant a right to counsel at his post-indictment lineup required exclusion of (1) all testimony as to the witness' identification of the accused at the lineup and (2) the witness' identification of the accused at trial if that identification was the fruit of the lineup identification. The *Wade* opinion noted that typical lineup practices made it very difficult to attack the credibility of the lineup identification at trial since it was almost impossible to develop fully the circumstances surrounding the lineup. Typically there was no picture of the lineup, nor was there a reliable nonprosecution observer who could recount any manipulation either in the lineup itself or the presentation of lineup to the eyewitness. Consistent with the approach taken in *Miranda*, *Wade*'s Sixth Amendment ruling required only that the accused be given the opportunity to seek the assistance of a lawyer. The police had to inform the accused of his right to an attorney (including the court appointed attorney for the indigent accused). The accused then could waive his rights, but the burden rested on the prosecution, as under *Miranda*, to prove waiver.

The *Wade* ruling resulted in a general reexamination of lineup procedures, producing more uniform, fairer procedures in most communities. It has not produced a great many lawyers at lineups since the ruling only applies after the suspect has reached the point where he is an "accused person" under the Sixth Amendment. Most lineups are held before the suspect's first appearance before a magistrate (the start of adversary judicial proceedings), and they therefore are not subject to the Sixth Amendment. They are, however, subject to due process limitations.

Due Process.   The due process guarantee prohibits the use at trial of any eyewitness identification procedure "unnecessarily suggestive and conducive to irreparable mistaken identification."[86] In determining whether an identification procedure violates due process, a court will consider the "totality of circumstances" surrounding the identification. This includes the suggestiveness of the procedure in pointing to the suspect, the existence of practical justifications for the suggestiveness, and the likely reliability of the witness' identification of the suspect

---

84.   *United States v. Ash*, 413 U.S. 300, 93 S.Ct. 2568, 37 L.Ed.2d 619 (1973).

85.   While the *Wade* ruling did not involve a showup, the Court's subsequent expressions of concern as to the reliability of the showup procedure suggest that it also would be viewed as a critical stage.

86.   *Manson v. Braithwaite*, 432 U.S. 98, 97 S.Ct. 2243, 53 L.Ed.2d 140 (1977).

apart from the suggestiveness of the procedure. Undoubtedly, the showup tends to be the most suggestive procedure since it asks the witness to look at only a single suspect. Yet showups have been upheld where dictated by the need for a prompt presentation of the suspect to the eyewitness. Thus, police may use "on-the-scene" showups in which a suspect is arrested at or near the scene of the crime and is immediately brought before an eyewitness for identification.[87] Where showups are delayed for a substantial period of time, so that a lineup may have been used instead, they are more likely to be held invalid. Even here, however, the Court may find that other factors, evidencing the reliability of the eyewitness, offset the suggestiveness of the procedure. These other factors would include the opportunity of the witness to get a good look at the criminal at the time of the crime, the accuracy of the witness' prior description of the criminal as it relates to the suspect, the level of certainty demonstrated by the witness in identifying the suspect, and the amount of time between the showup and the crime.

Foster v. California[88] affords a good illustration of the type of identification procedure that will be held to violate due process. In that case, there was only one eyewitness, the night manager of a robbed telegraph office. The first lineup contained only the defendant and two other men. Both were a foot shorter than the defendant and he was the only person wearing the kind of jacket that had been worn by the robber. When the night manager was unable to make a positive identification, the night manager was allowed to view the defendant alone in a small room. The manager still was tentative, and the police arranged another lineup several days later, with the defendant being the only participant who also was in the earlier lineup. This time there was a positive identification. The Court held that the use of that identification violated due process. "The suggestive elements in this identification procedure," the Court noted, "made it all but inevitable that [the manager] would identify the [defendant] whether or not he was in fact 'the man.'"[89]

---

87. See *Russell v. United States*, 408 F.2d 1280 (D.C. Cir. 1969). Although a lineup would be less suggestive, the delay involved in using a lineup could create disadvantages. If the suspect is presented on a prompt showup, the police will learn immediately if they have the right man. If they do not, the innocent person will be released sooner and the police can get back to their search for the right person sooner than if they had to wait for a lineup.

88. *Foster v. California*, 394 U.S. 440, 89 S.Ct. 1127, 22 L.Ed.2d 402 (1969).

89. For a more detailed analysis of the legal limitations on investigative practices, see the materials collected in Y. Kamisar, W. LaFave, J. Israel, *Modern Criminal Procedure*, St. Paul, Minn.: West Publishing Company, 1974, 4th ed. See also, with respect to constitutional limitations, D. Fellman, *The Defendant's Rights Today*, Madison, Wisc.: University of Wisconsin Press, 1976; W. Ringel, *Searches and Seizures, Arrest and Confessions*, New York: Clark Boardman Company, 1972; C. Whitebread, *Constitutional Criminal Procedure*, Washington, D.C.: American Academy of Judicial Education, 1978.

Chapter 11

The Accusation

Once the investigatory process has reached the point where a suspect is arrested, the focus of the criminal justice process soon shifts to the formal accusation to be made against the arrestee. In this chapter, we will consider various procedural steps that relate to the presentation and review of that accusation. We will examine the prosecutor's decision to charge, the review of that decision by the magistrate (at the preliminary hearing) and by the grand jury, and pretrial challenges to the accusation. Before turning to these procedures, however, we should consider the different tasks performed by the magistrate at the first appearance of the arrestee.[1] The first appearance serves a variety of functions relating both to the accusation and the trial.

THE FIRST APPEARANCE

Timing. All jurisdictions have provisions requiring that an arrested person be presented before a magistrate with reasonable promptness. Most state that the arrestee be presented "without unnecessary delay" or "without undue delay," although several refer to presentment "forthwith" or "immediately." A few states use a standard such as "without unnecessary delay," but also add a specific maximum time period.[2] No matter how the standard of prompt presentment is described, it does not require that the police take the arrestee directly to the magistrate. Delay due to normal station-house procedures (e.g., making an arrest

---

1. As we noted in our overview, p. 182 *supra*, states vary in their description of the first appearance, with some calling it the "initial presentment" or the "arraignment on the warrant."

2. See California Penal Code §825 (without unnecessary delay and, in any event, within two days excluding Sundays and holidays); Alaska R. Crim. P. 5(a)(1) (24 hours); Florida R. Crim. P. 3.130 (24 hours). The National Advisory Commission on Criminal Justice Standards and Goals, note 61 at p. 296 *infra*, recommended a normal limit of 6 hours in its Court Standard 4.5 and its Corrections Standard 4.5(1).

record, taking fingerprints and photographs, permitting a telephone call,[3] and preparing a complaint) is always accepted. Courts also have approved delays of several hours for such purposes as placing the arrestee in a lineup, matching fingerprints, or contacting the arrestee's alleged alibi witnesses. Finally, any delay due to the unavailability of a magistrate during evening hours also is viewed as justified. When these various permissible delays are added together, the presentment statutes often permit presentments as late as 24-48 hours after the time of arrest (with an even longer period commonly accepted over weekends). Several court have sought to enforce the prompt presentment requirement by excluding any confession obtained after the arrestee should have been presented.[4]

The Filing and Review of the Complaint.   Prior to the presentation of the arrestee, a formal accusation (usually a complaint) will be filed with the magistrate. In *Pugh v. Rainwater*, the Supreme Court held that where a person is arrested without a warrant and the arrestee is not released shortly thereafter,[5] a court shall promptly review the arrest to ensure that it was based on probable cause as required by the Fourth Amendment. Ordinarily, the magistrate performs this task either shortly before or at the start of the first appearance. His review of probable cause is similar to the determination that would be made in issuing an arrest warrant. The magistrate must decide, based on sworn statements of the arresting officer (usually contained in the complaint or the arresting officer's affidavit), that the officer had sufficient information to establish probable cause to arrest.

Magistrate Duties at the First Appearance.   Once the arrestee is before the magistrate, the magistrate's initial task is to make certain that the arrestee is the person whose name appears in the complaint. The magistrate then will inform the arrestee that he is now a defendant since charges have been filed against him. The magistrate will read the charges set forth in the complaint and, in some jurisdictions, will give the defendant a copy of the complaint. The magistrate also will inform the defendant of several of his rights. Ordinarily, he will be told of his right to remain silent and will be warned that any statement made by him may be used against him. He also will be told of his right to the assistance of counsel in all

---

3.   Many states have statutory provisions authorizing the arrestee to contact by telephone at least one "outside person" (usually a lawyer or relative). See, e.g., Illinois Stat. ch. 38, §103-3(a): "Persons who are arrested shall have the right to communicate with an attorney of their choice and a member of their family by making a reasonable number of telephone calls or in any other reasonable manner. Such communication shall be permitted within a reasonable time after arrival at the first place of custody." In other states, police permit calls to be made as a matter of local custom.

4.   The United States Supreme Court adopted such a rule for all federal courts in *McNabb v. United States*, 318 U.S. 332, 63S.Ct.608, 87L.Ed.819 (1943) and *Mallory v. United States*, 354 U.S. 449, 77 S.Ct.1356, 1L.Ed.2d 1479 (1957), but that position was rejected in the Omnibus Crime Control Act of 1968, 18 United States Code §3501. However, a similar rule has been adopted in several states, including Michigan, Maryland, and Pennsylvania. See *Johnson v. State*, note 23 at p. *supra*.

5.   This would occur if the arrestee was released upon issuance of a summons at the station-house or was released on station-house bail (see note 6 at p., 272 *infra*). These options are available primarily in misdemeanor cases. Where either is used, the arrestee still will come before a magistrate for a first appearance, but that appearance will not be scheduled for several days. Since the arrestee has been released, there is no urgency in getting him before the magistrate.

further proceedings. If the defendant is charged with a felony, the magistrate will set a date for a preliminary hearing. If the defendant is charged with a misdemeanor, he may be asked to enter a plea at this point if he is assisted by counsel or does not desire the assistance of counsel.

We will discuss the preliminary hearing later in this chapter and the entry of the plea will be considered in Chapter Twelve as to both misdemeanor and felony cases. There are two other key functions of the magistrate, however, that deserve our immediate attention. In informing the defendant of his right to counsel, the magistrate will tell him that he is entitled to court appointed counsel if he is indigent (i.e., unable to afford counsel). Ordinarily, the magistrate either will make the appointment for the indigent defendant or at least make the determination as to indigency so as to permit prompt appointment by the general trial court. The magistrate also will determine the conditions under which the defendant may obtain his release from custody pending trial—a task commonly described as "setting bail."

BAIL

Early Development of the Bail System.   The concept of bail probably dates back to the system of frankpledges adopted in England after the Norman Conquest of 1066. Under that system, if a member of the local community was alleged to have committed a crime, the community as a whole was required to pledge its property as security for the accused's appearance at trial. The prospect of imposing a property loss on others in the community could produce considerable pressure on the accused to remain in the area and stand trial. The concept of community responsibility eventually dissolved, but the capacity of the accused to retain his freedom pending trial by posting security (commonly called "bail") remained. By the time our country achieved its independence, release upon posting bail was available in Anglo-American law for all but capital cases.

The release of a defendant on bail in non-capital cases was justified on several grounds. Of course, the major justification was that it would avoid the possible incarceration of accused persons who were innocent. As Chief Justice Vinson once noted, if defendants were assumed to be guilty and denied their release pending trial, "the presumption of innocence, secured only after centuries of struggle, would loose its meaning." The availability of bail also was important in ensuring that the accused had ample opportunity to present his defense at trial. Not all defendants were represented by counsel and even those with counsel often were themselves responsible for collecting evidence and searching for witnesses to be presented at trial. A defendant who was in jail could suffer a serious disadvantage in preparing his case. Finally, even if the defendant would suffer no disadvantage in case preparation and obviously was guilty, the availability of bail ensured that he would not be incarcerated for a longer period than appropriate for the offense he committed. Very often several months spent in jail awaiting trial would be a greater punishment than that which was imposed under the law for the crime itself. Indeed, at the time, punishment for a non-capital offense often was a fine only.

While these advantages of pretrial release were given great weight, they obviously were not viewed as prevailing in every case. It was essential that the person be present at his trial. Bail was thought to be necessary to assure his appearance, and if he could not arrange for the posting of bail in an appropriate amount, he would not be released. Moreover, in the case of capital offenses, release was not available even if the accused could afford to post bail.

Professional Bondsmen. The initial American practice, inherited from the English, insisted that bail take the form either of a cash deposit or a bond secured by real estate (i.e., a promise to pay a certain amount supported by an interest in land that could be taken by the state if the amount came due). There were many people who were good risks, but lacked either the cash or real estate needed to post bail. Other persons with an ample supply of either soon began to post bail for such defendants for a fee. The states gradually recognized that a new business of "bail bonding" had been created and sought to regulate it.

Bail bonding companies today ordinarily must be licensed by the state. They then are authorized to issue bonds on behalf of their clients without posting cash or a secured interest in real property; their general financial resources serve as security for their bonds. The companies are allowed to charge a fee for the bonds, usually set in the range of 10 to 15% of the face value of the bond. Thus, where a court sets bail at $1,000, the defendant ordinarily can obtain a bail bond for that amount upon payment of a fee of $100. If the defendant appears in court for trial, he does not obtain the return of any part of his fee. If he fails to appear and the bonding company cannot locate him within a specified period (e.g., 6 months), then the company will forfeit $1,000. If the company later finds the defendant, it can seek to collect the $1,000 from him, but most defendants who have "skipped" will not have any assets (and they are not likely to acquire any if they are subsequently imprisoned for skipping, a separate offense in itself).

Bonding companies follow various practices to ensure that they do not suffer significant losses on their bonds. In most areas of the country, if the defendant appears to pose any significant risk of flight, many companies will refuse to issue a bond on his behalf even though he can pay the fee. Others will issue a bond only if the defendant can get other persons with assets, such as his parents, to sign an agreement to reimburse the bonding company if he should flee. Once a bail bond is issued, some bondsmen will keep contact with their clients, either through the telephone or personal visits, to ensure that they stay in the area. Ordinarily, such personal attention is limited to those clients for whom substantial bonds have been issued. If the defendant has skipped, the bondsman will try to locate him through a network of informants who may be willing to cooperate with the bondsman but not the police. Where the bonding company is facing possible forfeiture on a high bond, it may employ "skip-tracers," who are, in effect, modern "bounty hunters." The skip-tracers are not regulated by law, and they sometimes themselves operate within the shadows of the criminal justice system in seeking fugitives. In some areas, the unsavory reputation of the skip-tracers has carried over to the bondsmen as a result of various questionable practices (e.g., non-enforcement of forfeitures) suggesting collusive arrangements with court officials and counsel.

Reform Movement of the 1960's. During the 1960's, a nationwide bail reform movement led to the adoption of various alternatives to bail bonds posted by professional bondsmen. The reform movement was the product of two major concerns. First, studies showed that many defendants who were most unlikely to skip could not gain their release pending trial because they were too poor to afford even low level bonds. Thus, it was not unusual to find that half of the arrestees could not afford a bondsman's fee of $100 and therefore could not make bail set by the court at $1,000. Indeed, a substantial percentage could not make bail set at $500 or less. (The situation was not helped by bondsman's in some communities who refused to write bonds for small amounts). In many cases, when one looked to other relevant factors, such as ties to the community, the persons who were failing to make bail often were more likely to appear at trial than those who were making bail.

A second major concern that led to bail reform was the extreme overcrowding in local jails. More than half of the persons in those jails were defendants awaiting trial as opposed to convicted defendants serving jail sentences. Moreover, persons awaiting trial posed far greater difficulties for the jailers. Programs for such prisoners could not be tailored to a particular time period since the prisoner's stay, unlike that of the person serving a sentence, was not for a set term. Where space in training or work programs was available, the person awaiting trial could not be forced to participate. In the case of a convicted person, participation is viewed as a requirement of his sentence. Prisoners awaiting trial are kept in jail only to assure their appearance at trial, however, and they cannot be subjected to any restrictions that go beyond that limited function. Frequently the jailers simply operated the jail as a holding facility, providing almost no programs whatsoever for prisoners awaiting trial. Those prisoners presented still other difficulties because of their diverse backgrounds, ranging from first offenders charged with minor offenses to experienced criminals awaiting trial on serious felonies. In most jails, available facilities did not permit the separation of the more serious offenders. While other changes in the operation of the jails also were needed, it was generally believed (1) that elimination of the overcrowding would reduce serious disciplinary problems and (2) that the best method of attacking overcrowding was to reduce the number of persons, particularly minor misdemeanants, who were kept in jail pending trial.

The reform movement of the 1960's looked primarily to four alternatives to the traditional form of bail which would permit more defendants to gain their freedom pending trial: (1) release on summons; (2) release on personal recognizance; (3) release under the supervision of a third party; and (4) release under a ten percent bond.

Release on Summons. The first of the alternatives involves greater police use of the summons to release misdemeanant arrestees prior to their first appearance. In some instances, the person will be released on the street, as discussed in Chapter Ten, while in others, the person will be released at the police station after a quick check of his background. If that check shows that the person has strong community ties (e.g., local residence, job, family), indicating that he is likely to appear in court, the officer in charge has authority to release him at the station upon issuance of a summons. In most jurisdictions, this authority is used only for the most minor misdemeanors and is used in cases where the individual certainly would otherwise be released on his own recognizance at the first appearance.[6]

Release on Personal Recognizance.   The second alternative, release on personal recognizance, is not a new procedure for most jurisdictions. A "personal recognizance" is a personal pledge, and a person is released on his personal recognizance when he is put at liberty pending trial on the basis of his pledge to appear in court as scheduled. In some jurisdictions, he may also be required to sign a personal bond, but the bond need not be cosigned by a professional bondsman or supported by any security. His own word is enough to gain his release. Prior to the reform movement of the 1960's, most jurisdictions used release on personal recognizance (commonly called R.O.R.) only in rare cases. Various studies conducted in the early 1960's showed that extensive R.O.R. programs could be adopted with almost no risk. Under these programs, information is sought on defendant's stability in the community, as judged by his length of residence and employment, and the presence of family in the community. Consideration also is given to factors indicating the type of sentence that he might be facing if convicted (e.g., the seriousness of the charge, and the defendant's prior criminal record). Where this data suggests that the community ties are strong and the potential sentence is not very great, the likelihood that the individual will skip is viewed as sufficiently small to permit release on R.O.R.. In many jurisdictions today, over one-third of all arrestees presented before a magistrate are released on R.O.R.. This group includes many persons who previously would have gained their release by obtaining a bond from a professional bondsman, but it also includes many others who would not have been able to afford a bondsman's fee.

Supervised Release.   Another alternative, less commonly utilized, is the release of the defendant into the custody of a third person. This form of release is used for persons who do not qualify for R.O.R., but are likely to appear for trial if they are required to maintain constant contact with some third person responsible for their appearance. The third person can be a relative or local clergyman, but is usually a local community service agency. Very often, the agency will provide supportive counseling (e.g., job counseling) in addition to "keeping track" of the defendant's whereabouts. Another form of supervized release merely requires that the defendant report weekly to some representative of the court, such as a probation officer.

Ten Percent Bonds.   The final alternative, the ten percent bond, relies on the posting of security, but does away with the professional bondsman. Under the ten percent system, the defendant posts ten percent of the full amount of the bail with the court. The ten percent figure is derived from the common fee charged by bondsmen. The defendant is offered two advantages, however, over the use of

---

6.   See pp. 240-41 *supra* discussing the summons and the mandatory summons provisions adopted in some jurisdictions. Closely related to the use of the summons was the increased use of station-house bail. Under a station-house bail procedure, the local court establishes a bail schedule for various minor offenses. The bail for shoplifting, for example, might be $100. After the person is booked, fingerprinted, and photographed, he may obtain his release by posting the $100 with the police. Most of the persons using station-house bail would obtain bail at the first appearance if the station-house bail procedure were not available. However, the station-house bail procedure permits them to avoid spending time in jail while awaiting a first appearance.

bondsmen. First, if the individual can make the ten percent payment, he is certain that he can gain his release. A bondsman always has the option of refusing to accept him as a client or insisting that he post additional security. Second, if the defendant appears at his trial and other hearings, the court will retain a small service fee and return to him most of his ten percent fee. The bondsman, on the other hand, will keep the full fee in all cases. In some jurisdictions, the ten percent system is available only for misdemeanor offenses. At least three states not only utilize the ten percent system for all offenses, but make it the only permissible form of bond. These states have, in effect, eliminated the business of professional bondmaking.[7]

The Federal Bail Reform Act. The Federal Bail Reform Act of 1966, applicable to all federal courts, has served as a model for state legislation governing pretrial release.[8] The federal statute first makes it clear that the magistrate has only one function in setting bail: "Determining what conditions of release will reasonably assure the appearance of the person as required [by law]." While judicial decisions traditionally have noted that bail should be set with only this purpose in mind,[9] some magistrates obviously had been more concerned with other objectives. Thus, cases had been noted in which the magistrate apparently was seeking to keep the defendant in jail pending trial because of concern that he might engage in other crimes if released. In other situations, magistrates apparently had been concerned primarily with summarily punishing the accused. They believed that a "taste" of jail would "do him good," and knew that his inability to make bail would ensure that he had such a taste, without regard to the eventual outcome of his case. The federal act makes it clear that setting bail conditions for any purpose other than assuring the accused's appearance is illegal (at least in the absence of special provisions authorizing preventive detention, a subject we will discuss shortly). In this respect, it does not change the guiding rule, but sets it forth more clearly than did the previous statutes and the bail provisions in state and federal constitutions.

In determining what conditions of release are necessary to assure the accused's appearance, the federal act directs the court to take into account, on the "basis of available information," the following factors: "The nature and circumstances of the offense charged, the weight of the evidence against the accused, the

---

7. The states are Illinois, Oregon, and Kentucky. At the time this book was written, several other states were contemplating total replacement of bondsmen with the ten percent system.

8. 18 United States Code §3146. Some of the newer state provisions are closely patterned after the federal statute. See, e.g., Florida R. Crim. P. 3.130. Others use a somewhat different structure (see, e.g., Illinois Stat. ch. 38, § 110), but their basic thrust is similar to that of the federal act. Indeed, some courts have held that the federal act's emphasis on release upon conditions other than the posting of secured bonds is constitutionally compelled, at least as applied to persons too poor to afford a bondsman's fee. See *Pugh v. Rainwater*, 557 F.2d 1189, 572 F.2d 1053 (5th Cir. 1978).

9. Thus, in the leading Supreme Court case on the subject, decided in 1951, the Court noted: "The right to release before trial is conditioned upon the accused's giving adequate assurance that he will stand trial and submit to sentence if found guilty ... Bail set at a figure higher than an amount reasonably calculated to fulfill this purpose is 'excessive' under the Eighth Amendment." *Stack v. Boyle*, 342 U.S. 1, 4-5, 72 S.Ct.1, 3-4, 96 L.Ed.3 (1951).

accused's family ties, employment, financial resources, character and mental condition, the length of his residence in the community, his record of convictions, and his record of appearance at court proceedings or of flight to avoid prosecution or failure to appear at court proceedings." Note that several of the factors (e.g., weight of the evidence, and past convictions) relate to consideration of the possible sentence that will be imposed if the person is convicted. A substantial likelihood that the person will be found guilty and a severe sentence imposed provides a natural incentive for flight. On the other hand, even here, the magistrate is also to consider information relating to the individual's community ties (e.g., family and employment). Collecting information relating to community ties has been an administrative problem under the federal act and similar state provisions. In many areas, a special pretrial service agency has been established to assist the court in this regard. In others, courts have managed to operate successfully with information gathered by community volunteers, including college students.

Once the magistrate has considered all of the relevant factors, he must select the appropriate conditions for release from among those conditions recognized under the relevant statute. The federal act starts with a presumpton in favor of the release of the defendant upon either his promise to return or a personal bond (i.e., R.O.R.). If the magistrate finds that more restraints are necessary, he is directed to consider the possibility of placing non-monetary conditions upon release, such as placing the defendant in the custody of a third person, restricting his travel, association or place of abode, or placing him in partial jail custody so that he may work during the day and be confined at night. If these alternatives are unsatisfactory, the court is then directed to consider monetary conditions. Initially, the magistrate must consider the possibility that the individual pay ten percent of the amount of the bond into the court. Only after the magistrate finds that all of the above alternatives are inadequate may he turn to a bond posted by a bail bondsman.

Once the magistrate has set his conditions, the accused can seek review of those conditions in a higher court. Ordinarily, however, it is quite difficult to challenge the magistrate's discretion. The mere fact that the magistrate set conditions that the accused could not meet does not render those conditions excessive. The magistrate's determination is most likely to be overturned where he has made a mechanical decision, based largely on the seriousness of the offense charged, without regard to other factors noted in the bail statute. Because of their heavy caseloads, magistrates are sometimes tempted to routinize their bail setting determinations. However, the federal act and similar state provisions clearly require an individualized determination.

Capital Offenses.   At the time of the adoption of the federal constitution, it was firmly established that bail could be denied for offenses punishable by capital punishment. The Eighth Amendment traditionally has been viewed as incorporating this exception in its provision prohibiting "excessive bail." Over forty state constitutions recognize the same exception in providing that bail shall be available to all defendants except for "capital offenses when proof is evident or the presumption great."[10] Under these provisions, bail is not available in capital cases when the prosecution's evidence is sufficient to establish a "fair likelihood" that the defendant is in danger of being convicted.[11] The significance of this exception today is uncertain in light of the substantial constitutional restrictions placed on the state's authority to impose the death penalty. As we shall see in Chapter Thirteen, states may now impose the death penalty only for a limited group of murder convictions.[12] The question therefore arises as to whether bail still can be denied for offenses (primarily homicides) that formerly were punishable by capital punishment, but now are subject to a maximum punishment of life imprisonment. Some courts have construed the capital offense exception strictly, holding that it applies only to those offenses for which the death penalty is still possible. [13] They argue that the exception is based on the notion that a person threatened with possible loss of life is sure to flee. Where that threat no longer exists, they argue, the defendant has a constitutional right to bail set in accordance with the general bail statutes. Other state courts have argued that the capital offense exception was based on the gravity of the offenses involved, particularly murder. They continue to accept the denial of bail in such cases where there is a substantial likelihood of conviction.[14]

Preventive Detention. Preventive detention is the detention of an accused person without bail on the ground that he either will harm himself or the community if not incarcerated. Preventive detention was practiced by magistrates for many years without open acknowledgement. When they believed that the accused was too dangerous to be released pending his trial, they simply set conditions for release that they knew he could not meet. When a magistrate set bail in an amount of many thousands of dollars, he most frequently was seeking to preventively detain rather than to assure the accused's appearance at trial. Adoption of statutes like the Federal Bail Reform Act clearly established the illegality of preventive detention. This forced the legislatures to consider directly whether preventive detention should be permitted, and, if so, under what circumstances. Congress responded by adopting the Preventive Detention Act of 1971, applicable only to the District of Columbia.[15] The federal act permits the court to deny bail where the court concludes that pretrial release of the accused will pose a significant threat to the "safety of the community." The act applies primarily to persons who are charged with crimes of violence and have exhibited a pattern of behavior establishing their dangerousness (e.g., prior convictions for crimes of violence).

---

10. See, e.g., California Constitution, art. 1, §6.

11. *State v. Konigsberg,* 33 N.J. 367, 164 A.2d 740 (1960).

12. See pp. 334-37 *infra.*

13. See *In re Tarr,* 109 Ariz. 264, 508 P.2d 728 (1973); *State v. Johnson,* 61 N.J. 351, 294 A.2d 245 (1972).

14. See e.g., *Ex parte Bynum,* 294 Ala. 78, 312 So.2d 52 (1975); *Jones v. Sheriff, Washoe County,* 89 Nev. 175, 509 P.2d 824 (1973). See also *Covington v. Coparo,* 297 F.Supp. 203 (S.D.N.Y. 1969). In support of this position it is noted that states which long ago abolished capital punishment have continued to retain an exception denying bail in murder cases where the "proof is evident or the presumption great." See Michigan Constitution, art. 1, §15.

15. 84 Statutes-at-Large 644-50.

The court may not conclude that a person falls in this category without an adversary hearing in which the defendant is represented by counsel. If bail is denied on this ground, the prosecution of the defendant's case must be accelerated so that he is brought to trial within 60 days. The constitutionality of the preventive detention concept is debatable under the federal constitution. Proponents of preventive detention note that the Eighth Amendent prohibits the imposition of "excessive bail," but does not state that Congress must provide for bail in all cases. They rely heavily on the analogy provided by the capital offense exception. Opponents contend that the history of the Eighth Amendment indicates that it was designed to establish a right to bail in all cases except those involving offenses punishable by death.

Adoption of preventive detention probably would require a constitutional amendment in the many states with constitutions stating that bail shall be available for all but capital offenses. Supporters of such amendments argue that it would be better to bring preventive detention out in the open and authorize it under careful restrictions than to permit magistrates to continue to impose it informally by setting bonds which defendants obviously cannot meet. They argue that the community would still be protected and many defendants now being detained through high bail would be benefited since a hearing might establish that they were not actually dangerous.

COUNSEL

Timing. The defendant's right to the assistance of counsel is recognized in the Sixth Amendment and in similar provisions in almost all state constitutions. Originally, that right was viewed as primarily, if not exclusively, concerned with the presence of counsel at the trial. In *Powell v. Alabama,* [16] a famous Supreme Court decision of the 1930's, the Court concluded that this focus was too narrow. To obtain the effective assistance of counsel at trial, the defendant's opportunity to retain counsel could not be limited to the trial itself. Indeed, the Court noted, "the most critical period of the proceeding[s] against" defendants might be that period "from the time of their arraignment until the beginning of their trial, when consultation, thorough going investigation, and preparation [are] vitally important." Defendants are "as much entitled to . . . [counsel's] aid during that period as at the trial itself." Subsequent cases expanded upon the *Powell* analysis. They held that counsel's pretrial preparation also would be of little value if counsel did not participate at still earlier proceedings involving the defendant in which important steps were taken that might have a substantial impact upon his trial. Thus, as we have already seen, the *Wade* case held that an arrested person who had been formally accused (thereby giving rise to the Sixth Amendment's protection) was entitled to counsel at a lineup. Similarly, *Coleman v. Alabama* [17] held that the Sixth Amendment right applied to the preliminary hearing because here too the proceedings had an important bearing on the trial and "counsel's absence might derogate from the accused's right to a fair trial."

---

16. *Powell v. Alabama,* 287 U.S. 45, 53 S.Ct. 55, 77 L.Ed. 158 (1932).

17. *Coleman v. Alabama,* 399 U.S. 1, 90 S.Ct. 1999, 26 L.Ed.2d 387 (1970).

Decisions like *Wade* and *Coleman* have placed considerable pressure on the criminal justice process to ensure that counsel is brought into the process shortly after charges are filed. In many jurisdictions, the arrested person is given a right to call counsel from the police station, which permits him to arrange for counsel's presence at the first appearance.[18] In all jurisdictions, the magistrate has the obligation at the first appearance to inform the defendant of his right to counsel. This includes the defendant's right to hire his own attorney and his right to a lawyer appointed by the court if he cannot afford to hire an attorney. Many of the major developments in the right to counsel have been concerned with this latter right of the indigent defendant to counsel appointed at the state's expense.

Indigent Defendants. The Sixth Amendment simply notes that "the accused shall enjoy the right . . . to have the Assistance of Counsel for his defense." Most state constitutional provisions use quite similar language. They do not deal specifically with the situation presented by the defendant who wants to be represented by a lawyer but cannot afford to hire a lawyer (a financial status the law describes as *indigency*). Initially, the state and federal constitutional provisions were viewed as ensuring only that the person able to hire an attorney could utilize a lawyer's skills. This was a substantial advance in itself over the English practice that had been rejected by the framers of the constitution. The English generally permitted representation by counsel only in misdemeanor cases, while the Sixth Amendment applied to all criminal cases.

Even though the Sixth Amendment originally was viewed as applying only to privately hired counsel, the indigent defendant was not totally without assistance. The due process clause required a fair trial and the question soon arose as to whether the defendant could obtain such a trial, under our adversary trial system, without a lawyer. In *Powell v. Alabama,* the Supreme Court held that, at least in some cases, due process required that the court appoint counsel at the state's expense to assist the indigent defendant. In a statement that later served as the foundation for several dramatic extensions of the right to counsel, the Court emphasized the need for legal expertise and knowledge:

> *The right to be heard would be, in many cases, of little avail if it did not comprehend the right to be heard by counsel. Even the intelligent and educated layman has small and sometimes no skill in the science of law. If charged with crime, he is incapable, generally, of determining for himself whether the indictment is good or bad. He is unfamiliar with the rules of evidence. Left without the aid of counsel he may be put on trial without a proper charge, and convicted upon incompetent evidence, or evidence irrelevant to the issue or otherwise inadmissible. He lacks both the skill and knowledge adequately to prepare his defense, even though he may have a perfect one. He requires the guiding hand of counsel at every step in the*

---

18. See note 3 at p. 268 *supra*. Many jurisdictions also have provisions requiring the police to allow the arrestee to consult in private with his lawyer at the jail. See, e.g., Illinois Stat. ch. 38, §103-4: "Any person committed, imprisoned or restrained of his liberty for any cause whatever and whether or not such person is charged with an offense shall, except in cases of imminent danger of escape, be allowed to consult with any licensed attorney at law of this State whom such person may desire to see or consult, alone and in private at the place of custody, as many times and for such period each time as is reasonable."

proceedings against him. Without it, though he be not guilty, he faces the danger of conviction because he does not know how to establish his innocence.[19]

In the thirty-one years between the decisions in *Powell* and *Gideon v. Wainwright,* [20] the Supreme Court proceeded on a case-by-case analysis to determine under what circumstances appointment of counsel was necessary to ensure that an indigent defendant received a fair trial. In *Gideon,* the Court, now relying on the Sixth Amendment, held that a case-by-case approach was inappropriate. The reasoning of *Powell,* the Court noted, established the need for counsel in all felony cases. Lawyers in criminal cases were "necessities, not luxuries" and a defendant could not be denied their assistance simply because the defendant was poor. *Gideon* concluded that the Sixth Amendment right to counsel provided the indigent defendant with a right to appointed counsel in every felony case.

In *Argersinger v. Hamlin,* [21] the *Powell-Gideon* analysis was extended to misdemeanors, at least where the misdemeanor conviction resulted in a jail term. The Court noted that the legal problems presented in a misdemeanor case often could be just as complex as those presented in a felony case. The assistance of counsel acordingly could be just as essential to achieving a fair trial in the misdemeanor case as in the felony case. The Court found it unnecessary to decide, however, whether appointed counsel was constitutionally required where the statutory punishment for the misdemeanor offense was limited to a fine or where the offense was punishable by imprisonment but the defendant received a sentence of a fine only. It had to decide only the case before it, involving an indigent defendant who had been sentenced to jail. His constitutional rights had been denied by the imposition of that sentence after a proceeding in which the state had refused to appoint counsel to assist him.

By tying its ruling to the actual imposition of imprisonment, *Argersinger* placed a considerable burden on the magistrate in those jurisdictions that will appoint counsel only where required to do so by the *Argersinger* ruling. Theoretically, almost all misdemeanor defendants face possible jail sentences since almost all misdemeanor statutes provide for imposing a jail sentence at the judge's discretion. Whether an indigent misdemeanor defendant is constitutionally entitled to appointed counsel depends, as far as *Argersinger* took the law, upon whether he actually will receive a jail sentence. Counsel must be appointed, however, at the outset of the proceedings, and, at that time, it often is difficult to predict what sentence will be imposed if the defendant is convicted. If the magistrate fails to appoint counsel and later finds that a jail sentence is appropriate, his hands are tied; to impose such a sentence would result in an *Argersinger* violation. Moreover, many magistrates feel that it is inappropriate to even attempt such a prediction in advance of trial. A substantial number of states accordingly have gone beyond *Argersinger.* They require that counsel be appointed in all cases where the misdemeanor charged is punishable by imprisonment, without making any

---

19.   *Powell v. Alabama,* 287 U.S. 45, 68-69, 53 S.Ct. 55, 63-64, 77 L.Ed. 158 (1932).

20.   *Gideon v. Wainwright,* 372 U.S. 335, 83 S.Ct. 792, 9L.Ed.2d 799 (1963).

21.   *Argersinger v. Hamlin,* 407 U.S. 25, 92 S.Ct. 2006, 32 L.Ed.2d 530 (1972).

attempt to predict the ultimate sentence. Indeed, in several states, counsel is appointed as well for offenses punishable only by substantial fines.[22]

Determining Indigency. Although it has described indigent defendants as persons lacking funds to hire a lawyer, the Supreme Court has not indicated what sources of funds and what alternative expenditures must be considered in concluding that a defendant cannot "afford" to hire a lawyer. Lower courts generally have held that the separate financial resources of a spouse or relative cannot be considered. A court cannot conclude that college students who are "capable of tapping enough resources to finance their education" are therefore capable of tapping the resources of others to hire a lawyer. The key is the financial capacity of the defendant himself.[23] Moreover, the defendant may be indigent even though he has sufficient resources to hire counsel. For example, if he has just enough funds to either post bond or employ a lawyer, he cannot be made to choose between his personal liberty and representation at trial. So too, if he has an automobile, but he needs it to stay in a job training program, he may not be forced to sell it. As various courts have noted, an individual does not have to become 'destitute" in order to be classified as "indigent." Where the defendant appears to be temporarily poor (as in the case of students), the state may impose a requirement of recoupment—that is, requiring the defendant to reimburse the state when he is able to do so.[24] In most jurisdictions, approximately 60-70 percent of all felony defendants and 30-40 percent of all misdemeanor defendants will be classified as indigent.[25]

Methods of Appointing Counsel. There are essentially three systems used for the appointment of counsel to assist the indigent: the assigned counsel system, the public defender system, and a mixed system which uses elements of both of the other systems. Under the assigned counsel system, an individual attorney is selected by the court (often by the magistrate) to represent a particular indigent defendant. The attorney is paid by the state, but ordinarily the payment is substantially less than that earned in private practice. The public defender system relies upon a state-funded legal office which is, in many respects, the defense counterpart of the prosecutor's office. The legal staff of the office are full time government employees who represent all indigent defendants in the judicial district. The mixed system is basically an assigned counsel system except that some cases are assigned to individual attorneys and others are assigned to a defender

---

22. See New Hampshire Rev. Stat. §§604-A:1 and 604-A:2 (misdemeanors punishable by fine exceeding $500); *Alexander v. City of Anchorage,* 490 P.2d 910 (Alaska 1971) (counsel must be appointed "where the penalty upon conviction . . . may result in incarceration . . . the loss of a valuable license or a fine so heavy so as indicate criminality").

23. See, e.g., *March v. Municipal Court,* 7 Cal.3d 422, 102 Cal. Rptr. 597, 498 P.2d 437 (1972).

24. The constitutionality of recoupment programs was upheld in *Fuller v. Oregon,* 417 U.S. 40, 94S.Ct. 2116, 40 L.Ed.2d 642 (1974).

25. See L. Benner, B. Neory, R. Gutman, *The Other Face Of Justice: A Report Of The National Defender Survey,* Chicago, Ill.: National Legal Aid and Defender Association, 1973, and the sources cited there. Of course, the percentage of cases in which counsel is appointed may be somewhat lower, particularly in misdemeanor cases. Some indigent defendants will waive counsel (a topic discussed *infra*). Also, in misdemeanor cases, jurisdictions refusing to go beyond *Argersinger* will not appoint counsel in those cases where the indigent defendant obviously will not be sentenced to jail.

office. Under this system, the defender office is more likely to be a private non-profit organization rather than a state agency. It ordinarily will be paid a fee by the state for each appointment it is given.

There are advantages and disadvantages to each of the systems. A major difficulty of the assigned counsel system has been the misuse of the appointment process. Some judges have been known to appoint friends or political supporters who are not faring well in the practice of law and can use the additional business. Others have looked primarily to young, inexperienced lawyers who also are grateful for the additional income. In either instance, the lawyers may not be familiar with criminal practice. Some jurisdictions have avoided this difficulty by appointing counsel, largely in rotation, from a list of all of the criminal lawyers in the community. This system produces more experienced counsel, but not all are pleased to work for a lesser fee than they would receive in private practice. The mixed system, by permitting appointment of the defender office to the less serious cases, tends to alleviate the burden on private counsel while still providing experienced private counsel in significant cases.

The public defender system offers the advantages of expertise and efficiency. The public defender's office, like the prosecutor's office, is solely engaged in criminal practice. Its staff can take advantage of their specialization and familiarity with local court practice. The office often has a sufficient caseload to hire investigators and other para-professionals to assist in preparing cases. Since they are full time government employees, paid a regular salary, public defender attorneys do not have the incentive of trying to quickly dispose of a case so as to earn a fee as rapidly as possible. On the other hand, it has been suggested that clients may view a public defender with distrust. They know that they are being prosecuted by the state and that their attorney is an employee of the state rather than a "private attorney." Also, most defender offices carry huge caseloads, and some commentators suggest that defenders therefore are inclined to "trade off" their cases, encouraging guilty pleas in the hopeless cases so they will have more time for the stronger cases. On the other hand, because they are handling criminal cases constantly, defenders become accustomed to police practices and therefore may be more familiar with investigative deficiencies that might help their clients. Also, since the defenders automatically represent all indigent defendants, they often can begin representing defendants at an earlier stage than would be permitted under an assigned counsel system. Thus, a defender ordinarily will be available in the courtroom at the first appearance and can be of immediate assistance in such matters as the setting of bail. Under an assigned system, the appointment usually will not be made until after the first appearance.[26]

Waiver.   The defendant's right to the assistance of counsel, whether privately retained counsel or court appointed counsel, may be waived by a defendant who acts "knowingly and intelligently." The Supreme Court has emphasized, however,

---

26.   In recent years, there has been a growing trend toward use of public defenders. Today, almost every major metropolitan area is served by a public defender office. Statewide offices also are beginning to serve rural counties. Thus between 1961 and 1973, the percentage of counties served by public defender systems grew from 3% with 25% of the population to 25% with 64% of the population. See L. Benner et al., note 25 *supra* at p. 13.

that waiver will not be "lightly assumed." Thus *Carnley v. Cochran* held that a waiver could not be presumed from a "silent record"; the transcript of the proceeding must show that the defendant was informed specifically of his right to counsel and specifically rejected such assistance. [27] Moreover, even a specific rejection will not be sufficient unless the surrounding circumstances indicate that the defendant was acting knowingly and voluntarily. Most often a defendant will waive counsel when he intends to plead guilty. As we shall see,[28] before the court accepts a guilty plea, it ordinarily will inform the defendant of the nature of the charges against him, the maximum sentence that may be imposed, and the nature of the rights that will be relinquished by not going to trial. The court also will ask the defendant to state for the record that he is pleading guilty of his own free will. Where the defendant is without counsel, this procedure is expanded to include notification of defendant's right to counsel and information as to counsel's possible functions. If the defendant then indicates, in response to the court's questions, that he understands his rights and desires to waive counsel and plead guilty, the court ordinarily will have established a knowing and voluntary waiver of counsel.

A more difficult problem is presented where the defendant desires to waive counsel and proceed to represent himself at trial. In *Faretta v. California*, [29] the Court held that the Sixth Amendment guarantees to a defendant the right to proceed *pro se* (i.e., without counsel) in a criminal trial. Several state courts had suggested that a trial court could deny pro se representation when it concluded that the defendant's self-representation would put him at a serious disadvantage in opposing the prosecutor. [30] The Supreme Court rejected this viewpoint. It noted that the Sixth Amendment apparently placed the defendant's right to a "free choice" above his interest in a fair trial. Moreover, where the defendant was adamantly opposed to representation by a lawyer, there would be little value in forcing him to have a lawyer; his refusal to assist the lawyer would undermine many of the advantages that legal representation might otherwise give him. The *Faretta* opinion, while upholding the defendant's right of free choice, stressed that the trial court must take special care to ensure that the defendant is knowingly and intelligently giving up those "traditional benefits associated with the right to counsel":

> *'Although a defendant need not himself have the skill and experience of a lawyer in order competently and intelligently to choose self-representation, he should be made aware of the dangers and disadvantages of self-representation, so that the record will establish that 'he knows what he is doing and his choice is made with eyes open.'*

27. *Carnley v. Cochran*, 369 U.S. 506, 82 S.Ct. 884, 8␣L.Ed.2d 70 (1962).

28. See pp. 305-06 *infra*.

29. *Faretta v. California*, 422 U.S. 806 95 S.Ct.2525 45␣L.Ed.2d 562 (1975).

30. Many experts note that self-representation may not be as foolish as it might seem at first glance. They note that a defendant with a weak case may find his best chance of success in proceeding pro se in the hope that "the jury will be sympathetic toward a layman who pits himself against the Goliath of the state." *People v. Addison*, 256 Cal.App.2d 18, 63 Cal.Rptr. 626 (1967).

The *Faretta* opinion also noted that the right to self-representation "is not a license to abuse the dignity of the courtroom." Under *Illinois v. Allen*,[31] the judge may terminate self-representation by a defendant "who deliberately engages in serious and obstructionist misconduct."

Waiver Before the Magistrate. The role of the magistrate in dealing with the waiver of counsel will vary with the nature of the case involved. In felony cases, the magistrate ordinarily is not concerned with a final waiver since the trial or the guilty plea will be before the general trial court. The magistrate may have to deal with an initial indication of waiver, however, if the defendant is indigent but does not desire that counsel be appointed. Even though a magistrate determines that the indigent felony defendant has made a voluntary and knowing waiver of appointed counsel, that waiver will not be permanent. At the next stage in the proceeding, before the trial court, that court will again inquire as to whether the defendant truly desires to waive his right to counsel. In misdemeanor cases, the magistrate usually will be dealing with final waivers. Since the magistrate has trial jurisdiction in the misdemeanor case, [32] he may take a plea of guilty at the first appearance if the defendant has counsel or is willing to waive counsel. Traditionally, a very high percentage of misdemeanor cases are decided by guilty pleas. In most jurisdictions, the great bulk of those pleas will be taken at the first appearance, along with a waiver of counsel.

PROSECUTORIAL SCREENING

Procedure. In most jurisdictions, either shortly before or shortly after the first appearance, a prosecuting attorney will review the case to determine whether prosecution is appropriate. In some jurisdictions, as we have noted, this must be done before the first appearance because a complaint can be filed only with the prosecutor's approval.[33] Most prosecutors prefer to review cases before the complaint is to be filed, even if they are not legally required to do so. If the prosecutor, upon pre-complaint review, decides that the case does not merit prosecution, it can be dropped at that stage without occupying the time of the magistrate.[34] In some communities, however, time pressures make it impossible to review all cases before the first appearance. Prosecutors then commonly screen immediately before the preliminary hearing in felony cases or the trial in misdemeanor cases.[35] If the prosecutor decides at either stage that the case does not merit prosecution,

---

31. *Illinois v. Allen,* 397 U.S. 337, 90 S.Ct 1057, 25L.Ed.2d 353 (1970). Stand-by counsel frequently are appointed in pro se cases so that they may continue with the case if the defendant's self-representation is terminated for deliberate misconduct. Very often stand-by counsel also will be able to assist the defendant in his self-representation.

32. See p. 36 *supra.* We refer here only to those misdemeanors within the magistrate's trial jurisdiction. Others will be treated in much the same manner as a felony.

33. See p. 245 *supra.*

34. If the suspect was arrested without a warrant, he would, of course, be released upon the prosecutor's determination not to proceed. Where the police seek an arrest warrant prior to making an arrest, the prosecutor's decision not to seek the warrant simply ends the matter and avoids an unnecessary arrest.

35. If misdemeanor cases are reviewed after the first appearance, the prosecutor needs to consider far fewer cases than would be screened prior to the filing of the complaint. A substantial number of

he will make a motion to dismiss the complaint and terminate the case (called a motion of *nolle presequi*). Such motions will almost automatically be granted by the magistrate.

Legal Controls. As we saw in Chapter Eight, the prosecutor's screening of cases is one of the most important steps in the criminal process. The prosecutor eliminates more cases from the criminal process in the exercise of his discretion not to prosecute than does the magistrate at the preliminary hearing, the grand jury in its review, or the trial jury in its review. Moreover, the prosecutor eliminates not simply cases in which the evidence is weak, but also some in which criminal liability can be proved, but the prosecutor considers prosecution inappropriate. Notwithstanding the obvious importance of prosecutorial screening, the prosecutor's exercise of authority to refuse to prosecute is largely unregulated by the law. At common law, the prosecutor was recognized as a "minister of justice" with almost absolute authority not to proceed in a particular case. Courts today continue to recognize that same authority and largely refuse to review a prosecutor's decision not to prosecute. A court will not seek to force a prosecutor to proceed on a citizen's complaint no matter how important the case or how clear the evidence of guilt. The following statement by a federal court reflects the law in both federal and state courts:

> The federal courts are powerless to interfere with [the United States Attorney's] discretionary power. The court cannot compel him to prosecute a complaint, or even an indictment, whatever his reasons for not acting. The remedy for any dereliction of his duty lies, not with the courts, but, with the executive branch of our government and ultimately with the people.[36]

Appropriate Standards. On what grounds should a prosecutor refuse to proceed in a case? General agreement exists that a prosecutor should not proceed where the evidence is insufficient to confict.[37] Indeed, most prosecutors agree that they should not proceed, even though the evidence might be sufficient, if they personally have substantial doubts as to guilt (e.g., they do not believe the complaining witness). Where a case presents adequate evidence for conviction, appropriate grounds for refusing to proceed are not as readily apparent. The National District Attorney's Association has suggested three primary grounds for refusing

misdemeanor defendants are likely to have pled guilty at the first appearance, and those cases no longer need to be screened.

36. *Pugach v. Klein*, 193 F.Supp. 630, 634 (S.D.N.Y. 1961). The courts have recognized one exception to their general refusal to review the prosecutor's discretion. Where a defendant can show that persons who commit criminal acts identical to his ordinarily are not prosecuted, and the decision to prosecute him was based on his race, religion, or exercise of free speech, the court will dismiss the prosecution against him as a denial of equal protection. See *People v. Gray*, 254 Cal.App.2d 256, 63 Cal.Rptr. 211 (1967). See also *Dixon v. District of Columbia*, 394 F.2d 966 (D.C. Cir. 1968) (dismissing a traffic offense prosecution where the prosecutor originally agreed to drop charges, but later instituted charges after the defendant had filed a complaint against the arresting officer with the local Human Relations Council).

37. The American Bar Association, Code of Professional Responsibility, provides in Disciplinary Rule 7-103(A): "A public prosecutor or other government lawyer shall not institute or cause to be instituted criminal charges when he knows or it is obvious that the charges are not supported by probable cause."

to proceed in such cases.[38] First, it notes that the overbreadth of statutes may make certain acts criminal that the legislature probably did not view as crimes. A statute may prohibit all gambling, but it is unlikely that its framers desired that it be applied to a friendly poker game. Second, the lack of enforcement resources may require that certain minor offenses not be prosecuted so as to permit concentration on more serious cases. Where there is a shortage of manpower, cases that would be prosecuted at other times may now have to be dismissed with the offender warned that he will not be so lucky the next time. The refusal to prosecute minor victimless offenses, such as soliciting for prostitution or possession of a small quantity of marijuana, often is justified on this ground. Many prosecutors approach obscenity prosecutions with considerable caution for similar reasons relating to resource allocation. Obscenity prosecutions tend to involve long, complicated trials and multiple appeals, yet often produce little more, even when successful, than a shift from the sale of one pornographic publication to the sale of another.

The third ground noted as a legitimate basis for refusing to prosecute a provable case is the presence of "extenuating circumstances . . . which militate against strict enforcement." The National District Attorneys Association cites the following factors as those that might establish such circumstances: (1) "When the victim has expressed a desire that the offender not be prosecuted" (e.g., where one spouse, assaulted by other, now is opposed to prosecution); (2) "Where the mere fact of prosecution would, in the prosecutor's judgment, cause undue harm to the offender" (e.g., where a public figure, who will be ruined by the publicity, has committed a minor first offense not involving violence, such as petty theft); (3) "Where the offender, if not prosecuted, will likely aid in achieving other law enforcment goals" (e.g., the narcotics user who will testify against a supplier); and (4) "When the harm done by the offense can be corrected without prosecution" (e.g., reimbursement of victim by a first offender who destroyed another's property while somewhat intoxicated). The N.D.A.A. notes that these factors are not exclusive, nor are they necessarily controlling. They always must be considered in light of the nature of the offender and the offense. Some weight also must be given to keeping differential treatment of persons who committed the same crime within limits that will be accepted by the public. As the very nature of the various relevant factors suggests, deciding whether to charge a person with a crime often is one of the most delicate and complex responsibilities that may be imposed upon any public official.

Diversion.   The prosecutor's choice is not always between prosecuting and not prosecuting. In recent years a third alternative, participation in a diversion program, has received considerable attention, particularly in disposing of misdemeanor cases. Diversion refers to a process whereby potential defendants are not prosecuted if they agree to undertake an informal probation program. Conditions of the informal probation commonly include not committing crimes, participation in job or vocational training or counseling programs, and reimbursement of the victim of the crime (where feasible). The program usually is administered by a

---

38. National District Attorney's Association, *National Prosecution Standards*, Chicago, Ill.: N.D.A.A., 1977, pp. 125-128.

volunteer citizens group, or a special government agency attached to either the prosecutor's office or the probation department. If the individual successfully completes the program (which usually will last less than a year), charges are never brought. If he does not, then the prosecutor is free to institute charges. Diversion programs commonly are used for first offenders accused of committing non-violent crimes (e.g., shoplifting, fraud). In some communities, programs have been extended, with federal funding, to a wide range of offenses committed by narcotics users or alcoholics. Proponents of diversion programs note that the programs can reduce congested court dockets, achieve rehabilitation of offenders, and avoid the unnecessary imposition of the stigma of a criminal conviction. Opponents express concern that the programs ignore the rights of accused persons who may be innocent (counsel is not provided), too often operate so as to discriminate arbitrarily against certain offenders (e.g., persons with disadvantaged backgrounds), and provide few safeguards against prosecutorial arbitrariness in determining whether the individual has successfully completed his program. Some critics have suggested that the programs should be placed under judicial supervision or at least be subject to careful judicial review, but this would eliminate a major advantage of the programs in reducing congested court dockets.

Selecting the Charge. Once the prosecutor has decided that prosecution is appropriate, he must select the right charge. In many instances the decision is easy; the defendant has committed a single crime and that is the only one that can be charged. Very often, however, the defendant will have commited several crimes. In some cases he will have committed a series of separate offenses (e.g., a number of burglaries) prior to his apprehension. In other instances, a single course of criminal conduct may violate several statutes. Thus, the Supreme Court once found that a single sale of narcotics violated three separate federal statutes—(1) the sale of drugs without a prescription; (2) the sale of drugs in a package not marked with appropriate tax stamps; and (3) the sale of drugs with knowledge that they had been unlawfully imported.[39] Finally, even when a person commits a single crime (e.g. murder), he may have violated both a higher and lower level of the offense (e.g., the first and second degrees of murder). He cannot be convicted of both levels, and the prosecutor must choose between them in presenting the charge.

Some prosecutors take the position that crimes should be charged as fully as possible. Viewing the evidence in the light most favorable to the prosecution, the charge should include as many offenses at the highest level as the evidence will support. In defense of this position, it is noted that a charge at the highest level can always be reduced if the defendant's actions do not merit such a substantial penalty. On the other hand, if the prosecutor charges at a lower level and facts developed at the subsequent proceedings indicate the offense was more serious, it will be most difficult to raise the charge. (Indeed, once the case goes to trial, it usually will be impossible to so). Another factor that encourages prosecutors to charge as fully as possible is the practice of plea bargaining, which we will consider in the next chapter. Higher charges give the prosecutor more leeway in negotiating

---

39. *Blockburger v. United States,* 284 U.S. 299, 52 S.Ct. 180, 76 L.Ed. 306 (1931).

pleas, and place more pressure on the defendant to plead guilty in exchange for a reduced charge.

Many prosecutors try to exercise more discretion in selecting charges. They do not simply charge the highest offense in all cases. As in the decision to charge, they take into consideration the nature of the crime, the defendant's past record, and the cost of proceeding on multiple charges. Very often they will conclude that there is no extra benefit to be achieved by charging three burglaries rather than one. In other cases, they may find the total situation does not merit the highest possible offense even though it is technically applicable. Consider, for example, the case of a young man who uses a coat hanger to force open a car door and then steals a bottle of liquor lying in the front seat. Technically, the offense may be burglary, a medium level felony. If this was a first offense, a prosecutor exercising discretion may prefer the charge of theft from an automobile, a low level felony. If there were extenuating circumstances, the charge might well be reduced to petty larceny of property valued at less than one hundred dollars, a minor misdemeanor. In many such cases, the task of selecting an appropriate charge can present as many complexities as the decision to charge itself.

PRELIMINARY HEARING

Availability. Preliminary hearings are available in felony prosecutions in most, but not all jurisdictions. In those states where felonies are charged by information, there usually must be a preliminary hearing (or a waiver of the hearing) to proceed. State law commonly provides that the prosecutor may file an information with the trial court only if the magistrate has determined at a preliminary hearing that there is sufficient evidence to proceed or the defendant has waived his right to that determination. In those jurisdictions that prosecute by grand jury indictment,[40] a preliminary hearing is not as significant since the grand jury, not the magistrate, has the final word as to whether there is sufficient evidence to proceed. Preliminary hearings nevertheless often are available in indictment jurisdictions since they provide a more prompt, initial review of the evidence. Grand jury consideration of a defendant's case may not be available until several weeks after the defendant's arrest. The preliminary hearing, on the other hand, can be held within several days and can promptly dispose of those cases in which the evidence clearly will not support the offense alleged in the complaint. Accordingly, a defendant in an indictment jurisdiction often can have his case reviewed first by the magistrate at the preliminary hearing and then by the grand jury. The grand jury's determination will prevail, however. It may hold the evidence insufficient even though the magistrate has held otherwise. Similarly, if the magistrate holds that the evidence is insufficient to prosecute, the prosecutor still may take the case to the grand jury and request that it issue an indictment (although prosecutors rarely utilize this authority). If a grand jury should review a case before a scheduled preliminary hearing, then the preliminary hearing will not be held. Since the grand jury has the final word, holding a preliminary hearing at this point would be only a wasted motion. In many federal districts, United States Attorneys obtain

---

40.   See note 47 *infra*. See also p. 185 *supra* on the distinction between prosecution by indictment and prosecution by information.

indictments quite promptly and preliminary hearings therefore are rarely held. In several states, prosecuting attorneys similarly will by-pass preliminary hearings in certain types of cases (e.g., homicide prosecutions) by obtaining grand jury indictments shortly after the first appearance.

Procedure. There is considerable variation in the nature of the preliminary hearing. All jurisdictions hold the hearing before a magistrate within a short period (commonly five to twelve days) after the first appearance. The defendant will be represented by counsel (court appointed counsel if he is indigent)[41] and the state by the prosecutor. The burden is upon the prosecutor to show that there is sufficient evidence to justify continuation of the prosecution. As we saw in Chapter Nine, the usual standard of proof applied at the preliminary hearing is the probable cause standard. However, some jurisdictions grant the magistrate sufficient leeway in weighing evidence and judging the credibility of witnesses that the standard is, in effect, a preponderance of the evidence standard.[42] An equally important variable is the jurisdiction's rule regarding the evidence that may be used at the preliminary hearing. In the federal system, the prosecution may rely entirely upon hearsay evidence that would not be admissible at trial. Thus the prosecutor may simply put the investigating officer on the stand and let him summarize what various witnesses have told him. In other jurisdictions, the prosecutor is limited to evidence that could be used at trial. Here, the witnesses themselves must be called to testify. In some jurisdictions, the defense counsel can utilize the exclusionary rule at the preliminary hearing to bar evidence obtained through constitutional violations. Other jurisdictions follow the federal practice of permitting such objections to be raised only before the trial court. All jurisdictions permit the defense counsel to cross-examine prosecution witnesses, but they vary considerably in the allowable scope of the cross-examination. Some restrict the defense counsel to precisely those points noted by the witness in his original testimony, while others permit counsel to explore other matters that may be relevant to the case. All jurisdictions permit the defense to present its own witnesses, although defense counsel rarely take advantage of that right. (Common defense strategy advises against "tipping your hand" at the preliminary hearing by disclosing your likely trial defense unless the defense witnesses are so strong that they clearly will defeat the prosecutor's showing of probable cause). The length of the typical preliminary hearing tends to vary with the jurisdiction's rules relating to admissible evidence and cross-examination. In jurisdictions in which the prosecution may rely on hearsay evidence and cross-examination is limited, a preliminary hearing in a typical robbery case may last no longer than fifteen minutes.

The magistrate's function at the preliminary hearing is simply to determine whether the applicable standard of proof has been met. Unlike the prosecutor, he

---

41. In *Coleman v. Alabama*, 399 U.S. 1, 90 S.Ct. 1999, 26 L.Ed. 2d 387 (1970), the Supreme Court held that the preliminary hearing was a critical stage occurring after the initiation of the adversary judicial proceedings and the Sixth Amendment right of the indigent defendant to appointed counsel therefore applied. While the state was not constitutionally compelled to provide a preliminary hearing, it could not do so and then fail to provide the indigent defendant with appointed counsel.

42. See pp. 213-14 *supra*.

does not have discretion to reject a prosecution because he feels other alternatives (such as a diversion program) would be preferable. If the magistrate finds that the evidence is sufficient, he will "bindover" (i.e., send the case on) to the trial court (in an information state) or to the grand jury (in an indictment state). If the magistrate finds that the evidence supports a lesser felony than that alleged in the complaint, he will bindover on the lesser charge alone. If he finds that only a misdemeanor has been established, he will set the case for trial in the magistrate court on the misdemeanor charge. If the magistrate finds that there is not probable cause to support any charge, he will dismiss the complaint and order the defendant released if he still is in custody.[43] Where the defendant is boundover and has not made bail, the preliminary hearing also may be used to obtain a review of the bail by the magistrate. Since the magistrate now has more information concerning the offense, he may be willing to reduce the bail (particularly if the case was boundover on a lesser charge).

Functions of the Preliminary Hearing. The primary function of the preliminary hearing is to test the sufficiency of the prosecution's evidence. This is a very important function. The elimination of cases not supported by probable cause fulfills various objectives of the criminal justice process. As one court noted, it serves "to prevent hasty, malicious, improvident, and oppressive prosecutions, . . . to avoid both for the defendant and the public the expense of a public trial, and to save the defendant from the humiliation and anxiety involved in public prosecution."[44] The preliminary hearing also serves incidentally to perform other functions helpful to both prosecution and defendant. For the defense, it is a valuable "discovery technique"—a method of discovering in advance of trial the nature of the evidence that the prosecution intends to use at trial. It also serves to assist the defense counsel in preparing for the cross-examination of prosecution witnesses at trial. He has the opportunity for a "dry run" at cross-examining those witnesses called at the hearing. When those witnesses testify again at trial, they may be challenged on any inconsistencies between their trial testimony and their preliminary hearing testimony. For the prosecution, the primary advantage is the preservation of testimony. If a witness should testify at the preliminary hearing and then be unavailable to testify at trial (e.g., due to death), his preliminary hearing testimony may be introduced at trial.[45]

GRAND JURY

Availability. The grand jury is an ancient institution, dating back to the 1100's, though it has changed substantially in form and function over the years. Initially,

---

43. Of course, as noted previously, in a jurisdiction that utilizes prosecution by grand jury indictment, the prosecutor still may seek to have the grand jury indict the defendant.

44. *Theis v. State,* 178 Wis. 98, 189 N.W. 539 (1922).

45. Since the defendant had the opportunity to cross-examine the witness at the preliminary hearing, the use of that testimony at trial does not violate the Sixth Amendment right of confrontation (see p. 317 *infra*). The witness must be truly unavailable to testify at trial, however. If he cannot be found, the prosecution must show that it made a diligent effort to find him. If this is established, the witness' prior preliminary hearing testimony will be read to the jury and they may give it whatever weight they believe it deserves.

its function was to serve as an investigative agency, assisting the Crown in ferreting out crimes. Subsequently, it took on an additional role, acting as a shield against unjust prosecutions. When the federal constitution was adopted, it was this screening function that was preserved in the Fifth Amendment. The Fifth Amendment provides that, except in military cases, "no person shall be held to answer for a capital or otherwise infamous crime, unless on a presentment or indictment of a Grand Jury." As we have seen, the Fifth Amendment requirement of grand jury review has been held not to apply to the states under the Fourteenth Amendment due process clause.[46] While grand jury screening is a valuable function, other screening procedures, such as the preliminary hearing, are equally satisfactory in meeting the requirements of due process. About half of the states still require grand jury review as a matter of state law.[47] The remaining states prosecute by information and rely primarily upon the preliminary hearing to ensure against prosecutions not supported by probable cause.

Where grand jury review is required under state law, that requirement usually applies only to felony offenses.[48] The Fifth Amendment's reference to "infamous crimes" similarly has been held applicable only to felonies. Grand jury review ordinarily can be waived by the defendant (although some jurisdictions prohibit waiver in capital cases). If the defendant chooses to waive his right to grand jury review, the prosecutor then may present the felony charge in an information. Although the Fifth Amendment and many state provisions refer to both "indictments" and "presentments," charges approved for prosecution by a grand jury are presented today only in the form of an indictment. A presentment historically was a charge similar to an indictment except that it was prepared by the grand jury on its own initiative. Grand juries today rarely decide to issue charges except upon the request of the prosecutor. In the occasional cases where they do act on their own initiative, the charges are nevertheless presented in a formal accusation labeled as an indictment.

Selection. Although a state need not provide for grand jury review, if it does so, the jurors must be selected in a manner consistent with the due process and equal protection guarantees of the Fourteenth Amendment. Those guarantees prohibit discrimination in jury selection based on race, religion, or sex. They do not, however, prohibit the state from establishing reasonable qualifications for jury service that relate to a grand juror's duties. States commonly require that jurors be residents of the county, be of voting age, be able to read and write the English

---

46. See p. 221 *supra.*

47. The following states require prosecution by indictment for all felonies: Alabama, Alaska, Delaware, Georgia, Hawaii, Kentucky, Maine, Massachusetts, Mississippi, New Hampshire, New Jersey, New York, North Carolina, Ohio, Pennsylvania, South Carolina, Tennessee, Texas, Virginia, and West Virginia. Several other states require prosecution by indictment for various serious felonies (e.g., all offenses punishable by life imprisonment or death). These states are: Connecticut, Florida, Louisiana, Minnesota, and Rhode Island. The remaining states permit prosecution by information for all felonies.

48. South Carolina, Tennessee, and West Virginia require prosecution by indictment for a substantial group of misdemeanors. These states also are more restrictive than most indictment jurisdictions in dealing with waiver.

language, not suffer from physical disabilities that would interfere with jury service, have no prior felony convictions, and not be under a pending criminal charge. The selection of the grand jurors usually is delegated by law to a special government commission known as the jury commission. Ordinarily, each judicial district has its own jury commission with its members appointed by the general trial court. In most states, the jury commission will select grand jurors at random from voter registration lists. Some jurisdictions combine the voting lists with other lists that might include additional qualified persons who do not vote (e.g., lists of taxpayers, licensed drivers, utility customers). Several jurisdictions continue to utilize a "key man" system, under which prominent persons in the community nominate individuals that they believe to be of "sound mind and good moral character." The jury commission then selects the jurors at random from a list of the qualified nominees.

If a jurisdiction relies upon a voter registration list or a combined list, the process of selection is almost immune to a successful challenge. Use of the key man system, however, presents potential difficulties. The Supreme Court has held that the system is not unconstitutional in itself, but it is suspect. If a jurisdiction with a key man system regularly has a much smaller percentage of black grand jurors than the percentage of blacks in the community, it will be assumed that the system has been used unconstitutionally to discriminate against blacks. Indictments issued by a grand jury selected in such an unconstitutional manner then can be challenged by all defendants—that is both black and white defendants can have their indictments dismissed. The discrimination against prospective black jurors deprives all defendants, whether white or black, of their right to a grand jury selected from a fair cross section of the community.[49]

In selecting prospective grand jurors from a voter registration or other appropriate list, the jury commissioners ordinarily select substantially more people than the number required for jury service. This larger group of persons is sometimes called the jury "venire" or "array." Some of the people selected for the venire will not meet the necessary qualifications (e.g., they may be physically unable to serve). Others may hold positions entitling them to exemptions from jury service. Most jurisdictions give automatic exemptions to persons performing essential public service (e.g., physicians and firemen). Still others may be excluded by state law. Lawyers and police officers, for example, are automatically barred from jury service because of their relationship to the courts and the criminal justice process. The jury commissioners first must eliminate those persons who are unqualified, exempt, or excluded by law, and then randomly select from the venire the precise number of persons needed for a grand jury. That number will vary with state law.

At common law, the grand jury was composed of 23 persons with an affirmative vote of a majority (12) required for an indictment. In many jurisdictions, the minimum size was reduced, while the number required for an indictment was not

---

49. Among the leading cases dealing with jury discrimination, the key man system, and challenges by defendants are *Strauder v. West Virginia,* 100 U.S. 303, 25 L.Ed. 664 (1879); *Casteneda v. Partida,* 430 U.S. 482, 97 S.Ct. 1272, 51 L.Ed. 2d 498 (1977); and *Peters v. Kiff,* 407 U. S. 493, 92 S.Ct. 2163, 33 L.Ed.2d 83 (1972). See also *Taylor v. Louisiana,* 419 U. S. 522, 95 S.Ct. 692, 42 L.Ed.2d 690 (1975) (involving trial jury selection).

changed. The federal courts now use grand juries of 16-23 persons with 12 votes still necessary for an indictment. Some states use an even smaller grand jury, such as a 12 person jury with 9 affirmative votes required for indictment. The term of the grand jury varies from state to state, but it usually will be for at least several weeks, with terms of several months not uncommon. The frequency with which the grand jury meets will vary with the type of community involved. In rural areas, grand jurors sometimes meet for only one day a month and then not even for the full day. On the other hand, the District Attorney for the County of New York (Manhattan) generally uses five separate grand juries simultaneously, with each meeting five days a week, three hours each day.

The Function and Structure of the Grand Jury. The Supreme Court has described the screening function of the grand jury as follows:

> *[I]t serves the invaluable function in our society of standing between the accuser and the accused, whether the latter be an individual, minority group, or other, to determine whether a charge is founded upon reason or was dictated by an intimidating power or by malice and personal ill will.*[50]

The legal structure of the grand jury is designed largely to ensure that it can perform this function effectively. For example, the jurors receive evidence in secret session, which serves to insulate them from public pressure. A disappointed prosecutor, bound by the oath of secrecy, cannot publicly describe the evidence that he presented to the grand jury in the hope of stirring public opposition to its decision. The grand jury will discuss the case and vote on it outside the presence of the prosecutor, with the votes of individual jurors always kept secret.[51] Of course, the grand jury will receive legal advice and evidence from the prosecutor, but his word is not final. The jurors may seek further legal advice from the court, and they may require the prosecutor to subpoena witnesses not initially presented before them. In fact, if the prosecutor fails to cooperate with the grand jury, it may ask the court to replace him. The grand jury is established under the law as an "arm of the court," and the court has an obligation to preserve its independence.

As we saw in Chapter Nine, the standard of proof for grand jury indictment is probable cause in some jurisdictions and the higher, prima facie proof standard in others. Under the latter standard, the grand jury must conclude that the evidence before it, if unexplained or uncontradicted at trial, would lead a reasonable trial jury to find guilt beyond a reasonable doubt. In most jurisdictions, the grand jury (unlike the trial jury) also will be told by the court that it has the power to "nullify" the law. Even though the prosecution's evidence is sufficient and the grand jury believes the defendant committed a crime, the grand jury may refuse to indict if it concludes that prosecution would result in a "miscarriage of justice."

---

50. *Wood v. Georgia,* 370 U. S. 375, 390, 82 S.Ct. 1364, 8 L.Ed.2d 569 (1962).

51. The grand jury foreman reports the vote for and against each indictment proposed by the prosecutor, but does not report the vote of the individual jurors. If the grand jury approves the proposed indictment, the foreman will endorse it as a "true bill." If it rejects the proposed indictment, the foreman will record that it is "not a true bill."

Grand Jury Performance. How well does the grand jury perform its screening function? There has been an ongoing debate on this issue for the last fifty years. Critics of the grand jury argue that it is recognized legally as an independent body, but operates in fact as no more than the "rubber stamp" of the prosecutor. Although it has the authority to act on its own direction, its close association with the prosecutor, they argue, inevitably leads it to follow almost all of his recommendations. The critics note, for example, that prosecutors in many jurisdictions regularly obtain indictments solely on a police officer's description of the reports of various witnesses.[52] Moreover, even in those states that require the grand jury to hear the direct testimony of those witnesses, grand juries rarely reject more than ten percent of the proposed indictments placed before them. The critics also suggest that a large portion of that ten percent probably consists of cases in which the prosecutor has himself recommended that the grand jury refuse to indict. Prosecutors, they contend, sometimes seek to evade personal responsibility for refusing to prosecute by presenting to the grand jury weak cases that they expect it to reject.

Supporters of the grand jury contend that the low percentage of cases in which indictments are not returned (under 5% in some jurisdictions) is a meaningless statistic. They note that, with careful screening, the vast majority of cases presented by the prosecutor will be "open and shut" cases obviously requiring prosecution. The crucial question, they maintain, is how many weak cases are rejected during prosecutorial screening because the prosecutor knows that they could not "get by" the grand jury. Supporters point to the trial record on indictments, noting that an extremely small percentage of indictments are dismissed by the trial court for lack of a prima facie case. They also argue that the preliminary hearing, commonly championed by the critics of the grand jury, does not fare much better than the grand jury in terms of its screening statistics. In many information states, magistrates too dismiss charges in less than ten percent of the cases presented to them.

CHALLENGES TO THE ACCUSATION

Once the preliminary hearing magistrate issues a bindover order in an information state, or a grand jury finds a true bill in an indictment jurisdiction, the felony case moves to the general trial court. The indictment or information is filed with that court, and the defendant is arraigned on the information or indictment. In some respects, the arraignment is similar to the first appearance. The trial court establishes the identity of the defendant, and either reads to him or gives him a

---

52. Under the practice followed in the federal system and most states, a grand jury indictment may be based entirely on hearsay. Other states require indictments to be based only on evidence that would be admissible at trial, with minor exceptions. This position has been enforced most vigorously in New York, where a court will dismiss an indictment if not supported by legally admissible evidence establishing a prima facie case. See New York Criminal Procedure Law §210.30. In the federal system, on the other hand, the courts will not review the sufficiency of the evidence before the grand jury. See *Costello v. United States*, 350 U.S. 359, 76 S.Ct.406, 100 L.Ed. 397 (1956). The grand jury also may receive illegally seized evidence that would be barred from trial under the exclusionary rule. See *United States v. Calandra*, 414 U. S. 338, 94 S.Ct. 613, 38 L.Ed.2d 561 (1974).

copy of the information or indictment. If the defendant is still in custody, the trial court will review bail, and if the defendant appears without an attorney, the trial court will seek to determine why counsel is not present. If the defendant desires to waive counsel, the court will go through the same steps as the magistrate to ensure that the waiver is made knowingly and voluntarily. Unlike the first appearance, the trial court also will take the defendant's plea to the charge.[53] Before doing so, however, the defendant will be given an opportunity to present any legal challenges to the court's authority to proceed on the charge. The defendant here would raise any defects in the charging process (e.g., discriminatory selection of the grand jury) or in the accusation itself. Three of the more significant challenges are: (1) the inadequacy of the indictment or information in providing notice of the charge; (2) prosecution in violation of the double jeopardy prohibition; and (3) improper venue in the location of the charge.[54]

Notice. The Sixth Amendment provides that "in all criminal prosecutions, the accused shall enjoy the right . . . to be informed of the nature and cause of the accusation." To ensure that the accusation provides adequate notice, state laws commonly require that an indictment or information contain a statement of the facts constituting the offense, identify the offense by name or statutory citation, and indicate, to the extent practicable, the time and place of the offense. In determining whether an accusation provides sufficient notice, a court must assume that the defendant is innocent and knows nothing about the events in question. Assume, for example, that an indictment alleges that a defendant acted fraudulently in selling an unidentified item to John Jones on a certain date. The defendant then claims that the indictment does not provide adequate notice because it fails to identify the nature of the fraud or the item sold. The court cannot respond that the defendant made the sale so he must have known what was sold and must be aware of what representations he made in selling the item. The notice must be adequate to assist the defendant who may have been falsely accused even of making the sale. It must "sufficiently apprise . . . [a] defendant of what he must be prepared to meet."[55]

Prosecutors sometimes hesitate to be too specific in an indictment or information for fear that the facts disclosed at trial will not match those alleged in the accusation. The prosecutor cannot seek at trial to prove the offense in a manner other than that set forth in the accusation. If he were allowed to do so, the accusation would be valueless in providing notice to the defendant. On the other hand, minor variations which do not take the defendant by surprise are permitted in most, though not all, jurisdictions. In a Tennessee case, the court refused to permit the prosecution to prove that a robbery was committed with a rifle when

---

53. In many jurisdictions, the magistrate will take a plea at the first appearance to misdemeanor charges which are within the magistrate's trial jurisdiction. For such cases, the first appearance serves both as a first appearance and as an arraignment on the accusation. See note 14, p. 184 *supra.*

54. The timing in raising these objections will vary from jurisdiction to jurisdiction. Many states permit them to be raised at any time before trial.

55. *Russell v. United States,* 369 U. S. 749, 764, 82 S.Ct. 1038, 1047, 8 L.Ed.2d 240 (1962).

the indictment had charged that the robber used a pistol.[56] Fortunately, most jurisdictions today are not so technical.

Double Jeopardy. The Fifth Amendment provides that no person shall be "subject for the same offence to be twice put in jeopardy of life or limb." The most frequently quoted explanation of the purpose of this "double jeopardy" prohibition comes from *Green v. United States:*

> *The underlying idea . . . is that the State with all its resources and power should not be allowed to make repeated attempts to convict an individual for an alleged offense, thereby subjecting him to embarrassment, expense and ordeal and compelling hm to live in a continuing state of anxiety and insecurity, as well as enhancing the possibility that even though innocent he may be found guilty.*[57]

The double jeopardy clause's reference to "life or limb" has been held to encompass any form of criminal punishment, including imprisonment as well as capital punishment. The defendant is viewed as being placed in "jeopardy" of suffering such punishment as soon as he is put to trial on the criminal charge. Thus, read literally, the amendment prohibits any second trial for the same offense. The Supreme Court has held, however, that this literal interpretation must give way to several exceptions to the double jeopardy prohibition that were well accepted at the common law. The most prominent of these exceptions relate to cases in which the first trial does not result in a verdict of conviction or acquittal. Thus, if a person is put to trial but the trial cannot be completed because of some exceptional circumstance (such as the death of the judge), a retrial is permissible. Similarly, if the first trial resulted in a hung jury (i.e., the jury is divided and cannot reach a verdict), there may be a second trial. Where the trial is completed, however, and the defendant is acquitted, the prosecution is barred from retrying the defendant. Even though the verdict of acquittal may be erroneous, the prosecution cannot either appeal or seek to retry on a new indictment. An aquittal for this purpose includes both an acquittal on all charges and an acquittal on one of several charges. If a defendant is charged with first degree murder, but is convicted only of second degree murder, he is viewed as having been acquitted on the higher charge and double jeopardy absolutely bars reprosecution on that charge.

Where a defendant has been convicted, the application of the double jeopardy bar depends upon the defendant's response to that conviction. If he appeals the conviction and it is reversed due to some trial error, he may be tried again for the same offense. If the defendant does not challenge the conviction, the prosecution may not retry the defendant. The prosecution may later conclude that it should have proceeded on a higher charge for the same offense or it may dislike the sentence imposed by the court, but it is barred by the Fifth Amendment from starting over again. Similarly, after a court has imposed a sentence, it may not reconsider the matter and raise the sentence.

---

56. *State v. Brooks,* 224 Tenn. 712, 462 S.W.2d 491 (1970); *State v. Duncan,* 224 Tenn. 712, 462 S.W.2d 491 (1970); *Duncan v. Tennessee,* 405 U.S. 127, 92 S.Ct, 785, 31 L.Ed.2d 86 (1972) (refusing review of the retrial on an indictment alleging use of the rifle).

57. *Green v. United States,* 355 U.S. 184, 187, 78 S.Ct. 221, 223, 2 L.Ed.2d 199 (1957).

It should be emphasized that the double jeopardy prohibition applies only to a second trial for the same offense. The commission of the same criminal act against different victims or against the same victim at different times does not constitute a single offense even though the same statute is violated. Double jeopardy does not bar separate trials and separate punishments for the robbery of two persons at the same place or the robbery of the same person at two different times. Under the "separate sovereign" doctrine, federal and state offenses arising from the same criminal acts also are treated as separate offenses.[58] Thus, if a person robs a federally insured bank, he may be prosecuted separately by both federal and state governments and punished for both offenses. As a matter of prosecution policy, the federal government ordinarily will not bring a federal prosecution after a person has been tried for a state offense based on the same criminal episode. Almost half of the states follow a similar policy, refusing to permit state prosecutions following a federal prosecution for the same criminal acts.

Venue. *Venue* comes from a French word meaning neighborhood and refers, in the legal setting, to the place of the trial. A basic tenet of American criminal procedure is that criminal actions should be tried in the place where the offense occurred. This concept is recognized in two places in the federal constitution. Article III, Section 2 provides:

> *The trial of all Crimes, except in Cases of Impeachment, shall be by jury; and such Trial shall be held in the State where the said Crimes shall have been committed; but when not committed within the State, the Trial shall be at such Place or Places as the Congress may by Law have directed.*

The Sixth Amendment incorporates the same principle in describing the defendant's right to a jury trial. It notes that the accused is entitled to "an impartial jury of the state and district wherein the crime shall have been committed, which district shall have been previously ascertained by law." Because of these constitutional provisions, an offense committed in Iowa must be tried in Iowa and one committed in Wyoming must be tried in Wyoming. Moreover, where the state is divided into judicial districts, the offense must be tried in the district in which it was committed. The federal courts, as we have seen, are divided into districts in the more populous states.[59] State courts commonly are divided into districts consisting of a single county or group of counties. Many states have provisions requiring that the criminal trial be held in the county in which the offense occurred even where the judicial district contains several counties. If the venue is improper, the defendant may challenge the prosecution, insisting that it be brought in the right place or not at all.[60]

---

58. *Bartkus v. Illinois*, 359 U.S. 121, 79 S.Ct, 676, 3 L.Ed.2d 684 (1959).

59. See p. 40 *supra*.

60. It should be noted that venue requirements are not absolute. The defendant may force the prosecution to try him in the right district, but he also may waive his objection. Indeed, the defendant himself can request that the trial be moved to another district, one in which the crime did not occur. This request for a "change in venue" commonly is made when pretrial publicity makes it difficult for the defendant to obtain an unbiased jury or the convenience of the witnesses would be served by trial in another county. Granting such a motion lies in the discretion of the

Even though venue is limited to the district in which the offense was committed, there are situations in which the prosecution will have a choice of districts. Some offenses are committed in more than one district. Kidnapping, for example, is a "continuing offense" that is committed in very district into which the victim is taken. Even murder may be viewed, under special circumstances, as having been committed in more than one district. Where a man located in one district shoots across the district line and kills a person in the next district, the prosecution can be brought in either district. In those cases where it cannot be readily determined whether the offense was committed in one district or another (e.g., it was committed somewhere in the vicinity of the county line), either district ordinarily constitutes proper venue. Similarly, where even the general location of the offense cannot be determined, but evidence of the crime is found in one district (e.g., the body of a murdered person is found there), that district may used for the trial.[61]

---

court, unless it is clear that venue must be changed to guarantee the defendant's right to a fair trial.

61. For a more extensive legal analysis of the various topics described in this chapter, see *Modern Criminal Procedure*, note 89 at p. 266 *supra*. For excellent descriptions of the law and practice relating to various different preliminary steps in the criminal justice process, see L. Katz, L. Litwin, and R. Bamberger, *Justice Is The Crime*, Cleveland, Ohio: Case Western Reserve Press, 1972; F. Miller, *Prosecution: The Decision To Charge A Suspect With A Crime*, Boston, Mass.: Little, Brown, and Company, 1969. Another useful source, containing an extensive bibliography, is the National Advisory Commission on Criminal Justice Standards and Goals, report on *Courts*, Washington, D.C.: Government Printing Office, 1973.

Chapter 12

Adjudication

The term *adjudication* refers to the process of reaching a final judicial decision in a lawsuit. In descriptions of the American criminal justice process, that term commonly is reserved for the two methods of reaching a final decision on the merits of the criminal charge—the trial and the guilty plea. Of course, cases may be disposed of by other types of rulings (e.g., a dismissal for lack of a speedy trial), but the guilty plea and the trial are the only two dispositional procedures that provide a final decision based on the guilt or innocence of the accused.

GUILTY PLEAS

Form of Pleas. As we noted in the last chapter, the defendant will enter his plea at an arraignment before the court which has jurisdiction to try his case. In the felony case, this is the arraignment on the information or indictment before the general trial court. After informing the defendant of the contents of the information or indictment, the court will ask the defendant, "How do you plead"? In all jurisdictions the defendant has two choices, and in many he also has a third. A defendant always can plead "not guilty," which puts the prosecution to proving its case at trial.[1] He also can plead guilty, which admits the commission of the crime. The guilty plea results in the entry of a judgment of conviction, just as would a jury finding guilt. The plea of *nolo contendere* is the third option. It produces the same result as the guilty plea, though it is different in form. Nolo contendere means "no contest." The plea tells the court that it may accept the accusation as the basis for the entry of a judgment of conviction, but it does not acknowledge the truth of the

---

1. In most jurisdictions, defendant will have to go beyond a simple "not guilty" statement under limited circumstances. Thus, if he intends to rely upon an insanity defense, the proper form of the plea may be "not guilty by reason of insanity." In several jurisdictions, an objection based upon double jeopardy is also viewed as a matter to be noted in the plea (rather than simply raised through a motion to dismiss the accusation). Where these special pleas are used, the defendant may combine them with a plea of not guilty—e.g., pleading both not guilty and not guilty by reason of insanity. See California Penal Code §1016.

297

accusation. The defendant loses, in effect, by default. The plea is regularly available in only about half of the states. Moreover, most of those states give the court discretionary authority to deny to the defendant the option of pleading nolo contendere.

The primary legal advantage of the nolo contendere plea from the defendant's perspective is that the plea cannot be used in a civil case to prove that he committed a crime, while a guilty plea can be used for that purpose.[2] With respect to the imposition of sentence, the defendant's criminal record, and other matters relating to the criminal justice process, there is no difference between the nolo contendere and guilty pleas. Since our concern is with the criminal justice process, we will treat the two pleas as identical. Our discussion of guilty pleas is meant to encompass pleas of nolo contendere unless we indicate otherwise.

Guilty Plea Dispositions. Over the last few years, the frequent disposition of cases through guilty pleas has attracted considerable attention from the mass media. Guilty pleas and plea bargaining have been the primary focus of television specials and newspaper and magazine features on the criminal justice process.[3] While the media has made an important contribution to public awareness of the realities of the criminal justice process, it sometimes has tended to exaggerate the role played by guilty pleas in the disposition of criminal cases. Too often, we have been left with the impression that almost all criminal prosecutions result in a guilty plea. We have been told, for example, that over ninety percent of all criminal cases are disposed of by guilty pleas. Such statements err on two grounds. First, they confuse the ratio of guilty pleas to trials with the ratio of guilty pleas to all dispositions of cases. Second, they attempt to portray a nationwide pattern based on the experience of a few major cities.

In evaluating dispositions by guilty plea, one must always keep in mind that a significant number of criminal cases, particularly felonies, will be terminated without ever reaching the stage where disposition will be made by trial or guilty plea. Even if one assumes careful screening by the prosecutor before charges are filed, a substantial group of cases will be dismissed at preliminary proceedings (e.g., the preliminary hearing or grand jury review). Another substantial group will be dismissed by the trial judge on defense or prosecution motions before trial. The defense may gain a dismissal, for example, on a successful legal claim (e.g., double jeopardy) or by obtaining the exclusion of crucial evidence on a pretrial motion

---

2. The nolo contendere plea is used most frequently where the criminal law violation constitutes a civil wrong for which substantial damages may be recovered by the victim. The antitrust field is illustrative. If a defendant charged with a criminal antitrust violation pleads guilty, that plea may be used in a civil suit to automatically establish his liability for substantial damages to all persons injured by the violation. On the other hand, if he enters a plea of nolo contendere, that plea cannot be used in civil suits, and each civil litigant must establish independently that there has been a violation. Under such circumstances, it is likely that fewer parties will file a civil suit than they would were they able to "ride on the coattails" of a guilty plea or a guilty verdict obtained in the criminal prosecution.

3. The practice of plea bargaining received considerable coverage, in particular, after former Vice President Agnew entered a plea of nolo contendere to a tax evasion charge and received a sentence of probation as a result of a plea agreement. The Agnew agreement was particularly complex since it involved the Vice President's resignation from office as well as the government's agreement not to press a series of other charges.

challenging an illegal search. The prosecution may suddenly find a weakness in its case (e.g., a missing witness) that requires it to seek dismissal. As a result of the dismissals at the trial level and at the preliminary proceedings, a jurisdiction rarely will have more than eighty percent of its original felony cases left for adjudication by guilty plea or trial. Thus, even if all of the remaining defendants plead guilty, we could not have a guilty plea rate of more than eighty percent as measured against the disposition of all felony cases. When newspaper reports refer to guilty plea rates in excess of ninety percent, they are referring to the rate of guilty pleas as among those cases that are terminated by plea or trial. The percentage of guilty pleas *among all felony dispositions* rarely will exceed seventy-five percent, even in those judicial districts with the highest guilty plea rates.[4] Indeed, even for misdemeanors, where there is less screening, the percentage of guilty pleas among total dispositions should fall within the range of eighty to ninety percent.

If one looks only to felony cases decided either by trial or guilty plea, a guilty plea rate in excess of ninety percent still is not the norm throughout the country. Admittedly, there are some major urban areas, such as New York City, in which more than nine guilty pleas are received for every trial held,[5] but the larger urban communities, suffering from particularly heavy caseloads, tend to have a substantially higher percentage of guilty pleas than the smaller communities. Moreover, even among our major urban communities, the guilty plea rate for felonies is more likely to fall between seventy and eighty-five percent.[6]

---

4. M. Finkelstein, *A Statistical Analysis of Guilty Plea Practices in Federal Courts,* 89 Harvard L. Rev. 293 (1975), found a substantially lower percentage of guilty pleas in federal courts without even considering pre-arraignment dismissals. Guilty pleas were entered in only 60.5% of the 48,154 post-arraignment dispositions in the federal district courts (excluding the District of Columbia) in 1974. The highest percentage of pleas in post-arraignment dispositions over the previous 50 years was 85.8% in 1951. Reports from other jurisdictions are similar. See, e.g., *Report of the Administrative Director of the New Jersey Courts, 1976-77,* p. F-3 (14,002 guilty pleas out of 24,648 cases terminated); 1976 *Annual Report of the Administrative Office of the Illinois Courts,* p. 146 (17,032 guilty plea dispositions out of 38,408 felony defendants disposed of during the year, including pre-arraignment dispositions). See also note 5 *infra* describing the experience in New York City.

5. While New York is not the only district in this category, it is the most commonly cited example. The Vera Institute publication, *Felony Arrests: Their Prosecution and Disposition on New York City's Courts,* New York: Vera Institute of Justice, 1977, p. 7, relying on an extensive sample, offered the following estimate of the disposition of felony arrests in New York City's four major boroughs: out of 75,661 arrests reaching disposition, 41,488 would result in guilty pleas, 1,744 in trials and 32,429 in dismissals. Among the guilty pleas, 2,785 would be to original felony charged, 7,900 to a lesser felony, and 30,803 to a misdemeanor.

6. Statistics on guilty pleas and trials in several major cities are noted in D. McIntyre and D. Lippman. *Prosecutors and Early Disposition Of Felony Cases,* 56 American Bar Association Journal 1154 (1970); L. Katz, et al., note 61 at p.   *supra,* and various state reports such as those cited in note 4 *supra.* The extreme variation of the rates among different types of communities across the county makes it very difficult to generalize. Although major cities tend to have higher rates, there are some cities in which the plea rate is very low. Baltimore is the prime example, with a guilty plea rate of less than 20%. (Defendants there commonly waive jury trial, however, and have their cases tried by the judge alone). See D. McIntyre and D. Lippman, *supra.* On the other hand, there are some non-urban communities in which the ratio of guilty pleas to trials is very high. See, e.g., M. Heumann, *Plea Bargaining,* Chicago, Ill.: University of Chicago Press, 1978 (reporting on experiences throughout Connecticut). H. Kalven and H. Zeisel, *The American Jury,* Boston, Mass.: Little, Brown, and Company, 1966, p. 18, estimated a nationwide average of

The guilty plea rate in a particular community will be influenced by various factors, including bail policy, sentencing laws, and the perspective of the lawyers as to judge and juror attitudes. The most significant factor, however, will be the nature and extent of prosecutor-defense plea bargaining. We refer here to the prosecutor's granting of concessions relating to the charge or sentence in return for the defendant's agreement to plead guilty. Contrary to popular impression, extensive plea bargaining is not a universal practice. While almost all prosecutors will engage in some form of plea bargaining in at least some cases, they differ considerably as to the type of cases in which they will plea bargain. Some prosecutors are willing to plea bargain in almost all cases. Others will utilize plea bargaining only in a comparatively small group of cases (e.g., first offenders charged with lower level felonies).[7] Still others take a position between these extremes. They will, for example, consider plea bargaining in all offenses except certain crimes of violence (e.g., rape). During periods of a police "crack down" on certain crimes (e.g., burglaries), they may refuse to bargain on these crimes as well. Defendants viewed as career criminals similarly may be denied concessions or offered only very small concessions without regard to the crime involved. Finally, even in those districts where plea bargains are available in almost all felony cases, they rarely are used in minor misdemeanor cases since defendants commonly are willing to plead guilty in such cases without receiving concessions from the prosecutor.

The Nature of Plea Bargaining.   The nature of plea bargaining varies considerably from jurisdiction to jurisdiction, from prosecutor to prosecutor, and even from case to case. Differences relate to the style of the negotiations, the persons participating, and the type of concessions provided. The style of the negotiation can range from a series of lengthy conferences to a hurried conversation in a courthouse hallway. Most often, the negotiations will be between the prosecutor and the defense counsel, with the defendant informed of the final offer for his approval or disapproval. However, in some areas, it is not unusual for the defendant himself, the investigating police officer, or even the judge to be directly involved in the negotiations. The discretion granted the individual assistant prosecutor in striking his own arrangement with defense counsel will vary. In many prosecutors' offices, the nature and extent of the concessions granted will be tightly controlled by office guidelines. Indeed, in some offices, to ensure uniformity, permissible concessions are set for each case by a small group of prosecutors responsible solely for supervising plea bargaining.

The concessions offered in plea agreements tend to fall into two categories: *charge* concessions and *sentence* concessions. Both relate to sentencing, but the charge concession does so less directly. Under charge bargaining, the prosecutor will offer to reduce the crime charged to a lesser crime, or to drop one or more of a

---

75 percent guilty pleas, 15 percent jury trials, and 10 percent bench trials for all felonies, but the data relied upon is now outdated.

7.   Major urban prosecutor's offices that do not utilize "wholesale" plea bargaining include Philadelphia and Baltimore. In 1975, the District Attorney of Alaska issued a directive largely eliminating plea bargaining in that state. Of course, even when there is no formal plea bargaining between prosecution and defense, guilty pleas may be encouraged by the anticipated leniency of judges toward defendants who plea guilty. Defense counsel commonly are aware of those judges who almost automatically give a lighter sentence to a defendant pleading guilty than to a defendant convicted of the same crime after trial.

series of charges. Consider, for example, the case of a defendant who is charged with using a weapon to rob three participants in a card game. The defendant may be charged with three armed robberies, each carrying a maximum penalty of twenty years imprisonment. If he is convicted on all three charges, and is given consecutive sentences, the maximum sentence would be sixty years of imprisonment. The prosecutor may offer to proceed on only one charge if the defendant enters a plea of guilty (i.e., after the defendant pleads guilty to one armed robbery charge, the other charges will be dismissed on the prosecutor's motion). If the defendant is a first offender, the prosecutor may be willing to grant a greater concession. If the defendant pleads guilty to the lesser offense of unarmed robbery, carrying a maximum imprisonment term of fifteen years, then all of the other charges will be dismissed. Perhaps, under some circumstances, the prosecutor might even be satisfied with a guilty plea to the charge of larceny from the person, an offense that carries a maximum ten year sentence and also opens up the possibility of probation at the judge's discretion. If the defendant accepted that offer, he could be certain that his sentence could not exceed ten years, [8] but he could not be sure that he would receive probation. On that score, he would have to rely upon the best advice of his lawyer as to the judge's sentencing tendencies.

If the prosecutor in our hypothetical utilized sentence bargaining, the defendant would gain considerably more certainty as to his actual sentence. The most common form of sentence bargaining involves a negotiated sentence recommendation. In many jurisdictions, prosecutors are empowered or even required by local practice to make a sentence recommendation to the court. Where a plea negotiation turns on the prosecutor's recommendation, that recommendation ordinarily will be given great weight by the sentencing judge. The judge recognizes that if he too frequently rejects such a recommendation, the plea negotiation process simply will break down. Thus, in our armed robbery hypothetical, the defendant would seek to include as part of the bargain a prosecutorial recommendation of probation. Of course, the defendant still would be taking a chance. His case might be one of that small group in which the judge decides the prosecutor has gone too far and rejects the recommendation. Nevertheless, with the recommendation, the defendant usually will have a much more solid basis for anticipating probation than he would under a charge bargain alone.

In various parts of the country, sentence bargaining is conducted so as to give the defendant an absolute commitment as to sentence. Some jurisdictions achieve this through direct participation of the judge in the negotiation. Since the judge sets the sentence, he alone can state exactly what sentence will be imposed. Although many defense counsel prefer judicial participation in plea negotiation, that practice has been criticized by appellate courts as inconsistent with the judicial role. In various jurisdictions, including the federal judicial system, direct judicial participation is prohibited by court rule. In other states where it merely is

---

8. The defendant often may not be certain, however, that the ten year maximum is giving him a substantial benefit from pleading guilty. If the state law permits the judge to set the maximum sentence on an armed robbery charge anywhere within the twenty year limit set by the statute, it is at least theoretically possible that the defendant, if convicted after trial, would not receive a sentence higher than a ten year concurrent sentence on each of the three armed robbery charges. In weighing the prosecutor's offer, the defendant must balance the risk of receiving a sixty year sentence against the certainty of receiving no more than a ten year sentence.

frowned upon, many trial judges continue to participate in negotiations on a regular basis.

Other jurisdictions have used a "conditional" guilty plea procedure to give the defendant more certainty as to sentence. Under this procedure, the defendant and prosecutor negotiate a sentence without judicial participation. The guilty plea is then entered on condition that the defendant receive the negotiated sentence. If the court decides that a higher sentence is needed, the defendant may withdraw his plea and go to trial before a new judge. The procedure is similar to that involved in negotiating sentence recommendations except that the defendant here has an automatic right to withdraw his plea if the judge does not follow the recommendation.[9]

Justifications For Plea Bargaining. While the form of the plea concession offered by a particular prosecutor may be similar in all cases, the prosecutor's justification for offering the concession will differ dramatically from case to case. In some cases, the concession may be offered to obtain the defendant's cooperation in successfully prosecuting other offenders engaged in more serious criminal conduct. It is common practice in almost all jurisdictions to grant concessions to the defendant who is willing to plead guilty and testify for the state against an accomplice who is viewed as the more serious offender. In other cases, the concession may be offered because the prosecutor believes that the defendant, though guilty, has a fairly good chance of gaining an acquittal or dismissal. The prosecutor may be concerned, for example, that the defendant will gain exclusion of crucial evidence or that an uncooperative victim will refuse to testify. Gaining a guilty plea to a lesser crime might be preferable to running the risk of an acquittal on all charges. If the defendant pleads guilty to a lesser offense, he will be subject to some punishment. Admittedly, that punishment might be less than what the prosecutor views as appropriate for the defendant's actions, but it still is better from his viewpoint than an acquittal that results in no punishment at all. From the defendant's perspective, though he naturally would prefer an acquittal, a plea to a lesser offense might be preferable to running the risk that the prosecution will successfully prove its case on the higher offense. For both sides, accepting "half of a loaf" is better than running the risk that they will lose everything. Similar compromises to avoid the uncertainties of the trial process are responsible for the high percentage of settlements in civil cases.

Most plea concessions probably are given for reasons other than the two noted above. Ordinarily, the defendant's assistance is not needed to prosecute others and the prosecution's case is so strong that there is little likelihood of losing. Under such circumstances, why would the prosecutor offer the defendant a concession in return for a guilty plea? The American Bar Association has cited three basic justifications for offering either charge or sentence concessions to persons who will plead guilty in such situations.[10] First, the "defendant by his plea has aided in ensuring the prompt and certain application of correctional measures to him." Even with an "open and shut case," there is always the possibility, avoided

---

9.   Federal Rule 11, set forth in the addendum at the end of this chapter, provides for this type of procedure.

10.   American Bar Association, *Standards Relating To Pleas Of Guilty*, §1.8 (Approved draft, 1968).

by the guilty plea, that the prosecutor might run into unexpected trouble at trial. Moreover, with the usual crowded trial docket, considerable time would elapse before the defendant was convicted and a sentence imposed. The defendant who pleads guilty can be sentenced promptly, thereby adding to the impact of the sentence and lessening the need for a more severe sentence. Second, the A.B.A. notes, the defendant who has "acknowledged hs guilt and shown a willingness to assume responsibility for his conduct" is in less need of a severe punishment. The guilty person who pleads guilty is willing to confess his wrongdoing and accept his punishment. A plea of guilty "may also evidence a decision by the defendant not to abuse the system by attempting to prevent conviction at trial by perjury or subornation of perjury."

The third A.B.A. justification is summarized as follows: "[T]he defendant by his plea has aided in avoiding delay (including delay due to crowded dockets) in the disposition of other cases and thereby has increased the probability of prompt and certain application of correctional measures to other offenders." In most jurisdictions, heavy caseloads simply would not permit the trial of all cases within a reasonable time period. By pleading guilty and permitting scarce trial resources to be devoted more fully to cases in which there may be some question as to guilt, the obviously guilty defendant has assisted the process in avoiding the conviction of the innocent. He also has performed a service similar, in a fashion, to the individual who testifies on behalf of the state; he has assisted the state in gaining the conviction of those obviously guilty persons who go to trial by permitting their trials to be held more promptly. [11]

The justifications for plea bargaining offered by the American Bar Association have not convinced all criminal justice experts. Many oppose granting the defendant a concession simply because his guilty plea lightens an otherwise overwhelming caseload. The defendant should not be entitled to a sentence reduction, they note, merely because he saves us the cost of a trial. They also contend that the plea bargaining process, even if theoretically justified, has been a disaster in practice. They point to various abuses that they view as basically inherent in plea bargaining. In particular, they cite overcharging,[12] the favoring of defendants whose lawyers are regularly involved in the process, and disproportionate sentencing that treats an experienced offender who pleads guilty more leniently than a first offender who exercises his constitutional right to a trial. Plea bargaining also is blamed for giving the criminal justice process a harried, bargain-counter image.

---

11. A fourth justification offered by the A.B.A. relates more to the degree of the concession granted than the decision to grant a concession in the first instance. A charge reduction often is appropriate, the A.B.A. notes, to provide the court with "more meaningful sentence alternatives." For example, the prosecutor may conclude, based on the offender's background, that probation is appropriate, but the offense charged may not permit probation. A plea bargain can result in a reduction of the charge to an offense that is subject to probation. Of course, the prosecutor could enable the court to impose probation by reducing the charge initially without regard to the defendant's willingness to plead guilty. See p. 286 *supra.* The common practice in many prosecutor's offices, however, is to consider "more meaningful sentence alternatives" only where the defendant is willing to plead guilty.

12. The reference here is to a practice under which the prosecutor includes every conceivable charge in the initial accusation, and then reduces down to a more appropriate charge in return for a plea. The result, the critics contend, is that the persons who do not plead guilty, but go to trial, have to face the additional charges that were included as part of the overcharging.

Defendants become convinced, it is argued, that the system is basically corrupt, with their sentences depending as much on their ability to "wheel and deal" as the wrongfulness of their acts. Criticisms such as these led the National Advisory Commission to the Law Enforcement Assistance Administration to recommend that plea bargains be abolished. [13] While that recommendation has not received widespread support among prosecutors, it has produced intensified efforts to ensure that plea negotiations are conducted fairly and openly and produce results consistent with sound law enforcement policy.

The Constitutionality of Plea Bargaining.   The constitutionality of plea bargaining was upheld by the Supreme Court in *Brady v. United States,* decided in 1970.[14] Until that time, doubts as to the legality of the practice had often produced a distasteful charade in the acceptance of guilty pleas. Knowing full well that a plea bargain had been struck, the judge accepting the plea would ask the defendant whether any promises had been made and the defendant would dutifully respond that there had been none. The concern was that a plea induced by a promise might be viewed as involuntary, just as a confession induced by a promise is viewed as involuntary. *Brady* flatly rejected that analogy. The defendant who enters a negotiated guilty plea does so in open court on the advice of counsel. He has had the "full opportunity to assess the advantages and disadvantages of a trial as compared with those attending a plea of guilty." Under these circumstances, his plea is voluntary. He can rationally decide, the Court noted, that he would prefer to accept the "certainty . . . of a lesser penalty rather than face a wider range of possibilities extending from acquittal to conviction and a higher penalty authorized by law for the crime charged."

The *Brady* opinion also rejected the contention that plea bargaining serves to punish those who exercise their constitutional right to a trial. The Court previously had stated that a sentencing judge would violate due process if he imposed a sentence higher than that merited by the defendant's conduct simply because the defendant had persisted in going to trial. However, the plea bargaining process does not ask that a higher sentence than otherwise appropriate be imposed upon defendants convicted at trial; it simply provides a reduction in sentence to those who plead guilty. Relying upon the American Bar Association report, the *Brady* opinion stressed that this reduction was granted for legitimate reasons that served the overall interests of justice, and not to punish persons who decided to go to trial. "We cannot hold that it is unconstitutional," said the Court, "for the state to extend a benefit to a defendant who in turn extends a substantial benefit to the State and who demonstrates by his plea that he is ready and willing to admit his crime and to enter the correctional system in a frame of mind which affords hope for success in rehabilitation over a shorter period of time than might otherwise be

13.   National Advisory Commission on Criminal Justice Standards and Goals, *Report on Courts,* note 61 at p. 296 *supra,* provides in its Standard 3.1: "[N]egotiations between prosecutors and defendants—either personally or through their attoneys—concerning concessions to be made in return for guilty pleas should be prohibited. In the event that the prosecution makes a recommendation as to sentence, it should not be affected by the willingness of the defendant to plead guilty to some or all of the offenses with which he is charged. A plea of guilty should not be considered by the court in determining the sentence to be imposed."

14.   *Brady v. United States,* 397 U.S, 742 90 S.Ct.1463 25 L.Ed.2d 747 (1970).

necessary." The Court warned, however, that the plea bargain must be fulfilled, and that the prosecutor could not threaten prosecution on a charge "not justified by the evidence" in order to induce a defendant to plead guilty.

Responsibilities of the Court In Accepting a Plea of Guilty. Before accepting a guilty plea, a judge must make three determinations relating to the plea: first, that it is voluntary; second, that is is knowingly made; and third, that it has a factual basis. The judge will determine whether these three conditions exist primarily by questioning in open court the defendant, his attorney, and the prosecutor. As we noted previously, the judge must take particular care in cases where the defendant has waived an attorney and is entering the plea without legal representation.[15]

To determine that a plea is voluntary, the judge will ask the defendant whether he has been threatened or otherwise coerced. If the judge is satisfied with the defendant's answer, he then will ask whether the plea is based on any promises. In most jurisdictions today, the concessions granted for a negotiated plea are placed on the record. If the defendant can later establish that the plea was based on a promise that was not kept or was otherwise involuntary, the plea may be withdrawn. However, where the judge fully explored the background of the plea prior to its acceptance, it will be most difficult for the defendant to contend that the plea was not entered voluntarily. He must overcome his own previous statement that there was no coercion and that the only promises were those set forth in the record.

Besides being made voluntarily, the plea must be made with knowledge of both the rights that are being relinquished and the consequences that may follow from conviction on the plea. To ensure that such knowledge exists, the judge commonly will advise the defendant as to (1) the nature of the charge against him; (2) the rights he would have at trial if he were to contest the charge; and (3) the maximum sentence that may be imposed upon conviction. The precise scope of the judge's statement will vary somewhat from jurisdiction to jurisdiction or even from judge to judge. In describing the nature of the charges, for example, some judges will simply describe the crime in its statutory terms, while others will note the major elements of the offense and major defenses as well. What is a satisfactory notification may depend upon various factors, such as the complexity of the particular crime, the defendant's educational background, and whether the defendant is represented by counsel. Similarly, in describing the trial rights the defendant is relinquishing, some judges will describe only a few basic rights (e.g., self-incrimination, jury trial, and confrontation) while others will describe a wide range of rights (including, for example, the right to exclude unconstitutionally seized evidence). When informing the defendant as to the possible consequences of his plea, some judges will give only the maximum prison sentence while others will note other possible consequences as well (e.g., revocation of probation). After advising the defendant of his rights and the consequences of his plea, the judge usually will question the defendant to be certain that he understands what he has been told.

---

15. See p. 281 *supra*.

The final task of the judge is to determine that there is a "factual basis" for the plea. Ordinarily, the defendant will be asked in his own words to explain what he did. In this statement, the defendant must acknowledge facts indicating that he has committed the crime to which he is pleading guilty or, as is often the case on a negotiated plea, an even greater crime. In *North Carolina v. Alford,*[16] the question arose as to whether a court could accept a plea to a lesser charge where the defendant denied that he committed any crime but desired to plead guilty in order to avoid a possible conviction on a higher charge. The Supreme Court held that it was not necessary that the defendant admit his guilt, at least where the prosecution had submitted on the record a summary of available evidence that would establish a strong case against defendant. The *Alford* procedure is the ordinary procedure for nolo contendere pleas. The defendant will not make a statement as to what he did, but the prosecution will present the factual basis for the plea through its statement.

To ensure that all judges within the jurisdiction handle guilty pleas in a uniform fashion, many jurisdictions have adopted detailed provisions on the presentation and acceptance of guilty pleas. Federal Court Rule 11, set forth at the end of this chapter,[17] is typical of such provisions. It has served as the model for numerous state provisions.

TRIAL RIGHTS

If the defendant enters a plea of not guilty, he is entitled to a trial. We have already noted some of the basic trial rights of the defendant, such as his right to counsel and his right to insist that the prosecution prove his guilt beyond a reasonable doubt. We will here touch upon several other key trial rights. First, however, you should be aware of the general order of proceedings at the trial.

The Order of the Trial.   The initial step in the trial process ordinarily is the selection of the jury (or the waiver of the jury if the case is to be tried to the judge alone). The court then gives the jury preliminary instructions, describing the trial procedure and advising them that they should not discuss the case until they are ready to deliberate. The court also will read to the jury the charge as stated in the information or indictment (or a complaint in the case of a misdemeanor). The prosecution will then make an opening statement describing in general what the state intends to prove. The defense counsel may respond immediately with the defense's opening statement, or that statement may be postponed until the defense is ready to present its evidence. The opening statements are not evidence. They serve only to assist the jury in understanding the points that the prosecution and defense hope to establish at trial. Following the opening statements, the prosecution will present witnesses, who may be cross-examined by the defense counsel. The defense then will present its own witnesses, if it so desires. Those witnesses may be cross-examined by the prosecutor. The defendant may testify as a defense witness, but he need not do so. After the defense has presented its evidence, the prosecution may respond with additional witnesses (called rebuttal

---

16. *North Carolina v. Alford,* 400 U.S. 25 91 S.Ct.160 27 L.Ed.162 (1970).

17. See the addendum at p. 328 *infra.*

witnesses) to contradict the defense's case. The defense in turn may present its own rebuttal witnesses to contradict the prosecution's rebuttal. Ordinarily, this would end the presentation of the evidence. The order of the next few steps will vary considerably from state to state. In most, the prosecution and defense will make their closing statements and the judge will then instruct the jury as to the law. In some states, the instructions will be given before the closing statements are made. In their closing statements, each side will present its own view of the evidence. Ordinarily, the prosecution will make an initial closing statement, the defense will respond, and then the prosecution may respond to the defense. The prosecution is given the final word because it bears the burden of proving the case beyond a reasonable doubt.

Right to a Public Trial. The Sixth Amendment assures to the accused, in all criminal cases, the right to a "public trial." The right to a public trial was well established at common law. It reflected, in part, the distaste for the secret proceedings of the English Court of the Star Chamber, which also was responsible for the right against self-incrimination.[18] An open trial was viewed, for several reasons, as an essential guarantee against employment of the courts as an instrument of persecution. As one court noted:

> The knowledge that every criminal trial was subject to contemporaneous review in the forum of public opinion was regarded as an effective restraint on possible abuse of judicial power. It was also thought that if trials were public they might come to the attention of important witnesses unknown to the parties who might voluntarily come forward to testify, and that the conduct of trials in public would enable the spectators to learn about their government and acquire confidence in their judicial remedies.[19]

While the right to a public trial has been construed broadly by the courts, all recognize that the defendant's right to have the public present is subject to certain limitations. The court may limit public attendance to avoid overcrowding, exclude disorderly persons, and bar youthful spectators where testimony involves subjects (e.g., sexual matters) thought to be inappropriate for their ears. Statutes authorizing the exclusion of adult spectators in sex offense cases also have been upheld where they apply only to general spectators and not to relatives and friends of the parties and representatives of the press.[20] Some courts have held that, even though the right to a public trial is designed largely to protect the defendant, the defendant's waiver of the right does not thereby give the court authority to exclude all spectators, including representatives of the press.[21] While the presence of a large audience may well have an intimidating effect inconsistent with the defendant's right to a fair trial, the same could not be said of the presence of reporters alone.

---

18. See p. 230 *supra*.

19. *United States v. Kobli,* 172 F.2d 919 (3d Cir. 1949).

20. See 39 American Law Reports 3d 852 (1971).

21. Not all courts agree on this point. *State ex rel. Gore Newspaper Company v. Tyson,* 313 So.2d 777 (Fla.App. 1975) discusses the various cases. A somewhat different problem is presented with respect to reporters at preliminary proceedings, such as a preliminary hearing. Newspaper coverage of these proceedings in highly publicized cases may make it difficult to find jurors who have an open mind on the case.

Right to a Speedy Trial. The Sixth Amendment also guarantees to the accused a right to a speedy trial. This right compliments state statutes of limitation, which we discussed in Chapter Five. Those statutes bar the presentation of state charges based on offenses that occurred long before the prosecution.[22] The speedy trial guarantee serves a similar purpose but looks to a different aspect of delay. While the limitation statutes look to the time span between the commission of the offense and the initiation of prosecution, the speedy trial guarantee looks to the span between the initiation of the prosecution and the trial. It requires that the prosecution, once initiated, reach the point of final adjudication, the trial, with reasonable promptness. Failure to provide a speedy trial is fatal to the prosecution. Since the denial of defendant's right to a speedy trial can never be remedied, the prosecution must be terminated and the defendant released even though he may have been guilty of the crime charged.

Barker v. Wingo[23] is the leading case on the constitutional guarantee to a speedy trial. Under *Barker,* there is no specific period of delay that will automatically constitute a denial of a speedy trial. Even a delay of five years (as in *Barker*) does not necessarily violate the defendant's constitutional right. In each case, the delay must be analyzed in light of four factors: (1) the length of the delay; (2) the prejudice to the defendant caused by the delay; (3) whether the defendant objected to the delay; and (4) the reason for the delay. Initially, there must be a delay of a sufficient time period so as to suggest a possible violation. No precise time period is set for this purpose, [24] but it is usually assumed that the delay must approach a year before any serious problems are presented. If the delay has been significant, then the three other factors must be considered. In considering the factor of prejudice, a court will look to the three functions of the speedy trial guarantee noted in *Barker:* "(1) to prevent oppressive pretrial incarceration [where the defendant did not make bail]; (2) to minimize [the] anxiety and concern of the accused; and (3) to limit the possibility that the defense will be impaired." The third type of prejudice is the most significant. As a result of delay, defense witnesses may be lost (e.g., they may die or disappear) or the memory of those witnesses may fade.

Where the delay has been significant and the defendant's ability to present a defense has been impaired, a court is likely to find a constitutional violation unless the third or fourth factors under the *Barker* analysis excuse the delay—that is, unless the defendant knowingly failed to object to the delay or the state had a valid justification for the delay. The defendant's failure to object is an important factor because, as noted in *Barker,* many defendants prefer delay. Where the defendant has been released pending trial, delay may be to his advantage. As the prosecution's case grows stale, and the memories of the witnesses fade, the defendant's

---

22. See p. 125 *supra.* The statutes of limitation, as noted in Chapter Five, do not apply to all crimes. The speedy trial guarantee, on the other hand, does apply to all criminal prosecutions.

23. *Barker v. Wingo,* 407 U.S. 5149 2S.Ct.2182 33 L.Ed.2d 101 (1972).

24. As the Court noted, the period of delay that is acceptable for this purpose will vary with the nature of the case. A longer delay is to be expected for a complex conspiracy charge, which takes considerable prosecution preparation, then for an "ordinary street crime."

chances of winning at trial improve. If the defendant had an opportunity to object to the delay, but did not do so, his failure to object suggests that he did not view the delay as prejudicial. As the fourth factor suggests, there may be cases where the delay was justified even though the defendant did request a more prompt trial. Thus, in *Barker,* the Court noted that a delay to accommodate a prosecution witness who was ill and could not testify immediately was appropriate. Overcrowded dockets, on the other hand, was described as a "neutral reason" that would not work to the prosecution's benefit.

In sum, under *Barker,* the circumstances surrounding the delay must be examined with care in each case. In some cases, a delay of several years will be acceptable because the defendant failed to object to the delay and could not show specific prejudice to his presentation of a defense. In others, a much shorter delay may constitute a violation of defendant's Sixth Amendment rights because of the presence of prejudice, a defense demand, or an improper prosecutorial purpose in obtaining the delay.

Many jurisdictions have adopted speedy trial statutes requiring more prompt trials than the constitutional guarantee. The Federal Speedy Trial Act of 1974 is typical of those provisions.[25] That Act requires that cases be brought to trial within ninety days of the arraignment on the information or indictment unless special circumstances exist. [26] There are, however, various exceptions to this time period. Additional delay is justified, for example, for: (1) the disposition of various pretrial motions, such as the motion to suppress evidence; (2) the trial of other charges against the defendant; (3) an examination of the defendant to determine if he is competent to stand trial; and (4) a continuance (i.e., extension of time) granted at the request of a defendant or the prosecution if the court finds that "the ends of justice served by taking such action outweigh the best interests of the public and the defendant in a speedy trial." The Federal Speedy Trial Act has resulted in some improvement in the prompt disposition of cases, although many trials still are held beyond the ninety day limit as a result of the various exceptions noted above. One consequence of the emphasis upon providing speedy trials has been a greater delay in the trial of civil cases since criminal cases must be given first priority on the court's trial docket.

The Right to a Jury Trial. Trial by jury is so well established in this country that we sometimes forget how unique it is among the nations of the world. No nation places a greater emphasis on the use of the jury than the United States. In this country, the jury trial is not viewed simply as a method of providing accurate fact-finding. It adds an element of citizen control of government that reflects

---

25. 18 United States Code §§3161-3174.

26. Many state provisions are more lenient. The Illinois statute, for example, sets a basic time period of 120 days from the date of arrest for a defendant in custody and 160 days from the date of demand for defendants released pending trial. Illinois Stat. ch. 38, §103.5. It also recognizes various exceptions similar to those in the Federal Speedy Trial Act.

our democratic ideals. In *Duncan v. Louisiana,* the Supreme Court described the significance of the jury in this way:

> A right to jury trial is granted to criminal defendants in order to prevent oppression by the Government. Those who wrote our constitutions knew from history and experience that it was necessary to protect against unfounded criminal charges brought to eliminate enemies and against judges too responsive to the voice of higher authority. The framers of the constitutions strove to create an independent judiciary but insisted upon further protection against arbitrary action. Providing an accused with the right to be tried by a jury of his peers gave him an inestimable safeguard against the corrupt or overzealous prosecutor and against the compliant, biased, or eccentric judge. If the defendant preferred the common-sense judgment of a jury to the more tutored but perhaps less sympathetic reaction of the single judge, he was to have it. Beyond this, the jury trial provisions in the Federal and State Constitutions reflect a fundamental decision about the exercise of official power—a reluctance to entrust plenary powers over the life and liberty of the citizen to one judge or to a group of judges. Fear of unchecked power, so typical of our State and Federal Governments in other respects, found expression in the criminal law in this insistence upon community participation in the determination of guilt or innocence.[27]

Although the Sixth Amendment declares that the accused shall have the right to a jury trial "in all criminal prosecutions," [28] that provision has always been read in light of an historical exception for "petty offenses." At the time the Constitution was adopted, jury trials were not provided for minor offenses, and it appears that the draftsmen of the Sixth Amendment had no intention to alter that practice. The Court has not offered a complete definition of what constitutes a petty offense, but it has noted that any offense punishable in excess of six months imprisonment is not a petty offense. [29] Most states today go beyond the demand of the Constitution and provide jury trials in all criminal cases, including petty offenses. The size of the jury will vary, however. In misdemeanor cases, many states use a six person jury rather than the traditional twelve person jury used in felony cases.

In several states, a six person jury also is used in non-capital felony cases. The Supreme Court has upheld this practice. The Sixth Amendment does not

---

27. *Duncan v. Louisiana,* 391 U.S. 145 156 88 S.Ct. 1444 1451 20 L.Ed.2d 491 (1968). The Court also noted:

> We are aware of the long debate, especially in this century, among those who write about the administration of justice, as to the wisdom of permitting untrained laymen to determine the facts in civil and criminal proceedings. Although the debate has been intense, with powerful voices on either side, most of the controversy has centered on the jury in civil cases. Indeed, some of the severest critics of civil juries acknowledge that the arguments for criminal juries are much stronger. In addition, at the heart of the dispute have been express or implicit assertions that juries are incapable of adequately understanding evidence or determining issues of fact, and that they are unpredictable, quixotic, and little better than a roll of dice. Yet, the most recent and exhaustive study of the jury in criminal cases concluded that juries do understand the evidence and come to sound conlusions in most of the cases presented to them and that when juries differ with the result at which the judge would have arrived, it is usually because they are serving some of the very purposes for which they were created and for which they are now employed.

28. Similarly, Article III, section 2 declares: "The Trial of all Crimes, except in Cases of Impeachment, shall be by jury."

29. *Baldwin v. New York,* 399 U.S. 66 90 S.Ct.1886 26 L.Ed.2d 437 (1970).

demand that the jury have a specific number of jurors. It does require that the number "be large enough to promote group deliberation, free from outside attempts at intimidation, and to provide a fair possibility for obtaining a representative cross section of the community."[30] The Supreme Court also has upheld the practice in a few states of accepting non-unanimous jury verdicts. The Court reasoned that the functions of the Sixth Amendment could be satisfied by a non-unanimous verdict where the majority was substantial (e.g., 5 our of 6 or 9 out of 12), but it suggested that convictions on the vote of a less than seventy-five percent majority probably would be unconstitutional. While the state may structure its verdict requirement so that one or two jurors cannot stubbornly "hold-out" and thereby "hang" the jury, it may not structure it so as to reduce the need for deliberation to the point that a verdict is reached as soon as a slight majority favors one result or another.[31]

Selection of the Jury. The objectives of the Sixth Amendment, the Supreme Court has noted, require that the jury be selected from a "representative cross-section" of the community:

> [T]he selection of a petit jury [i.e., a trial jury] from a representative cross section of the community is an essential component of the Sixth Amendment right to a jury trial. . . . The purpose of the jury is to guard against the exercise of arbitrary power— to make available the common sense judgement of the community as a hedge against the overzealous or mistaken prosecutor and in preference to the professional or perhaps overconditioned or biased response of a judge. This prophylactic vehicle is not provided if the jury pool is made up of only special segments of the populace or if large, distinctive groups are excluded from the pool.[32]

The "cross-section requirement" of the Sixth Amendment is very similar in its impact to the constitutional limitations placed upon the selection of the grand jury.[33] Here too, the state cannot discriminate on the basis of race, sex, or religion, but it can establish reasonable qualifications for service. In most jurisdictions, the initial group of persons called for possible jury service (the *petit jury venire*) is selected in the same manner as the grand jury venire. The jury commissioners randomly select the venire from voter registration or other appropriate lists. They then eliminate those persons who do not meet the qualifications for jury service, are exempt from service, or are excluded because of their occupation. The remaining members of the venire are then available for selection to a particular trial jury.

---

30. See *Williams v. Florida,* 399 U.S. 78 90 S.Ct.1893 26 L.Ed.2d 446 (1970), upholding the use of six person juries in felony cases in Flordia. Other states using less than twelve person juries in felony cases are Louisiana, South Carolina, Texas, and Utah. Approximately two-thirds of the states use small juries in misdemeanor cases. See E. Prescott, *Facets Of The Jury System,* Denver, Colo.: National Center for State Courts, 1976. In *Ballew v. Georgia,* 435 U.S. 223 98 S.Ct.1029 55 L.Ed.2d 234 (1978), the Court held that a jury of five was too small to satisfy the Sixth Amendment.

31. See *Apodaca v. Oregon,* 406 U.S. 404 92 S.Ct.1628, 32 L.Ed.2d 184 (1972). upheld 10-2 verdicts in felony cases and *Johnson v. Louisiana,* 406 U.S. 356 92 S.Ct.1620, 32 L.Ed.2d 152 (1972), upheld 9-3 verdicts in felony cases. Two other states, Oklahoma and Texas, accept less than unanimous verdicts, but do so only in misdeameanor cases. See E. Prescott, note 30 *supra.*

32. *Taylor v. Louisiana,* 419 U.S. 522, 530 95 S.Ct.692, 697 42 L.Ed.2d 690 (1974).

33. See pp. 289-90 *supra.*

Unlike grand jurors, however, they are not automatically placed on a jury. They first must be screened to ensure that they meet another basic jury trial requirement—that the jurors not be biased.

Although the Sixth Amendment refers only to the defendant's right to an "impartial" jury, all jurisdictions seek to ensure that the jurors are unbiased as to both the prosecution and the defense. The procedure used to exclude potentially biased jurors varies from state to state, but the basic elements are similar in most states. Assuming that the jury will have twelve members, a somewhat larger group (e.g., twenty-five) will be drawn from the venire and will be brought before the court with the attorneys and the defendant present. The court will identify the defendant and the attorneys, read the names of prospective witnesses, and briefly outline the nature of the case. The prospective jurors will then be asked whether they know the defendant, the attorneys, or the witnesses, or have any special interest in the case. In every jurisdiction, certain specified relationships to a case are automatically sufficient to exclude a prospective juror from serving in that case. Typically, a person can be excluded if he was a witness to the crime, served as a juror in a closely related case (e.g., the prosecution of an alleged accomplice), or is a relative of the victim, the defendant, any witness or the attorneys. In automatically excluding persons who have such relationships, the law is saying that here a potential bias is sufficient to disqualify the prospective juror. Proof of actual bias is not necessary. It may be that, in some instances, such persons would be impartial, but the law recognizes, as Justice Frankfurter once observed, that "justice must satisfy the appearance of justice" as well as reach a just result.[34]

Of course, even if a prohibited relationship to the case is not present, a prospective juror will be exluded if actual bias can be shown. States typically describe actual bias as having a frame of mind that will prevent the prospective juror from rendering an impartial verdict, based solely upon the evidence in the case. Such bias often will be present when the prospective juror is acquainted with one of the participants, though lacking the family relationship that automatically permits his exclusion. The nature of the acquaintanceship will be controlling. For example, a prospective juror who is a close friend of one of the attorneys would be excluded on the ground that he is likely to give too much weight to that attorney's argument. On the other hand, a person would not be excluded simply because he and the attorney are members of a large service club and have met once or twice at meetings.

Actual bias also is established if it can be shown that the prospective juror is unwilling to accept the law governing his decision. Thus, the defense may require the exclusion of a prospective juror who refuses to accept the presumption of innocence, insisting that he will acquit only if the defendant can show he was not guilty. A prosecutor similarly can exclude a person who is opposed to convicting any defendant for the crime charged because he does not believe it should be a crime.[35] A biased frame of mind also might be the product of a juror's preconceived

---

34. *Offutt v. United States,* 348 U.S. 11, 14 75 S.Ct.11,13, 99 L.Ed.11 (1954).

35. Similarly, in a capital punishment case, a juror will be excluded if he states that he absolutely could not vote for capital punishment under any circumstances. However, since the law gives jurors considerable discretion in voting against capital punishment, see pp. 336-37 *infra,* a prospective juror will not be excluded simply because he generally is opposed to captial punishment

notions concerning the parties in the case. Thus, a juror could be excluded if he acknowledged he could not accept the testimony of several defense witnesses because he could never trust the word of someone of their ethnic background. So too, a prospective juror will be excluded if he has read about the case in the newspapers, and has come to a conclusive determination that the defendant is guilty or innocent. On the other hand, if the prospective juror has only a tentative opinion, and states that he can put it aside and decide the case solely on the evidence presented, he may be viewed as not sufficiently influenced to be excluded for bias.[36] The law recognizes that most persons have general predispositions toward believing or not believing certain types of persons. All it asks is that the juror put these aside, judge each witness individually, and make his decision based only on the evidence before him.

Most biased persons, if asked whether they are biased, will promptly deny it. The law accordingly provides for the questioning of prospective jurors concerning their knowledge of the case, viewpoint, background, and other factors that might be relevant in establishing a biased frame of mind. This process is called the *voir dire,* Norman French for "to tell the truth." In some jurisdictions, lawyers will directly question the prospective jurors. In others, the lawyers will give a list of proposed questions to the judge, who will screen them and then ask the questions himself. If a lawyer believes that the prospective juror's answers to the voir dire questions establish bias, the lawyer will *challenge* the juror *for cause*. A "challenge" is simply a lawyer's request that a prospective juror be excluded from the jury. A challenge "for cause" is a challenge based on a specific legal ground that requires the individual's exclusion. To show "cause," the lawyer ordinarily must establish the presence of either actual bias or a relationship conclusively presumed by the law to create bias. As we shall see, there is another form of challenge (the peremptory challenge) that does not require such a showing.

The law recognizes that it is not always easy to establish actual bias. Accordingly, it gives to both defense counsel and prosecutor the right to exclude a limited number of prospective jurors without offering any reasons for their exclusion. This authority is exercised through the *peremptory challenge*. As the term "peremptory" suggests, the challenge acts automatically to exclude the prospective juror. The judge has no discretion in the matter even though he may believe that the juror clearly is not biased. Indeed, as a matter of practice, attorneys often use peremptory challenges to exclude persons that they view as entirely capable of

---

and would consider imposing it only in the most extreme case. *Witherspoon v. Illinois*, 391 U.S. 510, 88 S.Ct.1770, 20 L.Ed.2d 776 (1968).

36. The American Bar Association, *Standards On Fair Trial and Free Press* (Approved Draft 1968), sets forth the appropriate guidelines for such cases in Standard 3.4(b): "If [a prospective juror] has seen or heard and remembers information that will be developed in the course of trial, or that may be inadmissible but is not so prejudicial as to create a substantial risk that his judgment will be affected, his acceptability shall turn on whether his testimony as to impartiality is believed. If he admits to having formed an opinion, he shall be subject to challenge for cause unless the examination shows unequivocally that he can be impartial. A prospective juror who has been exposed to and remembers reports of highly significant information, such as the existence or contents of a confession, or other incriminating matters that may be inadmissible in evidence, or substantial amounts of inflammatory material, shall be subject to challenge for cause without regard to his testimony as to his state of mind."

rendering an impartial verdict. Once the attorney has excluded, either through challenges for cause or peremptory challenges, all the persons he views as truly biased, he may exercise his remaining peremptory challenges to seek to ensure that the jury is as favorable to his position as possible. His objective will be to exclude persons who are less likely than others to be readily convinced of the rightness of his position. Attorneys have a vast body of folklore relating to the tendencies of jurors of certain cultural and religious backgrounds in favoring particular types of defendants in particular cases. In some major cases, defense attorneys have gone beyond folklore to use the services of psychologists, psychiatrists, and sociologists to identify those background factors suggesting that a person is likely to be favorable to their client. Of course, the attorney's ability to make effective use of peremptory challenges in gaining a favorable jury will depend upon the number of challenges available. The fewer the number of challenges, the less maneuverability available in shaping a favorable jury. Some jurisdictions will grant only five challenges in the typical felony case while others will grant twenty in the same type of cases. Also, some jurisdictions will give the prosecutor fewer challenges than the defendant.[37]

Preventing Pretrial Publicity.   Where a case has received considerable newspaper or television publicity, it often is difficult to find an impartial jury. Media coverage that "tries" a defendant in advance of trial also may intimidate or influence witnesses. The First Amendment guarantees to the press the right to publish what it knows. Accordingly, a court generally may not issue a "gag order" seeking to keep the press from publishing information relating to a criminal case even though the publication may make it more difficult to obtain a fair trial for the defendant. [38] The court may, however, keep the attorneys from waging a public relations battle that will contribute to the pretrial publicity. The American Bar Association's Code of Professional Responsibility, adopted in almost all states, restricts the comments to the media that may be made by both prosecutor and defense counsel. The Code applies primarily to comments prior to trial. (Once the jury is selected, it can be sequestered in separate living quarters where it will not have an opportunity to read newspapers or watch television). Basically the lawyers are directed not to go beyond the public record, noting the nature of the charge and the defendant's response to it. In particular, they may not make

---

37. The number of peremptory challenges allowed varies with several factors. Ordinarily, more challenges are granted in capital cases. Additional challenges also are given where alternate jurors are selected (i.e., extra jurors who will hear evidence with the jury and will be available as a substitute if any of the first twelve jurors become ill). On the other side, fewer peremptory challenges are given for six person juries. The Michigan and New York provisions are illustrative of state variations on peremptory challenges. Michigan allows five peremptory challenges for felonies punishable by less than life imprisonment; twenty challenges for the defense and fifteen for the prosecution in life imprisonment cases; and three challenges for each side in misdemeanor cases (tried before a six person jury). See Michigan General Court Rule 511.5, District Court Rule 511.5 New York provides the same number of challenges to both sides in all situations: for class A felonies, twenty plus two for each alternate juror; for class B or C felonies, fifteen plus two for each alternate juror; for all other cases, ten plus two for each alternate juror. See New York Criminal Procedure Law §270.25(2).

38. *Nebraska Press Association v. Stuart,* 427 U.S. 539, 96 S.Ct.2791, 49 L.Ed.2d 683 (1976).

reference to confessions, lie-detector tests, or similar matter that might be inadmissible at trial.[39] Police departments have been encouraged to adopt similar restrictions upon their public statements and several have done so.

Compelling the Attendance of Witnesses. The Sixth Amendment grants to the accused the right "to have compulsory process for obtaining witnesses in his favor." This means that the accused may obtain a court order (a *subpoena*) directing a witness to appear in court to testify. The prosecution is given similar authority. Neither side need rely on volunteers. Indeed, under legislation adopted in almost every state, a subpoena may be used to compel the appearance of witnesses residing outside the state. While the state issuing the subpoena lacks authority over persons outside its borders, the state in which the witness resides will use its authority to compel compliance with the subpoena. Under the states' reciprocal agreement to assist each other, witnesses ordinarily may be subpoenaed from throughout the United States. [40]

The authority to subpoena a witness does not necessarily ensure that the witness will be required by the court to testify. The witness may have a legal right

---

39.   A.B.A. Code of Professional Responsibility, Disciplinary Rule 7-107 provides:

   (B) A lawyer or law firm associated with the prosecution or defense of a criminal matter shall not, from the time of the filing of a complaint, information, or indictment, the issuance of an arrest warrant, or arrest until the commencement of the trial or disposition without trial make or participate in making an extradjudicial statement that a reasonable person would expect to be disseminated by means of public communication and that relates to:

   (1) The character, reputation, or prior criminal record (including arrests, indictments, or other charges of crime) of the accused.

   (2) The possibility of a plea of guilty to the offense charged or to a lesser offense.

   (3) The existence or contents of any confession, admission, or statement given by the accused or his refusal or failure to make a statement.

   (4) The performance or results of any examinations or tests or the refusal or failure of the accused to submit to examinations or tests.

   (5) The identity, testimony, or credibility of a prospective witness.

   (6) Any opinion as to the guilt or innocence of the accused, the evidence, or the merits of the case.

   (C) DR 7-107 (B) does not preclude a lawyer during such period from announcing:

   (1) The name, age, residence, occupation, and family status of the accused.

   (2) If the accused has not been apprehended, any information necessary to aid in his apprehension or to warn the public of any dangers he may present.

   (3) A request for assistance in obtaining evidence.

   (4) The identity of the victim of the crime.

   (5) The fact, time, and place of arrest, resistance, pursuit, and use of weapons.

   (6) The identity of investigating and arresting officers or agencies and the length of the investigation.

   (7) At the time of seizure, a description of the physical evidence seized, other than a confession, admission, or statement.

   (8) The nature, substance, or text of the charge.

   (9) Quotations from or references to public records of the court in the case.

   (10) The scheduling or result of any step in the judicial proceedings.

   (11) That the accused denies the charges made against him.

40.   The Uniform Act to Secure the Attendance of Witnesses from Without A State in Criminal Proceedings, West's Uniform Law Annotated, vol. 13, p. 1, has been adopted in all but two states (Alabama and Georgia). The act extends to any witness "material and necessary" to a criminal trial. The witness must be paid his travel expenses and an attendance fee set by state law.

(commonly called a *testimonial privilege*) not to testify as to certain matters. We already have discussed the prohibition against compulsory self-incrimination. If the witness believes that the answer to a question posed by prosecution or defense will furnish evidence that conceivably could be used against him in a criminal prosecution, he may refuse to testify under the protection of the Fifth Amendment.[41] State law commonly grants persons the right not to testify as to other matters where disclosure would interfere with the confidentiality of certain protected realtionships. Thus, one spouse may not be required to testify against the other spouse, a clergyman may not be required to disclose a confidential communication from a person he is counseling, and a lawyer may not be required to disclose certain communications with his client. Other privileges recognized in many jurisdictions relate to confidential communications between doctor and patient, newspaper reporter and confidential informant, and social workers or psychologists and their clients. The scope of each of these privileges will vary with the applicable state statute or court rule. A few of the privileges (e.g., the newspaper reporter's privilege) may not apply where the defendant is seeking disclosure of testimony that would be helpful in establishing his innocence.

Defendant's Right Not To Testify.   As we already have noted, the one person who cannot be subpoenaed to testify is the defendant.[42] Under the Fifth Amendment, the defendant has an absolute right not to testify. Moreover, no adverse comment on his failure to testify can be made by the prosecutor or the trial judge. Thus, the prosecutor may not argue in his closing statement to the jury that the "witness who knew the most has not testified." This is an obvious reference to the defendant's failure to testify and suggests to the jury that he did not testify because he had something to hide.[43] The Court may, however, give the jury an instruction informing it that the defendant has a right not to testify and his exercise of that right may not be taken against him. This instruction may be given even though the defense counsel would prefer that the instruction not be given so as to avoid calling attention to the defendant's failure to testify.[44]

Of course, a defendant may testify if he desires to do so. However, he is then subject to cross-examination just like any witness. Since cross-examination may be broader than his direct testimony, the defendant who takes the stand will not be able to tell just his part of the story. The prosecutor may question him as to all

---

41. Ordinarily, the prosecutor is authorized by statute to respond to a witness' exercise of the self-incrimination protection by granting the witness immunity from prosecution on any criminal charges disclosed by his testimony. Since the Fifth Amendment protects a person against criminal incrimination, the grant of immunity eliminates the application of that Amendment (i.e., the witness no longer can fear that his answers will be used against him in a criminal case since he is immune from prosecution). Once the witness is granted immunity, he then must testify or be held in contempt of court. Immunity ordinarily can be granted only with the approval of the court upon a showing that the immunization of the witness will be in the interest of justice under the circumstances of the particular case. In some jurisdictions, the immunity only extends to the prosecution's use of the witness' statement or evidence derived therefrom. The witness may still be prosecuted on the basis of independently acquired evidence. See *Kastigar v. United States,* 406 U.S. 441, 92 S.Ct.1643, 32 L.Ed.2d 212 (1972).

42. See p. 306 *supra.*

43. *Griffin v. California,* 380 U.S. 609, 85 S.Ct.1229, 14 L.Ed.2d 106 (1965).

44. *Lakeside v. Oregon,* 435 U.S. 333, 98 S.Ct.1091, 55 L.Ed.2d 319 (1978).

of the facts relating to the offense. Also, as with other witnesses, prior convictions may be noted to challenge his credibility.

Right Of Cross-Examination. The Sixth Amendment provides that the accused shall have the right "to be confronted with the witnesses against him." This provision provides a constitutional right to cross-examine opposing witnesses. State law gives the same right of cross-examination to the prosecutor. Either side may question a witness produced by the other side to test the accuracy of his observation and recollection. Each side may ask the opposing witness questions designed to show that he is confused as to the facts, lacked the opportunity to observe carefully the events in question, or has a faulty memory. Very frequently counsel also will seek to make these points by noting inconsistencies between the witness' current statement and his previous statements about the same events. In cross-examining the witness, an opposing attorney may ask leading questions, which are questions suggestive of an answer. "Now on the night in question," the cross-examiner may ask, "didn't you have several drinks"? (Lawyers joke about a famous leading question, phrased so as to catch the witness even with a denial: "When did you stop beating your wife"?).[45]

The process of challenging a witness' credibility is called *impeachment*. A witness may be impeached, as we have seen, by showing that his testimony is weakened by his faulty memory, his limited opportunity for careful observation, or his general incompetence as an observer. He also may be impeached by showing that he is a person who is likely to be telling a lie. Thus, the cross-examiner may attempt to show that the witness has an obvious bias that would lead him to lie. He also may show that the witness is a person who cannot be trusted. In this connection, he may show, through other witnesses, that the opposing witness has a reputation in his community as a person who tells lies. He may also show that the witness has been convicted of a serious offense in the past. Most jurisdictions do not limit such impeachment to crimes that directly cast doubt on credibility (e.g., perjury); they include any serious offense on the theory that a person capable of committing such an offense would also be capable of lying. The possibility of being impeached in this manner often leads a defendant with prior convictions to refuse to testify. Of course, if he testifies and his prior convictions are brought out on cross-examination, the jury will be told that those offenses lawfully may be considered only for impeachment purposes (i.e., only in judging his credibility). Nevertheless, there is always concern that the jury will disregard the instruction and assume that the defendant committed the crime charged because he has committed other crimes in the past.

THE RULES OF EVIDENCE

The presentation of information in a criminal or civil trial is governed by rules which are called the "rules of evidence." Since a trial in Anglo-American law is an adversary proceeding, a contest between opposing sides, the rules of evidence

---

45. Leading questions normally are not permitted in the examination of one's own witness; the witness should be able to tell his story without hints from the attorney presenting him. Cross-examiners are given greater leeway because the witness is an opposing witness and there is less danger that he will simply follow along with the examiner's suggestions.

resemble the rules of the contest, to be applied by the judge acting as an impartial referee. The rules are designed to serve several functions, but their primary objective is to help the fact-finder in reaching an accurate verdict based upon reliable information. On occasion, other interests may require that certain reliable information be kept from the fact-finder, as in the exclusion of items obtained through an unconstitutional search.

We cannot hope in an introductory text to enter into an in-depth study of the rules of evidence. All we can do is to get a general idea of the subject. We start by describing the various types of matter that fall within the definition of evidence.

Definition of Evidence and Kinds of Evidence.   Evidence is every species of proof legally presented in a court of law through the medium of witnesses, records, documents, objects, etc., for the purpose of inducing belief in the minds of the court or jury on the issues in the case. Evidence can be classified as real evidence, testimony, direct evidence, circumstantial evidence, and in other ways. *Real evidence* includes objects of any kind (guns, maps, fingerprints, etc.) placed before the court or jury; *testimony* is the statements of competent witnesses. *Direct evidence* is eyewitness evidence; *circumstantial evidence* is evidence of circumstances which tend to prove the truth or falsity of a fact in issue. To be acceptable in court, evidence must be relevant and competent.

Relevant Evidence.   Relevant evidence means evidence which is related to the issue and which will tend to prove or disprove an alleged fact. Thus, if the defendant is charged with murder, and the issue is whether or not he killed the deceased, evidence as to his motive, his ability to commit the offense, his opportunity to commit the offense, and his intention to commit the offense, are all relevant evidence. His fingerprints on the murder weapon, his sudden wealth after the deceased was robbed, the threats he made against the deceased, his attempt to flee or commit suicide, are also relevant evidence, as the proof of these facts would tend to prove the guilt of the defendant. Lawyers often speak of the "chain of evidence," which refers to the fact that evidence tends to develop bit by bit with one piece of evidence supporting and tending to prove another.

Competent Evidence.   Competent evidence means evidence given by a competent witness. Some evidence offered in court cannot be received for reasons of public policy or because it is patently unreliable. A person of unsound mind may not be a competent witness because it is apparent that he could not understand what he saw or heard or is not able to correctly relate it. Very young children are sometimes incompetent witnesses. However, there is usually no arbitrary age limit below which a child cannot testify. If it can be shown that the child was able to understand what he saw or heard, and knows the difference between right and wrong, he may be called as a witness and his testimony received. A convicted felon is a competent witness in most states, though the fact of his conviction may be shown to impeach his testimony. At one time, accomplices were declared to be incompetent witnesses against their fellow conspirators, but the approach today is simply to require that the accomplice's testimony be corroborated before it can serve to convict the defendant.

The mere fact that evidence is competent does not, of course, mean that the jury must believe it. Some competent evidence may be almost worthless in terms of inducing belief. A wife's alibi for her husband may be competent, but the jury may dismiss her testimony as not worthy of belief. While competency of the evidence is for the judge to decide, the weight of the evidence is for the jury to decide.

Proof of Special Facts.   Although a jury has great freedom in weighing evidence, there are some rules that bind the jury as to the proof of certain facts. The most significant are the rules governing judicial notice and presumptions. *Judicial notice* means that the court will take as proved certain facts of common knowledge without requiring that witnesses or other evidence be produced to prove the fact in court. Thus, a court will take judicial notice of the days of the week, the months of the year, the properties of matter (gas explodes, a skidding car will leave skid marks, etc.), historical facts (the dates of all the wars, the names of the Presidents of the United States, etc.), the usual dimensions (12 inches to a foot, the number of pounds in a ton, etc.), and similar commonly known facts. Once the court takes judicial notice of these facts, they also are accepted by the jury.

An *evidentiary presumption* exists when the law states that proof of one fact shall be sufficient proof of another fact. In effect, the existence of the second fact is presumed from the existence of the first. There are two types of presumptions, those that are conclusive and those that can be rebutted (shown to be untrue). The common law rule that a child under seven is incapable of committing a criminal act is a typical conclusive presumption. Even if the prosecution could prove that the child was wise beyond his years and fully capable of formulating a criminal intent, the child would still be immune from criminal prosecution. The status of the child presumed by the law is absolute.

Most presumptions may be rebutted. They are based on factual inferences, justified by the common pattern of events, and require the opposing side to prove otherwise. For example, a woman is presumed to be chaste, and man who is missing for over seven years is presumed to be dead. Either presumption can be contradicted by showing evidence to the contrary, but if no such evidence is introduced, the jury is to accept the presumed fact.[46]

Opinion and Expert Testimony.   Various rules of evidence limit the scope of the testimony received by a jury. One major rule in this category is the rule relating to opinion testimony. Under this rule, a lay (non-expert) witness may testify only to what he observed and cannot give his opinion on what happened. There are some exceptions to this position, but they are limited to matters of common experience based on personal observation. For example, a lay witness may testify that a man was drunk—which is an opinion—but he will be required to describe those actions of the man that led him to believe that the man was drunk.

---

46.   Still other presumptions do not bind the jury and therefore are described as "permissive" presumptions or inferences. These presumptions also may be rebutted by proof to the contrary, but even if they are not rebutted, the jury need not accept the presumed fact. For example, a jury may, but need not, conclude that a person intended the natural and probable consequences of his act.

An expert witness, unlike a lay witness, may give an opinion even though he had not been present at the event. The basis of the expert witness' testimony is that he is an expert in the field, and this must be shown before he can express an opinion. Though he was not present at the event, a psychiatrist may give his expert opinion that the defendant was suffering from delusions at the time he killed the victim; a police officer may testify that skid marks of a certain length show the driver was driving at 70 miles an hour when he applied the brakes; a jeweler may testify as to the value of the property stolen; or a real estate agent to the value of the real property sold. A psychiatrist who has never even examined a defendant may be asked to give his opinion of his mental condition solely on the basis of what he has observed of the defendant in court and the testimony presented in court about the event. Expert opinion may be brought out by means of the hypothetical question, which must be based on facts in evidence. In effect, the expert witness is asked: "If so and so happened in such and such a way with this and that result, what is your opinion as to the mental condition of the defendant at the time?" An expert, but not a lay witness, is permitted to answer such a question.

Hearsay Evidence.   The general rule is that hearsay evidence is not admissible (not competent evidence) to prove an issue in a court of law. Hearsay evidence is second-hand evidence in which a witness is telling not what he knows of his own knowledge but what somebody else told him. Since the person making the statement is not in court, there is no way that he can be confronted and cross-examined as to the truth of what he said. The law sees such evidence as denying the defendant the right to confrontation and also as unreliable. A woman may say, "I know the defendant was there that night because my brother told me he was there." If the defendant cross-examines only the woman, he can get no information as to when and under what conditions the brother saw the defendant, nor whether the brother had good eyesight, disliked the defendant, or any other fact that might discredit his testimony. The law therefore says that the woman's testimony is hearsay and not admissible. If the state wants the brother's testimony, it will have to call the brother to the witness stand, where he can be examined and cross-examined about the occasion when he saw the defendant.

There are many exceptions to the hearsay rule which we cannot consider here, except for the *res-gestae* exception, which is important to police investigation, and admissions and confessions which constitute important and sometimes crucial evidence against the defendant.

Res Gestae.   The Latin phrase *res gestae* means literally "things done." It might be translated in modern terms as "the happening." If existence of an event is in issue in a criminal case, then proof of all aspects of that event may be introduced into evidence, including statements made at the same time, even though those statements might otherwise be barred by the hearsay rule. For example, if a police officer witnesses an accident which he undertakes to investigate, he can testify in court as to what happened and also as to *what was said* during the course of his investigation at the scene. A bystander may say to the driver of the car, "You were driving 80 miles an hour," and the driver not deny it. The police officer can testify to what the bystander said and that the driver did not deny it, though the statement is hearsay since the bystander is not in court to be cross-examined. Declarations uttered spontaneously and simultaneously with an act which is admissible in evidence may be admitted as an exception to the hearsay rule, provided the utterances are so closely related to the event that the probability of their truth is high. The *res-gestae* exception thus is based, like many other hearsay rule exceptions, on the likely reliability of the evidence even without confrontation of the original source of the hearsay.

Admissions Against Interest.   Statements made by the defendant that are against his interest are also accepted into evidence as exceptions to the hearsay rule. These include both admissions and confessions. An admission connects the accused with the act; a confession admits that he committed that act. The defendant may say, "I was there when he was killed"—this is an admission which puts him at the scene, though it is not a confession that he killed the victim. A confession says, "I killed him"—but may go on to claim self defense or some other extenuating circumstance. Either type of statement against interest is admissible as an exception to the hearsay rule because the defendant can hardly object that he had no opportunity to cross-examine the speaker when he himself was that person. Of course, if the statement was obtained by the police, it also must meet the due process and *Miranda* standards noted in Chapter Ten.

Objections to the Admission of Evidence.   One of the main duties of an attorney in the trial of a case is to make a timely objection to the admission of evidence which, because of the rules of evidence, should not be heard by the jury. After the opposing side asks a question, and before the witness answers, the attorney will state his objections to the court. He will say, "I object to the admission of that evidence because it is irrelevant, or because it is hearsay, or immaterial, or because no proper foundation has been laid for its admission," and so on. The sing-song objection, "I object to the admission of the evidence because it is incompetent, irrelevant, and immaterial," is constantly heard in any trial. The court rules on the objection and thus permits the offered evidence to be admitted or refuses to permit its admission. If the attorney's objection is overruled by the court, the evidence is admitted; if the objection is sustained, the evidence is not admitted or must be presented in some other form.

PROCEEDINGS AT THE CLOSE OF THE EVIDENCE

Instructions to the Jury.   The jury decides the facts, but the court decides the law. Therefore, the court must instruct the jury in the law applicable to the facts in the case. For example, if the defense is insanity, the judge must instruct the jury as to how insanity is determined in that state—whether by the M'Naghten Rule, the Irresistible Impulse Rule, or the Model Penal Code formulation. Of course, the judge does not just say, "You must follow the M'Naghten Rule,"—he carefully states the M'Naghten Rule as it applies to the facts in the case.

Instructions to the jury are prepared by the judge and the attorneys in the case after all the evidence has been received and both the prosecution and the defense have "rested," (i.e., completed the introduction of evidence). The prosecution and the defense each draw up the instructions that they want given to the jury, stating their theory of the law applicable to the case. The judge chooses from these offered instructions or may prepare his own. The instructions are written out, signed by the judge, and read by the judge to the jury. The jury later takes the set of written instructions into the jury room with them to guide them in their deliberations.

Arguments to the Jury.   As we have seen, the closing arguments to the jury come before the judge instructs the jury in some states and after the instructions in others. The order of argument also is fixed by the law of the state; the usual sequence is for the state to present part of its argument, the defense to present its argument, and then the state to present the final argument. The argument of each side is an attempt to persuade the jury toward a favorable verdict. The prosecutor will carefully sum up the facts and discuss the instructions of the court, giving them an interpretation favorable to the state. He may also call upon the jurors to do their duty as citizens and punish the defendant who committed such a heinous crime. The defense attorney will recapitulate the evidence favorable to the defendant, criticize the witnesses for the state and show how they should not be believed, and will interpret the facts and the instructions to the jury in the way most likely to result in a verdict of not guilty. The defense will almost surely call upon the jurors to do their duty as citizens and reject the prosecution's case for its failure to prove guilt beyond a reasonable doubt. Closing arguments to a jury can be works of art on both sides, and to many people, they constitute the high point of any criminal trial.

Charging the Jury.   As his final instruction, the judge charges the jury to retire to the jury room and well and truly consider the facts of the case, the instruction of the court, and the argument of counsel, thereupon to return a just verdict. The court will instruct the jury on the possible verdicts, and give them a written form for each verdict, the appropriate one to be signed by the foreman and returned to the court after agreement has been reached. The usual forms of verdict in a criminal case are "Guilty" and "Not Guilty," though the jury in a particular case may have an option of deciding on the degree of the offense. In such case it will be given alternative forms of the guilty verdict for Murder in the First Degree, Murder in the Second Degree, and Manslaughter, together with the form for the verdict of "Not Guilty." Again the foreman will sign the appropriate verdict. A verdict of "Not Guilty by Reason of Insanity" may also be a possible verdict in the case, depending upon the defense and the evidence introduced to support it. If this is true, the jury will be supplied a form for returning this verdict.

After the judge has charged the jury, the jurors are put into the custody of the bailiff, and will remain sequestered (isolated from other people) until they reach a verdict, or until it becomes apparent that they are not able to reach a verdict and are discharged by the court. Some juries are sequestered throughout the entire trial, depending upon the nature of the case; others are sequestered only after the close of the evidence. The jurors "retire" under the custody of the bailiff to a jury room to deliberate on their verdict. They take with them the pleadings in the case, the instructions to the jury, and usually any exhibits admitted into evidence. If at any time they want to refresh their memory about the testimony of any witness, they may ask the court reporter to give them a transcript of his testimony on the point in question. The jury sometimes asks for additional instructions, or asks the court to further explain instructions already given by the court. In such case, the judge and the attorneys work out a new set of instructions, which are taken to the jury by the bailiff.

All communications between the jury and the court are through the bailiff—no juror is permitted to leave the jury room. (In small towns, however, where there are no facilities for preparation of meals, the jury is taken at meal-time to a public restaurant. They remain in the custody of the bailiff, whose duty it is to see that they are not approached by any person not a juror and that they do not receive material or communications of any kind which might influence their verdict.)

The Deliberations of the Jury. The duty of the jury is to consider the facts and the law of the case and arrive at a verdict. The foreman of the jury, chosen by the jury itself (or sometimes automatically the first juror accepted by both the state and the defense) frequently begins the deliberation by taking a vote of the jury. The vote may on rare occasions result in an immediate unanimous verdict. The usual situation, however, is that the first vote discloses that the jury is divided; some voting "guilty" and some "not guilty." Discussions then go on back and forth between the members of the jury, with votes being taken periodically, until the jury finally votes unanimously one way or another. If the jury cannot reach agreement after prolonged deliberations, they report this fact to the court. The court usually instructs them to stay for another stated period and keep trying. If at the end of this time they still have not reached a verdict, there is a "hung jury." The members of a hung jury come back into court and are dismissed by the judge. If the state believes it still can gain a conviction, it may retry the defendant. Sometimes he is released because the state decides that if it couldn't convict him the first time, it probably can't do it the second time around. Jury deliberations, at least in theory, are secret.

In some states, juries are charged not only with deciding on guilt or innocence but also must fix the sentence. This practice is particularly wide-spread in capital cases where the death penalty may be imposed. We will discuss jury sentencing in the next chapter.

Return of the Verdict. After the jury has reached an agreement on the verdict, the jury comes back into the courtroom. The judge, the attorneys for the state and the defense, and the defendant must be present. The judge inquires of the jurors as to whether or not they have reached a verdict. The jurors nod or reply, "We have, your honor." The bailiff goes to the foreman of the jury, takes from him the written verdict, which has been signed by the foreman and brought into court, and presents the verdict to the judge. The judge reads the verdict, and hands it back to the bailiff to be read aloud in court, or reads the verdict himself from the bench. The verdict will say, "We, the jury, duly impaneled and sworn, find the defendant guilty as charged," or, "We, the jury, duly impaneled and sworn, do find the defendant 'Not Guilty,' " or whatever particular form of verdict has been agreed upon by the jurors.

If the verdict of the jury is "Not Guilty," the defendant is immediately released from custody and the case is ended (the double jeopardy bar prohibiting the state from pursuing an appeal). If the verdict is "Guilty," the defendant is kept in custody. Defendants found guilty customarily make certain motions challenging the verdict which the court will rule upon prior to sentencing. Sentencing takes place several days after the verdict, the exact time depending, among other things, on whether or not the court requires a pre-sentence investigation and the condition of the court docket. We will discuss sentencing at length in the next chapter.

APPEAL OF THE CONVICTION

After sentence is imposed, the defendant may appeal his conviction. The laws of all states now provide for an appeal of a conviction from the magistrate court to a court of general jurisdiction, and from a court of general jurisdiction to an intermediate appellate court or the highest court in the state. In the federal system, appeals go from the District Court to the United States Court of Appeals. Finally, certain cases may be taken from the United States Court of Appeals and from the highest courts in a state to the United States Supreme Court. We discussed in Chapter Three the nature of the different appellate courts and the nature of the appellate process. We also noted the distinction between the initial appeal, which usually is granted as a matter of right, and subsequent appeals, which usually are available only at the discretion of the higher court.

Ordinarily, an appellate court will consider only those legal points that were presented before the trial court. In state cases before the Supreme Court, as we have seen in Chapter Three, the review is limited to issues of federal law. If the appellate court determines that a legal error was not committed, it will "affirm" the result below. If it finds there was an error, it must determine whether the error was harmless. An error deemed to be harmless does not require reversal of the conviction; the court can affirm on the ground that the defendant was not injured by the error. If the appellate court can say that beyond a reasonable doubt the jury would have reached the same conclusion even if the error had not been committed, it may find that the error was harmless. Otherwise, the error is too substantial to be disregarded, and the conviction must be reversed and the case remanded to the trial court. Ordinarily, the case can be retried following the reversal. A retrial is not permitted, however, when the appellate court reversed on the ground that there was insufficient evidence to convict the defendant. [47]

Though there is no constitutional right to appeal, if a state provides for an appeal (as all have done), the right of appeal must be available on an equal basis to all convicted persons without regard to their financial resources. Thus, it has been held that the state must furnish a free transcript and appointed counsel for an appeal filed by an indigent defendant.[48]

---

47. *Burks v. United States,* 437 U.S. 1, 98 S.Ct. 2141, 57 L.Ed.2d 1 (1978).

48. *Griffin v. Illinois,* 351 U.S. 12, 76 S.Ct. 585, 100 L.Ed. 891 (1956) (transcript); *Douglas v. California,* 372 U.S. 353, 83 S.Ct. 814, 9 L.Ed2d 811 (1962) (counsel); *Ross v. Moffitt,* 417 U.S. 600 94 S.Ct. 2437, 41 L.Ed.2d 341 (1974) (appointed counsel not needed for preparation of petition for certiorari on second-level appeal).

HABEAS CORPUS

AND POST-CONVICTION REVIEW

The Nature Of Habeas Corpus. The writ of habeas corpus is referred to as the "Great Writ of Liberty."[49] Its purpose is to obtain the release of a person illegally confined or restrained of his liberty. The literal meaning of habeas corpus is "you have the body" and the writ of habeas corpus commands the person "having the body" (i.e., restraining another) to bring the person into court and show cause as to whether or not the detention is legal.

Technically, the writ of habeas corpus is a civil remedy, but it often is used to challenge custody that has been imposed in connection with the criminal justice process. It is used primarily in two settings in the criminal process. First, persons who are arrested and not promptly presented before a magistrate may use the writ to gain a hearing as to the legality of their detention. Ordinarily, an application for the writ is filed on behalf of the arrestee in the general trial court of the judicial district in which the arrestee is being held. The jailer is named as the defendant since he is the person holding the arrestee in custody. If the application sets forth facts suggesting the arrestee is being detained in violation of the prompt presentment requirement, the court will issue the writ directing the jailer to bring the arrestee forward. The writ was designed originally to prevent the Crown from taking a person into custody and holding him there without initiating prosecution. It still serves that purpose.

Once prosecution has been intiated, the defendant may challenge the legality of his detention through the regular criminal process. If his arrest was illegal, he may raise that issue before the magistrate. If the prosecution lacks probable cause to proceed, he may challenge its case at the preliminary hearing. If he is being detained because the magistrate denied his right to bail, that issue can be raised before the trial court. Since these other remedies are available, the writ of habeas corpus cannot be used. The writ is an extraordinary remedy, unavailable where other remedies may be used. Once the criminal proceedings are over and all appeal rights have been exhausted, the writ again becomes the only available remedy. If a convicted defendant believes that his conviction was invalid, he may use the writ to gain a reexamination of the legality of his conviction. The application will be filed with the general trial court in the district in which he is imprisoned, with the warden of the prison or the director of the state department of corrections as the defendant. Since the challenge is really to the conviction, the warden or director often will be represented by the prosecuting attorney who obtained the conviction. The writ at this point is serving as a means of gaining a

---

49. The writ of habeas corpus played an important role in challenging abuses of the Crown during the seventeenth and eighteenth centuries. It accordingly was regarded as a great constitutional guarantee of personal liberty at the time of the adoption of the federal constitution. Article I, Section 9, Clause 2 of the United States Constitution guaranteed the availability of the writ in federal courts in providing: "The Privilege of the Writ of Habeas Corpus shall not be suspended, unless when in Cases of Rebellion or Invasion the public Safety may require it." Congress, in the First Judiciary Act of 1789, provided for use of the writ by persons "in custody under or by colour of the authority of the United States." It was this Act that was amended after the Civil War to include state prisoners. See the text at note 51 *infra*.

post-appeal review of his conviction. It is, however, limited to certain types of challenges.

Grounds for Post-Appeal Review. States vary as to the issues that may be raised in obtaining a post-appeal review of a conviction through the writ of habeas corpus. All agree that minor errors cannot be presented. Some will review only errors that go to the trial court's authority to proceed in the defendant's case (commonly described as "jurisdictional" errors). Thus, an imprisoned defendant can use the writ to challenge the constitutionality of the criminal statute under which he was convicted, but he cannot use it to challenge the sufficiency of the evidence to sustain his conviction or the admission of improper evidence at his trial. Many states have permitted the imprisoned defendant to go beyond jurisdictional errors. They allow the writ to be used to consider any "fundamental" error in the trial court proceedings that resulted in the defendant's conviction. This will include most (if not all) constitutional violations. However, the defendant ordinarily cannot present his claim of a fundamental error if the same claim was considered and rejected at his trial or on appeal (or, in many states, if the claim could have been raised at his trial or on appeal). The writ may not be used, the courts have stressed, as a substitute for procedures normally available for raising legal claims within the criminal justice process.

What kinds of issues are most likely to be viewed as appropriate for consideration in a habeas corpus application? One of the more common allegations is the prosecutor's violation of due process through the knowing use of perjured testimony at trial. A violation of this type commonly would not be discovered until well after the trial and could not be raised on appeal. Another claim commonly presented on habeas corpus is alleged coercion resulting in an involuntary guilty plea. Since the coercion existed at the time the plea was entered, the defendant could not reasonably have been expected to raise the issue before the trial judge. When an appropriate claim is raised in a habeas application, a hearing on the claim will be held. If the court concludes that there was a violation, it will order that the defendant be released unless the state initiates a reprosecution within a short period of time. Thus, the result is similar in practical impact to a reversal on appeal.

Statutory Post-Conviction Remedies. During the 1950's and 1960's, as the constitutional rights of defendants were expanded, the range of the issues that could be presented in post-appeal habeas corpus proceedings also expanded. Many jurisdictions concluded that the writ of habeas corpus provided an awkward procedure for permitting post-appeal challenges to convictions. The convicted defendant's legal action ideally should be brought against the prosecutor in the district of conviction rather than the warden in the district of imprisonment. Moreover, since the challenge is basically to the conviction, it logically should be available to all convicted defendants, rather than just those held in custody. The states generally were hesitant to alter the structure of the writ of habeas corpus to accommodate such changes since the writ served many functions aside from permitting post-appeal challenges to convictions. Accordingly, about half of the states adopted special statutes creating a simplified post-appeal procedure for challenging an illegal conviction. The legal actions created by these statutes commonly are described as a "post-conviction remedies" or "collateral attack proceedings."

Aside from procedural distinctions, the post-conviction remedies are quite similar to the habeas corpus proceedings of those states that give the broadest expanse to the "Great Writ." As with habeas corpus, the statutory remedies are available only after the convicted defendant has exhausted his normal criminal procedure remedies. If he still has the opportunity to appeal, for example, the remedy is not available. The statutory remedies also are limited to claims based on jurisdictional defects and constitutional violations at trial. Moreover, such claims ordinarily will not be considered if the defendant deliberately bypassed an opportunity to present these issues at trial or on appeal.[50]

Federal Habeas Corpus for State Prisoners. Following the Civil War, Congress, doubtful of the southern states' willingness to adhere to constitutional safeguards, made the writ of habeas corpus in federal courts available to persons held in custody by state officials. The federal writ formerly applied only to persons held in custody by the federal government, but Congress made it applicable to *any* prisoner held in custody "in violation of the Constitution or laws or treaties of the United States."[51] State prisoners raising valid federal claims were given the opportunity to eventually present those claims before federal courts (today, federal district courts) if they were ill-treated by state courts.

Over the years, a complicated body of law has developed as to the role of federal courts in considering habeas corpus applications of state prisoners. The main thrust of the various decisions is that the federal writ, though expanded at times, still will be limited by traditional standards of habeas corpus relief. Thus, the state prisoner cannot seek habeas relief until he first has exhausted his state remedies. Also, habeas corpus relief will be granted only where he shows that the state criminal proceeding was marred by a fundamental constitutional error. The admission of unconstitutionally seized evidence at his trial ordinarily will not be sufficient to gain habeas relief. On the other hand, violations that relate to the fairness of the defendant's trial (such as a denial of counsel), or the state court's authority to proceed (such as a double jeopardy violation), will be sufficient. Finally, even where the imprisoned state defendant raises a fundamental constitutional violation, federal habeas corpus relief will not be granted if the defendant purposely failed to raise that issue before the state courts or, in some instances, simply failed to comply with important state procedural rules.[52]

Federal and State Court Conflict. State prisoner applications for federal habeas corpus relief have been a source of considerable conflict between federal and state courts in recent years. As we have seen, in the normal appellate process,

---

50. A review of the state provisions is contained in American Bar Association, *Standards Relating To Post-Conviction Remedies* (Approved Draft, 1968).

51. 28 United States Code §2241.

52. The leading cases on the federal habeas corpus for state prisoners are *Stone v. Powell*, 429 U.S. 465, 96 S.Ct. 3037, 49 L.Ed.2d 1067(1976); *Wainwright v. Sykes*, 433 U.S. 72, 97 S.Ct. 2497, 53 L.Ed.2d 594 (1977); and *Fay v. Noia*, 372 U.S. 391, 83 S.Ct. 822 9 L.Ed.2d 837 (1963).

the decision of the highest state court will be subject to review only by the United States Supreme Court. Federal habeas corpus, however, permits a federal district court to order the release of a state prisoner after the highest state court has affirmed his conviction. After as many as three state courts (trial, intermediate appellate, and state supreme court) have held that the defendant's constitutional rights were not violated, a federal district court may hold otherwise and order the state to retry him (or release him if a retrial is impossible). Particularly irksome to some state courts is the fact that a single federal judge may reject an interpretation of the federal constitution adopted by a unanimous panel of several justices of the highest state court. Proponents of federal habeas corpus relief acknowledge that the federal habeas procedure creates an "awkward" pattern of review, but they claim that this is a "necessary evil." They note that there are too many state cases involving significant constitutional issues for the United States Supreme Court to review directly all of those cases. The review provided by federal habeas corpus is, in their opinion, an essential protection against state convictions that may violate the federal constitution. If a federal district court should improperly reject a state supreme court's interpretation of the federal constitution, the state may appeal that ruling to the United States Court of Appeals. Should the state lose there, it may then seek Supreme Court review by petition for certiorari. Supporters of federal habeas corpus contend that imposing such burdens on the state is a small price to pay for the additional protection of constitutional rights provided by the "Great Writ."[53]

ADDENDUM: THE FEDERAL RULE
OF CRIMINAL PROCEDURE ON PLEAS

RULE 11.

(a) Alternatives. A defendant may plead not guilty, guilty, or nolo contendere. If a defendant refuses to plead or if a defendant corporation fails to appear, the court shall enter a plea of not guilty.

(b) Nolo contendere. A defendant may plead nolo contendere only with the consent of the court. Such a plea shall be accepted by the court only after due consideration of the views of the parties and the interest of the public in the effective administration of justice.

(c) Advice to Defendant. Before accepting a plea of guilty or nolo contendere, the court must address the defendant personally in open court and inform him of, and determine that he understands, the following:

---

53. For additional information on plea bargains and guilty pleas, see J. Bond, *Pleas Bargaining and Guilty Pleas,* New York: Clark Boardman Company, 1978 (including an extensive bibliography). For further information on the criminal trial, see F. Bailey and H. Rothblatt, *Successful Techniques For Criminal Trials,* Rochester, New York: The Lawyers Co-operative Publishing Company, 1971; and *McCormick on Evidence* (E. Cleary, ed.), St. Paul, Minn.: West Publishing Company, 1972, 2nd ed.. For an extremely interesting description of a single trial, see P. Zimroth, *Perversions of Justice,* New York: The Viking Press, 1974. On appeals and post-conviction remedies, see P. Carrington, D. Meador, and M. Rosenberg, *Justice on Appeal,* St. Paul, Minn.: West Publishing Company, 1976; and R. Popper, *Post-Conviction Remedies In A Nutshell,* St. Paul, Minn.: West Publishing Company, 1978.

(1)   the nature of the charge to which the plea is offered, the mandatory minimum penalty provided by law, if any, and the maximum possible penalty provided by law; and

(2)   if the defendant is not represented by an attorney, that he has the right to be represented by an attorney at every stage of the proceeding against him and, if necessary, one will be appointed to represent him; and

(3)   that he has the right to plead not guilty or to persist in that plea if it has already been made, and that he has the right to be tried by a jury and at that trial has the right to the assistance of counsel, the right to confront and cross-examine witnesses against him, and the right not to be compelled to incriminate himself; and

(4)   that if he pleads guilty or nolo contendere there will not be a further trial of any kind, so that by pleading guilty or nolo contendere he waives the right to a trial; and

(5)   that if he pleads guilty or nolo contendere, the court may ask him questions about the offense to which he has pleaded, and if he answers these questions under oath, on the record, and in the presence of counsel, his answers may later be used against him in a prosecution for perjury or false statement.

(d)   Insuring That The Plea Is Voluntary.   The court shall not accept a plea of guilty or nolo contendere without first, by addressing the defendant personally in open court, determining that the plea is voluntary and not the result of force or threats or of promises apart from a plea agreement. The court shall also inquire as to whether the defendant's willingness to plead guilty or nolo contendere results from prior discussions between the attorney for the government and the defendant or his attorney.

(e)   Plea Agreement Procedure.

(1)   *In General.*   The attorney for the government and the attorney for the defendant or the defendant when acting pro se may engage in discussions with a view toward reaching an agreement that, upon the entering of a plea of guilty or nolo contendere to a charged offense or to a lesser or related offense, the attorney for the government will do any of the following:

(A)   move for dismissal of other charges; or

(B)   make a recommendation, or agree not to oppose the defendant's request, for a particular sentence, with the understanding that such recommendation or request shall not be binding upon the court; or

(C)   agree that a specific sentence is the appropriate disposition of the case. The court shall not participate in any such discussions.

(2)   *Notice of Such Agreement.*   If a plea agreement has been reached by the parties, the court shall, on the record, require the disclosure of the agreement in open court or, on a showing of good cause, in camera, at the time the plea is offered. Thereupon the court may accept or reject the agreement, or may defer its decision as to the acceptance or rejection until there has been an opportunity to consider the presentence report.

(3)   *Acceptance of a Plea Agreement.*   If the court accepts the plea agreement, the court shall inform the defendant that it will embody in the judgment and sentence the disposition provided for in the plea agreement.

(4)   *Rejection of a Plea Agreement.*   If the court rejects the plea agreement, the court shall, on the record, inform the parties of this fact, advise the defendant personally in open court or, on a showing of good cause, in camera, that the court is not bound by the plea agreement, afford the defendant the opportunity to then withdraw his plea, and advise the defendant that if he persists in his guilty plea or plea of nolo contendere the disposition of the case may be less favorable to the defendant than that contemplated by the plea agreement.

(5)   *Time of Plea Agreement Procedure.*   Except for good cause shown, notification to the court of the existence of a plea agreement shall be given at the arraignment or at such other time, prior to trial, as may be fixed by the court.

(6)   *Inadmissibility of Pleas, Offers of Pleas, and Related Statements.*   Except as otherwise provided in this paragraph, evidence of a plea of guilty, later withdrawn, or a plea of nolo contendere, or of an offer to plead guilty or nolo contendere to the crime charged or any other crime, or of statements made in connection with, and relevant to, any of the foregoing pleas or offers, is not admissible in any civil or criminal proceeding against the person who made the plea or offer. However, evidence of a statement made in connection with, and relevant to, a plea of guilty, later withdrawn, a plea of nolo contendere, or an offer to plead guilty or nolo contendere to the crime charged or any other crime, is admissible in a criminal proceeding for perjury or false statement if the statement was made by the defendant under oath, on the record, and in the presence of counsel.

(f)   Determining Accuracy of Plea.   Notwithstanding the acceptance of a plea of guilty, the court should not enter a judgment upon such plea without making such inquiry as shall satisfy it that there is a factual basis for the plea.

(g)   Record of Proceedings.   A verbatim record of the proceedings at which the defendant enters a plea shall be made and, if there is a plea of guilty or nolo contendere, the record shall include, without limitation, the court's advice to the defendant, the inquiry into the voluntariness of the plea including any plea agreement, and the inquiry into the accuracy of a guilty plea.

Chapter 13

Sentencing and Corrections

The imposition of sentence and the administration of sentence are two of the most important steps in the criminal justice process. Together they determine the degree of restraint that will be imposed upon the convicted defendant and how long that restraint will last. Many defendants are far more concerned about the nature of that restraint than they are about the possibility of conviction in itself. They recognize that public stigma attaches to a criminal conviction, but their primary concern is whether they will be incarcerated. Certainly, for those defendants, the processes of sentencing and corrections (i.e., the administration of the sentence) are as important as the process of the trial. As we shall see, however, sentencing and corrections are not nearly as tightly regulated by the law as are the trial and many pretrial proceedings.[1] In both sentencing and corrections, the law relies heavily upon the exercise of discretionary authority by the officials involved. The initial questions to be asked in analyzing either field are: (1) who has been given this discretionary authority, (2) exactly how broad is that discretion, and (3) what procedures apply to the use of that discretion? We start with these questions as applied to the process of sentencing.

---

1. There is, however, considerably more legal regulation of sentences and corrections today than there was ten years ago. The National Advisory Commission on Criminal Justice Standards and Goals, *Report on Corrections,* Washington, D.C.: Government Printing Office, 1973, pp. 8-9, aptly summarizes the state of law prior to 1960 and the developments since then:

   The United States has a strong and abiding attachment to the rule of law, with a rich inheritance of a government of law rather than men. This high regard for the rule of law has been applied extensively in the criminal justice system up to the point of conviction. But beyond conviction, until recently, largely unsupervised and arbitrary discretion held sway. This was true of sentencing, for which criteria were absent and from which appeals were both rare and difficult. It was true of the discretion exercised by the institutional administrator concerning prison conditions and disciplinary sanctions. It applied to the exercise by the parole board of discretion to release and revoke. Within the last decade, however, the movement to bring the law, judges, and lawyers into relationships with the correctional system has grown apace.

ALLOCATION OF SENTENCING AUTHORITY

Legislative Control.   We tend to view sentencing as the responsibility of the judge since it is the judge who formally pronounces the sentence. Actually, the initial responsibility for sentencing lies with the legislature, which commonly shares that responsibility with the judge. How the responsibility is shared varies from state to state. In all states, the legislature will make the initial determination as to whether a particular form of punishment can be imposed for a particular crime. The legislature's refusal to authorize a certain punishment is binding on the judge. The court has no common law power to impose fines, for example, where the legislature has not provided for the use of fines in sentencing. Ordinarily the legislature will authorize use of more than one punishment for a particular crime and will give the court some discretion in its selection of the appropriate punishment. The court will be given a choice, for example, between probation and imprisonment. Once that choice is made, the court then will have further discretion in shaping the form of the punishment (e.g., the length of imprisonment or the terms of probation). That discretion also will be subjected to at least some legislative control. For example, the legislature always will set a limit on the highest possible term of imprisonment for each offense.

The discretion granted to the judge in setting sentences usually varies with the type of sentence imposed. Legislatures tend to exercise different degrees of control over the imposition of capital punishment, imprisonment, probation, and fines. In the next several sections, we will examine the variations in judicial sentencing discretion as to each of these forms of punishment. But first, we should consider the role of other recipients of sentencing responsibility.

We have assumed so far that the responsibility for sentencing is being shared only by the legislature and the court. In most jurisdictions, for fines and probation, these are the only two agencies involved in determining the sentence. Sentences of imprisonment, on the other hand, often involve another agency, the parole board. While the board does not set the term of imprisonment, it often has authority to determine the length of time actually served in a prison. We will consider the parole board's function in connection with our discussion of the administration of corrections, in the latter part of this chapter. The jury is another body that may be given sentencing responsibility. The authority to impose capital punishment commonly is divided between the legislature (which sets guidelines) and the trier of fact in the particular case. As a practical matter, since most defendants in capital cases prefer a jury trial to a bench trial, the responsibility for determining whether the death sentence is to be imposed usually lies with the jury. For most states, this is the sole area of juror sentencing responsibility. In several states, however, the jury also occupies a central role in sentencing in noncapital cases.

Jury Sentencing in Noncapital Cases.   Nine states currently provide for jury sentencing in at least some noncapital cases tried to a jury.[2] In five of those states,

---

2.   These states generally do not provide for jury sentencing when the defendant pleads guilty or waives his right to a jury trial and is tried before the judge alone. However, the defendant may not have a unilateral right to waive a jury trial and thereby assure that he will be sentenced by the judge. In Virginia, for example, a defendant may waive a jury trial only with the approval of the court and the prosecutor. Virginia Code §19.2-257.

the jury has the authority to sentence for all offenses.[3] In two states, jury sentencing applies only to several specified crimes.[4] In two other states, the defendant has a choice between judge sentencing and jury sentencing.[5] Where jury sentencing is applicable, the nine states ordinarily still give the judge some control over the sentence. If the jury cannot agree as to sentence, several of the states permit the judge to fix the sentence by himself. Missouri permits the judge to impose a lesser prison sentence than that set by the jury. The judge also may have the power to grant probation or to suspend the sentence even though the jury has imposed a prison sentence.

Jury sentencing in noncapital cases originated in this country, probably as a result of colonial distrust of English judges appointed by the King. It never commanded the support of a large number of states, and the number of states using it has gradually diminished to the nine states noted above. In support of jury sentencing, it is argued that: (1) juror sentences are fairer because those sentences reflect the consensus viewpoint of several persons; (2) jurors are more sensitive than judges, who become calloused from constantly dealing with criminal cases; (3) jurors are less subject to public pressures than judges, particularly elected judges; and (4) jury-fixed punishment reduces popular distrust of official justice. The great weight of expert opinion has rejected these supposed advantages as more than offset by several disadvantages. First, juries are more likely to produce uneven sentences for essentially similar defendants. Each jury acts on its own sense of justice, having no idea as to the normal range of sentences usually given for a particular crime. Moreover, juries are shut-off from much of the information that is needed to make the sentence fit the character of the defendant as well as the harm caused. Information relating to the defendant's prior criminal record, employment record, and family responsibilities, for example, will not be admissible at trial because it is irrelevant to the issue of guilt or innocence. Finally, some critics are concerned that jury sentencing may undermine the protection of the reasonable doubt standard as to the issue of guilt. A jury given sentencing authority, they argue, will be tempted to compromise on a questionable case of guilt, holding the person guilty and then imposing an extremely light sentence.

Jury sentencing is such a unique practice today that we will largely ignore it in the remaining sections which deal with the division of sentencing responsibility. In analyzing the discretion available in imposing sentences of imprisonment, probation, or fine, we will assume that the sentencing official is a judge rather than the jury. Before turning to these areas, however, consideration should be given to the major constitutional limitation upon the type of punishment that may be authorized by the legislature—the Eighth Amendment prohibition against cruel and unusual punishment.

---

3. See Arkansas Stat. §41-802; Kentucky R. Crim. P. 9.84; Oklahoma Stat., tit. 22, §926; Tennessee Code §40-2707; Virginia Code §19.2-295.

4. See, e.g., Alabama Code §§13-1-92, 13-1-4, 13-6-222; Mississippi Code §§95-3-67, 95-3-70.

5. Texas Code of Criminal Procedure, art. 37.07 (defendant will be sentenced by a jury if he so requests); Missouri §557.036 (defendant will be sentenced by a jury unless he waives that right and requests to be sentenced by the judge).

Cruel and Unusual Punishment.   The Eighth Amendment was designed to prohibit certain forms of punishment, such as torture, that had been practiced in England and were widely viewed as reprehensible. The Supreme Court has noted, however, that the Amendment is stated in flexible terms that permit it to reach forms of punishment that were acceptable at the time of the constitution, but today may be viewed as comparable to torture. The term "cruel and unusual," the Court has said, "may acquire meaning as public opinion becomes enlightened by a humane justice."[6] It appears unlikely, however, that any of the forms of punishment used today would be held to violate the Eighth Amendment. Corporal punishment was finally abolished in 1972,[7] and capital punishment, as we shall see, was recently upheld as applied to appropriate cases. It should be noted, however, that the characterization of punishment as cruel and unusual is not dependent solely upon the form of the punishment. The Eighth Amendment prohibition also extends to punishment grossly disproportionate in severity to the seriousness of crime for which it is imposed. Thus in *Weems v. United States,*[8] a sentence of twelve years in chains at hard labor, surveillance for life, and a heavy fine was so disproportionate for the crime of embezzlement as to be unconstitutional. State courts, relying on this precedent, have invalidated other punishments as similarly excessive, including three years imprisonment for concealment of a gallon of whiskey, a minimum of 20 years for sale of marijuana, and the life imprisonment of a fourteen year-old convicted of rape.[9]

CAPITAL PUNISHMENT

The Need for Guidelines.   Although Michigan in 1847 was the first English-speaking government in the world to abolish capital punishment, the abolition movement has commanded only limited support in this country. In 1972, prior to the decision in *Furman v. Georgia,*[10] only nine states had abolished capital punishment.[11] In *Furman,* a sharply divided Supreme Court held that the death penalty as then administered constituted cruel and unusual punishment. The

---

6.   *Weems v. United States,* 217 U.S. 349, 378, 30 S.Ct. 544, 54 L.Ed. 793 (1910).

7.   The last statute providing for corporal punishment—a Delaware statute providing for whipping —was repealed in 1972. See S. Rubin, *Law of Criminal Corrections,* St. Paul, Minn.: West Publishing Company, 2d ed., 1973, p. 146. It is likely that such punishment would be held to constitute cruel and unusual punishment, although the Delaware provision was upheld in *Balser v. State,* 195 A.2d 757 (Del. 1963). See Rubin *supra* at p. 432. In *Ingraham v. Wright,* 430 U.S. 651, 97 S.Ct. 1401, 15 L.Ed.2d 711 (1977), the Supreme Court, in upholding the constitutionality of paddling as a form of school discipline, stressed that its ruling was not made under the Eighth Amendment since the prohibition against cruel and unusual punishment applied only to punishment imposed upon persons convicted of crimes. The "openness" of the public school and its "supervision by the community" resulted in the application of different standards to school discipline cases.

8.   *Weems v. United States,* 217 U.S. 349, 30 S.Ct. 544, 54 L.Ed. 793 (1910).

9.   See *Nowling v. State,* 151 Fla. 584, 10 So.2d 130 (1948) (whiskey concealment); *People v. Lorentzen,* 387 Mich. 167, 194 N.W.2d 827 (1972) (marijuana); *Workman v. Commonwealth,* 429 S.W.2d 374 (Ky.Ct.App., 1968) (youthful rape defendant).

10.   *Furman v. Georgia,* 408 U.S. 238, 92 S.Ct. 2726, 33 L.Ed.2d 346 (1973).

11.   Alaska, Hawaii, Iowa, Maine, Michigan, Minnesota, Oregon, West Virginia, and Wisconsin. Rhode Island had the death penalty only for murder committed by prisoners serving a life

Georgia statute before the Court was typical of most capital punishment statutes in force at the time. It simply called upon the trier of fact, after finding the defendant guilty of first degree murder, to consider the facts and choose between death and life imprisonment. Two of the five justices in the Supreme Court majority argued that capital punishment was always unconstitutional. The other three suggested that capital punishment could be permissible, but the prevailing statutes left so much unguided discretion with the judge or jury that the imposition of the penalty had become arbitrary. The Court could not uphold the penalty, they argued, where there was "no meaningful basis for distinguishing the few cases in which [death] is imposed from the many cases in which it is not."[12]

Furman cast serious doubt on the validity of the capital punishment statutes in each of the forty-one states that then had such provisions. Most of the states sought to amend their statutes to eliminate the arbitrariness in administration that had been the deciding factor in *Furman*. In 1976, in *Gregg v. Georgia*,[13] a majority of the justices (7-2) held Georgia had achieved this objective and its capital punishment statute was therefore constitutional.[14] The Georgia statute provided for a split (bifurcated) trial on the first degree murder charge. The jury (or judge, if a jury trial was waived) first determined guilt and then, in a separate proceeding, considered the issue of punishment. The statute required that the judge or jury consider a list of several aggravating circumstances, as well as any mitigating circumstances, in deciding whether the death penalty should apply.[15]

---

sentence. North Dakota had an almost equally limited provision. Several other states had abolished the death penalty and then restored it. Included in this group were: Delaware, South Dakota, Kansas, Missouri, Washington, Colorado, and Maine.

12. *Furman v. Georgia,* 408 U.S. 238, 313, 92 S.Ct. 2726, 33 L.Ed.2d 346 (1972) (Justice White concurring). Justice Stewart similarly noted: "The death sentences are cruel and unusual in the same way that being struck by lightning is cruel and unusual. For all people convicted of rape and murder in 1967 and 1968, many just as reprehensible as these, the petitioners are among a capriciously selected random handful upon whom the sentence of death has in fact been imposed . . . . [T]he Eighth and Fourteenth Amendments cannot tolerate the infliction of a sentence of death under legal systems that permit this unique penalty to be so wantonly and freakishly imposed." 408 U.S. at 309-10.

13. *Gregg v. Georgia,* 428 U.S. 153, 96 S.Ct. 2909, 49 L.Ed.2d 859 (1976).

14. The defendant in *Gregg* also argued that capital punishment was an excessive punishment (and therefore cruel and unusual) because it served no legitimate function of punishment that could not be served as well by life imprisonment. The majority of the Court also rejected this contention. The effectiveness of capital punishment as a deterrent was viewed as "a complex factual issue the resolution of which properly rests with the legislature." (The Court itself examined studies on the deterrent impact of capital punishment, but found them indecisive, neither establishing nor disproving the possibility that the death penalty deterred some prospective murderers). The majority further noted that the death penalty clearly brought an extra element to the punishment objective of retribution that was not provided by life imprisonment.

15. Among the aggravating factors were the following: (1) the defendant had a prior conviction for a capital felony or a "substantial history of serious assaultive criminal convictions"; (2) the murder was committed in the course of committing rape, armed robbery, kidnapping, burglary, or arson; (3) the defendant created a grave risk of death to more than one person; (4) the defendant killed for profit; (5) the victim was a judicial officer or prosecutor killed during or because of his exercise of official duty; (6) the victim was a police officer, corrections employee, or fireman who was engaged in the performance of his duties; (7) the defendant directed another to kill as his agent; (8) the murder was committed in a "wantonly vile, horrible, or inhumane" manner in that it involved "torture, depravity of mind or an aggravated battery"; (9) the defendant was a prison escapee; or (10) the murder was committed in an attempt to avoid arrest. In the *Gregg* case, the second and fourth factors were present.

The death sentence could not be imposed unless judge or jury found beyond a reasonable doubt that one or more of the aggravating circumstances was present in the case. That finding, set forth in the record, could then be challenged by the defendant on appeal. The Supreme Court found that the new Georgia statute eliminated the difficulties found in *Furman:*

> The new Georgia sentencing procedures, by contrast [to those in *Furman*], focus the jury's attention on the particularized nature of the crime and the particularized nature of the individual defendant. While the jury is permitted to consider any aggravating or mitigating circumstances, it must find and identify at least one statutory aggravating factor before it may impose a penalty of death. In this way is the jury's discretion channeled. No longer can a jury wantonly and freakishly impose the death sentence; it is always circumscribed by the legislative guidelines.[16]

In companion cases to *Gregg,* the Court approved two similar capital punishment provisions, but it later rejected a distinguishable Ohio provision. *Proffitt v. Florida*[17] upheld a statute which listed eight aggravating and seven mitigating circumstances and required the jury to find that the aggravating circumstances outweighed the mitigating before imposing the death sentence. *Jurek v. Texas*[18] upheld a statute which did not use a series of aggravating circumstances, but produced a similar impact in limiting discretion. The Texas statute defined a capital homicide as a killing committed in any of five situations, each of which involved aggravating circumstances (e.g., a killing in the course of a violent felony). It also required that the jury find proof beyond a reasonable doubt that (1) the killing was deliberate and (2) "a probability [exists] that the defendant would commit criminal acts of violence and would constitute a continuing threat to society." In *Lockett v. Ohio,*[19] the Court held unconstitutional an Ohio statute even though it required the presence of aggravating circumstances. This statute was deficient because, unlike the Georgia, Florida, and Texas statutes, it largely excluded jury consideration of mitigating circumstances (e.g., the fact that the defendant acted under the substantial domination of another person).

Other Constitutional Limitations. While insisting upon legislative guidelines that channel the jury's discretion, the Supreme Court has held invalid statutes that impose so much control that they deny to the jury the discretion to refuse to impose capital punishment. As we already have noted, the Court rejected an Ohio statute that listed aggravating circumstances, but prohibited consideration of various mitigating circumstances relating to "a defendant's character or record" or the nature of the homicide.[20] The Court also has held invalid statutes that automatically required the death penalty for certain types of homicides. *Roberts v. Louisiana,*[21] for example, found unconstitutional a statute automatically requiring the death penalty for any intentional killing of a police officer "engaged

---

16. *Gregg v. Georgia,* 428 U.S. 153, 206-7, 96 S.Ct. 2909, 49 L.Ed.2d 859 (1976).

17. *Proffitt v. Florida,* 428 U.S. 242, 96 S.Ct. 2960, 49 L.Ed.2d 913 (1976).

18. *Jurek v. Texas,* 428 U.S. 262, 96 S.Ct. 2950, 49 L.Ed.2d 929 (1976).

19. *Lockett v. Ohio,*   U.S.   , 98 S.Ct. 2954, 57 L.Ed.2d 973 (1978).

20. *Lockett v. Ohio,*   U.S.   , 98 S.Ct. 2954, 57 L.Ed.2d 973 (1978).

21. *H. Roberts v. Louisiana,* 431 U.S. 633, 97 S.Ct. 1993, 52 L.Ed.2d 637 (1977).

in the performance of his lawful duties."[22] The Court also rejected a death sentence imposed pursuant to a valid statute where the judge imposing the sentence relied in part on confidential information not disclosed to the defendant or his lawyer.[23] While confidential information often is used in sentencing in noncapital cases,[24] the Court noted that the "severity" and "finality" of capital punishment required that the defendant be given an opportunity to deny or explain any information relied upon in imposing a death sentence. Finally, relying on the Eighth Amendment prohibition against grossly disproportionate punishment, the Court held the death penalty could not be imposed for the crime of rape.[25] The Court strongly suggested that the capital punishment would be invalid as cruel and unusual punishment if imposed for an offense other than murder.

Current State Laws. Following the *Furman* decision, thirty-four states adopted new capital punishment provisions.[26] Some adopted mandatory death sentence provisions that clearly are unconstitutional. Most adopted statutes identifying aggravating or mitigating circumstances that the judge or jury are directed to consider in deciding whether to impose the death sentence. Not all have been as successful as Georgia, Florida, and Texas, however, in meeting constitutional standards. Until a particular state's provision is upheld by the Supreme Court, some doubt will remain as to its validity. As a result, the hundreds of prisoners on death row (over 450 as of December 31, 1978) will remain there until many more death penalty cases are decided by the Supreme Court.[27] Five years after *Furman,* there had been only one execution in the United States, and that case involved a defendant who refused to challenge his sentence before the Supreme Court.[28]

FINES

Legislative Authorization. Fines generally are viewed as the least severe of all possible punishments. It is for this reason, perhaps, that judges are given extremely broad discretion in setting fines. Criminal codes generally authorize the use of fines for most crimes. Some of the older criminal codes authorize the imposition of fines for all offenses except murder. The new codes, on the other hand, often do not authorize fines for the highest category of felonies (which

---

22. See also *Woodson v. North Carolina*, 428 U.S. 280, 96 S.Ct. 2978, 49 L.Ed.2d 944 (1976) and *S. Roberts v. Louisiana,* 428 U.S. 325, 96 S.Ct. 3001, 49 L.Ed.2d 974 (1976), also invalidating automatic capital punishment provisions.

23. *Gardner v. Florida,* 430 U.S. 349, 97 S.Ct. 1197, 51 L.Ed.2d 393 (1977).

24. See pp. 365-66 *infra.*

25. *Coker v. Georgia,* 433 U.S. 584, 97 S.Ct. 2861, 53 L.Ed.2d 982 (1977).

26. The thirty four states with such statutes, as of August 1, 1977, were: Alabama, Arizona, Arkansas, California, Colorado, Connecticut, Delaware, Florida, Georgia, Idaho, Illinois, Indiana, Kentucky, Louisiana, Mississippi, Missouri, Montana, Nebraska, Nevada, New Hampshire, New York, North Carolina, Ohio, Oklahoma, Pennsylvania, Rhode Island, South Carolina, Tennessee, Texas, Utah, Vermont, Virginia, Washington, and Wyoming.

27. Even then, many will not be executed since almost all states grant to the governor or special boards the authority to commute a death sentence to life imprisonment. See note 160 *infra* and pp. 381-82 *infra.*

28. See *Gilmore v. Utah,* 429 U.S. 1012, 97 S.Ct. 436, 50 L.Ed.2d 632 (1976).

commonly includes murder, kidnapping, rape, and certain other violent crimes). Where fines are authorized, they may be used as a supplement to imprisonment or probation or as the sole punishment where the offense does not require imprisonment or probation.[29]

Besides authorizing the use of a fine, the criminal code will set an upper limit as to the amount of the fine, which will vary with the class of offense. In Texas, for example, the limits are $10,000 for a second degree felony, $5,000 for a third degree felony, $2,000 for a class A misdemeanor, $1,000 for a class B misdemeanor, and $200 for a class C misdemeanor.[30] Older codes which have not been adjusted to take inflation into account may have somewhat lower limits. Since corporations cannot be imprisoned, some states have special provisions authorizing higher fines to be levied against corporate defendants. Arizona has the highest limit of one million dollars for a corporate defendant convicted of a felony.[31]

Legislative Guidelines. The Model Penal Code proposed the following legislative guidelines on the use of fines:

> (1) The court shall not sentence a defendant only to pay a fine, when any other disposition is authorized by law, unless having regard to the nature and circumstances of the crime and to the history and character of the defendant, it is of the opinion that the fine alone suffices for protection of the public.
>
> (2) The Court shall not sentence a defendant to pay a fine in addition to a sentence of imprisonment or probation unless:
>
> (a) the defendant has derived a pecuniary gain from the crime; or
>
> (b) the Court is of [the] opinion that a fine is specially adapted to deterrence of the crime involved or to the correction of the offender.
>
> (3) The Court shall not sentence a defendant to pay a fine unless:
>
> (a) the defendant is or will be able to pay the fine; and
>
> (b) the fine will not prevent the defendant from making restitution or reparation to the victim of the crime.
>
> (4) In determining the amount and method of payment of a fine, the Court shall take into account the financial resources of the defendant and the nature of the burden that its payment will impose.[32]

Many of the states that generally follow the Model Code did not adopt this provision. They preferred to leave the court's discretion unfettered by any specific legislative directions.[33] Thus, a substantial majority of jurisdictions today include no legislative directive as to how a judge should use his discretion when a fine is

---

29. See p. 76 *supra* as to offenses punishable only by a fine.

30. See Texas Penal Code §§12.33, 12.34, 12.21, 12.22, and 12.23.

31. See Arizona Revised Stat. §13-1004.

32. MPC §7.02.

33. Neither Texas nor Illinois, for example, adopted this provision. Several states make reference to the defendant's pecuniary gain in authorizing the judge to set the maximum fine for felonies at "double the amount of the defendant's gain from the commission of the crime." See, e.g., New York Penal Code §80.00.

authorized by statute. It generally is assumed, however, that judges are guided largely by the standards suggested in the Model Code.

Generally, the frequency of the use of fines decreases with the severity of the offense. Anyone who has paid a traffic ticket knows that a fine is almost the exclusive sentence of the traffic court. Fines also are the most common sanction applied in misdemeanor cases. In the magistrate courts of some major cities, fines have been used as the sole sentence in over 90% of the misdemeanor convictions. Where a magistrate court can make extensive use of a probation agency, fines are more likely to be combined with a sentence of probation. Even in such courts, however, most misdemeanor offenses still will be punished by a fine alone. On the other hand, in felony cases, courts rarely rely upon a fine as the sole punishment. Indeed, even if we consider fines that are combined with probation or imprisonment, the percentage of felony cases in which fines are imposed still is likely to be far below fifty percent.

Judicial Review. Fines within the statutory maximum ordinarily will be reversed on appeal only under the most unusual circumstances. The Eighth Amendment to the United States Constitution prohibits "excessive fines," but few fines have been held to violate this prohibition. The equal protection clause of the Fourteenth Amendment imposes a more important constitutional restriction when an offender cannot pay a fine. Magistrates in many communities commonly followed the practice of giving misdemeanor offenders the choice between paying a fine or serving a jail term—"thirty dollars or thirty days" was the common phrasing of the sentence. Of course, if the defendants were too poor to pay the fine, they simply went to jail. In *Tate v. Short*,[34] the Supreme Court relied on the equal protection clause to put an end to this practice. The Court held that a state could not incarcerate an offender in default of the payment of a fine where the offender was unable to pay the fine. A defendant could be imprisoned for his commission of a crime, but the state here was really incarcerating him because he was too poor to pay the fine. In light of *Tate*, magistrate courts today often use an installment plan that permits the indigent defendant to pay his fine over a period of several months.

PROBATION

Probation And Suspended Sentences. The authority to grant probation probably grew out of the traditional practice of judges of "suspending" sentences. The judge would simply fail to set a sentence or set the sentence and fail to direct that it be executed. The offender then would be released. If the offender's subsequent behavior was satisfactory, nothing more would be done. If he had further difficulty with the law, the judge, usually on request of the prosecutor, would revoke his freedom. This time the judge would set a sentence, or reinstate the previous sentence, and the sentence would be executed. The common law authority of a judge to suspend a sentence was questionable, but many judges regularly exercised that authority.

---

34. *Tate v. Short*, 401 U.S. 395, 91 S.Ct. 668, 28 L.Ed.2d 130 (1971).

Since the defendant released on a suspended sentence was not subject to formal supervision, judges tended to suspend sentences only in minor cases. During the late 1800's, courts began to experiment with a combination of a suspended sentence and careful supervision that could be applied to more serious offenses. This new procedure, called probation, soon was authorized by statute and provision was made for appointment of special "probation officers," who could supervise the released offenders. By 1915, thirty-three states authorized some form of probation. Today, all jurisdictions have probation statutes. These statutes control the availability of probation, the conditions that may be imposed upon the offender, and the procedures that must be followed in revoking the probation when the offender has violated those conditions.

With the widespread adoption of probation statutes, the use of the suspended sentences rapidly diminished. Indeed, many courts took the position that they lacked the authority to grant a suspended sentence where the state probation statutes made no reference to the use of suspended sentencing. Since the legislature had specifically authorized only release under supervision (probation), it would be inappropriate to utilize a procedure granting release without supervision (i.e., a suspended sentence). In 1962, the Model Penal Code recommended that states authorize both suspended sentences and probation.[35] Today, about half of the states have statutes authorizing judges to impose suspended sentences in cases where they otherwise could use probation. The provisions vary considerably, however. Some states adhere closely to the Model Code proposal, under which the primary distinction between the suspended sentence and the probation sentence is the lack of regular supervision. The period of suspension is essentially the same as that for probation and the same conditions may be imposed upon the offender. Many of these states describe this sentence as a "conditional discharge" rather than a "suspended sentence."[36] Other states permit a procedure (often described as "delayed sentencing") which is quite different from probation. The suspension is conditioned on a single factor—the offender's non-violation of the law during the term of the suspension—while probation usually is based on a variety of conditions. Also, the period during which the offender must comply with that condition is considerably shorter than the usual term of a probationary sentence. Under either procedure, suspended sentences are used in those cases where probation would otherwise be appropriate, but the offender's rehabilitation is so clear that he would gain no benefit from the assistance and supervision of a probation officer.

Availability Of Probation. States almost without exception deny the court the authority to grant probation to persons convicted of first degree murder. A substantial majority also impose a mandatory imprisonment term for persons

---

35. MPC §301.1.

36. See, e.g., a New York Penal Law §§65.05, 65.10; Illinois Stat. ch. 38, §§1005-6-1, 1005-6-3. Illinois adds a special sentencing procedure called "Disposition of Supervision," under which the defendant pleads guilty, the court defers further proceedings, the defendant is released, and no judgment of conviction is imposed if the defendant complies with conditions imposed by the court. See Illinois Stat. ch. 38, §1005-6-1(c).

charged as habitual offenders.[37] Beyond this point, however, there is little agreement as to what crimes should be non-probationable. Several states add only rape, kidnapping, and attempted murder.[38] Others include a substantial list of crimes. New York, for example, denies probation for almost all class A and B felonies and some class C felonies as well. Its list includes arson, robbery, burglary while armed, various drug offenses (with a special exception for persons who provide material assistance in the prosecution of other drug offenders), assaults with a weapon, bribery relating to the investigation of serious crimes, and conspiracies to commit various serious crimes.[39]

The use of "laundry lists" of non-probational offenses, as in New York, has been criticized by various distinguished reports on sentencing. The American Bar Association, for example, takes the position that the legislature should authorize probation for all offenses.[40] The A.B.A. notes:

> *[N]o legislative definition or classification of offenses can take account of all contingencies. However right it may be to take the gravest view of an offense in general, there will be cases comprehended in the definition where the circumstances were so unusual, or the mitigations so extreme, that a suspended sentence or probation would be proper. We see no reason to distrust the courts upon this matter or to fear that such authority will be abused.*[41]

On the other side, supporters of the New York approach stress that, as the A.B.A. itself recognizes, probation can properly be refused where granting it "would unduly depreciate the seriousness of the offense."[42] The issue presented, they argue, is not simply whether imprisonment is necessary to keep the offender from repeating his offense. If it were, then prison sentences would have been inappropriate for the Watergate defendants, for dozens of corrupt mayors, legislators, and businessmen, and even for some murderers. There is need to deter crime and reinforce community values by indicating that certain crimes will automatically result in imprisonment. Legislative authorization of probation for serious crimes, it is argued, diminishes public belief in the certainty of imprisonment. It suggests

---

37. See p. 352 *infra*.

38. See, e.g., Delaware Code ch. 11, §4204 (all class A felonies); Connecticut General Stat. §53a-29 (same).

39. See New York Penal Law §§60.05, 65.00. Illinois also has an extensive list of non-probational offenses. See Illinois Stat. ch. 38, §1005-5-3 (including murder, attempted murder, aggravated kidnapping, rape, deviate sexual assault, heinous battery, armed robbery, aggravated arson, various drug offenses, and various weapon offenses). California is another state with an extensive list, but it provides that probation shall not be granted for those offenses "except in unusual cases where the interests of justice would best be served if the person is granted probation." California Penal Code §1203(d).

40. See American Bar Association, *Standards Relating to Probation*, §1.1 (Approved Draft 1970). A similar position is taken in the Model Penal Code §6.02, and the National Council of Crime and Delinquency's Model Sentencing Act. The National Advisory Commission, note 1 *supra*, at §5.2, recommends that probation be considered for all offenders except those subject to an extended term as dangerous offenders.

41. A.B.A., *Standards Relating to Sentencing Alternatives and Procedures* (Approved Draft 1968) at p. 66, quoting from the Model Penal Code commentary to MPC §6.02.

42. A.B.A., *Standards Relating to Probation*, note 40 *supra* at §1.3(a)(iii).

to potential offenders that they have a "sporting chance" of escaping with a light sentence (i.e. probation).

So far, available data on the impact of mandatory imprisonment on potential offenders is unclear. Some argue that the offender who is sophisticated enough to be aware that the crime is not probationable is also sophisticated enough to be aware that he probably can use plea-bargaining to circumvent the mandatory imprisonment requirement. Others note that, even with plea bargaining, prohibitions against probation will result in more sentences of imprisonment for serious crimes. Judicial discretion, they note, has produced a system under which, in some communities, "a substantial percentage of individuals convicted of armed robbery (including many repeated offenders) receive no sentence of imprisonment."[43] The current trend appears to be in favor of the New York approach, as numerous states recently have added (or are considering adding) various drug offenses and offenses involving the use of weapons to their lists of non-probational offenses.

The Presumption Favoring Probation. Assuming that a judge is dealing with a crime that is probationable, he ordinarily is given broad discretion in determining whether to impose probation or imprisonment. The earlier probation statutes often were viewed, however, as suggesting that the judge should be somewhat cautious in his use of that discretion. They authorized the use of probation where the judge found that supervised release was in the best interests of the public and the defendant.[44] This suggested to some judges that the burden was on the defendant to show why he deserved probation rather than imprisonment. The judge started by assuming imprisonment was appropriate, and then looked for special circumstances that justified probation. Newer provisions, in contrast, are phrased so as to create a presumption in favor of probation. Thus, the Illinois statute provides:

> Except where specifically prohibited by other provisions of this Code, the court shall impose a sentence of probation ... unless, having regard to the nature and circumstance of the offense, and to the history, character and condition of the offender, the court is of the opinion that:
>
> > (1)   his imprisonment or periodic imprisonment is necessary for the protection of the public; or

---

43. Report of the Twentieth Century Fund Task Force on Criminal Sentencing, *Fair and Certain Punishment,* New York: McGraw-Hill Book Company, 1976, p. 4. The reference here is to a study disclosing that "only 27 percent of convicted armed robbers with substantial prior records received a prison sentence in Los Angeles County during 1970." Ibid. In other jurisdictions in which serious offenses like armed robbery are probationable, the percentage of offenders sentenced to prison is much higher. See, e.g., Michigan Department of Correctons, *Dimensions — 1975 Report,* p. 13-16 (1976) (88% of persons convicted of second degree murder; 78% of persons convicted of armed robbery).

44. The Texas provision, Texas Code of Criminal Procedure art. 42.12, is typical of such provisions: "The judges of the courts of the State of Texas ... when it shall appear to the satisfaction of the court that the ends of justice and the best interests of the public as well as the defendant will be subserved thereby, shall have the power, after conviction or a plea of guilty for any crime or offense, where the maximum punishment assessed against the defendant does not exceed ten years imprisonment, to suspend the imposition of the sentence and may place the defendant on probation ..."

(2) probation or conditional discharge would deprecate the seriousness of the offender's conduct and would be inconsistent with the ends of justice.[45]

Statutes of this type are viewed as suggesting that the judge should exercise his discretion in favor of a liberal use of probation. The judge is to consider probation first and to impose imprisonment only if he finds special circumstances that make probation inappropriate.

Should there be a presumption in favor of probation? The Model Penal Code, the American Bar Association, and the National Advisory Commission all favor the Illinois formula, particularly where the state already has excluded from probation most crimes of violence.[46] They stress the following advantages of probation in cases where the offender does not pose a continued threat to the community: (1) it "maximizes the liberty of the individual" while serving the public interest; (2) it "promotes the rehabilitation of the offender by continuing normal community contacts"; (3) it "avoids the negative and frequently stultifying effects of confinement which often severely and unnecessarily complicate the reintegration of the offender into the community"; (4) it "minimizes the impact of the conviction upon innocent dependents of the offender"; (5) it "greatly reduces the financial costs of an effective correctional system."[47]

Judicial Review. Whether or not a state establishes a presumption in favor of probation, a judge's decision to impose imprisonment rather than probation is unlikely to be reversed on appeal. The traditional view is that judge's decision will be reversed only if "probation was denied for some arbitrary reason wholly unrelated to the statutory standard to be applied in determining whether to grant probation."[48] The statutory standards, as we have seen, tend to be very broad. In many states, the standard is stated as whether probation would serve "the ends of justice and the best interests of the public as well as the defendant." [49] The Illinois standard, quoted previously, refers to the seriousness of the crime and the need for incarceration to protect the public. These standards grant the judge broad discretion to deny probation on the basis of a variety of factors relating to the defendant's background and character or the nature of the crime. Appellate judges will not attempt to second-guess the trial judge's evaluation of obviously relevant factors. The trial judge has had much closer contact with the case. He was in a far better position, for example, to evaluate the offender's current attitudes as they

45. Illinois Stat. ch. 38, §1005-6-1.

46. See MPC §7.01; A.B.A., *Standards Relating to Probation*, note 40 *supra*, at §1.2; National Advisory Commission, note 1 *supra*, at §5.2. As to the offenses excluded from probation in Illinois, see note 39 *supra*.

47. A.B.A. *Standards Relating to Probation*, note 40 *supra*, §1.2. While costs vary throughout the country, probation supervision typically costs less than one-fifth of the cost of housing a prisoner in a maximum or medium security prison. In Michigan, for example, the cost per prisoner exceeds $6,000 while the cost per probationer is less than $600. Moreover, the construction costs in Michigan for new prisons is $35,000 per medium security cell and $50,000 per maximum security cell. Several states, seeking to encourage wider use of probation, have adopted the California program of state subsidization of probation supervision costs (which otherwise are borne by the county).

48. *Whitfield v. United States*, 401 F.2d; 480 (9th Cir. 1968).

49. See note 44 *supra*.

relate to possible rehabilitation. Also, some appellate courts are influenced by the view that probation is granted as a matter of grace. The defendant cannot complain, they argue, simply because the trial judge refused to confer on him a "privilege" to which no offender has any legal "right". [50] Statutory provisions establishing a presumption in favor of probation would seem to override that viewpoint, but whether they produce closer appellate review of the denial of probation remains to be seen.

Length Of Probation. The sentencing judge ordinarily has discretion to set the specific length of the probation term, subject to any limits specified by statute. Older statutes set a minimum and maximum term of probation based on the statutory limits for terms of imprisonment for the same offense. Modern statutes, following the recommendation of the Model Penal Code, make no attempt to tie the term of probation to often lengthy terms of imprisonment. Instead, they set a probation term in the range of five years for felonies and two years for misdemeanors.[51] Proponents of the uniform, shorter maximum argue that the shorter term prevents unnecessary supervision of the probationer and lessens the uncertainty of the probationer and people dealing with him as to his future legal status. Most statutes authorize the court to extend the probation term if some doubt exists as to the probationer's progress toward rehabilitation.

Probation Conditions. Every sentence of probation carries with it certain requirements (called "conditions") relating to the offender's future behavior. The probationer must agree to these conditions, and his failure to comply with them can result in the revocation of his probation (a subject we will discuss later in this chapter). Probation conditions fall into two categories. First, there are those conditions required by state law to be included in every probation agreement. These conditions typically are few and simple. In Illinois, for example, the required conditions are: (1) that the probationer "not violate any criminal statute of any jurisdiction"; (2) that he report to his probation officer as directed by the court; and (3) that he "refrain from possessing a firearm or other dangerous item."[52] Many jurisdictions also include a standard condition that the probationer not leave the state without the permission of his probation officer.

The second group of probation conditions are those conditions imposed by the judge at his discretion. The statutes usually authorize the court to impose such conditions "as it deems reasonably necessary to insure that the defendant will lead a law-abiding life or to assist him to do so."[53] The statutes usually also list a series of the more common conditions that may be suitable for this purpose. Some are

---

50. This view was expressed by the Supreme Court in *Burns v. United States,* 287 U.S. 216, 220, 53 S.Ct. 154, 77 L.Ed. 266 (1932): "Probation is thus conferred as a privilege and cannot be demanded as a right. It is a matter of favor, not of contract. There is no requirement that it be granted on a specified showing."

51. MPC §301.2. See, e.g., Illinois Stat. ch. 38, §1005-6-2; New York Penal Code §65.00 (both using maximum terms that vary with the felony level, but do not exceed 5 years for the higher class felonies).

52. Illinois Stat. ch. 38, §1005-6-3.

53. New York Penal Code §65.10.

quite general (e.g., "avoid injurious or vicious habits"), but most involve specific obligations (e.g., make restitution to the victim). A typical statutory listing of permissible conditions is set forth below.[54] The list is not exclusive. A court may include other provisions as it deems appropriate.

Although the court's authority in fixing conditions is quite broad, there are some limits. Appellate courts have invalidated conditions as not being reasonably related to the rehabilitation of the offender. A Michigan court struck down a condition that prohibited the offender from continuing to play college basketball.[55] A Virginia court held invalid an attempt to banish the offender from the county, and a Washington court rejected a condition requiring a lower echelon drug dealer to reveal her sources in open court where that condition could have endangered her life.[56]

Probation conditions also have been rejected where they unduly infringe on the offender's constitutional rights, but it is recognized that a probationer can be required to relinquish those rights to some extent. A condition of probation forbidding the offender, a fanatical opponent of taxation, to speak, write, or circulate materials on that subject was held to violate the First Amendment guarantee of free speech.[57] On the other hand, using a legal standard similar to that applied to probation conditions, courts have upheld parole and commutation conditions that restrict First Amendment rights. Thus, they accepted conditions denying Philip and Daniel Berrigan the right to travel to North Vietnam, and forbidding Jimmy

---

54. New York Penal Code §65.10 lists the following permissible conditions:
    (a) Avoid injurious or vicious habits;
    (b) Refrain from frequenting unlawful or disreputable places or consorting with disreputable persons;
    (c) Work faithfully at a suitable employment or faithfully pursue a course of study or of vocational training that will equip him for suitable employment;
    (d) Undergo available medical or psychiatric treatment and remain in a specified institution, when required for that purpose;
    (e) Support his dependents and meet other family responsibilities;
    (f) Make restitution of the fruits of his offense or make reparation, in an amount he can afford to pay, for the loss or damage caused thereby. When restitution or reparation is a condition of the sentence, the court shall fix the amount thereof and the manner of performance.
    (g) If a person under the age of twenty-one years, (i) reside with his parents or in a suitable foster home or hostel as referred to in section two hundred forty-four of the executive law, (ii) attend school, (iii) spend such part of the period of the sentence as the court may direct, but not exceeding two years, in a facility made available by the division for youth pursuant to subdivision two of section five hundred two of the executive law, provided that admission to such facility may be made only with the prior consent of the division for youth, (iv) attend a nonresidential program for such hours and pursuant to a schedule prescribed by the court as suitable for a program of rehabilitation of youth, (v) contribute to his own support in any home, foster home or hostel;
    (h) Post a bond or other security for the performance of any or all conditions imposed;
    (i) Satisfy any other conditions reasonably related to his rehabilitation.
    Special additional conditions are set for narcotics addicts.
55. *People v. Higgins,* 22 Mich.App. 479, 177 N.W.2d 716 (1970).
56. *Loving v. Commonwealth,* 206 Va. 924, 147 S.E.2d 78 (1966); *State v. Langford,* 12 Wash.App. 228, 529 P.2d 839 (1974).
57. *Porth v. Templar,* 453 F.2d 330 (10th Cir. 1971).

Hoffa from participating in union activities for several years.[58] The courts are presently split over the constitutionality of a condition requiring the probationer to submit to searches by police officers at any time. A few courts have invalidated such a condition on the grounds that it was unconstitutionally coerced.[59] Various other courts have upheld blanket search provisions on the grounds that the "conditional nature" of probation and the "legitimate demands" of the probation process justify the loss of some traditional Fourth Amendment freedoms.[60]

Probation Combined With Incarceration.   Many jurisdictions authorize the judge to require, as a condition of probation, that the probationer spend a short period of time in jail. In some cases, the offender will serve his jail time before he returns to the community under probation supervision. In others, he will be released first and serve his time on weekends. The federal system uses a similar procedure involving a more substantial jail sentence. The judges impose a "split sentence" under which the probationer is imprisoned for a period up to six months and then is released on probation.[61] In 1974, approximately ten percent of the federal defendants committed to federal institutions were sentenced to a "split sentence" instead of straight incarceration.[62] In California, the combination of probation and jail sentence has been used in almost half of all cases in which probation has been granted. [63]

A recent innovation, "shock probation," provides a somewhat controversial form of probation/incarceration.[64] Under the pioneer Ohio statute, "shock probation" is available only when the offender has been denied probation and sentenced to imprisonment in one of the state correctional facilities (usually a state prison). When the offender has been incarcerated between thirty and sixty days, he may petition the sentencing court for suspension of the remainder of his prison sentence and the imposition of probation. The court may then grant or deny probation within its discretion. As the name suggests, shock probation can be used to give an offender a "stronger taste" of incarceration than a predetermined jail term; under shock probation, the offender is sent to a state institution without any certainty that he will be released on probation. Subsequent statistical analysis of "shock probation" in Ohio reveals that only 15% of 7,000 offenders granted probation under this program since 1972 have returned to prison because of further criminality or a probation violation. [65]

---

58.   *Berrigan v. Sigler,* 358 F.Supp. 130 (D.D.C. 1973); *Hoffa v. Saxbe,* 378 F.Supp. 1221 (D.D.C. 1974).

59.   *Tamez v. State,* 534 S.W.2d 686 (Tex.Cr.App. 1976); *People v. Peterson,* 62 Mich.App. 258, 233 N.W.2d 250 (1975); *United States v. Consualo-Gomez,* 521 F.2d 259 (9th Cir. 1975).

60.   *People v. Mason,* 5 Cal.3d 759, 97 Cal.Rptr. 302, 488 P.2d 630 (1971); *Himmage v. State,* 88 Nev. 296, 496 P.2d 763 (1972); *State v. Schlosser,* 202 N.W.2d 136 (N.D. 1972).

61.   18 United States Code §3651.

62.   *Sourcebook of Criminal Justice Statistics — 1976,* note 1, p. 1 *supra,* at p. 709.

63.   G. Killinger, H. Kerper, and P. Cromwell, *Probation and Parole In The Criminal Justice System,* St. Paul, Minn.: West Publishing Company, 1976, p. 76.

64.   Indiana Stat. §9-2209; Kentucky Revised Stat. §439.265; Ohio Code §2947.061.

65.   See J. Shoemaker and A. Harris, *Shock Treatment In Ohio—Pro And Con,* 50 State Government 2 (1977).

IMPRISONMENT

The term imprisonment, as we will use it, refers to incarceration in jails, prisons, prison farms, road camps, or any other type of correctional institution. As we saw in Chapter Four, imprisonment as a form of punishment is an American invention.[66] Contrary to popular impression, it is not the most common form of punishment, even for felonies. In discussing the "sieve effect" of the criminal justice process in Chapter Eight, we estimated that only one-third of the convicted felons in our "typical" jurisdiction would be sentenced to prison. The percentage might be higher in states with a long list of non-probationable offenses, but the majority of the felons would still be placed on probation.[67] We do not mean to suggest, of course, that the number of persons sentenced to imprisonment is insubstantial. As of 1972, there were almost 200,000 persons incarcerated in state and federal prisons and an additional 75,000 serving sentences in jails. The figures are probably higher today.[68]

Choosing the Term of Imprisonment. As we have seen, the choice between imposing imprisonment and imposing probation sometimes lies with the sentencing judge, and sometimes is determined by the legislature. We are concerned here with the decision made after imprisonment has been selected as the appropriate sanction—the decision as to the term of the imprisonment. The amount of discretion granted to the judge in setting the term of the imprisonment will vary with the level of the offense. In misdemeanor cases, the judge is given discretion to set the exact length of the jail term, provided it does not exceed a maximum specified by statute. The statutory maximum will vary with the level of the misdemeanor. As in the case of felonies, misdemeanors commonly are divided into several classes, with each class carrying its own maximum penalty. In New York, for example, the maximum term is one year for a class A misdemeanor, three months for a class B misdemeanor, and fifteen days for a violation.[69] The judge has authority to set a fixed term at any point between one day in jail and the statutory maximum for the misdemeanor for which he is sentencing. Moreover, in almost all states, the sentence set by the judge will be the sentence actually served by the defendant. Credits for "good time," which play a significant role in reducing felony sentences, do not apply to misdemeanors. If the judge sets the sentence at "thirty days in jail," the defendant will serve a full thirty days. Usually, misdemeanor jail sentences are quite short. Ordinarily jails have a limited capacity, if any, to provide the training and work programs needed for persons sentenced to a term of

---

66. See p. 62 *supra.*

67. See pp. 341-42 *supra.* Our estimate does not include defendants sentenced to a short jail term combined with probation. This additional group might raise the percentage of felony defendants sentenced to some form of incarceration above the fifty percent level.

68. The statistics for 1972 come from the *Sourcebook of Criminal Justice Statistics—1976,* note 1, p. 1 *supra,* at p. 632, 686. A more recent estimate puts the prison population as approximately 250,000. See 11 Corrections Magazine 10 (1976).

69. See New York Penal Code §70.15. As in the case of felonies, some states do not use penalty classes, but specify the maximum sentence for each crime in the code provision defining the crime. See p. 88 *supra.* Also, as noted at p. 76 *supra,* several states have a special category of misdemeanors for which the only sentence is a fine.

several months. In some jurisdictions, county farms or camps are available for persons receiving long misdemeanor sentences.

The judge's role in setting the length of the sentence in felony cases will depend in part on whether the state utilizes indeterminate or determinate sentences.[70] Indeterminate sentences provide for a maximum term, a minimum term, and parole board authority to release the prisoner on parole at any point between the minimum and maximum. Determinate sentences provide for a fixed term without any opportunity for early parole at the discretion of a parole board. Under either determinate or indeterminate sentencing, the court may have substantial or quite limited discretion in setting the length of the sentence. The nature of the judge's determinations under the two forms of sentencing is sufficiently different, however, to require separate consideration of each.

Indeterminate Sentencing.   Indeterminate sentencing currently is used in over forty states, but each state varies in the role that they assign to the judge in setting the minimum and maximum sentences. Some bind the judge to specific maximums and minimums set by statute, while others give him discretionary authority to set his own maximum and minimum terms within certain limits set by the statute. Where discretion is granted, some states leave the judge's authority very flexible, while others impose restrictions as to the relationship of the minimum and maximum sentences. The only common element in the sentencing structure of all of these states is the requirement of some degree of indeterminacy in the sentence.

Starting with the maximum sentence, we find that all states set a statutory maximum for each class of felony. Several states require that the judge impose exactly that maximum, but others grant him discretion to select a lower maximum. States denying judicial discretion take the position that the statutory maximum is the appropriate term for those offenders whose behavior in prison does not suggest that they are ready for parole. The test for release before that maximum is served, they believe, should be whether the individual has made some progress toward rehabilitation. Since the trial judge cannot be certain that the prisoner will make such progress, he should not be allowed to reduce the statutory maximum. Supporters of this position note that, in some cases, the prisoner may even grow more dangerous in prison. Leaving the statutory maximum intact will ensure that such prisoners remain incarcerated as long as the law will allow.

States granting the judge authority to reduce the maximum below that set in the statute take a considerably different view of the function of the statutory maximum. They stress that the maximum punishment should not exceed that which is appropriate for the offense as it was committed in the particular case. The statutory maximum does not always meet this limitation because the legislature tends to set it with the most heinous version of the crime in mind. An armed robber who uses a fake pistol cannot appropriately be sentenced to a statutory maximum set for all armed robbers, including the person who uses a loaded revolver. Supporters of judicial discretion also note that the maximums set in American indeterminate sentencing statutes are extraordinarily high as compared to the

---

70. See pp. 91-97 *supra* discussing determinate, indeterminate, and presumptive-determinate sentencing.

sentences provided in other countries. As a matter of practice, almost all prisoners are paroled long before their maximum terms are served. In state after state, 85-95% of all prisoners are paroled in less than five years even though over 60% are sentenced to terms substantially in excess of five years.[71] If the judge is given discretion to set the maximum below the statutory maximum, he may set a more realistic maximum in light of actual parole practices.

Turning to the judge's discretion in setting the minimum term, we find several variations. Most states permit the court to set its own minimum sentence. However, they differ initially as to how low that sentence may be. A majority of the states require a minimum of at least one year for all felonies. A few states do not set any limit, permitting the minimum to start, at least theoretically, at one day. As a practical matter, however, the limit in these states usually is at least several months because the parole board will not consider parole before then.[72] Where there either is no statutory limit or the limit is one year, the judge has considerable flexibility in setting the minimum term. Of course, he cannot go below the statutory minimum. However, he can leave the minimum at that level or he can set it at a slightly or substantially higher level. There may be some limit on the extent to which he may raise the minimum, but that limit still should provide considerable leeway. In most jurisdictions, he simply may not raise the minimum above a certain portion of the maximum sentence. The American Bar Association has recommended that the minimum sentence never exceed one-third of the maximum, but some states permit a minimum as high as two-thirds of the maximum.[73] Several apparently do not impose any limit on the minimum, so long as some indeterminacy exists. In these states judges occasionally set minimums that are fairly close to the maximum (e.g., a sentence of nine years minimum and ten years maximum).[74]

In recent years, there has been a movement toward "mandatory minimum" statutes that limit the judge's discretion to keep a low minimum. These statutes impose required minimum sentences that are substantially in excess of the traditional one year statutory minimum. In some cases the mandatory minimums are for three or four years, but others are for periods in excess of even ten years.[75]

---

71. See the National Advisory Commission's *Report on Corrections*, note 1 *supra*, at p. 143, 150-53. The *Report* recommends a maximum term of no more than five years of all felons not found to be dangerous. See also the A.B.A. Standard quoted at note 90 *infra*.

72. Thus, in the state of Washington, which has no minimum for most offenses, the parole board is given six months before they are required to set as the earliest possible parole date. See Washington Revised Code §§9.95.010, 9.95.040.

73. See American Bar Association, *Standards Relating To Sentencing Alternatives and Procedures*, §3.2(c)(iii) (Approved Draft 1968).

74. In Michigan, although the statute did not specify a particular gap between the minimum and maximum, the Court held that it was inconsistent with the objectives of indeterminate sentencing for the minimum to be greater than two-thirds of the maximum. See *People v. Tanner*, 387 Mich. 683, 199 N.W.2d 202 (1972). Other states without provisions requiring a specified gap have held only that the minimum and maximum cannot be identical. See *State v. Janiec*, 25 N.J.Super 197, 95 A.2d 762 (1953); *People v. King*, 1 Ill.2d 496, 116 N.E.2d 623 (1953) (upholding a sentence of 199 years to life).

75. New York, for example, imposes a mandatory minimum of 15 years for certain class A felonies, including first degree kidnapping, first degree arson, attempted murder, and sale of drugs. See New York Penal Code §70.00.

Some states impose substantial mandatory minimums for all of their more serious offenses. Others use it for specific crimes, most noteably drug sales and offenses involving the use of a weapon. Supporters of substantial mandatory minimums contend that there is no need for judicial discretion to impose lower minimum sentences where dangerous crimes are involved. Opponents argue that dangerous crimes do not always involve dangerous offenders. In appropriate cases, the individual may offer a true potential for a successful return to society after only one or two years of prison. If the judge feels that a particular defendant offers that potential, his hands should not be tied by a high, legislatively imposed minimum sentence. Opponents of mandatory minimums also argue that mandatory minimums commonly are circumvented through plea bargaining, and that only persons convicted at trial actually are forced to serve those minimum terms.

In several states, the judge is given no discretion over the minimum. In some, a specified minimum is set by statute for each offense, and the judge may not raise it. In others, the minimum automatically is set at a particular portion (e.g., one-third) of the maximum selected by the judge. In these states, the sentence usually does not even announce a minimum as such. The court sets a single term, which serves as the maximum, and the state law then provides that the defendant will be eligible for parole after serving the specified portion of that term.[76]

When the various alternatives are combined, we find basically four different structures for indeterminate sentencing: (1) both maximum and minimum terms are set by statute allowing the judge no discretion;[77] (2) the judge has discretion to set both the maximum and minimum terms, but may not violate the upper and lower limits set by statute;[78] (3) the maximum term is set by statute, but the judge has discretion to set the minimum within limits specified by statute;[79] (4) the judge has discretion to set the maximum within a statutory upper limit, but the minimum term is set by statute. [80] A substantial majority of the states appear to follow the second alternative. Their statutory structures still vary considerably, however, due to differences in their treatment of other key elements, such as

---

76. These states are sometimes described as using a "determinate" sentencing structure, but they do not have true determinate sentencing since the parole eligibility fixes a minimum sentence. Determinate sentencing usually is used to describe a sentencing structure that does not include a substantial discretionary parole authority.

77. Washington appears to be the only state that still retains this structure. See Washington Revised Code §§9.95.010, 9.95.040.

78. Included in this category are New York, New Jersey, Pennsylvania, and the current federal sentencing structure.

79. Michigan and Ohio both use this structure. See Michigan Compiled Laws §769.8 and Ohio Revised Code §2929.11. However, Ohio generally limits the judge to a choice among three statutorily specified minimum sentences, while Michigan provides considerable discretion in setting the minimum sentence.

80. This category includes states, such as Alabama, Delaware, and Georgia, in which the judge sets a maximum sentence and the minimum sentence is then set automatically by law. It also includes states, such as Texas, where the statute sets a minimum for each punishment category, and the judge (or the jury) sets the maximum. See Texas Penal Code §§12.32-12.34 and Texas Code of Criminal Procedure, art. 42.09.

substantial mandatory minimums and the degree of indeterminacy required between the minimum and maximum.

Determinate Felony Sentencing.   As we saw in Chapter Five, there has been a strong movement in recent years toward determinate sentencing.[81] Indeed, as this book goes into print, several of the states that we have cited as illustrating different indeterminate sentencing structures are seriously considering abandoning indeterminate sentencing in favor of determinate sentencing. While a major objective of determinate sentencing is to eliminate discretion and thereby ensure greater uniformity in sentencing, several of the new state provisions concentrate primarily on eliminating parole board discretion.[82] The judge retains considerable discretion in setting the single, fixed term of imprisonment. In Maine, for example, the court is merely directed to set a term of imprisonment that does not exceed twenty years for a class A crime, ten years for a class B crime, and five years for a class C crime.[83] The Illinois determinate sentencing statute provides a narrower range for its lower level felonies, but it permits the judge to set a fixed term anywhere within the range of 6-30 years and 4-15 years for its two highest categories of felonies (other than murder). Illinois does seek, however, to guide the judge's exercise of discretion by requiring consideration of specified mitigating factors and aggravating factors.[84]

Indiana utilizes a presumptive-determinate sentencing structure giving the judge so much discretion that it has been described as "presumptive sentencing as wide [open] as the prairie."[85] California, on the other hand, also uses a presumptive-determinate structure, and gives the judge very little discretion. The California statute, described previously,[86] requires the judge to accept the legislative

---

81.   See pp. 94-97 *supra*. Determinate sentencing has been adopted in Arizona, California, Indiana, Illinois, Maryland, and New Mexico.

82.   It should be noted that the states adopting determinate sentencing have varied in their treatment of parole discretion. Maine abolishes all discretionary parole but authorizes the Department of Corrections to petition the court for "resentencing" which would enable it to release a prisoner before he has completed his full term. See Maine Revised Stat., tit. 34, §1154. In Indiana the parole board's function is limited largely to computing good time allowances. Indiana Code §35-50-1-1. In California, the parole board, converted into a Community Release Board, still retains special discretionary authority for several offenses that automatically carry terms of life imprisonment with the possibility of parole. See note 22 at p.   *supra*. Arizona retains parole for first offenders after they have served one-half of the presumptive sentence, but repeat offenders must serve the full sentence. See Arizona Revised Stat. §13-704, 13-411.

83.   Maine Revised Stat., tit. 34, §1252.

84.   The Illinois ranges for determinate sentences for offenses other than murder are: class X felony (6-30 years); class 1 felony (4-15 years); class 2 felony (3-7 years); class 3 felony (2-5 years); class 4 felony (1-3 years). Additional extended terms are available as discussed in note 25 at p.   *supra*. Typical mitigating circumstances are: (1) the fact that defendant's conduct "neither caused nor threatened serious harm to others"; (2) the defendant's criminal conduct was "induced or facilitated by" another person; (3) the defendant's criminal conduct was the result of circumstances unlikely to recur. Aggravating circumstances include a prior record of criminal activity, receipt of compensation for committing the crime, and the fact that the conduct caused or threatened serious harm. See Illinois Stat. ch. 38, §§1005-5-3.1, 1005-5-3.2, 1005-8-1.

85.   See M. Zalman, *The Rise and Fall Of The Indeterminate Sentence,* 24 Wayne Law Review 857, 875 (1978). The Indiana range is somewhat more extensive than that in Illinois.

86.   See pp. 95-96 *supra*.

specified presumptive sentence unless he finds aggravating or mitigating circumstances. Even then, only one year will be added to or subtracted from the presumptive sentence. Enhancements can add several more years, but the judge here merely determines whether the specified factors justifying the enhancement (e.g., use of a firearm) were present. In sum, the contrast between California, Illinois, Maine, and Indiana shows that determinate sentencing, like indeterminate sentencing, can cover a wide spectrum as to the discretion granted the judge in setting the length of imprisonment.

Habitual Offender Statutes. Most states have statutes (commonly called "habitual offender" or "recidivist" statutes) that provide for increased prison sentences for repeat offenders. These statutes rest on the theory that persons who have repeatedly demonstrated their inability to comply with the law are more likely to commit crimes again and therefore should be incapacitated for a longer period of time than the first offender. The variation among these statutes is immense. Some apply only to persons committing crimes of violence who have committed previous crimes of violence. Others apply to all types of felonies. Some become applicable on the second offense, while others are triggered by a third or fourth offense. Some count only those past offenses for which the defendant served a prison term. Many prohibit probation for the habitual offender, while others simply provide for a longer prison term if the judge imposes a sentence of imprisonment. Some deal only with the minimum sentence, imposing a substantial mandatory minimum. Others control the maximum and minimum sentence (or the single determinate sentence). The increased sentence under some statutes is measured by the crime currently committed (e.g., one-half of the maximum for that crime is added). Other statutes provide for an automatic life term for third or fourth offender without regard to the usual maximum for the current offense. In most states, the extended term must be imposed by the court if the statute applies, but others grant the judge discretion not to impose that term.[87]

The current state of the habitual offender laws in this country has been widely condemned. Studies show that these statutes are used primarily in plea negotiations. Prosecutors encourage (some say "coerce") defendants to plead guilty to the current offense in exchange for a withdrawal of the habitual offender

---

87. A survey of the various state habitual offender provisions is contained in L. Sleffel, *The Law and The Dangerous Criminal*, Lexington, Mass.: Lexington Books, 1977, pp. 1-28. The procedures used under habitual offender provisions tend to be somewhat less varied. Initially, the prosecutor must charge the defendant as a habitual criminal. In some states this is done in the information or indictment charging the current offense, while others use a supplemental information or indictment. Under either procedure, the defendant should be aware of the pending habitual offender charge before he pleads guilty or is tried on the current offense. If he goes to trial, the jury should not be aware of the habitual offender charge when they try the case. A special problem is presented, however, in states using jury sentencing. In *Spencer v. Texas*, 385 U.S. 554, 87 S.Ct. 648, 17 L.Ed.2d 606 (1967), the Supreme Court held that it did not violate due process to present the second offender charge to a sentencing jury at the same time that it determined guilt. Ordinarily, however, jury sentencing states will split the two issues; the jury first determines guilt, and then is informed of the habitual offender charge and asked to set the sentence in light of that charge. Whether the sentencing is by jury or judge, the defendant only can be sentenced as a habitual offender after the prosecution has established that he falls within the statute. Ordinarily, introduction of the official record of the prior convictions is all that is needed.

charge. [88] The American Bar Association has recommended that continued use of extended term provisions be tied to several reforms. Section 2.5 of its *Standards Relating to Sentencing Alternatives and Procedures* provides:

> As stated in section 21.(d), many sentences authorized by statute in this country are, by comparison to other countries and in terms of the needs of the public, excessively long for the vast majority of cases. Their length is undoubtedly the product of concern for protection against the most exceptional cases, most notably the particularly dangerous offender and the professional criminal. It would be more desirable for the penal code to differentiate explicitly between most offenders and such exceptional cases, by providing lower, more realistic sentences for the former and authorizing a special term for the latter. The Advisory Committee would endorse a special term in such a context, but only on the following assumptions:
>
> > (i) Provision for such a special term will be accompanied by a substantial and general reduction of the terms available for most offenders; and
> >
> > (ii) Adequate criteria will be developed and stated in the enabling legislation which carefully delineate the type of offender on whom such a special term can be imposed;[89] and
> >
> > (iii) Precautions will be taken, such as by the requirement of procedures which assure the adequate development of information about the offender and by provision for appellate review of the sentence, to assure that such a special term will not be imposed in cases where it is not warranted; and
> >
> > (iv) The sentence authorized in such cases will be structured in accordance with the principles reflected in section 3.1(c) [providing for judicial discretion and an 'outside limit for extreme cases' of a 25 year maximum term]
> > . . . . [90]

Youthful Offenders.   Many states have special provisions for sentencing "youthful offenders," commonly defined as persons under the age of twenty-one.[91] These

---

88. In *Bordenkircher v. Hayes,* 434 U.S. 357, 98 S.Ct. 663, 54 L.Ed.2d 604 (1978), the Supreme Court upheld this practice.

89. Several jurisdictions have started in this direction with "dangerous offender" provisions. See, e.g., 18 United States Code §3575; New York Penal Code §70.10. The federal provision is aimed at dangerous offenders generally and is not limited to habitual offenders. The court must find, based on the defendant's past and current behavior, that an extended term is needed to protect the public and that he falls in one of three categories:

    1. The defendant has two previous convictions for offenses punishable by death or imprisonment for more than one year, and was imprisoned for at least one of these offenses, and the present offense was committed within five years of a previous offense or within five years of his release from imprisonment for a previous offense.

    2. The present offense was part of a pattern of criminal conduct 'which constituted a substantial source of his income, and in which he manifested special skill or expertise.'

    3. The present felony involved a conspiracy with three or more other persons, and the defendant did, or agreed to do, one of the following: "initiate, organize, plan, finance, direct, manage, or supervise all or part of such conspiracy or conduct, or give or receive a bribe or use force as all or part of such conduct." L. Sleffel, note 50 *supra* at p. 23.

90. See A.B.A. Standards note 41 *supra* at §2.5. The standards also requested certain procedural reform in sentence hearings.

91. See S. Rubin, note 7 *supra*, at p. 495. There is considerable variation, however, as to the applicable age. New York imposes a limit of 19 at the time the offense was committed. See New York Criminal Procedure Law §720.10. The Federal Youth Corrections Act, 18 United States Code §§5005-5024 applies to offenders under the age of 22, but also permits the court to include "young adults" between the ages of 22 and 25. See 18 United States Code §4209.

statutes provide for imprisonment in special institutions and permit substantially earlier release than would be provided under the usual determinate or indeterminate sentence for the offense involved. Ordinarily, they may be used at the discretion of the court. If the judge finds that the offender "will not derive benefit from treatment" as a youthful offender, he may sentence him as an adult.[92] If the defendant is sentenced as a youthful offender, a special youth authority will determine the point of his release. There is no mandatory minimum sentence and he may be released within a short period. In most states, he must be released before he reaches a certain age (e.g., twenty-five). Under some state statutes, it is possible that the youthful offender will remain incarcerated longer than he would have if sentenced as an adult, but such cases are rare. In many jurisdictions, youthful offenders convicted of certain crimes may later have the record of their conviction expunged if they have not been convicted of other crimes.[93]

Concurrent and Consecutive Sentences.   As we saw in Chapter Eleven, a single indictment or information can charge the defendant with the commission of several separate crimes.[94] If the defendant then is convicted for the separate crimes, he will be sentenced individually on each crime. When the individual sentences imposed are imprisonment, the terms for each sentence can run *concurrently* or *consecutively*. Concurrent sentencing means that the terms will be served simultaneously. Consecutive sentencing means that the terms must be served in sequence, one following the other. Consider, for example, the case of a defendant charged with burglarizing two gasoline stations and robbing the attendant at another. Assume that the sentences on the burglaries are 2-10 years and the sentence on the robbery is 3-20 years. If the sentences are to be served concurrently, the defendant will be serving his burglary sentences at the same time that he is serving his robbery sentence. At the end of three years, when he is eligible for parole on the robbery sentence, he will also have served the minimum sentence on each of the burglary sentences. Basically, the defendant's sentence will have been the highest of the three concurrent sentences, the 3-20 years for robbery. The parole board will be aware of the other convictions, however, and these convictions may make it more reluctant to grant parole.

If the sentences are imposed consecutively, the defendant's situation will be quite different. He will not be eligible for parole at the end of three years. He must serve at least four more years to complete the two year minimums on each of the two burglaries. Also, his maximum term is not twenty years, but forty (20+10+10). The defendant in our hypothetical could not have been charged as a habitual offender; those statutes apply only to persons who have been previously convicted, not to persons charged with several offenses at the same time. Nevertheless, by using consecutive sentences, the court could impose the same kind of extended term that would be available under a habitual offender statute.

---

92.   See, e.g., 18 United States Code §4209.

93.   See pp. 383-84 *infra*.

94.   See p. 285 *supra*.

A 1974 study of state sentencing provisions reported that almost all states permit consecutive sentencing under some circumstances.[95] Several allow it only for certain crimes (e.g., jail break). Over forty states allow consecutive sentencing for almost all crimes.[96] Almost all of those states grant the judge discretion to impose either consecutive or concurrent sentences. Many, however, also include a provision suggesting that sentences ordinarily will be concurrent (sometimes described as a legislative presumption in favor of concurrent sentencing). This position is in accord with the recommendations of various advisory groups on sentencing policies.[97] In most jurisdictions, the court also has discretion to make the term imposed for a current conviction run concurrently with the remaining term of a previous conviction. This authority often is used where defendant's conviction results in a parole violation and recommitment to serve the remainder of a prior sentence. In some instances, a sentence in one jurisdiction may run concurrently with a sentence being served in another jurisdiction.

THE DILEMMA OF DISCRETION

As we have seen, judges usually have substantial discretion in sentencing. Most states give them considerable leeway in choosing between probation and imprisonment, in setting the term of imprisonment under either an indeterminate or determinate sentencing structure, in deciding whether a young offender will be given the special benefits of a youthful offender statute, and in determining whether to impose consecutive or concurrent sentences for multiple convictions. In some jurisdictions, judges even have the final say as to whether an extended term will be imposed under a habitual offender charge. Judicial discretion in sentencing is one of the most hotly debated subjects in the criminal justice field today. Few experts are satisfied with the present system, but there is a sharp division among the critics as to what reforms are needed. Some argue that extensive judicial discretion is basically correct, but minor modifications would be valuable so as to more carefully control the exercise of that discretion. Others argue that the discretion must be taken away from the judges and either placed elsewhere or largely eliminated from the sentencing process. To fully appreciate the issues in this crucial debate, one most have some answers to at least three questions. Why did we give judges extensive sentencing discretion in the first place? What have been the advantages and disadvantages of judicial discretion? What alternatives are available, and what are their advantages and disadvantages? After lengthy discussions, experts remain in disagreement as to the

95. R. Hand and R. Singer, *Sentencing Computation Laws and Practice,* Washington, D.C.: American Bar Association Commission on Correctional Facilities, 1974.

96. The New York provision is typical. It allows consecutive sentencing for all crimes unless the offenses involved were "committed through a single act or omission or through an act or omission which in itself constituted one of the offenses and also was a material element of the other." New York Penal Code §70.25.

97. Both the National Advisory Commission, note 1 *supra,* and the A.B.A., note 41 *supra,* urge that the use of consecutive sentences be limited to cases in which the court finds substantial indication that the maximum sentence for the most severe offense is not long enough to protect the public safety.

appropriate responses to these questions. We will attempt merely to summarize some of the more substantial points they have made.

Individualizing Sentences: The Need For Discretion. We noted in Chapter Five that the movement toward indeterminate sentences (and judicial discretion) reflected an interest in accommodating the several objectives of punishment. Indeterminate sentencing was designed to achieve rehabilitation as well as deterrence, to avoid needless incapacitation while still obtaining a punishment sufficient to serve the legitimate needs of retribution.[98] The development of probation reflected these same concerns, although the primary emphasis here clearly was on rehabilitation. The overall objective of our sentencing philosophy was to make the punishment fit the offender as well as the offense. This was an objective that required individualized sentencing based upon the facts of the individual case. It was an objective that lent itself naturally to broad judicial discretion.

There are those today who contend that our emphasis on rehabilitation has been misplaced—not because it is an inappropriate goal, but because it remains largely beyond our capacity. Yet even if this controversial premise is accepted, the need for individualized sentencing hardly disappears. If one looks to incapacitation, deterrence, or even retribution, there is still need for individualization. Let us consider, for example, five cases of kidnapping. No. 1 is a woman whose baby died, and who took another woman's baby from the hospital. No. 2 is a young man whose girl-friend said she was breaking up with him. He put her in a car and drove her around for 24 hours trying to persuade her to change her mind, while her frantic parents tried to locate them and the girl did everything she could to get away. No. 3 is a divorced man who took his own child from its mother who had legal custody and refused to tell the mother where the child was. No. 4 is a kidnapper for ransom who kept a young woman buried in a box fitted with air tubes for breathing in order to make it impossible for searchers to find her, and who demanded $200,000 from her wealthy father. No. 5 is a woman accomplice of the kidnapper for ransom. She assisted in the kidnapping because she was in love with the kidnapper and was also threatened by him. She did everything she could to keep the kidnapped girl alive when it was possible for her to do so.

The offense charged in each of our five cases is identical— kidnapping. The legislature has drawn some general distinctions in defining that crime, but it can hardly take into consideration all of the factors that distinguish one kidnapping from another and one person's participation from that of his accomplice. Even if one were concerned only with retribution, somebody must be given authority to distinguish between these five cases. The evil in each is hardly equivalent to the others even though the same crime is involved. A sanction as severe as imprisonment should not be imposed without drawing more careful lines that relate to our retribution objective. Of course, once we add consideration of deterrence and some degree of rehabilitation, we must consider more factors and there is even greater need for individualization. In sum, individualization probably would not be as essential if we had fewer punishment objectives and they did not so frequently clash, but even if we shifted our focus so that deterrence or retribtuion

---

98.   See pp. 93-94 *supra.*

became the dominant theme — as some say we should—a certain amount of individualization (and hence discretion) would still be needed.

Factors Affecting Judicial Discretion.   How in fact have judges utilized the discretion they have received? Have they emphasized factors that relate to the several goals of punishment? Most experts believe that they have done so, although many would say that there has been too much emphasis on one factor or another. While the weight given to particular factors varies with the judge, almost all judges have tended to look to the same basic elements. The first, and probably the most signficant, is the seriousness of the offense as it was carried out. As we saw in our five kidnapping cases, the gravity of the actor's wrongdoing is not always revealed simply by the punishment category in which the legislature places the particular crime. A sentencing court will want to know if the case involved special aggravating circumstances that made the defendant's conduct more serious than that of other offenders who commit the same crime. Though a violent act is not a formal element of the crime charged, did the defendant here actually threaten harm to his victim? Did he involve minors in the commission of the crime? Did he pick upon a victim who was particularly vulnerable? Did the planning, sophistication or professionalism of the crime indicate premeditation? On the other side, the court also will want to know if the case involved special mitigating factors that suggest a lower sentence: the defendant may have been a passive participant or may have played a minor role in committing the crime; the defendant may have exercised special caution to avoid harming the victim; the defendant may have acted under the influence of alcohol or extreme emotional stress; or the victim may have been an initiator or provoker of the incident. Our list of mitigating and aggravating factors is not complete, but only illustrative. As we have noted, several of the recently adopted determinate sentencing provisions include lists of specific aggravating and mitigating factors to be considered by the judge.[99]

Judges also will look to the character and background of the defendant. Has he been convicted of previous offenses? Has he "served time" before? Has he engaged in a pattern of violent conduct which suggests that he poses a serious danger to society? What is his attitude towards this crime—has he plead guilty, made restitution to the victim, assisted the police in convicting his accomplices? Does he have social stability indicating that he may be able to stay out of trouble? Relevant factors here include his family ties, employment record, possible addiction to drugs, and the character of his friends and associates. Many judges are concerned that such factors tend to discriminate among socio-economic classes, favoring in particular the defendant from a middle-class community. However, available evidence suggests that such offenders are less likely to repeat certain types of offenses (e.g., burglaries) then other prisoners who have far less to look foward to when they are returned to the community.

Another factor likely to influence the judge is the community attitude toward the crime and the offender. If there is special community fear of the particular type of crime, or outrage as to the particular case before the court, the judge may feel that the community's demand for retribution or deterrence should

---

99.   See note 23 at p. 96 *supra;* note 84 *supra.*

be reflected in his sentence. Reviewing a sentence of two years imprisonment and five years suspended sentence for two counts of forcible rape, the Supreme Court of Alaska rejected that sentence because it failed to give sufficient weight to "community condemnation of the offender's anti-social conduct." The trial court had relied primarily upon the defendant's potential for rehabilitation, but the Alaska Supreme Court stressed that that interest did not justify ignoring the need for "the reaffirmation of societal norms, for the purpose of maintaining respect for the norms." In light of that need, the sentence was too lenient: "A substantially longer period of actual confinement was called for . . . [so as to] bring home to [the defendant] the serious nature and consequences of his crime and to reaffirm society's condemnation of violent and forcible rape."[100]

The judge's exercise of discretion in sentencing also is likely to be influenced by his perspective of the state's corrections system. The nature of prison life and prison programs may be a deciding factor in choosing between probation or imprisonment or in setting the term of imprisonment. When there still is some hope for rehabilitation, and the judge views the prison system as almost inevitably having a negative impact on an offender, the judge is more likely to turn to probation. Where the judge has decided on imprisonment, the conditions under which time will be served may influence his determination as to the appropriate minimum term. Life in an antiquated, maximum security prison obviously is somewhat different than life in a modern, minimum security institution. The judge may be impressed (or depressed) by the prison system's rehabilitative programs. Where he has some confidence in those programs, he may hesitate to impose a high minimum for fear that it will interfere with the parole of the prisoner at that point when he is most likely to achieve a successful return to the community. Judges are aware that holding a prisoner beyond that point may be counterproductive. It can lead to bitterness and a reinforcement of the attitudes which led the offender to prison in the first place. On the other hand, if the judge believes that the corrections system offers little hope of rehabilitation or that the parole board takes too many unjustifiable risks, he may be inclined to impose a higher minimum sentence.

Judges also take into consideration the impact of the sentence upon the administration of an overburdened criminal justice system. They recognize that if concessions are not given for guilty pleas, the backlog of cases to be tried may grow so heavy as to almost cause the system to collapse. They also recognize that, where prisons are overcrowded and new prisons are not being built, the parole board may be in a position where it is forced to release a prisoner for every new prisoner it receives. In such situations, high maximum terms are meaningless. Prisoners will be released long before their full terms are served (even without consideration of liberal good time allowances). Indeed, a high minimum may be unwise even though the judge is confident that this offender should be incapacitated for a substantial period of time. The judge has no way of comparing this offender to others that the parole board also must consider for possible release. Assuming that overcrowding will require the parole board to release some prisoners who are far from good risks, the judge may hesitate to tie the board's hands with a high

---

100. *State v. Lancaster,* 550 P.2d 1257 (Alaska 1976).

minimum, thereby possibly forcing it to take an even greater risk in paroling a less deserving prisoner.

Improper Factors. While judges are divided as to the weight that should be given to some factors (e.g., a guilty plea), all agree that certain factors should not be considered. A sentence clearly should not be based on the race, sex, or the social status of the offender. Yet we frequently hear of studies that supposedly show that sentences are strongly influenced by these clearly irrelevant factors. One particularly disturbing study presented by counsel in the Supreme Court's death penalty cases pointed out that the capital punishment was more often imposed on black defendants than white defendants.[101] Other studies, however, suggest that if all other factors are kept constant, race and sex have little if any significant impact on sentencing. Studies conducted by the Institute of Contemporary Corrections at Sam Houston State University show, for example, that where differences in offenses, previous criminal record, number of counts and some thirty-two other factors are kept constant, no disparity attributable to race alone can be shown. A similar result was obtained as to sex, which may mean that the shorter sentences received by women as a group are a function of less serious offenses and shorter criminal histories rather than the result of sexism in sentencing.[102] Before one concludes that sentence differentials are based on irrelevant factors, a careful study must be made of the individual cases. A major difficulty is that race and sex can be determined from a surface analysis, but underlying factors that explain differences in sentencing often are found in presentence reports not available to the public.

Disparity In Sentencing. A major complaint leveled against judicial discretion in sentencing is that it produces "sentencing disparity." Unfortunately, the label "sentencing disparity" is used in many different ways. If it refers simply to different sentences for persons convicted of the same crime, then it is not necessarily an evil. A prisoner who receives a higher sentence than a fellow prisoner convicted of the same crime quite naturally complains that the system is not "fair." Fairness, however, must be judged in light of the proper objectives of sentencing. The prisoner's higher sentence may be the product of a variety of factors relevant to those objectives, such as his extaordinary violence in the commission of the crime or his long criminal record. Disparity justified by such factors is not a cause of concern, although further efforts may be needed to educate the public as to the reasons for its existence.

Disparity due to sentencing based on irrelevant factors is, on the other hand, an evil that should be eliminated. We already have noted the disagreement as to the existence of disparities based on race, sex, or social status. Many argue that such disparities have not yet been shown to be a major problem. There is general

---

101. See *Furman v. Georgia,* 408 U.S. 223, 250, 92 S.Ct. 2726, 33 L.Ed.2d 346 (1971).

102. These studies, reported in unpublished Master's Theses of degree candidates at Sam Houston State University in Huntsville, Texas, are cited and described more fully in the first edition of this book. See H. Kerper, *Introduction To The Criminal Justice System,* St. Paul, Minn.: West Publishing Company, 1972, p. 336. A similar analysis might be made of social status. Consider W. Seymour, Jr., *Social and Ethical Considerations In Assessing White-Collar Crime,* 11 American Criminal Law Review 821 (1973).

agreement, however, that another form of unfortunate disparity does exist—namely sentencing disparities produced by the differences in the sentencing philosophies of individual judges. Different judges will take different views of the gravity of the same crime. One judge may abhor narcotic violations and "come down hard" on all narcotics offenders. Another may view narcotics users as victims of the "pushers" and reserve harsh sentences for major dealers. Judges also differ as to the weight to be given to particular sentencing objectives. One judge may emphasize the possibilities of rehabilitation, while another may be concerned primarily with making the offender "pay his debt to society." Thus, the individual judge's value judgments obviously play some role in sentencing. We are uncertain, however, as to how greatly sentences are influenced by these variations among judges. Are we talking about an occasional disparity produced by the idiosyncratic views of a "hanging judge" or is this an everyday problem influencing sentences in many cases?

Sentencing institutes held throughout the country suggest that differences in judicial philosophies may have an impact in a significant number of sentencing decisions. At these institutes, various trial judges are given hypothetical cases and asked to indicate what sentence they would impose. They have not seen the defendant, of course, but they are given a fairly complete picture of the offense plus all of the information as to the defendant's background that would be available in the ordinary case (age, prior record, drug use, education, etc.). While the proposed sentences do tend to cluster at certain points, they also disclose considerable disparity between some judges. For example, in one bank robbery case presented to 48 federal district judges, the average maximum term proposed was slightly over ten years, but the responses of individual judges ranged from five to eighteen years. In a hypothetical heroin possession case considered by the same group of judges, 36% would have granted probation, while the remainder would have imposed incarceration ranging from three months to the statutory maximum of two years.[103] After participating in such institutes and noting the different approaches of his colleagues in sentencing, one federal judge concluded: "[O]ur laws characteristically leave to the sentencing judge a range of choice that should be unthinkable in 'a government of law, not of men.'"[104]

Alternatives: Assisting Judges. How should improper disparity in sentencing be eliminated? Some commentators argue that judicial discretion is a basically sound idea requiring only minor modifications to eliminate the more extreme disparities. They suggest the use of sentencing guidelines, more sentencing institutes where judges share ideas, and stronger appellate review of sentences. Such programs, they argue, will produce greater uniformity without eliminating the opportunity for individualizing sentences. As they see it, the primary need is to increase communications among judges and between judges and the correctional system.

One of the more innovative programs for increasing the information shared by judges utilizes statistical analysis of sentences currently imposed by judges.

103. See A. Partridge and W. Elridge, *The Second Circuit Sentencing Study,* Washington, D.C.: Federal Judicial Center, 1974.

104. M. Frankel, *Criminal Sentences: Law Without Order,* New York: Hill and Wang, 1975, p. 5.

Sentences are analyzed in light of a series of variables to determine the weight being given to each. Then the key variables are arranged on a grid that produces a series of different sentencing categories for each offense. Looking to the variables in the case before him, which include such factors as the offender's educational level and age at the time of his first conviction, the judge can place the case in a particular category, which will tell him what sentence commonly is given to this type of defendant in this type of case. While current guideline programs do not go far,[105] some commentators argue that there should be a presumption against sentences outside the guidelines. If the judge should impose a sentence that does not fit within the guidelines, he would be required to state his reasons for deviating from the guidelines and his decision would then be subject to careful appellate review. A major criticism of this proposal is that it might lead to "robot sentencing." Judges could become so hesitant to go outside the guidelines that they might sentence without regard to the unique circumstances of individual cases.

Alternatives: Parole Boards and Sentencing Commissions.

Some critics of judicial discretion contend that the suggested modifications, even if they could produce greater uniformity, would not be satisfactory. The problem, as they see it, is that the modifications only would produce more consistent adherence to sentencing policies that reflect a consensus judgment of the judiciary. These critics share the doubts, expressed by many judges themselves, as to whether judges are well equipped to set sentencing policies. They agree with Justice Frankfurter, who once noted:

> *We lawyers who become judges . . . are not very competent, are not qualified by experience, to impose sentences where any discretion is to be exercised. I do not think it is in the domain of the training of lawyers to know what to do with a fellow after you find out he is a thief. I do not think legal training gives you any special competence.*[106]

Assuming one accepts this view, the question arises as to who should be the recipient of the discretion currently given to judges. The two most common suggestions are the parole board and a special sentencing commission.

At one time, most opponents of judicial discretion argued that more authority should be granted to the parole board. The ideal, as they saw it, was a system under which there was no minimum sentence and the maximum was set by statute. The key was to provide as much indeterminancy as possible so as to increase parole board discretion. The advantages of parole board sentencing supposedly were: (1) parole boards are centralized agencies and thus more likely to provide statewide uniformity of treatment of similar cases; (2) the parole board could be staffed with experts on human behavior; (3) parole boards are more likely to use a

---

105. Guideline programs are now used in individual counties in several state courts. See Zalman, note 85 *supra,* at p. 860, 866-872. They are based in part on techniques developed in the parole decision guidelines formulated by the Federal Parole Commission. See note 153 *infra.*

106. Justice Frankfurter's comment is quoted in E. Celler, *Legislative Views On The Importance Of The Sentencing Institute,* 30 Federal Rules Decisions 471 (1962). For a contrary view, see Frankel, note 104 *supra,* at p. 56. Judge Frankel notes: "[F]or all the wretchedness of our performance to date, I think vital aspects of the sentencing function are peculiarly *legal,* and peculiarly within the special competence of people legally trained."

scientific approach in sentencing, considering many variables; and (4) parole board sentencing might decrease the control that prosecutors exercise over the sentencing process through plea bargaining. Of course, even if parole board sentencing provided a successful alternative to judicial discretion in setting the term of imprisonment, it did not furnish a complete solution for those opposed to judicial discretion. The judge still would retain discretion over the issue as to whether or not to grant probation since a parole board deals only with imprisonment.

Broadened parole board discretion was promoted in many states until the mid-1960's. Then, the tide seemed to turn. Today, as we saw in our discussion of determinate sentencing, there probably is more opposition to parole board discretion than to judicial discretion. The complaints against parole board discretion are many, but the most significant is that parole boards tend to emphasize the wrong factors in determining whether a prisoner should be released. They place too little emphasis on the nature of the crime, it is argued, and too much emphasis on how well the defender has done in prison. The latter factor, critics suggest, has little predictive value. Prisoners participate in "rehabilitative" programs in prison because they know they must do so to obtain their early release. Prisons are, in effect, drama schools that force persons to act as if they were rehabilitated according to our sterotyped views of proper behavior. Moreover, the critics continue, it is questionable whether prisoner behavior is a good predictor of community behavior in any event. Professor Hans Mattick once noted, in discussing the role of prisons: "It is hard to train an aviator in a submarine." His colleague Norval Morris then added: "It is even harder to predict his flying capacity from observing his submarine behavior."[107]

In recent years, the sentencing commission has replaced the parole board as the primary candidate for assuming discretionary authority in sentencing. So far, no jurisdiction has adopted the commission proposal, but Congress, in particular, is giving it serious consideration. The commission would be composed of a variety of persons with something to contribute to sentencing—penologists, lawyers, clergymen, sociologists, and perhaps, ex-convicts. The function of the commission would not be to sentence in each case. Rather, it would issue guidelines based upon policies that it had developed. In many respects these guidelines would be similar in form to the judicial guidelines previously noted. The primary difference is that the commission's guidelines would be based on policies formulated by the commission rather than policies reflected in current sentences set by judges. To preserve some flexibility, judges would be given limited discretion to depart from the guidelines in exceptional cases. It is anticipated, however, that the guidelines would be controlling in 85-90% of all cases. Departures from the guidelines would be subject to appeal.

The supporters of the sentencing commission claim that it would bring the following strengths to the sentencing process: (1) greater uniformity in sentencing without loss of flexibility; (2) centralization of policy-making authority in a single body; and (3) greater professional expertise. Critics raise the possibility that it too

---

107. N. Morris, *The Future Of Imprisonment,* Chicago, Ill.: University of Chicago Press, 1974, p. 16.

would lead to "robot sentencing." They doubt that true individualization of sentencing can be obtained by a weighted analysis of variables. Actuaries may use that technique in setting life insurance rates, but sentencing requires consideration of too many intangibles. Only the judge who is close to the case and the community, they argue, can appropriately evaluate the sentencing needs of the particular offense and offender.

Alternatives: Legislative Controls. Another group of critics of judicial discretion would like almost to eliminate discretion altogether. Individualization, they argue, is not a worthwhile objective. More emphasis should be placed on uniformity and certainty of punishment. In their view, the legislature should exercise primary control over the sentence. This group favors legislative classification of various crimes as non-probationable. It also favors fairly tight legislative control over the terms of imprisonment, as provided in the California presumptive-determinate sentencing structure. Opponents view this approach as reflecting an almost total rejection of the rehabilitative goal. Moreover, they question the legislature's capacity to properly assess sentences even from the perspective of retribution and deterrence. The legislature, they note, is too far removed from the criminal justice process to set specific guidelines. If it miscalculates, it is not in a position to make a quick adjustment. The passage of new legislation is a time consuming process.

SENTENCING PROCEDURES

Presentence Reports. If the trial judge is to consider even half of the factors that may be relevant to the multiple objectives of sentencing, he obviously must have considerably more information than is disclosed in the process of determining guilt. Neither the trial nor the guilty plea procedure is likely to reveal much pertinent information as to the defendant's background, and the guilty plea procedure may not even disclose all of the relevant information concerning the offense itself. Ordinarily, the needed additional information will be provided by the presentence report, which is prepared by the probation staff attached to the court. Presentence reports are used fairly regularly in felony cases in almost all states. In many states they also are used for those misdemeanor cases that do not almost automatically result in a sentence of a fine. While the presentence report is designed primarily to aid the court in determining the appropriate sentence, it also may be useful to prison authorities in classifying prisoners, parole boards in evaluating the prisoner's possibilities, and probation officers in supervising probationers.

Many states do not require presentence reports, but give the court discretion to order the report.[108] They assume that the court will ordinarily request a report, but anticipate that there will be a fair number of cases in which the report will not be useful. These would be cases in which the judge has very little sentencing discretion or the disposition is obvious from the nature of the crime. Other states give the court discretion to require a report in any case, but require that he obtain

---

108. Presentence reports are not used in jury sentencing. The jury relies solely upon the information received at trial. See pp. 333-34 *supra*.

it on certain types of cases. Most frequently, these states require a report for all felony cases in which the judge has discretion to grant probation.[109] Finally, several states, following the Model Penal Code, require presentence reports in all felony cases.[110]

The content of the presentence report usually varies with the nature of the case. Reports commonly include a description of the circumstances attending the commission of the crime, the defendant's history of delinquency or criminality, and the defendant's "social history," which includes such matters as family situation, employment history, education, and personal habits. Ordinarily the report also will include the probation officer's analysis of possible dispositions and his recommendation. In some reports, the probation officer will include his own evaluation of the defendant's motive and character. Illinois requires by statute a particularly comprehensive report that includes, among other things, a review of all resources within the community which might be available to assist the defendant's rehabilitation.[111]

Preparing a presentence report often is a time consuming task. The probation officer will interview the defendant for basic data and then check school and employment records. He may talk to the victim of the crime, the defendant's family, and other persons in the community who know the defendant. Where the court has requested a physical or mental examination, he will arrange for these examinations. The F.B.I. and state crime records must be checked for prior

---

109. See California Penal Code §1203. The emphasis on probationable offenses may stem from the fact that the judge's broadest discretion in sentencing often lies in his choice between probation and imprisonment. In some states, however, presentence reports are required only where the judge actually grants probation. See Ohio Revised Code §2951.03.

110. See MPC §7.07 (also requiring the report in misdemeanor cases in which the defendant is under the age of 22). States requiring reports in all felony cases include Illinois and New York. See Illinois Stat. ch. 38, §1005-3-1 (exempting certain cases where prosecutor and defense agree that a report is not needed); New York Criminal Procedure Law §390.20. New York also requires reports for misdemeanor cases in which the court imposes a sentence in excess of ninety days imprisonment or a sentence of probation.

111. Illinois Stat. ch. 38, §1005-3-2 provides that the presentence report "shall set forth":
    (1) the defendant's history of delinquency or criminality, physical and mental history and condition, family situation and background, economic status, education, occupation and personal habits;
    (2) information about special resources within the community which might be available to assist the defendant's rehabilitation, including treatment centers, residential facilities, vocational training services, correctional manpower programs, employment opportunities, special educational programs, alcohol and drug abuse programming, psychiatric and marriage counseling, and other programs and facilities which could aid the defendant's successful reintegration into society:
    (3) the effect the offense committed has had upon the victim or victims thereof, and any compensatory benefit that various sentencing alternatives would confer on such victim or victims;
    (4) information concerning the defendant's status since arrest, including his record if released on his own recognizance, or the defendant's achievement record if released on a conditional pre-trial supervision program;
    (5) when appropriate, a plan, based upon the personal, economic and social adjustment needs of the defendant, utilizing public and private community resources as an alternative to institutional sentencing; and
    (6) any other matters that the investigatory officer deems relevant or the court directs to be included.

offenses and arrests. The report then must be written and submitted to the judge. The probation officer will not start on the report until after the defendant is convicted, and he usually will be carrying a heavy caseload of probation supervision assignments at the same time. As a result, the next stage in the process, the sentencing hearing, may not be scheduled until several weeks after the proceeding in which the defendant was found guilty. In the meantime, the defendant may continue to be released on bail, or he may await sentencing in the local jail.[112]

Confidentiality of the Presentence Report. Should the presentence report be a confidential document, unavailable to the prosecutor and defense counsel? States vary in their treatment of this issue. A few states, most noteably California, make the report a public record, available to anyone.[113] Several states require that the report be disclosed to defense counsel and the prosecutor.[114] Other jursidictions make the report available to counsel except for the "recommendation as to sentence," and any "diagnostic opinion which might seriously disrupt a program of rehabilitation, sources of information obtained upon a promise of confidentiality, or . . . other information which, if disclosed, might result in harm, physical or otherwise, to the defendant or other persons."[115] Most states simply leave disclosure of all or part of the report to the discretion of the court.[116] Disclosure is required as a matter of federal constitutional law in capital punishment cases.[117]

Mandatory disclosure requirements have been opposed on several grounds: disclosure may allow defense counsel to delay the sentencing process interminably by challenging everything in the report; disclosure would hamper the collection of information from persons who are fearful of the defendant; disclosure may deter the probation officer from expressing his well informed, but necessarily speculative estimate of the defendant's chances for rehabilitation; and disclosure of certain matters, such as psychological reports, might discourage the defendant's rehabilitative efforts. Supporters of full disclosure respond that, unless disclosure is made, the defendant will not be able to correct any errors or misleading information in the presentence report. It is too easy, they argue, for a person who dislikes

---

112. The Federal Bail Reform Act includes a separate standard on bail after conviction, which has been followed in many states. It provides that bail shall be granted "unless the court . . . has reason to believe that no one or more conditions of release will reasonably assure that the person will not flee or pose a danger to any other person or to the community." 18 United States Code §3148. In other states, there is no presumption in favor of bail once the defendant has been convicted. In those states, the courts ordinarily will grant bail only in cases where there appears to be a reasonable chance that the defendant will receive probation. If the defendant is sentenced to imprisonment, he ordinarily will be given credit for time served in jail awaiting trial or sentence.

113. California Penal Code §1203. In most states the report is not included as part of the court record available to the public even if it is disclosed to the prosecuting attorney and the defense counsel. The report will be disclosed only to counsel (where such disclosure is ordered by the court or required by law) and any agency that is involved in corrections, such as the parole board. See New York Criminal Procedure Law §390.50.

114. See, e.g., Illinois Stat. ch. 38, §1005-3-4.

115. Federal Rules of Criminal Procedure, Rule 3.2(c)(3). See also New York Criminal Procedure Law §390.20; Michigan General Court Rules, Rule 785.12.

116. See Rubin, note 7 *supra,* at p. 102. Where the state statute is silent on the issue of disclosure, most courts hold that disclosure is at the discretion of the trial judge.

117. See *Gardner v. Florida,* discussed at p. 337 *supra.*

the defendant to give erroneous information and then claim that his remarks must be kept confidential because he fears retaliation. Some proponents of disclosure also quarrel with the assumption that probation officers will prepare the report from a neutral perspective. Many probation officers, they contend, have stereotyped views of certain offenders, which should not be passed on to the court without full opportunity for a defense response.

Presentence Hearings. The announcement of sentence by the judge will occur in open court in the presence of the defendant, his counsel, and, usually, the prosecutor. Before the judge announces sentence, he is required in almost all jurisdictions to recognize the defendant's *right of allocution*—that is, the defendant's right to speak to the court on his own behalf. In most places, the judge also will allow defense counsel to make a brief statement. Traditionally, this was the total extent of the presentence hearing. More and more jurisdictions have been moving, however, towards a more substantial hearing in which both prosecution and defense are allowed to present their own information relating to the appropriate sentence and to rebut information in the presentence report (where it has been disclosed). In these states, counsel ordinarily will submit factual information through their own written memoranda or through the affidavits of their informants. Testimony will not be heard, and neither side will have the opportunity to cross-examine under oath the persons whose statements are cited to the court in counsels' memoranda or affidavits or the presentence report.

While the informal hearing described above goes substantially beyond the practice of ten or twenty years ago, various advisory groups have suggested that these hearings do not go far enough in ensuring a full development of relevant facts. The National Advisory Commission to the Law Enforcement Assistance Administration has recommended, for example, that defense counsel be allowed to call as a witness and cross-examine "the person who prepared the presentence report and any persons whose information, contained in the presentence report, may be highly damaging to the defendant."[118] The American Bar Association similarly recommends that where either party disagrees with factual information noted in the presentence report, "evidence offered by the parties on the sentencing issue should be presented in open court will full rights of confrontation, cross-examination, and representation by counsel."[119] A few states have adopted procedures that move in the direction of these recommendations. Illinois, for example, requires the court to "consider evidence . . . offered by the parties on aggravation and mitigation," and allows cross-examination at the trial court's discretion.[120] Most states appear to be fearful that the proposals of the National Advisory Commission and the A.B.A. would turn the sentencing proceeding into a mini-trial.

The Supreme Court has noted that the presentence hearing must comply with the requirements of due process, but those requirements have been held so

118. National Advisory Commission, note 1 *supra.* at §51.7.

119. A.B.A., *Standards Relating To Sentencing Alternatives and Procedures,* note 41 *supra,* at §5.4.

120. Illinois Stat. ch. 38, §1005-4-1. *People v. Drewniak,* 105 Ill.App.2d 37, 245 N.E.2d 102 (1969).

far only to bar reliance on clearly erroneous factual information. In *Townsend v. Burke*,[121] the sentencing procedure was held to violate due process where the trial court misread the defendant's criminal record to contain five prior convictions when defendant had only three prior convictions. While the defendant there was not represented by counsel, the *Townsend* ruling would appear to apply to any sentencing proceeding in which the court refused to consider defense information that could aboslutely rebut information cited by the court as relevant to its sentencing determination. On the other hand, *Townsend* does not require that the court allow the defense to cross-examine the sources of the information cited by the court. In *Williams v. New York*,[122] the Court held that due process did not extend the rights of confrontation and cross-examination to the sentencing proceeding. The trial judge could rely upon information contained in a presentence report even though the persons supplying that information had not testified in court. The determination as to sentence, the Court noted, was constitutionally distinguishable from the determination as to guilt: While "tribunals passing on the guilt of a defendant have always been hedged in by strict evidentiary procedural limitations," the tradition in sentencing, established long before the adoption of the federal constitution, was to grant the sentencing judge "wide discretion in the sources and types of evidence used to assist him in determining the kind and extent of the punishment to be imposed." [123]

Sentencing Councils. The United States is unique among modern nations in that, except for jury-sentencing, we give only one person the power to set the appropriate sentence in a criminal case—the sentencing judge. In many civil law countries the sentencing decision is shared by a panel of judges who hear the case. In several judicial districts, American judges do seek to share the consideration of possible sentences, although not the ultimate responsibility of sentencing, through sentencing councils. The council procedure simply consists of meetings of a group of judges within a single district at which they discuss proposed sentences in individual cases so as to assist the sentencing judge. The first sentencing council was instituted in the United States District Court for the Eastern District of Michigan in 1960. Ordinarily, the judges participating in the sentencing council meet once a week to discuss sentences that they will impose in the next week. Several days before the council meets each judge receives a copy of the presentence report prepared for each defendant and records his recommendation of sentence. The recommendations are then discussed and differences of opinion

---

121. *Townsend v. Burke,* 334 U.S. 736, 68 S.Ct. 1252, 92 L. Ed. 1690 (1948).

122. *Williams v. New York,* 337 U.S. 241, 69 S.Ct. 1079, 93 L.Ed. 1337 (1949).

123. 337 U.S. at 246. The Court also stressed that "modern changes in the treatment of offenders," made it "more necessary now . . . [that] the distinctions in the evidential procedure in trial and sentencing processes" be retained:

> Under the practice of individualizing punishments, investigational techniques have been given an important role. Probation workers making reports of their investigations have not been trained to prosecute but to aid offenders. Their reports have been given a high value by conscientious judges who want to sentence persons on the best available information rather than on guesswork and inadequate information. To deprive sentencing judges of this kind of information would undermine modern penological procedural policies that have been cautiously adopted throughout the nation after careful consideration and experimentation.

are expressed. The role of the council is purely advisory, however, for the sentencing judge in every case must make the final decision. The recommendations of his colleagues are not binding. The American Bar Association has urged that courts having more than one judge make substantial use of the sentencing council procedure as a means of gaining the advantage of "group judgment."[124] A major drawback of the procedure is that it consumes far more time than the traditional procedure involving a single judge.

Appellate Review Of Sentencing. We have noted previously that all jursidictions provide for an appeal by a convicted defendant. On that appeal, the defendant may challenge the trial judge's exercise of discretion with respect to any issue relating to the trial. In many jurisdictions, he may not do the same with respect to all aspects of sentencing. All jursidictions will permit the defendant to challenge his sentence on appeal on the ground that: (1) the judge failed to follow proper procedure in imposing the sentence, (2) the sentence exceeded the maximum sentence authorized by law, or (3) the sentence constituted cruel and unusual punishment in violation of the federal constitution. Whether he also may challenge his sentence on the ground that it was far too severe depends upon the law of the particular state. In a majority of the states he can raise that claim, but a substantial minority will not consider a claim of excessive severity so long as the sentence is within the authorized statutory limits. In the states that deny such review, the defendant sentenced by the harshest sentencing judge in the state simply must bear the burden of the draw that brought his case before that judge. If the defendant received a minimum sentence twice that usually recieved by persons convicted under similar circumstances, he can gain no relief on appeal (assuming that the minimum does not exceed statutory limits). The fact that his accomplice sentenced by another judge received a much lower sentence, notwithstanding a more substantial criminal record, similarly is irrelevant on appeal.

At one time, almost all state appellate courts refused to consider challenges to the severity of a sentence (although an unjust sentence may well have influenced the court as it reviewed other alleged errors in the case). The common law took the position that any sentence within the limits provided by statute could not constitute an abuse of discretion and therefore there was no possible error for the appellate court to review. Gradually, concerned by obvious disparities in sentences, the courts moved toward limited review of the severity of sentences. In some cases, the appellate courts were authorized by statute to reduce excessive sentences. A New York provision states, for example, that the intermediate appellate courts may consider on appeal whether "a sentence imposed upon a valid conviction is . . . unduly harsh or severe."[125] In other instances, the state appellate court rejected the common law rule as inconsistent with its ability to review an abuse of discretion in all other areas of the criminal law. Other appellate courts

---

124. A.B.A., *Standards Relating To Sentencing Alternatives and Procedures,* note 41 *supra,* at §7.1.

125. New York Criminal Procedure Law §470.15. See also Illinois Stat. ch. 38, §121-9 (also authorizing review). In other states the statutes are not so clear. Statutes authorizing the appellate court to "reverse, affirm, or *modify*" the judgment below have been held to authorize sentence review in several states, including California. See California Penal Code §1260.

have refused to take this step, arguing that the common law rule should be overturned only by specific legislative directive.[126] One advantage of legislation is that it may authorize appellate challenges to sentences by the prosecutor as well as the defendant, as is done in Alaska. [127] Another legislative possibility is to use a special court, composed of experienced trial judges, to review challenges to sentences. A court of this type is used in Connecticut and Massachusetts.[128]

In those states that have sentence review, the appellate courts vary somewhat in the standard they apply to allegedly excessive sentences. The basic thrust of the approach followed in all states, however, is to avoid "second-guessing" the judge. The appellate court will have before it the presentence report and the record of the trial and presentence hearing, but the trial judge is closer to the community and he has seen the defendant. The Alaska court will reverse a trial judge only if it finds the sentence clearly excessive in light of the nature of the crime, the defendant's background, and the need to protect the public. Other courts describe the applicable standard as whether the sentence was clearly at variance with the purpose and spirit of the law. Some courts will reverse only if the sentence is so extreme that it can be explained only by partiality, prejudice, or an oppressive motivation.[129] In some states, the appellate court will only reverse and remand for the trial court to set a new sentence in light of the policies noted in the appellate court opinion. In others, the appellate court may impose a new sentence itself. Experience with appellate review in those states that have had it for a substantial number of years indicates that it results in the rejection of sentences in a small percentage of all cases.

Having discussed the division of authority in the setting of the sentence, the factors considered, and the procedure followed, we now are ready to turn to the administration of the sentence. Here again, we see a heavy emphasis on discretion, with a recent movement towards more substantial legal regulation of the exercise of that discretion. We start our examination of the administration of the sentence with the administration of probation.

THE ADMINISTRATION OF PROBATION

Probation Supervision. A universal condition of probation is that the probationer report regularly to his probation officer. Most probationers are required to meet with their probation officers once every month, but where the officer feels

---

126. The various decisions are noted in American Bar Association, *Standards Relating To Appellate Review Of Sentences* (Approved Draft 1968). The American Bar Association takes the position that appellate review of sentences is desirable as a means of correcting injustices, promoting respect for the law, and developing uniform sentencing criteria.

127. Alaska Stat. §12.55.201. Other states do not authorize appeal by the prosecutor, but they do give the court authority to raise a sentence if it finds, on defendant's appeal, that the sentence should have been higher. See, e.g., Massachusetts Gen. Laws ch. 278, §§28A-28D.

128. See Connecticut Gen. Stat. §51-194-6; Massachusetts Gen. Laws ch. 278, §§28A-28D. See also Montana Revised Code §95.2501.

129. The leading cases include *State v. Lancaster,* note 100 *supra; State v. Chaney,* 477 P.2d 441 (Alaska 1970); *State v. Fogle,* 181 S.E.2d 483 (S.C. 1971); *People v. Wright,* 56 Ill.2d 523, 309 N.E.2d 537 (1974).

that more intensive supervision is needed, he may require more frequent meetings. Although traditional probation supervision emphasizes a close one-on-one relationship between the probationer and the officer, where the officer's caseload is heavy, he may meet jointly with several probationers to discuss their common problems. The meetings between the probationer and officer serve two main functions; to provide control and supervision of the probationer and to provide the probationer with counseling.

The traditional model of probation counseling emphasizes individual casework by the officer. The officer is supposed to create a therapeutic relationship, employing various counseling skills to rehabilitate and modify the behavior of the probationer. The traditional model is extremely time consuming, however, and it often cannot be achieved because of the heavy caseloads carried by most probation officers.[130] In many areas, the traditional model of the probation officer is gradually being replaced by the model of the probation officer as a "community resource manager."[131] Under this role model, the officer's goal is to deliver services to the probationer rather than to perform individualized casework. The probation department will develop specific counselling programs under the direction of specially trained officers and also will attempt to utilize fully community service agencies. The supervising officer relinquishes his responsibility as a primary counselor and seeks instead to provide information and referrals to the various programs that might assist the probationer. The new model, it is hoped, will allow officers to take on a larger number of probationers while at the same time improving the effectiveness of probation through the use of specialized programs.

The probation officer also carries the initial responsibility for determining whether the probationer is complying with the conditions set forth in the probation order. This responsibility casts the probation officer in the role of an investigator. He will seek information from the probationer as to his current behavior and check those responses through inquiries directed to employers, family members, and local police. The permissible scope of the officer's investigative authority is not always clear. As we saw in a previous section, courts are divided as to the officer's power to search the probationer at any time, without probable cause, pursuant to a probation condition authorizing such searches.[132] When the probation officer discovers that the probationer has violated a condition of probation, he assumes a role similar to that of the prosecutor in a criminal proceeding. He is given considerable discretion in determining whether to press for probation revocation based upon the violation. Using his good judgment, he may decide to overlook minor or excusable violations. If he does decide that probation revocation is justified, he must present the matter to the court. Since it was the court that placed the offender on probation, only the court can revoke probation.

---

130. See p. 199 *supra* as to the heavy caseload borne by probation officers. In the federal system, the average caseload at one point reached 76 probationers per probation officer. It subsequently was reduced to 44 probationers per officer by almost tripling the number of probation officers over a ten year period. See *Sourcebook Of Criminal Justice Statistics—1976*, note 1, p. 1 *supra*, at p. 663. A recent survey reported an average caseload throughout the country of 107 adult probationers per officer, 9 Criminal Justice Newsletter, No. 11, p. 6-7 (May 22, 1977).

131. See National Advisory Commission, note 1 *supra*, at p. 311-330.

132. See p. 346 *supra*.

Judicial Authority To Revoke Probation. The court may revoke probation based on a finding that the probationer violated any condition of his probation. Even a relatively minor or technical violation may be grounds for revocation. However, the court is not required to revoke simply because it finds a violation. Other alternatives are available. The court may simply reprimand the probationer and issue a warning. It may add further probation conditions, requiring the probationer to refrain from certain conduct (e.g., to stop associating with certain persons). Some jursidictions authorize the court to impose "jail therapy," whereby the probationer is jailed for a short time and then continues on probation. If the court does revoke probation, the defendant is then sentenced to imprisonment.

By far the most common ground for probation revocation is the commission of another offense. The court need not wait until the defendant is tried and convicted of the other crime (although courts frequently do wait). It may make its own independent determination at a revocation hearing held even before the probationer has been charged with the other offense. Very often the court may find that other probation conditions have been violated without having to resolve the issue of guilt as to the new offense. Consider, for example, the case of a probationer who has been involved with a stolen car ring. His involvement becomes known to his probation officer and the police, but his criminal liability will be difficult to establish in court. Evidence of the probationer's involvement is entirely circumstantial; the probationer has been living with people, believed to be operating the ring, who have long criminal records; he has been spending large amounts of money gambling and drinking in local bars although he has no present employment. Rather than prosecute the probationer for car theft, the police may convince the probation officer to seek revocation on the basis of the probationer's involvement with the car theft ring. Even if the court finds the evidence insufficient to establish that the probationer violated the law, it may revoke probation based on the clearly established violation of various other conditions (failure to keep steady employment, association with convicted felons, patronizing bars, etc.).

Probation Revocation Procedures. Prior to the Supreme Court's decision in *Morrissey v. Brewer*,[133] many lower courts had stated that the probationer was not entitled to a full hearing on the revocation of his probation. As they saw it, the probationer had been granted a "privilege" when he was placed on probation, and he could not complain when the state withdrew that privilege on its own terms. *Morrissey* flatly rejected this analysis as applied to both probation and parole revocation proceedings. The Court stressed that the probationer or parolee suffers a "grievous loss" when his liberty is withdrawn. Admittedly, the state does not have to grant him his liberty in the first instance, but neither does it have to grant in the first instance various other benefits that cannot be taken away without a fair hearing (e.g., public employment and welfare payments). The Sixth Amendment does not apply to probation or parole revocation because that Amendment refers only to the "criminal prosecution" itself. However, both revocations involve deprivations of liberty and therefore, *Morrissey* concluded, are subject to the requirements of due process.

---

133. *Morrissey v. Brewer*, 408 U.S. 471, 92 S.Ct. 2593, 33 L.Ed.2d 484 (1972).

Although the *Morrissey* opinion clearly indicated that a probationer was entitled to a fair hearing at a probation revocation proceeding, the opinion was concerned primarily with parole revocation proceedings. Many of the due process standards announced in the opinion were geared to special aspects of the parole revocation process, but the Court did describe certain basic requirements of a fair hearing that seemed to be equally applicable to a probation revocation proceeding. In *Gagnon v. Scarpelli*,[134] the Supreme Court held, as most had anticipated, that the basic requirements noted in *Morrissey* did indeed apply to the probation revocation proceeding. Basically, those requirements are: (1) the probationer must be given written notice of the claimed violation in advance of the proceedings; (2) the court cannot rely on information not disclosed to the probationer at the proceeding; (3) the probationer must have an opportunity to be heard in person and to present witnesses and other evidence; (4) the probationer must have the opportunity to confront and cross-examine the persons presenting information against him unless there is "good cause" justifying acceptance of their affidavits in lieu of their live testimony; (5) the court must set forth the grounds for its decision in a written opinion; (6) the probationer may not be held in custody awaiting a probation revocation proceeding without a reasonably prompt initial inquiry, similar to a "preliminary hearing," to determine whether there is probable cause to believe that he committed the alleged violation; and (7) the revocation hearing must be held within a "reaonsable time" after the probationer is taken into custody.[135] Although many of these rights are similar to those available in a criminal trial, the Court stressed that the revocation proceeding could be far more flexible. It noted in particular that the judge could consider various types of evidence that would not be admissible in a criminal trial.

Counsel. All jursidictions permit the probationer to be represented by retained counsel at the probation revocation proceeding. Many, however, will not automatically provide counsel for the probationer who cannot afford to retain a lawyer. As you recall, the Sixth Amendment grants to the indigent defendant the assistance of court appointed counsel in all felony cases and any misdemeanor case resulting in imprisonment. The parole revocation process certainly results in imprisonment, but it is not governed by the Sixth Amendment. Only the due process clause applies to the revocation proceeding, and the Supreme Court has held that due process does not necessarily require that the indigent be assisted by counsel. Whether counsel must be appointed depends upon the nature of the issues posed in the particular revocation proceeding. First, a distinction has been drawn between revocation proceedings that consider revocation alone and those that may involve revocation and sentencing. The latter type of proceeding is presented where the judge initially imposed probation without determining what sentence of imprisonment would apply if probation were revoked. In such a situation, once the court decides to revoke probation, the probation revocation proceeding becomes,

---

134. *Gagnon v. Scarpelli*, 411 U.S. 778, 93 S.Ct. 1756, 36 L.Ed.2d 656 (1973).

135. *Gagnon* involved an unusual Wisconsin procedure under which probation was revoked by the Wisconsin Department of Public Welfare rather than the sentencing court, but the standards announced in *Gagnon* have been viewed as equally applicable to the traditional revocation proceeding before the trial court.

in effect, a presentence hearing. Here, the Court has held, the assistance of a lawyer definitely is required, just as it would be required at an original presentence hearing.[136]

In many revocation proceedings, no separate sentencing issues are presented. The court has set the imprisonment term before placing the defendant on probation, and that term is automatically imposed if probation is revoked. In these cases, the probationer's constitutional right to appointed counsel depends upon the probationer's need for a lawyer to make effective use of his hearing rights. *Gagnon v. Scarpelli* established a presumption that counsel is needed where the probationer requests counsel on the basis of a "colorable claim" that (1) he did not commit the alleged violation or (2) circumstances existed that "justified or mitigated the violation" and those circumstances are "complex or otherwise difficult to develop or present." In such cases, the probationer presents significant issues that can only be developed fully with the aid of counsel. On the other hand, if the violation charged is the commission of a serious crime and the probationer has already been convicted of committing that crime, the probationer has little need for a lawyer. Revocation is likely to be automatic, and any plea for mercy can be advanced by the probationer himself. To ensure that indigent probationers receive lawyers in all cases where counsel might conceivably be helpful, *Gagnon* requires that the Court make a careful inquiry and place its reasons for refusing to appoint counsel in the record.

THE ADMINISTRATION OF INCARCERATION

Assignment To An Institution. Depending upon the organization of the state correctional system, the court commits a felony offender to the director of the state department of corrections or to the warden of a particular state penal institution. Once the order of commitment is entered, the court loses all control over the convicted man. The decisions as to place and conditions of confinement are made by the correctional authority or by the warden of the institution to which the offender has been committed. States with state-wide correctional departments operate many different kinds of penal institutions for adult felons. Hardened professional criminals are placed in maximum security institutions; first offenders are placed in minimum security or open institutions; and specialized institutions may be provided for sexual offenders or youthful offenders.[137]

The large states usually have a separate facility to which the newly convicted felon is sent while decisions are being made as to the place and nature of his confinement. Some of these facilities, variously called Reception Centers, Diagnostic Centers, and the like, serve only to isolate the prisoner until any danger of his carrying a communicable disease into a prison has passed. Other centers carry on extensive diagnostic procedures to determine the best treatment plan for the prisoner in terms of his background and needs. A prisoner will be given complete physical and mental examinations, his educational level will be assessed, and his

---

136. *Mempa v. Rhay*, 389 U.S. 128, 88 S.Ct. 254, 19 L.Ed.2d 336 (1968).

137. Of course, this is not true of all states. Some of the smaller states have a single prison. Special prisoners, such as female prisoners or prisoners requiring maximum security, are housed in the more specialized prisons of larger states, with the home state paying the costs.

work skills inventoried. An extensive social history will be developed, based in part on the presentence report. The final treatment plan will designate the facility in which the prisoner will be placed, his work assignments there, and any special training or treatment programs in which he will participate. The federal government even provides excellent plastic surgery at one of its centers, since it has been found that the correction of physical deformities contributes greatly to an inmate's rehabilitation.

The prisoner's stay in the receiving facility may run anywhere from a week to a few months depending upon the type of testing and analysis applied there. At the end of that time, he is assigned to one of the regular units in the corrections system and he is likely to stay there until ready for release. Due to overcrowding, changes in programs, or behavioral difficulties, transfers sometimes are made. As with the original assignment of the prisoner, transfers are largely at the discretion of the corrections department. The Supreme Court has held that a prisoner transferred to a less favorable institution is not constitutionally entitled to a hearing on the transfer where state law leaves the transfer in the discretion of the corrections officials.[138] The Court indicated, however, that a hearing would be needed if state law limited transfers to cases in which the prisoner had engaged in acts of misconduct.

Restrictions Imposed Upon Inmates. Are the range and severity of the restrictions imposed upon inmates also a matter left largely to the discretion of corrections officials? For a long time, there were very few legal limits on the administration of prisons. State statutes dealt with limited aspects of the subject. They commonly prohibited the imposition of corporal punishment, but said little else as to what restraints might be imposed upon inmates. Correctional associations developed more comprehensive standards, but those standards were not legally enforceable. The courts basically took a "hands off" position. Indeed, one early case described the prisoner as "a slave of the state" with no legal rights.[139] Most courts simply noted that they could not assume responsibility for reviewing actions taken by prison officials. Incarceration necessarily carried with it a deprivation of rights, and courts had no basis for determining which deprivations were valid and which were not—aside from the extreme case of physical punishment that violated the Eighth Amendment prohibition against cruel and unusual punishment.

During the late 1960's, the courts (primarily the federal courts) began to reject the "hands off" approach. Initially, the courts were concerned with infringement of First Amendment freedoms. Black Muslim prisoners were not allowed to hold religious meetings. All prisoners were being denied access to the courts by a series of prison restrictions (e.g., inmates were not allowed to assist each other in preparing petitions). Such restrictions were invalidated as imposing unnecessary and unreasonable restraints on inmates, and the courts recognized that this same standard could be applied to various other prison regulations. A full review of the

---

138. *Meachum v. Fano*, 427 U.S. 215, 96 S.Ct. 2532, 49 L.Ed.2d 451 (1976).

139. *Ruffin v. Commonwealth*, 62 Va. 790, 796 (1811).

subsequent decisions would occupy a book in itself.[140] Relying on the First Amendment, the Eighth Amendment, and the due process clause of the Fourteenth Amendment, a wide variety of regulations have been held invalid. Under the First Amendment, the courts have restricted (though not eliminated) the censorship of mail, protected a prisoner's right to publish articles and write books, ensured fair treatment of minority religious groups (though not to the extent of requiring prison officials to change the food they serve), and guaranteed prisoners ready access to the courts to file suits. Relying on the Eighth Amendment, courts have restricted somewhat the use of solitary confinement, have prohibited physical abuse, and have required the state to eliminate overcrowded, unsanitary physical conditions. In one noteable case, the entire Arkansas penal system was declared to violate the Eighth Amendment because of the conditions in that state's prisons.[141] The due process rulings have related primarily to procedures used in imposing prison discipline. In *Wolff v. McDonnell,*[142] for example, the Supreme Court held that the prisoner could not be deprived of good time credits unless he was given written notice of his alleged violation, a statement of the evidence against him, and the opportunity to respond (including the right to call witnesses when that would not be unduly hazardous to institutional safety or correctional goals). In response to the various judicial decisions, corrections officials in various states have sought to develop guidelines as to what restraints are permissible under what circumstances. The guidelines stress, in particular, the need for uniformity and fairness in the administration of prison rules.[143]

Treatment Programs. The nature and number of prison treatment programs vary widely from state to state. Since statistics show that the average inmate is apt to be a school drop-out, and, in an alarming number of cases, is functionally illiterate, the traditional emphasis has been on educational programs. Some corrections departments provide instruction at every grade level from the first

---

140. See, e.g., S. Krantz, *Corrections and Prisoners' Rights In A Nutshell*, St. Paul, Minn.: West Publishing Company, 1976; H. Kerper and J. Kerper, *Legal Rights Of The Convicted*, St. Paul, Minn.: West Publishing Company, 1974: H. Hoffman, *Prisoners' Rights*, New York: Mathew Bender, 1976. These books collect citations to all of the cases described in our discussion.

141. *Holt v. Sarver*, 309 F.Supp. 362 (E.D. Ark. 1970).

142. *Wolff v. McDonnell*, 418 U.S. 539, 94 S.Ct. 2963, 41 L.Ed.2d 935 (1974).

143. See, e.g., *Model Rules and Regulations On Prisoners' Rights and Responsibilities*, St. Paul, Minn.: West Publishing Company, 1973 (rules prepared for the Massachusetts Department of Corrections). In several states, comprehensive correction codes have been adopted by the legislature. The Illinois Code, for example, places various limitations upon disciplinary sanctions. It prohibits corporal punishment and denial of food or bedding, limits solitary confinement to 15 days (except in cases of violence), and limits disciplinary restrictions on visitations and participation in prison programs. See Illinois Stat. ch. 38, §1003-8-7.

A Department of Justice Corrections Task Force has proposed even more comprehensive standards for possible adoption by Congress. See 9 Criminal Justice Newsletter, No. 14 (July 3, 1978). The standards cover physical facilities (e.g., requiring a minimum of 60 square feet of dormitory space per inmate) as well as inmate rights and discipline. The inmate rights' provisions include requirements that: (1) inmates have the right to refuse to participate in programs, except work assignments; (2) inmate mail not be read or censored, except where there is "clear and convincing evidence that a particular item of correspondence threatens the safety or security of the institution, a public official, or any other person, or is being used in furtherance of illegal activities"; and (3) inmates be permitted to send sealed letters to courts, counsel, and government officials.

through college. The corrections system often will have the authority to award a high school diploma or its equivalent. In some areas, more advanced student-inmates may attend nearby colleges. Other programs usually include vocational training, psychological counseling, recreational activities, and work in prison industries. The range of prison industries across the United States is extensive, going far beyond the traditional stamping of license plates.

In recent years, treatment programs have been criticized on various grounds. Many note that they will not work where prisons are overcrowded, understaffed, and filled with racial tension. They argue that, in such a setting (which they view as inevitable), there should be less emphasis on treatment programs and more on simply humanizing prisons. The key, they say, is to put our limited resources into making prisons more civilized places that can be governed effectively by the corrections department. Other critics argue that the programs will only work if they become voluntary programs. Currently, an inmate recognizes that early parole often rests on successful completion of the programs outlined in his "treatment plan." He is, in effect, coerced to participate in the program. Supporters of the current programs claim that they have not been given a fair trial. They point to numerous individual success stories, notwithstanding high recidivism rates. The standards of the American Correctional Association seek to obtain the best of all worlds—excellent rehabilitative programs, reasonable living accommodations, and recognition of the individuality of prisoners.[144] The major obstacle faced by all corrections systems in attempting to meet these standards has been a shortage of funding. In ranking their priorities for distributing government funds, the American people (and their legislatures) traditionally have placed corrections toward the bottom of their list.

Good Time Allowances.   To provide a tangible incentive to prisoners to conform to prison regulations, almost all states have "good time" laws that permit a prisoner to earn credits that reduce the time he must serve in prison.[145] If he maintains good behavior, the prisoner may serve his time at an accelerated pace. Every day of good behavior may earn him credit for as many as two days served on his sentence. Moreover, good behavior requires no more than compliance with prison regulations and participation in programs as directed. Indeed, in most states, good time credits are automatically deducted unless the prisoner is charged with a violation of prison regulations.

States vary both in the extent of the good time credit allowed and the way in which it will be applied against the sentence. Typically, good time will be earned at different rates depending upon the number of years served. Thus, for the first year served, the credit may be sixty days; for the second, it will be raised to 120 days; by the fifth or sixth year, the prisoner may be earning a credit of six months for every year served. In some states, the prisoner earns more good time if he is a first-offender. In Texas, prisoners who achieve the status of trusty receive a better good

---

144. American Correctional Association, *Manual of Correctional Standards,* Washington, D.C., 1966.

145. Hand and Singer, note 95 *supra,* lists the various state good time laws as of 1974. At that time, only Hawaii, Pennsylvania, and Utah had no such laws. See also *Sourcebook of Criminal Justice Statistics—1976,* note 1, p. 1 *supra,* at p. 262.

time rate. In many jurisdictions, additional good time can be earned for "meritorious conduct." This may include a blood donation, excellent performance in a prison industry, or excellent attendance at school.

In about twenty states, good time is deducted from both the minimum and maximum terms of an indeterminate sentence. The remaining states credit good time against only the maximum or only the minimum. Where good time is credited against the minimum, it advances parole eligibility. As good time builds, it places considerable pressure on the prisoner to maintain his good behavior. A serious breach of discipline (e.g., an act of violence or an attempted escape) can result in the loss of all previously accrued good time credits. As we saw in a previous section, the Supreme Court has held that good time credits cannot be denied without giving the prisoner an opporunity to defend his behavior.[146]

Detainers.   A detainer is a kind of "hold order" filed against an inmate by another jurisdiction. It requests that, upon release, the inmate be "detained" so he can be brought to the other jurisdiction to stand trial. (In practice, the inmate would not be physically detained, but the two jurisdictions would cooperate so that an officer from the state filing the detainer could take the prisoner into custody just as he is released from prison). Detainers commonly are filed by prosecutors from other states who have charges pending against the inmate. Unfortunately, many prosecutors file detainers with no intention of proceeding on the detainer (at least not if the defendant remains in prison for a few more years). Studies show that almost half of all detainers are never acted upon by the requesting state. In the meantime, the presence of the detainer can have a significant impact upon the inmate's status in prison. Because of the detainer, he may be held under maximum security or be denied opportunities open to other prisoners, such as being made a trusty. Since the detainer makes the prisoner's future uncertain, the prison may put less effort into his rehabilitation program. In some jurisdictions, parole boards are hesitant to grant parole to a prisoner under the cloud of a detainer.

Two fairly recent developments may relieve some of the difficulties presented by detainers. All but a few states have now adopted the *Interstate Agreement On Detainers.*[147] Under that agreement, once a detainer is received, the warden must promptly inform the prisoner of the detainer and his right to demand a trial on the pending charge in the other state. The Supreme Court has held that, if such a demand is made, the requesting state's failure to provide a prompt trial may constitute a denial of the defendant's right to a speedy trial.[148]

---

146. See p. 375 *supra. Sourcebook of Criminal Justice Statistics—1976,* note 1, p. 1 *supra,* at p. 271, lists the administrative procedures as of 1973 for forfeiture or denial of good time. A substantial majority of the states provided for a hearing before a discipline committee, at which the inmate could present witnesses and be represented by an inmate representative or counsel substitute. These states also provided for an appeal to the corrections authority. About half also provided for an appeal to the courts.

147. The Interstate Agreement and a list of the states adopting it are contained in West's Uniform Laws Annotated, vol. 11, p. 323. As of 1977, the agreement had been adopted in all states except Alabama, Alaska, Louisiana, Mississippi, and Oklahoma. It also had been adopted by the federal government.

148. See *Smith v. Hooey,* 393 U.S. 374, 89 S.Ct. 575, 21 L.Ed.2d 607 (1969); *Dickey v. Florida,* 398 U.S. 30, 90 S.Ct. 1564, 26 L.Ed.2d 26 (1970). These decisions are based on the assumption that the

Moreover, the Interstate Agreement itself requires that the prisoner be brought to trial within six months after he has demanded his right to disposition of the pending charges. Of course, not every prisoner will be willing to risk the possibility that the prosecutor might respond to his demand by actually providing a prompt trial rather than dismissing the pending charges and withdrawing the detainer. If the prisoner is tried and convicted, then he faces the certainty of serving an additional sentence after he completes his current sentence.[149] If he does not object to the detainer, the possibility exists that the prosecutor may not be willing to proceed a few years from now when the prisoner finishes his current sentence.

PAROLE AND RELEASE

Availability.   As we have seen, the states which have adopted determinate sentencing structures have either eliminated or drastically restricted parole.[150] In states with indeterminate sentencing, however, parole remains an essential element of the sentencing structure. Parole involves the release of the prisoner subject to conditions similar to those imposed on the probationer. Parole may be granted by the responsible state agency (usually called a parole board) after the prisoner has served his minimum sentence.[151] The parole board usually has several members, who are either interested citizens appointed by the governor or corrections department personnel selected by the head of that department. Frequently, the board will be assisted by special hearing officers who hold hearings and make recommendations to the board. Most parole boards automatically schedule hearings for every inmate as soon as he becomes eligible for parole.[152] If he is not released at that point, subsequent hearings will be scheduled at regular intervals.

Ordinarily, there are no statutory guidelines as to what circumstances justify granting or denying parole to a prisoner who is eligible for parole. The Federal Parole Commission has published comprehensive administrative guidelines on parole that emphasize what the Commission describes as "offense (severity) and offender (parole prognosis) characteristics."[153] In many respects these are the same factors emphasized by the sentencing judge, except that the parole board can

---

holding state will temporarily release the prisoner for trial in the state filing the detainer. Ordinarily, the states will cooperate in this regard. The prisoner's demand for a trial is viewed under the interstate agreement as waiver of extradition to the receiving state. See note 3 at p. 226 *supra.*

149. Of course, this may not be true if the two sentences run concurrently. See p. 354 *supra.*

150. See note 82 *supra.*

151. This will be the minimum sentence less good time credit where that credit is deducted from the minimum. See p. 377 *supra.* As noted at p. 350 *supra,* some indeterminate sentencing states do not set a minimum as such, but simply provide that parole eligibility begins upon completion of a specified portion (e.g., one-third) of the sentence set by the court. It also should be noted that the parole board does not always have final authority to grant parole. In two states (Oklahoma and Texas), the governor has final authority, but acts on the parole board's recommendation.

152. Not all inmates will become eligible for parole. Persons convicted of first degree murder, for example, commonly are sentenced to a life term without any chance of parole. In many states, other life-termers will be eligible for parole after serving a certain term specified by statute (e.g., fifteen years). In some jurisdictions, parole eligibility is lost, notwithstanding service of the minimum sentence, if the prisoner attempts to escape or engages in certain violent acts. See V. O'Leary and K. Hanrahan, *Law and Practice In Parole Proceedings,* 13 Criminal Law Bulletin 181 (1977).

153. 28 United States Code of Federal Regulation, §2.20.

look to the individual's recent performance in evaluating his personal qualities. Many jurisdictions give substantial weight to the prisoner's completion of programs that will assist him in gaining employment. Indeed, in some jursidictions, it is common practice for the board to enter into a "social contract" with the prisoner; if he maintains good behavior and accomplishes certain training goals (e.g., obtains his high school diploma), he will be released at a certain point after becoming eligible for parole.

Parole Hearings. The procedures of parole hearings vary from state to state. Indeed, not all states regularly hold hearings. A few prefer simply to review the files in the case, permitting the prisoner to submit a statement on his own behalf. Ordinarily, hearings are rather informal affairs held before a hearing officer or one or more board members. The prisoner usually will be informed of the material in his parole file, which relates primarily to his offense, his prior criminal record, and his performance in prison. The prisoner also will be given the opportunity to state his own case for parole and to ask any questions about the parole process. In almost half of the states, he may be assisted by an attorney, and several states will appoint an attorney upon request of an indigent prisoner.[154] The remaining states prohibit representation by an attorney on the ground that it interferes with the board's evaluation of the prisoner's statements and demeanor at the hearing. Shortly after the hearing, most boards will provide the prisoner with a written explanation of its decision. If the prisoner is not released on parole, he must be released after he has served his full sentence.

Pre-release Programs. An inmate about to be released on parole or nearing the end of his sentence often is transferred to a special institution where security measures are relaxed and special programs (e.g., daytime work-release) help to prepare him for his return to the community. In many jurisdictions these pre-release facilities are "half-way houses" located in the community. At a typical pre-release center, the correctional officers and inmates wear street clothes; liberal family visits are permitted; and trained counselors help the inmate with such matters as straightening out his social security record and obtaining a driver's license.

Parole Supervision. The prisoner who is released on parole will be subject to a variety of conditions similar to those imposed upon probationers.[155] Like the probationer, he will be required to attend regular meetings with a supervising parole officer. The function of the parole officer is basically the same as that of the probation officer. Indeed, in some jurisdictions probation officers will supervise parolees as well as probationers.[156] The parolee ordinarily will remain on parole through the balance of the maximum term of his sentence. If the parolee successfully completes his parole term, he is discharged as a matter of law and the parole board loses all jurisdiction over him.

---

154. The various state parole hearings are reviewed in O'Leary and Hanrahan, note 152 *supra*.

155. See pp. 344-46 *supra*.

156. Where the parolee or probationer has reason to move to another state, his parole or probation will be supervised by an officer in that state pursuant to the Interstate Compact on the Supervision of Parolees and Probationers.

Parole Revocation.   If the parolee violates a condition of parole, his parole may be revoked. Parole revocation is similar to probation revocation except that the decision is made by the parole board rather than the judge. As noted previously, *Morrissey v. Brewer*[157] held that certain minimum procedural rights must be granted in the parole revocation process. Initially, the Court noted, due process requires a reasonably prompt informal inquiry conducted by an impartial hearing officer near the place of the parolee's arrest. The function of this hearing is to determine whether probable cause exists to believe the parolee violated a parole condition. The parolee may present his case and may question the persons supplying adverse information (absent offsetting security considerations). If probable cause exists, the parolee may then be returned to prison. At the prison, he will receive a reasonably prompt full hearing on this alleged violation. Under *Morrissey,* that hearing must contain the following elements:

> (a) written notice of the claimed violations of parole; (b) disclosure to the parolee of evidence against him; (c) opportunity to be heard in person and to present witnesses and documentary evidence; (d) the right to confront and cross-examine adverse witnesses (unless the hearing officer specifically finds good cause for not allowing confrontation); (e) a 'neutral and detached' hearing body such as a traditional parole board, members of which need not be judicial officers or lawyers; and (f) a written statement by the factfinder as to the evidence relied on and reasons for revoking parole.

In light of the *Gagnon v. Scarpelli* ruling,[158] the indigent parolee is not automatically entitled to be represented by a lawyer in this proceeding. The nature of both the claimed violation and the parolee's defense will determine the need for counsel. Many states, however, automatically appoint counsel, while almost all permit representation by retained counsel without regard to the nature of the issues in the case.

PARDONS

Availability.   What can be done for the inmate who appears to merit release but is not eligible for parole and has many years left on his sentence? Consider, for example, the first degree murderer, sentenced to life imprisonment, who has been in prison for thirty years and has displayed outstanding character and industry. Another example might be the aged embezzler who is suffering from a terminal illiness but will not be eligible for parole for several years. In cases such as these, the state's power to grant clemency may be used to release the prisoner. That power dates back to a practice of the English kings. Since a crime was viewed as a breach of the king's peace, the king had the authority to forgive (grant "clemency"). The order of clemency granted by the king traditionally was known as a *pardon.* Today, clemency may take several forms, including some that are not technically pardons, but the state's authority to grant clemency is still described as its "pardoning power."

---

157. See note 133 *supra.*

158. See note 134 *supra.* The state practice under *Gagnon* is described in O'Leary and Hanrahan, note 152 *supra.*

Every state recognizes the pardoning power by statute or constitutional provision. The federal constitution, in Article 2, similarly notes the authority of the President to grant "pardons for offenses against the United States, except in cases of impeachment." As the pardon of President Nixon illustrated, many jurisdictions permit pardons to be granted before the recipient is convicted or even charged. Our concern here is with the use of the pardoning authority to release incarcerated defendants who are not eligible for release under the state's parole and sentencing provisions. This is by far the most common use of the pardoning authority. In some cases, such pardons are granted on the ground that the prisoner was an innocent victim of a mistaken conviction. Most pardons, however, are based simply on the ground that further imprisonment would be unjust. Such pardons typically have been granted in cases presenting the following circumstances: (1) an extremely excessive original sentence, considering the nature of the crime and the sentences imposed on others for the same offense; (2) a recent change in the criminal code that will eliminate or sharply reduce the level of criminal liability in future cases for the offense committed by the prisoner; (3) the ill health of the prisoner; and (4) some heroic or self-sacrificing conduct by the prisoner while in custody.

State provisions vary in their placement of the pardoning power.[159] Almost forty states grant the pardoning power to the governor. In several of these states, however, he may grant clemency only upon the recommendation of special boards. Often, even where the governor may act on his own, he will adopt a policy of granting pardons only on the recommenation of the parole board. In ten states, the pardoning power is granted to a special state board. That board usually is appointed by the governor, but he has no control over its decisions.

In all states, the pardoning authority is viewed as a politically sensitive power. Pardons are not subject to judicial review, and there is need to ensure that they are granted for appropriate reasons. In large part, the states rely upon the glare of publicity as a restraining influence. Where the governor is given exclusive pardoning power, most states require that he make a report to the legislature on each pardon, noting the reasons for his action. About half the states require that notice of each pending pardon application be given to the prosecuting attorney, the sentencing judge, and other interested parties.

Forms of Clemency. The basic form of clemency granted today are the full pardon, the conditional pardon, and commutation. The full or absolute pardon releases an individual from the consequences of conviction without any conditions. In some jurisdictions, a full pardon serves to restore civil rights lost through the conviction. Governors or pardon boards in those states frequently are hesitant to grant a full pardon unless the pardon is granted on the ground that the prisoner was mistakenly convicted. They ordinarily will use either a conditional pardon or commutation. A conditional pardon may serve the same function as a parole release. The prisoner may be pardoned on condition that he comply with certain conditions relating to his future behavior (e.g., that he obey all laws of the state). If the pardoned prisoner violates the condition, he may lose his pardon and be

---

159. A National Center for State Courts' publication, *Clemency: Legal Authority, Procedure, and Structure*, Williamsburg, Virginia, 1977, contains a detailed description of the law in each state.

returned to prison to serve the balance of his original sentence. If the prisoner complies with the pardon conditions over a period of years, the conditional pardon may then be converted to a full pardon.

Commutation consists of a reduction in penalty. Its best known use is in the reduction of the death penalty to life imprisonment.[160] However, it more frequently is used to reduce the prisoner's term of imprisonment and thereby make him eligible for immediate parole. It often is the preferred form of clemency because the legal standards applicable to the supervision of parolees and revocation of parole are much clearer than those applicable to persons released on a conditional pardon.

CIVIL DISABILITIES

Rights Automatically Lost Upon Conviction.   In almost all states, a felony conviction carries with it the loss of certain civil and political rights. In some states, the rights are lost only upon conviction for an offense in that state. In other states, rights are lost even though the conviction is by another state or the federal government. The most severe civil disability was the imposition of "civil death," a status that has largely disappeared from the American law. A felon declared civilly dead lost all rights under the civil law; he could not make a contract, marry, or leave a will. Disability provisions in force today usually relate to two areas, citizenship rights and occupational restrictions.[161] In the area of citizenship rights, states commonly provide that felons will lose the right to vote, hold public office, and serve as a juror. Occupational restrictions may relate to a wide variety of occupations. A convicted felon in most states cannot obtain the license necessary to be a barber, beautician, real estate broker, chiropractor, embalmer, nurse, physician, or stock broker. Felons commonly cannot obtain liquor licenses or work in establishments where liquor is sold. Restrictions upon public employment are particularly prevalent. Several states have provisions that either automatically exclude or create a presumption against hiring felons in any government position.

---

160. A closely related form of clemency is the reprieve, which merely postpones execution of the sentence. Reprieves most commonly are granted while the governor is considering commutation of a death sentence. In most jurisdictions, the governor will not consider an application for commutation in a death penalty case until after the death penalty is upheld by the courts on appeal. At this point, a reprieve may be necessary to prevent immediate execution of the sentence.

    The rate of commutation in death penalty cases varies widely from governor to governor. Some governors opposed to capital punishment have regularly commuted all or almost all death sentences during their term of office. Executions in the United States dropped sharply during the mid-1960's following the initiation of legal challenges that eventually led to the *Furman* decision. See p. 335 *supra*. For the period of the 1940's and 1950's, when the annual number of executions in the United States ranged from 153 (in 1947) to 49 (in 1959), the commutation rates for various key states were: California (156 executions and 28 commutations between 1944-63); Georgia (146 executions and 41 commutations bewteen 1946-63); Maryland (57 executions and 35 commutations between 1936-61); and Texas (94 executions and 22 commutations between 1950-62). See E. Abramowitz and D. Paget, *Executive Clemency In Capital Cases,* 39 New York University Law Review 136 (1964).

161. Various state provisions are surveyed in *The Collateral Consequences of Criminal Conviction,* 23 Vanderbilt Law Review 929 (1970), and National Clearinghouse on Offender Employment Restrictions, *Reviewing Offender Employment Restrictions,* Washington, D.C. (1973). These articles also survey the provisions on the restoration of rights noted in the next section.

The current provisions on civil disabilities have been soundly criticized as overbroad and inconsistent with policies followed in corrections programs. While prisons emphasize job training, disability provisions reinforce the natural reluctance of employers to hire felons by delcaring that ex-convicts cannot engage in as many as fifty different occupations. The National Advisory Commission to the Law Enforcement Assistance Administration recommends that only three disabilities flow from a felony conviction; (1) denial of public office during the period of actual confinement; (2) restriction of jury service during actual confinement; (3) denial of a "license or governmental privilege to selected criminal offenders when there is a direct relationship between the offense committed or the characteristics of the offender and the license or privilege sought."[162]

Few states have gone as far as the National Advisory Commission recommends, but many have liberalized their licensing provisions. The newer provisions do not automatically bar convicted felons from various professions, but still permit the conviction to be considered by the licensing board in determining whether the applicant meets the statutory standard as to "moral character."

Restoration of Rights. Traditionally, the civil disabilities resulting from a conviction lasted forever. They could be removed only by a full pardon, and even a pardon did not have that impact in many states. In recent years, however, a substantial group of states have adopted legislation providing for a "restoration of rights." In several states, the restoration operates automatically upon the offender's completion of his prison sentence, probation, or parole. These provisions restore political rights (e.g., the right to vote), but they do not restore eligibility to receive an occupational license. Other states provide somewhat broader restoration upon special application. New York, for example, permits the sentencing court or parole board to issue a Certificate of Relief From Disabilities which overrides statutory prohibitions against issuing licenses to felons and denies other agencies the discretion to refuse license applications based solely upon prior convictions.[163] Provisions of this type ordinarily are limited to a certain class of felons (e.g., first offenders) and may impose a waiting period of several years after completion of the sentence. The court or parole board is given broad discretion to grant or deny the application in the "public interest."

Approximately a dozen jurisdictions also authorize the expungement of a conviction under limited circumstances. The term "expungement" suggests that the conviction is erased or struck from the records, but this is not entirely the case. An expungement permits the individual to answer "No" to an employment application asking the question, "Have you ever been convicted of a crime"? However, the expunged conviction still exists for use in a subsequent criminal prosecution. It may be considered for such purposes as determining eligibility for probation or applying a habitual offender statute. Expungement statutes often are limited to youthful offenders, although some states make them available to all first offenders. The effectiveness of expungement statutes is debatable. The prior conviction

---

162. National Advisory Commission, note 1 *supra*, at §16.17.

163. New York Corrections Code §700. A related procedure provides for issuance of a certificate of "Good Conduct." See also California Penal Code §4852.21 providing for a Certificate of Rehabilitation.

still may be revealed through sources other than the official record of convictions (e.g., prison records), but most employers should not have ready access to those sources.

THE PROBLEM OF RECIDIVISM

The stated objective of the correctional process is to return the offender to society as a law-abiding citizen. The success of corrections in achieving that objective commonly is measured by the recidivism rate of convicted offenders. The recidivism rate attempts to measure the percentage of offenders who become recidivists (i.e., repeat offenders) by committing at least one additional crime. We sometimes hear that the recidivism rate is as high as 70% or as low as 20%. These figures mean nothing unless we know how they are computed. First, while most rates measure only recidivism among offenders who were imprisoned, some also include offenders who were placed on probation. Since persons placed on probation ordinarily pose a lesser risk of continuing criminality, recidivism rates naturally are lower when probationers are included in the group being measured. Second, all recidivism rates are based on offenses committed within a specified time period after the offender was convicted (where probationers are included) or was released from prison. A longer time period usually produces a higher rate of repeaters. More persons who repeat are likely to be caught in a five year period than a two year period. Finally, some rates count the offender as a recidivist if he is arrested again, others if he is prosecuted again, and still others only if he is convicted again. Some rates include all subsequent offenses, while others use only subsequent felonies.

How high are the recidivist rates? The F.B.I., using a four year period and a sample drawn from its Computerized Criminal History file, showed the following rearrest rate among persons released from prison during 1972: 81% for persons initially convicted of burglary, 70% for those initially convicted of assault, and 28% for those initially convicted of embezzlement.[164] The rearrest rate for all persons released on parole over the four year period was 71%, while that for persons receiving probation or a suspended sentence was 51%. These rates are somewhat higher than rates based only on those subsequent arrests that produced convictions or probation or parole revocations. Applying that standard over a three year period to all inmates released or paroled in Georgia, the Georgia Corrections Department reported rates in the area of 49 to 53 percent.[165] The National Council on Crime and Delinquency suggests a figure below 20% based on parolees who were convicted of serious crimes or had their parole revoked for commission of a crime within a three year period of their parole.[166]

Whatever the shortcomings of the methods used to arrive at recidivism rates, no informed person would deny that too many offenders pass through the criminal

---

164. *Uniform Crime Reports—1975* (see note 29, p. 80 *supra*) at p. 42-45.

165. Corrections Digest, June 11, 1975, at p. 4.

166. See *Sourcebook of Criminal Justice Statistics—1966,* note 1, p. 1 *supra,* at p. 757. Michigan statistics similarly show a below 20% rate of probation violations (including violations based on subsequent offenses that result in conviction or probation revocation) over a four year period. See *Dimensions,* note 43 *supra,* at p. 115.

justice process, are released, and within a very short period are beginning the process over again. A major goal of corrections has to be the development of a more accurate means of predicting who will fall in this category and who will not.[167] In the meantime, relying on the premise that the best predictor is past behavior, prosecutors in many parts of the country have developed "career criminal" units. These units place special emphasis upon obtaining prompt convictions and high sentences (usually under habitual criminal statutes) against persons with long criminal records. A major difficulty left unresolved, however, is what the over-crowded correctional system is expected to do with these prisoners. Some argue that such "career criminals" must be viewed as basically not amenable to rehabilitation. The primary function of prisons, they argue, should be to keep these prisoners out of the community until they reach the point of middle age, when, as statistics tell us, they will pose far less of a threat of recidivism. Certainly the prison system of today is not structured to serve such a function. Indeed, one of the most urgent tasks in criminal justice reform is to determine what functions prisons are to play and how they must be reshaped to effectively fill that role.[168]

---

167. A recent Michigan program, based on the records of parolees, has had success using the following factors to predict a high risk of violent crime: (1) currently serving time for robbery, sexual assault, murder or a similar crime; (2) found guilty of major misconduct while in prison or "involuntarily placed in administrative segregation" by the prison's security classification committee; (3) first arrested before 15th birthday. See 9 Criminal Justice Newsletter, No. 3 (January 30, 1978).

168. For further information on the subjects covered in this chapter, see Rubin, note 7 *supra*; Killinger, Kerper and Cromwell, note 63 *supra*; R. Goldfarb and L. Singer, *After Conviction*, New York: Simon and Schuster, 1973; and R. Dawson, *Sentencing*, Boston, Mass.: Little, Brown and Company, 1969.

Chapter 14

The Juvenile Court Process and Juvenile Corrections

JUVENILE COURTS

Strictly speaking, the juvenile court is not part of the criminal justice system.[1] The juvenile court is not a criminal court, though it has many characteristics of a criminal court. Neither is the juvenile court an ordinary civil court, though it is called a civil court. The juvenile court is a *special statutory court* given jurisdiction over cases involving juveniles who are alleged to have committed criminal acts. If the juveniles are found to have committed such acts, they are not "convicted," but are declared to be delinquent children in need of the care and protection of the court. The significance of the juvenile justice system in dealing with crime should not be underestimated. As we saw in Chapter Eight, a substantial portion of those arrested for various felony offenses are juveniles.[2]

A juvenile court's authority ordinarily is not limited to delinquency cases. The court usually also is vested with authority to hear cases concerning abused or neglected children whose condition is such that intervention of the court is necessary for their care and protection. This invokes the "dependency jurisdiction" of the juvenile court. Our discussion will be limited to the court's "delinquency

---

1. We use the term juvenile court to refer to all courts with juvenile delinquency jurisdiction. In some states these courts may be known as the Family Court or the Juvenile Division of the Probate Court. In about half of the states the juvenile court is on the same level as the general trial court. In the other states, it is an inferior court, with its rulings subject to review by the general trial court rather than an appellate court. In several states where the juvenile court is an inferior court, juvenile judges, like magistrates, need not be lawyers. The structure of the juvenile court is reviewed in the working papers of the National Advisory Commission, note 8 *infra,* Volume III, and M. Levin and R. Sarri, *Juvenile Delinquency: A Comparative Analysis of Legal Codes in the United States,* Ann Arbor, Mich.: University of Michigan Project on the National Assessment of Juvenile Corrections, 1974.

2. See p. 190 *supra.*

jurisdiction" since it is that jurisdiction which involves, among others, those juveniles who have violated the criminal law.

The Development of Separate Institutions for Juveniles. You will remember that the early law imposed criminal responsibility on all persons who committed an offense regardless of age, sex, or mental condition. When the church declared that no child under seven could be guilty of sin, the king's court went along with the same rule and did not hold a child under seven criminally liable. However, children over seven were treated exactly as adults—they were tried in the same courts and suffered the same punishments—if it could be shown (from ages 7-14) that they understood the nature and quality of their act and that it was wrong.

As society became more enlightened, people became upset over the severe punishments inflicted upon children. As a result, though children continued to be tried in adult courts, they were gradually exempted from the more severe punishments. At about the same time, the church and private individuals established institutions for the care of homeless children, which on occasion admitted children who had transgressed against the law. These institutions, though far from ideal by our standards, were a great improvement over the prisons of the same period. Special institutions for young offenders later were established by the state itself, and were given names which reflected the main purpose of the institutional programs. The very earliest were called "Workhouses" because the object of the institution was to see that the errant child did useful work. Later, they were named "Reform Schools" to reflect the newly articulated purpose of reform. When it was decided that one of the best ways to reform a young offender was to teach him a trade, the juvenile institutions became "Industrial Schools." Today, institutions for children who have been adjudicated delinquent are usually called "Training Schools" or simply "Schools." This is partly because almost all such institutions have complete educational programs and are accredited schools, but also because the name "school" reflects the fact that the institutions are places for care and treatment, and not for punishment.

The First Juvenile Court. The less severe punishments and the special institutions were a great step foward in the treatment of juvenile offenders. However, adult criminal courts that applied the same standards of accountability to young offenders, and followed the procedures used in the adult criminal courts, continued to hand down what many people considered to be unconscionable sentences against juveniles. It was also felt that many children did not need to be sent to an institution; they could be "reformed" right in their own communities if given the proper care and direction. The movement for a special court to handle juvenile cases was begun by the women who worked in the Settlement Houses of Chicago. The Settlement Houses were charitable organizations devoted to the welfare of immigrants who came into this country, helping them to find homes and jobs and ways to learn the new language. In this work, the women witnessed many instances of unreasonably harsh treatment of young offenders. The women got the support of the Chicago Bar, and in 1900, the first juvenile court was established in Cook County, Illinois. Gradually, other states set up this new court. Wyoming, in 1945, was the last state in the Union to add juvenile courts to its court system.

The Doctrine of Parens Patriae. The philosophy of this new court was unlike that of any other court in history, though it had some resemblance to the old "Court of the King's Conscience." The Chancellor's Courts of early England had often intervened on behalf of fatherless children to require accountings of their money from their guardians and in other ways to protect their interests. The doctrine of the law was that the king had the right and duty to do this because he was "the father of his country." The Latin phrase *parens patriae* means "father of his country," and this doctrine and this phrase became associated with the new court.

The jursidiction of the juvenile court rested upon the doctrine of *parens patriae*—the duty of the state to protect its children. The purpose of this court was not to judge and punish the child for his misbehavior but to provide for him the care and treatment he needed to grow up into a useful and law abiding citizen. If the child's own parents failed or neglected to train him properly, then the state had a duty to take the place of his parents. This new juvenile court would act toward the errant child "as a kind and loving father."

Since the stated objective of this court was to provide the conditions under which the child brought before it could grow up as a useful citizen, the right of the court to act with respect to the child did not depend upon his having committed an act which, if committed by an adult, would be a crime. The state had a duty to protect the child against other kinds of harmful acts as well. The juvenile court was thus given the power to declare a child delinquent, and so take him under its protection, for such things as habitual truancy, frequenting places of ill repute, keeping bad company, and engaging in conduct harmful to himself or others.

Parens Patriae Reconsidered. The *parens patriae* philosophy of the juvenile court had a profound effect on juvenile court procedures. In its original conception, the juvenile court was viewed as a non-adversary court. There was no participant in the juvenile court who was supposed to be "against" the juvenile; everyone, from the judge on down, was "for" the juvenile. Since the only objective was to provide the juvenile with the kind of care and treatment that he would receive from a kind and loving parent, juvenile court procedures could be informal so as to put the juvenile at ease. This approach would serve his best interests. There was no need for the juvenile to be represented by counsel—an attorney would be superfluous in light of the nature of the proceedings. Of course, the juvenile's identity would not be disclosed to the public and an adjudication of delinquency would cast no stigma upon him.

Unfortunately, the noble objective of the juvenile court was not realized. In *Kent v. United States*,[3] the Supreme Court suggested that frequently the juvenile was getting "the worst of both worlds"; he was receiving "neither the [procedural] protections accorded to adults nor the solicitious care and regenerative treatment postulated for children." The landmark case of *In re Gault*[4] sought to remedy this situation. The Court there held that the basic elements of due process applied to

3.   *Kent v. United States,* 383 U.S. 541, 556, 86 S.Ct. 1045, 1054, 16 L.Ed.2d 84 (1966).

4.   *In re Gault,* 387 U.S. 1, 87 S.Ct. 1428, 18 L.Ed.2d 527 (1967).

juvenile courts. The juvenile in *Gault* was charged with the commission of an act that violated the criminal law and was subject to possible committment in a state juvenile institution if adjudicated a delinquent. "It would be extraordinary," the Court noted, "if our Constitution did not require [in such a proceeding] the procedural regularity of care implied in the phrase due process." The concept of *parens patriae* could not justify the state's failure to observe those elements of procedure necessary to secure a fair fact-finding proceeding.

The *Gault* opinion cited four procedural requirements as essential to providing due process in juvenile "adjudicatory hearings." (The adjudicatory hearing is the hearing at which the determination as to delinquency is made; it is similar to the trial in the criminal case and is to be distinguished from various pretrial hearings that also may be used in the juvenile process). The first *Gault* requirement is that notice of the delinquency charges be given to the child and his parents. That notice must inform them "of the specific issues that they must meet" and must be given sufficiently in advance of the delinquency hearing to permit adequate preparation for the hearing. Second, the child and his parents must be advised of their right to be represented by counsel. If they are unable to afford counsel, a lawyer must be appointed at state expense to represent the child (unless there is a knowing and voluntary waiver of the right to counsel). Third, the child must be afforded his right to remain silent under the Fifth Amendment's self-incrimination clause. Although technically classified as civil proceedings, "[delinquency] proceedings . . . which may lead to commitment to a state institution must be regarded as 'criminal' for purposes of the privilege against self-incrimination." Fourth, the child is entitled to confront any witnesses against him and to subject them to cross-examination. Later cases supplemented the *Gault* ruling. *In re Winship,*[5] held that "proof beyond a reasonable doubt" is another "essential of due process" when the "juvenile is charged with an act which would constitute a crime if committed by an adult." *Breed v. Jones*[6] held that due process also protects the juvenile against twice being placed in jeopardy in the course of juvenile proceedings. However, *McKeiver v. Pennsylvania*[7] held that a state need not provide a jury trial. A jury, the Court noted, was not a "necessary component of accurate fact-finding." With the other protections provided, a trial before a judge alone meets the standard of due process.

JUVENILE COURT JURISDICTION

The Juvenile Court Age. The "juvenile court age" is the age within which a child is subject to the delinquency jurisdiction of the juvenile court. Both a minimum and maximum age are involved. Only six states set forth a minimum age in their statutory law. Four use the age of ten and two use the age of seven. The remainder of the states set no minimum age, but it is assumed that their courts would apply the age limit of seven based upon the common law rule that children

---

5. *In re Winship,* 397 U.S. 358, 90 S.Ct. 1068, 25 L.Ed.2d 368 (1970).

6. *Breed v. Jones,* 421 U.S. 519, 95 S.Ct. 1779, 44 L.Ed.2d 346 (1975).

7. *McKeiver v. Pennsylvania,* 403, U.S. 528, 91 S.Ct. 1976, 29 L.Ed.2d 647 (1971).

under seven were incompetent to commit crimes. Available arrest statistics indicate that children under ten rarely are charged as delinquents, and the National Advisory Commission to the Law Enforcement Assistance Administration has recommended that all states set the minimum age at ten.[8]

The upper age limit for initially exercising juvenile court jurisdiction varies from 15 to 17. Six states use 15, twelve use 16, and thirty-three use 17. Thus, an 18 year old must be prosecuted as an adult throughout the United States. There no longer are any states in which original jursidiction extends to 21, as was true until recently in California.[9]

Once the juvenile is adjudicated a delinquent, the court can continue to exercise control over the juvenile beyond the maximum age for originally exercising jurisdiction. If the age limit for exercising control were not extended, the court's hands would be tied in dealing with juveniles who were just below the maximum age when found to be delinquent. The maximum age for continuing to exercise control (called continuing jurisdiction) also varies among the states. Several states with initial maximum age limits below 17 permit continuing jurisdiction only until the delinquent reaches the age of 18. Several others use 20. Over forty states permit continuing jurisdiction until the delinquent is 21. Three states place no maximum age limit on the continuing jurisdiction for juveniles adjudicated delinquent as a result of certain serious crimes, like homicide and rape.

Where the delinquent has engaged in activity that constitutes a serious crime, the court ordinarily will exercise control over him for a shorter period of time than would a criminal court over an adult convicted of committing the same offense. On the other hand, a juvenile who committed an act constituting a misdemeanor may be subject to control over a longer period than would an adult who committed the same crime. For example, a 15 year old who violated a one year misdemeanor provision might be subject to the control of a juvenile court for six years, until he reaches the age of 21. A few states have adopted provisions prohibiting the institutionalization of the juvenile for a longer period than the maximum imprisonment of an adult for the same offense. However, since juvenile corrections is supposed to be entirely rehabilitative and in the juvenile's best interest, most states take the position that the length of imprisonment for a criminal conviction has no relationship to the appropriate period for keeping a juvenile in an institution.

In most states, the juvenile court age is determined as of the date of the offense; in other states, the jurisdiction of the juvenile court is determined by the age of the defendant at the time of the adjudicatory hearing. If the uppermost juvenile court age is 15, a boy who commits an offense the day before his sixteenth birthday would be tried in the one state in a juvenile court; in the other state, since the case cannot be prepared for trial in one day, he would be tried in an adult court.

---

8.   National Advisory Commission on Criminal Justice Standards and Goals, *Report on Juvenile Justice and Delinquency Prevention,* Washington, D.C.: Government Printing Office, 1976, §9.2. The various state age limitations (both maximum and minimum ages) are surveyed in the National Advisory Commission Working Papers, Volume IV, and Levin and Sarri, note 1 *supra.*

9.   See Levin and Sarri, note 1 *supra,* listing the various states.

Acts of Delinquency: Crimes.   The states initially define delinquency as encompassing any act by a juvenile that would constitute a federal or state crime (including ordinance violations) if committed by an adult. However, most states then create one or more exceptions to this definition.[10] The primary exception is the traffic offense. Over thirty states require that minor traffic offenses be handled in the traffic court, while more serious traffic offenses (e.g., driving while intoxicated) remain in the jurisdiction of the juvenile court. Twelve states also exempt one or more serious offenses, requiring that juveniles committing these offenses be prosecuted in the criminal courts. In eight of these states, a juvenile must be tried in the criminal courts if charged with homicide or certain other offenses that carry mandatory life-terms (e.g., kidnapping). In four other states, a distinction is drawn based upon the age of the juvenile. Thus, in Louisiana, the juvenile court loses jursidiction over juveniles who are alleged to have committed rape or homicide only if the juvenile is 15 or older.

Twelve states give the prosecutor discretion to send a case to the criminal courts rather than the juvenile courts under certain circumstances. In some, this authority is limited to offenses carrying a significant maximum sentence (e.g., twenty years imprisonment). In others, if the juvenile is over a certain age, the prosecutor has authority to take the case to the criminal courts in all felony cases.[11] A few states permit the prosecutor to bring a criminal prosecution in any case in which the juvenile has fled the state to avoid prosecution.

In addition to those cases involving juveniles that must be prosecuted in the criminal courts and those that may be presented there at the prosecutor's option, the criminal courts may receive cases involving juveniles that have been "waived" by the juvenile court. In all but two states, the juvenile court has authority under certain circumstances to waive its jurisdiction and thereby transfer a juvenile case to the criminal system. In most states, the court may waive jurisdiction only if the juvenile is above a certain age. That age varies among the states from thirteen to sixteen. If a juvenile court is considering waiver, it ordinarily will hold a full hearing, similar to an adjudicatory hearing, on the issue of waiver alone.[12] The judge's initial function at that hearing will be to determine whether probable cause exists to believe that the juvenile committed the alleged offense. If probable cause is established, the judge then is directed to consider two factors in determining whether waiver is appropriate: the seriousness of the offense and the "suitability of the juvenile" for treatment. In some jurisdictions, waiver is permitted only if

---

10.   The various state provisions are surveyed in Volume IX of the National Advisory Commission Working Papers, note 8 *supra,* and Levin and Sarri, note 1 *supra.*

11.   It should be noted, however, that where states prosecute felonies by indictment, the prosecutor's authority is only to take the case to the grand jury, which may refuse to indict on the ground that a juvenile court proceeding would be preferrable. Also, in some states, the statutes do not refer to the prosecutor's discretion as such, but simply state that the juvenile court and the criminal court shall have "concurrent jurisdiction" in certain cases. These provisions effectively give the prosecutor discretion to choose betweeen a criminal prosecution and a delinquency proceeding. As the initiator of proceedings, the prosecutor may pick the court with concurrent jurisdiction to which he will present the case.

12.   *Kent v. United States,* 383 U.S. 541, 86 S.Ct. 1045, 16 L.Ed.2d 84 (1966) suggests that such a hearing may be constitutionally required. See *Bouge v. Reed,* 254 Or. 418, 459 P.2d 869 (1969).

the judge finds that both factors justify waiver. In other states, additional limitations may be imposed on the judge's discretion. Waiver may be allowed only for the most serious offenses or only upon the request of the prosecuting attorney. In most jurisdictions, waiver appears to be a rather infrequent practice. A juvenile usually will not be viewed as unsuitable for juvenile treatment unless juvenile corrections has made a substantial attempt to rehabilitate him in the past and has failed. Accordingly, waiver cases tend to involve serious juvenile offenders with a long record of juvenile offenses. On occasion, however, the violent nature of the crime may lead to a waiver notwithstanding the absence of a significant prior juvenile record.

Acts of Delinquency: Non-Criminal Acts.   Since the purpose of the juvenile court is to give care and protection to the child, most states extend delinquency jurisdiction to various activities that would not constitute crimes if committed by an adult. Among these are truancy, running away from home, violating a curfew, consuming liquor, and being incorrigible or beyond the control of a parent. Some states include a "catch-all" provision applicable to juveniles who are "wayward," "idling" or simply " in need of supervision."[13] Such non-criminal activities generally are described as "status offenses" since it is only the actor's status as a juvenile that makes such actions subject to judicial control. The exercise of juvenile court jurisdiction on the basis of status offenses has been severely criticized by many groups. In recent years, several advisory commissions or committees have recommended that such jurisdiction be eliminated.[14] Most significantly, the Juvenile Justice and Delinquency Prevention Act of 1974 provides that a state receiving federal funding must adhere to the principal that "juveniles who are charged with . . . offenses that would not be criminal if committed by an adult . . . shall not be placed in juvenile detention or correctional facilities."[15] In the future, it is likely that status offenders will be removed from delinquency jurisdiction in most states. They either will be handled entirely outside of the juvenile court (e.g., by the state department of social services) or will be viewed as coming within the court's quite separate jurisdiction over neglected children in appropriate cases.

THE JUVENILE PROCESS

The Police and the Juvenile Offender.   In all states, a police officer can arrest a juvenile for the commission of a crime. In addition, states generally authorize an officer to take a juvenile into custody if the officer has reasonable cause to believe that the juvenile would be subject to juvenile court jurisdiction on other grounds

---

13.   For a survey of these provisions, see Volume V of the Working Papers of the National Advisory Commission, note 8 *supra,* and the Report of the Joint Commission on Juvenile Justice Standards of the Institute of Judicial Administration and the American Bar Association, *Standards Relating to Non-Criminal Misbehavior* (Tentative Draft 1977), Cambridge, Mass.: Ballinger Publishing Company.

14.   These include the International Association of Chiefs of Police, the National Council of Crime and Delinquency, and the National Advisory Commission. See the National Advisory Commission Working Papers, note 8 *supra,* p. 3 and the National Advisory Committee Report, note 8 *supra,* at §9.1.

15.   42 United States Code §5633.

(e.g., a status offense). In most jurisdictions, the officer is required by law to notify the child's parents as soon as possible after he has been taken into custody. In many cases, the police will hold the child at the station until the parents arrive and then release him into their custody. Very often, the officer will drop the matter at this point, and charges will not be filed with the juvenile court. The police play a very important screening function in determining which juveniles will be taken before the juvenile court and which will be returned to their parents with a warning. Ordinarily, the police department will have no formal guidelines governing this decision, although a general "rule of thumb" may be understood to apply. Thus, the general practice might be to charge the juvenile with delinquency if (1) he has several prior arrests, (2) he has committed a felony, or (3) an officer in the "youth division" knows the juvenile and believes he is "headed for trouble."

Detention. Although the officer intends to charge the juvenile, he need not place him in a detention facility pending his appearance before the juvenile judge. Most states allow the officer to release a juvenile upon a signed promise of the parent or guardian to bring the child before the court when required to do so.[16] Many states also permit release upon posting of station-house bail. If the juvenile is to be detained, many states require that he be detained in a special juvenile facility rather than a jail. Some, however, prohibit detention in a jail only if the juvenile is under a certain age (e.g., 15). Others permit detention in a jail if separate juvenile facilities are not available. Some of these states may require that the juveniles be kept in a separate section of the jail. The National Advisory Committee recommended that jails never be used for the detention of juveniles. It noted "frequent and tragic stories of suicide, rape, and abuses" of juveniles held in jail. Nevertheless, a substantial number of juveniles (conservatively estimated as exceeding 100,000 per year) are still being detained in jail for lack of alternative facilities.[17]

Many jurisdictions require a detention hearing within a certain time after the juvenile is initially taken into custody. It generally is assumed that the detention hearing should be held as promptly as possible, but the outside limit set by statute often may be 48 hours or even longer. The function of the detention hearing is to determine if the juvenile should remain in detention pending the adjudicatory hearing. The issue here is not simply whether the juvenile will flee (as it would be in a bail hearing in a criminal case), but also whether release of the juvenile to his parents or guardian is feasible.[18] In some cases, the most appropri-

---

16. The various provisions relating to release, detention, and detention hearings are surveyed in Levin and Sarri, note 1 *supra.*

17. See National Advisory Commission, note 8 *supra*, at p. 667-668 and the authorities citing there.

18. The National Advisory Commission, note 8 *supra*, at §22.4, suggests that pre-adjudicatory detention may be imposed where clearly necessary for the following purposes:
    1. To insure the presence of the juvenile at subsequent family court proceedings;
    2. To provide physical care for a juvenile who cannot return home because there is no parent or other suitable person able and willing to supervise and care for the juvenile adequately;
    3. To prevent the juvenile from harming or intimidating any witness, or otherwise threatening the orderly process of the family court proceedings;
    4. To prevent the juvenile from inflicting bodily harm on others; or
    5. To protect the juvenile from bodily harm.

ate disposition may be placement in "shelter-care" facility (e.g., a group boarding home). In some jurisdictions, before the court can approve detention or shelter-care pending an adjudicatory hearing, it must determine at the detention hearing that probable cause exists as to the charge. In those states that do not require a detention hearing, the court still must grant specific approval of detention that lasts beyond a few days.

Filing of the Petition.   The petition in a juvenile case is similar to a citizen's complaint in a criminal case. Generally, the state codes place no restriction on who may file a petition. Any person may do so if he has "reasonable cause" to believe that the juvenile has committed a delinquent act. Most petitions are filed by the police following their decision to press charges. However, petitions also are filed by truant officers, school officials, parents, and victims of offenses when they go directly to the court rather than to the police. In most of these cases, the juvenile will not have been arrested, so a court order must be issued directing that he appear before the court. This order is usually called a "summons."

Intake.   A major step in the juvenile process is the administrative screening of complaints, usually by an officer known as the "intake officer." In one sense, this officer performs the same screening function as a prosecutor in determining whether to prosecute, but the intake officer's full role is somewhat more complicated. The intake officer may approve the complaint and refer it to the court for an adjudicatory hearing or dismiss it and release the child from any further obligations. He also has another option, however, that involves dismissal of the complaint but requires the child to participate in a rehabilitative program. Long before diversion programs received significant attention in the criminal justice process, they were commonly used in the juvenile justice process. Delinquency petitions were dismissed on condition that the child seek the assistance of a community service agency, return to school, or participate in some community service programs. In some areas, special youth service bureaus, attached to the court, provided various counselling services for youths referred by the intake workers. Today, many juvenile courts rely far more heavily on diversion than adjudication in the disposition of cases.

The screening process of the intake officer usually tends to be more thorough than that of the prosecutor in the criminal justice system. Ordinarily, the intake officer will interview the juvenile, his parents, and the arresting officer or other complainant. In some instances, the case will be referred to a probation officer for an investigation. Of course, in evaluating this information, the intake officer's perspective is likely to be somewhat different than that of the prosecutor. While the intake officer also is concerned with the protection of society and deterring unjustifiable conduct, he will give considerably more weight to the "best interests of the child" than would most prosecutors. In recent years, some prosecutors have expressed concern as to their lack of participation in the intake process. In many jurisdictions, the prosecutor ordinarily took no interest in a case until after the petition was approved for an adjudicatory hearing. Today, consultation between the intake officer and the prosecutor is more common. In some jurisdictions, moreover, the prosecutor is given the final authority to force a case to the adjudicatory stage.[19]

Appointment of Counsel.   Traditionally, retained counsel was allowed to participate in the juvenile process from the very outset, but counsel was not appointed to represent the indigent until after the petition had been approved at the intake proceeding. In recent years, some courts, using a juvenile defender service, have provided counsel at the intake stage. Of course, the juvenile can waive a lawyer, if the waiver is made knowingly and voluntarily. The National Advisory Commission, concerned as to the juvenile's exercise of intelligent choice, suggests that a waiver should not be accepted unless the juvenile has first consulted with a lawyer.[20] In cases where the interests of the parent and the child appear to be adverse, the court must make sure that the appointed or retained counsel represents the child alone. Such situations arise, for example, where the parent is the complainant or the offense involved is a status offense relating to the control of the parents. Indeed, in some cases involving offenses relating to the parents' control of the child, it may be necessary to have separate counsel for the parents in addition to the counsel for the child.

The Adjudicatory Hearing.   The adjudicatory hearing is held as soon as possible after the child has been charged, leaving sufficient time for the defense counsel to prepare his case. The purpose of the hearing is to determine whether or not the child did in fact commit the delinquent act with which he is charged. In an adult court, this would amount to a determination of guilt or innocence. Just as an adult can plead guilty, a juvenile can admit to the facts alleged in the petition. Prior to accepting the admission, the juvenile judge will determine that it is made voluntarily and knowingly. Very often, the judge will conduct an inquiry similar to that conducted by a criminal court judge in accepting a guilty plea.

Since the *Gault* decision, the proceedings in an adjudicatory hearing in juvenile court closely resemble a trial in an adult criminal court. The adjudicatory hearing is before the juvenile judge and is attended by the child, his parents, the prosecuting attorney, and defense counsel. Several states provide for juries. Otherwise, the hearing is closed. The witnesses against the child appear in court and testify under oath as in an adult court. The prosecuting attorney represents the state and examines and cross-examines witnesses. The lawyer representing the child cross-examines the state's witnesses and presents witnesses on behalf of the child. The case against the child must be proved to the same level of proof required in criminal cases—beyond a reasonable doubt.

After hearing all of the evidence, the court may dismiss the case or make an adjudication of delinquency, which is a finding that the child is a delinquent child

---

19.   See Levin and Sarri, note 1 *supra.* We assume, of course, that there is at least probable cause to support the charge. In some jurisdictions, a probable cause hearing, similar to a preliminary hearing, will be held prior to the adjudicatory hearing. See Volume VII of the Working Papers of the National Advisory Commission, note 8 *supra.*

20.   See National Advisory Commission, note 8 *supra,* at §16.1.

in need of the further supervision of the court. If the child is found to be delinquent, the court sets a date for the dispositional hearing and asks that a Social History Report be prepared.

The Social History Report. The Social History Report is very similar to the presentence report used in adult criminal courts. The report is prepared by a juvenile court probation officer who makes an extensive investigation of the child's background, family relations, mental and physical health, school performance, work record, and prior delinquent history. The probation officer often starts the preparation of the report at the time of the intake decision, but the judge does not look at the report until after the adjudication of delinquency. As with presentence reports, judges often rely heavily upon the Social History Report and upon the recommendations of the probation officer.

The Dispositional Hearing. The dispositional hearing is the equivalent of a sentencing hearing, but it usually has retained many of the informal aspects that developed in the juvenile court prior to *Gault*. At no other point in the juvenile court process is the basic philosophy of the juvenile court more in evidence. The judge, probation officer, prosecutor, defense attorney, the child's parents, and the child, enter into informal discussions as to the best disposition for the child—the stated objective being not to punish him for his wrongdoing but to provide for his care and rehabilitation.

Depending upon community facilities, the judge may have a considerable range of dispositional alternatives. At this late date in the proceedings, he still has authority to dismiss the case against the child. He may continue the case (i.e., postpone the order of disposition) or release the child into the custody of his parents. He may place the juvenile on probation, send him to a foster home, place him in a private institution for children, or as a last resort, commit the child to a state correctional authority or institution. The prevailing guideline in selecting among dispositions is the principle of the "least restrictive alternative." The National Advisory Commission states that guideline as follows:

> *In choosing among statutorily permissible dispositions, the court should employ the least coercive category and duration of disposition that are appropriate to the seriousness of the delinquent act, as modified by the degree of culpability indicated by the circumstances of the particular case, age and prior record of the juvenile.*[21]

JUVENILE CORRECTIONS

Probation. Once a child has been adjudicated a delinquent, the most frequent disposition is probation rather than commitment to a state correctional institution. A fully organized and staffed juvenile court has a probation department. Except in a few states, Juvenile Probation Departments are locally organized and financed. Typically, however, fully organized juvenile courts exist only in the

---

21. National Advisory Commission, note 8 *supra*, at §14.4

metropolitan areas; in smaller cities and rural areas, no adequate supervisory services for juvenile offenders are available.

Juvenile probation, like adult probation, is a judicial function. The juvenile on probation continues in the custody of the juvenile court under the supervision of the probation officer. If there is a fully staffed Juvenile Probation Department, the probation officer will be a college educated professional with training and experience in social casework or in juvenile corrections. If there is no juvenile probation department, the probation officer may be the sheriff, an interested citizen, or the juvenile judge himself.

Terms and Conditions of Probation.   The juvenile judge in the dispositional hearing sets the term and conditions of probation. Typical conditions require that the juvenile attend school regularly; obey all the laws; be at home every night by a certain hour; remain in a certain locality; and report regularly to the probation officer. Special conditions may prohibit the juvenile from driving a car, associating with the members of a juvenile gang, getting married without the consent of the probation officer, or require that the juvenile make restitution to the victim of his offense. The probation term may extend until the juvenile reaches the maximum age for the court's continuing jursidiction. In practice, however, the term of probation usually does not exceed one or two years.

Revocation of Probation.   Probation can be revoked by the court if the juvenile violates any of the terms of his probation. Typically, probation is not revoked for minor transgressions, but is usually revoked if the juvenile commits another offense, absconds from the jurisdiction, or fails to report regularly. The juvenile has a right to a hearing on revocation of probation and is also entitled to be represented by counsel at the revocation hearing. The juvenile whose probation is revoked is committed to the juvenile correctional authority, or, in some states, directly to a juvenile correctional institution.

Commitment To an Institution.   If the juvenile is to be committed to an institution, either directly or as a result of a probation violation, a variety of procedures may be available. In most states, the court may place the juvenile with a private institution (e.g., a group home) that has been certified by the state. If this alternative is used, the court may make the placement directly. If a public institution is used, the court may have the authority to select a particular camp, ranch, or school. Frequently, however, the commitment must be made by a state-wide agency (commonly called a Youth Authority), that performs a function similar to the state corrections commission. That agency will then determine which state institution is appropriate for the juvenile. The agency also will determine when the juvenile should be released from the institution, although he must be released upon reaching the maximum age for continuing jurisdiction.

Treatment Programs in Juvenile Institutions.   A large state will have many types of juvenile institutions and provide a variety of programs for the rehabilitation of delinquents. Early training schools focused on suffering and hard work; modern schools emphasize continued academic education and counseling. Work camps, often called forestry camps, have been found effective in many states, though the boys sent to such camps are usually carefully selected from the general training school population.

Parole. Some youth authorities provide for parole from a juvenile institution which is similar in all respects to adult parole. The juvenile is released into the community under the supervision of a parole officer who is employed by the youth authority or is sometimes a probation officer attached to a juvenile court. He can be returned to the institution for violation of his parole conditions.

Aftercare. Many authorities working with delinquent juveniles believe that all juveniles need supervision when released from an institution. Aftercare supervision may be similar to parole supervision or may consist of assignment to a "halfway house." Halfway houses are located in the community, and provide a place where a youth may live while he is readjusting to life in a free society. Authorities in the halfway house assist the youth in obtaining a job which he may work at during the day, returning to the halfway house at night. When the youth and his counselors feel that he is able to "go it on his own," he is given his complete release from the youth authority and moves out of the halfway house.

The Effect of an Adjudication of Delinquency. The founders of the juvenile court took great precautions to protect the juvenile from any adverse effects from an adjudication of delinquency. Statutes provide that the civil disabilities commonly following criminal convictions cannot be applied to delinquency adjudications. Moreover, disclosure of a juvenile record is limited by law to specifically authorized persons. Fingerprints are to be taken for identification purposes or to connect the juvenile with other offenses; they should not later be placed in central fingerprint files such as the F.B.I.'s files, but are to be destroyed. Publication of the names of the juveniles in the public press is forbidden in some states, and, in others, the press has agreed to refrain from such publication.

In spite of these precautions, juvenile records frequently are disclosed. Only half of the states require that the police arrest record be expunged or otherwise kept from public disclosure. Most permit the juvenile judge to release the records and this is commonly done where the records are desired in connection with a subsequent criminal case. Indeed, the Supreme Court has held that a defendant, in seeking to impeach an opposing witness, may refer to his juvenile delinquent probationary status.[22] In recent years, further efforts have been made to guard the confidentiality of juvenile records. It is a difficult objective to achieve, however, since there are some purposes (e.g., law enforcement use) for which disclosure is deemed appropriate. Once the records are disclosed to some sources, the task of ensuring that there is no further disclosure requires many more safeguards than are currently applied.

REVIEWING THE OVERALL PROCESS

The chart on page 401 should help you in understanding the juvenile court process and give you an idea of the number of people who are involved in helping the dependent or delinquent child who is referred to the juvenile court. The chart

---

22. *Davis v. Alaska*, 415 U.S. 308, 94 S.Ct. 1105, 39 L.Ed.2d 347 (1974).

shows the organization of a juvenile court in a city of approximately 275,000 people. Not all juvenile courts have the same organization and few outside of large metropolitan areas provide the services that are offered by this progressive court. In smaller communities, the entire juvenile court may consist of one part-time judge.

Depending upon the offense and the needs of the child, services of any of the persons attached to the court can be called upon. Investigation will begin with intake and may involve detention in the child care center and examination by a physician, psychiatrist, psychological consultant or clinical psychologist. The chaplain acts as spiritual advisor and counselor to both the child and his parents.

Continued investigation is available through the services of the Probation Department under the direction of the Director of Probation Services. If the case is filed upon, the attorney for the court will present the case against the juvenile. This attorney acts in the same capacity as a prosecutor in a criminal court except that he is generally better informed about and more involved in the dispositional procedures (sentencing). A Public Juvenile Defender staff headed by an attorney and using the services of part-time paid and volunteer law students is a unique feature of this court which will be more and more frequently found in the larger juvenile courts.

The juvenile judge, in this case the judge of a district court, must approve the detention of children held in the Child Care Center for longer than 24 hours. He presides over all hearings in the court, and makes all of the decisions as to the disposition of children who are brought before the court. Only the juvenile judge may order a disposition which involves taking a child away from his parents.

The dispositional alternatives of the juvenile judge include placing the child in the custody of the Youth Council or putting him on probation in his court. The Youth Council may incarcerate the child in a juvenile correctional institution, and after a period in the institution, release him on parole. The juvenile on probation or parole is under the supervision of a probation or parole officer under the direction of the Director of Probation.

A juvenile with a drug problem would be assigned to the Drug Treatment Program under a specialized probation officer who could call upon the psychiatric social worker, the community worker, the counselor-therapist, and the community Child Guidance Clinic.

The Chief Probation Officer is the administrative head of the juvenile court and works closely with the juvenile judge. In this court, the Chief Probation Officer is employed by a Juvenile Board set up by statute and consisting of the county judge and the five district judges. Funds for the operation of the court are provided by the county commissioners. In this state, the county judge is chairman of the board of county commissioners. The Citizens Advisory Committee is a liaison between the juvenile court and the community.

The Internship and special programs bring young professionals into the court for training. The undergraduate interns work in the court during the summer between their junior and senior years and have an opportunity to put into practice the theories they have learned in school. Graduate students are on supervised field placement assignments. Law students are learning about the legal procedure of the court, and young psychologists are given clinical experience.

Juvenile Court Organization

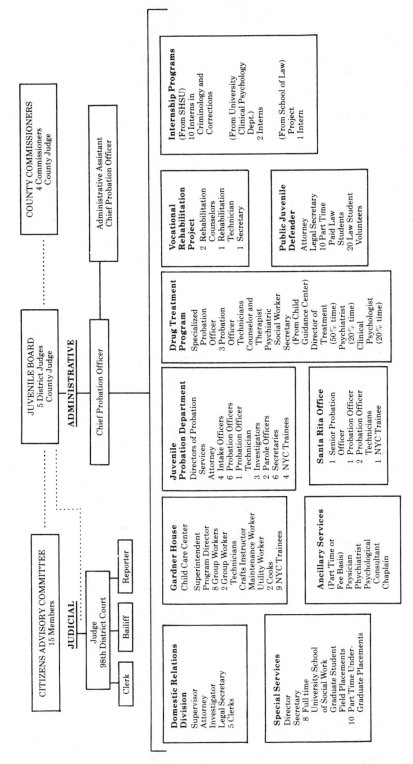

As you can see, many highly trained people are involved in the juvenile court process, and many specialized services are available for the purpose of helping children in trouble.

The Success of the System.   The juvenile court process has its critics and its supporters. Very often we find that the position from which one views the process has considerable bearing on his analysis of its strengths and weaknesses. This point was illustrated, in part, in the testimony of various experts before the Senate Juvenile Delinquency Subcommittee in its hearings on serious juvenile crime. A former defense counsel saw the system as basically inept. He suggested:

> (1) very little rehabilitation is taking place; (2) no one knows which children are in need of either habilitation or rehabilitation; (3) all children receiving similar sentences tend to be treated in basically the same manner rather than in an individualized manner; (4) no one presently can differentiate between a dangerous and nondangerous juvenile offender; (5) because no one can differentiate, many children are unduly punished while others are prematurely set loose to prey on the community; and (6) the so-called 'successes' of the juvenile system probably occur for reasons other than the juvenile system.

A chief of police thought that the system could distinguish between offenders and its major deficiency was its failure to do. He noted:

> My concern is that we have failed to accept and overlooked the premise that there is such a thing as a 'juvenile criminal.' My own perception . . . is that if we could remove a certain hard core of serious juvenile offenders from our jurisdictions, we would realize a noticeable reduction in many offenses. We are failing miserably in providing meaningful institutionalization for these offenders within the juvenile justice system.

A prosecutor suggested that the problem cited by the police chief was produced, in part, by the lack of strong participation in the juvenile process by prosecutors:

> Vigorous representation of the state's interest by the prosecutor—as opposed to social workers and other non-attorneys—would . . . do much to protect the public's interest and safety in cases of violent offenders and nonviolent chronic offenders. Unfortunately, many states have been slow to abandon the informal, nonadversarial nature of their juvenile court proceedings and have made very limited or no provisions for representation of the state's interest, i.e., representation by prosecutors.

The Director of the New York Division for Youth expressed concern about "the current fashion of saying 'rehabilitation' has 'failed'" and should be abandoned:

> While it is obvious that there are youth committing serious acts which hurt others, there is no 'new breed' of 'remorseless, cold-eyed' youth who do violence to the old and the weak without a second thought and are therefore unreachable. When youth say they do not care, or offer outrageous excuses for their behavior, that is only the beginning; for when youngsters are confronted by strong, caring, active, able staff in an atmosphere of close supervision and intensive individual attention, breakthroughs can occur.

The director cited programs that provided such intensive individual attention and had been successful even in treating juveniles involved in violent acts. The treatment approach of these programs, he noted, was not especially startling or bizarre.

It consisted of a heavy emphasis on indivdiual therapy, group therapy, highly individualized education and recreation. Major emphasis was placed on working with the families of the youngsters as well.

Finally, a juvenile judge also expressed continued confidence in rehabilitation:

> The pragmatic question is has this nonpunitive system worked with juvenile felons? The answer is an astonishing and resounding yes. A study of over 800 juveniles found delinquent in Cook County, Illinois in 1974 for committing violent offenses (rape, robbery, homicide, assault and battery) has been recently completed. The study reveals the following:
>
> — Of the 606 juveniles in the base group, 84 had findings for new offenses, violent or nonviolent. In other words, *the proportion with any overall recidivism was one in seven, or 14%* ... For almost half (31) of all 84 recidivism, the new findings were violent offenses. This makes a violent recidivism rate of 7%, or 1 in 14 of the total base group.
>
> ... There is a rush to treat children involved in crime as adults either through reduction in juvenile court jurisdiction or by importing adult criminal justice philosophy and methods into the juvenile justice system. This stands the nation's response to crime on its head. We should be transferring juvenile justice methods, which we know from empirical evidence work, into the troubled adult system.[23]

---

23. The persons quoted are Wallace J. Mlyniec (defense attorney); Col. Robert O. Mathews (chief of police, Howard County, Maryland); Robert F. Leonard (prosecutor, Genesee County, Michigan); Peter B. Edelman (director, New York State Division for Youth); and William S. White (president-elect, National Council of Juvenile and Family Court Judges). Their statements are quoted in 9 Criminal Justice Newsletter, No. 10, p. 4-5 (May 8, 1978).

    For further information on the juvenile justice system, see the National Advisory Commission Report, note 8 *supra*; F. Faust and P. Brantingham (editors), *Juvenile Justice Philosophy,* St. Paul, Minn.: West Publishing Company, 1974; T. Johnson, *Introduction to the Juvenile Justice System,* St. Paul, Minn.: West Publishing Company, 1975.

Part Four

The Professionals in the Criminal Justice System

INTRODUCTION

A profession is characterized by organization, learning, and a code of ethics by which the behavior of its members is judged and regulated. In a fully recognized profession the following characteristics can be identified.

1. A recognized body of knowledge which is systematically transmitted to new members.
2. A professional organization to which the members belong or with which they identify themselves.
3. A Code of Ethics regulating the conduct of members.
4. A special process of licensing or admissions administered by the government or the group itself, which grants the privileges of the profession to persons thought to be qualified and denies them to others who seek to engage in the profession.

Of those persons working in the criminal justice system, the members of the legal profession belong to one of the classical professions. Legal knowledge is formally transmitted in approved law schools and tested in bar examinations. The American Bar Association and Bar Associations in each state, district, county or city are professional organizations of lawyers. Lawyers are bound by a comprehensive Code of Professional Responsibility, which is enforced by the State Bar Associations and by the courts. Only lawyers licensed by the state may practice law. Also, lawyers, in common with many professionals, are expected to perform a variety of public service functions, including donation of legal services to indigents, as part of their professional responsibilities.

While the lawyers are the only regular workers in the criminal justice system (except for the prison doctors and chaplains) who belong to one of the classic professions, other participants in the system meet most, if not all the criteria which characterize a profession. They have specialized training and skills derived from a recognized body of knowledge which is systematically transmitted to new members; they have professional organizations; many of these organizations have adopted codes of ethics; and members of some of the groups must be licensed or "certified". We have, therefore, elected to label as professionals in the criminal justice system not only the prosecutor, the defense attorney, and the lawyer-judge, but also the police officer, the correctional administrator, the probation and parole officer, the institutional correctional officer, and the court administrator. Many social scientists would disagree with our characterization of some or all of these criminal justice participants as professionals.[1] Technically, these critics may be correct, but each of these groups has made sufficient effort to achieve the standards of professionalism, particularly in the past decade, that we feel justified in describing them as professionals.

With respect to each group of professionals in the criminal justice system, we will explore their method of selection, their education and training, and their roles in the criminal justice process. We will also consider the inter-relationships among the professionals in the system. As we have pointed out previously, understanding and cooperation among all persons associated with the criminal justice system is an imperative if the criminal justice system is to fulfill its crucial role in a modern society.

---

1.   Police work, for example, has been described as more of a craft, or skilled trade, than a profession. Consider, for example, J. Wilson, *Varieties Of Police Behavior*, Cambridge, Mass.: Harvard University Press, 1968, p. 30:

> [M]embers of professions tend to govern themselves through collegial bodies, to restrict the authority of their nominal superiors, to take seriously their reputation among fellow professionals, and to encourage some of their kind to devote themselves to adding systematically to the knowledge of the profession through writing and research. The police are not in any of these senses professionals. They acquire most of their knowledge and skill on the job, not in separate academies; they are emphatically subject to the authority of their superiors; they have no serious professional society, only a union-like bargaining agent; and they do not produce, in systematic written form, new knowledge about their craft.

Chapter 15

The Police

THE POLICE AGENCIES

Fragmentation. In the United States, the police function is performed by a variety of agencies at all levels of government. Altogether, there are over 20,000 police agencies.[2] Less than 100 of these agencies are federal agencies, and only about 200 are state agencies. The remaining 19,700 or so police agencies are units of a county, city, village, township, or other local governments. The wide distribution of police authority among various different agencies reflects two basic concerns of the American people. First, we view centralized police authority as posing an inherent threat to our political liberties. The concept of a single national police force, with total police authority, is associated with the national police forces found in almost all totalitarian regimes. Undoubtedly, a single national police force or even fifty statewide police units would offer various advantages, in terms of cost and efficient use of manpower, over the current division of police authority. But we are more than willing to pay the price of fragmented police authority in order to avoid the dangers to democracy of a centralized police authority.

Of course, the opposition to an all-powerful centralized police force does not explain why we often have as many as 500 different police agencies within a single state. One can avoid the dangers of centralization without dividing police authority as extensively as we do in this country. The extreme fragmentation of American police authority also is explained, in part, by our desire for local control as a means of shaping police policy. The police department which is a unit of a small city is more likely to reflect the viewpoints of the citizens in that city than a

---

2. Unless otherwise indicated, the statistics cited in this chapter come from *The Sourcebook Of Criminal Justice Statistics—1976*, note 1, p. 1 *supra*, and the *Uniform Crime Reports—1976*, p. 80 *supra*.

department that polices the entire county in which that city is located. Local control may affect the police department's hiring policies, its allocation of resources, and even the exercise of its discretion in enforcement of the law. The attitudes of the local community often may be a primary factor in persuading a local police department to place greater emphasis on hiring officers with college experience, to increase patrols in particular areas of the community, or to refuse to press charges on certain minor offenses.

Over the years, many experts have suggested that our concern for local control has led to far too much fragmentation of police authority. Substantial waste results from the fact that most local departments are not large enough to gain any of the economies of size in such areas as purchasing equipment or training specialists. There also is some overlap in the functions performed by police units operating in nearby communities. So far, however, the only substantial movement toward reducing the fragmentation of police authority has centered on eliminating very small departments consisting of only a few officers.[3]

Federal Police Agencies.   Although we tend to hear mostly about the Federal Bureau of Investigation, there are almost fifty different federal agencies with police authority. Of these agencies, the F.B.I. has the broadest jurisdiction since it is responsible for enforcement of all federal criminal laws outside of those special fields where enforcement is assigned to other, specialized federal police agencies.[4] The other agencies, limited to particular groupings of federal offenses, include the following: the Drug Enforcement Administration (responsible for enforcing federal laws relating to controlled substances); the Immigration and Naturalization Service (responsible for enforcing laws relating to the admission, deportation and naturalization of aliens, and also including the Border Patrol); the Internal Revenue Service (responsible for enforcing the criminal and civil provisions of the federal tax law); the Alcohol, Tobacco, and Firearms Division (enforcing various federal provisions, including criminal laws, relating to the distribution of alcohol, tobacco, firearms, and explosives); the Secret Service (responsible for the suppression of counterfeit currency as well as protection of the President and other specified persons); the Bureau of Customs (enforcing various criminal provisions relating to imports and smuggling); the National Park Service (providing law enforcement in national parks through the Park Rangers and the U.S. Park

---

3.   Thus, the National Advisory Commission on Criminal Justice Standards and Goals, *Report on Police*, Washington, D.C.: Government Printing Office, 1973, §5.2 sets forth a basic policy urging only limited consolidation:

> Every State and local government and every police agency should provide police services by the most effective and efficient organizational means available to it. In determining this means, each should acknowledge that the police organization (and any functional unit within it) should be large enough to be effective but small enough to be responsive to the people. If the most effective and efficient police service can be provided through mutual agreement or joint participation with other criminal justice agencies, the governmental entity or the police agency immediately should enter into the appropriate agreement or joint operation. At a minimum, police agencies that employ fewer than 10 sworn employees should consolidate for improved efficiency and effectiveness.

4.   The F.B.I. also is the largest of the federal police agencies, although it contains fewer sworn officers (approximately 8,000 "special agents") than several of our largest city police departments.

Police); and the Postal Inspection Service (charged with enforcing a wide range of criminal violations—e.g., improper use of mails, burglaries, employee theft—insofar as they relate to postal services).

The various federal police agencies are scattered through a variety of departments almost as varied as their law enforcement activities. For example, the Federal Bureau of Investigation, the Drug Enforcement Administration, and the Immigration and Naturalization Service all are part of the Justice Department; the Internal Revenue Service, the Alcohol, Tobacco and Firearms Division, the Secret Service, and the Customs Bureau all are part of the Treasury Department; the National Park Service is part of the Interior Department; and the Postal Inspection Service is part of the United States Postal Service. Other federal departments, such as Agriculture, and Labor, also have inspection units with law enforcement authority.

Achieving coordination among the various federal police agencies has always presented a problem because of their scattered location throughout the government. One major positive force has been the central role played by the Department of Justice in the enforcement of all federal criminal laws. While investigative authority is divided, all prosecutions must be brought through the United States Attorneys or other prosecuting divisions within the Justice Department, and each case presented by the investigative agency must meet guidelines for prosecutions set by that department. In recent years, the Justice Department has sought to obtain greater coordination of investigative efforts by encouraging the use of joint task forces involving several investigative agencies. The most noted of these groups has been the organized crime strike forces which have been assigned to approximately 20 major metropolitan areas. The strike forces ordinarily consist of representatives of several agencies, including the Federal Bureau of Investigation, the Drug Enforcement Administration, the Internal Revenue Service, the Secret Service, the Alcohol, Tobacco, and Firearms Division, and the Securities and Exchange Commission. In many areas, the strike force has established close liason with local authorities. A major objective of the strike force concept is to ensure that each agency has established consistent investigative priorities that will permit the total investigative effort to be more successful.

Perhaps more difficult problems in achieving coordination result from the overlap with state and local police activities. As we noted in discussing the federal criminal law, many violations of that law also constitute violations of state law. Also, the same persons frequently are involved in separate violations of federal and state law. Three major approaches have been emphasized to avoid duplication of effort and inconsistencies in approach by federal and state and local officials. Initially, the federal government has sought to maintain a strong relationship with state and local departments by providing them with various support services. Thus, the F.B.I. provides a scientific laboratory and a fingerprint identification service that is heavily used by various state and local departments. The Bureau's annual report on crime in the United States (the Uniform Crime Reports) serves a somewhat similar function. Second, the federal agencies generally have sought to carefully confine their activities to the investigation of federal crimes. In the area of kidnapping, for example, the F.B.I. will only intervene in an investigation when, based upon relevant factors (e.g., a significant period of disappearance), there is a reasonable likelihood that the kidnapper has violated a federal law by taking the victim across state lines. Finally, efforts have been made to maintain an open line of communications between local and federal police officials. Notwithstanding such efforts, the degree of coordination achieved often has depended, in the end, upon the attitudes of the particular individuals in charge of the local police department and the office of the federal agency in the particular community.

State Police Agencies. Each state has one or more police agencies that are part of the state government. The basic state police agency ordinarily is called the "state police department" or "state highway patrol." In some states, the authority of this agency is limited primarily to traffic control. In others, the state police have general law enforcement authority, although policing the highways is one of their basic responsibilities. Where the state police department operates as an all-purpose police force, it commonly will provide specialized services for the smaller municipal departments, such as training programs, scientific laboratories, and computerized information services. A state department with general police authority also will lend its assistance to smaller local departments in the more difficult criminal investigations. Theoretically, the state police department could conduct its own independent investigation of any crime committed anywhere within the state. Thus, where a crime is committed in a city, both the state police and the city police could investigate separately. Both would have the power to act in the area, and neither could exclude the other's operations. As a matter of practice, however, state police departments almost always avoid duplicating local police operations by concentrating their efforts in rural areas which do not have local police departments.

In addition to its basic police agency, the state usually will have several specialized police agencies. These may include a state bureau of narcotics enforcement, a state park police force, various licensing agencies with inspectors possessing police authority, and even special campus police forces for the state universities. Where the agencies are confined to a particular geographic area (e.g., parks), there ordinarily is little overlap with local police departments. Where the state agency concentrates on a particular class of offenses (e.g., narcotics), there may be considerable duplication of effort and even some competition between the state and local agencies. Overall, the manpower of the various state police agencies will be substantially less than the total manpower of all of the various local agencies. Typically, the local agencies combined will have six or seven times as many officers as the state agencies. On the other hand, the basic state agency will be larger than most of the individual local departments.

Local Police Agencies. Local police agencies commonly are found at the county, city, and township levels of government. At the county level, the primary police agency is the sheriff's department.[5] There are basically two different styles of sheriff's offices. In certain states, the sheriff's responsibility is limited almost

---

5.   The term sheriff, comes from a combination of two early English terms, "shire" and "rieve." The "shire" was the counterpart of the county and the "rieve" was the chief enforcement officer of the county. The term "constable" originally referred to an official who assisted the sheriff, but gradually was used to describe a local official who had law enforcement responsibilities, but also served various other functions.

exclusively to civil functions (e.g., service of process) and administration of the county jail. In other states, the sheriff's department is a full-time law enforcement agency. Such departments usually concentrate their law enforcement efforts in those localities within the county that lack local police departments (usually villages and small townships). However, the sheriff's authority actually extends to the entire county (including areas policed by city police departments), and the sheriff's department could enforce laws within the cities if it so desires. Thus, in many states, the state police, the sheriff's department, and the local city or township police have overlapping enforcement authority within the city or township, although they commonly distribute their efforts so as to limit the likelihood of duplication.

Below the county level, most cities and many townships have their own police departments. Indeed, of the more than 520,000 police employees in this country,[6] more than two-thirds are employed in city and township police departments. Each department is largely limited to enforcement of criminal laws in the particular municipality or township that it serves, although officers often may move into other districts in pursuit of persons who committed crimes in their districts. The size of city and township departments vary tremendously. Over half of those departments have the full-time equivalent manpower of three officers or less. On the other hand, the largest police department, the New York City police department, has over 20,000 officers. Typically, in a major metropolitan area, composed of a large city and numerous suburbs, there is likely to be over 100 different police departments, and those departments are likely to range in size from one officer to several thousand officers.

In recent years, neighboring communities have sought to foster cooperation among their respective police departments by establishing county-wide training programs, coordinating their schedules for patroling their mutual boundaries, and developing joint task forces for investigation of particular types of crimes, such as narcotics distribution. It is difficult, however, to eliminate entirely the overlap in the investigations performed by local police in neighboring communities; crime simply does not stop at local borders and often independent investigations will relate to the same individuals.

SELECTION AND TRAINING

Entrance Requirements. Police recruits must meet several basic entrance standards. Ordinarily, they must be citizens, be within certain age limits (e.g., 21-35 years old), possess good health, and meet certain requirements as to weight, height, and vision. In most jurisdictions, they may not have a criminal record. Educational requirements vary, but the vast majority of agencies do not require educational achievement beyond a high school diploma. The F.B.I. is the most noteable exception, requiring at least a college degree for all recruits.[7] If the

---

6. The reference is to full-time employees and includes approximately 100,000 civilian employees as well as 420,000 law enforcement officers.

7. F.B.I. agents must be graduates of a law school, graduates of a four year college with a degree in accounting, or meet other special qualifications (e.g., a college graduate with experience in a related field). Several local police departments, following the F.B.I.'s lead, have sought to employ

applicants meet these basic standards, they then must take and pass a civil service examination. In many jurisdictions they also must pass psychiatric/psychological appraisals designed to screen out potentially "unstable" persons. Applicants who pass these tests then are added to the force, as openings arise, in the order of their civil service scores.[8]

Raising Educational Standards. In the last twenty years, police departments throughout the country have sought to upgrade the educational requirements for recruits. They have recognized that college training can be very helpful to a police officer. The very complex police role, which we will discuss shortly, requires an understanding of psychology, sociology, and government that goes beyond high school training. Moreover, individuals who have attended college ordinarily have a greater intellectual capacity than those who stopped their education at the high school level. Available studies indicate that "police officers with a college background generally perform significantly better than police officers without a college degree."[9] The National Advisory Commission accordingly has recommended that, "Every police agency should, no later than 1982, require as a condition of initial employment the completion of at least 4 years of education . . . at an accredited college or university."[10] Perhaps no recommendation of the Commission offers *less* chance of fulfillment. Based on past performance, it will be many years before most police departments are able to find enough applicants with even two years of college work to meet all of their manpower needs.

Police departments have to face various obstacles in attempting to recruit persons who have a college education. For many years, most colleges paid little attention to preparing their students for work in the criminal justice field. This situation fortunately has changed. Criminal justice programs have been developed in junior colleges and four year colleges throughout the country. Another difficulty faced by the police recruiters—low salaries—also is changing. Salary structures in many major departments are now the equivalent of those for teachers, social workers, and other government employees in public service positions. Excellent health programs and retirement benefits also tend to make police work more competitive economically with these other occupations. Police recruiters still must overcome the non-professional image of police work in the eyes of college students. As the National Advisory Commission noted, the low minimal educational requirements has led "police work . . . to be regarded as a second class occupation, open to anyone with no more than a minimum education, average intelligence, and good health."[11] The Commission anticipated that the raising of educational standards would make the profession more appealing to college students. Still another difficulty, however, is the concern of many young graduates

only college graduates, but this group does not include any of the very large departments in major urban areas.

8. Where police departments have engaged in the past in illegal discrimination against certain groups (e.g., women, blacks), they may be required by court order to hire applicants from those groups ahead of persons from other groups with higher test scores.

9. National Advisory Commission, note 3 *supra*, at p. 367.

10. National Advisory Commission, note 3 *supra*, at §15.1.

11. National Advisory Commission, note 3 *supra*, at p. 367.

that police work will not be challenging. To encourage application of college students, the police departments may have to assure prospective applicants that they will not spend a substantial portion of their career directing traffic, checking parking meters, or working in record bureaus. A trend toward shifting most such functions to civilian personnel will help in this regard.

Some experts suggest that the educational level of officers can more easily be raised by placing greater emphasis on courses taken by officers after they are hired than by imposing higher entrance requirements. Various departments now are offering incentive pay increases designed to encourage officers to continue their education. Colleges and universities have sought to cooperate by scheduling classes at times when they might be taken by working officers. Some police departments also have developed programs authorizing an academic leave to permit an officer to complete his education. The federal Law Enforcement Education Program (LEEP) should spur further development of these programs.

Recruitment of Women and Minorities. Recruitment of minority and female candidates has been a major problem for police departments throughout the United States. The absence of a substantial number of minorities and women in police work over the years has worked against recent recruitment efforts. There is no tradition that leads a member of a minority group or a woman to look naturally to police work as a profession. Moreover, many members of minority groups and many women are not convinced that they really are wanted, notwithstanding the new recruiting efforts. In some instances, physical requirements relating to height and weight naturally work against women and certain minority groups. The National Advisory Commission has suggested several steps that may be taken to recruit more successfully without departing from relevant qualifications: (1) "special abilities, such as the ability to speak a foreign language, strength, and agility, or any other compensating factor should be taken into consideration in addition to height and weight requirements"; (2) special recruitment efforts should be spearheaded by officers from the groups being recruited; (3) emphasis should be placed on the community service aspect of police work; (4) a policy of non-discrimination should be announced and vigorously enforced.[12]

Police Training. The emphasis in police training programs is quite the opposite of the educational efforts of a college program. At college, the prospective officer studies such subjects as crime and deviant behavior, the psychology of offenders, urban problems, and the policies underlying legal regulations. The typical police training program, operated by the police department itself, concentrates basically on "how-to-do-it" subjects such as accident investigation, use of firearms, administration of first-aid, legal rules relating to search and seizure, etc. In recent years, more emphasis has been placed on those areas where the officer must play an especially delicate role, such as the intervention in family disputes. Almost half of the states require at least 200 hours of classroom training covering the traditional "how-to-do-it" curriculum. Many departments in larger cities now

---

12. See National Advisory Commission, note 3 *supra*, at §13.3.

exceed the standard of 400 hours recommended by the National Advisory Commission.[13] Cooperative training programs involving several departments may reduce costs sufficiently that more of the smaller departments can meet this goal in the future.

Most police departments add a few weeks of formal field training to the prescribed classroom work. Field training programs usually involve the performance of police work in the field under the direct supervision of another officer who serves as an instructor. Many departments that do not have formal field training programs will assign new officers to work with more senior officers who can assist them. Also, new officers are placed on a probationary status for periods commonly ranging from six months to one year, and, at least theortically, this status should encourage closer supervision.

In the past, once an officer finished his probationary period, that ended his formal training requirements, unless he desired a promotion. In recent years, however, more attention is being given to continued in-service training to keep officers abreast of new developments. Most states still do not require in-service training, but more and more individual departments, particularly in large cities, are themselves requiring anywhere from 40 to 100 hours of in-service education each year. Also, supervisory personnel commonly must fulfill even more stringent continuing education requirements.

The more extensive police training programs are viewed as adequate by some experts and inadequate by others. Some critics of the programs appear to be concerned primarily by the lack of general educational requirements for police recruits. They believe that the training programs should place a greater emphasis on the social and psychological significance of what officers do since so many recruits will not be college trained. Other critics stress the most critical functions performed by the police officer. They argue, for example, that "a physician is an authority with the power of life and death in situations involving physical disorder, [while] a policeman is a life and death authority in situations of social disorder"; yet, physicians are trained on the average of 11,000 hours while many policemen are trained for no more than 200 hours.[14]

Supporters of the current training programs note that those programs cannot be expected to compensate for inadequate educational requirements. There is, they note, a distinction between "education," a function for the colleges, and "training," a function for the police academy. They also reject the view that police training must be tested by the occasional life and death decision of the ordinary officer. The training must focus primarily on the everyday task of the officer. It would make little sense, they note, to put every officer through a series of simulated exercises on the use of deadly force. When and if the ordinary officer ever faced that decision, the value of the training might well be lost through the passage of time. Although the patrol officer may deal with almost every type of problem presented by police work, specialized training must be limited, in their view, to

---

13. See National Advisory Commission, note 3 *supra*, at §16.3 and p. 393-399.

14. See American Bar Association, *Standards Relating to the Urban Police Function* (Approved Draft 1973) at p. 203.

those officers in special units who are most likely to be presented with a particular problem.

Promotions. The promotion of police personnel is marked by a sharp division between the procedures followed in selecting the highest ranking police officials and the remainder of the officers. Political considerations commonly enter into the selection of the highest officials and those officials often are given limited job security. Sheriffs, for example, are directly elected in partisan elections for terms of office that rarely run more than four years. Police chiefs in municipal departments commonly are appointed by the mayor or city council and serve at the pleasure of one or the other. In most places, their appointment, unlike the sheriff's election, is not based on partisan political grounds. Very frequently the appointees have had no experience in politics, but simply are officers who have advanced in the ranks of the department from their initial entry as patrolmen. Still, in choosing a chief from among several high ranking officers, the mayor or council is likely to give weight to certain political considerations, such as whether the candidate's appointment is likely to be supported by particular ethnic groups. Of course, the degree of emphasis placed upon such factors will vary from community to community, and the tenure of the appointee will vary in a similar fashion. Since the highest ranking officers (e.g., the assistant chiefs) commonly are appointed by the chief, their appointment and tenure frequently will involve considerations similar to those governing the appointment and tenure of the chief himself.

Beneath the very highest positions, promotion of police personnel ordinarily is based on civil service or a similar merit system. Applicants for positions compete by examinations. These officers, like the average patrolman, are given typical civil service job security—that is, they can be fired only if good cause for their discharge is established in an administrative hearing. Accordingly, most officers and partolmen view their job as an assured career position, and they tend to stay until they have earned retirement.

THE ROLE OF A POLICE OFFICER

Multiple Functions. The traditional image of police work—the image conveyed over the years in countless television dramas, comic strips, and newspaper articles—is that of the officer who outwits or outwrestles a dangerous criminal in the course of investigating serious crimes. The investigation of serious crime is, however, only one of many aspects of police work. Indeed, in a typical police department, a comparatively small portion of the department's total activity is spent on the investigation of major felonies. Far more time will be spent on general patrol or even on performing various social services. Police are responsible for directing traffic, issuing licenses, and handling various emergencies, both minor and major. If a city gas main springs a leak, the police cordon off the area, and go from house to house warning the residents. If a child's pet can't get down out of the tree, the police are called to help. Police aid the sick, free passengers from stalled elevators, and comfort lost children. They also are expected to perform an essentially social service function in dealing with various minor offenses. Thus, they are called upon to settle family quarrels and to handle the misbehaving drunks.

Even with respect to serious crime, much of the police work does not involve investigation. Police work with the community in various ways to prevent serious crime. They sponsor programs for delinquent youth, organize citizen volunteers who will provide escort service for senior citizens, and advise citizens on the installation of locks to secure their homes. Most significantly, the police patrol—which uses most of the police manpower—provides a police presence that hopefully deters the commission of crimes as well as permitting a prompt response in the investigation of crime.

Police Organization.   The multiple responsibilities of the police also are reflected in the typical organization of a police department. Most police departments are divided into three major segments—patrol, services and administration, and investigation. Of the three, the division responsible for services and administration is the farthest removed from criminal investigation. It performs a variety of tasks, including community relations, record keeping, maintenance of equipment, and police training.[15] In very large departments, this division may also include the office of police legal adviser and a research and planning office.

The primary allocation of departmental manpower will be to the patrol division. Its basic function is to patrol—that is, to move through an assigned area on foot or by vehicle and to respond to specific calls for assistance or particular situations requiring police intervention. Patrolmen do get involved in investigation of serious crime. On occasion, the patrolman will make a dramatic arrest of a robber or rapist, but most of his arrests will be for minor offenses. The vast portion of the time spent on patrol will be occupied simply with moving from one place to another, handling social service functions (helping to find a lost child), handling traffic problems, helping in preventing crime (checking to be sure that shop doors are locked), or dealing with minor misdemeanors (assaults in the course of family disputes, shoplifters caught by store owners, etc.). It is unlikely that the patrolmen will devote more than one-tenth of their time to investigating major felonies.[16]

The detective division is the only major division devoted primarily to the investigation of crimes.[17] Where the offender is not apprehended in the act or immediately identified, the case ordinarily will be turned over to a detective unit

---

15. The police internal investigations unit, which may be located in this division, does have an investigative role. Its function is to investigate complaints against police officers, which often may involve allegations of ciminal violations.

16. See P. Greenwood and J. Petersilia, *The Criminal Investigation Process*, Santa Monica, Cal.: The Rand Corporation, 1975. The time devoted by patrol officers to investigation of major felonies will depend in part on the precise division of duties between detectives and patrol officers. In many departments, the patrol officer will immediately turn the investigation over to the detective division unless the patrol officer makes the arrest at the scene of the investigation or the perpetrator has been indentified and can be apprehended without great difficulty. In other areas, patrol officers may take considerably more responsibility for investigation of various types of crimes, and may not turn such cases over to detectives until a substantial investigative effort has proven unsuccessful.

17. Some police departments use vice squads and tactical squads that seek out offenders through aggressive decoy programs (posing as easy victims for muggers or possible clients for prostitutes). In a sense, their work also is investigative in nature. Where those squads are part of a separate division, that division may be characterized as another division primarily concerned with investigation.

for further investigation. In some police departments, the detective division is subdivided into groups specializing in particular crimes. There almost always will be a separate homicide unit and many departments have special units for sex offenses, robbery and burglary, organized crime, narcotics, and crimes involving fraud (confidence games, bad checks, etc.). Even detectives do not spend all of their time investigating crimes. They may have responsibilities in working with the community on crime prevention programs.[18] They also may be involved in filing numerous reports. The detective division is a comparatively small division (commonly no more than one-tenth the size of the patrol division) operating with a caseload which experts invariably view as too heavy. Ordinarily, the key to a successful investigation by detectives is the presence of a "lead" pointing to a specific person. Without it, the chances of a successful investigation are very slim.

Multiple Functions and Law Enforcement Responsibilities. The multiple functions of the police department tend, in several ways, to restrict the effectiveness of the police in the investigation of crime and the enforcement of the law. First, the resources available to the police must be spread over all of its responsibilities; police manpower cannot be concentrated solely on law enforcement functions. Second, the diversity of police responsibilities may require some compromise in the selection of officers. The qualities needed in criminal investigation are not necessarily the same qualities required to perform other police functions.[19] It often is difficult, for example, to find people who will act effectively and courageously in apprehending a felon, yet have the ability to endure the long periods of monotony involved in routine patrol. Similarly, the social-service functions of the police may not always be compatible with the investigation functions. Officers servicing people in times of stress may develop an informality and flexibility in approach that is somewhat inconsistent with their adherence to the formalistic legal requirements often imposed in the area of ciminal investigation.

In various situations, the officer also may be torn between his social service and law enforcement responsibilities. Consider, for example, the role of an officer called to the scene of a family altercation. Is it the function of the officer to arrest the family member who obviously has committed an assault? If the officer makes an arrest, he may be destroying all possibilities of reconciliation. In some instances, the strong family ties make it likely that an arrest will cause the family members to redirect their anger toward the police officer, possibly leading to even more violence. Many argue that the proper police role in dealing with family disturbances is first to restore and maintain order and then to act as mediator. The

---

18. Even the Federal Bureau of Investigation, which is commonly viewed as a basically investigative police force, has numerous other obligations. The F.B.I. is required, for example, to gain background information on prospective government employees, to collect crime statistics, and to gather information that may relate to civil suits involving the government.

19. The diverse qualities required by the multiple functions of the officer are suggested by the typical list of qualities that should be sought in police recruits: (1) courage, physical skill, and personal integrity; (2) the intelligence necessary to follow complex legal requirements; (3) the ability to endure long periods of monotony in routine patrol, and still react quickly in emergencies; (4) the ability to deal with extremely divergent human situations that may call for friendliness and persuasion or firmness and force; and (5) objectivity in dealing with special interest groups.

test of success, they argue, is not whether the officer makes a successful arrest, but whether he can assist in restoring family harmony so as to avoid further violence.[20]

In recent years, various proposals have been advanced to eliminate some of the multiple functions of police departments. These proposals seek to make the police department a streamlined law enforcement agency and not a community service organization. The proposals suggest that offenses such as drunkenness and drug abuse be handled in detoxification centers and drug abuse clinics, removing police responsibility for these offenders. It also is suggested that many domestic disputes be turned over to trained social workers, and that various existing offenses, such as homosexual conduct between consenting adults, be removed from the criminal code. Special traffic departments could be staffed with persons trained for traffic control but not trained for criminal investigation; only when a traffic offense required more than routine investigation would the fully trained police officer be called. Parking meters could be monitored by metermaids, and school crossings could be protected by men and women hired for that service. Several of these proposals have been instituted, but the change in the role of the police has not been dramatic. Public drunkenness is no longer a crime in many jurisdictions, but it is still the police who pick up the drunks and take them to the detoxification centers rather than the jails.

Complexities in Law Enforcement. Aside from reconciling its social service and law enforcement responsibilities, the police department must deal with various complexities presented by the law enforcement system alone. First among these is the obvious need to exercise discretion in determining the extent to which various criminal laws will be enforced. The officer must deal with the fact that we pass many laws that we do not expect to be enforced at all, or at least not to their full extent. The speed limit may be 70 miles an hour, but the officer is not supposed to give a ticket to the citizen doing 72 on the freeway. Gambling and prostitution are forbidden, but red light districts flourish and are tacitly accepted by the community. Stealing is illegal, but the police officer is not supposed to arrest the conventioner who takes a couple of towels from the motel.

Where the offense involved is one that society clearly wants enforced, the police role is filled with other complexities. We do not simply tell the police to enforce the law in the most effective and efficient manner possible. We do not approach law enforcement as a "war against crime" with "no holds barred." The law enforcement officer must abide by legal restrictions designed to protect the rights of individuals. Although police officers are not lawyers and often must make quick decisions under tense and rapidly changing conditions, we require that they adhere to legal standards that sometimes are so unclear that they produce a 5-4 division among the justices of the Supreme Court. Some have suggested that the difficulties faced by the police in adhering to legal standards are partly of their own making. The National Advisory Commission has suggested, for example, that

---

20. The various approaches to the handling of domestic disputes are noted in Chapter One of the Texas Criminal Justice Council, *Model Rules For Law Enforcement Officers*, Gaithersburg, Md.: International Association of Chiefs of Police, 1974. Among the non-arrest remedies noted in the *Model Rules* are: (1) mediation (2) referral to appropriate social, medical, or legal counseling (3) temporary voluntary separation (4) issuance of a warning (5) mention of a peace bond or complaint procedure (6) confiscation of weapon and (7) physical restraint.

police would have far less difficulty in understanding and applying legal standards if they made an effort to formulate specific operational rules, relating to arrests, searches, and other activities, that are based upon the various judicial decisions. [21] Even with such guidelines, however, there will be many areas in which police officers will be dealing with legal uncertainties.

The police are expected not only to adhere to the law, but to do so in a manner that does not alienate the community. They are expected to act with fairness, but without "throwing their weight around." They are given discretion to arrest or not arrest, to release on a citation or retain in custody, and to use or not use deadly force, but we expect them to exercise that discretion on the basis of sound judgment that gives no weight to personal prejudices. Persons are to be treated the same way without regard to their race, ethnic background, or general life style. Police officers are told that they must display the same even-handed approach in communities that welcome them and communities that resent them. The police are asked to maintain their calm while dealing with persons who are often angry, desperate, and violent. These are not easy tasks, and in many respects, they require personality traits that are not readily found in persons who fill the other image we have of the effective law enforcement officer — that of the aggressive, individualistic man of action who views law enforcement as more than "just another job." Indeed, very often, the officer is forced to deal with conflicting public images of the police officer's role as well as the competing values reflected in the governing law.

Public Attitudes.   Over the years, the police have had their good periods and their bad periods in terms of public esteem. During the late 1960's, for example, the public image of police hit a distinct low. It was, perhaps, the worst period for that image since the pre-civil war days when police jobs were distributed as part of political patronage. Many of the factors that have contributed to an adverse police

---

21. See National Advisory Commission, note 3 *supra* at p. 25:

> Police agencies on the whole have attempted to maintain investigative authority at its outer limits as defined by court decisions and, through training, to instruct its officers in those limits. There has been little attempt to reduce the numerous court decisions dealing with aspects of police investigation to a clear outline of police, procedures, and rules embodied in a general order format; this has been done in other matters, such as the custody of evidence and the processing of prisoners.

> Police agencies should develop clear rules to help police officers understand court rulings on criminal investigations. Policy then will emanate from the administrative level of the police hierarchy instead of from the operational level. Agencies that have done this illustrate the areas of need for policy guidelines. As reported in the President's Commission on Law Enforcement and Administration of Justice, the New York State Combined Council of Law Enforcement Officials developed comprehensive guidelines for officers to follow in implementing that State's 'stop and frisk' legislation. That policy, in effect since 1964, has undoubtedly been a factor in defending the legislation from constitutional attack. More recently, the Metropolitan Police Department of the District of Columbia, in two general orders, provided explicit guidelines for officers engaged in automobile searches and eyewitness identification. Those orders, based on judicial rulings and police experience, provide examples that explain the intent of their provisions, and they are written clearly and concisely.

> Police guidelines governing criminal investigations have other advantages. By taking the initiative, police agencies can provide courts with thoroughly considered policies expressing police investigative needs that courts may recognize when ruling on the propriety of police investigations.

image flow from specific police actions, but an unrealistic public view of the role and responsibility of the police has also been a contributing factor. Too frequently, antagonism toward specific laws is carried over to antagonism toward the police, although they have no special responsibility for those laws. In some instances, the police become the focus for a general discontent with the policies of the community. Police difficulties in the ghettoes, for example, arise in part from the fact that the police are the most visible symbol of the middle class society that ghetto residents view as largely ignoring their problems.

Similarly, the police image will almost certainly suffer during periods when crime appears to be rising rapidly and disrespect for the law appears widespread. Unfortunately, most people tend to overestimate the role of the police in crime prevention. The police do not create and they cannot resolve the social conditions that stimulate crime. They do not start, nor can they control, the dramatic social changes that so often result in widespread challenges to laws that fail to keep up with these changes. Yet, because the police are the most visible element of the criminal justice process, they tend to bear the responsibility for the difficulties suffered by the criminal justice system as a result of these factors.

Finally, the police image is subject to the high standards of responsibility that flow from the special role of police in our society. One of the factors that has plagued the police community over the years has been the occurrence of police scandals in many major cities. Bribery and misuse of authority for personal profit is not unique to the police profession. Corporate businessmen and union leaders also have had their share of scandals. But crime by people who are themselves engaged in the law enforcement process causes special public concern. It is viewed as undermining respect for the law itself. Similarly, misuse of authority to trample on individual rights causes far more concern when the misuse is by the police rather than by some other governmental agency. During the 1960's, when there was a great clamor for civilian review boards that could investigate citizen complaints against government officials, the focus was primarily on complaints against the police.[22] In a democratic society, there is special concern as to misuse of police authority because only the police have such direct control over individual liberty. While the police are our official protectors, they also are the possessors of the kind of authority as to which there is the greatest fear of misuse.

RELATIONSHIP TO OTHER PROFESSIONALS

The Problem.   Sociologists frequently comment upon a sense of alienation—and in some instances actual antagonism—between the police and the other professionals in the criminal justice system. The police work with the other professionals, they note, but there is not an active spirit of cooperation. Indeed, in some instances, there appears to be very minimal coordination, or even purposeful conflicts produced by professional rivalries. The lack of cooperation between the police and the other professionals should not be overexaggerated. We cannot really

---

22.   Such boards never gained widespread acceptance. Today, complaints against the police commonly are subject to a police review board or a board composed of representatives of higher-level city officials. See National Advisory Commission, note 3 *supra*, at p. 469-491.

expect substantial coordination, for example, between the police and defense counsel. Once the prosecution is initiated, they are on opposite sides of an adversary process. The most that can be expected is that police and defense attorneys respect each other and abide by the legal rules in dealing with each other. In many jurisdictions, such respect and adherence to the law is present.

The judge similarly performs a role that does not lend itself to coordination with police activities. The judge must be an impartial supervisor of an adversary trial system. It is important that he be neutral and maintain an image of neutrality. Again, the most that can be expected is that each of the professionals appreciate the role of the other. In many jurisdictions, that appreciation can be found among most police officers and most judges.

Police cooperation with the local prosecutor is essential to the successful operation of the criminal justice system, and, in many jurisdictions, a healthy spirit of cooperation does exist. The prosecutor and police cooperate in the investigation of crimes and the presentation of cases in court. The opportunities for cooperation with correction officials are less frequent, but here too, there is often a healthy spirit of cooperation. In sum, the sense of alienation and lack of cooperation noted by the commentators is not present everywhere. Yet, it does exist in some jurisdictions, and it is important that we understand why it exists. Four factors relating to the police role are especially significant in this regard — the police perspective of the crime, the police perspective of the criminal, the close contact between the police and the community, and the differences in the background and training of the police and the other professionals.

Perspective of the Crime. The police officer's role in investigating crime gives him a viewpoint of the criminal justice process quite different from that of other criminal justice professionals. Police see crime, so to speak, "in the raw." Unlike the judge, defense attorney, and prosecutor, police see crime as it is committed in the street rather than as reported in law offices or courtroom. The police officer is the only criminal justice professional who regularly sees the victim and the damage that the criminal act has caused. The police officer talks to the molested child, sees the results of a brutal beating, and views the bloody dead body of the filling station operator who has been ruthlessly killed by the robber. He must identify the young girl killed or mutilated by a drunken driver, and notify her parents. It is the police officer who must try to confront the old couple defrauded of their life savings or deal with the angry victim who has had his car stolen for the third time. No other person in the criminal justice system comes into such constant direct contact with the victim.

The officer's close contact with the victim naturally influences his attitude as to the proper goals of the criminal law. His orientation tends to be toward retribution and incapacitation rather than rehabilitation. He is naturally concerned about the fact that the others in the process (particularly the judge and the corrections officer) will not have seen the extent of the victim's suffering and therefore may give little weight to that factor in sentencing and corrections. It is not surprising, therefore, that he may view the judge as acting in a "dream world," far removed from crime as it appears on the street. Neither is it surprising that he may have difficulty in understanding how defense counsel can so vigorously defend persons who have caused such great harm.

Perspective of the Criminal.   The police officer also has a somewhat different perspective of the defendant than the other participants in the process. The other participants usually see the defendant in the controlled setting of the witness stand, the jail, or the office interview. The police officer sees the defendant in his "natural setting," sometimes only moments after he has committed a crime. In some cases, this perspective may give the officer a somewhat more compassionate viewpoint then the other professionals. He has listened to the heroin addict as he pleaded for a "fix." He knows the difficult family situation that has produced the youthful car thief. In many instances, however, the officer's dealings with the offender will lead him to view any disposition that releases the defendant, even temporarily, as potentially dangerous. This is particularly true when the arrest of the accused required the use of force or a threat of force. While the court views the release of such a defendant on bail as a mere recognition of the defendant's rights, the officer views it as a potential threat to his personal safety. If, as the officer believes, the accused is likely to commit more crimes, the officer will only be forced to arrest the accused again, and the officer may not again be so fortunate as to avoid personal injury in making that arrest.

Community Pressures.   Since the police have the most direct contact with the community, they also tend to be more responsive to community pressures to solve crime. Frequently they view themselves as caught in a conflict between an afraid and angry community that wants efficiency in investigations, and a legal structure that demands that they recognize various rights of suspects that interfere with efficient enforcement. Similarly, police may view themselves as caught in a conflict between a community that views a particular illegal activity as harmless, and a legal structure that treats it as a serious crime and encourages its enforcement. In many instances, officers may view the community's response as more realistic than that of the legal system. Thus, many officers feel that the community is more tolerant then the law of the occasional mistake that flows from the need to make snap judgments in situations calling for immediate action. Indeed, when officers feel that they have community support, they may be inclined to simply ignore legal standards, arguing that they are unrealistic. Thus, studies have suggested that officers in certain communities will give false testimony to justify productive searches that would otherwise be illegal. Having operated on a hunch and having discovered incriminating evidence, they will now testify to circumstances that did not exist in the hope of establishing probable cause and thereby gaining use of the evidence in a criminal prosecution.[23] As they see it, their actions are consistent with the community's true concerns and merely evade an overly technical legal limitation.

Professional Differences.   Alienation between the police and other professionals in the criminal justice process also stems from the differences in the training and background of the different professionals. Police often complain that the lawyers in the system do not treat them as professionals. They note, for example, that they often are the "forgotten man" in the scheduling of cases. Frequently, they may spend several hours waiting to testify and then discover that they will

---

23.   See F. Graham, *The Self-Inflicted Wound*, New York: The MacMillan Company, 1970, p. 136-37.

not testify that day because the case has been postponed or it was disposed of by a guilty plea. Police also note that the legal professionals, particularly the defense counsel, are constantly complaining about the officer's lack of training. Professionals who have finished college and obtained an advanced degree are simply unwilling, police claim, to recognize that police officers also can be professionals, notwithstanding their more limited educational background. For their own part, the police may have doubts as to the true professionalism of the lawyers in the system. They note that politics often plays a part in the selection of judges and prosecutors. While the police officer views his job as a career position, the prosecuting attorney frequently views his as a stepping stone to private practice or other political office. Police may have doubts as to whether the prosecutor's committment to law enforcement matches their committment. Differences in the background and training of the police officer and the correctional officer produce similar difficulties. The two are more likely to view each other as professionals, but the police, in particular, have little understanding of the correctional process. The police officer has not been trained in the correctional process and he is far removed from the imprisonment aspect of the process. His contact is primarily with the failures of the process—those who have not been rehabilitated. His skepticism of the correctional process under such circumstances is quite natural, and the opportunity for communication that would create understanding is limited. The police officer will complain (but not usually to the probation officer) that when they take a juvenile offender to the juvenile court, the court releases them so fast that "the kids beat us home." The juvenile probation officer reply (but seldom directly to the police officer) that "home was the best place for the boy, and besides we had no other place to put him—the detention home is full, the institution for boys is full, and the probation caseloads ae impossibly high."

Improving Understanding. Other professionals in the system would do well to be sensitive to the police officer's experience at the scene of the crime, and appreciate the reasons for his "be tough on criminals" attitude. The police should be consulted on penal reform, and should be listened to when they talk about community problems. The police officer, on the other side, should expand his knowledge of the other segments of the criminal justice system. He should have an understanding of what the probation and parole officer is trying to accomplish, and realize that while incarceration may remove the offender from the neighborhood for a time, he will almost surely return, since few men are kept in prison for life. Police training should include an explanation of basic legal principles so that the law is not viewed as composed merely of technical legal rules. The officer should be made aware of the special role of the defense counsel in the adversary system, perhaps by permitting defense counsel to participate, along with the prosecutor, in some police training programs. Hopefully, as education standards for police officers are raised, police officers will gain a better understanding of the total process through more extensive college preparation and continuing education programs.[24]

---

24.   More complete materials on police organization and administration may be found in the National Advisory Commission Report, note 3 *supra*; H. More, *The American Police,* St. Paul, Minn.: West Publishing Company, 1976; O. Wilson and R. McLaren, *Police Administration,* New York; McGraw-Hill Book Company, 1972.

Chapter 16

The Legal and Judicial Professionals

Three professionals in the criminal justice system—prosecutors, defense counsel and judges—will be lawyers.[1] While each performs a somewhat different role, all are concerned with the judicial process and the interpretation of the law. The lawyer-professionals all will be graduates of law schools, and they all will have passed an examination establishing their knowledge of the law and their ability to utilize legal analysis.[2] As persons admitted to the practice of the law (which is described as admission to the "bar"), they all are subject to that profession's Code of Professional Responsibility.[3] These similarities in educational background, skills, and professional standards will serve as the starting point for our analysis of the three professionals in this chapter. We will concentrate primarily on the

---

1. As noted in Chapter Three (p. 44 *supra*), non-lawyer judges serve in the magistrate courts in many states. However, all general trial court judges and appellate court judges will be lawyers. Moreover, in those states in which magistrates need not be lawyers, the defendant often has a right to a trial *de novo* before the general trial court, which will provide him with a fresh trial before a lawyer-judge. See p. 39 *supra*.

2. There are a few states in which graduates of the state law school are automatically admitted to practice law in that state without taking the bar examination. There are also a few states in which a person can qualify to take the examination by learning law while clerking in a law firm rather than by attending law school. However, this route to the taking of the examination is rarely utilized.

3. Each state has its own Code of Professional Responsibility, but those codes all follow closely the American Bar Association's *Code of Professional Responsibility* (Approved Draft 1970, with subsequent amendments). The A.B.A.'s *Code* consists of "Cannons," "Disciplinary Rules," and "Ethical Considerations." The Cannons are statements of general concepts (e.g., that a lawyer "should exercise independent professional judgment on behalf of a client"). The Disciplinary Rules are specific guidelines, violation of which will result in the imposition of sanctions. The state codes commonly consist solely of the Cannons and the Disciplinary Rules. The Ethical Considerations are statements of principles designed to assist the attorney in resolving ethical issues presented in particular situations. They are described by the A.B.A. as "aspirational in character and represent[ing] the objectives toward which every member of the profession should strive."

differences in their roles, their methods of selection, their training, and their relationship to the non-lawyer professionals in the criminal justice process. We start with a description of the various officials who may serve as prosecutors.

THE DIVISION OF PROSECUTING AUTHORITY

State Prosecutions.   The authority to prosecute is divided among various state and federal officials. The state officials are responsible for prosecutions under state law and the federal officials for prosecutions under federal law. The division of prosecuting authority at the state level varies from state to state. Ordinarily, the official with primary responsibility for prosecutions under state law is the local prosecuting attorney (also called the "district attorney," "county attorney," or "state's attorney"). The local prosecutor is selected either from a single county or from a group of counties that are combined to form a prosecutorial district in a sparsely populated area. The local prosecutor has the primary responsibility for bringing prosecutions for all violations of state law committed within his county or district. There are approximately 2,600 local prosecuting attorneys in the United States.[4] Most serve only part-time and do not have any full-time staff attorneys to assist them.[5] The prosecuting attorney offices in urban areas tend to be quite large, however, and often have more lawyers than the largest local law firm. The office of the District Attorney of Los Angeles County, for example, has over 500 staff attorneys.

In many states, the local prosecutor's prosecutions are subject, at least theoretically, to the superceding authority of the state attorney general. Some dozen states allow the attorney general on his own initiative to replace the prosecuting attorney in any pending prosecution, and several other states permit the attorney general to intervene in a pending prosecution upon direction of the governor. This authority permits the attorney general to intervene and dismiss a case which he believes to have been initiated for improper purposes, or to intervene and press forward in a case where he feels the prosecuting attorney is not exercising sufficient diligence. In practice, however, intervention for either purpose is rare. By and large, attorneys general intervene only in cases where the local prosecutor has a potential conflict of interest (e.g., prosecution against a former staff member) and would prefer that an outside officer prosecute.

In fourteen states, the attorney general may himself initiate prosecution. Most often, attorneys general use their power to initiate prosecutions with respect

---

4.   The statistics on prosecuting attorneys used in this chapter come from the *Sourcebook of Criminal Justice Statistics—1976*, note 1 at p. 1 *supra*, and the National District Attorney Association, *National Prosecution Standards*, Chicago, Ill., 1977.

5.   Part-time prosecutors ordinarily spend the remainder of their time in the private practice of law. That practice may affect in various respects the prosecutor's handling of his public role, although statutes ordinarily bar the prosecutor from private practice in situations presenting a direct conflict with his public position. (Most part-time prosecutors limit their private practice to civil matters, although some handle criminal defense work in adjoining counties). In recent years, considerable effort has been made to make the prosecutor's position a full-time position, with private practice barred.

only to a limited class of offenses, such as tax fraud and criminal antitrust violations, as to which local prosecutors are likely to lack sufficient expertise.[6] In these areas, they often create special units that will deal with almost all such offenses committed throughout the state. The success of these units has led several states that do not permit the general initiation of prosecution by the attorney general to authorize initiation for limited groups of crimes, like antitrust, that often have a statewide impact and require special expertise to prosecute.

The prosecuting attorney and the attorney general ordinarily are the only officials with authority to prosecute violations of state law. Public attorneys at other levels of government, such as a city or township attorney, cannot enforce state provisions. They may, however, bring prosecutions to enforce local ordinances, and such ordinances frequently duplicate state misdemeanors both in substance and authorized punishments. Where the city attorney and the prosecuting attorney follow different policies as to the treatment of minor offenses (e.g., whether plea bargaining will be used in drunk driving cases), the result often is disparate treatment of defendants depending upon whether the local police present their case to the city attorney for prosecution as an ordinance violation or to the local prosecutor for prosecution as a state misdemeanor.

The Advantages and Disadvantages of Divided State Prosecuting Authority. One major concern relating to the division of state prosecuting authority is the inconsistency in the application of the law resulting from the different policies of different prosecutors. As we just saw, this can occur within a single county where particular conduct constitutes both a misdemeanor and an ordinance violation. For felony level crimes, the central authority of the local prosecuting attorney ensures a consistent county-wide prosecution policy, but differences arise between counties. Different prosecutors in different counties can follow quite different policies on such matters as the decision to charge, the use of diversion programs, plea bargaining, and use of certain trial tactics.[7] In recent years, various efforts have been made to eliminate such inconsistencies. To achieve closer communications among local prosecutors, state prosecuting attorney associations and some state attorneys general have established special programs designed to keep local prosecutors informed of the various policies being followed across the state. Programs have also been developed to assist prosecutors in using new prosecution procedures that have proven successful in other districts and to develop general guidelines as to prosecution policies. While such efforts have helped to lessen the differences in the policies followed by the various prosecutors, those policies still remain far from uniform—particularly with respect to plea negotiation.

---

6. The reference here is only to states that utilize local prosecutors. In addition, there are three states, described at note 9 *infra*, in which the attorney general bears responsibility for all local prosecutions.

7. There are various aspects of litigation as to which the prosecutor may have considerable discretion, providing he meets the minimum legal standards. Thus, the prosecutor may choose between prosecuting on several different offenses in a single prosecution or in separate prosecutions. He may prosecute accomplices separately or in a joint trial. He may give defense counsel substantially more advance notice of the nature of the prosecution's case than is legally required (usually, this is done if the defense counsel is willing to give reciprocal disclosure). In a few jursidictions, the prosecutor may insist upon a jury trial even though the defendant desires to waive a jury trial.

Another problem presented by the fragmentation of prosecuting authority is that many offices are too small to be efficient. Again, state attorneys general and prosecuting attorney associations have sought to offset this deficiency by providing various support services to the smaller offices, such as legal research assistance, office management programs, and shared use of computer facilities. Also, almost a third of the states have moved to a district selection system, which permits them to create multiple county districts large enough to support a full-time prosecutor with part-time assistants in each county. These reforms have been only partially successful, however, and the inefficiency of the smaller offices remains a major difficulty in most states.

Over the years, various proposals have been advanced for adoption of a single, statewide prosecutorial authority, vested in the Attorney General.[8] So far, only three states have adopted such a program, Alaska, Delaware, and Rhode Island.[9] Adoption of a statewide system of prosecution has been opposed on the ground that it would place too much power in a single official. Proponents of the current system also note that the political accountability of the prosecuting attorney to his local district ensures that local conditions will be considered in formulating prosecution policies. They contend that, in a criminal justice system that lacks the resources to provide full enforcement of all laws, it is extremely important that community sentiment be considered in allocating the resources of the prosecutor's office and in appraising the disposition appropriate to particular offenses and offenders. Insofar as the division of prosecuting authority among a large number of local prosecuting officials results in inconsistency and inefficiency, those costs are viewed as more than offset by the benefits of local autonomy.

Federal Prosecutions.   In the federal system, the final authority over all prosecutions rests with the Attorney General. Of course, the Attorney General does not personally supervise individual prosecutions; he relies heavily on various subordinate officials who are given the primary responsibility for prosecutorial decisions. For most federal offenses, that responsibility lies with the United States Attorneys. There are 94 United States Attorneys, one for each of the federal judicial districts. Their offices range in strength from a single Assistant U.S. Attorney (in Guam) to over 150 Assistants (in the District of Columbia). Over half of the offices have fewer than ten attorneys. The U.S. Attorneys are given considerable discretion, but they must operate within general guidelines prescribed by the Attorney General. For certain types of cases (e.g., civil rights prosecutions), they must receive specific approval from the Attorney General or the Deputy Attorney General in charge of the Criminal Division of the Department of Justice. The Criminal Division operates as the arm of the Attorney General in coordinating the enforcement of federal laws by the U.S. Attorneys. In various areas—most

---

8.   One of the earlier recommendations was that advanced by the Wickersham Commission in 1931. More recently a similar proposal was made by the Committee for Economic Development, composed of a distinguished group of businessmen. Both proposals are discussed in National Association of Attorneys General, *The Prosecution Function*, Raleigh, North Carolina, 1974, p. 37.

9.   In each of these states, all prosecutions are conducted under the direction of the Attorney General. In Alaska, local prosecutors are used, but they are appointed by the attorney general, and he is responsible for their performance.

notably white collar crime and public corruption—the Criminal Division provides substantial assistance to United States Attorneys in the investigation and presentation of cases. In a few specialized areas (e.g., antitrust), the initial responsibility for enforcement is given to other divisions of the Justice Department. If any conflicts arise between the policies followed by those divisions and the U.S. Attorneys, they can be resolved by the Attorney General.

THE SELECTION AND TRAINING OF PROSECUTORS

Selection of the Prosecuting Attorney.   With few exceptions, local prosecuting attorneys are elected in a partisan election in the district they serve.[10] They are elected for a fairly short term of office, usually four years, with eleven states having terms of only two years. Two states provide for the appointment of local prosecutors, but political considerations also are said to play a part in their selection.[11] United States Attorneys are appointed by the President, with the consent of the Senate. The Presidential appointees ordinarily have been recommended by the Senators from the state in which they will serve. The United States Attorneys tend to be of the same political party as the President and usually are replaced when a new President from another party takes office.

As one might expect, with the minimal job security provided by the political selection process, most prosecuting attorneys do not view their office as a career position. Indeed, this attitude carries over even to jurisdictions in which incumbents ordinarily are reelected, so that the prosecutor could assume that he would have a fairly long tenure if he so desired. Studies conducted in various states have produced such statistics as: (1) almost 50% of the local prosecutors were serving their first term; (2) most former prosecuting attorneys had left office voluntarily rather than because of an election defeat; (3) almost 50% of the prosecutors interviewed were interested in seeking other government positions.[12] Of course, there are exceptions to this general pattern. In almost every state, one can point to prosecutors who have remained in office for twenty or thirty years and have rejected countless opportunities to become judges or enter private practice. The number of prosecutors following such a career pattern appears to be growing slightly, but it still represents only a small portion of the 2,600 local prosecutors in this country.

---

10. As noted *supra*, state attorneys general may also have significant prosecutorial authority. Attorneys general are elected in forty-two states, appointed by the governor in six states, appointed by the legislature in one state, and by the state supreme court in another.

11. Prosecuting attorneys are appointed by the court in Connecticut and by the governor in New Jersey. The National District Attorneys Association, *National Prosecution Standards*, note 4 *supra*, at §1.1, favors local election, as opposed to appointment, on the ground that appointment eliminates the prosecutor's "direct authority from and responsibility to, the voters of his district." The commentary to the standard further notes, however, that nonpartisan elections may be desirable in some settings.

12. See *National Prosecution Standards*, note 4 *supra*, at p. 11-12. These statistics also are explained, in part, by the fact that the post of prosecuting attorney is not a full-time position in many areas of the country. See note 5 *supra*.

Assistant Prosecutors. The selection and tenure of assistant prosecutors generally rests in the sole discretion of the prosecuting attorney.[13] The standards employed by the prosecuting attorney in hiring assistants will vary with the individual office. At one time, many offices relied heavily upon the applicant's political affiliation. New prosecutors, upon entry into office, would make an almost "clean sweep" of the assistants of a former prosecutor of an opposing party. Today, many more offices hire on a strictly nonpartisan, merit-oriented basis. Moreover, while the assistants are not protected by civil service, they often do have a substantial degree of job security as a practical matter. Nevertheless, the assistants generally do not view the job as a career position. Most assistant prosecutors are hired during the early stages of their careers, stay several years, and then leave for higher paying positions outside the government. The high turnover in many prosecutor offices often is a source of concern among judges and police officers. They view the typical assistant prosecutor as a young attorney who is willing to spend a couple of years handling an overload of cases at a low salary in order to get some criminal trial experience. Too often this produces, they argue, something less than a fully dedicated public servant.

Training. Most states impose only a single qualification for selection to the post of prosecutor or assistant prosecutor—that the individual be a member of the state bar. Several states also require that the local prosecutor have several years experience in the practice of law, though none of these require that that practice be in the field of criminal law. In states where experience is not mandated by law, lawyers elected to the office of local prosecutor nevertheless usually have had some previous practice experience. Assistant prosecutors, on the other hand, commonly are hired directly upon their admission to the bar. While practice experience generally is viewed as helpful, the underlying assumption is that the basic tools required for effective practice are the legal skills learned in law school. Other skills, relating primarily to the exercise of judgment, can be learned on the job.

While new prosecutors or assistant prosecutors may have only limited knowledge of the criminal field, law school training is designed to permit a lawyer to enter a new field and educate himself.[14] In many states, the attorney general's office or the state prosecuting attorney association will assist the new prosecutor or assistant prosecutor in this process of self-education by providing special training programs. The larger prosecutor offices often will operate their own programs. In addition, the job assignments of new assistants in such offices will be geared to permit the assistant to move from less serious to more serious cases as he gains

---

13. The discretionary aspect of the appointment process commonly carries over to the promotion process. Although weight is given to seniority, there ordinarily is no firm policy on promotions. Indeed, unlike police departments, which rely entirely on internal promotions, high level vacancies in prosecutor offices often are filled by attorneys hired from outside the office.

14. The typical law school graduate will have taken 24-30 courses in law school. Most schools offer from 3-7 courses directly related to the practice of criminal law, but will require that the student take only one such course. (Other criminal law courses may be elected at the student's option). The basic teaching philosophy of most law schools is to emphasize general skills (e.g., legal argumentation, statutory interpretation), rather than the laws applicable to a particular field in a particular jurisdiction. Excellent treatises are available that provide a good introduction to the law governing most major fields.

experience. Continuing education programs also are available. The National College of District Attorneys offers, in particular, a wide variety of courses covering topics ranging from office management to the newest legal developments.

THE ROLE OF THE PROSECUTING ATTORNEY

The Broad Range of the Prosecutor's Authority. The range of the prosecutor's authority in making crucial decisions probably exceeds that of any other professional in the criminal justice system. Perhaps the most significant series of decisions made by the prosecutor, in terms of their implications for both the individual involved and the community, are the decisions relating to the charge. The prosecutor must determine initially whether or not to charge. If he decides to proceed, he then must select the appropriate charge or series of charges. While the law sets the maximum charge, it does not prohibit charging at a level lower than that maximum if the prosecutor feels that is appropriate. Later, the prosecutor also may decide to reduce the charge in return for a guilty plea. In all of these decisions, there are very few legal limitations upon the prosecutor. His decision not to charge, in particular, is largely unreviewable. He is responsible primarily to the electorate that put him in office, rather than to the courts.[15]

While the prosecutor's decisions relating to the charge are enough in themselves to establish the crucial nature of the prosecutor's role, his responsibility also extends to various other important steps in the criminal justice process. His functions start at the point of the investigation of the crime and continue through to the imposition of sentence. If the police desire to conduct a search requiring a warrant, the prosecutor usually will be involved in obtaining that warrant. If they desire to utilize electronic surveillance, he must be involved in obtaining court approval for such surveillance. In some cases, the prosecutor will be consulted prior to the arrest for the purpose of obtaining an arrest warrant. Following the arrest, he may be involved in various aspects of the investigation having a bearing on the decision to charge and the conduct of the prosecution. He talks with the arresting officer, interviews witnesses, goes to the scene of the crime, and studies ballistics tests, blood tests, and other physical evidence. He acquaints himself with the previous criminal history of the accused; often makes recommendations on bail; maintains an action against the bail bondsman in case of forfeited bail; cooperates with law enforcement officers from sister states who seek to apprehend and extradite fugitives; and obtains extradition of fugitives from his own state who must be brought back for trial or imprisonment.

The prosecutor prepares the accusation—the grand jury indictments or information. He presents the case before the grand jury when he seeks an indictment; establishes the prima facie case at the preliminary hearing; and appears for the state at the arraignment. He defends against motions to dismiss the prosecution. If the case is not resolved by a guilty plea, the prosecutor must present the case at trial. Conducting a trial requires very special skills, many of which are acquired only through experience. Prosecutors will gain that experience more rapidly than lawyers in almost any other field of law. In large offices, the assistant

---

15. See p. 283 *supra*. See also note 7 *supra* as to other discretionary decisions of the prosecutor relating to the charge.

prosecuting attorneys are given specialized assignments that permit them to capitalize on their experience. An attorney who is particularly successful with a certain type of case—homicide or robbery, for example—may try a majority of those cases that go to trial in his jurisdiction. Successful prosecutors become familiar with the abilities and also the idiosyncracies of the trial judges. In some jurisdictions, they can arrange their dockets so as to have cases set before the judges they believe will be most favorable to the type of case they are presenting. Prosecutors (along with defense attorneys) often investigate the background of the members of the jury panel, seeking to determine profession, social status, and other matters that might be valuable in the exercise of peremptory challenges.

If the case results in a conviction, either through a guilty verdict or guilty plea, the prosecutor will participate in the sentencing hearing. In many jursidictions, he will make a recommendation on sentence. In all jurisdictions, he is responsible for presenting to the court any special information bearing on the sentence that is not likely to be in the presentence report. If there is a subsequent appeal, or a collateral proceeding (e.g., a habeas corpus petition), he will represent the state in that proceeding as well.

In many communities, the prosecutor serves still other functions in the criminal justice system. He often is the foremost spokesman for law enforcement in the community. He goes before the legislature to recommend or oppose penal reform. He is called upon to make speeches on crime and law enforcement before various groups. He participates in police training programs. In highly publicized cases, he often supervises the release of information to the media so as to minimize the possibility that prejudicial pretrial publicity will deny the defendant a fair trial.

In most jurisdictions, the prosecutor also will have significant responsibility in civil matters involving the county government. Thus, the prosecutor ordinarily represents the county in all suits against it. He also may be involved in negotiations relating to accident claims, contract claims, and labor relation problems involving the county.[16] Ordinarily, the prosecutor's civil obligations do not interfere with his primary responsibility of presenting criminal prosecutions. There are some situations, however, in which conflicts may arise. Thus, in a particular case, the prosecutor may be forced to consider not only the need for enforcement of the criminal law against a likely defendant, but also that defendant's ability to press a civil suit against the local government arising from excessive use of police force. The resulting trade-off may be one that would not have been arrived at if the prosecutor's perspectives were not shaped by his civil as well as his criminal responsibilities.

The Duty To Seek Justice.   In exercising his extensive authority within the criminal justice process, the prosecutor is not simply the adversary of the defense counsel. Unlike the defense counsel, his duty is not to "win" wherever he can do so

---

16. In recent years, there has been a movement towards relieving the prosecutor of responsibility for handling civil matters. In about one-fourth of the states, the local prosecutor now is responsible only for criminal cases. In several other states, prosecutors in large urban areas have been divested of civil responsibilities, which have become the province of special county counsel. The federal prosecutors—the United States Attorneys—still have very substantial responsibilities for representation of the United States government in civil litigation.

within the limits of the law. The prosecutor also must be satisfied that the result reached in a particular case is a correct one and that the government has not treated the accused unfairly. The interest of his client—the state—is not equivalent to the narrow self-interest of the defendant. His overall objective is to "seek justice" within the law. The Code of Professional Responsibility sets forth this obligation, and the reasons for its existence, as follows:

> The responsibility of a public prosecutor differs from that of the usual advocate; his duty is to seek justice, not merely to convict. This special duty exists because: (1) the prosecutor represents the sovereign and therefore should use restraint in the discretionary exercise of governmental powers, such as in the selection of cases to prosecute; (2) during trial the prosecutor is not only an advocate but he also may make decisions normally made by an individual client, and those affecting the public interest should be fair to all; and (3) in our system of criminal justice the accused is to be given the benefit of all reasonable doubts.[17]

The A.B.A. Standards. What does a prosecutor's obligation to "seek justice" mean as applied to the various functions noted at the outset of this section? Perhaps the most complete answer to this question is found in the American Bar Association's *Standards Relating to the Prosecution Function.*[18] The *Standards* project provides guidelines for the performance of most basic prosecutorial functions. It includes standards as to preferred conduct and as to conduct (described as "unprofessional") so clearly inconsistent with the prosecutor's responsibilities as to call for disciplinary action.[19] Throughout, it views the prosecutor as a "minister of justice," occupying what is described as a "quasi-judicial" role rather than simply the role of an advocate. This view has a bearing on the prosecutor's actions as an administrator, as a litigant, and as an adviser to the police.

As an administrator, the *Standards* stress that the prosecutor should develop a statement of general principles to guide the exercise of prosecutorial discretion in his office. Those principles should assist in providing fair, efficient, and consistent enforcement of the law. The prosecutor also should sharply restrict the private practice of himself or his assistants (if private practice is allowed) to avoid any appearance of a conflict of interest as well as any actual conflict of interest. He should work for the prompt disposition of cases; it is unprofessional conduct to use procedural devices for delay where there is no legitimate basis for delay. As an adviser to the police, the prosecutor is directed to provide legal advice and aid in the training of the police in the performance of their functions in accordance with the law. It is the obligation of the prosecutor also to investigate suspected illegal activity when the traditional investigative agencies will not deal with it. This includes investigation of allegations of police illegality when such allegations are not adequately investigated by the police. In his investigations, it is

---

17. A.B.A., *Code of Professional Responsibility*, note 3 *supra*, Ethical Consideration 7-13.

18. American Bar Association, *Standards Relating to the Prosecutor Function and The Defense Function* (Approved Draft 1971).

19. Disciplinary action ordinarily consists of temporary suspension from the practice of law or disbarment (revocation of license to practice law). In most jurisdictions, a lawyer charged with violation of the standards of professional responsibility is entitled to a hearing before a committee of the bar, with an appeal of any adverse decision to the highest state court.

unprofessional conduct for a prosecutor to use illegal means to obtain evidence or to instruct or encourage others to use such means.

In considering whether to charge, the standards suggest that the prosecutor consider the availability of non-criminal dispositions, including rehabilitation programs. Prosecutors should be familiar with social agencies that can assist in the evaluation of cases for diversion from the criminal process. The *Standards* note that the prosecutor should not charge in a case unless he first determines there is evidence which would support a conviction. Even then, it continues, the prosecution is not obliged to prosecute, but may decline to do so "for good cause consistent with the public interest." Among the factors that may be considered in making that decision are the prosecutor's own reasonable doubt as to the accused's guilt and the disproportion of the authorized punishment in relation to the particular conduct of the offender. Among the factors that should not be considered are the personal or political advantages or disadvantages that might be involved in prosecution and the prosecutor's desire to enhance his record of conviction.

Once the decision to prosecute has been made, the prosecutor must recognize the validity of the processes designed to screen his decisions. He should not encourage an uncounselled waiver of the preliminary hearing. He should present to the grand jury only evidence which he believes properly admissible at the trial, and should disclose to the grand jury any evidence which he knows will tend to negate guilt. The prosecutor also must recognize the procedural rights of the defendant and the basic objective of avoiding the erroneous conviction of the innocent. He should cooperate, when asked, in obtaining counsel for the accused. He should cooperate as well in arrangments for release of the accused pending trial under the prevailing state system for release. It is unprofessional conduct for the prosecutor to advise a prospective witness to decline to give information to the defense. It also is unprofessional conduct for a prosecutor to fail to disclose to the defense at the earliest feasible opportunity evidence that would tend to negate guilt or reduce the degree of the offense. The prosecutor is never justified in avoiding the pursuit of evidence because he believes it will damage his case or aid the accused.

In the area of plea negotiations, the *Standards* state that the prosecutor should make known a general policy of willingness to consult with defense counsel concerning entry of a guilty plea. It is unprofessional conduct to engage in plea discussions directly with an accused when the accused is represented by counsel (except with counsel's approval). It is unprofessional as well for a prosecutor knowingly to make false statements or representations in the course of plea discussions. It also is unprofessional conduct for a prosecutor to make any promise or commitment concerning the sentence which will be imposed by the judge, but he may properly discuss with the defense what recommendation he will make concerning the sentence. If the prosecutor finds he is unable to fulfill an understanding arrived at in plea discussions, he should give notice to the defendant and cooperate in securing leave of the court for the withdrawal of the plea of guilty.

The *Standards* require high professional conduct from the prosecutor in the course of a trial. He must act with dignity in the courtroom and support the authority of the court. It is unprofessional conduct for a prosecutor to engage in tactics or behavior purposefully calculated to irritate or annoy the opposing counsel. It is unprofessional conduct also to attempt to communicate privately with the jury or any person called for jury service. In his opening argument, his presentation of evidence, his examination of witnesses, and his arguments to the jury, he must abide by the rules of evidence and refrain from arguments calculated to inflame the jury. He should not make any public comments critical of a verdict, whether rendered by a judge or jury.

The prosecutor should not make the severity of the sentences the index of his effectiveness; he should seek to assure that a fair and informed judgment is made on sentence and to avoid unfair sentence disparities; he should assist the court in obtaining full and accurate information in the presentence report and should disclose all information in his files which is relevant to the sentencing issue.

The Prosecutor in Relation to Other Professionals in the Criminal Justice System. The prosecutor works closely with the police, with the judge, and with defense attorneys. His relationships with the police are usually amicable. Where difficulties arise, they often are the product of the different perspectives of the police and prosecutor produced by their distinct roles in the system. A prosecutor understandably resents police illegalities that result in the exclusion of evidence and thereby prevent the conviction of a guilty person. Prosecutors also may quarrel with police over the use of arrest authority in settings suggesting the arrest was used for purposes other than prosecution. Similarly, prosecutors expect police to successfully stay on the proper side of the sometimes narrow line that divides investigative encouragement of a criminal act from actual entrapment. Police do not necessarily defend illegal actions on their part, but they often tend to view the law as too technical and the prosecutor's expectations as far too high considering the conditions under which they must operate.

The police, for their part, sometimes have grievances against the prosecutor. They suspect that political reasons occasionally enter into the decision of the prosecutor to prosecute or not to prosecute. They think that the prosecutor's acquiescence in the setting of low bail for dangerous offenders is unjustifiable. Police see some prosecutors as just plain incompetent, and believe that good police work is sometimes frustrated by bungled prosecution. Many police also believe that plea bargaining works against the safety of the community and good law enforcement. Here again, the major difficulty often lies in the failure of the different professionals to appreciate the problems faced by the other professionals. Burdened by a chronic case overload, prosecutors and police may be so preoccupied with their own problems that neither is able to recognize the administrative realities of the other's situation.

Most judges and prosecutors work harmoniously together. Judges and prosecutors share a common caseload problem and accommodate each other in resolving it. Thus, judges often are willing to accept sentence recommendations that are part of a plea bargain even though they personally view the sentence as too lenient. Similarly, prosecutors may grant the defendant certain concessions at the urging of a judge who says the point is "not worth arguing about." On issues such as pretrial disclosure of evidence, a judge may take the position that the prosecutor would best serve the interests of justice by granting disclosure rather than challenging every defense request for disclosure, winning some and losing others, and taking up a considerable amount of everybody's time. While the prosecutor has a right to insist on litigating every issue, he is likely to respond affirmatively to a judge's suggestion that he concede the point and go on to more important matters.

Judges, prosecutors, and defense counsel, all being lawyers, tend to have a better appreciation of each other's role than do the other professionals in the process. The police and prosecutor, because of their constant contact, gradually should develop a fair understanding of each other's role. The greatest communication gap involving the prosecutor lies between the prosecutor and the corrections official. Prosecutors typically concern themselves very little with the correctional process, and usually have little knowledge about it. Their chief contact with a correctional institution is with the jail—they interview witnesses and talk with accused persons being held in the jail. Their contact with probation and parole officers is cursory; they recommend probation but sometimes may know very little about the supervisory functions performed by probation officers. Many prosecutors lack a full understanding of the case work method used in probation, parole, and social case work, and some prosecutors are actively antagonistic to its use with the offender. In recent years, law schools have developed courses on corrections and prosecutors have participated more heavily in the probation revocation process. The result has been increased awareness of the problems faced in corrections, although the prosecutors, like the police, often approach the area from a considerably different perspective than many corrections officials.

THE DEFENSE ATTORNEY

Selection. Where the defendant has the means, he simply hires a lawyer, usually on recommendation of a friend or another lawyer who does not handle criminal work. Where the defendant is indigent, counsel will be appointed through one of the three methods that we discussed in Chapter Eleven.[20] As we noted there, the growing trend across the country is towards use of either the "mixed" or "public defender" methods of appointment, as opposed to the traditional assigned counsel method. This trend has produced a dramatic increase in the number of public defender agencies. As of 1974, there were approximately 500 such agencies.[21] The defender agencies usually are part of the state or county government, although there are some local defender offices supported by municipalities. About one-third of the states have statewide public defender agencies. Those statewide agencies that handle trials ordinarily have branch offices throughout the state, and those offices often have considerable independence.[22]

While the local public defender's office is likely to be somewhat smaller than the prosecutor's office, it can, nevertheless, have a fairly large staff. The Defender Association of Philadelphia, for example, has over 100 attorneys, 24 investigators,

---

20. See p. 279 *supra.*

21. *Sourcebook of Criminal Justice Statistics—1976*, note 1, p. 1 *supra*, at p. 38. The organization of various defender agencies is described in the report of the National Study Commission on Defense Services, *Guidelines For Legal Defense Systems in the United States*, Chicago, Ill.: National Legal Aid and Defender Association, 1976.

22. Some statewide agencies serve only on appeals, with county defender agencies or court appointed private counsel providing representation at trial.

15 social workers, and a psychiatrist on its staff. The chief public defender of a local agency commonly is appointed by the county or city council, the local judges, or a nonpartisan advisory board. The chief defender of a statewide agency commonly is appointed by the state supreme court or a nonpartisan advisory board. Ordinarily partisan politics will not enter into the selection process, but the appointing body certainly may consider various "political" factors, such as community support for the candidate. The assistant defenders are then selected on a nonpartisan basis by the chief defender. As with assistant prosecutors, they usually are young lawyers interested in obtaining trial experience. Most will not make their career in the public defender office, although they may stay in the criminal field as private defense lawyers.

Estimates of the number of lawyers who specialize in criminal defense work vary, but it generally is assumed that that group is composed of less than 5% of the more than 400,000 lawyers in the United States. If we define the specialist as the lawyer who spends most of his time in the criminal field, the defense specialists probably are divided about equally between private attorneys and public defenders. Of course, there are far more private attorneys who will take criminal cases on a regular basis, but spend most of their time in other fields. The vast majority of attorneys view criminal defense work as a most undesirable field for specialization. The financial rewards are not nearly as great as in most other legal fields. Lawyers in defender offices, like lawyers in prosecutor offices, are poorly paid as compared to private practitioners generally. Private lawyers specializing in defense work, moreover, may be even more poorly paid. Most non-indigent criminal defendants can pay only a moderate fee, and only organized crime can provide the steady business comparable to a prosperous businessman-client in the field of civil law. Moreover, the conditions under which the defense attorney works, whether private practitioner or public defender, are unappealing to most lawyers. Counsel for the defendant must expect to lose more cases than he wins, not for any reason related to his legal capabilities, but simply because most prosecutions that are not dismissed early in the process will be well founded. The defense counsel must expect to spend most of his time in overcrowded courtrooms, dealing with people who have committed questionable acts, and attempting to place those acts in the best possible light.

Finally, the public image of the defense lawyer tends to be quite poor as compared to other lawyers. To some extent, the criminal defense lawyer is identified unjustifiably with the client he represents. Also, particularly in large cities, a small segment of the defense bar is of low legal and dubious ethical quality. These are the private practitioners who operate on a volume basis, pushing their clients towards a guilty plea and collecting a quick fee. Unfortunately, the poor reputation of this portion of the bar often rubs off on all criminal defense lawyers. To some extent, the working conditions and the public esteem of the defense attorney have improved with the growth of the public defender agencies. Nevertheless, both factors are still far below that which is available to lawyers practicing in many fields of civil law.

Training. The training of the defense counsel is similar in most respects to that of the prosecutor. There are no legal qualifications for handling criminal defense work other than admission to the bar. Most defense lawyers enter the field immediately upon receiving their license to practice. They have the legal skills learned in law schools, but must acquire other skills "on the job." Private practitioners often suffer from the disadvantage that they are not associated with a group of more experienced lawyers. In defender offices, as in prosecutor offices, the new lawyer can learn from his seniors. He also can be moved along from the less serious to the more serious cases as he gains experience. Training programs for new defenders, similar to those provided for new prosecutors, are available in many areas. Continuing education programs also are available to all criminal defense counsel. The National College of Criminal Defense Lawyers and Public Defenders serves as a counterpart in this area to the National College of District Attorneys.

The Role Of Defense Counsel.   The defense counsel's role, simply put, is that of an advocate for his client. As the Code of Professional Responsibility notes, his obligation is to represent his client "zealously" within the "bounds of the law."[23] The defense counsel's function is to employ all legal means to secure the acquittal of his client, and, if that is not possible, to make every effort to have his client convicted of some lesser offense or to have the court impose the lightest possible sentence. The defense attorney is not a policeman or a prosecutor, and he cannot be expected to assist these professionals (except where doing so will help his client). He is, of course, an officer of the court, as is any lawyer. He must abide by the rules of procedure and the ethical standards of his profession. Thus, like any attorney, he cannot knowingly use perjured testimony or false evidence or advance a legal point that cannot be supported by good faith argument. Neither can he counsel a client in the commission of a future crime. On the other hand, he has no obligation to reveal his client's past crimes. Indeed, with few exceptions, the Code of Professional Responsibility prohibits a lawyer from revealing, without the client's authorization, confidential information received from the client.[24]

A question frequently asked by non-lawyers is, "How can a lawyer in good conscience defend a guilty person at a trial"? Different defense lawyers offer different answers to this question, but they all agree that they can justifiably contest the guilt of a client even when the client has told them that he is guilty. Some argue that it is inappropriate for a lawyer ever to assume that his client is guilty. The fact that his client appears to be guilty, indeed that he has confessed to the crime, does not necessarily mean that he is guilty. The determination as to guilt can only be made by the judge or jury. Other lawyers argue that it does not matter whether the client is guilty. All defendants, guilty or not, have a right to insist that the state prove its case. The function of defense counsel, they note, is to protect that right by going to trial if the client desires to do so. Still other lawyers stress that the defense of a guilty defendant at trial should not be viewed as an act simply benefiting the defendant, but as an act benefiting the criminal justice

---

23. See A.B.A., *Code of Professional Responsibility*, note 3 *supra*, Cannon 7 and Ethical Consideration 7-19.

24. A.B.A., *Code of Professional Responsibility*, note 3 *supra*, at Disciplinary Rule 4-101. A major exception permitting disclosure without client approval, refers to information needed by authorities to prevent a future crime.

process itself. The Code of Professional Responsibility advances this theory in its Ethical Consideration 7-19:

> An adversary presentation counters the natural human tendency to judge too swiftly in terms of the familiar that which is not yet fully known; the advocate, by his zealous preparation and presentation of facts and law, enables the tribunal to come to the hearing with an open and neutral mind and to render impartial judgments. The duty of a lawyer to his client and his duty to the legal system are the same: to represent his client zealously within the bounds of the law.[25]

The duty of the legal profession to represent all defendants, the unpopular as well as the sympathetic, is clear. No lawyer need accept employment from a defendant he would rather not represent, but he must recognize that the fulfillment of the obligation of the profession requires that he accept his share of unpopular clients. When he is appointed by the court to represent a client who could not otherwise obtain counsel, he cannot lightly refuse that appointment. As Ethical Consideration 2-29 notes:

> When a lawyer is appointed by a court . . . to undertake representation of a person unable to obtain counsel, whether for financial or other reasons, he should not seek to be excused from undertaking the representation except for compelling reasons. Compelling reasons do not include such factors as the repugnance of the subject matter of the proceeding, the identity or position of a person involved in the case, [or] the belief of the lawyer that the defendant in a criminal proceeding is guilty . . .[26]

A.B.A. Standards. The American Bar Association's *Standards Relating to the Defense Function*[27] sets forth basic guidelines for a defense counsel in fulfilling his obligation to his client. While recognizing counsel's duty to zealously represent his client within the bounds of the law, the *Standards* admonish against excesses. Defense counsel is to avoid unnecessary delay, to refrain from misrepresentations of law and fact, and to avoid personal publicity connected with the case. Fees must be set on the basis of the time and effort required by counsel, the responsibility assumed, the novelty and difficulty of the question involved, the gravity of the charge, the experience, reputation and ability of the lawyer, and the capacity of the client to pay a fee. The lawyer may not obtain literary rights from the accused to publish books, plays, articles, interviews, or pictures relating to the case.

The defense lawyer is required to conduct a prompt investigation of the circumstances of the case relative to guilt and degree of penalty, to keep his client informed of developments in the case, and to take prompt action to preserve all of the legal rights of the accused. Certain decisions relating to the conduct of the case are ultimately for the accused and others are ultimately for the defense counsel. The decisions which are to be made by the accused, after full consultation with counsel, are: (1) what plea to enter; (2) whether to waive jury trial; and (3) whether to testify in his own behalf. The decision on what witnesses to call, whether and

---

25. A.B.A., *Code of Professional Responsibility*, note 3 *supra*, Ethical Consideration 7-19.

26. A.B.A., *Code of Professional Responsibility*, note 3 *supra*, Ethical Consideration 2-29.

27. See note 18 *supra*.

how to conduct cross-examination, and all other strategic and tactical decisions tend to be the exclusive province of the lawyer after consultation with his client.

The defense lawyer is instructed to explore the possibility of an early diversion of the case from the criminal process through the use of other community agencies. If it appears desirable, he is to secure the permission of his client to enter into plea discussions with the prosecutor. High standards of ethical conduct in the presentation of evidence, examination of witnesses, argument to the jury, and in other courtroom proceedings also are imposed upon the defense attorney.

The defense attorney should be familiar with the sentencing alternatives available to the court, and these alternatives should be fully explained by the lawyer to his client. Defense counsel should present in court any argument that will assist it in reaching a proper sentence; he also should check the facts in the presentence report and be prepared to challenge or supplement them if necessary. After conviction, the lawyer should explain to the defendant the meaning and consequences of the court's judgment and his right to appeal. Appellate counsel should not seek to withdraw from a case solely on the basis of his own determination that the appeal lacks merit. After a conviction is affirmed on appeal, appellate counsel should determine whether there is any ground for relief under other post-conviction remedies, such as habeas corpus, although he has no duty to represent his client in such proceedings unless he has agreed to do so.

The *Standards* place a duty on the bar to encourage through every available means the widest possible participation in the defense of criminal cases by experienced trial lawyers; lawyers active in general trial practice should be encouraged to qualify themselves for participation in criminal cases both by formal training and through experience as associate counsel; qualified trial lawyers should not announce a general unwillingness to appear in criminal cases, and law firms should encourage partners and associates to appear in criminal cases.

The duties of the lawyer to his client are said to be the same whether he is privately employed, judicially appointed, or serving as part of a defender system. Every jurisdiction is urged to guarantee by statute or rule of court the right of an accused to prompt and effective communication with a lawyer, with reasonable access to a telephone and other facilities for that purpose. There should be a referral service which maintains a list of lawyers willing and qualified to undertake the defense of a criminal case which is organized to provide prompt service at all times. Personnel of jails, prisons, and custodial institutions should be prohibited by law or administrative regulations from examining or otherwise interfering with any communication or correspondence between a client and his lawyer relating to legal actions arising out of criminal charges or conditions of incarceration.

Defense Role and Client Relationships.   A defense lawyer often finds that, notwithstanding his substantial efforts to serve as an effective advocate for his clients, many losing clients will be dissatisfied with his services. A study of over 2,000 applications for writs of habeas corpus filed by prisoners in Florida prison system disclosed that such dissatisfaction often is the product of the defendant's unrealistic notion of his lawyer's function. Basically, the offender sees it as his lawyer's duty to "get him off," no matter how guilty he may be of the offense. In the process, the offender wants his attorney to act in a highly aggressive manner with which he can identify. The "fighting" criminal lawyer is the one who is appreciated by his clients, even when counsel's conduct may antagonize judge and jury and actually result in a more severe sentence. Offenders take literally the ethical admonition given to a lawyer to represent his client's interest "exclusive of all others." Lawyers interpret this to mean "exclusive of all other whose interests may be adverse to those of the client;" the offender insists that it means "exclusive of all others—period." Many an inmate complained in his habeas application that his lawyer was handling cases for other clients when he should have been devoting *full time* to *his* case. An attorney who fraternized with the prosecutor or spoke well of the judge was suspected by his client of a "sell-out." A substantial number of prisoners insisted that they were victims of a "frame-up," participated in by the prosecutor, the judge, and their own counsel. It was interesting to note that the inmates complained as often of lawyers whom they had selected and paid as they did of appointed counsel.[28] Other studies suggest, however, that defendants who had privately retained counsel tend to rate their counsel somewhat more highly.[29] Defendants are naturally suspicious of lawyers who don't cost them anything and are selected for them by the court.

The Defense Attorney in Relation to Other Professionals in the Criminal Justice System. The defense attorney often finds himself in conflict with the police, the prosecutor, and the corrections officer. As an advocate for the defendant, he must put to one side any sympathies he may have for the problems faced by the other professionals in the performance of their roles. He cannot ignore legal objections that will assist his client's case simply because those objections are based upon "technicalities." Neither can he ignore police violations of his client's rights because these violations are "understandable" in light of the pressures placed upon the police. He must challenge the probation officer's request for probation revocation even though he knows that the officer also has concern for the best interests of the probationer. In sum, much of the "conflict" is the inevitable product of the different functions of the defense attorney and the other participants in the process. The prosecutor usually will understand that defense counsel's obligation differs from his, and he will not think less of defense counsel for his honest efforts to represent his client. The police and corrections officers tend to be less appreciative of the adversary system, and they therefore tend to view the defense counsel more harshly. Here again, a broader understanding of the total system by all of the professionals involved would be helpful in improving their working relationships.

THE JUDGE

Functions of the Judge. We already have examined, in Chapter Three, the structure of the court system and the role of the courts in determining and applying the law. Various rulings that must be made by judges have been noted throughout Part Three. Accordingly, we need only briefly review here the functions of

---

28. H. Kerper. *Development of a Theoretical Foundation for the Use of "Writs" in the Resocialization Process in the Correctional Setting,* (Unpublished Master's Thesis, Florida State University, December, 1965. Major Professor, Dr. Vernon Fox); H. Kerper. *"On 'Writs' and 'Resocialization'"* American Journal of Correction (November/December, 1967).

29. See J. Casper, *Criminal Courts: The Defendant's Perspective,* Washington, D.C.: Government Printing Office, 1978, p. 30-37.

judges of the different courts in the judicial hierarchy. The magistrate court, as we have seen, serves as the basic trial court for lower-level misdemeanors in some jurisdictions and for all misdemeanors in others. In addition, the magistrate court conducts the preliminary hearing for those cases beyond its trial jurisdiction. The magistrate also performs several important preliminary functions for all criminal cases, such as issuing search and arrest warrants and setting bail. The general trial court serves an appellate function in reviewing rulings of the magistrate. Its most significant authority is its trial jurisdiction in all felony cases and such misdemeanors as might be beyond the magistrate court's jurisdiction. The general trial court also will have jurisdiction over various miscellaneous actions, such as habeas corpus applications and requests for extradition. The intermediate appellate court will review the decision of the trial court. The state supreme court will review the decisions of the intermediate appellate court, or the decisions of the trial court where there is no intermediate appellate court. [30]

Discretion and Judicial "Neutrality."   In performing the functions associated with their court, the judges will, of course, be bound by the applicable rules of law. However, as we have seen, legal standards often are far from precise. In some areas, as in the standards governing bail, the applicable law sets forth a general objective and tells the judge to consider a variety of factors in reaching that objective. In other areas, the law may use a very flexible guideline for determining legality, such as a standard of "reasonableness." In still other areas, the applicability of one rule of law as opposed to another may be unclear. The end result is that a judge at almost every stage of the criminal proceeding is given considerable discretion in making some decisions. Perhaps the broadest discretion exists in the field of sentencing, where the judge will have authority to impose any sentence within a broad range specified by the legislature. Yet, discretion is also present in areas more closely regulated by the law, such as the trial. If the jury is waived and the judge sits as the trier of fact, he has considerable discretion in making factual determinations based upon his personal evaluation of the credibility of witnesses. Even if the case is tried to the jury, the judge has considerable discretion, under several of the rules of evidence, in determining whether particular information will be brought to the attention of the jury.

Because of the broad discretion granted judges in making some very crucial rulings, it is extremely important that judicial decisions be based on what lawyers call "neutral principles." Neutrality in judicial decision making does not require that the judge balance evenly all of the factors that are relevant to a particular ruling. One judge in interpreting a statute may place primary emphasis on the statutory language while another may stress legislative history, but both will be acting on the basis of neutral principles. "Neutral" or "impartial" judicial decision making requires only that the judge's rulings be based on legally relevant factors and that those factors be applied in an even-handed manner to all similar cases.

---

30. The state supreme court also usually has authority to act as the administrative supervisor of the entire state judicial system. It may prescribe standards for the internal administration of the courts, relating to such matters as the scheduling of cases and the recording of court proceedings. The court may have authority to temporarily reassign trial judges or magistrates to other districts in order to reduce case backlogs. These administrative decisions quite often are delegated to a professional court administrator. See pp. 451-52 *infra*.

This requires in many instances that the judge ignore his personal views as to the desirable objectives of the law. When the rule set down by the legislature is clear, the judge cannot reject it because he views the law as unwise. When the precedent of the supreme court is clear, the trial judge may not disregard it because he would have ruled otherwise if he had been on the supreme court. There are, however, situations in which the law permits the judge to give weight to his personal view as to the appropriate objectives of the law. We discussed in Chapter Three the role of the judge's personal viewpoint in dealing with the creation of new common law standards. An even more direct invitation to rely on personal philosophy may exist in sentencing. Thus, in a jurisdiction that grants the judge broad discretion under indeterminate sentencing, the law clearly permits one judge to place more emphasis on rehabilitation and another on deterrence.

While neutral principles often provide room for application of personal philosophies, they never permit reliance upon personal prejudices. It clearly is contrary to judicial ethics to let a decision rest on the judge's personal antagonism toward a person involved in a lawsuit. The judge may not consider the race, sex, or religion of the defendant or the victim unless the law requires consideration of that factor (as in an employment discrimination case). In a case where he feels that he has a personal bias or prejudice or a personal stake in the outcome of the case, the judge should disqualify himself. Indeed, most judges will disqualify themselves when there is a potential for an appearance of partiality in his decision (e.g., where the judge formerly served as a lawyer on the same case or a closely related matter). Also, the judge should never be influenced by outside pressures. As the *Code of Judicial Conduct* concludes, the judge must remain "unswayed by partisan interests, public clamor, or fear of criticism."[31]

Another important aspect of principled decision making is the judge's full recognition of the adversary process. Thus, a judge must rely essentially on information presented in the hearing before him. He cannot base his decision on his personal knowledge of disputed evidentiary facts. He should not engage in discussions of the case with the lawyers on either side without the other side being present. He should not seek advice on a case from an outside expert without first notifying both parties and giving them a chance to respond to the expert's comments. Above all, the judge should never penalize a client for the misconduct of his counsel.

Judicial Qualifications.   When one considers all of the aspects of judging that require the exercise of some degree of discretion, it is not surprising that so many distinguished jurists have themselves noted that the quality of justice rests heavily on the quality of the individual judge. As Justice Arthur Vanderbilt of the New Jersey Supreme Court once noted: "[Highly qualified] judges can after a fashion make even an inadequate system of substantive law achieve justice; on the other hand, judges who lack ... qualifications will defeat [even] the best system of substantive and procedural law imaginable."[32] But what makes for a highly qualified judge? Experts disagree as to the weight given to any one trait, but they

---

31.   American Bar Association, *Code of Judicial Conduct,* Cannon 3(A) (1972).

32.   A. Vanderbilt, *The Challenges of Judicial Reform,* Princeton, New Jersey: Princeton University Press, 1955, p. 11-12.

generally are in agreement as to the total package of necessary skills. Justice Vanderbilt described that package as follows:

> *We need judges learned in the law, not merely the law in books but, something far more difficult to acquire, the law as applied in action in the courtroom; judges deeply versed in the mysteries of human nature and adept in the discovery of the truth in the discordant testimony of fallible human beings; judges beholden to no man, independent and honest and— equally important—believed by all men to be independent and honest; judges, above all, fired with consuming zeal to mete out justice according to law to every man, woman, and child that may come before them and to preserve individual freedom against any aggression of government; judges with the humility born of wisdom, patient and untiring in the search for truth and keenly conscious of the evils arising in a workaday world from any unnecessary delay.* [33]

Obviously the qualities noted by Justice Vanderbilt cannot be prescribed by statute as legal qualifications for office; the statutes governing selection must be satisfied with listing formal, easily measurable criteria, such as age, possession of a law degree, local residency, and, perhaps, experience in the practice of law. Many jurisdictions do not include even all of these potentially relevant criteria.[34] Almost all states impose a minimum age requirement, usually the same as that required for service in the state legislature (commonly 18 or 21). Almost all also require that appellate judges and judges of the general trial court be lawyers. [35] About half of the states have specific legal experience requirements for the general trial court and higher courts. Ordinarily, these requirements will be a specified number of years (ranging from 3 to 10) in a legal position. Aside from these minimal requirements, the task of ensuring that our judges are qualified persons is left largely to the selection process.

Methods of Selection. There are four different methods that are utilized to select judges in the United States: (1) appointment, with or without confirmation by another agency; (2) partisan political election; (3) nonpartisan election; and (4) a combination of nomination by commission, appointment, and periodic reelection that was originated in Missouri and commonly is described as the "Missouri plan." These four methods reflect the basic differences in selection procedures. There are, in addition, numerous minor variations that may be found in the use of any one method. In states using nonpartisan elections, for example, there may be

---

33. Vanderbilt, *The Challenge of Law Reform,* note 32 *supra,* at p. 12.

34. The various state qualifications are listed in Council of State Governments, *Book of States — 1978-79,* Lexington, Ky., 1978, p. 88 and *Sourcebook of Criminal Justice Statistics — 1976,* note 1, p. 1 *supra,* at p. 160. The same sources also list the terms of office and methods of selecting judges in individual states.

35. Some state provisions simply note that the judge must be "learned in the law," but that phrase has been viewed as requiring admission to the bar. Even where the governing statute or constitutional provision fails to require legal training, judges at the general trial court and higher levels traditionally have been lawyers. As we noted in Chapter Three, nonlawyer judges are found almost exclusively in the magistrate court.

significant differences in the procedures that must be followed to have one's name placed on the ballot. In states employing the Missouri plan, there are numerous differences in the composition of the nominating commissions. For our purposes, it is sufficient to concentrate on the basic differences; we will describe the four selection methods in their "typical" form, without regard to the many minor variations.

While some states utilize one or another of the four methods to select all of their judges, many employ different methods to select judges at different levels in the judicial hierarchy. In Oklahoma, for example, three different selection methods are used. The Missouri plan is used in selecting supreme court judges and judges of the criminal appellate court. Judges of the trial courts of general jurisdiction are elected on a nonpartisan ballot. Municipal judges are appointed by the governing body of the municipality. In some jurisdictions, different selection methods even are utilized for courts on the same level located in different parts of the state. Thus, in Missouri, judges of the general trial court in the three largest counties are appointed pursuant to the Missouri plan, but judges of the same court in other counties are elected in partisan elections. Though the states' use of combinations of selection methods varies, there is one common pattern found in many states. Where a state utilizes the Missouri plan or appointment by the state's governor or legislature, neither method is likely to be carried through to the selection of magistrates. Both methods require a considerable investment of time and effort by high ranking state officials and therefore tend to be cumbersome as applied to the magistrate court, which usually has many more judges than the other courts. Accordingly, in those states, judges of the magistrate court usually are either elected or appointed by the general trial court or local city council (when the court is a municipal court).

The jurisdictions also vary as to the length of the terms for which their judges are selected. In the federal system, judges are appointed to "hold their Offices during Good Behavior."[36] For all practical purposes, this is an appointment for a lifetime term. Only four states provide for the equivalent of a lifetime term.[37] The remaining states utilize terms that range between four and sixteen years. Frequently, the term for an appellate court is longer than that for a trial court. The most common term for trial courts is six years, which is used in approximately half of the states. At the appellate level, six years is the shortest term, with over twenty states using terms of ten years or more.

Appointment Of Judges. The appointment method has achieved prominence primarily because it is the exclusive method for selection of federal judges. Justices of the Supreme Court, judges of the court of appeals, and all district court judges are appointed by the President with the advice and consent of the Senate. Federal magistrates are appointed, in turn, by the district court. Several states

---

36. United States Constitution, Article III, section I. This does not apply to Federal magistrates, who are appointed for an 8 year or 4 year term.

37. Rhode Island provides for a life term, while New Jersey provides for an initial term of seven years with possible reappointment for life. Massachusetts and Delaware provide for tenure until the age of seventy.

similarly provide for appointment of general trial or appellate judges by the governor with the consent of the state legislature or an executive council. Most of the states using a gubernatorial appointment system, however, combine it with the nominating commission and reelection that are features of the Missouri plan. Five states retain the practice, common in the early days of the Republic, of appointment by the legislature. However, one (Rhode Island) uses the system to select only supreme court justices, and another (Connecticut) has added the element of nomination of candidates by the governor. The appointment of magistrates is fairly common among the states, although it ranks behind selection by election. Appointment will be made by the general trial court if the magistrate court is a state or county court and by the local municipality if it is a municipal court.

Whether the appointment is made by the chief executive, the legislature, or a combination of the two, the appointment process tends to have a political flavor. The federal appointment process is illustrative. There, as a result of the Senate's power to block an appointment by refusing to confirm the President's appointee, individual Senators have acquired substantial influence over the appointment of district court and court of appeals judges who come from their states. Under the practice known as "senatorial courtesy," the Senate will refuse to confirm a presidential appointee who is opposed on any ground by a Senator from the state in which the appointee would sit. This means the individual Senator can "veto" a presidential appointee whose politics he finds particularly distasteful. Indeed, where the Senator comes from the President's political party, he will have even greater power. Traditionally those Senators have managed informally to turn the appointment process around; it is the Senator who will informally nominate a candidate to the President, with the President almost automatically appointing that nominee unless the local bar association rates the person as unqualified. Senatorial nominees almost always have been affiliated with the political party of the President and Senator, and frequently they have been active political supporters of the Senator making the nomination. In recent years, there has been some movement away from senatorial control over judicial appointments, but political affiliation has remained an important criterion for selection. For several years during the 1970's, Congress refused to create any new judgeships notwithstanding crushing court backlogs. The Democrats who controlled the Congress simply were not eager to create judgeships for a Republican President to fill.

Election of Judges.   The election of judges is a legacy of the populist movement that flourished in this country in the latter half of the nineteenth century. Judges were policy-makers, it was argued, and they accordingly should be subject to the election process. At one time the election of judges was even more popular than it is today. Most of the states that have moved to the Missouri plan previously had an elective system. Today, approximately fifteen states elect judges in contested elections in which they run under a party label (usually Democratic or Republican). Approximately the same number of states use nonpartisan elections in which the candidate runs on his name alone without party label. Where a partisan election is used, the candidate obtains a place on the ballot by gaining his party's nomination at its convention or by winning the party's primary. Where a nonpartisan election is used, the candidate must collect a certain number of signatures to gain a place in a nonpartisan primary and then must be among the top group in the primary to be included on the final ballot.

In most jurisdictions electing their judges, a judge running for reelection may be designated on the ballot as the current officeholder. This "incumbency label" gives a sitting judge a considerable advantage, particularly in a nonpartisan election, and it helps to explain the special significance of the process for filling vacancies resulting from the death or resignation of a judge during his term. Several studies have shown that, in a typical elective state, half of the trial judges were originally appointed by the governor to fill a vacancy and then were elected to office. While these appointees were required to run in the next election, they then were sitting judges and had a substantial advantage in running as the incumbent. Accordingly, political scientists have noted that the elective method may turn out in practice to be influenced as much by appointments as it is by elections.

The election of judges generally has been condemned by groups interested in improving the quality of the judiciary. Where partisan elections are used, the true judge-makers are said to be the leaders of the dominant political party who select that party's candidates. All too frequently, it is argued, the selection process is aimed more at rewarding lawyers who have made contributions (some financial) to the party than in selecting the most qualified people. Nonpartisan elections eliminate the party influence but substitute other disadvantages. Whatever responsibilities the political parties might have to produce at least minimally qualified candidates are lost. Qualified persons might be willing to run in an election as the nominee of the party that usually wins, yet not be willing to risk the vagaries of an election in which they must run primarily on their name. It is difficult in a campaign for judge to develop any substantive issues. Moreover, voters generally are not that interested in the judicial election. Research shows that many voters go to the polls without adequate information concerning the candidates. Too often, it is argued, voters in a nonpartisan election will look primarily to the candidate's name, relying on such factors as the name's indication of ethnic origin or its familiarity as a common "political name" in the community.

The Missouri Plan. In 1913, the American Judicature Society, an organization dedicated to the promotion of the efficient administration of justice, sought to devise a method of judicial selection that would maximize the benefits and minimize the weaknesses of both the appointment and election processes. Reform was difficult to achieve, however, and it was not until 1940 that the first state, Missouri, adopted the Judicature Society's approach to judicial selection. That approach contained five basic elements: (1) a nonpartisan selection commission, composed of lawyers and laymen, would nominate a list of several candidates for each vacant judicial post; (2) the governor would appoint to the post one of the persons nominated by the commission; (3) the appointed judge then would serve a probationary period of one or two years before being required to run in an election; (4) the judge would run in the election without an opponent, the voters being asked to vote only on whether the judge should be retained or rejected; (5) there would be periodic voter review of the judge's performance through approval/disapproval elections at the end of each subsequent term of office. Today, approximately a dozen states utilize the Missouri plan for the selection of at least some of their judges.[38] As we noted previously, the plan generally is not used for selection of magistrates, and some states do not use it for the selection of the general trial court judges.

Objections to the Missouri plan have focused primarily on the role of the nominating commission. Proponents of the elective system argue that the undemocratic nature of the nominating committee may result in elitist control of the judiciary. The lawyer members of the commission ordinarily are selected by the state bar and frequently are lawyers from leading law firms. Critics claim that these members will dominate the commission and their nominees will tend to be lawyers whose careers have been spent in large business law firms or government service rather than individual practitioners in such areas as criminal law. It also is argued that minority group representation will not increase under a Missouri plan. Studies of the Missouri plan's actual operation in several states tend to reject the fear that the nominating commissions will reflect an elitist philosophy. The studies reveal a diversified group of nominees selected from various segments of the bar, including individual practitioners. They also show, however, a low minority group representation. Of course, that statistic simply may reflect the fact that over 97 percent of all lawyers are Caucasian, but the federal government, which uses an appointive system, and certain states with elective systems do have higher percentages (e.g., seven or eight percent) of minority judges.

In part, the debate over the different selection methods reflects basic disagreements as to the comparative importance of the various traits cited by Justice Vanderbilt in describing the ideal jurist. Everybody wants a selection system that produces highly qualified judges, and everybody agrees that political donations, for example, do not establish the individual's qualifications. There is far less agreement, however, as to the weight that should be given to a variety of other factors, such as ethnic and economic background, in evaluating merit. Those systems of selection that are most likely to give weight to clearly irrelevant factors (such as financial contributions) may also be the systems that are most likely to reflect the pluralistic interests of our society.

Judicial Training. In some foreign countries, a law student decides upon a career as a judge shortly before he graduates and then pursues an extensive period of training for the judiciary. He begins his service at the lowest level of the judiciary and gradually rises in the ranks. This has never been the practice in the United States. Judges at all levels frequently come to the judiciary directly from the practice of law. They must learn the skills of judging while on the bench. Many argue that this is not a formidable task. Judges, they note, apply the same legal skills that they used as lawyers, but simply no longer act as adversaries. Others argue that just as baseball players require special training to become umpires, lawyers should obtain further training to assist them in moving to their new role. Numerous states have developed limited training programs (rarely exceeding 40

---

38. In addition, several states have adopted significant variations of the plan. Thus, California utilizes gubernatorial appointment, confirmation by a commission, and a substantial initial term of office followed by an approval/disapproval election. Massachusetts utilizes a nominating commission and gubernatorial appointment, but does not require a subsequent election. Several states utilize a nominating commission and gubernatorial appointment to fill interim vacancies, but then require the appointee to run in a partisan or nonpartisan election.

classroom hours) for new judges.[39] In addition, a substantial majority of the states have mandatory continuing education programs for all judges. These programs typically are limited, however, to a few conferences each year. The National College of State Trial Judges provides an extensive continuing education program for judges that has been widely praised.

The Judge in Relation to Other Professionals in the Criminal Justice System. Lawyers customarily treat judges with deference and respect. Instances of lawyers verbally abusing a judge during a trial are infrequent, although they receive considerable publicity when they do occur. The power of the court to hold the lawyer in contempt is a persuasive deterrent to such conduct. Moreover, most lawyers fully understand the judge's role, just as the judge fully understands their role. The lawyer need not agree with the court's ruling, but he knows he must abide by it for the time being and that he may challenge it again on appeal.

Police officers, on the other hand, sometimes have been openly contemptuous of court decisions. They have complained that certain rulings hamper police investigation and give the offender what they consider to be an unfair advantage *vis a vis* the lawabiding citizen. Sentencing judges as a group often are criticized by police as being too lenient. A major problem in this area is a lack of communications between the courts and the police. Judges speak to the police (and the public generally) only through their opinions. The opinions are written for lawyers and do not contain the kind of direct, non-technical explanation that might help the police officer understand exactly why the judge ruled the way that he did. Most judges feel that they cannot go beyond their opinions to provide such an explanation. Even if the police make public pronouncements reflecting a misconception of the content of a recent decision, a judge cannot, they argue, seek to clarify his decision. A responding letter to the police would involve a revision of the court's opinion outside of the judicial process. If the judges step beyond that process, they become, in effect, legal advisers rather than judges.[40] Insofar as the position of the court is misunderstood by the police, the courts must rely upon the prosecutor, as the police legal adviser, to set the record straight.

The difficulties that judges have in dealings with correctional officers stem from a similar communications problem and another source as well. Judges too frequently lack familiarity with the correctional system. Their lack of familiarity with the prisons is understandable, though not justifiable, in light of the isolation of most prisons. It is more difficult to understand why so many judges are unfamiliar with the operations of probation and parole officers, who are working in the community. Judges who regularly use presentence reports tend to have better working relationships with individual probation officers, though the judge's knowledge about the supervisory function performed by the probation officer may

---

39.   States utilizing non-lawyer judges in the magistrate courts almost always impose mandatory education programs for newly selected non-lawyer judges. These programs often run several days and are supplemented by compulsory continuing education requirements.

40.   For similar reasons, courts consider it inappropriate, when holding that a particular practice is invalid, to even comment on the possible legality of procedures the police might adopt as alternatives to the invalid practice.

still be woefully inadequate. The probation officer feels that he gets little understanding and support from the judge in the performance of his difficult task, and some judges are openly antagonistic to the social work concepts which form the basis for the case work techniques commonly used by the probation officer. Organizations of judges and individual judges are attempting to bridge this information gap between the courts and corrections. Some judges have even had themselves committed to a penal institution to learn first-hand what happens to the convicted man.

THE COURT ADMINISTRATORS

Clerks of court, bailiffs, and court reporters also are involved in the administration of criminal justice. The *Clerk of Court* is an appointed official when attached to a federal or appellate court. At the state superior court level, Clerks of Court are traditionally elected county officials. Clerks of Court in many areas are County Clerks as well, with duties in addition to those related to the court. A deputy is usually assigned the chief responsibility for acting as Clerk of Court where the two offices of County Clerk and Clerk of Court are combined.

The Clerk of Court is responsible for keeping all the records of the court. The returns on arrest and search warrants are made to the Clerk. In some courts, the Clerks are authorized by court rule to issue arrest warrants. The indictment, the information, all of the pleadings filed by the prosecutor or defense attorney, the instructions to the jury, the verdict, and the sentence are kept in the files by the Clerk. Such documents are also transcribed into large bound volumes comprising permanent court records. Clerks of Court issue subpoenas for witnesses, notices about jury service, keep track of the fees due jurors and witnesses, and attend upon the court during trials to swear witnesses and produce court records needed by the judge or the attorneys in the case. Clerks keep a record of all cases filed, of all cases dismissed, of all cases tried, and of all cases appealed, having special responsibilities in the preparation of the record for the appeal.

There is a general lack of standardization of court records, which contributes to the inefficiency of the court system, but professional organizations of Clerks of Court often work toward more uniformity. (One state department of corrections regularly receives over twenty different forms of the judgment, sentence, and commitment, the basic documents committing a man to prison, from the courts throughout the state. It is estimated that a standardized commitment form would save the department thousands of dollars a year in record keeping expense).

Bailiffs usually are permanent court employees in the large metropolitan courts, that try cases daily. In smaller communities, a bailiff is usually appointed by the judge for the duration of a trial, with one or two persons making themselves regularly available for the post. The bailiff's duties are to see to the security and decorum of the court; he keeps an eye on the defendant after he has been delivered to the court, and summons witnesses when it is their turn to testify. He is responsible for the protection and care of the jury during the trial and during the jury deliberations. If the jury is sequestered, he accompanies the jurors, and reports to the court attempts by any person to contact a juror. He also watches for improprieties committed by a juror, such as making forbidden telephone calls, or buying the daily newspaper which contains an account of the trial. The bailiff returns the jury to the courtroom when a verdict has been reached, and assists the judge in keeping order in the courtroom if an unseemly outbreak is likely upon announcement of the verdict.

Court reporters are highly paid professionals whose duty it is to take down, and then transcribe, the testimony at the trial or other court proceedings. Some reporters use shorthand, others use stenotype machines. In some states, tape recorders have been used to record proceedings in certain courts. The use of tape recordings permits the hiring of reporters (at much lower salaries) without stenographic skills. However, stenographers claim that the transcriptions made from the tapes are not likely to be as accurate as those made from a stenographer's shorthand. Stenographers are in short supply, and stenographic transcription is a time consuming process. As a result, long delays often occur in the preparation of trial transcripts, to the detriment of both the defendant and the prosecution. Court reporters also are charged with the care and preservation of the physical evidence introduced during the trial, though permanent responsibility belongs to the Clerk of Court. Guns and other such evidence are kept in a special safe provided for that purpose. Authority is given for disposal of the weapon after the time for appeal has passed or after a stated number of years.

The professional *court administrator* is a newcomer in the criminal justice system. The first class of court administrators graduated from the Institute of Court Management at the University of Denver in 1970. Their assignments were to highly paid positions with the federal courts. Court administrators have also been hired in various state courts.

The trained court administrator will take many of the duties of court administration off the shoulders of an over-worked chief justice or presiding judge. He is expected to bring up-to-date management techniques into the court and to greatly increase the efficiency of court operation. Some courts are already experimenting with the use of computers in the docketing of cases, with the computer preparing the notices which must be sent out to jurors, witnesses, and attorneys. Trained court administrators are expected to accelerate this trend and find additional uses for business machines in court management.

In the Congressional Act providing for the appointment of administrators for each of the eleven federal circuits, the duties of the court administrators were set out as follows:

1. Exercising administrative control of all non-judicial activities of the courts of appeals of the circuit in which he is appointed.
2. Administering the personnel system of the court of appeals.
3. Administering the budget of the court.
4. Maintaining a modern accounting system.
5. Establishing and maintaining property control records and undertaking a space management program.
6. Conducting studies relating to the business and administration of the courts within the circuit and preparing appropriate recommendations and reports to the chief judge, the circuit council, and the Judicial Conference.
7. Collecting, compiling, and analyzing statistical data with a view to the preparation and presentation of reports.
8. Representing the circuit as liaison to other courts and agencies.

9. Arranging and attending meetings of the judges and other officers of the circuit.

10. Preparing an annual report, including recommendations for more expeditious disposition of the business of the circuit.

The Act also provides, however, that all duties delegated to the administrator "shall be subject to the general supervision of the chief judge of the circuit."[41] A similar pattern is followed in the state courts using court administrators.

Upon the graduation of the class of the Institute for Court Management, Chief Justice Warren E. Burger commented:

> I hope that from now on judges will encourage the more promising young people in court clerk's offices to secure special training. Only by this process is there any hope of escaping from the "management morass" that now afflicts most large court systems. No other course offers any hope of bringing court operations into the 20th century in terms of management that will match other developments in the law and the urgent needs of the courts.[42]

---

41. The Circuit Court Executive Act, 28 United States Code §332.

42. As quoted in American Bar News, Vol. 16, No. 2, (February, 1971) p. 7. For further information on the material in this chapter, see the *National Prosecution Standards*, note 4 *supra*; *Guidelines for Legal Defense Systems in the United States*, note 21 *supra*; and Abraham, note 33, p. 55 *supra*.

Chapter 17

The Correctional Officer

Corrections includes a wide variety of officials involved in the administration of sentences. Some are persons belonging to other professions (e.g., physicians) who simply practice their profession in the special context of the correctional institution. We will concentrate in this chapter on persons who are involved in the special rehabilitative mission of corrections. This concludes the correctional administrator, the probation and parole officer, and some, but not all, of the officials working in correctional institutions. Before examining the functions of these various correctional officials, it would be helpful to understand the structure of the various corrections agencies. We accordingly start with a discussion of those agencies.

THE DIVISION OF CORRECTIONS AUTHORITY

State Corrections. Corrections authority tends to be divided according to three basic corrections responsibilities—administration of correctional institutions (i.e., prisons, jails, half-way houses, etc.), probation supervision, and parole supervision. A 1974 survey noted over 5,000 agencies charged with administration of correctional institutions (including both adult and juvenile facilities).[1] Those agencies are scattered throughout the state, county, and municipal levels of government. The primary facility administered by county and municipal governments is the local jail. In almost every county, there is a jail operated by the local sheriff. In addition, many major municipalities have their own jails. Altogether, there are more than 4,000 jails in the United States, and almost all are operated by a different local government agency. In most states, the jails must meet various minimal standards specified by the State Department of Corrections, but the local agencies otherwise are free from any central control. In some jurisdictions, local

---

1. See *Sourcebook of Criminal Justice Statistics—1976*, note 1, p. 1 *supra*, at p. 38. Unless otherwise indicated, the statistics cited in this chapter come from the *Sourcebook* and National Advisory Commission on Criminal Justice Standards and Goals, *Corrections*, Washington, D.C.: Government Printing Office, 1973.

agencies also operate other institutions, such as half-way houses and farms, that are used for misdemeanants.

There is considerably more unification in the administration of those facilities in which felons commonly serve their sentences. Such facilities, whether prisons, camps, or half-way houses, ordinarily are administered by a single state agency, usually the State Department of Corrections. In some states, central authority is rather loosely exercised, and each prison or other correctional institution is operated largely as a separate entity. In others, the central administrators impose extensive guidelines and reporting requirements designed to provide uniformity in the operation of the various units.

Parole authority also tends to be placed in a single agency at the state level, but the nature of that agency varies. Since the parole decision concerns the release of felons from state institutions, about two-thirds of the states place parole authority in a separate branch of the same state agency that administers the state institutions. In the other third of the states, however, parole authority is placed in an entirely separate agency, usually one having responsibility only for the decision on parole and parole supervision. (Whichever agency grants parole usually is responsible also for parole supervision, administered through its field offices).

The allocation of responsibility for probation supervision tends to follow one of three common patterns. In almost half of the states, the probation authority is located in the same agency that administers the parole authority, usually the Department of Corrections. In the remaining states, probation authority is either shared between local and state agencies or is vested entirely in local agencies. The primary local agency is a probation department that is an adjunct of the local court. Such agencies are usually associated with courts of general jurisdiction and therefore are located at the county level of government. However, some municipalities have their own probation agency. In some states, courts in the more heavily populated counties have their own probation departments while courts in sparsely settled counties use probation services supplied by the state. In some states, the division is between felony probation services (supplied by the state) and misdemeanor probation services (supplied by the local government).

Over the years, various proposals have been advanced toward achieving some substantial degree of unification in the organization of corrections.[2] These proposals generally have been more favorably received than the various proposals urging consolidation of police or prosecution agencies. Five states, Alaska, Connecticut, Delaware, Rhode Island and Vermont, now have a totally unified corrections system, with a single agency exercising control over the administration of all correctional institutions and probation and parole supervision. Several other states have granted a single state agency authority over all adult correctional

---

2.   Thus, National Advisory Commission, note 1 *supra*, provides at §16.4: "Each State should enact legislation by 1978 to unify all correctional facilities and programs. The board of parole may be administratively part of an overall statewide correctional services agency, but it should be autonomous in its decision-making authority and separate from field services. Programs for adult, juvenile, and youthful offenders that should be within the agency include: (1) Services for persons awaiting trial; (2) Probation supervision; (3) Institutional confinement; (4) Community-based programs, whether prior to or during institutional confinement; (5) Parole and other aftercare programs; and (6) All programs for misdemeanants including probation, confinement, community-based programs, and parole."

activities except the administration of jails, which is left to the counties. Moreover, more states appear to be looking in this direction, with gradual absorption of various corrections functions by the state departments of corrections.

Federal Corrections. The federal corrections authority is divided between the Board of Parole and the Bureau of Prisons, which are separate agencies within the Department of Justice, and the Federal Probation Service, which is supervised by the Administrative Office of the United States Courts. The Board of Parole considers all applications for parole by federal prisoners and has jurisdiction over all parolees. The Bureau of Prisons is responsible for over 30 correctional institutions and approximately 15 community treatment centers (half-way houses) in the federal prison system.[3] The Board and Bureau operate in close coordination and their regional offices often are located in the same building to facilitate that coordination. Where any conflicts in approach arise, they are resolved by the Attorney General.

The Probation Service, on the other hand, is divided into field offices which operate independently of each other. Each field office is subject to the control of an individual district court and tends to reflect the view of that court. The Administrative Office of the Federal Courts does provide assistance to the various field offices and thereby facilitates the adoption of uniform procedures.

THE CORRECTIONAL ADMINISTRATOR

The highest-level correctional administrators include the director of a state department or division of corrections, the director of any separate parole agency, and the superintendents of major state correctional institutions in jurisdictions where those institutions are not administered by a single state agency. The highest-level officers ordinarily are appointed by the governor or a state corrections commission whose members are appointed by the governor. The high-level correctional administrator serves at the pleasure of the governor or commission that appoints him. His position is not viewed as "political," however, and he will not be replaced automatically whenever there is a change in the political party that controls the state government. In jurisdictions in which the highest-level administrator is the director of corrections, the departmental heads below him, including the wardens of major institutions, are usually selected by the director. They are protected by civil service, but they serve in the high-level posts only at the discretion of the director.

Correctional officers holding high-level positions must be persons of outstanding administrative abilities. Their employees are numbered in the hundreds; the offenders under their care are counted in the thousands; the public property for which they are responsible is valued at many millions of dollars. One of their main duties is to prepare the budget for the operation of their agency, which must be defended before the appropriate executive and legislative committees. Since

---

3. It also operates several detention centers that house federal defendants who have been unable to post bail and are awaiting trial. In regions without such centers, federal defendants awaiting trial are housed in local jails.

correctional funding budgets are notoriously inadequate, this often is a frustrating task.

The high-level administrator also must be a public relations expert of high order. He is given the assignment of rehabilitating offenders, and meaningful work is an important rehabilitative tool. Yet the administrator may well run into public relations problems if prisoners are given work outside a correctional institution that is competitive with union labor or manufacture items within the institution that compete with local businesses. (Indeed, such work programs may even be prohibited by law.) Similarly, when the administrator encourages use of parole, he must be able to defend that position every time a parolee commits a new offense. The administrator also must be able to deal with the media during very difficult periods following prison disorders or highly publicized escapes.

THE PROBATION AND PAROLE OFFICER

Selection of the Probation and Parole Officer. Assuming that the parole officer is an employee of a state parole agency, he probably will be selected on the basis of a civil service exam. As a practical matter, though not necessarily a legal requirement, he usually must be a college graduate. The same hiring procedure will apply to probation officers who are employed by a state agency. Indeed, the same state officers often are made responsible for both probation and parole supervision. Where probation officers are employees of the local court rather than the state corrections system, the appointment process commonly is not governed by civil service. Often appointment lies entirely within the discretion of the court. As with court appointments of attorneys to represent indigent defendants, instances have been noted where court appointments of probation officers appear to have been based upon factors other than the professional qualifications of the applicant. Most courts, however, seek to emphasize merit, and they often rely primarily upon the recommendations of their professional staff in making appointments. Moreover, once appointed by the court, those probation officers commonly remain in their posts so long as they perform satisfactorily. Thus, whether appointment is by civil service or by judicial discretion, the probation officer generally is viewed as a career professional.

Education and Training of the Probation and Parole Officer. Until recently, there has been no consensus as to the kind of education and training needed by a probation and parole officer, although, as noted, most states require in practice that the person have a college degree. There is increasing agreement that training for correctional work is properly grounded in the behavioral sciences and related fields. The areas of knowledge which the probation or parole officer needs include casework, group work techniques, sociology, psychology, law, and public administration. Previous familiarity with community resources and skill in basic research are also important assets. Some departments accordingly have looked for persons with a Masters of Social Work degree and some practical experience in casework technique. There are not enough persons with such qualifications, however, to fill all of the openings. The new view of the officer as more of a "community resource manager" than a caseworker-counsellor should lead to a broadening of acceptable qualifications.[4]

Probation and parole departments are also providing extensive in-service training for employees, with some departments having special training sections. In-service training acquaints the new officer with the policies and procedures of the agency and instructs him on how to prepare a presentence report and how to present a case in court. Group discussions of actual cases teach him techniques of casework and offer him help in problem solving by acquainting him with community resources available to an offender. Attendance at workshops and conferences dealing with crime and delinquency is encouraged and financially assisted by the agency.

The Role of the Probation and Parole Officer.   The role of the probation and parole officer varies somewhat depending upon where he is employed, whether he is handling probation, parole, or both, and whether he is working with juveniles or adults. All probation and parole officers are concerned, however, with one basic problem—helping the offender to change his behavior in such a way as to avoid further conflict with the law. The probation and parole officer must accomplish this feat under limitations imposed by the conditions of probation and parole, including time limitations. We discussed the nature of parole and probation supervision in Chapter Thirteen. As we saw there, the probation officer or parole officer will be asked to accomplish a good deal with an unrealistic case load and with few community resources to fall back upon in time of need. The parole officer will have a particularly difficult task because he will be dealing with offenders who have the extra burden of readjusting to an open society after a period of incarceration.

The good parole officer may be a friend to the parolee, but he also must maintain a proper professional distance. If the parolee violates the conditions of his parole, the parole officer must consider community concerns as well as the interests of the parolee in making his decision as to whether or not to recommend revocation of the parole. As we learned in Chapter Thirteen, a parole officer usually does not recommend revocation for a minor violation. A parolee may miss one reporting period, or violate restrictions on going into a bar or tavern, or fail to request permission to buy a car; such "technical" violations will not in most cases result in revocation. Indeed, the commission of petty offenses often may not result in a revocation recommendation, although the commission of a felony or serious misdemeanors ordinarily will result in such a recommendation. The discretion of the parole officer in this area almost parallels that of the prosecutor in deciding whether to prosecute, but the parole officer acts from the disadvantageous position of not being an elected official. The probation officer sits in a similar position

---

4.   See p. 370 *supra.* The National Advisory Commission, note 1 *supra*, notes at p. 415: "Both the Corrections Task Force in 1967 and the Joint Commission in 1969 agreed that a baccalaureate degree should be the basic education requirement for a parole officer, and persons with graduate study might be used for specialized functions. Both also stressed the need to create opportunities for greater use of persons with less than college-level study. Many tasks carried out by a parole officer can be executed just as easily by persons with much less training, and many skills needed in a parole agency are possessed by those with limited education. As observed earlier, persons drawn from the [communities] to be served are good examples of staff with needed specialized skills. Ex-offenders also are an example of a manpower resource needed in parole agencies."

in determining whether to recommend probation revocation. In some jurisdictions, he also will be given considerable discretion by the judge in determining what goes into a presentence report.

The Probation and Parole Officer in Relation to Other Professionals in the Criminal Justice System.

Parole officers have relatively little contact with other professionals in the system except for the police. Relationships between the policeman and the parole officer are often fraught with dissension and misunderstanding. Some parole officers complain that the police harrass parolees. Thus, the police practice of "rounding-up" all ex-convicts to question them about unsolved crimes was a frequent source of dispute between parole officers and police before the practice was sharply curtailed by judicial decisions. Parole officers complained that such practices interfered with the rehabilitation of parolees. Just as the parolees were making progress, they would be taken into custody and relatives and employees would begin to doubt them. The police responded that there was always a distinct possibility that a parolee committed a crime, as evidenced by the high recidivism rates. Police and parole officers also may take different views of parole counseling techniques. Police officers dislike programs which bring ex-convicts together while parole officers often find such programs, including group therapy, very helpful in the management of their parolees.

Police and probation officers have similar areas of conflict. Police officers tend to believe that probation officers have unrealistic notions about changing the behavior of the offender. Some police officers believe that probation officers ignore the welfare of the community and of law-abiding citizens when they fail to report minor violations of probation conditions. Probation officers, on the other hand, stoutly defend their decisions on the basis that incarceration will only change the offender's behavior for the worse, and that the offender's best chance for rehabilitation often remains in the community. In some communities, probation officers extensively consult with police officers in preparing presentence reports. The result often is improved communications and less disagreement as to other aspects of the probation officer's role.

We have previously touched upon the lack of understanding between judges and probation and parole officers; a similar condition often exists between prosecutors and probation and parole officers. As we also have noted previously, some of the tension between the different professionals is a natural by-product of their different roles, but some comes from a lack of appreciation of each other's role. When judges, prosecutors, police, and probation and parole officers are brought together at a workshop or conference and engage in frank discussions about their job responsibilities, it is not difficult to improve relationships. The participants in such dialogues discover their common goals and many common problems, and begin to realize the degree to which the criminal justice system functions as a system with interacting and mutually dependent parts. It is particularly important that police, prosecutors, and judges recognize that their actions and attitudes may have a profound effect on the rehabilitation of the offender. Corrections is not the task only of the corrections officer.

THE INSTITUTIONAL CORRECTIONAL OFFICER

There is some disagreement as to just who is a "correctional officer." In the broad sense, everyone who works in a correctional institution is a correctional officer. The corrections continuum begins with the first contact of the offender with institution and continues until he is released back into a free society; hence, everyone who comes in contact with him in the institution has a bearing on his rehabilitation. However, for the purposes of our discussion in this chapter, we will limit the term "institutional correctional officer" to persons who are assigned duties that relate to the rehabilitation of the offender, as opposed to duties strictly limited to the maintenance of the institution. Under this standard, the term "correctional officer" is not limited to psychologists, counselors, and others who are involved directly in formal rehabilitation programs. As we shall see, some custodial officers also may be heavily involved in the "treatment program" of the institution.

Jails and Misdemeanant Institutions. We generally have refrained from characterizing the staff of jails and lock-ups as "correctional officers," which is unfair to some truly fine jail administrators. The jail administrator may be, but seldom is, a trained corrections specialist. County jails are under the supervision of the sheriff, who may be a good law enforcement officer but whose knowledge of correctional administration often is zero. As to staff members who actually operate the jails, few can be called correctional officers by the widest extension of the meaning of the term. Indeed, in some areas, jails are manned by non-deputies. Most commonly, jailors, whether deputies or non-deputies, view their responsibility as entirely custodial.

In fairness, it must be pointed out that jailors often are dealing with an aged, run down institution, overcrowded with offenders of all types, as well as with a great many persons awaiting indictment or trial. Since even decent living accommodations are not provided, an attempt to develop in such a place recreational, educational, or rehabilitative programs of any kind would be useless, if not ludicrous. In other areas, however, there are new jails being operated by trained jail administrators, who are making a career out of jail administration. These jails tend to place a higher priority on recreational and educational programs. Of course, the mixed nature of their population and the short terms they serve still imposes serious limits upon what can be done.[5]

Felony Corrections Institutions. Our focus in this section will be on correctional officers working in various adult corrections institutions for felons. This category covers a wide range of institutions with a total population of approximately 250,000[6] It includes some traditional maximum security prisons, where inmates live in tiered cells, eat at long tables in a large dining room, and are involved primarily in simple prison industries. It also includes modern, minimum security institutions that resemble a college campus, with inmates living in private

5.   See p. 271 *supra.*

6.   See note 68 at p. 347 *supra.*

rooms and spending most of their time in educational or vocational training programs. It includes institutions limited to youthful offenders and those with inmates of all ages who have committed all kinds of crimes. It includes institutions that place primary emphasis on regimentation and control and even those that condone the use of physical brutality to achieve those objectives. On the other hand, it also includes institutions that seek to recognize the individuality of each inmate and permit diversity to the greatest extent feasible. It includes institutions in which, as a practical matter, the most powerful inmates exercise a substantial influence over the operation of the institution. It also includes institutions in which the correctional personnel are firmly in control and exercise that control without creating an authoritarian atmosphere. In sum, there is tremendous diversity among the various corrections institutions and the performance of the corrections professional will be shaped to a large extent by the nature of the institution. This makes it very difficult to discuss the "role" of a corrections officer. An official described as a "vocational counselor" in one institution may be asked to work individually with inmates to increase their vocational capacity, while a "vocational counselor" in another institution may be asked to serve as no more than a foreman in a prison shop.

The role of the custodial staff is one that varies most significantly with the nature of the institution. In some institutions, to describe the custodial officers as "corrections officers" is a contradiction in terms. Their function has no relation whatsoever to "treatment" or "corrections." (Indeed, even describing some institutions as "corrections institutions" is a misnomer since their focus almost seems designed to make the inmates more anti-social than they were when they arrived). In other institutions, custodial officers are viewed as a crucial link between the inmate and the various counselors and teachers engaged in the corrections program. Custodial officers are constantly reminded that, if they treat the prisoners in a dehumanizing manner, if they arbitrarily enforce rules and play favorites, or if they fail to keep some inmates from preying on others, they will undercut completely the efforts of other correctional officers in treatment or training programs. Their role, as seen by these institutions, is both to maintain security and to maintain an atmosphere conducive to the overall rehabilitative program of the institution.

Unfortunately, the custodial officers today are too frequently the weakest link in the correctional process. In most jurisdictions, they come to their post with no prior experience in the field. They commonly must pass a civil service exam, but that test requires no special expertise beyond that of the typical high school graduate. While an in-service training program is provided, that training may run only a few weeks and usually will concentrate on the mechanics of the job. Little effort is spent in gaining an understanding of the psychology of the inmates. In many respects, the persons attracted to the job of custodial officer are among those least likely to understand the inmate's difficulties. While the inmates often are members of minority groups who grew up in the city, the custodial officers commonly are Caucasions from the rural communities in which prisons typically are located. The National Advisory Commission has suggested that concentrated efforts be made to recruit a more diverse, better qualified group of custodial officers. It advocates active recruitment among minority groups and making greater use of ex-offenders and women.[7] However, with the traditional low pay and the physical isolation of many institutions, the recruitment of better qualified personnel is likely to continue to be a very difficult task.

The Role Of the Correctional Officer.   As we have noted, the role of the correctional officer will vary according to the type of institution in which he works. His role also will vary according to his particular job assignment. A custodial officer obviously has somewhat different functions than a vocational counsel. Yet, whatever the type of institution or the type of job, the institutional correctional officer, like his community based counterpart, is an agent of behavior change. He is charged with the duty of sending the inmate back into society as a law-abiding and contributing member of that society, as a person who will obey the law, not because he is afraid not to but because he desires to do so. Psychologists talk about helping the inmate to "internalize the values of the larger society," by which they mean accepting those values as valid guides to his own conduct. This clearly is a major task of correctional treatment.

That the correctional officer fails in this task at least as often as he succeeds is by no means the sole fault of the correctional officer or even of the correctional system. Techniques simply do not exist that will ensure change in the behavior of a 40 year old man who has spent his life in criminal pursuits, nor even in a 20 year old youth who is serving time for his first offense. If you will think how difficult it is for you to stop smoking or to stay on a diet, you will have some appreciation of the magnitude of the correctional task which often requires the restructuring of a person's personality and value system.

Knowledgeable correctional administrators often state that a substantial percentage of their charges should never have been sent to prison—some form of supervision and treatment in the community would have had a much greater chance of success. But those of us on the "outside" often see incarceration as a "cure all." What we really want, of course, is simply to hand the problem of criminal behavior over to somebody who will keep the offender out of our city and out of our neighborhood. Thus, we place upon the corrections department two, often inconsistent tasks, rehabilitation and incapacitation. And when it comes to

---

7.   National Advisory Commission, note 1 *supra,* at p. 465, notes:

    Emergence of racial strife is a major concern in all correctional programs. . . . Minorities are found disproportionately in the ranks of corrections: overrepresented as clients and under-represented as staff. Unfortunately, there are no reliable national figures on minority group clients in the correctional system. Estimates place the percentage high but vary with geographical regions and urban-rural distribution of the population. For example, in California almost half of the 20,800 inmates are blacks or Chicanos. In the total New York State system, 56 percent of all inmates are blacks or Puerto Ricans. . . . In most States, the proportion of minority group members confined is much greater than the proportion of such persons living in the State. . . . Obviously it is immediately necessary to increase the number of correctional personnel who come from minority groups. . . . Corrections needs to look at other groups as well as minorities for the additional manpower it needs. More ex-offenders, women, and volunteers should be used. . . . While corrections once was an operation to control, hold, survey, and regiment the behavior of its wards, today it is oriented increasingly to behavior modification. When the emphasis was on physical control, physical strength was a primary prerequisite for positions. This long-cherished tradition has been challenged and is giving way. As the social distance between the keepers and the kept has decreased, a push to utilize once-untapped resources has surfaced. Utilization of ex-offenders, women, and volunteers will introduce different skills, as well as help change the custodial image of the corrections system.

the allocation of resources, we usually make it clear that we are more interested in incapacitation than rehabilitation.

The Institutional Correction Officer in Relation to Other Professionals in the Criminal Justice System. The institutional correctional officer's relations with the other professionals in the criminal justice system are dominated by two factors. The first is the isolation of that officer from the remainder of the system. He does not have an everyday working relationship with any of the other professionals. Very often he is working in a setting that is physically remote from their base of operations. Aside from occasional conferences, there is little opportunity for an exchange of viewpoints. The second factor is the somewhat different perspective of the corrections officer. His emphasis is much more heavily on treatment than most of the other professionals. The end result is that the other professionals and society at large, often treat the correctional institution (and the correctional officer) as the "scapegoat" of the system. We have noted previously the need for increased communications and understanding among all professionals in the criminal justice system. Certainly, the status of the correctional officer would improve with a greater appreciation of the handicaps under which he operates. Perhaps, however, the first step toward improving his relationship with other professionals must be the more precise definition of his role. We must determine what it is that we can realistically expect from our correctional institutions and the officials who work in those institutions.[8]

---

8. See e.g., the discussion at p. 376 *supra.* See also Morris, note 107 at p. 362 *supra*; J. Conrad, *We Should Never Have Promised A Hospital*, 34 Federal Probation 3 (December 1975).

   For further material on the subjects discussed in this chapter, see National Advisory Commission, note 1 *supra*; R. Minton, ed., *Inside Prison American Style*, New York: Vintage Books, 1971; Goldfarb and Singer, note 168 at p. 385 *supra*; G. Killinger and P. Cromwell, *Penology—The Evolution Of Corrections In America*, St. Paul, Minn.: West Publishing Company, 1973; G. Killinger and P. Cromwell, *Corrections In The Community: Alternatives To Imprisonment*, St. Paul, Minn.: West Publishing Company, 1974.

Appendix A

How to Find and Cite the Law

The law as we know it in the United States is derived principally from two sources (1) legislation (Constitutions, statutes, municipal ordinances, rules of court or administrative agencies, etc.) and (2) case law (the opinions of courts and decisions of administrative agencies). What follows is a description of the materials containing those sources and the form used in referring to them.[1]

Federal Statutes.   The basic law of the United States is, of course, the United States Constitution. It appears in many types of publications. The acts of Congress appear as (a) Slip Laws; (b) Statutes at Large; (c) Revised Statutes; (d) United States Code. The United States Code is divided into 50 titles covering particular subject matter. For example, Title 18 covers Crime and Criminal Procedures, and Title 28 covers the Judiciary and Judicial Procedures. There is also an annotated set of the United States Code entitled "United States Code Annotated" in which the text of the law is followed by an abstract of pertinent decisions.

State Statutes.   The Constitution of a State can be found in many forms. It may be set out in full in a separate bound volume, or it may appear as a volume of the statutes. Any beginning textbook on state government will have in it a copy of the State constitution.

The legislature passes laws (or statutes) as they come to them on the legislative calendar. At the close of a particular session of the legislature, the laws passed at that session are published in a bound volume (usually paperback) entitled "Session Laws." The Session Laws are identified by the name of the state and the year. Individual statutes are identified by number or by chapters. At a later date, the laws will appear in bound volumes arranged according to the subject matter.

---

1.   Much of the material in this chapter is taken from M. Cohen, ed., *How to Find The Law*, St. Paul, Minn.: West Publishing Company, 1976, 7th ed.. The student who wants to become proficient in legal research should acquaint himself with that publication.

The Session Laws will first appear arranged according to subject matter as "pocket parts" to a set of laws already published. After a certain length of time the laws will be consolidated, compiled, revised, or codified. At that time new permanently bound volumes will appear incorporating all of the statutes to the date of publication. These bound volumes are called variously Statutes, Statutes at Large, Revised Statutes, Compiled Statutes, and Consolidated Statutes and Codes. (There are some technical differences in these terms which we will not consider here). Codes typically provide a topical arrangement of broad subjects of the law such as Penal Code, Code of Criminal Procedure, Traffic Code, Juvenile Code, Corrections Code, and so forth. There are also sets of annotated statutes. An annotated set of laws or statutes are arranged in such a manner that the text of the statute is followed by notes concerning the cases which have decided something about the statute or referred to it. For example, a statute defining the crime of burglary as breaking and entering a building will be followed by the cases that decide what constitutes a building that may be burglarized.

Local Ordinances.   Local law is to be found in Municipal Charters and County and Municipal Ordinances. There is usually a printed pamphlet of some kind setting out the Municipal Charter, or it may be found in the state laws. County and Municipal Ordinances are usually to be found in permanent or semi-permanent form. The most recent enactments can be found in the Minutes of the County Commissioners or the Municipal Council.

HOW STATUTES ARE CITED

To "cite" a statute (or the decision of a court) means to give information as to where it can be found. Reference is made to the title of the volume (Session Laws, Revised Code, Consolidated Statutes, etc.), the article, section, and sub-section numbers. In some jurisdictions, the same title is used for all statutory volumes. Thus, all volumes of the federal statutes are titled United States Code and all volumes of the Michigan statutes are titled Michigan Compiled Laws. In several states, volumes take the title of the Codes they contain. Thus, New York has separate volumes entitled Criminal Procedure Law, Penal Law, Banking Law, etc. Various abbreviations may be used in citing statutes. The sign § refers to "section," "ch." refers to chapter, and "art." refers to article. While some jurisdictions include references to chapters and articles in their official citation form, others use only the section numbers.

The *United States Constitution* is cited to article and clause for which the § sign is used. Abbreviations are accepted. Thus

U.S. Const. art. 1, § 9

State Constitutions are cited in the same way. Thus

Const. Ore. art. 1, § 10 *or* N.H.Const. art. 1, §15

Federal Statutes are cited to the Statutes-at-Large, the Revised Statutes, or the United States Code. Since 1936, the *Statutes-at-Large* have been published at the end of each Congress. The Statutes-at-Large are arranged in chronological order by approval date and represent the official records of the laws contained therein. They are cited to the volume and page. Thus

> 40 Stat. 1551

The *Revised Statutes* consist of 74 titles and 5,601 sections and represent the first codification of federal law. They are cited by section. Thus

> Revised Statutes, Section 5596 *or* Rev.Stat. § 5596

A compilation of the laws of the United States was authorized by Congress in 1925, to be entitled the Code of Laws of the United States. It is referred to and cited as the *United States Code.* If the statute has been amended and is located in the pocket part or supplement to the Code, this fact is reflected in the citation. Thus

> 10 U.S.C. § 936 (1958) as amended *or* 10 U.S.C. § 936 (1958 supp.)

A parallel citation to the Statutes-at-Large and the United States Code would read

> 37 Stat. 315; 7 U.S.C. §§ 151-154, 156-164-a, 167

The *United States Code Annotated* is an annotated set of the United States Code. It is cited

> 26 U.S.C.A. §§ 5081-6300

The *Federal Rules of Criminal Procedure* are cited

> Fed.Rules Crim.Proc. 46(f)

State Session Laws (sometimes called Acts, Statutes, Resolves, etc.) are cited by identifying the state, followed by the title, and the date. The particular statute is identified by chapter or section number. Thus

> N.J.L.1964, ch. 75

In citing other *state statutes*, the Code, Statutes, Revised Statutes, Compiled Statutes, etc. are identified by the name of the state and the title. The number of the particular statute is then given, followed by the article, section and sub-section numbers. Abbreviations may be used. Thus

> Calif.Welf. & Inst.Code, § 564—sub. c
> New York Penal Law, § 1932
> Ill.Rev.Stat., ch. 38 §§ 666-668
> D.C.Code, § 22-1301 (1951)
> Mich.Comp.Laws, § 28.1133
> Texas Rev.Civ.Stat., Art. 2338

The date is given on statutes cited if this is necessary for identification. If the citation is to an annotated work, however, no date need be given since the annotations are kept up to date with pocket parts inserted at the back of the book.

Annotated statutes may bear the name of the person or persons preparing the annotations whose name is set out in the title. Abbreviations may be used. Thus

> Smith-Hurd Ill.Ann.Stat. ch 28, 81-2
> West's Ann.Penal Code of Calif. § 1203.7
> Purdon's Pa.Stat.Ann. tit. 19 § 1081

or

> Fla.Stat.Ann. § 948.01
> Ann.Pub.Laws of Md., 1957, art. 27 § 24
> Vt.Stat.Ann. tit. 28 § 1010

Municipal charters and ordinances are cited by title, article and section number, the name and location of the city always being shown. Thus

> Philadelphia (Pa.) City Chater § 10-107
> Philadelphia (Pa.) Code § 10-819
> Philadelphia (Pa.) Civil Service Regulations, § 29
> Revised Code of the Civil and Criminal Ordinances of the City of Dallas, Texas, 1960, Chapter 37, Section 6, p. 883.

CASE LAW

Decisions of Federal Courts.   The official reports of the decisions of the United States Supreme Court are published in the United States Supreme Court Reports, now designated the *United States Reports*. (Certain early decisions are in special volumes named after the reporter who compiled them, as Dallas, Cranch, Wheaton, etc.)

The decisions of the United States Supreme Court are also published in the *Supreme Court Reporter* and the *Lawyer's Edition of the Supreme Court Reports*. The Lawyer's Edition of the Supreme Court Reports contains selected cases which are fully reported together with the briefs filed by counsel.

The decisions of the United States Courts of Appeals are published in the *Federal Reporter*. Selected decisions of the United States District Courts are published in *Federal Supplement*, and there is another set of books called *Federal Rules Decisions*. Prior to 1932 the decisions of the District Courts and of the Court of Claims and of Custom and Patent Appeals and of the Court of Appeals of the Distrct of Columbia were included in the Federal Reporter. The Supreme Court Reporter, Federal Reporter, Federal Supplement, and Federal Rules Decisions are part of the *National Reporter System* which is explained in the discussion of State court decisions. A court decision is cited by giving the names of the parties, the name and number of the reporter, the page on which the case begins, and the date of the decision.[2] The names of the parties are often underlined or appear in italics.

---

2.   If a second page number appears in a citation, the second number gives the page on which the matter quoted or under discussion can be found in the opinion. A citation written *Commonwealth v. Thomas*, 391 Pa. 486, 491 would indicate that the matter quoted or under discussion can be found on page 491.

Since the cases of the United State Supreme Court are reported in three series of reports—United States Reports, Supreme Court Reporter, and Lawyer's Edition of the Supreme Court Reports, a complete citation of a United States Supreme Court case would include all three reporters. Thus

Gideon v. Wainwright, 372 U.S. 335, 83 S.Ct. 792, 9 L.Ed.2d 799 (1963)

Some authorities maintain that citation to the United States Reports alone is sufficient. The system you will adopt will depend upon the use to which the citation is to be put. For your own notes, the United States citation serves to correctly identify the case. Thus

Gideon v. Wainwright, 372 U.S. 335 (1963)

The decisions of the federal courts, other than those of the United States Supreme Court, are published in two series known as the *Federal Reporter* and *Federal Supplement*. The *Federal Reporter* covers the decisions of the United States Courts of Appeals (formerly the United States Circuit Courts of Appeals). A correct citation to the Federal Reporter includes the name of the case, the volume and page of the Reporter, and identification of the circuit in which the case was decided, and the date. Thus

Smayda v. United States, 352 F.2d 251 (9th Cir. 1966)

The opinions of the District Courts which appear in *Federal Supplement* are cited the same way, except that the District Court is identified. Thus

Books Inc. v. Leary, 291 F.Supp. 622 (S.D.N.Y. 1968)

The letters S.D.N.Y. stand for the "Southern District of New York," which means the case was decided by the United States District Court for the Southern District of New York.

Both state and federal decisions appear in sets of specialized reports. The *American Law Reports* are annotated and contain the full text of selected decisions under which cases on the same point are noted. The American Law Reports 2d contain a detailed treatise on a practical point of current law preceded by a report in full of a modern case from a state or federal appellate court involving the problem annotated. When a case has been annotated in the American Law Reports, this information is given in the citation. Thus

Mosco v. United States, 301 F.2d 180 (9th Cir. 1962), 89 A.L.R.2d 715

Decisions of State Courts. Most of the decisions of the appellate courts of a state are written. The decisions of the highest court of the state are published in books known as the state reports, which bear the name of the state. In some states, decisions of an intermediate appellate court may appear in the same set as the decisions of the highest court, particularly if the intermediate appellate court is a court of last resort for a particular kind of action. In other states, the opinions of the intermediate appellate courts will appear in a separate set.

The great need for a comprehensive and unified system of reports lead to the development of the National Reporter System. The *National Reporter System* includes all of the decisions of the highest court in each state published in the state reports. The Reporter System also includes the decisions of all intermediate appellate courts. These are usually incorporated in the regional reporters, except that there are separate units in the Reporter System for the decisions of the lower New York and California courts.

The Reporter System reports the state decisions by regions. There are seven regional reporters, Pacific, North Western, South Western, North Eastern, Atlantic, South Eastern, Southern. The *Atlantic Reporter* covers the states of Connecticut, Delaware, Maine, Maryland, New Hampshire, New Jersey, Pennsylvania, Rhode Island, and Vermont. The *North Eastern Reporter* reports the decisions of the states of Illinois, Indiana, Massachusetts, New York, and Ohio. The *North Western Reporter* includes the decisions from Nebraska, North Dakota, South Dakota, Minnesota, Iowa, Michigan and Wisconsin. The *Pacific Reporter* reports the decisions from Arizona, California, Colorado, Idaho, Kansas, Montana, Nevada, New Mexico, Oklahoma, Oregon, Utah, Washington, and Wyoming. Alaska and Hawaii are also included in the Pacific Reporter. The *South Eastern Reporter* covers the states of Georgia, South Carolina, North Carolina, Virginia, and West Virginia. The *South Western Reporter* covers the states of Arkansas, Kentucky, Missouri, Tennessee, and Texas. The *Southern Reporter* includes the approved decisions from Alabama, Florida, Louisiana, and Mississippi.

The *New York Supplement* contains reports from the New York Court of Appeals and decisions of the lower courts of New York. The *California Reporter* was founded in 1960 and includes all California Supreme Court decisions and the approved decisions of lower California appellate courts no longer published in the Pacific Reporter.

The volumes in each set of Reporters are numbered in sequence; as new decisions are announced, a new volume is published. In the National Reporter System, and in some state reports, the consecutive numbers were ended at a certain point and a new set of numbers beginning with volume 1 were introduced. The volumes in the second series are identified by the use of "2d" following the name of the reporter. Thus, there is a volume 100 of California Reports and a volume 100 of California Reports 2d. There is a volume 65 of the Pacific Reporter, and a volume 65 of the second series. All of the regional reports have begun a second series, as has the Federal Reporter.

As we have said, a case is cited by giving the name of the parties, the name and number of the Reporter in which it appears, the page on which the case begins, and the date of the decision.

The case of Commonwealth v. Thomas appearing in the Pennsylvania State Reports, would be cited as

Commonwealth v. Thomas, 391 Pa. 486 (1958)

The case of Commonwealth v. Thomas is also reported in the second series of the Atlantic Reporter. If only the National Reporter system citation is given, the state is identified. Thus

Commonwealth v. Thomas, 137 A.2d 472 (Pa.1958)

The better practice in reporting state decisions is to give both the state report and the National Reporter System citations. Thus

Commonwealth v. Thomas, 391 Pa. 485, 137 A.2d 472 (1958)

When a state decision has been presented to the Supreme Court of the United States in an application for writ of certiorari (writ of review), the disposition of that case in the Supreme Court sometimes is noted. Action by a higher state court is reported in the same way. Thus

People v. Anderson, 397 Ill. 583, 74 N.E.2d 693 (1947) certiorari denied 333 U.S. 833, 68 S.Ct. 485, 92 L.Ed. 1117 (1948)

Fielden v. People, 128 Ill. 595 (1889) 21 N.E. 684, affirmed 143 U.S. 452, 12 S.Ct. 528, 26 L.Ed.. 224 (1892)

People v. Tananevics, 285 Ill. 374, 120 N.E. 766 (1918), affirming 208 Ill.App. 473; error dismissed, 252 U.S. 568, 40 S.Ct. 346, 64 L.Ed. 720 (1920).

When a state court decision has been annotated in the American Law Reports this fact is indicated in the citation. Thus

Nuchols v. Commonwealth, 312 Ky. 171, 226 S.W.2d 796 (1950), 13 A.L.R.2d 1478

LEGAL PUBLICATIONS

It is beyond the scope of this introductory work to set out the many sources of legal materials. There are the encyclopedias, *American Jurisprudence* (Am.Jur. and Am.Jur.2d) and *Corpus Juris—Corpus Juris Secundum* (C.J.—C.J.S.). Each is made up of over 400 alphabetically arranged topics or titles designed to cover the entire field of American law. Many states have encyclopedias of state law, which contain a text statement devoted to the law of the particular state with supporting cases confined to those from that state or to federal court decision construing the state laws. *Texas Jurisprudence* (Tex.Jur.) is an example of a state encyclopedia.

State and local *Digests* are a device for isolating pertinent case law to be used as authority for any given legal proposition. In a set of books known as *Words and Phrases*, the word or phrase is set out alphabetically, and is followed by a list of state and federal citations defining it. *Blacks Law Dictionary Fourth Revised Edition*, published by West Publishing Company, is another source of definitions. *Blacks* also gives judicial definitions with citations to the appropriate case.

Shephard's Citations provide a "history" of each reported case, i.e., shows whether the case was affirmed, reversed, modified, or dismissed. To "Shephardize" a case means to locate it in one of the units of Shepard's Citations (developed for each state, and for each unit in the National Reporter System). The case is located by volume and page number. Under the page number will be found the citation of other cases which have dealt with the cited cases. Symbols indicate whether the case was affirmed, overruled, cited in a dissenting opinion, followed in another case, and so on. Only by "Shephardizing" a case can the legal researcher be sure that the rule announced in the case is still "the law."

Articles in law journals or law reviews are an important source of information for the student and legal researcher. *Law Reviews* are published by the leading law schools. The leading articles may be authored by judges, lawyers, or law professors, but a law review also contains articles researched and authored by law students as part of their educational program. The reviews are published as periodicals.

Appendix B

Glossary of Legal Terms

ACCOMPLICE. An individual who voluntarily and knowingly assists another in committing an offense and thereby becomes criminally liable for the offense.

ACCUSED. The generic name for the defendant in a criminal case.

ACCUSATORY INSTRUMENT. A legal document, filed with the court, charging a person with the commission of a crime. The initial accusatory instrument commonly is known as a complaint. In felony cases, the final accusatory instrument, on which the defendant is tried, is usually an information or indictment. See also Charge.

ACCUSATORY STAGE. That stage in the criminal process that follows the filing of the accusatory instrument, as opposed to the investigatory stage (which refers to investigation for the purpose of determining whether to file an accusatory instrument).

ACQUITTAL. A final determination, after trial, that the accused is not guilty of the offense charged.

ACTUS REUS. The criminal act; the act of a person committing a crime.

ADJUDICATE. To determine finally; to adjudge.

ADVERSARY. An opponent. The opposite party in a lawsuit.

ADVERSARY PROCEEDING. A proceeding in which the opposing sides have the opportunity to present their evidence and arguments. In contrast, an *ex parte* proceeding is one in which only one side presents its case to the court.

ADVERSARY SYSTEM. The practice of conducting legal proceedings as a battle between opposing parties, with the judge acting as an impartial umpire and with the outcome determined by the pleadings and evidence introduced in court by the two sides.

ADVOCATE.   One who assists, defends, or pleads for another.

AFFIDAVIT.   A written or printed declaration or statement of facts, taken before an officer having authority to administer oaths.

AGGRAVATED ASSAULT.   An assault which results in a greater physical injury or poses a threat of more serious injury than a simple assault. This category of offense may include an assault with the intent to kill or to inflict severe bodily injury or an assault with a deadly weapon. See also the definitions of Assault and Simple Assault.

ALLOCUTION.   The court's inquiry of a convicted person as to whether he has anything to say on his behalf before sentence is imposed.

AMICUS CURIAE.   Literally, a friend of the court. A person who has no right to appear in a suit but is allowed to introduce argument, authority or evidence to ensure that the court receives all relevant information.

APPEAL.   The removal of a case from a lower court to a higher court for the purpose of obtaining a review of the legality of the proceedings in the lower court.

APPEARANCE TICKET.   A written notice, issued by a public servant, requiring a person to appear before a local criminal court in connection with an accusatory instrument to be filed against him. Also called a citation in some jurisdictions, particularly where issued by a police officer. See also Summons.

APPELLANT.   The party who takes an appeal from one court to a higher court. In criminal cases, this usually is the defendant convicted in the lower court.

APPELLATE JURISDICTION.   The authority of a court to review the decision of a lower court; the power to hear cases appealed from a lower court.

APPEARANCE.   The coming into court as party to a suit. In a criminal case, the initial appearance ordinarily occurs where the arrested person is brought before the magistrate.

APPELLEE.   The party in a case against whom an appeal is taken; in criminal cases, usually the state or the United States.

ARRAIGN.   To bring a prisoner before the court to answer the indictment or information. In practice, sometimes used also to refer to the appearance of the accused before a magistrate, at the point of first appearance (then called an arraignment on the complaint or warrant).

ARRAY.   The whole body of jurors summoned to attend a court. See also Venire.

ARREST.   The taking of a person into custody for the purpose of charging him with a crime or having him answer to a charge already brought.

ARREST WARRANT.   A court order authorizing a police officer to arrest a particular person.

ARSON. The intentional and unlawful burning of property. At common law, the malicious burning of the house or outhouse of another.

ASPORTATION. The removal of things from one place to another, which in many states is a required element of the offense of larceny.

ASSAULT. An attempt to inflict a battery upon another (see the definition of assault and battery) through the use of unlawful force. In some states, it also includes an action intended to put another in fear of a battery. In some states also, the distinction between assault and battery has been eliminated and both are called assaults.

ASSAULT AND BATTERY. A battery is an unlawful touching of the person of another. See Assault.

ATTEMPT. An overt act, beyond mere preparation, moving directly toward the actual commission of a substantive crime and for which criminal liability may be imposed.

B

BAIL. Traditionally, the property an arrested person had to leave with the court as security to obtain his release while awaiting a trial. The bail served to "guarantee" his appearance at the trial since it would be forfeited if he failed to appear. Today the term "bail" is used to refer to any condition that must be fulfilled to obtain the accused's release pending a judicial proceeding, not just the posting of property as security.

BAIL BOND. A document that obligates a person to forfeit a certain sum of money if the accused fails to appear as he promised in obtaining his release on bail. The bond is an alternative to posting the money itself. The persons who issue the bond and suffer the forfeiture are known as "sureties."

BAILMENT. A delivery of good or personal property by one person (the bailor) to another (the bailee) to carry out a special purpose and redeliver the goods to the bailor.

BATTERY. See Assault and Battery.

BENCH. A reference to the court or judges composing the court. A trial before a judge alone, sitting without a jury, is known as a bench trial.

BENCH WARRANT. An order issued by the court itself, or "from the bench," for the arrest of a person; usually in cases where the individual has violated a court order to appear in court. It differs from an arrest warrant in that it is not based on a probable cause showing that a person has committed a crime, but is based only on the person's failure to appear in court as directed.

BEYOND A REASONABLE DOUBT. It is proof to the degree required by law to permit the jury to convict in a criminal case.

BILL OF ATTAINDER. A legislative act that directs that punishment be imposed on a particular person without giving the person an opportunity to contest his guilt in a judicial trial.

BINDOVER.   The decision of the preliminary hearing judge holding that there is sufficient evidence to send the case on ("bind" it over) to the next stage in the proceeding.

BOOKING.   The clerical process involving the entry on the police "blotter" or arrest book of the suspect's name, the time of the arrest, the offense charged and the name of the arresting officer; often used in practice to refer to the police station-house procedures that take place from arrest to the initial appearance of the accused before the magistrate.

BREACH OF THE PEACE.   A violation or disturbance of the public tranquility and order.

BREAKING AND ENTRY.   In some jurisdictions burglaries (see definition below) are described as a "breaking and entry" or a "B and E." The breaking and entry, in fact, is only one element of a burglary.

BURDEN OF PROOF.   The obligation to introduce evidence establishing a fact so clearly as to meet the legal standard of proof (e.g., proof beyond a reasonable doubt).

BURGLARY.   Breaking and entering with intent to commit a felony or theft, or in some states, with intent to commit any offense.

C

CALENDAR.   As used in connection with judicial administration, a court calendar is a listing of the various cases filed in a court and the order in which they will be heard. This listing is also referred to as the court's "docket."

CAPITAL PUNISHMENT.   The use of the death penalty (i.e., execution) as the punishment for the commission of a particular crime.

CARNAL KNOWLEDGE.   Sexual intercourse; the slightest penetration of the sexual organ of the female by the sexual organ of the male.

CASE.   As used in connection with judicial proceedings, a general term for an action, cause, suit, or controversy contested before a court. As used in connection with investigation, a set of circumstances that are under investigation for possible legal action.

CASE LAW.   The body of law created by judicial rulings deciding particular cases. The standards explaining the law established by a particular decision are usually set forth in a statement of the court (called an "opinion") explaining the court's decision on the law in that case.

CERTIORARI, WRIT OF.   An order (writ) directed by a superior court to an inferior court asking that the record of a case be sent up for review by the superior court. This is the common method for obtaining a review of a case by the United States Supreme Court.

CHALLENGE.   As used in connection with the selection of jurors, the objection of counsel to the acceptance of a prospective person as juror. If the objection is based on a showing of bias, it is described as a "challenge for cause." See also the definition of Peremptory Challenge.

CHANGE OF VENUE. The removal of an action begun in one county or district to another county or district for trial.

CHARGE. To "charge" a person is to bring an accusation against him. A "charging document" is the legal document, filed with the court, accusing the defendant of a crime. See Accusatory Instrument. A judge's "charge" to the jury is his instructions to the jury as to their obligation in deciding the case.

CIRCUMSTANTIAL EVIDENCE. All evidence of an indirect nature; the existence of a principal fact is inferred from circumstances.

CIVIL ACTION. A lawsuit brought to obtain redress for some wrong in a manner other than imposing punishment. Compare the definition of Crime.

CIVIL LAW. The law having to do with civil actions. The term "civil law" also is used to describe the legal system, placing primary emphasis on statutory codes, that was derived from the Romans and presently prevails in most Western European countries. Compare the definition of Common Law.

COMMON LAW. The system of law, derived from the English, under which courts have authority to create new standards through their rulings in cases and future cases are decided on the basis of rulings in past cases.

COMPLAINT. In criminal law, a charge, preferred before a magistrate having jurisdiction, that a person named has committed a specified offense. Usually the first document filed in court charging the offense.

CONCURRENT SENTENCES. Running together; contemporaneous. Concurrent sentences run at the same time and each day served by the prisoner is credited on each of the concurrent sentences.

CONSECUTIVE SENTENCES. Sentences which are served one after the other; inmates refer to such sentences as "stacked."

CONSPIRACY. A separate offense based upon a combination of two or more persons to commit a crime. In some jurisdictions, it also includes a combination to commit an unlawful act in a manner that will have a substantial adverse impact on the public.

CONTEMPT OF COURT. Any act which is calculated to embarrass, hinder, or obstruct the court in the administration of justice, or which is calculated to lessen its authority or dignity. Direct contempts are those committed in the immediate view of the court (e.g., violence in the courtroom). Constructive (or indirect) contempts are those which arise from matters not occurring in the presence of the court, such as the failure to obey a lawful directive of the court to no longer engage in certain activities.

CONTRABAND. Any material object which it is unlawful for a private individual to possess.

CONVICTION. In a general sense, the result of a criminal trial which ends in a judgment that the person is guilty. Formally, the conviction is the official record of the finding of guilt.

CORPORAL PUNISHMENT. The infliction of bodily harm as form of punishment (such as whipping).

CORPUS DELICTI. The body of the crime; the essential elements of the criminal act; the substantial fact that a crime has been committed. The actual commission by someone of the offense charged.

COUNT. The several parts of an indictment or information each charging a distinct offense. Often used synonymously with the word "charge."

COURT ABOVE, COURT BELOW. In appellate practice, the "court above" is the one to which a case is removed for review, while the "court below" is the one from which the case is removed.

COURT NOT OF RECORD. A court, usually a magistrate court, whose judicial acts and proceedings are not recorded and therefore cannot be reviewed on the record by an appellate court. When decisions of this court are appealed, the higher court commonly will provide a completely new trial (a trial *de novo*).

CRIME. An act in violation of penal law; an offense against the law of the state.

CROSS-EXAMINATION. The examination of a witness upon a trial or hearing, by the party opposed to the one who produced him, to test the truth of his testimony or to further develop it for other purposes.

CULPABLE. Blameworthy; subject to criminal liability.

D

DECREE. The judgment of the court; a declaration of the court announcing the legal consequences of the facts found.

DEFENDANT. The party against whom relief or recovery is sought in an action or suit. In criminal law, the party charged with a crime.

DEFINITE SENTENCE. A sentence that provides for a specific term of incarceration; sometimes referred to as a flat-time, fixed-time, or determinate sentence.

DELIBERATE. As applied to a jury, the weighing of the evidence and the law for the purpose of determining the guilt or innocence of a defendant.

DELINQUENT CHILD. A person of no more than a specified age who has violated any law or ordinance or, in some jurisdictions, is deemed incorrigible; a person who has been adjudicated a delinquent by a juvenile court.

DE NOVO. Anew, afresh. A trial *de novo* is a retrial of a case, usually before a higher court. (See Courts Not Of Record).

DETAINER. A kind of "hold order" filed against an incarcerated person by another state or jurisdiction which seeks to take him into custody to answer to another criminal charge whenever he is released from his current imprisonment.

DETERMINATE SENTENCE. See Definite Sentence.

DIRECT EVIDENCE. That means of proof which tends to show the existence of a fact in question without the intervention of the proof of any other fact (e.g., the testimony of a witness as to events he witnessed). Direct evidence is distinguished from circumstantial evidence, which is often called "indirect."

DIRECT EXAMINATION. The first interrogation or examination of a witness by the party on whose behalf he is called.

DISCOVERY. A procedure whereby one side, in advance of trial, can learn of the evidence to be introduced by the other side at trial.

DIVERSION. Procedure for removing an offender from the criminal justice process and disposing of his case by alternative means.

DRIVING UNDER THE INFLUENCE. See Driving While Intoxicated.

DRIVING WHILE INTOXICATED. Driving or operating any motor vehicle while drunk or under the influence of liquor or narcotics, sometimes referred to as D.W.I.

DUCES TECUM. From the Latin "bring with you." A subpoena duces tecum requires a party to appear in court and bring with him certain documents, pieces of evidence, or other matters to be inspected by the court.

DUE PROCESS OF LAW. The fundamental rights necessary to provide a fair legal proceeding; the safeguards and protections of the law given to one accused of a crime. In substantive criminal law, the right to have crimes and punishments clearly defined in the law.

E

EMBEZZLEMENT. Misappropriation or misapplication of money or property entrusted to one's care, custody, or control.

EN BANC. Refers to the hearing of a case before all of the members of an appellate court. Some appellate courts of several judges will divide into panels of three or more judges in hearing cases. In a court that sits *en banc*, the full court will consider the case.

EVIDENCE. Any species of proof, presented at the trial, for the purpose of inducing belief in the minds of the court or jury.

EVIDENTIARY PRESUMPTION. A rule of law that permits a factfinder (judge or jury) to assume the existence of one fact upon proof of another, related fact.

EXCLUSIONARY RULE. The rule which excludes from the trial of an accused evidence illegally seized or obtained.

EXPERT WITNESS.   One who has skilled experience or extensive knowledge in his calling or in any branch of learning; person competent to give expert testimony.

EXPERT EVIDENCE.   Testimony given in relation to some scientific, technical, or professional matter by experts, i.e. persons qualified to speak authoritatively by reason of their special training, skill, or familiarity with the subject.

EX REL.   By or on the information of. Used in case title to designate the person at whose instance the government or public official is acting.

EX PARTE.   On one side only; by or for one party; done for, in behalf of, or on the application, of one party only.

EX POST FACTO LAW.   A law passed after the commission of an act which retrospectively changes the legal consequences by making the act criminal or increasing the criminal penalty for its commission.

F

FEDERAL QUESTION.   A case which contains an issue involving the United States Constitution or statutes presents a federal question.

FELONY.   Generally, an offense punishable by death or imprisonment in the penitentiary (or, as defined in some states, any term of imprisonment in excess of one year). At early common law, an offense occasioning total forfeiture of either land or goods to which capital or other punishment might be added according to the degree of guilt. A crime of graver or more atrocious nature than those designated as a misdemeanor.

FORCIBLE RAPE.   Rape by force or the threat of force. See also Rape.

FRUITS OF A CRIME.   Material objects acquired by means of and in consequence of the commission of a crime, and sometimes constituting the subject matter of the crime.

G

GOOD TIME.   Credit allowed on the sentence for exemplary conduct in confinement.

GRADING OF OFFENSES.   Grading refers to the legislative assignment of punishment within a hierarchy of penalties. The different grades of penalties often are designated by letters (e.g., class A, B, C felony) or degrees (e.g., first, second, and third degree felony). Where one offense carries a higher penalty than another, it commonly is described as being "graded" higher than the other offense.

GRAND JURY.   A jury selected from the community with the authority to conduct its own investigation into possible crimes and with the obligation to review cases presented by the prosecutor to determine if there is sufficient evidence to charge the accused with a crime. The charging instrument issued by the grand jury, if it decides the evidence is sufficient, is called an indictment.

GRAND LARCENY.   Larceny of the grade of felony.

H

HABEAS CORPUS.   Literally, "you have the body." See Writ of Habeas Corpus.

HALFWAY HOUSE.   A community correctional facility that provides a less structured environment, and less secured custody, than a prison. Halfway houses are often used to provide a transitional period for offenders being released from prison.

HARMLESS ERROR.   In appellate practice, an error committed by the trial court which is viewed as not affecting the substantial rights of the appellant and therefore not requiring reversal of the trial court's judgment.

HEARING.   A proceeding in which evidence is presented and arguments are heard for the purpose of making a determination on some factual or legal issue. A trial is a hearing, but not all hearings require the formalities of a trial.

HEARSAY.   Evidence not proceeding from the personal knowledge of the witness, but from the mere repetition of what he has heard others say.

HOMICIDE.   The killing of one human being by another.

HUNG JURY.   A jury so irreconcilably divided in opinion that it cannot agree upon any verdict.

I

IMPEACHMENT OF A WITNESS.   An attack on the credibility of a witness, usually made through cross-examination of the witness.

INADMISSIBLE EVIDENCE.   That which, under the rules of evidence, cannot be received for consideration in making a legal determination. Sometimes called "incompetent evidence."

INCARCERATION.   Confinement. As used in the criminal law, "incarceration" refers to imprisonment in a prison, jail, or similar correctional facility.

INDETERMINATE SENTENCE.   A sentence setting a minimum term and a maximum term of imprisonment (e.g., "not less than 3 years nor more than 10 years"), with the parole authority determining the exact point of release within the minimum and maximum limits.

INDEX CRIMES.   The crimes used by the Federal Bureau of Investigation in reporting the incidence of crime in the United States in the Uniform Crime Reports.

INDICTMENT.   An accusation in writing found and presented by a grand jury, charging that a person therein named has been guilty of a crime. See also the definition of Grand Jury.

INDIGENCY.   As used in the context of criminal procedure, lacking the funds to hire counsel.

INDIRECT EVIDENCE.   See Circumstantial Evidence.

INFAMOUS.   Shameful or disgraceful. See Infamous Crimes.

INFAMOUS CRIMES.   A crime which entails infamy upon one who has committed it; crimes punishable by imprisonment in the state prison or penitentiary. At common law, all felonies were considered to be infamous crimes.

INFERIOR COURTS.   A term sometimes used to refer to magistrate courts (i.e., courts of limited jurisdiction).

INFORMATION.   A charging instrument, similar in form and effect to an indictment except that it is issued by the prosecuting attorney rather than the grand jury.

IN FORMA PAUPERIS.   In the form of a pauper; as a poor person or indigent. Permission to bring legal action without the payment of required fees for writs, transcripts, and the like.

INFRACTION.   The name given in many jurisdictions to minor offenses, usually punishable by fine but not incarceration.

INITIAL APPEARANCE.   The first appearance of the accused before a magistrate. Where the accused is arrested, he must be presented before the magistrate, without unnecessary delay, for his initial appearance. See also Presentment.

INJUNCTION.   A writ prohibiting an individual or organization from performing some specified action.

IN RE.   In the affair; in the matter of; concerning. This is the usual method of entitling a judicial proceeding in which there are no adversary parties. For this reason, used in the title of cases in a juvenile court.

INVESTIGATORY STAGE.   The stage of investigation of a crime before any person has been formally charged with the offense. See also Accusatory Stage.

INQUEST.   A proceeding, often conducted by a coroner, to determine whether a death could have been caused by criminal homicide.

J

JAIL.   A local correctional institution in which are kept (1) persons awaiting trial who are unable to make bail; (2) persons convicted but awaiting sentence; (3) persons convicted of misdemeanors and sentenced to terms of imprisonment of one year or less; (4) persons convicted of felonies and sentenced to probation plus a term of imprisonment in jail of no more than a few months; and (5) persons arrested and awaiting their first appearance before a magistrate.

JAIL TIME.   Credit allowed on a sentence for the time spent in jail awaiting trial or mandate on appeal.

JUDGMENT. In general, the official and authentic decision of a court of justice upon the respective rights and claims of the parties to the action or suit therein litigated and submitted to its determination. In a criminal case, a judgment is comprised of a conviction and the sentence imposed thereon.

JUDICIAL PROCESS. The sequence of steps taken by the courts in deciding cases or disposing of legal controversies.

JURISDICTION. The authority to take certain action. As used with respect to a court, it refers to the authority to hear and decide a particular case. As used with respect to the adoption of legislation, it refers to a government (e.g., state or federal) having authority to pass such legislation.

JURY. A group of persons summoned and sworn to decide on facts at issue. The use of the word "jury" by itself refers to the petit (i.e., trial) jury rather than the grand jury.

JURY PANEL. This term is used in different ways in different jurisdictions. Some use it to refer to the group of persons selected to sit as the jury in the particular case. Others use it to refer to all those persons who are summoned to serve as jurors for a particular term of court (the "venire").

JUVENILE DELINQUENT. See Delinquent Child.

L

LARCENY. The taking of property from the possession of another with intent of the taker to convert it to his own use. Depending upon the value of the property taken, the offense is a felony or a misdemeanor. See Theft.

LAW. Law is the formal means of social control that involves the use of rules that are interpreted, and are enforceable, by the courts of a political community.

LEADING QUESTION. A question which is suggestive of the answer; one which instructs witness how to answer or puts into his mouth words to be echoed back; one which suggests to witness the answer desired.

LEGAL. Conforming to the law; according to a law; required or permitted by law; not forbidden or discountenanced by law; good and effectual law.

LEGISLATION. Legislation is rules of general application, enacted by a law-making body in a politically organized society. In its generic sense, legislation includes constitutions, treaties, statutes, ordinances, administrative regulations, and court rules. Most often the term is used to refer to a statute.

LESSER INCLUDED OFFENSE. When it is impossible to commit a particular crime without also committing, by the same conduct, another offense of lesser grade, the latter is, with respect to the former, a "lesser included offense." For example, a person who commits armed robbery also commits the crime of robbery itself. The elements of robbery are a part of armed robbery. Thus, robbery is a lesser included offense of armed robbery.

LESSER OFFENSE.   Sometimes used synonymously with a "less serious offense," or "minor offense."

LIMITATION OF ACTIONS.   The time at the end of which no action at law can be maintained; in criminal law, the time after the commission of the offense within which the indictment must be presented or the information filed. The statute setting that time limit is called a "statute of limitations."

LINEUP.   A police identification procedure during which a suspect is exhibited, along with others of similar physical characteristics, to witnesses to determine whether or not they can identify him as the offender.

LOCAL CRIMINAL COURTS.   A popular name for magistrate courts, particularly when the court is a municipal court rather than a county court.

M

MALA IN SE.   Wrong in themselves; acts immoral or wrong in themselves.

MALA PROHIBITA.   Crimes *mala prohibita* embrace actions prohibited by statute as infringing on other's rights, though no moral wrongdoing is involved.

MANSLAUGHER.   The lowest degree of criminal homicide; often divided into two categories: voluntary (non-negligent, usually intentional with provocation) and involuntary (unintentional, negligent or reckless).

MAXIMUM SECURITY PRISON.   A correctional facility designed for maximum control of inmates; usually constructed with outside perimeter controls, inside cell blocks, and patrolled by armed guards.

MENS REA.   The mental element required for criminal liability. The required mens rea varies from crime to crime, but traditionally requires a mental element suggesting a wrongful purpose.

MINIMUM SECURITY PRISON.   A correctional facility which is relatively open, with substantially less security measures than the traditional prison. Compare Maximum Security Prison.

MINOR.   A person or infant who is under the age of legal competence; under twenty-one in some states and under eighteen in others.

MIRANDA WARNING.   The warning which must be given to the suspect when subjected to custodial interrogation. The officer must warn the suspect (1) that he has a right to remain silent; (2) that if he talks, anything he says will be used against him; (3) that he has a right to be represented by counsel and a right to have counsel present at all questioning; and (4) that if he is too poor to afford counsel, counsel will be provided for him at state expense.

MISDEMEANOR.   Any crime which does not fall within the state definition for felony — usually an offense punishable by imprisonment of one year or less and imprisonment only in a jail (as opposed to a penitentiary).

MORAL TURPITUDE. An act of baseness, vileness, or depravity in the private and social duties which man owes to his fellow men, or to society in general, contrary to the accepted and customary rule of right and duty between man and man.

MURDER. The highest degree of culpable homicide.

N

NARCOTIC OFFENSES. Offenses relating to narcotic drugs, such as unlawful possession, sale or use. Also used to describe any substance abuse offense.

NEGOTIATED GUILTY PLEA. A guilty plea given in response to a concession made by the prosecutor on condition that the defendant plead guilty. The concession usually involves a reduction of the charge or a recommendation of leniency in sentencing.

NOLLE PROSEQUI. A motion of the prosecutor stating that he wishes to drop the prosecution and have the charges dismissed. Literally, a declaration that he will "not further prosecute" the case.

NOLO CONTENDERE. A pleading by the defendant, having the impact of a guilty plea in permitting a judgment of conviction to be entered by the court and sentence to be imposed, but not admitting guilt. Literally, a declaration that the defendant "will not contest" the charge.

NO-KNOCK ENTRY. Entry by police into a building, for the purpose of making an arrest or conducting a search, without first attempting to notify those within the building of the presence of the police and without requesting admission to the building; acceptable only under limited circumstances.

O

OBJECTION. Counsel's act of taking exception to some statement or procedure at trial.

ORIGINAL JURISDICTION. Jurisdiction in the first instance, commonly used to refer to trial jurisdiction as compared to appellate jurisdiction.

OVERCHARGING. A practice by which a prosecutor charges the defendant at a higher level than appropriate with the expectation that the charge will be reduced, in return for a guilty plea, to a lesser charge.

P

PARDON. An exercise of the power of the govenment to grant mercy by excusing an individual from the legal consequences (particularly the punishment) that follow from commission of a crime.

PARENS PATRIAE. Literally, "father of his country." The doctrine that the juvenile court treats the child as "a kind and loving father."

PAROLE.   The release of a prisoner from imprisonment, but not from the legal custody of the State, for rehabilitation outside of prison walls under such conditions and supervision as the Board of Parole may determine.

PENITENTIARY.   A correctional facility for housing persons convicted of felony offenses. Often used interchangeably with "prison."

PER CURIAM.   By the court. An opinion of the court which is authored by the justices collectively.

PER SE.   By itself; in itself, taken alone.

PEREMPTORY CHALLENGE.   Self determined, requiring no cause to be shown. As applied to selection of jurors, challenges allowed by law to both the state and defense to remove a prospective juror without cause from the panel of jurors. See also Challenge.

PETIT JURY.   A trial jury as distinguished from a Grand Jury.

PETITION FOR CERTIORARI.   An application to an appellate court requesting review by the certiorari procedure. See Certiorari.

PETTY LARCENY.   Larceny of the grade of misdemeanor.

PLEA BARGAINING.   See Negotiated Plea.

PLEA OF GUILTY.   A confession of guilt in open court.

PLEA OF NOT GUILTY.   A plea of defendant denying guilt as to the offense charged and putting the state to the proof of its charge.

PRECEDENT.   An adjudged case or decision of a court that serves as a standard for reaching the same result in later cases presenting the same legal issue. See *Stare Decisis*.

PRELIMINARY EXAMINATION.   Same as Preliminary Hearing.

PRELIMINARY HEARING.   An adversary hearing before a magistrate to determine whether there is sufficient evidence supporting a charge against the accused to send the case onto the next stage — grand jury review or the filing of an information by the prosecutor.

PRELIMINARY JURISDICTION.   A term commonly used to refer to judicial jurisdiction to deal with earlier processing steps in a case (e.g., the setting of bail, the holding of a preliminary hearing). Thus, magistrates are said to have "preliminary jurisdiction" but not "trial jurisdiction" in felony cases.

PREPONDERANCE OF THE EVIDENCE.   Greater weight of evidence: the preponderance of the evidence rests with the evidence which produces the stronger impression and is more convincing as to its truth when weighed against the evidence in opposition.

PRESENTENCE INVESTIGATION.   An investigation conducted by a probation officer to gather information relating to the background of the offender and other matters relevant to sentencing. A summary of the investigation is presented to the sentencing judge in the form of a presentence report.

PRESENTMENT. The initial appearance by the accused before the magistrate after arrest. Also, a written notice taken by a grand jury of any offense, from their own knowledge or observation, without any bill of indictment laid before them by the prosecutor.

PRESUMPTIONS. See Evidentiary Presumptions.

PRESUMPTIVE SENTENCING. A sentencing structure under which a particular sentence is presumed to be typical for a particular offense. The trial judge is allowed to depart from that typical sentence, within limited ranges, upon finding present certain mitigating factors (justifying a decrease in the sentence) or aggravating factors (justifying an increase in the sentence).

PREVENTIVE DETENTION. The denial of pretrial release (usually involving a refusal to set bail) on the ground that the accused poses a threat of danger to the community.

PRIMA FACIE CASE. A case developed with such evidence that it will justify a verdict favoring the person establishing the case unless that evidence is contradicted and overcome by other evidence.

PRIMA FACIE EVIDENCE. Evidence good and sufficient on its face; such evidence as is sufficient to establish a given fact, or the group of facts constituting the party's claim, and which, if not rebutted or contradicted, will remain sufficient.

PROBABLE CAUSE. Reasonable cause. An apparent state of facts which would induce a reasonably intelligent and prudent man to believe, in a criminal case, that the suspected person had committed the crime in question. More than suspicion, less than certainty.

PROBATION. The release of a convicted defendant by a court under conditions imposed by the court for a specified period of time, with the court reserving the right to impose a sentence of imprisonment if the probationer violates the conditions it imposed.

PROCEDURE. The mode of proceeding by which a legal right is enforced, as distinguished from the law which gives or defines the right; the machinery, as distinguished from its product.

PROSECUTOR'S INFORMATION. See Information.

PROSTITUTION. Sex offenses of a commercialized nature.

PROXIMATE CAUSE. That which, in a natural and continuous sequence, unbroken by any independant intervening cause, produces the injury, and without which the result would not have occurred.

PUBLIC DEFENDER. An official in the employment of the government who is responsible for representing indigent persons accused of crime within the particular jurisdiction.

R

RAPE.   The unlawful carnal knowledge of a woman against her will. See also Statutory Rape, Forcible Rape, and Carnal Knowledge.

REAL EVIDENCE.   Evidence furnished by things themselves on view or inspection, as distinguished from a description of them given by a witness.

REASONABLE CAUSE.   See Probable Cause.

REASONABLE DOUBT.   See Beyond A Reasonable Doubt.

REBUTTAL.   The introduction of rebutting evidence; the showing that a statement of witnesses as to what occurred is not true; the stage of a trial at which such evidence may be introduced; also the rebutting evidence itself.

REBUTTABLE PRESUMPTION.   A presumption that is to be taken as given unless rebutted by contrary evidence. Thus, it is presumed that a child between the ages of 7 and 14 lacks the capacity to understand the true nature of his criminal act and to distinguish right from wrong, but that presumption can be overcome by contrary evidence in the particular case.

RECIDIVISM.   Repeated acts of criminal conduct by an individual.

RECORD.   A written account of all of the acts and proceedings in an action or suit in a court of record.

RELEASE ON OWN RECOGNIZANCE.   A form of release pending trial or appeal. (See also Bail). The accused person is released either on his own promise to appear in court or upon posting a personal bail bond (i.e., a bond not guaranteed by sureties) as security for his appearance.

RESPONDENT.   The party who is the defendant on an appeal; the party who contends against an appeal.

REVOCATION.   The cancellation or withdrawal of a benefit as in the revocation of probation or parole.

RIGHT OF ALLOCUTION.   See Allocution.

ROBBERY.   Taking anything of value from the person of another by force or violence or by putting in fear.

S

SCIENTER.   Knowingly, with guilty knowledge.

SENTENCE.   The judgment, formally pronounced by the court after defendant's conviction, setting forth the punishment to be inflicted.

SERVICE OF PROCESS.   The service of a writ, summons, or other court order directing that a person appear in court or take other action; service is achieved when the court order is delivered to or left with the party designated in the order.

SEQUESTER. To keep a jury together and in isolation from other persons, under charge of the bailiff, during the pendency of a trial, sometimes called"separation of the jury." To keep witnesses apart from other witnesses and unable to hear their testimony. In the case of witnesses, sometimes called "putting the witness under rule."

SHOW-UP. Similar to a lineup except that only the suspect is shown to the witness (rather than the suspect and a group of other persons, as in a lineup).

SIMPLE ASSAULT. Assault which is not of an aggravated nature. See Aggravated Assault.

STANDING. The qualifications needed to bring a legal action or to raise a certain legal objection.

STARE DECISIS. To abide by, or adhere to decided cases; doctrine that, when a court has once laid down a principle of law as applicable to a certain state of facts, it will adhere to that principle, and apply it to all future cases where facts are substantially similar.

STATUTORY LAW. See Legislation.

STATUTORY RAPE. Carnal knowledge of a female child below the age fixed by statute. The child lacks the *legal* capacity to consent so the crime can be committed where no force is used and child consents in fact. See Rape.

SUBPOENA. A process issued by a court to cause a witness to appear and give testimony. When the person is required to bring with him records or other real evidence, the subpoena is described as a subpeona *duces tecum*. See Duces Tecum.

SUMMONS. A legal order of the court directing a person to appear in court to answer certain charges. In some jurisdictions, a citation issued by a peace officer directing a person to appear in court is also called a summons. See Appearance Ticket.

SUSPECT. A person who is suspected of having committed an offense, or who is believed to have committed an offense, but has not been formally charged with the offense or arrested. (Once arrested, the suspect commonly is described as an arrestee).

T

TESTIMONY. Evidence given by a competent witness, under oath or affirmation; as distinguished from evidence derived from writings, and other sources. Testimony is one species of evidence, but the words "testimony" and "evidence" are often used interchangeably.

TESTIMONIAL PRIVILEGE. A right of a person to refuse to give testimony himself or to prevent another from giving testimony of a certain type. Illustrative are the right to refuse to answer incriminating questions (privilege against self-incrimination) and to bar testimony concerning confidential communications between lawyer and client (lawyer-client privilege).

THEFT.   A popular name for larceny. See Larceny.

THE GREAT WRIT.   A name given to the Writ of Habeas Corpus.

TORT.   A civil wrong or injury; a legal wrong committed upon the person or property, independent of contract violation, which is redressed in a civil court.

TRANSCRIPT OF RECORD.   The printed record as prepared for review of a case by a higher court. In referring to the written documents on appeal, the words "transcript," "record" and "record on appeal" are used interchangeably.

TRIAL *DE NOVO.*   See *De Novo*, Court Not Of Record.

TRIAL JURISDICTION.   See Original Jurisdiction.

V

VANDALISM.   Willful or malicious destruction, injury, disfigurement, or defacement of property without consent of the owner or person having custody or control.

VENIRE.   To come, to appear. The name given to the writ for summoning the jury, and also to the body of prospective jurors summoned to court for possible selection as jurors. See also Jury Panel, Array.

VENUE.   The neighborhood, area, or locality in which an injury is declared to have been done, or fact declared to have happened. "Venue" designates the particular county or city in which a court with jurisdiction may hear the case. In criminal cases this ordinarily is the county or city in which the offense occurred.

VERDICT.   The formal decision or finding made by a jury, reported to the judge, and accepted.

VICTIMLESS CRIME.   A crime in which all persons involved are willing participants and none views himself as having suffered harm at the hands of another. The crimes of prostitution and gambling would fall in this category.

VOIR DIRE.   Literally, "To speak the truth." The preliminary examination of a prospective juror as to his competency, interest in the case, etc..

W

WAIVE.   To abandon or throw away; in modern law, to abandon or surrender a claim, a privilege, a right, or the opportunity to take advantage of some defect, irregularity, or wrong.

WARRANT.   A written order of the court (usually a magistrate) directing a peace officer to arrest a certain person (an arrest warrant) or to search a certain place (search warrant).

WRIT OF CERTIORARI.   See *Certiorari*.

WRIT OF HABEAS CORPUS.   A writ directed to a person detaining another and commanding him to present the person detained before the court so that the court may determine the legality of the detention.

Appendix C

Selected Sections
of the United States Constitution

Preamble

We the People of the United States, in Order to form a more perfect Union, establish Justice, insure domestic Tranquillity, provide for the common defence, promote the general Welfare, and secure the Blessings of Liberty to ourselves and our Posterity, do ordain and establish this Constitution for the United States of America.

Article I.

Section 6.   The Senators and Representatives shall receive a Compensation for their Services, to be ascertained by Law, and paid out of the Treasury of the United States. They shall in all Cases, except Treason, Felony and Breach of the Peace, be privileged from Arrest during their Attendance at the Session of their respective Houses, and in going to and returning from the same; and for any Speech or Debate in either House, they shall not be questioned in any other Place.

Section 9.   The privilege of the Writ of Habeas Corpus shall not be suspended, unless when in Cases of Rebellion or Invasion the public Safety may require it.

No Bill of Attainder or ex post facto Law shall be passed.

Article III.

Section 1.   The judicial Power of the United States, shall be vested in one supreme Court, and in such inferior Courts as the Congress may from time to time ordain and establish. The Judges, both of the supreme and inferior Courts, shall hold their Offices during good Behaviour, and shall, at stated Times, receive for their Services a Compensation which shall not be diminished during their Continuance in Office.

Section 2.   The judicial Power shall extend to all Cases, in Law and Equity, arising under this Constitution, the Laws of the United States, and Treaties made, or which shall be made, under their Authority;—to all Cases affecting Ambassadors, other public Ministers and Consuls;—to all Cases of admiralty and maritime Jurisdiction;—to Controversies to which the United States shall be a Party;—to Controversies between two or more States;—between a State and Citizens of another State;—between Citizens of different States;—between Citizens of the same State claiming Lands under Grants of different States, and between a State, or the Citizens thereof, and foreign States, Citizens or Subjects.

In all Cases affecting Ambassadors, other public Ministers and Consuls, and those in which a State shall be a Party, the supreme Court shall have original Jurisdiction. In all the other Cases before mentioned, the supreme Court shall have appellate Jurisdiction, both as to the Law and Fact, with such Exceptions, and under such Regulations as the Congress shall make.

The trial of all Crimes, except in Cases of Impeachment, shall be by Jury; and such Trial shall be held in the State where the said Crimes shall have been committed; but when not committed within any State, the Trial shall be at such Place or Places as the Congress may by Law have directed.

Article IV.

Section 2.   The Citizens of each State shall be entitled to all Privileges and Immunities of Citizens in the several States.

A Person charged in any State with Treason, Felony, or other Crime, who shall flee from Justice, and be found in another State, shall on Demand of the executive Authority of the State from which he fled, be delivered up, to be removed to the State having Jursidiction of the Crime.

No person held to Service or Labour in one State, under the Laws thereof, escaping into another, shall, in Consequence of any Law or Regulation therein, be discharged from such Service or Labour, but shall be delivered up on Claim of the Party to whom such Service or Labour may be due.

The Bill of Rights

Amendment I. [1791]

Congress shall make no law respecting an establishment of religion, or prohibiting the free exercise thereof; or abridging the freedom of speech, or of the press; or the right of the people peaceably to assemble, and to petition the Government for a redress of grievances.

Amendment II. [1791]

A well regulated Militia, being necessary to the security of a free State, the right of the people to keep and bear Arms, shall not be infringed.

Amendment III. [1791]

No Soldier shall, in time of peace be quartered in any house, without the consent of the Owner, nor in time of war, but in a manner to be prescribed by law.

Amendment IV. [1791]

The right of the people to be secure in their persons, houses, papers, and effects, against unreasonable searches and seizures, shall not be violated, and no Warrants shall issue, but upon probable cause, supported by Oath or affirmation, and particularly describing the place to be searched, the persons or things to be seized.

Amendment V. [1791]

No person shall be held to answer for a capital, or otherwise infamous crime, unless on a presentment or indictment of a Grand Jury, except in cases arising in the land or naval forces, or in the Militia, when in actual service in time of War or public danger; nor shall any person be subject for the same offence to be twice put in jeopardy of life or limb; nor shall be compelled in any criminal case to be a witness against himself, nor be deprived of life, liberty, or property, without due process of law; nor shall private property be taken for public use, without just compensation.

Amendment VI. [1791]

In all criminal prosecutions, the accused shall enjoy the right to a speedy and public trial, by an impartial jury of the State and district wherein the crime shall have been committed, which district shall have been previously ascertained by law, and to be informed of the nature and cause of the accusation; to be confronted with the witnesses against him; to have compulsory process for obtaining witnesses in his favor, and to have the Assistance of Counsel for his defence.

Amendment VII. [1791]

In Suits at common law, where the value in controversy shall exceed twenty dollars, the right of trial by jury shall be preserved, and no fact tried by a jury, shall be otherwise re-examined in any Court of the United States, than according to the rules of common law.

Amendment VIII. [1791]

Excessive bail shall not be required, nor excessive fines imposed, nor cruel and unusual punishments inflicted.

Amendment IX. [1791]

The enumeration in the Constitution, of certain rights, shall not be construed to deny or disparage others retained by the people.

Amendment X. [1791]

The powers not delegated to the United States by the Constitution, nor prohibited by it to the States, are reserved to the States respectively, or to the people.

Other Amendments

Amendment XIV. [1868]

Section 1.   All persons born or naturalized in the United States and subject to the jurisdiction thereof, are citizens of the United States and of the State wherein they reside. No State shall make or enforce any law which shall abridge the privileges or immunities of citizens of the United States; nor shall any State deprive any person of life, liberty, or property, without due process of law; nor deny to any person within its jurisdiction the equal protection of the laws.

Table of Cases

References are to Pages

Index

F

H

K

L

M

N

O

P

T

U

V